walk
BRITAIN2005

Supported by

THE HANDBOOK AND ACCOMMODATION
GUIDE OF THE RAMBLERS' ASSOCIATION

www.ramblers.org.uk

Compiled by the Ramblers' Association
Editor: Dan French
Deputy Editor: Sarah Bove
Information Editor: Des de Moor

Design and production by Think Publishing
Project Editor: Emma Jones
Art Director: Lou Millward
Designers: Susannah Hall and Chris Gregory
Picture Research: Stuart Fance
www.thinkpublishing.co.uk

Cover photograph
Robert Morris/ Alamy

Printed and bound by BGP, Colchester, Essex
walk BRITAIN 2005 is printed on UPM Cote which is
manufactured using wood products certified by the
Forestry Stewardship Council.

Trade distribution by Cordee Ltd
3a de Montfort Street
Leicester LE1 7HD
☎ 0116 254 3579
sales@cordee.co.uk

Accommodation Advertising
The Editor
The Ramblers' Association
☎ 020 7339 8585
yearbook@london.ramblers.org.uk

Commercial Advertising
Think Publishing
The Pall Mall Deposit
124-128 Barlby Road
London W10 6BL
☎ 020 8962 3020
advertising@thinkpublishing.co.uk

Published by
The Ramblers' Association
2nd Floor, Camelford House
89 Albert Embankment
London SE1 7TW
☎ 020 7339 8500
Fax 020 7339 8501
ramblers@london.ramblers.org.uk
www.ramblers.org.uk
Registered charity no. 1093577, and a company
limited by guarantee in England and Wales
(no. 4458492)

Ramblers' Association Scotland
Kingfisher House
Auld Mart Business Park
Milnathort
Kinross KY13 9DA
☎ 01577 861222
Fax 01577 861333
enquiries@scotland.ramblers.org.uk
www.ramblers.org.uk/scotland

Ramblers' Association Wales
1 Cathedral Road
Cardiff CF11 9HA
☎ 029 2034 3535
Fax 029 2023 7817
cerddwyr@ramblers.org.uk
www.ramblers.org.uk/wales
www.ramblers.org.uk/cymru

Ramblers Holidays
Box 43, 2 Church Road
Welwyn Garden City AL8 6PQ
☎ 01707 331133
Fax 01707 333276
info@ramblersholidays.co.uk
www.ramblersholidays.co.uk

ISBN 1 901184 67 6

ENGLAND

SOUTH WEST
Cornwall, Devon, Dorset, Gloucestershire, Somerset, Wiltshire

SOUTH
Berkshire, Buckinghamshire, Hampshire, Isle of Wight, Kent, London, Oxfordshire, Surrey, East Sussex, West Sussex

EAST
Bedfordshire, Cambridgeshire, Essex, Hertfordshire, Norfolk, Suffolk

EAST MIDLANDS
Derbyshire, Leicestershire, Lincolnshire, Northamptonshire, Nottinghamshire, Rutland

WEST MIDLANDS
Birmingham and the Black Country, Herefordshire, Shropshire, Staffordshire, Warwickshire, Worcestershire

NORTH WEST
Cheshire, Cumbria, Lancashire

NORTH EAST
Durham, Northumberland, Tyne and Wear

YORKSHIRE
East Yorkshire, North Yorkshire, South Yorkshire, West Yorkshire

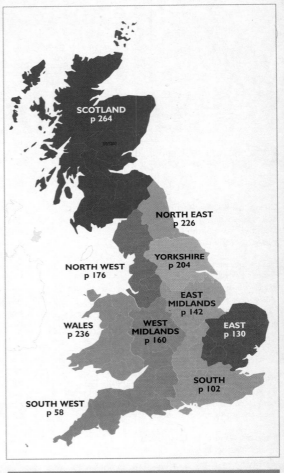

WALES

Anglesey
Carmarthenshire
Ceredigion
Conwy
Gwynedd
Monmouthshire
North East Wales (Denbighshire, Flintshire, Wrexham)
Pembrokeshire
Powys
South Wales (Blaenau Gwent, Bridgend, Cardiff, Caerphilly, Merthyr Tydfil, Newport, Neath Port Talbot, Rhondda Cynon Taff, Swansea, Torfaen, Vale of Glamorgan)

SCOTLAND

Argyll & Bute
Central Belt (Ayrshire, Clackmannanshire, Dumbartonshire, Dundee, Edinburgh, Falkirk, Fife, Glasgow, Inverclyde, Lanarkshire, Lothian, Midlothian, Renfrewshire & East Renfrewshire)
Dumfries & Galloway
Highland
Scottish Islands (see individual entries in Scotland)
Perth & Kinross
North East Scotland (Aberdeen, Aberdeenshire, Angus & Moray)
Scottish Borders
Stirling

CONTENTS

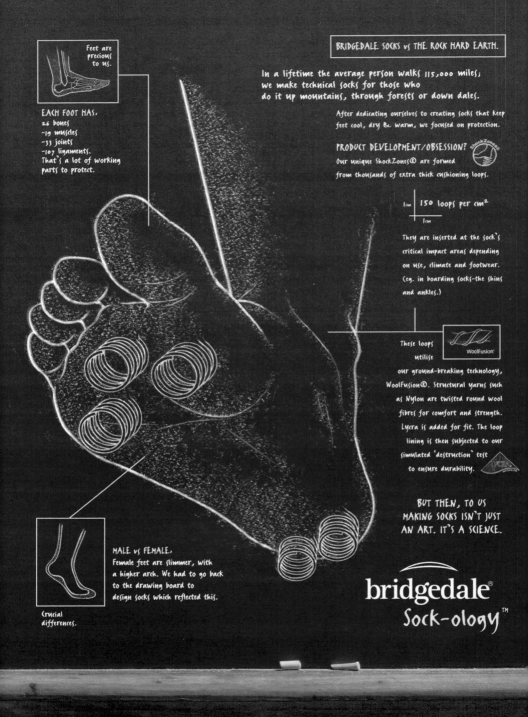

BRIDGEDALE SOCKS vs THE ROCK HARD EARTH.

Feet are precious to us.

EACH FOOT HAS:
26 bones
-19 muscles
-33 joints
-107 ligaments.
That's a lot of working parts to protect.

In a lifetime the average person walks 115,000 miles; we make technical socks for those who do it up mountains, through forests or down dales.

After dedicating ourselves to creating socks that keep feet cool, dry & warm, we focused on protection.

PRODUCT DEVELOPMENT/OBSESSION?
Our unique ShockZones® are formed from thousands of extra thick cushioning loops.

1cm | 150 loops per cm²
1cm

They are inserted at the sock's critical impact areas depending on use, climate and footwear. (eg. in boarding socks-the shins and ankles.)

These loops utilise our ground-breaking technology, WoolFusion®. Structural yarns such as Nylon are twisted round wool fibres for comfort and strength. Lycra is added for fit. The loop lining is then subjected to our simulated 'destruction' test to ensure durability.

WoolFusion®

BUT THEN, TO US MAKING SOCKS ISN'T JUST AN ART. IT'S A SCIENCE.

MALE vs FEMALE.
Female feet are slimmer, with a higher arch. We had to go back to the drawing board to design socks which reflected this.

Crucial differences.

bridgedale®
Sock-ology™

HOW TO USE THIS GUIDE

The annual handbook and accommodation guide of the Ramblers' Association has been redesigned to celebrate its 70th edition. For the first time, the new-look **walk BRITAIN** is divided into eight English regions, Wales and Scotland. Each contains a full colour map showing long distance paths, a short introduction to walking in the area, contact details for local Ramblers Groups, a list of useful walking publications and Millets' equipment shops, followed by accommodation divided into B&B, Self-catering, Groups, Hostels, Bunkhouses & Campsites, and Pubs & Tearooms.

Local Ramblers Groups

The Association's Groups carry out conservation work in their localities and walk and socialise together. Each Group listed organises its own programme of led walks. Most walks are now listed on the Group Walks Finder on our website; otherwise you can request a programme by sending a SAE to the Group Secretary. Many work from home and all are volunteers, so if you telephone, please do so at reasonable times. Many Groups also publish upcoming walks on their own websites and where relevant, these are listed. The websites can also be found at www.ramblers.org.uk.

Most Groups are mixed but some specialise; for examples some offer shorter walks or walks for families. There are also a number of Groups for enthusiasts in their 20s-30s – we've highlighted these in blue. All details were correct on publication of this book, but changes may take place during the year.

Publications

The books and guides listed cover a huge range of walks, from short circular strolls to long distance paths, and are prepared by local walkers with local knowledge. They're available by mail order directly from the addresses shown. Where no p&p charge is shown, this is included in the price. Further publications and information can be found in the Long Distance Paths section.

The Ramblers' Bookshop on p 34 stocks many other publications available from our main office.

Accommodation

The listings in this guide are organised by country/region and then by county or unitary authority order. Sometimes we have banded together authorities that are small in size or where there are fewer listings – see the contents page for details, and below for a full introduction to the accommodation listings.

Useful Contacts

Throughout the guide we refer to various other organisations; the contact details for these are contained in the Useful Contacts section on p 291.

THE ACCOMMODATION

BED & BREAKFAST

B&B entries are all listed under a 'place'. That place might be a village, a town or even a hamlet. The choice is determined by a number of elements, such as the proximity of the accommodation to a long distance path or national park, or on occasion, it is added on the request of an advertiser. If the place is situated in or bordering a national park, or is within two miles of one of the long distance paths, the name of that national park or path is given after the place name, with the national park listed first.

Many of the entries in this guide come from readers' recommendations. As we are not able to vet the establishments, this is a most valuable resource. Please keep your recommendations coming in.

SELF-CATERING

Prices for self-catering accommodation vary considerably by season; we give the lowest and highest cost, usually per week. Where a proprietor lets more than one property, the price of the cheapest in low season and the most expensive in high season are given. You are advised to make full enquiries before booking.

Tourist board awards may be different for each property let – in these cases we give the range of classifications awarded.

GROUP ACCOMMODATION

The group accommodation entries include many places tried and tested by Ramblers Groups and recommended to us. There is a variety of types, standards, prices, and sizes. Some are self-catering (SC), others provide meals (B&B), breakfast, lunch, dinner or all three. They include hotels, hostels, university halls of residence, cabins in the woods and farmhouses – hopefully something for everyone.

HOSTELS, BUNKHOUSES & CAMPSITES

Some centres listed here are primarily for groups, but are also open to individuals as well. In each case we state prices per night, and whether meals (B&B) and/or self-catering facilities (SC) are available. Many hostels accept children at a reduced rate.

Categories of establishments include:

BB = Bunkhouse Barn

A converted farm building, better equipped than the camping barn. Stoves and cooking facilities are provided. Toilets may be chemical. Separate sleeping areas available for males and females but little privacy. Bunk beds are provided.

B = Bunkhouse

Other kinds of converted buildings, simply but comfortably furnished. They can be run by hotels, sporting estates or individuals. Cooking facilities and utensils provided. Separate sleeping areas for males and females with beds or bunks. Showers and drying facilities provided.

C = Campsite

Some may be for tents only, welcome tourers, or have hook-up facilities for caravans. In some sites, static caravans are available. Some provide meals on-site.

CB = Camping Barn

A redundant farm building converted to provide basic shelter. Little or no privacy. Limited facilities. Toilets may be chemical. Sleeping areas are usually not divided between the sexes and there are wooden sleeping platforms. Camping barns are often described as 'stone tents'.

IH = Independent Hostel

A privately run hostel. The standards and conditions will vary from hostel to hostel. Some provide meals but the majority are self-catering. Sheet sleeping bag liners usually required.

OC = Outdoor Centre

Often available to groups only. See also Group Accommodation.

YHA = Youth Hostel

A hostel that's a member of the Youth Hostels Association.

PUBS & TEAROOMS

All these establishments have been recommended by Ramblers Groups and members.

TOURIST BOARD CLASSIFICATIONS

The AA, RAC and VisitBritain have agreed a common standard for rating accommodation: ★-★★★★★

for hotels and ◆-◆◆◆◆◆ for smaller guest accommodation. Self-catering establishments are rated ★-★★★★★. In addition, each organisation has its own special award scheme: RAC's sparkling diamond or warm welcome award; AA's red diamond award; VisitBritain's silver and gold awards. Classifications are stated for establishments that have been awarded them, however, we only display VisitBritain's silver Ⓢ and gold Ⓖ awards in this guide.

In Scotland and Wales all establishments are graded by stars (the AA and RAC have separate ratings).

In 2004 VisitBritain worked with the Countryside Agency, the Ramblers' Association and the CTC and others to produce a national scheme to meet the specific needs of walkers and cyclists. Ⓦ indicates a member of The Walker's Welcome scheme, Cyclist's Welcome scheme, or both.

RAMBLERS' DISCOUNT

Each establishment marked with a ▶◀ offers a discount to readers of **walk** BRITAIN 2005.

To qualify for the discount, the reader must produce a copy of the current year's guide upon settlement of their bill; you should also check upon booking. The amount of the discount is decided by the proprietor but will not be less that 5% off the standard price for B&B per person per night (not including other meals or any other services).

The discount may not be applicable if used in conjunction with other discount offers or if the customer has booked through means other than **walk** BRITAIN 2005.

FURTHER INFORMATION

Any reference to a path beneath the place name indicates there is information about that path in the section beginning on p 45.

Six-figure grid references are given for each entry and the maps referred to are the OS Landranger series, scale 1:50,000. These are mostly generated from the postcode and can be inaccurate in some sparsely populated areas.

We have been asked to point out that any deposit paid is not returnable in all circumstances and in particular that any amount paid by credit card may not be returnable.

DISCLAIMER

Finally, a disclaimer. The information in **walk** BRITAIN 2005 is based on details received from proprietors during 2004. The Ramblers' Association cannot be held responsible for errors or omissions.

KEY TO ABBREVIATIONS & SYMBOLS

Accommodation

A   Price per person per night under £20
B   Price per person per night £20 – £35
C   Price per person per night £35 or over

These prices are based on occupancy of a single room, per night. However, if no single room is available two prices may be shown to indicate single and shared occupancy.

☛◄	Ramblers Discount offered (see p 6)
☆	A box display advert
B&B	Bed & Breakfast accommodation
SC	Self-catering accommodation
✕	Evening meal normally available (unless 'book first') with average price/time served
✕ nearby	Evening meal available within a 10-minute walk
S, D, T, F	Number of single, double, twin or family rooms
ⅅ	Clothes drying facilities available
Ⅴ	Vegetarian evening meals are always available
⊗	No smoking throughout the establishment
ⅬB	At least one room has private bath/shower and/or toilet
⚏	A railway station is within 2 miles
(Stroud)	(the station)
🍴	A packed lunch can be arranged
☕	Tea/coffee making facilities in the bedrooms
⬦	Lifts are available by arrangement
ⅼ	Luggage transfer services can be arranged

🐕	You may be able to take a dog having first consulted with the proprietor
★	VisitBritain star rating (hotels and self-catering properties)
◆	VisitBritain diamond rating (B&Bs, guesthouses and inns)
Ⓢ Ⓖ	VisitBritain silver or gold award
Ⓦ	Walkers' Welcome scheme or Cyclists' Welcome scheme
Ⓜ	The proprietor is a member of the Ramblers' Association
Cairngorms	National park
South Downs*	Proposed national park
Offa's Dyke	Long distance path. For further details please refer to p 45

Pubs & Tearooms

�🍺	Pub
☕	Tearoom
✕	Food served
Ⅴ	Vegetarian food available
⋔	Reservations can be made for groups
♫ (Live)	Music policy
Ⅼ	Log fire
Ⅾ	Beer or tea garden
⊗	Pubs with a non-smoking area
↩	Accommodation is also available
Ⓑ(L)	Leave muddy boots at the door
Ⓑ(D)	Dry muddy boots by the fire
Ⓑ(G)	Muddy boots only in the garden
Ⓑ(☺)	Don't mind muddy boots

KEY TO THE MAPS

National Trail or Long Distance Route (Scotland)

Other long distance path

County boundary

National Park boundary

Today it's all a game for Rannoch, but for a walker or climber in trouble on Scotland's mountains he needs to be able to pla
it well. The dog's speed and superior sense of smell allow him to search many square miles a day in the sort of condition
that make human senses virtually useless.

Together with Kenny's knowledge of the mountains and handling skills, they make an expert team. The trust between them i
complete and built over many years. It certainly makes you think, in these days of avalanche transceivers and therma
imaging, that for many people when it's crunch time, a dog is still 'a man's best friend'.

TRUST IS EARNED berghaus

ABOUT US

WWW.BRITAINONVIEW.COM

THE RAMBLERS' ASSOCIATION...

- is Britain's biggest organisation working for walkers, a registered charity with 142,000 members across England, Scotland and Wales. We've been looking after Britain's footpaths and defending its beautiful countryside for over 70 years
- **provides information to walkers and works with central and local government to promote the health, recreation and environmental benefits of walking**

- increases access for walkers – our work is helping to establish statutory rights of access to our countryside
- **safeguards the countryside from unsightly and polluting developments so that walkers can enjoy its tranquillity and beauty**
- protects Britain's unique network of public paths – all too often, they are illegally blocked, obstructed and overgrown. We work with local authorities to make them a pleasure to walk on

BENEFITS OF MEMBERSHIP INCLUDE...

- **walk BRITAIN**, our annual handbook and accommodation guide
- **walk, our quarterly colour magazine**
- discretionary discounts at equipment shops
- **an annual membership card**
- up to four local/regional Area newsletters a year, where published
- **members can join a local Group of their choice and take part in its programme of walks and social events. Members may also participate in events and walks run by any other Group**

- access to the Ramblers Map Library. The Library stocks all OS Landranger and Explorer maps, and members can borrow up to 10 maps at a time for a small fee plus p&p. Contact the Map Library Service at our main office for details

On joining the Ramblers' Association each member agrees 'to respect the countryside, its beauty and wildlife'.

There is a special discounted rate for readers on p 11.

SUPPORTING US...

The Ramblers' Association is much more than a walking club. We are a registered charity – the only one dedicated to working for walkers to expand access to and protect our countryside.

Because we receive no money from central government, we are entirely dependent upon the generosity of our members and supporters. Here are some ways you can help us today WITHOUT putting your hand in your pocket:

ALAN BARBER

Gift Aid – If you 'Gift Aid It', we can claim an extra 28p per pound donated, even on membership fees. This accounted for £300,000 last year, but this could double if all our supporters registered. So, if you pay income tax or capital gains tax, please Gift Aid today, or ☎ 020 7339 8511 for a form.

Direct Debit – Over 50% of members pay their subscriptions by Direct Debit, which saves them trouble and greatly reduces our administration costs and bank charges. Members can, of course, cancel this arrangement at any time.

Ramblers' Association credit card – If you switch to our card, run by ethically-guided Co-operative Bank, we receive £15 for every account opened, a further £2.50 when first used plus a further 25p per £100 spent on the card. ☎ 0800 002 006 to apply, quoting reference 64309, or see the advert on p 22.

Ramblers' Insurance – We receive up to 10% of the premium for every home, travel or motor policy taken out with UIA Insurance – the insurer with principles. ☎ 0800 013 0064, quoting reference RAM2, visit www.ramblersinsurance.co.uk, or see the advert on p 21.

Following in your footsteps – Once you have provided for your loved ones, why not leave the world a better place and include the Ramblers in your will? For a copy of our free guide to making and updating your will, please ☎ 020 7339 8511, or see the advert on p 16.

Ramblers Holidays was set up in 1946 to support the work of the Ramblers' Association, and still makes a very significant donation to the Ramblers' Association every year. For a brochure ☎ 01707 331133, or see inside the back cover of this guide.

Our thanks go to Millets for their continuing support and sponsorship of this guide and we would like to draw your attention to their advertising contained on pages 40–44.

Special Discount Membership Offer

If you are not yet a Ramblers' member, use this coupon to get 20% off your first year's subscription, plus one month extra free for joining by Direct Debit. And if you are already a member why not introduce a friend to this special offer and give them this form? For your support you'll get a terrific range of benefits to help you to get the most out of walking:

- **walk BRITAIN, our handbook and accommodation guide**
- **A lively colour magazine, walk**
- **Membership of your local Ramblers Group**
- **Access to our Ordnance Survey map library**
- **Discretionary discounts on outdoor clothing and equipment**

Your support will ensure we can keep working for walkers:

Registered charity number 1093577

- **Protecting Britain's unique network of public paths**
- **Increasing access for walkers**
- **Safeguarding the countryside**
- **Providing information, advice and support**

IT IS A CONDITION OF THIS OFFER THAT YOU PAY BY DIRECT DEBIT

Yes, I/we would like to join the Ramblers' Association

Title_____ **Name(s)**_____

Address_____

_____

_____ **Postcode** _____

Date(s) of Birth _____ _____ **RA Group (if you have a preference)**_____

If you have no preference you will be placed in a group according to your postcode

| B |

Tick the box that suits you best: ☐ **Individual £19.20** (normally £24) ☐ **Joint/Family* £25.60** (normally £32)

☐ **Reduced Individual+ £14**   ☐ **Reduced Joint/Family*+ £18**

*Joint membership is available for two adults living at the same address,

+Reduced rates are available and are intended for people who, through whatever circumstances, cannot afford the standard rates.

The offer is vaild until December 2005. The offer is not open to existing members.

We occasionally exchange member's names and addresses with other like-minded organisations, which may be of interest to you. These are for use once only, and will not lead to further mailings. However, if you would prefer to be excluded from any such exchanges, please tick this box. ☐

Instruction to your Bank or Building Society to pay by Direct Debit

Please fill in the whole form and send it to: The Ramblers' Association, FREEPOST SW15, London SE1 7BR

Details of the Bank/Building Society

To: The Manager   Bank/Building Society

Address

Postcode

Name(s) of Account Holder(s)

Bank/Building Society account number

DIRECT Debit

Originator's Identification Number 9 2 2 6 7 0

Branch Sort Code

Reference Number (for office use)

Instruction to your Bank/Building Society — Please pay The Rambler' Association Direct Debits from the account detailed in this Instruction subject to the safeguards assured by the Direct Debit Guarantee.

Signature(s)

Date

Banks/Building Societies may not accept Direct Debit Instructions for some types of account.

Contour Navigator:

now you can **really** afford to put your feet up...

The perfect British walking boot. Crafted from rich, dark ruby 2.6mm calf leather uppers with a dual density rubber sole for outstanding grip and underfoot support. And all for just **£69.99**

The Mountain Boot Co. Ltd.   Tel: 0191 296 0212   www.mountainboot.co.uk

[CONTOUR

FREEDOM TO ROAM IN ENGLAND AND WALES

ALAN BARBER

19 September 2004 was an historic day in the history of the Ramblers' Association, as the new right of access contained in Part I of the Countryside and Rights of Way Act 2000 – a statutory freedom to roam – was implemented in two English regions, the South East and the Lower North West.

This marked the culmination of a campaign for increased access to the countryside that had lasted for over a century, but had come to the public eye following the Kinder Scout Mass Trespass in 1932, when six ramblers were imprisoned for leading the trespass. In 1935, the Ramblers' Association was formed, and the campaign for increased access to the countryside was integral to the organisation from the beginning.

The National Parks and Access to the Countryside Act 1949 secured access to some areas of open countryside, although in practice the Act had little effect outside the Peak District National Park.

The new right
In 1985 the Ramblers' Association launched its 'Forbidden Britain' campaign with a view to securing a new legal right of access. This brought the issue into the public eye once more and, after years of ceaseless campaigning by the Ramblers' Association, the Labour government elected in 1997 pledged to introduce a new statutory right of access to open countryside and registered common land across England and Wales. The resulting legislation – the Countryside and Rights of Way Act (CRoW) – finally received royal assent in November 2000.

The new right only provides a right of access on foot, although any existing rights on the land will remain unaffected. Walkers are required to observe certain restrictions, whilst landowners who obstruct anyone seeking to exercise their new right will be committing a criminal offence. For more information and the latest news on commencement of access please refer to our website.

Finding out more
Information on walkers' new rights and responsibilities, as well as the updated Countryside Code, can be obtained from the Countryside Agency's website (see Useful Contacts), or see our website and factsheet *Freedom to Roam* (see p37).

Now the new right of access is coming into force, the responsibility for managing access locally passes to the relevant access authority. It is important that access authorities (see Local Authorities) use their new powers to ensure, for example, misleading signs are removed and there are means of access to the newly accessible areas. Walkers should contact the relevant access authority and the Ramblers' Association if they encounter any problems with misleading notices or getting access to land.

FREEDOM TO ROAM – YOUR QUESTIONS ANSWERED

Where does the new legislation apply?
CRoW provides a legal right of access to approximately 4,000,000 acres of open, uncultivated countryside, which is defined in the legislation as mountain, moor, heath and down, as well as registered common land.

How can I find out where I can walk?
Since CRoW became law in November 2000 the Countryside Agency and the Countryside Council for Wales have been working to produce maps showing what land qualifies as either open countryside or registered common land. Only three of the final 'conclusive' maps have been published at the time of writing – for the South East, Lower North West and Central Southern England. However, these 'conclusive' maps will show open countryside even where the new right of access may not apply (such as on military training land) and walkers are advised to continue to use OS Explorer maps, which are being relaunched as soon as possible after access in each region has commenced.

When is the new access coming into force ?

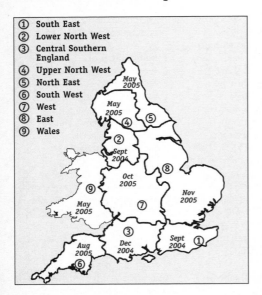

① **South East**
② **Lower North West**
③ **Central Southern England**
④ **Upper North West**
⑤ **North East**
⑥ **South West**
⑦ **West**
⑧ **East**
⑨ **Wales**

What am I allowed to do on access land?
The new law provides a right of access for walkers only, and does not confer any additional rights for cyclists or horse-riders (though where additional rights are currently allowed or tolerated, they are likely to continue). Dogs are permitted on some areas of open country, but must be kept on a lead on access land between 1 March and 31 July

and at any time in the vicinity of livestock. Furthermore, dogs may be banned temporarily or permanently from some areas of land. Access at night is permitted but may be subject to local restrictions. Walkers are responsible for their own safety at all times.

How is access managed locally?
Access is managed by local authorities or, in national parks, by the national park authority. They have the power to enact and enforce by-laws that will apply to open access land in their jurisdiction subject to consultation with the relevant local access forum and countryside body. They also have powers to set up the necessary infrastructure to make the new access land easily available to walkers including the power to appoint wardens, erect and maintain notices and improve means of access.

What is a local access forum?
Local access forums, made up of landowners, users and others with an interest in the land, have been established to advise access authorities on the local application of the new law. This may mean commenting on access management or the need for signage or the necessity or otherwise of a proposed long-term local access restriction.

Are owners able to close their land for any reason?
The Act allows landowners to close their land for up to 28 days a year (including some Saturdays and Sundays) for any reason. The Countryside Agency and the Countryside Council for Wales should be informed of these closures and can make the information publicly available online. Landowners may apply for further closures or restrictions, on a temporary or permanent basis, for health and safety, land management or fire risk. There may also be closures to protect wildlife or areas of historic interest or on the grounds of national security.

What should I do if I see a misleading notice?
If the notice is about a local restriction then call the Open Access Contact Centre on 0845 100 3298 and they will advise you. For any other notices please contact your Local Authority and then inform the Ramblers' Association.

What if there is no way onto the access land?
Access authorities must provide means of access to access land, ideally in consultation with the landowner but by order if necessary. If you find there is no way of getting to the access land, then please contact your local authority and then inform the Ramblers' Association on 0207 339 8500, though remember that not all access points will be available immediately.

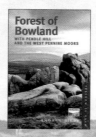

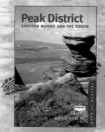

simple
pleasures

The world is ever-changing, but the simplest pleasures remain the same.

At the Ramblers' Association, we want to make sure that these pleasures can be enjoyed forever.

Once you have provided for your loved ones, remembering the Ramblers in your will is a wonderful way to preserve for tomorrow the countryside that gives you such pleasure today.

www.ramblers.org.uk

The Ramblers' Association is a member of the Legacy Promotion Campaign

---

Please tell me how I can remember **The Ramblers** in my Will

☐ Please send me a free guide to making and updating my will

The Ramblers

Registered charity number 1093577

Name _____

Address _____

_____

Postcode _____

I am a Ramblers member: Yes ☐   No ☐

Please return to:
John Wightman, The Ramblers' Association,
FREEPOST SW15, London SE1 7BR.

B

FOOTPATHS IN ENGLAND AND WALES

Britain's intricate web of rights of way gives intimate access to the furthest reaches of our countryside, but it is only as a result of 70 years' unstinting effort by the Ramblers' Association that many of these paths – 140,000 miles (225,000km) in England and Wales – have survived for use today.

The Ramblers' Association's key priority when it was established in 1935 was to secure legislation requiring the production of definitive maps of rights of way. These maps would provide conclusive evidence that any path shown on them was open to the public. This goal was achieved with the National Parks and Access to the Countryside Act 1949, but years of painstaking work by Ramblers' volunteers and others was needed to ensure that as many paths as possible were included on the maps.

Later, we successfully pressed for the rights of way information on definitive maps to be shown on Ordnance Survey maps. This invaluable information can be seen today on Explorer and Landranger maps.

Lobbying efforts continued over the years with support for statutory signposting, introduced by the Countryside Act 1968. During the passage of the Wildlife and Countryside Act through Parliament in 1981, we persuaded the House of Lords to defeat government proposals to abolish the right of appeal against path closures, and we played a key role in securing the Rights of Way Act 1990, which gives local authorities clear powers to enforce the law on keeping paths unobstructed where they cross cultivated fields.

More recently, with the Countryside and Rights of Way Act 2000, we supported the government's introduction of provisions to enable any member of the public to serve notice on a highway authority to secure the removal of obstructions.

How can I help?

Sadly, Acts of Parliament are not enough and vigilance is still needed because much rights of way law is ignored or poorly enforced by local highway authorities. These councils have a duty to see that public rights of way are:

- properly maintained
- kept free from obstructions
- signposted where they meet surfaced roads
- waymarked where necessary along their route
- recorded on the official (definitive) map

Yet it is estimated that there are over 200,000 obstacles and more than 110,000 missing signposts in England and Wales. That means a walker is likely to encounter an obstruction or problem every 1.25 miles (2 km). So next time you are out walking and you encounter a problem please report it to the local authority with responsibility for that path. We try to make it as simple as possible for everybody to do this. We've produced a *Reporting Path Problems* leaflet (available from our main office) or you can complete the form on p 23, or on our website.

Additionally the Ramblers' Association has many local footpath campaigns running up and down the country and we are always on the look-out for volunteers who would like to:

- conduct path surveys
- write to your local councillor
- write to your local newspaper
- be interviewed by local media
- carry out research concerning ancient paths

For more information about how you can help footpath campaigns, please contact The Footpath Campaigns Team at our main office or email openpaths@london.ramblers.org.uk.

The Footpath Campaigns Team produces *Notes on Footpath Campaigning* a comprehensive guide to all aspects of footpath campaigning as well as a monthly newsletter *Footpath Campaigner* that contains brief news of campaigning developments in England and Wales. To receive either or both please contact our main office.

Rights of Way
a guide to law and practice

by John Riddall and John Trevelyan. 3rd edition published June 2001, by the Ramblers' Association and Open Spaces Society. This accessible guide puts the law into practice for the benefit of the millions who walk, ride and cycle in the countryside. It is an invaluable reference work for path enthusiasts, local authority officials and lawyers.

Price £20 plus £4.50 p&p, order from Ramblers main office.

You can also order by phone: 020 7339 8500 or through www.ramblers.org.uk

RIGHTS OF WAY – YOUR QUESTIONS ANSWERED

Here we answer some of the most commonly asked questions on public rights of way. A fuller version of this text is available as a factsheet (FS7 – see p 37) and on our website.

What is a right of way?

A right of way is a path that anyone has the legal right to use on foot, and sometimes using other modes of transport.

 Public footpaths are open only to walkers, and may be waymarked with yellow arrows

 Public bridleways are open to walkers, horse riders and pedal cyclists, and may waymarked with blue arrows

 Byways Open to All Traffic (BOATs) are open to all traffic including motor vehicles, although they may not be maintained to the same standard as ordinary roads, and may be waymarked with red arrows.

Legally, a public right of way is part of the Queen's highway and subject to the same protection in law as all other highways, including trunk roads.

What are my rights on a public right of way?

Your legal right is to 'pass and repass along the way'. You may stop to rest or admire the view, or to consume refreshments, providing you stay on the path and do not cause an obstruction. You can also take with you a 'natural accompaniment', which includes a pram, pushchair or wheelchair (though you may find the surface of the path is not always suitable), or a dog. However, you should ensure that dogs are under close control. Note that there is no requirement for stiles to be suitable for use by dogs.

How do I know whether a path is a public right of way or not?

The safest evidence is the official 'definitive map' of public rights of way. These maps are available for public inspection at the offices of local surveying authorities (see Local Authorities). In addition, public rights of way information derived from them is shown by the OS on its Explorer and Landranger maps (see our factsheet, FS2 – p 37).

Some rights of way are not yet shown on definitive maps. These can quite properly be used, and application may be made to surveying authorities for them to be added to the map. The inner London boroughs are not required to produce definitive maps, though this does not mean there are no rights of way in inner London.

How does a path become public?

In legal theory most paths become rights of way because the owner 'dedicates' them to public use. In fact very few paths have been formally dedicated, but the law assumes that if the public uses a path without interference for some period of time – set by statute at 20 years – then the owner had intended to dedicate it as a right of way.

A public path that has been unused for 20 years does not cease to be public (except in Scotland). The legal maxim is 'once a highway, always a highway'.

Paths can also be created by agreement between local authorities and owners or by compulsory order, subject, in the case of objection, to confirmation by the Secretary of State for the Environment, Food and Rural Affairs, or the National Assembly for Wales.

Can a landowner put up new gates and stiles where none exist presently?

No. Not without seeking and getting permission from the highway authority and then complying with any conditions to that permission. Maintaining stiles and gates is primarily the owner's responsibility, but the highway authority must contribute 25% of the cost if asked and may contribute more if it wishes. If stiles and gates are not kept in proper repair the authority can, after 14 days' notice, do the job itself and send the bill to the owner.

How wide should a path be?

The path should be whatever width was dedicated for public use. This width may have arisen through usage, or by formal agreement, or by order, for example if the path has been diverted. The width may be recorded in a statement accompanying the definitive map but in many cases the proper width will be a matter of past practice on that particular path.

Is it illegal to plough up or disturb the surface of a path so as to make it inconvenient to use?

Yes, except where the path is a footpath or bridleway that runs across a field (as opposed to alongside a field edge). In this case the landowner can plough or otherwise disturb the path surface provided it is not reasonably convenient to avoid doing so. The path must be restored within 24 hours of the disturbance, or within two weeks if this is the first such disturbance for a

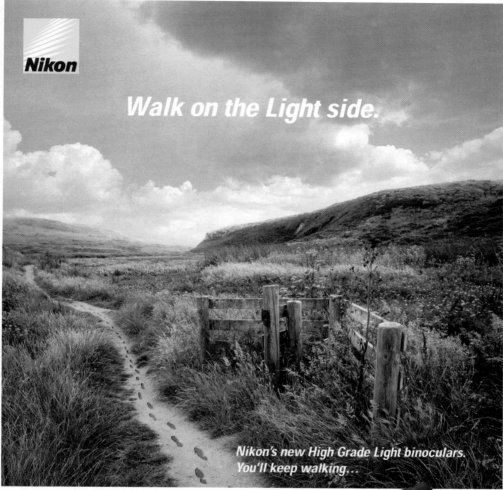

Walk on the Light side.

Nikon

Nikon's new High Grade Light binoculars.
You'll keep walking...

... and you'll love it. Because Nikon's new HGL binoculars are so light you'll hardly notice them until you look through them. Multilayer coating makes for the brightest, sharpest images, even where there's little light. Waterproof, fog-free construction ensures you see your way through, wherever your walk takes you. The new HGL binoculars from Nikon. Time to enjoy the wild side.

10x42 HG L DCF

particular crop. The restored path must be reasonably convenient to use, have a minimum width of 1m for a footpath or 2m for a bridleway, or the legal width (see earlier) if known, and its line must be clearly apparent on the ground.

What about crops growing on or over a path?

The landowner has a duty to prevent a crop (other than grass) from making the path difficult to find or follow. The minimum widths given earlier apply here also, but if the path is a field-edge path they are increased to 1.5m for a footpath, 3m for a bridleway. You have every right to walk through crops growing on or over a path, but stick as close as you can to its correct line. Report the problem to the highway authority (see Local Authorities): it has power to prosecute the landowner or cut the crop and send the owner the bill.

Can a farmer keep a bull in a field crossed by a public path?

Only a bull of up to 10 months in age. Bulls over 10 months of a recognised dairy breed (Ayrshire, British Friesian, British Holstein, Dairy Shorthorn, Guernsey, Jersey and Kerry) are banned from fields crossed by public paths under all circumstances. All other bulls over 10 months are banned unless accompanied by cows or heifers. If any bulls act in a way that endangers the public, an offence may have been committed under health and safety legislation.

What is an obstruction on a path?

Anything that interferes with your right to use it, for example a barbed wire fence across the path or a heap of manure dumped on it. Dense undergrowth is not normally treated as an obstruction but is dealt with under path maintenance. Highway authorities have a duty 'to prevent as far as possible the stopping up or obstruction' of paths.

Can I remove an obstruction to get by?

Yes, provided that you are a bona fide traveller on the path and have not gone out for the specific purpose of moving the obstruction, and that you remove only as much as is necessary to get through. If you can easily go round the obstruction without causing any damage, then you should do so.

Are horses allowed on public paths?

Horse riders have a right to use bridleways and byways. They have no right to use footpaths, and if they do they are committing a trespass against the owner of the land, unless the use is by permission. If use of a footpath by riders becomes a nuisance the local authority can ban them with a traffic regulation order or by-law. This makes such use a criminal offence rather than an act of trespass.

Are pedal cyclists allowed on public paths?

Pedal cyclists have a right to use bridleways and byways, but on bridleways they must give way to walkers and riders. Like horse riders, they have no right to use footpaths and if they do so they are committing a trespass against the owner of the land, unless use is by permission. As with horse-riding (see above), use of any right of way by cyclists can be controlled by traffic regulation orders and by-laws imposed by local authorities. Infringement of by-laws or orders is a criminal offence. Under the Highways Act 1835, it is an offence to ride a bicycle on the pavement at the side of a road, and under the Fixed Penalty Offences Order 1999 a person who rides on a pavement can be fined on the spot by a police officer.

Is it illegal to drive cars or motorcycles on public paths?

Anyone who drives a motor vehicle on a footpath or bridleway without permission is committing an offence. This does not apply if the driver stays within 15 yards of the road, only goes on the path to park and does not obstruct the right of passage. The owner of the land, however, can still order vehicles off even within 15 yards from the road. Races or speed trials on paths are forbidden. Permission for other types of trials on paths may be sought from the local authority, if the landowner consents.

What is trespass?

A person who strays from a right of way, or uses it other than for 'passing and repassing' commits trespass against the landowner.

In most cases, trespass is a civil rather than a criminal matter. A landowner may use 'reasonable force' to compel a trespasser to leave, but not more than is reasonably necessary. Unless injury to the property can be proven, a landowner could probably only recover nominal damages by suing for trespass. But of course you might have to meet the landowner's legal costs. Thus a notice saying 'Trespassers will be Prosecuted', aimed for instance at keeping you off a private drive, is usually meaningless. Criminal prosecution could only arise if you trespass and damage property. However, under public order law, trespassing with an intention to reside may be a criminal offence under some circumstances. It is also a criminal offence to trespass on railway land and sometimes on military training land.

Why do they deserve cheaper home insurance?

Because, like you, they're supporters of the Ramblers' Association. And like every supporter, they value security, peace of mind and being part of an organisation that's trustworthy. These values are shared by everyone at UIA. We have always operated with principles and we will only ever work with like-minded organisations.

Saving you up to £100

As a supporter of the Ramblers' Association you and your family can enjoy preferential home insurance rates and a saving of up to £100. We are able to offer you this because we reinvest all profits so our policyholders' money is used to benefit them. The table below illustrates just how much you could save with UIA.

Taking care of the small things

Apart from saving you money, we also know how important it is to look after the smaller details. That's why we offer free accidental damage cover on audio and computer equipment, optional matching suite cover, free delivery of replacement goods and discounts of at least £20 if you take out a combined buildings and contents policy.

A special 'thank you' to Ramblers

And, if you decide to take out a home insurance policy with UIA, we'll donate £15 to the Ramblers' Association, now and each time you renew your policy with us*.

So why not call UIA today to find out how much you deserve to save?

	London NW3 1	Bristol BS6 7	Birmingham B24 8	Liverpool L40 8
UIA Premium	£407.51	£286.68	£311.51	£226.09
Average Market Premium	£604.14	£424.47	£382.83	£307.93
Saving	£196.63	£137.79	£71.32	£81.84

Premiums illustrated (including Insurance Premium Tax at the current rate) are for standard cover for combined buildings and contents insurance for a buildings sum insured of £110,000 and a contents sum insured of £25,000. These premiums are calculated for a 37 year old, living in a 3 bedroom semi-detached house, built in 1970. Market average is based on a selection of 5 leading competitors. (Source: Whatif October 2004)

The Ramblers

0800 013 00 64**
ramblersinsurance.co.uk
(quoting ref. RYB05)

insurance with principles

Support the Ramblers
every time you spend

- You can apply for either a Platinum or Standard Visa card

- Both have balance transfer facilities*

- Every account opened raises money for the interests of regular walkers:

  - **£15** for every new account goes towards protecting public footpaths - encouraging walking for health and pleasure

  - A further **£2.50** is raised if the card is used within the first six months

  - Plus **25p** for every **£100** you spend using the card

Phone for further details and an instant decision

0800 002 006

Lines are open Monday - Friday 8am - 9pm, Saturday 8am - 8pm, Sunday 9am - 6pm
Please quote **64318** when you phone

www.ramblers.org.uk
Reg. Charity No: 1093577

in association with

The CO-OPERATIVE BANK
Customer led, ethically guided

The Co-operative Bank p.l.c.,
Head Office, P.O. Box 101,
1 Balloon Street,
Manchester M60 4EP
www.co-operativebank.co.uk

Path Problem Report Form

Please complete this form to report footpath problems and send it to the address below

WHERE WAS THE PROBLEM? Please give as much information as you can.

County/unitary authority _____

District_____

Parish/Community_____

From (place) _____

_____Grid ref._____

To (place)_____

_____Grid ref._____

Path number if known_____

Date problem encountered_____

WHAT WAS THE PROBLEM?
Be precise and quote a grid reference for any specific point. Draw a sketch map if you think it will help. If anyone spoke to you, please give details,
including their name and address if known.

WHAT TO DO NEXT? Give us your details

Name_____

Address_____

_____

Email_____

Telephone_____**Tick box for more Report Forms** ❏

Send this form to
Your local Ramblers representative or the Ramblers' Association,
2nd Floor, 87-90 Albert Embankment, London SE1 7TW.
☎ 020 7339 8500 • Fax 020 7339 8501.

supports you all the way

COUNTRYSIDE PROTECTION

Back in the 1930s when the Ramblers' Association was in its youth, it was part of a movement not only to secure access to the countryside but also to protect it. This is no less true today and our charitable objective 'to defend the beauty of the countryside' is just as relevant now as the pressures of development become ever greater.

Getting the message across

Governmental and media attention on issues such as house building, renewable energy, road building, aviation and sustainable development have provided us with opportunities to get messages across that demonstrate the need for greater countryside protection for the health and well-being of the nation. Significant changes to the planning system, enshrined in the Planning and Compulsory Purchase Act 2004, have challenged us to change the way we campaign on these issues, in particular by focusing on regional and local-level decision-making, rather than what happens at county level. Nationally we continue to respond to consultations on planning guidance, work closely with a range of like-minded organisations through Wildlife and Countryside Link (see Useful Contacts) and provide newsletters, training and advice to volunteers on how they can make a difference locally.

Much of our countryside work came to fruition in 2004: the government announced its decision not to allow the building of a deep sea terminal on the edge of the New Forest because of the environmental impacts that such a development would have; the decision to create a New Forest National Park was made following the public inquiry that ran throughout 2003; and the public inquiry into the designation of the South Downs as a national park began. In each of these cases we combined local knowledge and expertise with national clout and support to present clear, united and competent contributions to the debates that have surrounded them.

The forthcoming year looks interesting for the environmental movement. The government has failed on many counts to fulfil its promises, yet the possibility of a general election, the hosting of the G8 summit and the holding of the EU presidency could be opportunities to force its hand and get some real results. We shall be doing our bit by undertaking research into renewable energy and using it to inform our policy and campaigns. We shall also be pushing for more Area and Group walks to be accessible to everyone and we'll be working with other organisations and government to influence the transport agenda. As two new Bills on improving local communities and services come forward we shall add our voice through lobbying and by facilitating local involvement.

How to get involved

Countryside protection is dear to all walkers, and as such we intend to make it easier for everyone to be involved. If you mind about a local road-widening scheme, or would like to know how you can influence the decisions made in your local area, please contact the Countryside Team at our main office for advice.

"It has been prophesied that, as an outcome of the increasing congestion in towns and the universal use of motor cars and bicycles and lifts and moving stairways, our people will, in the year 2033, be atrophied in brain and body, herd-minded and legless. But the prophets have not reckoned with the Rambling Clubs. This vast and rapidly increasing Brotherhood of the Open Air is countering the menace by taking the youngmen [sic] and maidens out of the roar and the carbon-monoxided air of the cities to enjoy healthier surroundings among the beauties and interests of the countryside."

Extract from *The Ramblers Handbook 1933*, written by Basen Povey [If anyone knows of Basen Povey, the editor would be interested to hear from you.]

PROMOTING WALKING

Our central aim is to encourage walking. Whatever the motivating factor – to improve health, walk to work or school, spend time with friends or simply to unwind – we believe everyone can benefit from this activity. We're putting more resources into fulfilling this aim by expanding our Promoting Walking team and launching the Feet First initiative to promote walking to a wider range of people.

Discover the benefits

In 2004 we ran the innovative Walking Out projects in Stoke, Lincoln and Sheffield, working in partnership with community groups to reach people who, for whatever reason, have not yet had the opportunity to discover the benefits of walking. We've taken out hundreds of new walkers on easy, local and accessible walks, including refugees who are new to their surroundings and can benefit from the social integration that the walks offer. In Fife, Scotland, we're working with partners to deliver the successful Bums Off Seats programmes of short, local healthy walks. In Wales the ongoing Lonc a Chlonc (Walk and Talk) programme is one of Britain's longest established healthy walking projects.

Big campaigns and events can have a huge impact: in September 2004 we were a key partner in ITV's Britain on the Move campaign promoting physical activity to millions. Our annual Welcome to Walking Week, built around In Town Without My Car day, was even busier than usual as it also coincided with ITV's National Day of Walking and the launch of new access in the first two English regions. Everyday activities, such as the hundreds of walks organised every week by Ramblers volunteers, don't grab the headlines in the same way but are just as vital to our work.

Getting children walking is another matter of great concern. We already have several successful specialist groups of family walkers, and Welcome to Walking Week (17-25 September 2005) offers a good range of family walks. Our website and factsheets give practical advice and information on getting the kids on their feet. We hope that if children catch the walking bug young, it will stay with them all their lives.

At the same time we're busy lobbying national and local governments and health agencies to deliver desperately needed resources for promoting walking, and working to ensure that walking is recognised for its vital role in promoting healthy activity. After many years of lobbying by the Ramblers and like-minded organisations, the Department for Transport finally produced an action plan for walking and cycling in 2004 which, although it falls short of what is needed, at least recognises the importance of walking and the difficulties faced by people on foot. New walking strategies in Wales, Scotland and London have also been devised with the help of the Ramblers' Association.

Our authoritative information service is freely available to everyone. The information section of our website is an outstanding, extensive and very popular resource: you'll find sections on getting started, walking for health, gear, walking for people with disabilities and access for walkers as well as more and more local walks suggestions and our Group Walks Finder with listings of led walks. Non-web users are not forgotten with our range of factsheets and guides (see p 34), and booklets such as *Take 30*, a colourful introduction to walking for health. We offer an individual enquiry service too.

Walking Out project, Sheffield

SARAH BOVE

The Countryside Code

Be safe – plan ahead and follow any signs

Even when going out locally, it's best to get the latest information about where and when you can go; for example, your rights to go onto some areas of open land may be restricted while work is carried out, for safety reasons or during breeding seasons. Follow advice and local signs, and be prepared for the unexpected.

Leave gates and property as you find them

Please respect the working life of the countryside, as our actions can affect people's livelihoods, our heritage, and the safety and welfare of animals and ourselves.

Protect plants and animals, and take your litter home

We have a responsibility to protect our countryside now and for future generations, so make sure you don't harm animals, birds, plants, or trees.

Keep dogs under close control

The countryside is a great place to exercise dogs, but it's every owner's duty to make sure their dog is not a danger or nuisance to farm animals, wildlife or other people.

Consider other people

Showing consideration and respect for other people makes the countryside a pleasant environment for everyone – at home, at work and at leisure.

"The thing I enjoy about the countryside the most is the peace. quietness. space. fresh air... scenery. It's really beautiful."

PLEASE LEAVE GA AS YOU FIND IT

www.countrysideaccess.gov.uk

takes the rough ....with the smooth

Does your outdoor footwear perform effectively outside but let you down badly
when you want to look your best at the end of the day?
We happen to think that all work and no play makes for very dull footwear.
Which is why we designed the Dartmoor walking shoe.
Packed with technical features including a leather upper
with waterproof, breathable membrane
and durable slip and shock-proof Vibram outsoles,
they offer the highest levels of protection in the roughest terrain.
And the filthiest conditions.
Yet staying stylishly smart and fashionable in other challenging environments.
Handmade in Italy, and priced around £60, these shoes are the
essential choice for any James Bond.
Or Dirty Harry.

grisport®
FOOTWEAR

www.grisport.co.uk
Brochure Hotline: 0191 2090741

G R S

THE RAMBLERS' ASSOCIATION IN SCOTLAND

WWW.WALKINGWILD.COM

There are almost endless opportunities to explore Scotland on foot, and new arrangements for outdoor access mean things are set to get even better in the coming years.

New access legislation, the Land Reform (Scotland) Act 2003, will introduce access arrangements that promise to be amongst the best in Europe.

Ramblers' Association volunteers and staff have played a key role in securing better protection for footpath networks, clearer rights of access to the wider countryside and conservation of some of our most beautiful landscapes.

There has long been a general presumption of access to all land unless there is a very good reason for the public to be excluded. The Land Reform (Scotland) Act 2003 confirms this presumption, and walkers in Scotland will now have a statutory right of access to all land, except for areas such as railway lands, quarries, harbours, airfields and defence land where other laws apply.

During 2005 we will be working to ensure the effective implementation of the access legislation.

Local authorities have new duties and powers to develop Core Path Networks by adopting and improving existing paths and creating new ones. Councils have three years to produce plans for these networks. Core paths will eventually appear on OS Explorer maps. Scottish Natural Heritage and local authorities have developed The Scottish Paths Record database as a tool to help develop path networks.

Paths for all

Ramblers Scotland is a founding partner in Paths for All Partnership (see Useful Contacts), launched in 1996, to promote paths in Scotland for people of all ages and ability, for walking, cycling and horse riding. The key objectives of the Partnership are to achieve a significant increase in well-managed and welcoming paths close to where people live, and to promote their use.

Rights of way are less extensive in Scotland than in England and Wales

because there is a tradition of access to most land. Rights of way do exist, but there is no legal obligation on local authorities to record them, so they don't appear on OS maps, though paths and tracks are shown on these maps as geographical features and you have a right to walk on most of these. ScotWays (the Scottish Rights of Way and Access Society) keeps a catalogue of rights of way, signs many of them and maps and describes the major rural routes in its publication *Scottish Hill Tracks*. It is expected that Core Paths will largely supersede the existing arrangements for rights of way.

Please follow the Scottish Outdoor Access Code published by Scottish Natural Heritage:
- Respect the interests of other people
- Take care of the environment
- Take responsibility for your own actions

The full text of the Code, as approved by the Scottish Parliament is available at: www.snh.org.uk/pdfs/access/ApprovedCode050604.pdf.

GREAT OFFERS FROM GREAT MAGAZINES!

Whatever your passion for the outdoors we have a magazine to suit you.

6 ISSUES FOR THE PRICE OF 5

Country Walking – 6 issues for £16.50

Love walking? Let Britain's best-selling walking magazine be your companion and your guide.

Every month, *Country Walking* brings you all the information you need to enjoy your walks, including 27 regional walks with maps and step by step directions

TRAIL – 6 issues for £16.50

If you live for the outdoors, you need the UK's best-selling hill-walking magazine: *TRAIL*. Each month, Trail brings you all the information and inspiration you need to get out more in the mountains, including 15 tried and tested routes with detailed directions and maps and the toughest gear tests and kit buying guides in the UK.

Bird Watching – 6 issues for £17.00

If you're passionate about wild birds, let *Bird Watching* magazine help you get more out of your interest. Whether you want to know more about the birds in your garden or the whole of the UK this is the magazine for you.

Starting your subscription is easy.
Click on www.greatmagazines.co.uk/ramblers or call us on 0870 124 1010
and quote reference 'STEP'
Our lines are open Mon-Fri 8am – 9.30pm and Saturday 8am to 4pm.

NATIONAL PARKS – JOHN MUIR'S VISION BECOMES A REALITY

A Scot from Dunbar, John Muir, campaigned over 100 years ago in his adopted country, the USA, for public and political support for his vision that the nation's finest landscapes should be protected as 'national parks'. Now virtually every country in the world has its own national parks system.

Muir's vision is as relevant today as it was when Muir led the debate to protect Yellowstone and Yosemite.

In the late 1940s the Ramsey Committee, set up by the post-war government, recommended that a national park system, distinct from the system being set up in England and Wales, should be established in Scotland. Those proposals were abandoned after intense lobbying by a handful of members of the House of Lords.

Now the people of Scotland have a fledgling national parks system of their very own – bringing John Muir's vision to life in his native land.

Three national parks for Scotland?

We welcomed the creation of Scotland's first national park in Loch Lomond and the Trossachs and urged the Board to ensure that the special recreational qualities of the area are maintained and enhanced in the future. The Park was established on 8 July 2002 and covers 720 square miles.

The second park – the Cairngorms National Park – was officially opened on 1 September 2003. Although this is the biggest national park in Britain there are serious concerns because Highland Perthshire was excluded from the park boundary for political reasons. We have joined forces with other organisations to form PARC (Perthshire Alliance for the Real Cairngorms) to campaign for the inclusion of this area of Perthshire. If the Cairngorms are to achieve World Heritage Site status there needs to be integrated planning and management, and the widest possible boundary is needed to achieve this.

During 2005 Ramblers Scotland will also continue to press for a third national park – possibly centred on Harris, in the Western Isles – encompassing both coastal and marine areas.

The great outdoors:
take a refresher
course

REGATTA

GREAT OUTDOORS ™

fresh air clothing

ORDNANCE SURVEY MAPS

The best and most comprehensive walkers' maps of Britain are the 1:25 000 scale OS Explorer series in orange covers. They include a range of geographical features and landmarks at a high level of detail, including field boundaries, heights shown as contours and 'spot heights', railway stations and tram stops. They also show rights of way (except in Scotland), permissive paths, many long distance paths, off-road cycle paths, open access land (including new access land in England and Wales), locations of shorter circular walks and nature trails, information centres and visitor attractions.

Another OS series, 1:50 000 Landranger maps in pink and silver covers, also include rights of way and selected tourist attractions, but show less detail; OS are now marketing them as maps for planning days out rather than navigating on the ground.

Bookshops, information centres, larger newsagents and even some garages stock their local OS sheets. Maps can also be bought over the internet or direct from the OS, who can also supply a free Mapping Index showing all the sheet numbers. If you buy online from the OS by following the links from our website, we receive a donation for every map sold to assist in our work.

OTHER PAPER MAPS

While no other publisher covers all of Britain at detailed scales, a number of other specialist publishers do offer maps of use to walkers. The most important is Harvey who produce very clear specialist walkers' maps of certain popular upland areas and long distance paths at 1:25 000 and 1:40 000 scales. The maps also usually include useful information and addresses, and most are printed on weatherproof paper.

In urban areas street atlases can be more useful than OS maps: the Philips series is probably the best for walkers since most rights of way and other off-road paths, parks and open spaces and even some long distance walking routes are clearly shown. Available locally, or ☎ 020 7531 8459, www.philips-maps.co.uk.

ELECTRONIC MAPS

Electronic mapping systems for home PCs enable you to print OS maps at a variety of scales, to plan and annotate routes and link up to a GPS or pocket PC to take out on your walk – but make sure your hardware is compatible with the system you want to buy. The main suppliers of electronic maps are listed on p 295.

Mapping websites, allowing you to view extracts from Landranger and street maps by grid reference, postcode or place name, include www.streetmap.co.uk, www.multimap.com, www.map24.co.uk and the OS site. Explorer mapping is also gradually becoming available in electronic form.

LEARNING ABOUT MAPS

Map Reading Made Easy, free from the OS or downloadable from their website, is an excellent brief introduction. See also our Maps and navigation factsheet (FS2 – p 37), available on our website, which lists course providers and suggestions for further reading. Two particularly useful books are available from us. *Navigation and Leadership: a manual for walkers* (£4 + p&p) is the Ramblers' official 'bible' on the use of map and compass and leading group walks. Julian Tippett's *Navigation for Walkers* (£8.99 + p&p) is a great beginners' guide which includes OS map extracts.

PUBLIC TRANSPORT

Help avoid pollution and congestion by combining walking and public transport, and forget worries like parking, car crime and whether or not you should have a pint along the way.

Use National Rail for information about services and fares, their website also has an online journey planner. For long distance coaches, use National Express and Scottish City Link. Traveline has information on local bus, metro/underground, tram/light rail and ferries. When planning a walk have a map of your route to hand. The Traveline website has area journey planners, though these can be awkward to use if you need to cross a boundary; it also has a list of direct dial codes for the call centres. In London contact Transport for London.

There are an increasing number of services for countryside visitors, especially in popular areas during the summer; they often run on Sundays and bank holidays and offer economical ticket deals for those planning linear walks. See the information section of the Ramblers website, and www.countrygoer.org. Travel information for people with disabilities is available from Tripscope.

We encourage our Areas and Groups to organise walks by public transport wherever possible. Ramblers walk leaders in need of advice on organising walks by public transport should contact the Countryside team at our main office, who can put you in touch with our network of regional transport contacts.

THE RAMBLER'S BOOKSHOP
WALKING IN BRITAIN

walk BRITAIN 2005
Our annual yearbook and accommodation guide.
Packed with useful information and details of
2,000 places to stay
£5.99 (free to members)

Walking in Britain
Excellent Lonely Planet guide with background
notes and walk routes £13.99

Walking in Scotland
Indispensable Lonely Planet guide £11.99

Long Distance Walkers' Handbook:
7th edition comprehensive directory of trails
in UK £12.99

Long Distance Path Chart
Colour map of UK network £9.95

Ramblers' Regional Guides
Directories of places to walk
London (all of Greater London) £1.50
West Midlands (Hereford, Worcs,
Shrops, Staffs, Warks) £1.50
Yorkshire (including Dales and Moors) £1.50

An older series of free guides is available covering
other areas: please enquire for details.

Land's End to John O'Groats
Walk route suggestions and advice by
Andrew McCloy £11.99

Walk South East England
Colour booklet FREE

Independent Hostel Guide 2004
Special price £2.50

Collins Rambler's Guides
30 walks in each colour volume:
Ben Nevis and Glen Coe
by Chris Townsend £9.99
Chilterns & Ridgeway by Martin Andrew £9.99
Connemara by Paddy Dillon £9.99
Dartmoor by Richard Sale £9.99
Isle of Skye by Chris Townsend £9.99
Lake District by John Gillham
and Ronald Turnbull £9.99
North Wales by Richard Sale £9.99
Peak District by Roly Smith £9.99
Yorkshire Dales by David Leather £9.99

Walking in Britain (FSI)
Outline of access arrangements,
transport, accommodation, parks etc FREE

PATHS AND ROUTES

Angles Way
Norfolk Broads-Suffolk Brecks: route guide with
accommodation by RA Norfolk/Suffolk £2.70

Birmingham Greenway
Sutton Park to Bournville by Fred Willits £4.95

Calderdale Way
Around Calderdale, W Yorks £4.99

Cambrian Way
S-N Wales by Tony Drake £5.50

Capital RING Inner London Circular
Official guide to whole route by
Colin Saunders £12.99

Walking the Ceredigion Coast FREE

Chiltern Way from Hemel Hempstead £9.99

Cleveland Way
Around North York Moors and coast.
National Trail Guide by Ian Sampson £12.99
Accommodation and information guide FREE

Clwydian Way Circular from Prestatyn £6.95

Coast to Coast Walk
St Bees to Robin Hood's Bay
Harvey strip map and guide west:
St Bees to Keld £9.95
Harvey strip map and guide east to
Robin Hood's Bay £9.95
Accommodation guide £4.95

Cotswold Way Chipping Campden to Bath
Guide by Mark Richards £4.95
Harvey strip map and guide £9.95
Handbook: Accommodation list and
practical information £2.00

Cumbria Way Ulverston to Carlisle
Guide by Philip Dubock, including accom £5.95
Harvey strip map and guide £9.95
Accommodation guide also
available separately £1.25

Dales Way
Leeds, Bradford or Ilkley to Bowness
Harvey strip map and guide £9.95
Handbook and accommodation list £1.50

Ebor Way
Helmsley to Ilkley route card pack £4.99

Essex Way Epping to Harwich £3.00

Glyndwr's Way
Knighton to Welshpool £12.99
For accommodation guide see Offa's Dyke Path

Great Glen Way
Fort William to Inverness
Long distance route guide by
Jacquetta Megarry £10.99
Harvey strip map and guide £9.95
Accommodation and services guide FREE

Greater Ridgeway See under Ridgeway

Green Chain Walk
Thames Barrier, Thamesmead, Erith to Chislehurst,
Crystal Palace £3.50

Gritstone Trail Disley to Kidsgrove FREE

Hadrian's Wall Path Wallsend to Bowness
National Trail guide by Anthony Burton £12.99
Essential guide to walking the trail £3.50
Harvey strip map and guide £8.95
Accommodation guide FREE

Heart of England Way Stafford to Bourton
on the Water: Guide by John Roberts £7.50
Accommodation list FREE

Icknield Way See under Ridgeway

Isle of Anglesey Coastal Path
route card pack £1.50

Isle of Wight Coastal Path
and inland trails £3.00

Jubilee Trail (Dorset)
Forde Abbey to Bokerley Dyke £4.50

Jubilee Walkway
Central London map/guide FREE

London Loop
Near-circular walk around outer London. Official
guide to whole route by David Sharp £12.99

Macmillan Way Boston to Abbotsbury £9.00

Macmillan Way West
Castle Cary to Barnstaple £6.25

Monarch's Way Worcester to Shoreham
1 The Midlands: Worcester to Stratford £5.95
2 The Cotswolds, Mendips & Sea,
to Charmouth £6.95
3 The South Coast, The Downs and Escape £6.95

Nene Way
Badby to Wansford, leaflet pack £3.00

New River Path Islington – Hertford FREE

Nidderdale Way circ around
Nidderdale, N Yorks
Route card pack and accommodation list £2.95
Harvey strip map and guide £6.95

North Downs Way Farnham to Dover
National Trail guide £12.99
Harvey strip map and guide west,
to the Medway £9.95
Harvey strip map and guide east, to Dover £9.95

Offa's Dyke Path Chepstow to Prestatyn
National Trail Guide south, to Knighton £12.99
National Trail Guide north, to Prestatyn £12.99
Offa's Dyke/Glyndwr's Way
Accommodation list £4.00

**Walking the Peddars Way & Norfolk
Coast Path** with Weavers Way
Guidebook with accommodation £2.70

Pembrokeshire Coast Path
Amroth to Cardigan
National Trail Guide by Brian John £12.99
Accommodation list £2.50

Pennine Bridleway
Derbyshire to the South Pennines
National Trail Guide £12.99
Harvey strip map and guide £9.95
Accommodation and
information guide FREE

Pennine Way Edale to Kirk Yetholm
National Trail Guide south to Bowes £12.99
National Trail Guide north to Kirk Yetholm £12.99
Accommodation and transport pack FREE

Pilgrim's Trail
Winchester to Portsmouth £2.99

Ridgeway/Greater Ridgeway
(see also Peddars Way)
Ridgeway National Trail Avebury
to Ivinghoe £12.99
National Trail Companion:
accommodation, practical information £3.95
Greater Ridgeway Guide covering Wessex
Ridgeway, Ridgeway National Trail, Icknield Way,
Peddars Way: Lyme Regis to Hunstanton £12.95
Wessex Ridgeway Marlborough
to Shaftesbury £4.50
Icknield Way Ivinghoe to Knettishall Heath £4.50
Icknield Way accommodation list £1.00

Rob Roy Way Drymen to Pitlochry £10.99

Robin Hood Walks
Nottingham to Edwinstowe £4.95

Saints Way Padstow to Fowey £3.99

Sandlings Walk
Ipswich to Southwold £4.75

Sandstone Trail
Frodsham to Whitchurch FREE

Shropshire Way circular from Wem £6.99

Solent Way outline leaflet FREE

Pub Walks along the Solent Way
including full linear route Christchurch to
Emsworth £7.95

South Downs Way
Eastbourne to Winchester. Along the
South Downs Way in both directions £6.00
Harvey strip map and guide £9.95
Accommodation Guide £2.50

South West Coast Path Guide
Concise route directions, accommodation,
practical information £6.00

Southern Upland Way
Portpatrick to Cockburnspath. Long
distance route guide by Anthony Burton £12.99
Accommodation leaflet FREE

Speyside Way
Buckie to Craigelachie, Tomintoul, Aviemore
Long distance route guide £10.99
Accommodation and information FREE

St Cuthberts Way
Lindisfarne to Melrose £9.99

St Swithun's Way
Winchester to Farnham £3.99

Staffordshire Way Mow Cop to Kinver Edge
Official guide £5.00
Accommodation list
(with Way for Millennium) FREE

Stour and Orwell Walk
Felixstowe to Manningtree,
linking with Suffolk Coast and Heaths Path £4.00

Suffolk Coast and Heaths Path
Felixstowe to Lowestoft £4.00

Test Way Inkpen Beacon to Totton FREE

Thames Path Thames Barrier to Source
Official National Trail Guide by
David Sharp £12.99
Thames Path Companion: accommodation,
practical information £4.75

Three Castles Path Windsor to Winchester
Route guide by RA East Berkshire £2.95
Accommodation guide FREE

Trans Pennine Trail (E8)
Map/guide West Irish Sea – Yorkshire £4.95
Map/guide Central Derbyshire & Yorkshire £4.95
Map/guide East Yorkshire – North Sea £4.95
Accommodation and visitor guide £4.95

Two Moors Way Dartmoor to Exmoor
Route guide by Two Moors Way Association £4.95
Accommodation list 50p

Vanguard Way Croydon to Newhaven:
Route guide by Vanguards Rambling Club £2.95

Viking Way
Barton upon Humber to Oakham £3.95

The WaLK round Warwick,
Leamington and Kenilworth 75p

Way for the Millennium
(Staffs) Newport to Burton upon Trent £3.50
For accommodation guide see Staffordshire Way

Wealdway Gravesend to Eastbourne £5.00

Weavers Way See under Peddars Way

Wessex Ridgeway See under Ridgeway

West Highland Way Glasgow to Fort
William. Long distance route guide £14.99
Accommodation, practical information FREE

Wye Valley Walk Chepstow to Plynlimon,
including accommodation guide £9.00

Yorkshire Wolds Way Filey to Hull
National Trail Guide by Roger Ratcliffe £12.99
Harvey strip map and guide £8.95
Accommodation and information guide FREE

WALKING FOR EVERYONE

Walking for Health
by Dr W Bird & V Reynolds. Comprehensive and
accessible full-colour guide £14.99

Take 30
Practical booklet on walking for health FREE

Take 30 Poster
10-week healthy walking plan FREE

Walking for health factsheet (FS18) FREE

Walking for everyone (FS11)
Includes advice on finding easier walks, walking
with children and access to the outdoors for people
with disabilities FREE

Walking: getting started (FS16) FREE

Walking: a useful guide Booklet answering

common questions about walking, with useful
addresses and contacts FREE

Walking facts and figures (FS12) FREE

Preparing Walks Guidebooks £2.50

Discovering new routes
A report of the Volunteers' Conference 2000 on
outreach work FREE

PLEASE NOTE
Postage and packing is charged even on free items. Please see order form on p 38 for details.

Active joints need protecting from the inside as well. Jointace® is an advanced supplement specially designed to safeguard and maintain healthy joints. With Glucosamine, Omega-3 Fish Oil and ten specific vitamins and minerals, Jointace® capsules help keep joints cushioned, supple and flexible. Trust Jointace® to help maintain health and fitness in joints that work out as hard as you do.

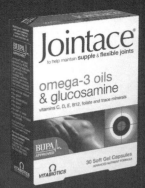

YOU'LL NEED MORE THAN THIS TO PROTECT YOUR JOINTS

ADVANCED NUTRITIONAL SUPPORT FOR JOINTS

Jointace Capsules are part of the jointace family including Jointace® Chondroitin & Glucosamine Tablets, Jointace® Gel and Jointace® Fizz.

www.jointace.com

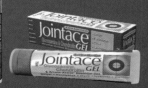

VITABIOTICS

*BUPA
APPROVED

FROM LARGER BOOTS, SUPERDRUG, LEADING SUPERMARKETS, CHEMISTS, HOLLAND & BARRETT, GNC AND HEALTH STORES

'Bupa Approved' logo applies to Jointace Capsules and Jointace Tablets.

TECHNICAL & LEADERSHIP ADVICE

Navigation and Leadership
Practical and official Ramblers' Association guide
for planning and navigating group walks   **£4.00**

Navigation for Walkers
by Julian Tippett, with colour illustrations and
OS map extracts, ideal for beginners   **£8.99**

Maps and navigation (FS2)   **FREE**

Clothing, equipment and safety (FS3)   **FREE**

Leading group walks (FS6)   **FREE**

Leading group walks in remote areas or
demanding conditions (GWSP1)   **FREE**

Walk leader's checklist on laminated
card   **FREE**

Let's Get Going
Advice on leading group walks for people with
disabilities and other special needs
   FREE

Guidelines for Events:
Manual from the Long Distance Walkers
Association on organising challenge walks and
events   **£1.70**

FOOTPATHS, ACCESS, COUNTRYSIDE

Rights of Way:
A guide to law and practice ('Blue Book') 3rd edn
full guide to law in England & Wales   **£20**

Footpath Worker
Authoritative journal on footpath law and related
matters, including regular updates to Rights of Way
4 issues £12   **(free to Groups/Areas)**

Animals and Rights of Way (CAN4)
Walking with your dog, dangerous animals on
paths etc   **FREE**

Basics of Footpath Law (FS7)
Introduction in question and answer form   **FREE**

Defending public paths
What the RA does to defend public paths and how
you can help.   **FREE**

**The Economic and Social Value of
Walking in England**
A report for the Ramblers' Association   **FREE**

Footpath erosion (FS14)
How serious is the problem, and what can walkers
do about it?   **FREE**

Freedom to Roam
A celebratory supplement   **FREE**

**Freedom to Roam in England and
Wales (FS8)**
The Countryside and Rights of
Way Act explained   **FREE**

Golf Courses (CAN2):
Their impact on paths   **FREE**

**Managing conflict over access to
open country**
A case study of the Peak National Park   **FREE**

**Meeting the challenges of the new
millennium**
A proposal for a wider New Forest
National Park   **FREE**

Paths for people
for parish and community councils. Also in
bilingual Welsh/English version   **FREE**

Reporting path problems
Includes a report form and general guidance.
Also available in Welsh
   FREE

**Rights of Way and Development
(CAN3)**
Planning permission and proposed
path changes   **FREE**

**Roads used as Public Paths and
Byways Open To All Traffic (CAN1)**
A detailed guide   **FREE**

You're Either Quick or Dead
Locations where walkers need safe,
convenient road crossings
   FREE

ABOUT THE RAMBLERS

About the Ramblers' Association (FS4)	**FREE**
Annual report 2002/3	**FREE**
Legacies How to remember the Ramblers' Association in your will	**FREE**
Waymarking the future A strategic framework for the growth and development of the RA 2002–2007	**FREE**

Wally Smith 1914-2001 Tribute to a veteran campaigner   **FREE**

Tom Stephenson: A 1970s tribute   **60p**

MAPS: We do not sell walker's maps, but we do maintain a map library which
members can use for a small fee. Please contact us for details.

WALKING INFORMATION ONLINE
An expanding range of the material listed on this page, and more, is available to
download from www.ramblers.org.uk/info

CLOTHING AND BADGES

Sweat shirt green, XL only, half price to clear	**£5.00**
Pin badge oval brass with colour RA logo	**£1.00**
Cloth badge (free with orders over £20)	**£1.00**

PLEASE NOTE
Postage and packing is charged even on free items. Please see order form on p **38** for details.

THE RAMBLERS' BOOKSHOP ORDER FORM

Item	Quantity	Price

Continue on a plain piece of paper if necessary

POSTAGE CHARGES

Please add these as follows:

● **UK Addresses**

Orders up to £4, add £1

Orders over £4 add £1.70 for first item, then £1.50 per item

Orders including Rights of Way (the 'Blue Book'): Minimum p&p charge £5

● **Other European addresses**

Orders up to £4, add £1.50

Orders over £4 add £2.20 for first item, then £1.70 per item

Orders including Rights of Way (the 'Blue Book'): Minimum shipping charge £6.50

● **All other addresses**

Orders up to £4, add £2.20

Orders over £4 add £4 for first item, then £1.70 per item

Orders including Rights of Way (the 'Blue Book'): Minimum shipping charge £12

FREE PUBLICATIONS

● Up to 2 free publications can be ordered without any additional charge when ordered with paid-for items only

● You can order up to two free publications sent on their own to a UK address on payment of a 50p p&p charge.

● Otherwise postage charges per 5 items are: UK addresses £1.50, European addresses £2.50, all other addresses £3.50.

PAYING BY CHEQUE & POSTAL ORDER

We can accept cheques or postal orders in UK pounds, made payable to the Ramblers' Association. We cannot accept cheques in any other currency, including Euro. Please don't send cash in the post.

PAYING BY CREDIT OR DEBIT CARD

We accept Visa, Mastercard, Switch and Delta cards only.

Telephone orders Please call us on 020 7339 8500 (international +44 20 7339 8500) on Mondays to Fridays 10:00–17:00 hrs. You can also take out a membership subscription by telephone.

Internet shopping You can order books and merchandise, make donations and join the Ramblers by credit or debit card at our website, **www.ramblers.org.uk**. You can also view a range of our free literature online at the site.

Total cost of items _____

Total postage (shipping) charges _____

Donation to Ramblers' Association _____

Grand total _____

Name _____

Address _____

Postcode _____   Country _____

Send this form and your payment to:
Ramblers' Association (Sales), 2nd Floor Camelford House, 89 Albert Embankment, London SE1 7TW, UK Please allow 14 days for delivery to UK, 28 days to rest of the world.

Special offer to Readers - 10% off
your first order at Hawkshead

◉ hawkshead

Main Street, Hawkshead Village, The Lake District

www.hawkshead.com

To request a catalogue call 0870 543 4000 or complete the voucher below and hand it in to a store.

✂ -

To claim your 10% discount:

Online - visit www.hawkshead.com and quote 04LQ when prompted at the checkout.
Catalogue - Telephone 0870 543 4000 and quote 04LQ to the operator when ordering.
In store - Complete the voucher below and bring to a store to claim your discount.

Email Address	Name
Address	
Postcode	Tel (incl STD code)

Terms and Conditions: this offer cannot be used in conjunction with any other offer. If you do not wish to be informed of our special offers, promotions and events please tick. ☐ From time to time we make our mailing list available to other reputable, carefully selected companies whose products may interest you. If you do not wish to receive such mailings please tick. ☐

OUR WALKING RANGE IS A STEP AHEAD.

If you're planning on going rambling or walking - for a great range of equipment, head for Millets. For jackets, boots, gloves, hats, compasses, backpacks and much, much more, we have it all. If it's the middle of winter or the height of summer, if it's for a leisurely countryside ramble or a more serious walking trip - if it's for the great outdoors, come and speak to us. You'll find that we know what we're talking about.

millets
THE OUTDOORS STORE

for all walks of life.

Our staff are the best in their field.

Mac, Blacks Norwich,
McMurdo Parka

We've been there and got the base layer.

THE OUTDOOR EXPERTS

The UK's *largest* walking festival *Tel:* 01983 813818

the
Isle of Wight   *7th-22nd May*

walking
festival

ISLE OF WIGHT
2005
WALKING FESTIVAL

LONG DISTANCE PATHS

These pages give information on a selection of long distance walking trails in Britain, offering many thousands of miles of excellent walking through a dramatic variety of landscapes. The trails are cross-referenced with the B&B section. Accommodation within 3.2km/2 miles of paths listed here is indicated as such under its location. Nearly all of them can be used as the basis of shorter walks, or walked in sections as well as in one go on a longer trip.

Some of the routes shown are National Trails and Scottish Long Distance Routes, nationally recognised and funded routes that are signed and maintained to a high standard with quality guides. The other trails have been created by various organisations and individuals, often in cooperation with local authorities and other bodies, and are signed unless otherwise stated, though standards vary. We recommend you always take a path guide and map even when following a well-signed trail.

Map sheet numbers refer to OS Explorer 1:25,000 maps. Explorer and Landranger maps now show the exact line of route for almost all the trails below. For more on maps see p 33.

Luggage carriers and hostel providers are listed at the end of the section. Many accommodation providers are also willing to transfer your luggage: look for the ! symbol in the accommodation section.

Please note we only have room for a selection of routes: there are now many hundreds of promoted walking routes in Britain and every year we regrettably have to delete some entries in order to include new ones while trying to maintain a good spread across the country. The paths and routes section of our website lists many more paths and in much more detail – see ww.ramblers.org.uk/info/paths – and you will find more complete lists in our regional guides (see p 34). The *Long Distance Walkers'*

Publications This year we have expanded the range of books sold from Ramblers main office and guides to most of the trails listed can be obtained from us: see p 34 for details. Publications with ISBN numbers can be ordered from bookshops and internet retailers; otherwise, full ordering details are shown, with TIC indicating a Tourist Information Centre. Guides include at least sketch maps and those marked (OS) have extracts from Ordnance Survey mapping, but taking the relevant OS sheets as well will give you wider view of the area. We have tried to recommend at least one comprehensive guide for each path; others may be available, but space restricts us from listing them all.

If you are planning your first extended walking trip on a long distance route we recommend you practice on day walks before setting out to make sure you can comfortably walk the distance you intend to cover each day. Don't forget that unless you have arranged luggage transfer you will probably be carrying a heavier pack than you would on a day walk.

EASY routes offer generally level walking through areas where transport and assistance are usually close at hand, and while attractive to all, they are especially recommended for the less experienced or energetic.

CHALLENGING routes have sections across difficult or remote terrain, which should only be attempted by those who have a little experience and navigational skill and are properly equipped, especially in bad weather. The majority fall somewhere in between.

Handbook and its accompanying *Long Distance Path Chart*, compiled by the Long Distance Walkers Association, provide a comprehensive overview of routes over 32km/20 miles: both are available from our main office.

Symbols and abbreviations
✳ new listing (may have been included in past yearbooks, but not in recent years).

🔱 National Trail (England and Wales). For more information see www.nationaltrail.gov.uk

🔰 Long Distance Route (Scotland)
(OS) Publication includes Ordnance Survey map extracts

Angles Way
See Peddars Way

Calderdale Way
Circular from Clay House, Greetland
80km/50 miles
Follows old packhorse routes and
moorland paths, circling high up
around the Calder Valley, close to
Halifax, Todmorden and Hebden
Bridge.
MAPS OL21, 288
PUBLICATIONS GUIDE £4.99 + P&P FROM
RAMBLERS MAIN OFFICE
USER GROUP CALDERDALE WAY ASSOCIATION,
16 TRENANCE GARDENS, GREETLAND
HALIFAX HX4 8NN

Cambrian Way
Cardiff to Conwy 440km/274 miles
CHALLENGING
A spectacular but demanding coast to
coast route through Wales, via the
Brecon Beacons, Cader Idris and
Snowdonia, originally proposed by
Ramblers' Association members.
Unsigned.
MAPS OL12, OL13, OL17, OL18, OL23, 151, 152,
187, 213, 215
PUBLICATIONS GUIDE INCLUDING
ACCOMMODATION LISTINGS £5.50 + P&P FROM
RAMBLERS MAIN OFFICE

Capital Ring
See London Loop

Ceredigion Coast Path
See Pembrokeshire Coast Path

Chiltern Way ✳
Circular via Hemel Hempstead with
alternative routes 275km/172 miles
total
Meandering, varied and largely rural
trail stretching from north to south
across the Chilterns AONB and
offering a good cross-section of the
characteristic Chiltern scenery.
Extended with new north and south
loops in 2003.
MAPS 171, 172, 181, 182, 192, 193
PUBLICATIONS GUIDE £9.99 + P&P FROM
RAMBLERS MAIN OFFICE. BOOKS OF CIRCULAR
WALKS AVAILABLE FROM THE BOOK CASTLE,
☎ 01582 605670, WWW.BOOK-CASTLE.CO.UK.

Cleveland Way 🍃
Helmsley to Filey Brigg 177km/110
miles
Horseshoe shaped route around the
northern edge of the North York
Moors to Saltburn, then along coastal
tracks south via Whitby and

Scarborough, all accessible by public
transport. Walkers can continue south
along the Yorkshire Wolds Way. The
Link Through the Tabular Hills
completes the circuit between
Helmsley and the coast near Scalby
(77km/48 miles).
LUGGAGE CARRIERS COAST TO COAST
HOLIDAYS, SHERPA VAN, SPOTLIGHT, YORKSHIRE
WALKING
MAPS OL26, OL27, 301. FOOTPRINT ROUTE MAP
ISBN 1 871149 09 6, £3.50.
PUBLICATIONS GUIDE (OS) £12.99 + P&P,
ACCOMMODATION GUIDE FREE + P&P FROM
RAMBLERS MAIN OFFICE. THE LINK THROUGH THE
TABULAR HILLS WALK ISBN 0 907480 44 6, £3.95
+ £1.25 P&P FROM NORTH YORK MOORS NATIONAL
PARK INFORMATION CENTRES.
CONTACT NATIONAL TRAIL OFFICER
☎ 01439 770657

Clwydian Way
Circular from Prestatyn 195km/122
miles
A circuit around Denbighshire through
splendid but little known walking
country in the Clwydian Hills.
Alternative routes and links give three
shorter circular routes of 67-141km/
42-88 miles.
MAPS 255, 256, 264, 265
PUBLICATIONS GUIDE (OS) £5.95 + P&P
FROM RAMBLERS MAIN OFFICE.
WWW.CLWYDIANWAY.CO.UK

Coast to Coast Walk
St Bees to Robin Hood's Bay
304km/190 miles
CHALLENGING
Famous unsigned route devised by A
Wainwright to link the Irish and North
Seas via remote and spectacular
countryside, including three National
Parks: the Lake District, Yorkshire Dales
and the North York Moors.
LUGGAGE CARRIERS BRIGANTES, COAST TO
COAST HOLIDAYS, COAST TO COAST PACKHORSE,
INSTEP, SHERPA VAN, SPOTLIGHT
HOSTEL BOOKING YHA
MAPS OL4, OL5, OL19, OL26, OL27, OL30, 302,
303, 304. HARVEY ROUTE MAPS ST BEES TO KELD;
AND KELD TO ROBIN HOOD'S BAY. £8.95 + P&P
EACH FROM RAMBLERS MAIN OFFICE.
PUBLICATIONS GUIDE £11.99 + P&P,
ACCOMMODATION GUIDE £4.95 + P&P FROM
RAMBLERS MAIN OFFICE.

Cotswold Way 🍃
Bath to Chipping Campden
163km/101 miles
Scenic, undulating route along the
Cotswold escarpment first proposed
by Gloucestershire Ramblers in the

1950s. Due to be relaunched as a
National Trail in spring 2005: for latest
news about route improvements see
National Trails website. Part of the
Cotswold Round, a lengthy circular
walk (see Macmillan Way).
LUGGAGE CARRIERS COMPASS, SHERPA VAN,
SPOTLIGHT
MAPS OL45, 155, 167, 179. HARVEY ROUTE MAP
£8.95 + P&P FROM RAMBLERS MAIN OFFICE
PUBLICATIONS GUIDE £3.95 + P&P,
HANDBOOK WITH ACCOMMODATION, FACILITIES
AND TRANSPORT £2 + P&P; BOTH FROM RAMBLERS
MAIN OFFICE.
CONTACT NATIONAL TRAIL OFFICE
☎ 01453 827004

Cowal Way ✳
Portavadie to Ardgartan near Arrochar
75km/47 miles
A trail opened in 2003 across the Cowal
peninsula from Loch Fyne to Loch Long,
with grassy hills, heather moorland,
forest plantations, prehistoric heritage
and rich wildlife all within easy reach of
Glasgow. Includes some more remote
and strenuous sections.
MAPS 362, 363, 364
PUBLICATIONS GUIDE £4.99 + P&P FROM
DUNOON VISITOR INFORMATION CENTRE
☎ 08707 200629, OR VIA WEBSITE BELOW.
CONTACT COLINTRAIVE AND GLENDARUEL
COMMUNITY COUNCIL ☎ 01700 841311,
WWW.COLGLEN.CO.UK

Cumbria Way
Ulverston to Carlisle 112km/70 miles
Through the heart of the Lake District
National Park via Langdale and
Borrowdale, Coniston, Derwent
Water and Caldbeck with plenty of
scope for high-level detours. A good
introduction to the area keeping mainly
to the valleys, with some higher
exposed ground.
LUGGAGE CARRIERS BRIGANTES, SHERPA VAN
HOSTEL BOOKING YHA BOOKING BUREAU
MAPS OL4, OL5, OL6, OL7, 315
HARVEY ROUTE MAP £8.95 + P&P FROM RAMBLERS
MAIN OFFICE.
PUBLICATIONS GUIDE £5.95 + P&P FROM
RAMBLERS MAIN OFFICE

Dales Way
Leeds, Shipley or Harrogate to
Bowness-on-Windemere 205km/128
miles total
Originally inspired by local Ramblers,
this fairly easy-going trail links the
Yorkshire Dales and the Lake District.
The 'classic' route runs from Ilkley to
Bowness, and three links connect with
the big towns of the lower Dales.

LUGGAGE CARRIERS BRIGANTES, SHERPA VAN, SPOTLIGHT
MAPS OL2, OL7, OL10, OL30, 297 (MAIN ROUTE), 288 (SHIPLEY), 289 (LEEDS). HARVEY ROUTE MAP INCLUDING ALL THREE LINKS £9.95 + P&P FROM RAMBLERS MAIN OFFICE
PUBLICATIONS GUIDE ISBN 1 870141 53 9, HILLSIDE £6.99. HANDBOOK INCLUDING ACCOMMODATION, FACILITIES AND TRANSPORT £1.50 + P&P FROM RAMBLERS MAIN OFFICE.
USER GROUP DALES WAY ASSOCIATION, 3 MOORFIELD ROAD, ILKLEY LS29 8BL, WWW.DALESWAY.ORG.UK

Essex Way
Epping to Harwich 130km/81 miles
Pioneered by Ramblers and CPRE members, the trail strikes out across quiet countryside via Dedham Vale and Constable country to finish at the Stour estuary. The unwaymarked 24km/15-mile Epping Forest Centenary Walk, created to celebrate the centenary of saving the Forest for public enjoyment, then connects Epping to Manor Park in east London.
MAPS 174, 175, 183, 184
PUBLICATIONS GUIDE £3 + P&P FROM RAMBLERS MAIN OFFICE. CENTENARY WALK GUIDE £1 + 30P P&P FROM EPPING FOREST INFORMATION CENTRE ☎ 020 8508 0028, EPPING.FOREST@CORPOFLONDON.GOV.UK

Fife Coastal Path
North Queensferry to Newport on Tay 107km/67 miles
Around the firths of Forth and Tay, through historic towns and villages, excellent countryside and attractive beaches, combining surfaced seaside promenades and rougher coastal tracks.
MAPS 367, 370, 371
PUBLICATIONS GUIDE £12.99 + P&P FROM RAMBLERS MAIN OFFICE. ROUTE DESCRIPTIONS ON WEBSITE BELOW.
WEBSITE WWW.FIFECOASTALPATH.COM

Glyndwr's Way
Knighton to Welshpool 206km/128 miles
A beautiful route through mid Wales visiting many sites associated with the 15th-century hero Owain Glyndwr. Forms a rough triangle with Offa's Dyke Path as the third side and Machynlleth as its westernmost point.
MAPS 201, 214, 215, 216, 239
PUBLICATIONS GUIDE (OS) £12.99 + P&P FROM RAMBLERS MAIN OFFICE. ACCOMMODATION GUIDE SEE OFFA'S DYKE PATH.
CONTACT NATIONAL TRAIL OFFICER ☎ 01654 703376

Great Glen Way
Fort William to Inverness 117km/73 miles
From the West Highland Way along Glen Mor and the northwest shores of Loch Lochy and Loch Ness, following the course of the Caledonian Canal.
LUGGAGE CARRIERS ABERCHALDER, EASYWAYS, WALKING SUPPORT
INDEPENDENT HOSTELS HIGHLAND HOSTELS, IBHS
MAPS 392, 400, 416. HARVEY ROUTE MAP £9.95 + P&P FROM RAMBLERS MAIN OFFICE.
PUBLICATIONS GUIDE £10.99 + P&P, ACCOMMODATION AND SERVICES GUIDE FREE + P&P FROM RAMBLERS MAIN OFFICE.
CONTACT GREAT GLEN WAY RANGER SERVICE ☎ 01320 366633, WWW.GREATGLENWAY.COM

Hadrian's Wall Path
Newcastle to Bowness on Solway 130km/81 miles
The route along this famous monument, built in AD 122 to mark the northern limit of the Roman empire and now a World Heritage Site, has quickly become one of Britain's most popular long walks.
LUGGAGE CARRIERS SPOTLIGHT, WALKERS BAGGAGE TRANSFER, WALKING SUPPORT
HOSTEL BOOKING YHA
MAPS OL43, 314, 315, 316. HARVEY ROUTE MAP £9.95 + P&P FROM RAMBLERS MAIN OFFICE.
PUBLICATIONS GUIDE (OS) £12.99 + P&P, ESSENTIAL GUIDE TO HADRIAN'S WALL PATH (FACILITIES, TRANSPORT, SUGGESTED ITINERARIES ETC) £3.50 + P&P FROM RAMBLERS MAIN OFFICE. SHORTER AND CIRCULAR WALKS GUIDES FROM INFORMATION LINE (BELOW)
CONTACTS NATIONAL TRAIL OFFICER ☎ 0191 269 1600, HADRIAN'S WALL INFORMATION LINE ☎ 01434 322002, WWW.HADRIANS-WALL.ORG
USER GROUP HADRIAN'S WALL PATH TRUST C/O NATIONAL TRAIL OFFICER

Heart Of England Way
Milford near Stafford to Bourton on the Water 161km/100 miles
A green route across the West Midlands linking Cannock Chase with the Cotswolds, through mainly gentle low-lying country with woodlands, canals and agricultural land.
MAPS OL45, 204, 205, 219, 220, 232, 244
PUBLICATIONS GUIDE £7.50, ACCOMMODATION LIST FREE + P&P FROM RAMBLERS MAIN OFFICE
USER GROUP HEART OF ENGLAND WAY ASSOCIATION, 50 GEORGE ROAD, WATER ORTON, BIRMINGHAM B46 1PE, WWW.HEARTOFENGLANDWAY.ORG

Icknield Way Path
Bledlow to Knettishall Heath near Thetford 206km/128 miles
Follows prehistoric trackways from the Chilterns into East Anglia, passing many sites of archaeological interest and connecting the Ridgeway and Peddars Way as part of a lengthy off-road route along ancient ways between the Dorset coast and the Wash. The historic walker's route runs from Ivinghoe Beacon but there are now alternative multi-user sections from Bledlow to Ivinghoe, running parallel to the Ridgeway, and from Aldbury to Pegsdon (Icknield Way Trail).
MAPS 181, 193, 208, 209, 210, 226, 229
PUBLICATIONS GUIDE (FROM IVINGHOE) £4.50 + P&P, ACCOMMODATION LIST £1 + P&P FROM RAMBLERS MAIN OFFICE. GREATER RIDGEWAY GUIDE: SEE RIDGEWAY. LEAFLET (BLEDLOW - IVINGHOE) FROM BUCKINGHAMSHIRE COUNCIL. ICKNIELD WAY TRAIL LEAFLET FROM NORTH CHILTERNS TRUST, ☎ 01582 412225.
USER GROUP ICKNIELD WAY ASSOCIATION, 9 BOUNDARY ROAD, BISHOPS STORTFORD CM23 5LE, WWW.ICKNIELDWAYPATH.CO.UK

Isle Of Anglesey Coastal Path
Circular via Llanfaethlu, Amlwch, Beaumaris, Holyhead 200km/125 miles
Fairly easy walking through diverse coastal scenery almost entirely within an AONB, with many attractive villages. Easily accessed by bus (details in publication).
MAPS 262, 263
PUBLICATIONS ROUTE CARD PACK £1.50 + P&P FROM RAMBLERS MAIN OFFICE, ALSO VIEWABLE ONLINE (SEE BELOW). NOTE THIS COVERS MOST, THOUGH NOT ALL OF THE PATH AND SHOULD BE USED IN CONJUNCTION WITH MAPS ABOVE. CIRCULAR WALKS LEAFLETS FREE FROM MENTER MÔN (BELOW).
CONTACT MENTER MÔN ☎ 01248 752495, WWW.ANGLESEYCOASTALPATH.COM

Isle Of Wight Coastal Path
Circular from Ryde 105km/65 miles
Attractive island circuit, via chines, saltmarshes, cliffs and holiday resorts, with plenty of accommodation and good public transport links. Connects with a number of other routes heading inland including the 22km/14-mile Tennyson Trail from Carisbrooke to Alum Bay and the 18km/11-mile Bembridge Trail from Shide to Bembridge.
LUGGAGE CARRIER BAG TAG
PUBLICATIONS COASTAL PATH AND INLAND TRAILS GUIDE £3 + P&P FROM RAMBLERS MAIN

OFFICE, OR VIEWABLE ONLINE (SEE BELOW).
CONTACT ISLE OF WIGHT TOURISM
☎ 01983 813800, WWW.ISLANDBREAKS.CO.UK

Jubilee Trail (Dorset)
Forde Abbey to Bokerley Dyke
145km/90 miles

A west-east route across the county
created by local Ramblers, avoiding the
most popular paths to seek out quiet
villages and views of rolling downs and
secret valleys.
MAPS OL15, 116, 117, 118
PUBLICATIONS GUIDE (OS) £4.50 + P&P
FROM RAMBLERS MAIN OFFICE.

Link through the Tabular
Hills Walk See Cleveland Way

London Loop
Erith to Rainham via Kingston, near
circular around Greater London
241km/150 miles EASY
The London Outer Orbital Path,
pioneered by the London Walking
Forum, is a fascinating mix of waterside,
parkland, nature reserves and
countryside on the urban fringe, within
easy reach of central London by public
transport. Sister path the inner orbital
Capital Ring runs for 115km/72 miles
via Woolwich, Crystal Palace,
Richmond and Finsbury Park. Both are
now Transport for London strategic
walking routes.
MAPS 160, 161, 162, 172, 173, 174
PUBLICATIONS LOOP AND RING GUIDEBOOKS
(OS) £12.99 + P&P EACH FROM RAMBLERS MAIN
OFFICE. FREE LEAFLETS FOR SOME SECTIONS ALSO
AVAILABLE: ☎ 0870 240 6094 OR SEE
WWW.TFL.GOV.UK/WALKING

Macmillan Ways
Macmillan Way: Boston to
Abbotsbury 464km/290 miles
Macmillan Way West: Castle Cary
to Barnstaple 163km/102 miles
Abbotsbury-Langport Link:
38.5km/24 miles
Cross-Cotswold Pathway: Banbury
to Bath 138km/86 miles
Cotswold Link: Chipping Campden
to Banbury 33.5km/21 miles
A network of attractive routes
linking the south coast, Bristol channel
and North Sea coast of England,
taking in the Cotswolds, the
Quantocks and the Fens The main
route runs diagonally across England
from south to east, while the western
route links the north Devon coast to
the east coast, or to the south coast
via the Langport link. The Cross-

Cotswold option uses one of the
most popular sections of the main
route with additional town links
providing public transport
connections, while the Cotswold Link
connects with the Cotswold Way
(see above) to create the Cotswold
Round, a 331km/207-mile circuit via
Chipping Campden, Banbury,
Cirencester and Bath.
MAPS MAIN ROUTE/ABBOTSBURY LINK: OL15,
OL45, 117, 129, 142, 156, 168, 191, 206, 207, 223,
233, 234, 248, 249, 261
WEST: OL9, 129, 140, 141, 142
CROSS-COTSWOLD PATHWAY/LINK: OL45, 155, 156,
168, 179, 191, 206
PUBLICATIONS MACMILLAN WAY GUIDE £9 +
P&P, MACMILLAN WAY WEST GUIDE £6.25 +
P&P FROM RAMBLERS MAIN OFFICE. NORTH-SOUTH
SUPPLEMENT FOR THE MAIN ROUTE, GUIDES
TO OTHER LINKS AND SPURS, PLANNERS,
ACCOMMODATION LISTS AND NUMEROUS OTHER
PUBLICATIONS AND MERCHANDISE FROM
CONTACT BELOW.
USER GROUP MACMILLAN WAY ASSOCIATION
☎ 01789 740852, WWW.MACMILLANWAY.ORG

Mary Towneley Loop
See Pennine Bridleway

Midshires Way ❋
Princes Risborough to Stockport
363km/230 miles
A walking link between southern and
northern England, from the Ridgeway
in the Chilterns to the Pennine
Bridleway and Trans Pennine Trail via
historic estates, farmland and the Peak
District National Park. Generally
gentle walking incorporating sections
of numerous other trails including the
North Bucks Way, Brampton Valley
Way and High Peak Trail.
MAPS OL1, OL24, 181, 192, 207, 223, 233, 244,
246, 259, 260, 269
PUBLICATIONS WALKING THE MIDSHIRES WAY,
ISBN 1 850058 778 7. SIGMA £7.95.

Monarch's Way
Worcester to Shoreham 982km/610
miles
Britain's second-longest promoted
route follows in the footsteps of
Charles II on his flight from the Battle
of Worcester, a meandering course
from the West Midlands to the south
coast taking in many historic sights.
MAPS OL45, 116, 117, 119, 120, 121, 122, 129, 130,
131, 132, 141, 142, 143, 155, 167, 168. 204, 205,
218, 219, 220, 221, 242
PUBLICATIONS GUIDE IN THREE VOLS: 1 THE
MIDLANDS £5.95 + P&P; 2 THE COTSWOLDS, THE
MENDIPS AND THE SEA £6.95 + P&P; 3 THE SOUTH

COAST, THE DOWNS AND ESCAPE £6.95 + P&P
FROM RAMBLERS MAIN OFFICE.
USER GROUP MONARCH'S WAY ASSOCIATION
☎ 0121 429 4397
WWW.MONARCHSWAY.50MEGS.COM

Nene Way
Badby to Sutton Bridge 177km/110
miles EASY
Along the valley of the river Nene
as it first meanders through quiet
Northamptonshire countryside
then straightens out onto a canalised
section towards Lincolnshire and
the Wash.
MAPS 207, 223, 224, 227, 234, 235, 249
PUBLICATIONS LEAFLET PACK BADBY TO
WANSFORD £3 + P&P FROM RAMBLERS MAIN
OFFICE. LEAFLET WANSFORD TO WHITTLESEA FREE
FROM PETERBOROUGH COUNCIL PUBLIC RIGHTS
OF WAY OFFICE. LEAFLET WHITTLESEA TO SUTTON
BRIDGE FREE FROM CAMBRIDGESHIRE COUNCIL
PUBLIC RIGHTS OF WAY OFFICE.

Nidderdale Way
Circular from Pateley Bridge 85 km/53
miles
Around the valley of the river Nidd, an
AONB on the edge of the Yorkshire
Dales, including gritstone outcrops and
rough, open moorland.
MAP 298,
HARVEY ROUTE MAP £6.95 + P&P FROM RAMBLERS
MAIN OFFICE.
PUBLICATIONS WALK CARD PACK £2.95 + P&P
FROM RAMBLERS MAIN OFFICE.
CONTACT NIDDERDALE AONB WHO CAN ALSO
GIVE INFORMATION ABOUT BUS SERVICES FOR
WALKERS IN NIDDERDALE.

North Downs Way 🧍
Farnham to Dover 245km/153 miles
Along the chalk ridges and wooded
downland of Surrey into Kent, with
an optional loop via Canterbury, often
running parallel to the ancient
trackway of the Pilgrim's Way. The
55km/24-mile St Swithun's Way
continues along the line of the
trackway from Farnham to
Winchester.
MAPS 137, 138, 145, 146, 147, 148, 150 (AND 132,
144 FOR ST SWITHUN'S WAY)
HARVEY ROUTE MAPS: WEST (FARNHAM TO THE
MEDWAY), EAST (MEDWAY TO DOVER), £9.95 EACH
FROM RAMBLERS MAIN OFFICE.
PUBLICATIONS GUIDE (OS) £12.99, ST
SWITHUN'S WAY GUIDE £3.99 + P&P FROM
RAMBLERS MAIN OFFICE. ACCOMMODATION AND
TRANSPORT DETAILS ON NATIONAL TRAILS
WEBSITE.
CONTACT NATIONAL TRAIL OFFICE
☎ 01622 221525

RICHMOND, LONDON LOOP LONG DISTANCE PATH

Offa's Dyke Path 🔒

Chepstow to Prestatyn 283km/177 miles **CHALLENGING**

A varied walk from the Severn estuary to the Irish Sea through the border country of England and Wales via Knighton, Welshpool and Llangollen, with around 100km/60 miles alongside the 8th century earthwork of Offa's Dyke itself. Although not as challenging as more mountainous routes, there are some remote sections with rough paths and many descents and climbs.

LUGGAGE CARRIERS BYWAYS BREAKS, SPOTLIGHT

MAPS OL13, OL14, 201, 216, 240, 256, 265 STRIP MAPS, OFFA'S DYKE SOUTH TO NORTH AND OFFA'S DYKE NORTH TO SOUTH, FROM OFFA'S DYKE ASSOCIATION (SEE BELOW), £5 + 50P P&P EACH

PUBLICATIONS GUIDES (OS) SOUTH CHEPSTOW TO KNIGHTON AND NORTH KNIGHTON TO PRESTATYN £12.99 + P&P EACH, ACCOMMODATION LIST £4 + P&P FROM RAMBLERS MAIN OFFICE; ROUTE DESCRIPTIONS SOUTH TO NORTH AND NORTH TO SOUTH, A CAMPING AND BACKPACKING GUIDE, CIRCULAR WALKS BOOKS AND NUMEROUS OTHER ITEMS FROM OFFA'S DYKE ASSOCIATION (BELOW).

USER GROUP/CONTACT OFFA'S DYKE ASSOCIATION ☎ 01547 528753

Peddars Way And Norfolk Coast Path

Knettishall Heath near Thetford to Cromer 146km/91 miles **EASY**

Effectively two routes: the Peddar's Way runs northwards through the Norfolk countryside to near Hunstanton, connecting with the Icknield Way path to form the last link in a continuous chain of ancient trackways from the south coast. The coast path then runs eastwards via Sheringham. Many sections are suitable for people with special access needs: more information from the National Trail office (below). Two other easy routes connect to provide a lengthy circuit of Norfolk, the 90km/56-mile Weavers Way from Cromer to Great Yarmouth via the Broads, and the 123km/77-mile Angles Way eastwards along the Waveney and Little Ouse rivers back to Knettishall Heath.

MAPS 229, 236, 250, 252, 252 (AND OL40, 238 FOR WEAVERS WAY; OL40, 230, 231 FOR ANGLES WAY)

PUBLICATIONS PEDDARS WAY/COAST PATH/WEAVERS WAY GUIDE INCLUDING ACCOMMODATION LIST AND ANGLES WAY GUIDE £2.70 + P&P EACH FROM RAMBLERS MAIN OFFICE. NATIONAL TRAIL GUIDE (OS) ISBN 1 85410 852 2, AURUM £12.99. GREATER RIDGEWAY GUIDE: SEE RIDGEWAY. EASY ACCESS INFORMATION ONLINE AT

WWW.NORFOLKCOASTAONB.ORG.UK

CONTACT NATIONAL TRAIL OFFICE ☎ 01328 850530

Pembrokeshire Coast Path 🔒

Amroth to Cardigan 299km/ 186 miles

Some of the most spectacular coastal walking in Britain, mainly along clifftops and almost all within the Pembrokeshire Coast National Park, including Wales' only marine nature reserve and 17 Sites of Special Scientific Interest (SSSIs). Some steep climbs but also sections suitable for people with special access needs. At Cardigan the Path links with the 101km/63-mile Ceredigion Coastal Path, which is still under development but already walkable; both paths will eventually form part of a continuous walking route around the Welsh coast.

LUGGAGE CARRIERS PEMBROKESHIRE DISCOVERY, TONY'S TAXIS

MAPS OL35, OL36 (CEREDIGION COAST OL23, 198, 213)

PUBLICATIONS PEMBROKESHIRE COAST PATH GUIDE (OS) £12.99 + P&P, ACCOMMODATION GUIDE £2.50 + P&P FROM RAMBLERS MAIN OFFICE. EASY ACCESS GUIDE £2.95 + P&P, WALK LEAFLETS FOR INDIVIDUAL SECTIONS AND CIRCULAR WALKS, VARIOUS OTHER PUBLICATIONS FROM PEMBROKESHIRE COAST NATIONAL PARK. WALKING THE CEREDIGION COAST FREE + P&P FROM RAMBLERS MAIN OFFICE. WALKING THE CARDIGAN BAY COAST FROM CARDIGAN TO BORTH, ISBN 1 902302 09 5, KITTIWAKE £3.95.

CONTACT PEMBROKESHIRE COAST NATIONAL PARK

Pennine Bridleway 🔒

Hartington or Middleton Top to Byrness 560km/350 miles

Despite its name, this new National Trail also provides a great route for walkers as well as horse riders and cyclists, running roughly parallel to the Pennine Way but along easier paths to the west of the hilltop. The first substantial section, 188km/117 miles from the Peak District to the South Pennines, opened in 2004, running roughly parallel to the Pennine Way but along lower-lying paths to the west of the hilltops. It includes the Mary Towneley Loop, a 68km/42-mile circuit through the South Pennines around Todmorden and Bacup. The rest is mainly walkable already, though as yet unsigned: see

National Trail website for the latest situation.

MAPS SOUTHERN SECTION OL1, OL21, OL24; NORTHERN SECTION OL2, OL19, OL41 HARVEY ROUTE MAP (SOUTHERN SECTION) £9.95 + P&P FROM RAMBLERS MAIN OFFICE

PUBLICATIONS GUIDE DERBYSHIRE TO THE SOUTH PENNINES £12.99 + P&P, ACCOMMODATION AND SERVICES GUIDE FREE + P&P, FROM RAMBLERS MAIN OFFICE.

CONTACT PENNINE BRIDLEWAY TEAM ☎ 0161 237 1061

Pennine Way 🔒

Edale to Kirk Yetholm 429km/268 miles **CHALLENGING**

Pioneered by Ramblers' campaigner Tom Stephenson and opened in 1965 as Britain's first long distance route, a high and wild trail along the backbone of England from the Peak District to the Scottish borders.

LUGGAGE CARRIERS BRIGANTES, SHERPA VAN, SPOTLIGHT

HOSTEL BOOKING YHA (ASK ABOUT PENNINE HIGHLIGHTS AS A SHORTER ALTERNATIVE TO THE WHOLE WALK)

MAPS OL1, OL2, OL16, OL19, OL21, OL30, OL31, OL42, OL43

PUBLICATIONS GUIDES SOUTH AND NORTH (OS), £12.99 + P&P EACH, INFORMATION PACK INCLUDING TRANSPORT AND ACCOMMODATION, FREE + P&P FROM RAMBLERS MAIN OFFICE.

CONTACT NATIONAL TRAIL OFFICE ☎ 0113 246 9222

USER GROUP PENNINE WAY ASSOCIATION, LANGRIG, SCRABSTER BRAES, THURSO KW14 7UQ WWW.PENNINEWAYASSOCIATION.CO.UK

Ribble Way 🔒

Dolphin Inn, Longton to Gavel Gap, near Hawes 111km/69 miles

A mouth to source walk along this attractive Lancashire river, via Preston, Clitheroe and Settle.

MAPS OL2, OL41

PUBLICATIONS LEAFLET £2.70 FROM SETTLE TIC ☎ 01729 825192, WWW.SETTLE.ORG.UK. A NEW OFFICIAL GUIDE FROM LANCASHIRE COUNCIL IS FORTHCOMING IN 2005.

The Ridgeway 🔒

Overton Hill, near Avebury to Ivinghoe Beacon 137km/85 miles

A route along 'Britain's oldest road' past the ancient hillforts of the North Wessex Downs, across the Thames and through the wooded countryside of the Chilterns. With the Wessex Ridgeway, Icknield Way and Peddars Way it forms a continuous 583km/363-mile walking

route following ancient ways from the south coast to the Wash, the complete route of which is described in the 'Greater Ridgeway' guide below.
MAPS 157, 170, 171, 181
HARVEY ROUTE MAP £9.95 FROM RAMBLERS MAIN OFFICE
PUBLICATIONS GUIDE (OS) £12.99 + P&P, COMPANION (ACCOMMODATION AND SERVICES) £3.95 + P&P, GREATER RIDGEWAY GUIDE (OS) £12.95 + P&P FROM RAMBLERS MAIN OFFICE.
CONTACT NATIONAL TRAILS OFFICE TEL 01865 810224
USER GROUP FRIENDS OF THE RIDGEWAY, 18 HAMPTON PARK, BRISTOL BS6 6LH, WWW.RIDGEWAYFRIENDS.ORG.UK

Rob Roy Way
Drymen to Pitlochry 126km/79 miles
Connecting the West Highland Way with the Tay valley, this unsigned route includes rich woodlands, remote moors and heaths, dramatic mountain views, impressive built heritage and sites connected with Scotland's most famous outlaw, Rob Roy MacGregor (1671–1734).
LUGGAGE CARRIER BIKE AND HIKE, EASYWAYS, LEAPFROGZ, WALKING SUPPORT
MAPS 347, 365, 378, 386
PUBLICATIONS GUIDE £10.99 + P&P FROM RAMBLERS MAIN OFFICE.
WEBSITE WWW.ROBROYWAY.COM

Robin Hood Way
Nottingham Castle to Edwinstowe, with circular alternatives 168km/105 miles
Following in the footsteps of the legendary figure after which it is named, this trail wanders through Sherwood Forest and the Dukeries.
MAPS 260, 270
PUBLICATIONS GUIDE £4.95 + P&P FROM RAMBLERS MAIN OFFICE. EIGHT CIRCULAR WALKS ARE DOWNLOADABLE FROM THE WEBSITE BELOW.
USER GROUP ROBIN HOOD WAY ASSOCIATION 28 WALKER CLOSE, NEWARK NG24 4BP, WWW.ROBINHOODWAY.CO.UK

Sandstone Trail
Frodsham to Whitchurch 51km/32 miles
An airy walk following the sandstone ridge that rises dramatically from the central Cheshire plain, including rock outcrops, woodlands, castles and historic churches. Can be walked easily in three sections of around 17km/10.5 miles each, with a seasonal weekend bus service.

LUGGAGE CARRIER BYWAYS BREAKS
MAPS 257, 267
PUBLICATIONS GUIDE LEAFLET FREE + P&P FROM RAMBLERS MAIN OFFICE, EXPLORER PACK (ACCOMMODATION ETC) FROM CHESHIRE COUNCIL COUNTRYSIDE SERVICES OR SEE WWW.CHESHIRE.GOV.UK/COUNTRYSIDE/WALKING/SANDSTONE_TRAIL.HTML

Saints' Way
Padstow to Fowey 42km/26 miles
Attractive coast to coast trail across Cornwall, following a route possibly taken by the Celtic saints.
MAPS 106, 107
PUBLICATIONS GUIDE £3.99 + P&P FROM RAMBLERS MAIN OFFICE.

Saxon Shore Way
Gravesend to Hastings 261km/163 miles
Intriguing walk around the Roman-era coastline of Kent, along the Thames Estuary, down the Wantsum Channel, along the White Cliffs and on into Sussex.
MAPS 124, 125, 138, 149, 150, 163
PUBLICATIONS AURUM PRESS GUIDE TEMPORARILY OUT OF PRINT AT TIME OF GOING TO PRESS, THOUGH ROUTE IS SHOWN ON OS MAPPING. CONTACT KENT COUNCIL COUNTRYSIDE ACCESS FOR FURTHER INFORMATION AND DETAILS OF CIRCULAR WALKS.
WEBSITE WWW.RURALWAYS.ORG.UK

Severn Way
Plynlimon to Bristol 360km/225 miles
Britain's longest riverside walk follows the Severn from its source in the wild mid Wales moorlands to its wide estuary on the Bristol channel via Welshpool, Shrewsbury, the World Heritage Site at Ironbridge, Worcester and Gloucester. The Way ends officially at Severn Beach (337km/210.5 miles) where a link path continues into central Bristol.
MAPS OL14, 167, 179, 190, 204, 214, 215, 216, 218, 241, 242
PUBLICATIONS GUIDEBOOK £6.95 FROM RECREATION DEPARTMENT, ENVIRONMENT AGENCY MIDLANDS REGION, HAFREN HOUSE, WELSHPOOL ROAD, SHELTON, SHREWSBURY SY3 8BB.
WEBSITE WWW.SEVERNWAY.COM

Shropshire Way
Circular from Shrewsbury with spur to Grindley Brook 264km/164 miles total
A tour devised by local Ramblers, including some of the county's most celebrated landscapes and spectacular views, combining the hilly country of Wenlock Edge, the Long Mynd and the Wrekin with gentler, more pastoral walking in the valleys.

MAPS 203, 216, 217, 241, 242
PUBLICATIONS GUIDE £6.99 + P&P FROM RAMBLERS MAIN OFFICE.

Solent Way
Christchurch to Emsworth 112km/70 miles
Across the south of Hampshire via beaches, clifftops, marshes, heaths, ancient woodlands, riverside villages and the historic waterfronts of Southampton and Portsmouth. The Way is waymarked from Milford but the Pub Walks title describes a route from Christchurch; a further link from Sandbanks (Poole) to Milford, signed as European path E9, connects with the South West Coast Path.
MAPS OL22, 119, 120 (AND OL15 FOR POOLE)
PUBLICATIONS PUB WALKS ALONG THE SOLENT WAY (INCLUDES COMPLETE LINEAR ROUTE) £7.95 + P&P, LEAFLET WITH ROUTE OVERVIEW, FREE + P&P FROM RAMBLERS MAIN OFFICE.
WEBSITE WWW.HANTS.GOV.UK/WALKING/SOLENTWAY

South Downs Way
Eastbourne to Winchester 161km/101 miles
Exhilirating route along the rolling chalk downs of Sussex and Hampshire, through the heart of the future National Park.
MAPS 119 (VERY SMALL PART), 120, 121, 122, 123, 132, HARVEY ROUTE MAP £9.95 + P&P FROM RAMBLERS MAIN OFFICE
PUBLICATIONS ALONG THE SOUTH DOWNS WAY GUIDE IN BOTH DIRECTIONS WITH ACCOMMODATION £6 + P&P, ACCOMMODATION GUIDE £2.50 + P&P FROM RAMBLERS MAIN OFFICE. NATIONAL TRAIL GUIDE (OS) ISBN 1 85410 966 9, AURUM £12.99
CONTACT NATIONAL TRAIL OFFICER ☎ 023 9259 7618

South West Coast Path
Minehead to Poole 1014km/630 miles
Britain's longest national walking route, a spectacular and massively popular continuous path around almost all of the southwest peninsula. Although never too remote, there are some arduous cliff top sections with steep climbs and descents.
LUGGAGE CARRIER RIO'S TAXIS (PART OF ROUTE)
MAPS OL9, OL15, OL20, 102, 103, 104, 105, 106, 107, 108, 110, 111, 115, 116, 126, 139
PUBLICATIONS GUIDEBOOK/ACCOMMODATION £6 + P&P FROM RAMBLERS MAIN OFFICE. NATIONAL TRAIL GUIDES IN FOUR VOLUMES, AURUM £12.99 EACH (OS): MINEHEAD TO PADSTOW

ISBN 1 85410 977 4, PADSTOW TO FALMOUTH. ISBN 1 85410 850 6, FALMOUTH TO EXMOUTH. ISBN 1 85410 768 2, EXMOUTH TO POOLE BY ROLAND TARR, ISBN 1 85410 988 X. SOUTH WEST COAST PATH THE OTHER WAY ROUND, ROUTE DESCRIPTION FROM POOLE TO MINEHEAD TO BE USED IN CONJUNCTION WITH OTHER GUIDES, £3.50 FROM SOUTH WEST COAST PATH ASSOCIATION (SEE BELOW) WHO CAN ALSO SUPPLY OTHER LITERATURE AND MERCHANDISE.
CONTACT NATIONAL TRAIL OFFICER ☎ 01392 383560
USER GROUP SOUTH WEST COAST PATH ASSOCIATION ☎ 01752 896237, WWW.SWCP.ORG.UK

Southern Upland Way ⊕
CHALLENGING
Portpatrick to Cockburnspath
341km/212 miles
Scenic coast to coast trail through southern Scotland via Sanquar, Moffatt and Melrose, combining some remote and demanding stretches with sections suitable for families.
LUGGAGE CARRIERS SOUTHERNUPLANDWAY.COM, WALKING SUPPORT, WAY FORWARD
MAPS OL32, OL44, 309, 310, 320, 321, 322, 328, 329, 330, 345, 346
PUBLICATIONS GUIDEBOOK (OS) £12.99 + P&P; ACCOMMODATION LEAFLET FREE + P&P FROM RAMBLERS MAIN OFFICE. SHORTER WALKS LEAFLETS FROM RANGER SERVICES OR DOWNLOADABLE FROM WEBSITE (SEE BELOW).
CONTACT WESTERN SECTION: DUMFRIES AND GALLOWAY RANGER SERVICE ☎ 01387 260184, EASTERN SECTION: SCOTTISH BORDERS RANGER SERVICE ☎ 01835 830281
WWW.DUMGAL.GOV.UK/SOUTHERNUPLANDWAY

Speyside Way ⊕
Buckie to Craigelachie, Tomintoul or Aviemore 135km/84 miles (total)
Following the fast-flowing river Spey south from the Grampian coast through classic malt whisky country, along forest trails and an old railway track to the famous Highland resort of Aviemore.
MAPS 403, 419, 424
HARVEY ROUTE MAP £9.95 + P&P FROM RAMBLERS MAIN OFFICE
PUBLICATIONS GUIDEBOOK £10.99 + P&P, ACCOMMODATION GUIDE FREE + P&P FROM RAMBLERS MAIN OFFICE.
CONTACT SPEYSIDE WAY RANGER'S OFFICE ☎ 01340 881266, WWW.SPEYSIDEWAY.ORG.UK

St Cuthbert's Way
Melrose to Lindisfarne 100km/62 miles
Pilgrimage path on the border between England and Scotland, following in the footsteps of a 7th century saint and linking the Pennine and Southern Upland Ways. Easy except for a remote upland stretch between Kirk Yetholm and Wooler.
LUGGAGE CARRIERS CARRYLITE, EASYWAYS, SHERPA VAN, SPOTLIGHT, WALKING SUPPORT
MAPS OL16, OL44, 339, 340. HARVEY ROUTE MAP £7.95 (INCLUDED WITH GUIDE BELOW)
PUBLICATIONS GUIDE £9.99 + P&P FROM RAMBLERS MAIN OFFICE. ACCOMMODATION DETAILS ONLINE AT WEBSITE BELOW.
CONTACT BERWICK UPON TWEED TIC ☎ 01289 330733; JEDBURGH TIC ☎ 01835 863435
WEBSITE WWW.STCUTHBERTSWAY.NET

St Swithun's Way
See North Downs Way

Staffordshire Way
Mow Cop Castle to Kinver Edge
148km/93 miles
A north-south route across the county, from gritstone hills on the edge of the Peak District via the steep wooded slopes of the Churnet Valley ('Staffordshire's Rhineland'), Cannock Chase and more gentle pastoral scenery and parkland to the sandstone ridge of Kinver Edge. New sister path The Way for the Millennium, designed for easier walking, crosses at Shugborough on its way from Newport to Burton upon Trent (65km/41 miles).
LUGGAGE CARRIERS OLD FURNACE
MAPS OL24, 219, 242, 244, 259, 268
PUBLICATIONS STAFFORDSHIRE WAY GUIDE £5 + P&P, WAY FOR THE MILLENNIUM GUIDE £3.50 + P&P, ACCOMMODATION LEAFLET FOR BOTH PATHS FREE + P&P FROM RAMBLERS MAIN OFFICE.

Suffolk Coast And Heaths Path
Manningtree to Lowestoft 106km/92 miles **EASY**
Through the tranquil landscapes of an Area of Outstanding Natural Beauty in a less-visited part of England: beaches, estuaries and wild heaths. The original route starts at Felixstowe, while an extension, the Stour and Orwell Walk, negotiates the river estuaries via Ipswich to Manningtree. The 96km/60-mile Sandlings Walk provides an inland alternative through the heathland between Ipswich and Southwold.
MAPS OL40, 197, 212, 231
PUBLICATIONS SUFFOLK COAST & HEATHS AND STOUR & ORWELL GUIDES INCLUDING PUBLIC TRANSPORT AND ACCOMMODATION DETAILS, £4 + P&P; SANDLINGS WALK GUIDE, £4.75 + P&P FROM RAMBLERS MAIN OFFICE.
CONTACT SUFFOLK COAST AND HEATHS PROJECT ☎ 01394 384948, WWW.SUFFOLKCOASTANDHEATHS.ORG

Teesdale Way
Tees Bay, Redcar to Dufton
161km/100 miles
Along the Tees from mouth to source, combining remote Pennine countryside with the Teesside towns, including 10 circular walks. A shorter path, the Tees Link, connects Middlesbrough Dock to High Cliff Nab, Guisborough (17km/10.5 miles) via Guisborough Forest.
MAPS OL26, OL31, 304, 306
PUBLICATIONS LEAFLET GUIDE FREE FROM DARLINGTON COUNCIL; TEES LINK LEAFLET FROM TEES FOREST

Test Way �֎
Inkpen Beacon to Totton (Southampton) 70.5km/44 miles
A north-south route across Hampshire from the dramatic escarpment at Inkpen along the course of the river Test, one of southern England's finest chalk streams, to its tidal marshes at Southampton Water via Stockbridge, Romsey and Totton. Divided into eight sections, all but one of which are linked by buses.
MAPS OL22, 131, 158
PUBLICATIONS LEAFLET TO BE USED IN CONJUNCTION WITH OS MAPS, FREE + P&P FROM RAMBLERS MAIN OFFICE; DETAILED ROUTE DESCRIPTION AT WWW.HANTS.GOV.UK/WALKING/TESTWAY

Thames Path 🚶
Thames Head near Kemble to Dartford Marshes 310 km/194 miles **EASY**
A splendid and massively popular riverside walk pioneered by Ramblers members from the remote Cotswolds to the heart of Britain's biggest city, through world-famous sites such as Oxford, Windsor, the central London riverfront and Greenwich. The National Trail ends officially at the Thames Barrier where a well-signed 16km/10 mile extension continues eastwards towards Erith and the marshes.
MAPS 160, 161, 168, 169, 170, 171, 172, 173, 180
PUBLICATIONS GUIDE (OS) £12.99 + P&P, COMPANION (ACCOMMODATION AND PRACTICAL INFORMATION) £4.50 + P&P FROM RAMBLERS MAIN OFFICE; GUIDE FROM BARRIER TO SOURCE, ISBN 1 85284 270 9, CICERONE £7.99.
CONTACT NATIONAL TRAIL OFFICE ☎ 01865 810224

AVIEMORE, SPEYSIDE WAY LONG DISTANCE PATH

Trans Pennine Trail
Southport to Chesterfield, Leeds, York or Hornsea 560km/350 miles (total)
Multi-user route from Merseyside to Humberside via Stockport (Manchester) and Doncaster, with connecting spurs to Chesterfield via Sheffield, Leeds via Wakefield, York and Beverley linking all the major cities of northern England, interestingly mixing rural and urban walking. Much of the route is wheelchair and pushchair accessible and easily reached by public transport. Walkers following the linear coast to coast route from Southport to Hornsea now need only route maps 1 and 3 below, while map 2 covers the central north-south spurs.
MAPS OLI, 268, 275, 276, 277, 278, 279, 285, 288, 289, 290, 291, 292, 293, 295
ROUTE MAPS:1 IRISH SEA   YORKSHIRE; 2 DERBYSHIRE & YORKSHIRE; 3 YORKSHIRE   NORTH SEA; £4.95 + P&P EACH FROM RAMBLERS MAIN OFFICE.
PUBLICATIONS ACCOMMODATION AND VISITOR GUIDE £4.95 + P&P FROM RAMBLERS MAIN OFFICE, TO BE USED IN CONJUNCTION WITH MAPS ABOVE.
CONTACT TRANS PENNINE TRAIL OFFICE ☎ 01226 772574,
WWW.TRANSPENNINETRAIL.ORG.UK
USER GROUP FRIENDS OF THE TRANS PENNINE TRAIL, 32 DALEBROOK COURT, SHEFFIELD S10 3PQ, RICHARD@HAYNES1.FSNET.CO.UK

Two Moors Way
Ivybridge to Lynmouth 166km/103 miles
Appealing south north route through Devon, linking Dartmoor to Exmoor and the north coast. Unsigned across the moors.
LUGGAGE CARRIERS CAN BE ARRANGED BY ACCOMMODATION PROVIDERS LISTED IN THIS GUIDE
MAPS OL9, OL20, OL28, 113, 114, 127
ILLUSTRATED ROUTE MAP, £1.50 + 50P P&P FROM TWO MOORS WAY ASSOCIATION (SEE BELOW)
PUBLICATIONS GUIDEBOOK £4.95 + P&P; ACCOMMODATION LIST 50P + P&P; BOTH FROM RAMBLERS MAIN OFFICE.
USER GROUP TWO MOORS WAY ASSOCIATION, COPPINS, THE POPLARS, PINHOE, EXETER EX4 9HH

Usk Valley Walk ✳
Caerleon (Newport) to Brecon 77km/48 miles EASY
Along the broad and beautiful valley of the river Usk, between the Brecon Beacons and the Black Mountains. While there are a few short, sharp climbs the route is generally on the level, particularly along the canal sections.
MAPS OL13, OL14, 152
PUBLICATIONS GUIDE £6.95 + 50P P&P FROM MONMOUTHSHIRE COUNTY COUNCIL COUNTRYSIDE

Valeways Millennium Heritage Trail
Circular from St Fagans 111km/ 69 miles
Meandering route through the Vale of Glamorgan, a little-visited but often beautiful area rich in history in the southernmost part of Wales. Circular via Peterston Super Ely, Barry, Cowbridge, Llantwit Major, St Bride's Major and Llanharry with spurs to Ewenny Priory near Bridgend and St Fagans. There are numerous circular walks using parts of the trail, detailed on the Valeways website (below).
MAP 151
PUBLICATIONS ROUTE CARD AND BOOKLET PACK £6.99 + £1.50 P&P FROM VALEWAYS (SEE BELOW).
CONTACT VALEWAYS ☎ 01446 749000, WWW.VALEWAYS.ORG.UK

Vanguard Way
See Wealdway

Viking Way
Barton upon Humber to Oakham 225km/140 miles EASY
From the Humber Bridge south along the Lincolnshire Wolds through territory once occupied by Vikings to Horncastle and Lincoln, finishing near Rutland Water.
MAPS 234, 247, 272, 273, 281, 282, 284
PUBLICATIONS GUIDEBOOK £3.95 + P&P, FACTSHEET INCLUDING ACCOMMODATION FREE + P&P FROM RAMBLERS MAIN OFFICE.

Way for the Millennium
See Staffordshire Way

Wealdway
Gravesend to Eastbourne 129km/ 80 miles
Attractive and surprisingly quiet walk originally devised by local Ramblers from the Thames estuary to the south coast via the Kent and Sussex Weald and Ashdown Forest. The southern section runs parallel and sometimes together with the Vanguard Way, an 107km/66-mile route from Croydon to Newhaven. At Croydon you can continue along the Wandle Trail for 19km/12 miles to join the Thames Path at Wandsworth.
MAPS 123, 135, 147, 148, 163 (AND 146, 161 FOR VANGUARD WAY/WANDLE TRAIL)
PUBLICATIONS WEALDWAY GUIDEBOOK (OS) £5 + P&P, VANGUARD WAY GUIDEBOOK £2.95 + P&P FROM RAMBLERS MAIN OFFICE. WANDLE TRAIL FREE LEAFLET FROM SUTTON LIBRARY ☎ 020 8770 4700, OR SEE WWW.WANDLETRAIL.ORG.

Weavers Way
See Peddars Way

Wessex Ridgeway
Marlborough to Lyme Regis 219km/136 miles
From deepest Wiltshire along ancient paths via the edge of Salisbury Plain and Cranbourne Chase to the Dorset Coast. Connects with the Ridgeway as part of a series of trails linking Wessex and East Anglia.
LUGGAGE TRANSFER RIO'S TAXIS (PART OF ROUTE)
MAPS 116, 117, 118, 130, 143, 157
PUBLICATIONS WILTSHIRE SECTION GUIDE £4.50 + P&P FROM RAMBLERS MAIN OFFICE. COMPLETE GUIDE ISBN 1 85410 613 9, AURUM £12.99 (OS). GREATER RIDGEWAY GUIDE SEE RIDGEWAY.

West Highland Way ⬤
Milngavie, Glasgow   Fort William 153km/95 miles CHALLENGING
A handsome trail, often busy in summer, via Loch Lomond and Rannoch Moor, ending at the foot of Ben Nevis and the start of the Great Glen Way. At the southern end, the 21km/13-mile Kelvin-Allander Walkway connects the Way with central Glasgow.
LUGGAGE CARRIERS AMS, EASYWAYS, LEAPFROGZ, ROBERTSON'S, SPOTLIGHT, TRAVEL-LITE
INDEPENDENT HOSTELS HIGHLAND HOSTELS
MAPS 347, 348, 364, 377, 384, 392 (AND 342 FOR THE WALKWAY)
HARVEY ROUTE MAP £9.95 (INCLUDED WITH GUIDE BELOW)
PUBLICATIONS GUIDE £14.99 + P&P, ACCOMMODATION LEAFLET FREE + P&P FROM RAMBLERS MAIN OFFICE. FIT FOR LIFE! MAP INCLUDING ALL GLASGOW WALKWAYS, FREE FROM GLASGOW TIC, TEL 0141 204 4400
CONTACT WEST HIGHLAND WAY RANGER ☎ 01389 722199,
WWW.WEST HIGHLAND WAY.CO.UK

Wye Valley Walk
Chepstow to Plylimon, Hafren Forest 218km/136 miles
Along the the river Wye via Monmouth, Hereford, Builth Wells

and Rhayader to the source deep in rugged and remote Hafren Forest, crisscrossing the border of England and Wales along dramatic limestone gorges and through rolling countryside and uplands.
MAPS OL13, OL14, 188, 189, 200, 214
PUBLICATIONS GUIDE £9 + P&P FROM RAMBLERS MAIN OFFICE.
WEBSITE WWW.WYEVALLEYWALK.ORG

Yorkshire Wolds Way 🚶

Hessle, Kingston upon Hull to Filey
127 km/79 miles

Formerly known as the Wolds Way, this route through rolling chalk hill country in a little-visited part of Yorkshire links the North Sea coast to the Humber and connects with the Cleveland Way. An Explorer bus runs along the route on summer Sundays and bank holidays: more information from National Trail Office.
MAPS 293, 294, 300, 301
PUBLICATIONS GUIDE (OS) £12.99 + P&P,
ACCOMMODATION GUIDE FREE + P&P FROM RAMBLERS MAIN OFFICE. CIRCULAR WALKS GUIDES AVAILABLE FROM NATIONAL TRAIL OFFICE (SEE BELOW)
CONTACT NATIONAL TRAIL OFFICER
☎ 01439 770657

EUROPEAN LONG DISTANCE PATHS

E-paths, designated by the European Ramblers' Association (ERA), form an international network across the whole of Europe, linking the national and local path networks of member countries. In Britain, they are implemented by the Long Distance Walkers Association, using ferries to connect with other European countries. The E-paths largely follow sections of existing trails and are not waymarked in their own right except at major junctions.

For details of trails shown in bold in the descriptions below, see under the main entries above. For an overview of the E-paths, visit the ERA website (see Useful Contacts p 291). See also the E-paths section at www.ramblers.org.uk/info/paths.

E2 Atlantic – Mediterranean

Stranraer Harwich or Dover
1400km/875 miles

An epic journey taking in the Southern Uplands, Pennines, Yorkshire coast, Wolds and Fens to connect with the ferry for Hoek van Holland. An alternative western route visits the Peak District, Cotswolds, Thames Valley and North Downs on its way to Dover (this western route continues from Oostende on the other side of the English channel but unfortunately there is currently no ferry connection: however it is possible to take the ferry to Calais and follow the E9 coastal path to Oostende). The two routes rejoin in the Belgian Kempen and continue along the famous GR5 via the Ardennes, Lake Geneva and the French Alps to the Mediterranean coast at Nice. An Irish section to the Galway coast is planned, making a total length of 4,850km/3,030 miles.

FROM STRANRAER:
SOUTHERN UPLAND WAY TO MELROSE 258KM/161 MILES
ST CUTHBERT'S WAY TO KIRK YETHOLM 51KM/32 MILES
PENNINE WAY TO MIDDLETON IN TEESDALE 180KM/113 MILES
EASTERN ROUTE VIA HARWICH
TEESDALE WAY AND TEESDALE LINK TO GUISBOROUGH 125KM/77.5 MILES
CLEVELAND WAY TO FILEY 99KM/62 MILES

YORKSHIRE WOLDS WAY TO HESSLE THEN VIA HUMBER BRIDGE TO BARTON UPON HUMBER 131KM/82 MILES
VIKING WAY TO RUTLAND WATER 233KM/146 MILES
HEREWARD WAY TO ELY 117KM/73 MILES BETWEEN STAMFORD AND PETERBOROUGH THE HEREWARD WAY IS NOT THOROUGHLY SIGNED AND THE GUIDE IS CURRENTLY OUT OF PRINT: FOLLOW THE TORPEL WAY OVER ROUGHLY THE SAME ROUTE (SEE BELOW)
FEN RIVERS WAY TO CAMBRIDGE 27KM/17 MILES
ROMAN ROAD LINK TO LINTON 18KM/11 MILES NOT YET SIGNED AND NO GUIDE, BUT THE ROMAN ROAD IS OBVIOUS ON OS MAPS.
ICKNIELD WAY PATH TO STETCHWORTH 15KM/9.5 MILES
STOUR VALLEY PATH TO STRATFORD ST MARY 83KM/52 MILES
ESSEX WAY TO RAMSEY THEN LINK PATH (NOT YET WAYMARKED) TO HARWICH INTERNATIONAL 28KM/17.5 MILES
WESTERN ROUTE VIA DOVER
PENNINE WAY TO STANDEDGE 200KM /125 MILES
OLDHAM WAY TO MOSSLEY 15KM/9.5 MILES
TAMESIDE TRAIL TO BROADBOTTOM 13KM/8 MILES
ETHEROW-GOYT VALLEY WAY TO COMPSTALL 8KM/5 MILES
GOYT WAY TO MARPLE 4KM/2.5 MILES
PEAK FOREST CANAL TO DISLEY 4KM/2.5 MILES
GRITSTONE TRAIL TO RUSHTON SPENCER 33KM/20.5 MILES
STAFFORDSHIRE WAY TO CANNOCK CHASE 76KM/47.5 MILES
HEART OF ENGLAND WAY TO BOURTON-ON-THE-WATER 159KM/99.5 MILES

OXFORDSHIRE WAY TO KIRTLINGTON 41KM/25.5 MILES
OXFORD CANAL WALK TO OXFORD 16KM/10 MILES
THAMES PATH TO WEYBRIDGE 146KM/91 MILES
WEY NAVIGATION TO GUILDFORD 25KM/15.5 MILES
NORTH DOWNS WAY TO DOVER 193KM/120.5 MILES

PUBLICATIONS
HEREWARD WAY OAKHAM TO STAMFORD LEAFLET FREE FROM RUTLAND COUNCIL
TORPEL WAY SEE COUNTRY WALKS AROUND PETERBOROUGH VOL 1, £3 FROM PETERBOROUGH COUNCIL
HEREWARD WAY PETERBOROUGH TO ELY LEAFLET 30P FROM CAMBRIDGESHIRE COUNTY COUNCIL COUNTRYSIDE SERVICES TEAM, ☎ 01223 717445
FEN RIVERS WAY GUIDE £4.50 FROM CAMBRIDGESHIRE RAMBLERS OR SEE WWW.FENRIVERSWAY.ORG.UK
STOUR VALLEY PATH ROUTE CARD PACK £3.50 FROM DEDHAM VALE & STOUR VALLEY COUNTRYSIDE PROJECT ☎ 01473 583176, WWW.DEDHAMVALESTOURVALLEY.ORG
OIDHAM WAY GUIDE £3.49 + STAMP FROM OLDHAM BOROUGH COUNCIL COUNTRYSIDE SERVICES, STRINESDALE CENTRE, HOLGATE STREET, WATERHEAD, OLDHAM OL4 2JW, ☎ 0161 620 8202
TAMESIDE TRAIL ROUTE CARD PACK £3.30 FROM TAMESIDE COUNTRYSIDE SERVICE, PARK BRIDGE HERITAGE CENTRE, THE STABLES, PARK BRIDGE, ASHTON UNDER LYNE OL6 8AQ, ☎ 0161 330 9613, WWW.TAMESIDE.GOV.UK
ETHEROW GOYT VALLEY WAY BOOKLET £2 FROM STOCKPORT RANGER SERVICE, ETHEROW COUNTRY PARK, GEORGE STREET, COMPSTALL, STOCKPORT SK6

5JQ, ☎ 0161 427 6937

GOYT WAY LEAFLET 10P FROM STOCKPORT RANGER SERVICE AS ABOVE.

GRITSTONE TRAIL LEAFLET FREE FROM CHESHIRE COUNCIL OR SEE WWW.CHESHIRE.GOV.UK/COUNTRYSIDE/WALKING/GRITSTONE_TRAIL.HTML

OXFORDSHIRE WAY GUIDE £5.99 + 50P P&P FROM OXFORDSHIRE COUNCIL

OXFORD CANAL FREE LEAFLETS FROM BRITISH WATERWAYS OXFORD CANAL OFFICE ☎ 01788 890666, WWW.YOUROWNTOWPATH.COM

WEY AND GODALMING NAVIGATIONS BOOKLET £3 + 41P P&P FROM NATIONAL TRUST RIVER WEY AND GODALMING NAVIGATIONS OFFICE, DAPDUNE WHARF, WHARF ROAD, GUILDFORD GU1 4RR, ☎ 01483 561389

E8 Atlantic – Istanbul
Liverpool to Hull 300km/188 miles
In Britain this path entirely follows the Trans Pennine Trail (see above), connecting via the Dublin ferry with the Irish Waymarked Ways network. From Rotterdam it strikes out towards the Rhine Valley, the Romantische Straße, the Northern Carpathians and the Bulgarian Rodopi mountains to Svilengrad on the Turkish border, a total of 4,390km/2,750 miles, though some

of the Eastern section of the route is incomplete.

E9 European Coastal Path
Plymouth to Dover 711km/444 miles, plus Isle of Wight loop 68 km/43 miles
Along or parallel to the south coast of England, including some of its most famous coastal sites and two future National Parks. The path provides an alternative to the mainland route of the E9, with which it connects by ferry at Roscoff, Calais and several points between. Additionally, it links the Saxon Shore Way and South West Coast Path to provide a continuous waymarked route of almost 1,000 miles around southern England from Gravesend to Minehead. The complete route will eventually stretch 5000km/3125 miles from Capo de São Vincente in the southwest corner of Portugal to Narva-Jõesuu on the Baltic coast at the Estonian-Russian border.

FROM PLYMOUTH
SOUTH WEST COAST PATH AND FERRY TO POOLE 343KM/214 MILES
E9 (SEE SOLENT WAY) TO MILFORD ON SEA 30KM/19 MILES
SOLENT WAY TO LYMINGTON 11KM/7 MILES

ISLE OF WIGHT LOOP VIA FERRY TO YARMOUTH
ISLE OF WIGHT COASTAL PATH TO THE NEEDLES 11KM/7 MILES
TENNYSON TRAIL (SEE IOW COASTAL PATH) TO CARISBROOK 21KM/13 MILES
E9 LINK TO NEWPORT 5KM/3.5 MILES
BEMBRIDGE TRAIL (SEE IOW COASTAL PATH) TO BEMBRIDGE 18KM/11 MILES
ISLE OF WIGHT COASTAL PATH TO RYDE 13KM/8 MILES THEN FERRY TO PORTSMOUTH

MAIN ROUTE
SOLENT WAY TO PORTSMOUTH, REJOINING ISLE OF WIGHT ALTERNATIVE 60KM/37.5 MILES.
SOLENT WAY TO LANGSTONE HARBOUR, HAVANT 16KM/10 MILES
STAUNTON WAY TO QUEEN ELIZABETH COUNTRY PARK 19KM/12 MILES
SOUTH DOWNS WAY TO JEVINGTON 111KM/69.5 MILES
1066 COUNTRY WALK TO RYE 56KM/35 MILES
SAXON SHORE WAY TO DOVER 65KM/39 MILES

PUBLICATIONS STAUNTON WAY LEAFLET FREE FROM HAMPSHIRE INFORMATION CENTRES ☎ 0800 028 0888 OR SEE WWW.HANTS.GOV.UK/LEISURE/WALKS/STAUNWAY 1066 COUNTRY WALK GUIDE ISBN 1 903568 00 5, CHALLENGE £4.95 (TO BE USED WITH OS MAPS). LEAFLET FROM BATTLE TIC ☎ 01424 773721, OR SEE WWW.1066COUNTRY.COM

LUGGAGE CARRIERS AND HOSTEL BOOKING

Aberchalder ☎ 01809 501411

AMS ☎ 01236 722795, www.amstransfers.com

BAG TAG ☎ 01983 861559, www.bagtagiow.co.uk

Bike and Hike ☎ 01877 339788, www.bikeandhike.co.uk

Brigantes ☎/fax 01729 830463, www.pikedaw.freeserve.co.uk/walks

Byways Breaks ☎/fax 0151 722 8050, www.byways-breaks.co.uk

CarryLite ☎ 01434 634448, www.carrylite.com

Coast to Coast Holidays ☎ 01642 489173, www.coasttocoast-holidays.co.uk

Coast to Coast Packhorse ☎ 017683 42028, www.cumbria.com/packhorse

Compass ☎ 01242 250642, www.compass-holidays.com

Easyways ☎ 01324 714132, www.easyways.com

Highland Hostels fax 01397 772411, www.highland-hostels.co.uk

IBHS www.hostel-scotland.co.uk

InStep ☎/fax 01903 766475, www.instephols.co.uk

Leapfrogz ☎ 01360 660466, www.leapfrogz.co.uk

Old Furnace ☎ 01538 703331, www.oldfurnace.co.uk

Pembrokeshire Discovery ☎ 01437 710720, www.pembrokeshirediscovery.co.uk

Rio's Taxis ☎ 07976 779407, www.lymeregis.com/taxis

Robertson's ☎ 01855 821428, www.lochaberinternet.co.uk/robertsons/westhighlandway.htm

Tony's Taxis ☎ 01437 720931, www.tonystaxis.co.uk

Travel-Lite ☎ 0141 956 7890, www.travel-lite-uk.com

Sherpa Van Project ☎ 0871 520 0124, www.sherpavan.com

southernuplandway.com ☎ 0870 835 8558, www.southernuplandway.com

Spotlight ☎ 0845 661 7131, www.muddybootswelcome.com

SYHA ☎ 0870 155 3255, www.syha.org.uk

Walkers' Baggage Transfer ☎ 0870 990 5549, www.walkersbags.co.uk

Walking Support ☎ 01896 822079, www.walkingsupport.co.uk

Way Forward ☎ 01750 42271, www.thewayforward.org

YHA Booking Bureau ☎ 0870 770 8868, www.yha.org.uk

Yorkshire Walking ☎ 01947 810096

Premier Retailers

Páramo Directional Clothing Systems are only available through selected independent outdoor retailers. Why?

To ensure that you get the best possible service and advice about the Páramo range and its suitability for your needs.

ENGLAND

AMBLESIDE
S.R. Cunningham
Outdoor Centre,
015394 32636,
The Mountain Factor,
015394 32752
ASHTON-UNDER-LYME
Outdoor Action,
0161 343 2151
AYLESBURY
Ramblers,
01296 420163
BACKWORTH
C.W.Tents,
0191 268 0110
BAMFORD
Hitch & Hike,
01433 651013
BAMPTON
Outwear,
01993 851418
CANLEY
Go Outdoors,
02476 671280
CHESTER
Camp & Climb,
01244 311174
CONISTON
Laeking Outdoors,
015394 41733
EXETER
Moorland Rambler,
01392 432681
GLENRIDDING ON
ULLSWATER
Catstycam,
017684 82351

GRASSINGTON
The Mountaineer,
01756 752266
HALIFAX
Hill & Dale,
01422 833360
HARROGATE
Out & About,
01423 561592
HAWES
S.R. Cunningham
Outdoor Centre,
01969 667595
HEMEL HEMPSTEAD
Complete Outdoors,
01442 873133
HOPE VALLEY
CCC Outdoors,
01433 659870,
Hitch & Hike,
01433 623331
HUDDERSFIELD
N.Blackburn,
01484 531561
IPSWICH
Action Outdoors,
01473 211647
KENDAL
Kentdale Outdoor,
015397 29188
KESWICK
Rathbones,
01768 772722
LEEDS
Chevin Trek,
01943 851166
LOUGHBOROUGH
At the Mountain,
01509 212868

MANSFIELD
W.Slack & Sons,
01623 624449
MORPETH
Northumbria
Mountain Sports,
01670 513276
NEWCASTLE-UPON-TYNE
Wildtrak,
0191 261 8582
PICKERING
Ryedale Rambler,
01751 475183
RICHMOND
Altberg,
01748 826922
SETTLE
Castleberg Sports,
01729 823751
SHEFFIELD
CCC Outdoor Equipment,
0114 272 9733,
Foothills,
0114 258 6228
STOCKPORT
Base Camp,
0161 480 2945
STOKE-ON-TRENT
Hi-Peak Leisure,
01782 268102
TAVISTOCK
Kountry Kit,
01822 613089
WAKEFIELD
Mitchells Practical Camping,
01924 272877
WHALLEY,
Whalley Warm & Dry,
01254 822220

WALES
BETWS-Y-COED
S.R. Cunningham
Outdoor Centre,
01690 710454

SCOTLAND
ABOYNE
Hilltrek Clothing,
01339 886062
DUNFERMLINE
Summits Ltd,
01383 620172
FORT WILLIAM
West Coast
Outdoor Leisure,
01397 705777
INVERNESS
W.D. Macpherson & Sons,
01463 711427
PAISLEY
Summits,
0141 887 5536
PEEBLES
Out & About,
01721 723590
STIRLING
C-N-Do Scotland,
01786 445703

IRELAND
BELFAST
Jackson Sports,
02890 238572

PÁRAMO® – *Leaders in comfort and performance*

To find your nearest Páramo Retailer ring us on **01892 786444** or go online at
www.paramo.co.uk and click on 'where to buy' (quote ref: M.RH.04/05)

Páramo Directional Clothing Systems – Unit F, Durgates Industrial Estate, Wadhurst, East Sussex, TN5 6DF

CORNWALL

BRITAINONVIEW/MARTIN BRENT

LYME REGIS, DORSET

The stunning coastline, the rolling countryside, the wild moors, and mild climate, all combine to make South West England a favourite walking destination.

To the north, the Cotswolds extend across Gloucestershire's wide spaces, valleys and woodlands, dotted with typical yellow stone villages, prehistoric monuments and Roman ruins.

Moving south into Wiltshire, the Wessex Ridgeway joins the Ridgeway National Trail at the Avebury Stone Circles. The path then snakes south across the chalky grasslands of Salisbury plain, and down through the rolling wooded landscape of Cranborne Chase to the coast.

Lining Dorset's World Heritage Coast, strewn with 200-million-year-old fossils, are Durdle Door, Lulworth Cove and the Isle of Portland. The Jubilee Trail traverses Thomas Hardy's rustic county, home to such jewels as the castles of Corfe and Portland.

A member says:

"If you're lucky enough, you might see badgers and otters on the Teign River, and looking out from the Salcombe Estuary onto the hilly, green and woody South Hams County is beautiful in its own right".

Somerset is characterised by its timeless villages, secret harbours, and the deer and ponies of Exmoor. The fenland and lakes of the Somerset Levels, with its willow wicker industry and superb wildlife, promise interesting walking, while the quiet wooded valleys of the Quantocks and the Mendip Hills offer views as far as Wales.

Exeter's canal walks, the Tarka Trail and the Two Moors Way, link the moors of Devon through a red sandstone landscape strewn with stone circles. Excellent walking is found on Exmoor and Dartmoor along packhorse trails once used by sailors, monks and smugglers!

Cornwall's rugged coastal cliffs stretch westward, and the sandy beaches to the south sweep across the beautiful estuaries of Camel and Fowey. Windswept Bodmin Moor, wooded valleys, granite outcrops and Bronze Age villages on the Lizard peninsula are natural havens of peace.

Almost all of this region's spectacular coastline can be explored along the South West Coast Path, Britain's longest promoted route.

Long Distance Paths

Cotswold Way	CWD
Heart of England Way	HOE
Jubilee Trail	JBD
Macmillan Way	MCM
Monarch's Way	MON
Offa's Dyke Path	OFD
Ridgeway	RDG
Saint's Way	STW
Severn Way	SVN
Solent Way	SOL
South West Coast Path	SWC
Thames Path	THM
Two Moors Way	2MS
Wessex Ridgeway	WXR
Wye Valley Walk	WVL

Public paths:
37,251km/ 23,133 miles

Mapped access land:

153.4 square miles (Area 3, Central Southern) to date

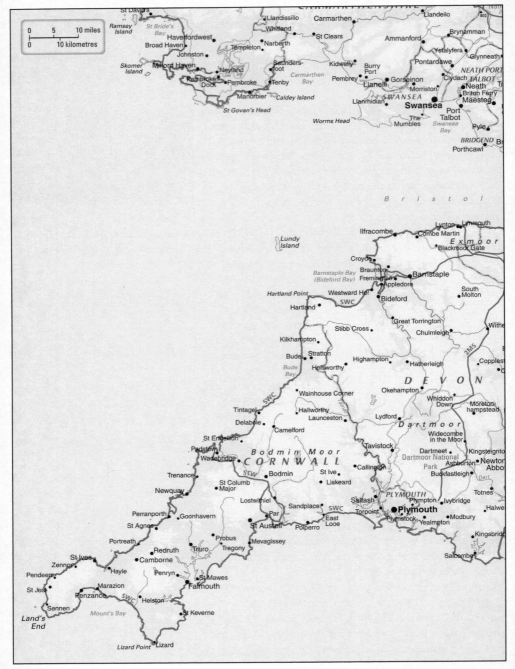

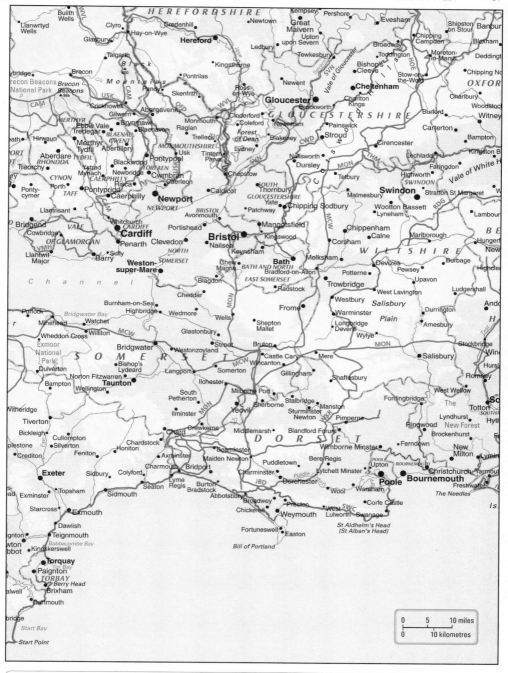

SOUTH WEST
LOCAL RAMBLERS CONTACTS

AVON
AREA SECRETARY
Mrs Julie Dollin, 13 Mountbatten Close, Yate, Bristol, BS37 5TD
julie.dollin@blueyonder.co.uk
http://avon-area.members.beeb.net

GROUP SECRETARIES
Bath Mr E Mcgaul, 24 Heathfield Close, Weston, Bath, BA1 4NW
☎ 01225 313126
www.tompson.demon.co.uk/Bath
ramblers/Bathhome.htm

Bristol Mr John Wrigley, 14 Archfield Road, Cotham, Bristol, BS6 6BE
☎ 0117 924 0125
www.bristolramblers.freeserve.co.uk

Brunel Walking & Activity Ms P M Richardson & Mr A Roberts, 11 Mill Steps, Winterbourne Down, Bristol, BS36 1BT
http://brunelwalking.org.uk

Kingswood Mrs A Page, 8 Northfield Avenue, Bristol, BS15 3RB
www.kingswoodramblers.pwp.
blueyonder.co.uk

Norton Radstock Mrs S Haddon, 4 Dymboro Close, Midsomer Norton, Bath, BA3 2QS

Severnside Jill Fysh, 43a Springfields, Ableton Lane, Severn Beach, Bristol, BS35 4PP ☎ 01454 633001
http://severnside.members.beeb.net

Southwold (Yate) Miss S S Naqui, 3 Brake Close, Sherbourne Park, Bradley Stoke, Bristol, BS32 8BA
☎ 01179 697246
www.bigwig.net/southwold

CORNWALL
AREA SECRETARY
Mrs C James, Chy-Vean, Tresillian, Truro, Cornwall, TR2 4BN ☎ 01872 520368
www.racornwall.org.uk

GROUP SECRETARIES
Bude/Stratton Mr P Judson, Meadowcroft, Bagbury Road, Bude, Cornwall, EX23 8QJ ☎ 01288 356597

Camel District (Wadebridge) Mr R Sheppard, Bramleys, Marshall Road, Nanstallon, Bodmin, Cornwall, PL30 5LD ☎ 01208 832136
www.racamelgroup.org.uk

Caradon Mrs E M Honey, Penyoke Lodge, Church Lane, Cargreen, Saltash, Cornwall, PL12 6NS ☎ 01752 841361

Carrick Mr J B Jennings, 7 Moresk Close, Truro, Cornwall, TR1 1DL
☎ 01872 278317

Newquay Mrs D Hanks, 2 Brewers Road, St Clement Vean, Truro, Cornwall,

TR1 1AJ ☎ 01872 222 367

Restormel Mrs J C Sloan, Westering, Old Hill, Grampound, Truro, TR2 4RY
☎ 01726 883413

West Cornwall (Penwith & Kerrier) Mrs Sylvia Ronan, Trebant, Ludgvan, Church Town, Penzance, TR20 8HH
☎ 01736 740542.

DEVON
AREA SECRETARY
Mrs E M Linfoot, 14 Blaydon Cottages, Blackborough, Cullompton, Devon, EX15 2HJ ☎ 01884 266435
http://website.lineone.net/
~devon.ramblers

GROUP SECRETARIES
Bovey Tracey Mrs P Bray, 17 St Andrews Road, Paignton, Devon, TQ4 6HA ☎ 01803 392182

Devon Bootlegs
Please contact our main office or visit
http://100bootlegs.mysite.freeserve.com

East Devon
Please contact our main office or visit
www.ramblers.org.uk for current details.

Exeter & District Mrs J D Fly, Volant, 53 Bilbie Close, Cullompton, Devon, EX15 1LG ☎ 01884 839 080

Moorland Mr E Smith, 20 Sunningdale Road, Saltash, Cornwall, PL12 4BN
☎ 01752 840491

North Devon Mrs Pauline Newbound, Mauretania, Town Bridge, Burrington, Umberleigh, Devon, EX37 9LT
☎ 01769 520421
http://website.lineone.net/
~northdevon.ramblers

Plymouth
Please contact our main office or visit
www.plymouthramblers.org.uk

South Devon Mr R A Woolcott, The Lodge, 43 Seymour Drive, Watcombe, Torquay, TQ2 8PY ☎ 01803 313430

South Hams Mr Peter Boult, Bridge Cottage, Frogmore, Kingsbridge, Devon, TQ7 2NU ☎ 01548 531701

Tavistock Mrs Rosemary Clarke, 39 Anderton Court, Whitchurch, Tavistock, Devon, PL19 9EX ☎ 01822 615564

Teignmouth & Dawlish Mrs A Mccallister , 21 Southdowns Road, Dawlish, Devon, EX7 0LB
☎ 01626 864046

Tiverton Mrs M A Cox, 18 Anstey Crescent, Tiverton, Devon, EX16 4JR
☎ 01884 256395

Totnes Mrs Thelma Bickford, 9b Headland Park Road, Paignton, Devon, TQ3 2EN ☎ 01803 553310

DORSET
AREA SECRETARY
Mr David Riches, 43 Wyke Rd, Weymouth, Dorset, DT4 9QQ
☎ 01305 784672
www.dorset-ramblers.co.uk

GROUP SECRETARIES
Dorset Younger Walkers
Miss A Coles, 16 Victoria Road, Dorchester, DT1 1SB
www.dorsetyoungwalkers.org.uk

East Dorset Mrs M H Kettlewell, 12 Limited Road, Bournemouth, BH9 1SS ☎ 01202 522467
(membs Enqs J Mcdonald 01202 691709) emkettl@tesco.ne

North Dorset Mr A T Combridge, Green Bushes, North Rd, Sherborne, Dorset, DT9 3JN
☎ 01935 812809

South Dorset Mr Stan Faris, 4 Long Acre, New Street, Portland, Dorset, DT5 1HH ☎ 01305 820957

West Dorset Mr M Green, 17 Hollymoor Lane, Beaminster, Dorset, DT8 3NG

GLOUCESTERSHIRE
AREA SECRETARY
Mrs J M Byrne, 60 Long Mynd Avenue, Cheltenham, Glos, GL51 3QN
☎ 01242 519608

GROUP SECRETARIES
Cirencester
Please contact our main office or visit
www.ramblers.org.uk for current details.

Cleeve Mrs Annie Clement, 22 Denham Close, Woodmancote, Cheltenham, Glos, GL52 9TX ☎ 01242 674866

Forest of Dean Mr C Bolton, Greenbank, Watery Lane, Minsterworth, Gloucester, GL2 8JQ ☎ 01452 750471
http://website.lineone.net/~fredgray/
website.lineone.net/~fredgray

Gloucester Mrs Jean Richards, 26 Hurcombe Way, Brockworth, Gloucester, GL3 4QP
☎ 01452 864451

Gloucestershire Walking Group Ms R James, 25 Highwood Avenue, Cheltenham, Glos, GL53 0JJ
☎ 01242 516 368

Mid-Gloucestershire Mrs E Sutcliffe, 21 Fortina Close, Cheltenham, GL50 4RB ☎ 01242 700525

North Cotswold Mr J D Clark, Stone Cottage, The Green, Lower Brailes, Banbury, Oxford, OX15 5HZ
☎ 01608 685 597

South Cotswold Mr B Smith &
Mrs J Smith, 139 Thrupp Lane, Thrupp,
Stroud, GL5 2DQ ☎ 01453 884 013
www.southcotswoldramblers.org.uk

HAMPSHIRE
AREA SECRETARY
Mr G Clift, 124 Anmore Road,
Denmead, Waterlooville, PO7 6NZ
☎ 023 92241812
www.hants.gov.uk/hampshireramblers

GROUP SECRETARIES
Alton Mrs G M Siddall, Peachings,
South Town Road, Medstead, Alton,
Hampshire, GU34 5ES
☎ 01420 564339

Andover Mr P L & Mrs M Wood,
9 Kingsmead, Anna Valley, Andover,
Hampshire, SP11 7PN
☎ 01264 710 844
www.hants.gov.uk/raag

Eastleigh Mrs P D Beazley, 16
Windover Close, Bitterne, Southampton,
SO19 5JS ☎ 02380 437443
www.hants.org.uk/eastleighramblers

Hampshire 20s & 30s Walking Group
Miss R V Lee, 8 Clare Court, 67 Howard
Road, Southampton, SO15 5BG
☎ 023 8033 2069
[membs Enqs 0798 6655660]
www.hants.gov.uk/hantswalk2030

Meon Mrs C Coxwell, 19 New Road,
Fareham, Hants., PO16 7SR
☎ 01329 827790)
claire.coxwell@talk.co.uk

New Forest Mrs Audrey Wilson,
16 West Road, Dibden Purlieu,
Southampton, SO45 4RJ
☎ 023 8084 6353

North East Hants Mr Brian Austen,
Kappa Crucis, Hillside Road, Farnham,
Surrey, GU9 9DW
☎ 01252 314826

North Hampshire Downs
Mr Mike Taylor, 19 Inkpen Gardens,
Lychpit, Basingstoke, Hants, RG24 8YQ
☎ 01256 842468

Portsmouth Mrs M G Haly,
95 Winstanley Road, Stamshaw,
Portsmouth, Hants, PO2 8JS
☎ 023 92693874

Romsey Mr T W Radford,
67 Rownhams Lane, North Baddesley,
Southampton, SO52 9HR
☎ 02380 731279
www.romseynet.org.uk/ramblers/
ramblers.htm

South East Hants Mr D Nixon,
27 Brading Avenue, Southsea, Hants,
PO4 9QJ ☎ 023 9273 2649
www.hants.org.uk/sehantsramblers

Southampton Mrs Janet Foskett,
2 Ambleside, Sholing, Southampton,
SO19 8EY ☎ 02380 363177
www.hants.gov.uk/sotonram

Waltham Mrs W E Bassom, 3 Mayfair
Court, Botley, Southampton, SO30 2GT
☎ 01489 784946

MENDIP HILLS, SOMERSET

Wessex Weekend Walkers
Ms H E Stacey, 18 Langham Close,
North Baddesley, Southampton,
SO52 9NT ☎ 07884 486676
www.wessexweekendwalkers.org.uk

Winchester Mr D Mason, Berkswell,
Rewlands Drive, Winchester, Hants,
SO22 6PA ☎ 01962 883135
www.hants.gov.uk/wramblers

SOMERSET
AREA SECRETARY
Mrs M Henry, 22 Linden Grove,
Taunton, Somerset, TA1 1EF
☎ 01823 333369
www.somersetramblers.org.uk

GROUP SECRETARIES
Clevedon Mrs Sue Shewan,
25 Honeylands, Portishead, Bristol,
BS20 6RB
☎ 01275 848075
www.somersetramblers.org.uk

Family Countryside Walkers
Stephanie Griffitts, 37 Hamlyn Road,
Glastonbury, BA6 8HT
☎ 01458 837818

Mendip Mrs M M Lugg, Tumbleweed,
4 Keward, Glastonbury Road, Wells,
Somerset, BA5 1TR ☎ 01749 674030

Sedgemoor Mrs M Thomas, Ashford
Lodge, Cannington, Bridgwater,
Somerset, TA5 2NL
ashfordlodge@aol.com

Somerset Walking & Activity
Miss H F Morrall, 73 Eaton Crescent,
Taunton, TA2 7UE

South Somerset Mr I L Rendall,
3a Tintern, Abbey Manor Park, Yeovil,
Somerset, BA21 3SJ
☎ 01935 421235
www.manatons.nildram.co.uk

Taunton Deane Mr A F Welsman,
Stonegallows House, Stonegallowshill,
Taunton, Somerset, TA1 5JS
☎ 01823 461811
www.tauntonramblers.org.uk

West Somerset Dr L A M Evans,
Woodpeckers, Bossington Lane, Porlock,
Minehead, TA24 8HD ☎ 01643 862170

Woodspring Julie Westgarth,
20 Ivybridge, Tavistock Road, Weston-
Super-Mare, BS22 6LP ☎ 01934 518537

WILTSHIRE & SWINDON
AREA SECRETARY
Mrs Pat Crabb, Frenshams, Turnball,
Chiseldon, Swindon, SN4 0LJ
☎ 01793 741471
www.ramblers-wilts.org.uk

GROUP SECRETARIES
Chippenham Mrs Kath Parkinson,
6 Silbury Road, Curzon Park, Calne,
Wiltshire, SN11 0ES ☎ 01249 811445

Mid Wiltshire Mrs Linda Gilder,
1 Moggs Lane, Calstone, Calne,
SN11 8QD ☎ 01249 814008
www.ramblers-wilts.org.uk

North East Wilts Mrs Joan Crosbee,
2 Kennet View, Fyfield, Marlborough,
Wiltshire, SN8 1PU ☎ 01672 861359

South Wiltshire Mrs Sue Austen,
8 Harnwood Road, Salisbury, Wiltshire,
SP2 8DD ☎ 01722 339755

West Wiltshire Mrs Jill Elliott, 152 Bath
Road, Bradford-On-Avon, Wilts, BA15
1SS ☎ 01225 862566

Wiltshire Wanderers Mr S M Nation,
21 Brynards Hill, Wootton Bassett,
Swindon, Wiltshire, SN4 7ER
☎ 01793 852327
http://homepage.ntlworld.com/
ron-di/ypg.htm

LOCAL RAMBLERS PUBLICATIONS

A Rambler's Guide to the Dorset Jubilee Trail

A comprehensive guide with maps to this 145km/90-mile walk. ISBN 1 901184 04 8, £4.50 + 50p p&p from Jubilee Trail Contact, 19 Shaston Crescent, Dorchester DT1 2EB. Cheques to Ramblers Association – Dorset Area.

Bristol Triangular City Walk

A 28km/18-mile circuit of the easily walked as three sections of between 6 km/4 miles and 13km/8 miles connected by public transport. Developed by Bristol Ramblers in association with the City Council.
£1.50 from 57 Somerset Road, Bristol BS4 2HT. Cheques to Bristol Group Ramblers' Association. Free from local outlets.

Bristol Backs: Discovering Bristol on Foot

compiled by Peter Gould, jointly published with Bristol City Council, ISBN 1 901184 52 8. 27 walks of between 3km/2 miles and 17.5km/11 miles in the city.
£6.99 + £1.50 p&p from 57 Somerset Road, Bristol BS4 2HT, bristolbacks@aol.com. Cheques to Bristol Group Ramblers' Association.

Channel to Channel Seaton-Watchet

by Ken Young: 80km/50-mile rural walk across the southwest peninsula.
£2 + 50p p&p from K Young, 14 Wilton Orchard, Taunton TA1 3SA. Cheques to K Young.

Cirencester Circuit

A moderate 16km/10 mile walk around Cirencester, £1 + 40p p&p; and Walks Around Cirencester, a moderate 9.5km/6 mile walk from Cirencester to Duntisbourne, 80p + 40p p&p from 80 Melmore Gardens, Cirencester GL7 1NS. Cheques to Cirencester Ramblers.

Cotswold Way Handbook & Accommodation List

ISBN 1 901184 62 5. £2 + 50p p&p from Mail Order Secretary, Tudor Cottage, Berrow, Malvern WR13 6JJ. Cheques to Ramblers' Association Gloucestershire Area.

Forest of Dean East

40p + 30p p&p from Mail Order Secretary, Tudor Cottage, Berrow, Malvern WR13 6JJ. Cheques to Ramblers' Association Gloucestershire Area.

The Glevum Way

42km/26 mile circular walk around Gloucester. 50p + 30p p&p from The Knoll, Crifty Craft Lane, Churchdown GL3 2DH. Cheques to Ramblers Association Gloucester Group.

The Kennet & Avon Wiggly Walks Guide

Three walks 3km/2 miles to 19km/12 miles, along the Vale of Pewsey and the Kennet and Avon Canal. Produced by the Kennet and Avon Canal Rural Transport Partnership with assistance from the Ramblers. Free from 01249 460600.

More Favourite Walks in the South Cotswolds

15 fully graded and illustrated walks of between 3km/2 miles and 22.5km/14 miles. £3.50 + 45p from Southcot, The Headlands, Stroud GL5 5PS. Cheques to South Cotswold Ramblers. See also www.southcotswoldramblers.org.uk for online updates of the book.

North Cotswold Diamond Way

30 sparkling short walks by Elizabeth Bell (North Cotswold Ramblers): recently revised edition presenting this 96km/60-mile circular route via Moreton-on-Marsh, devised to celebrate the Ramblers' diamond jubilee in 1975, as 30 linked shorter (around 8km/5 mile) circular walks. £6.95 + £2 p&p from Holly Tree House, Evenlode GL56 0NT. Cheques to Ramblers' Association North Cotswold Group.

Northeast Wiltshire Ramblers Publications:

Eleven Half-day Walks in N.E. Wiltshire by Phil Claridge. Circular walks of 7km/4.5 miles to 9km/5.5 miles. £1.80
Nine Downland Walks between Swindon and Marlborough: between 5km/3 miles and 12km/7.5 miles on the Downs. £1.80
Ten walks from village pubs near Swindon by Pat Crabb. Short circular walks of 2km/1.5 miles to 8km/5 miles with bus routes given where appropriate. £2
Twelve Walks around Marlborough between 5.5km/3.5 miles and 14.5km/9 miles. £1.80
20 Walks around Swindon between 3km/2 miles and 12km/7.5 miles, within a 30km/20-mile radius of Swindon. £2.30
All from 21 Brynards Hill, Wootton Bassett, Swindon SN4 7ER. Cheques to Ramblers' Association NE Wilts Group.

Rambles in the Roseland

(6 walks 4km/2.5 miles to 9km/5.5 miles)

Six Circular Coast and Country Walks on the Lizard
(6.5km/4 miles to 11km/7 miles)
Six Coastal Walks with Inland Returns in or on The Lizard
(5.5km/3.5 miles to 13km/8 miles)
Six Coastal Walks with Inland Returns in Penwith 1
(3km/2 miles to 11km/7 miles)
Six Coastal Walks with Inland Returns in Penwith 2
(3km/2 miles to 11km/7 miles)
Six Walks around Falmouth 1
(3km/2 miles to 11km/7 miles)
Six Walks around Falmouth 2
(3km/2 miles to 11km/7 miles)
Six North Cornwall Walks 1
(5km/3 miles to 9.5km/6 miles)
Six North Cornwall Walks 2
(5.5km/3.5 miles to 13km/8 miles)
Six Walks from Truro
(6.5km/4 miles to 11km/7 miles)
Wendron's Church and Chapels Walks (6 walks 6.5km/4 miles to 8km/ 5 miles)
All £1.25 each from Publicity Officer, 2 Lanaton Road, Penryn TR10 8RB. Cheques to Cornwall Area, Ramblers' Association.

Samaritans Way South West

by Graham Hoyle. Linking Bristol with the Cotswold Way National Trail and the South West Coast Path, 160km/100 miles. £5.45 from Samaritans Way SW Association, 6 Mervyn Road, Bristol BS7 9EL or email samaritansway@aol.com. Cheques to Samaritans Way SW.

Sarum Way A circular walk around Salisbury and Wilton.

Booklet £3.50 from 27 Richard Way, Salisbury SP2 8NT. Cheques to South Wilts Ramblers Group.

Six Walks in Chipping Sodbury

by South Gloucestershire Council and Southwold Ramblers. Leaflets are: Work and Play, Golf Course and Common, The Sodbury Round, Old Sodbury and Kingrove Common, Kingrove Common and Codrington, Paddocks and Ponds. Free from Chipping Sodbury Tourist Information Centre, The Clock Tower, Chipping Sodbury BS37 6AH ☎ 01454 888686.

Somerset Walks

by Taunton Deane Ramblers, illustrated by Ann Sharp, ISBN 1 901184 69 2. 16 circular walks 6.5km/4 miles to 22.5km/14 miles. (New this year)
£2.95 + 50p p&p from Greenway Thatch, North Curry, Taunton TA3 6NH. Cheques to Taunton Deane Ramblers.

Wiltshire
Why walk anywhere else?

- Stunning scenery to enjoy
- 3,800 miles of paths to walk
- 9 brand new walks on Salisbury Plain to discover, plus many, many more
- Great accommodation to suit all pockets
- Super pubs, restaurants and coffee shops to indulge in - after the walk!

Make sure you stay a while in
Wiltshire

Please go to
www.visitwiltshire.co.uk
to download walks from the interactive map,
book accommodation online, or order a walking book.
Or ring the brochure line on **0870 240 5599**

South Wiltshire Ramblers Publications:
8 easy walks in the Salisbury Area
10 shorter walks in the Salisbury Area
10 longer walks in the Salisbury Area
Card packs in plastic wallet
All £3.50 each from 27 Richard Way, Salisbury SP2 8NT. Cheques to South Wilts Ramblers Group.

Walks Around Dawlish
by Teignmouth and Dawlish Ramblers, published with Dawlish Town Council. Leaflet pack of seven illustrated walks around the town.
£2 from Dawlish Town Council, The Manor House, Old Town Street, Dawlish EX7 9AP ☎ *01626 863388. Cheques to Dawlish Town Council*

Walk West *and* Walk West Again
by Geoff Mullett (Avon Ramblers): 30 country walks of between 6.5km/4 miles and 22.5km/14 miles, and second volume (ISBN 1 901184 61 7) of walks from 6.5km/4 miles to 19km/12 miles, within easy reach of Bristol and Bath.
£7.99 each from 12 Gadshill Drive, Stoke Gifford, Bristol BS34 8UX. Cheques to Geoff Mullett.
For information and updates visit walk-west.members.beeb.net

Waymarked Trails in the Forest of Dean and Highmeadow Woods
Leaflet describing two circular walks, the Beechenhurst Trail and the Highmeadow Trail.
60p + 30p p&p as North Cotswold Diamond Way above.

West Wiltshire Ramblers Publications:
Ten Walks in West Wiltshire
10 circular walks between 6.5km/4 miles and 17.5km/11 miles, including some near railway stations. *£2.50.*
Walking in West Wiltshire Book 2 10 circular walks between 6.5km/4 miles and 11km/7 miles, including some near railway stations. *£1.25.*
Walking in West Wiltshire Book 3 10 circular walks between 8km/5 miles and 16km/10 miles, including some near railway stations, with sketch maps. *£1.25 All from 68 Savernake Avenue, Melksham SN12 7HE. Cheques to West Wilts Ramblers' Association.*

Yate Walks Leaflets
by Yate Town Council and Southwold Ramblers. Three leaflets: Brimshaw Manor Walk, Stanshawes Walk and Upstream & Downstream Walk. *Free from Yate Town Council, Poole Court, Poole Court Drive, Yate BS37 5PP.*

Ten Walks Around Devizes Varied walks of between 6.5km/4 miles and 11km/7 miles starting at Devizes market place. *£1.50 + 40p p&p from 1 Copings Close, Devizes SN10 5BW. Cheques to Ramblers' Association Mid Wilts Group.*

12 Walks Around Chippenham by Chippenham Ramblers, ISBN 1 000 3388 6. Varied selection of 4km/2.5-mile to 11km/8-mile walks, all using public transport. (New this year)
£2 from 11A High Street, Sutton Benger SN15 4RE. Cheques to Ramblers' Association Chippenham Group.

PORLOCK, SOMERSET

BARNSTAPLE	91 High Street X31 1HR
BATH	"6 Southgate Centre, The Mall" BA1 1QF
BODMIN	27/31 Fore Street PL31 2HT
BOSCOMBE	13 Sovereign Centre BH1 4SX
BRIDGWATER	5 Fore Street TA6 3NQ
BRISTOL	10 Broadmead BS1 3HH
CHELTENHAM	117 High Street GL50 1DW
CHIPPENHAM	17/18 High Street SN15 3ER
CIRENCESTER	6 Dyer Street GL7 2PF
DEVIZES	29 The Brittox SN1 01AJ
DORCHESTER	16 Cornhill DT1 1BQ
EXETER	207 High Street EX4 3EB
EXMOUTH	42 Chapel Street EX8 1HW
FALMOUTH	11 Market Strand TR11 3DB
GLOUCESTER	4 Southgate Street GL1 2DH
NEWTON ABBOT	2 Queen Street TQ12 2EF
PAIGNTON	37/39 Victoria Street TQ4 5DD
PENZANCE	105 Market Jew Street TR18 2LE
PLYMOUTH	39/40 New George Street PL1 1RW
POOLE	9 Kingland Crescent BH15 1TA
SALISBURY	38/39 Old George Mall SP1 2AF
SHREWSBURY	6/7 Mardol Head SY1 1HD
STROUD	34 Kendrick Street GL5 1AQ
TAUNTON	20 East Street TA1 3LP
TORQUAY	49 Union Street TQ1 1ET
TROWBRIDGE	40 The Shires BA14 8AT
TRURO	11 Pydar Street TR1 2AX
WESTON-S-MARE	98 High Street BS23 1HS
WEYMOUTH	74 St Mary Street DT14 8PJ
YATE	5 West Walk BS37 4AX
YEOVIL	22 Middle Street BA20 1LY
GUERNSEY	9 The Pollett GY1 1WQ
JERSEY	29/31 King Street JE2 4WS

BED & BREAKFAST

CORNWALL

● **Boscastle**
South West Coast Path

The Old Coach House, Tintagel Road, PL35 0AS
☎ 01840 250398   www.old-coach.co.uk   Map 190/098906
BB **B**   ✕ nearby   D4 TI F3   🅱 🅳 ⊛ 🐾👜👟🎒! ⛺   ◆◆◆◆

◥◣◢ Trerosewill Farm, Paradise , PL35 0BL   ☎ 01840 250545
(Mrs Cheryl Nicholls) www.trerosewill.co.uk   Map 190/098904
BB **B**   ✕ nearby   D3 TI F2
🅱 🅳 ⊛ 🐾👜👟🎒!⛺(M)   ◆◆◆◆◆(S)

Lower Meadows, Penally Hill, PL35 0HF   ☎ 01840 250570
(Anne & Adrian Prescott) www.lowermeadows.co.uk   Map 190,200/101913
BB **B/C**   ✕ nearby   D4 TI   🅱 🅳 ⊛ 🐾👜👟!   ◆◆◆◆

● **Bude**
South West Coast Path

◥◣◢ Pencarrol Guest House, 21 Downs View, EX23 8RF ☎ 01288 352478
(M & E Payne)   pencarrolbude@aol.com   Map 190/207071
BB **B**   ✕ nearby   S2 D3 TI FI   Closed Dec
🅱 🅳 ⊛ 🐾👜👟! ◆◆◆◆

◥◣◢ St Merryn, Coast View, Stratton, EX23 8AG ☎ 01288 352058
(Eileen Abbott) www.stmerryn.org.uk   Map 190/223062
BB **A**   ✕ nearby   SI DI TI FI
🅳 ⊛ 🐾👜👟🎒!⛺   Disabled access.

Links Side, 7 Burn View, EX23 8BY   ☎ 01288 352410 (Beryl Thomas)
www.linksside.co.uk   Map 190/219066
BB **B**   ✕ nearby   SI D/T/S5 F2   🅱 🅳 ⊛ 🐾👜⛺   ◆◆◆◆

◥◣◢ Tee-side Guest House, 2 Burn View, EX23 8BY ☎ 01288 352351
(Mrs June Downes) www.tee-side.co.uk   Map 190/208066
BB **B**   ✕ book first £14, 6:30pm   D2 T2
🆅 🅱 🅳 ⊛ 🐾👜👟   ◆◆◆◆

◥◣◢ Conna-Mara, Maer Down Rd, EX23 8NG ☎ 01288 356340
www.visitwestcountry.com/connamara   Map 190/205072
BB **B**   ✕ book first £10, 6:30pm   TI F2
🆅 🅱 🅳 ⊛ 🐾👜👟!⛺   ◆◆◆

◥◣◢ Riverview B&B, 2 Granville Terrace, EX23 8JZ ☎ 01288 359399
(Ann & Martin Venning) vennings@beeb.net Map 190/207065
BB **B**   ✕ nearby   D2 TI   🅱 🅳 ⊛ 🐾👜👟🎒   ◆◆◆◆

The Greenhouse, 16 Burn View, EX23 8BZ   ☎ 01288 355587
(Kevin & Yvette Queen) www.greenhousebude.co.uk   Map 190/210066
BB **B**   ✕ nearby   DI TI FI   🅱 🅳 ⊛ 🐾👜👟!⛺

┌─────────────────────────────
☆ **Harefield Cottage**
Upton, EX23 0LY ☎ 01288 352350 (Sally-Ann Trewin)
www.coast-countryside.co.uk   Map 190/202048
BB **B**   ✕ book first £10-£11, 6:30pm   DI TI FI
🆅 🅱 🐾👜👟🎒   ◆◆◆◆(S)

Only 250 yards from coastal footpath and
1/2 mile from the Natural Cycle Network. We
offer 3 en-suite bedrooms with luxurious
beds, TV, hospitality tray and hairdryer.
Excellent home-cooked evening meals are
available on request, using local and fresh
produce. All special diets catered for.
└─────────────────────────────

● **Camelford**
◥◣◢ The Countryman Hotel, Victoria Road, PL32 9XA ☎ 01840 212250
(Mrs Deborah Reeve) www.cornwall-online.co.uk/countryman Map 200/108839
BB **B**   ✕ book first £10, 7-8:30pm   S2 D3 T2 F3
🆅 🅱 🅳 ⊛ 🐾👜👟🎒!⛺   ◆◆◆   Guided walks.

Kings Acre Hotel, PL32 9UR ☎ 01840 213561 (Lynda & Graham)
www.kings-acre.com   Map 200/100842
BB **B**   ✕ £6, until 8:30pm   S2 D3 TI FI
🆅 🅱 🅳 ⊛ 🐾👜👟🎒!   ◆◆◆◆

● **Carbis Bay (St Ives)**
South West Coast Path
◥◣◢ Coast Vegetarian B&B, St Ives Rd, TR26 2RT ☎ 01736 795918
www.coastcornwall.co.uk   Map 203/524385
BB **B**   ✕ £6.45-£12.95, 6-8pm   D5 TI F2   ∞(Carbis Bay)
🆅 🅱 🅳 ⊛ 🐾👜

● **Coverack (Helston)**
South West Coast Path
Mellan House, TR12 6TH ☎ 01326 280482 (Mrs Muriel Fairhurst)
hmfmdcov@aol.com   Map 204/780186
BB **B**   ✕ nearby   SI DI TI   🅱 🅳 ⊛ 🐾👜👟!⛺

● **Cury (Mullion)**
South West Coast Path

┌─────────────────────────────
☆ **Cobblers Cottage**
Nantithet, TR12 7RB ☎ 01326 241342 (Mrs Hilary Lugg)
Map 203/681223
BB **B**   ✕ book first £14, 6:30pm   D2 TI
🅱 🅳 ⊛ 🐾👜👟   ◆◆◆◆◆(S)

This picturesque 17th century
riverside cottage, set in an acre of
beautiful gardens is situated just
2 1/2 miles from the SW Coast
Path. All bedrooms en-suite.
Evening dinner optional. Colour
brochure available.
└─────────────────────────────

● **East Looe**
South West Coast Path
Marwinthy Guest House, East Cliff, PL13 1DE ☎ 01503 264382
(Eddie Mawby) www.marwinthy.co.uk   Map 201/256533
BB **B**   ✕ nearby   D2 TI FI   Closed Nov-Jan   ∞(Looe) 🅱 🅳 👟🎒

● **Falmouth**
South West Coast Path
The Grove Hotel, Grove Place, TR11 4AU ☎ 01326 319577
www.thegrovehotel.net   Map 204/814323
BB **A**   ✕ book first £9, 7-9pm   S2 D3 T6 F4   ∞(Falmouth Town)
🆅 🅱 🅳 🐾👜👟🎒!(M)   ◆◆◆◆

Lerryn Hotel, De Pass Road, TR11 4BJ ☎ 01326 312489 (Ann Picken)
www.thelerrynhotel.co.uk   Map 204/813319
BB **C**   ✕ book first £16, 6:30-8pm   S4 D6 T8 F2   ∞(Falmouth Town)
🆅 🅱 🅳 ⊛ 🐾👜👟🎒!⛺

Wickham, 21 Gyllyngvase Terrace, TR11 4DL ☎ 01326 311140
(Steve & Jenny Lake) www.wickham-hotel.co.uk   Map 204/810318
BB **B**   ✕ nearby   S2 D2 T/F2   Closed Nov-Feb   ∞(Falmouth Town)
🅱 ⊛ 🐾👜   ◆◆◆

● Fowey

South West Coast Path & Saints Way

4 Daglands Road, PL23 IJL ☎ 01726 833164 (John & Carol Eardley)
www.jabedesign.co.uk/keverne Map 200/123518
BB **B** ✕ nearby D2 Closed Dec-Jan 🄱 🄳 ⊛ 🐾🛏🚗! 🥾 Ⓜ

☆ **Wringford**
Golant, PL23 ILA ☎ 01726 83220 (Liz Barclay)
Map 200/114548
BB **B** ✕ book first £12, 7-8pm SI TI Closed Dec-Jan
Ⓥ 🄱 🄳 ⊛ 🐾🛏🚗 🥾

Organically run smallholding in the Fowey River Valley, on the Saints Way, 3 miles from the south coast. No television. Evening meals for walkers only and by arrangement. Privacy and atmosphere. 1 twin en-suite £28 pp, 1 single £25pp. The kettle is always on!

● Golberdon (Callington)

🚌🚲 Keadeen, PLI7 7LT ☎ 01579 384197 (Mrs Geraldine Parkyn)
family@parkyn.charitydays.co.uk Map 201/329714
BB **B** ✕ nearby SI DI TI 🄱 🄳 ⊛ 🐾🛏

● Hayle

South West Coast Path

54 Penpol Terrace, TR27 4BQ ☎ 01736 752855 (Mrs Anne Cooper)
annejohn@cooper827.fsnet.co.uk Map 203/558374
BB **B** ✕ nearby SI DI TI Closed Dec 🚌(Hayle)
🄳 🐾🛏🚗! Ⓜ

● Helston

South West Coast Path

Lyndale Cottage Guest House, 4 Greenbank, Meneage Road, TRI3 8JA
☎ 01326 561082 (Mrs Sarah Payne) Map 203/663267
BB **B** ✕ nearby SI D3 TI FI 🄱 🄳 ⊛ 🐾🛏 Ⓜ ◆◆◆

🚌🚲 Carmelin, Pentreath Lane, The Lizard, TRI2 7NY ☎ 01326 290677
(Mrs Jane Grierson) www.bedandbreakfastcornwall.co.uk Map 203/699126
BB **B** ✕ £10.50, 7-8pm SI DI Ⓥ 🄱 🄳 ⊛ 🐾🛏🚗!🥾

● Lanivet (Bodmin)

Saints Way

Willowbrook, Old Coach Road, Lamorick, PL30 5HB ☎ 01208 831670
(Annie & George Miles) mileswillowbrook@onetel.com Map 200/037646
BB **B** ✕ nearby SI D2 TI 🄳 ⊛ 🛏🚗 ◆◆◆◆

Rosehill Cottage Guest House, Rosehill, PL30 5ES ☎ 01208 831965 (Nick & Fiona Bruckin) www.rosehillcottage.freeserve.co.uk Map 200/038648
BB **B** ✕ nearby D2 TI FI 🄱 🄳 ⊛ 🛏🥾

● Liskeard

Elnor Guest House, I Russell Street, PLI4 4BP ☎ 01579 342472
(Mr & Mrs B J Slocombe) elnor@btopenworld.com Map 201/250642
BB **B** ✕ nearby S4 DI TI F3 🚌(Liskeard)
🄱 🄳 ⊛ 🐾🛏

● Luchett (Callington)

🚌🚲 Higher Trowes, PLI7 8LH ☎ 01579 370890 (Jan & Phil Roper)
higher_trowes@btopenworld.com Map 201/383737

BB **B** ✕ book first £5-£12, 6-9pm SI T/FI
Ⓥ 🄱 🄳 ⊛ 🐾🛏🚗!🥾

● Luxulyan (Bodmin)

Saints Way

🚌🚲 Tor View, Corgee Farm, PL30 5DS ☎ 01726 850340 (Clare Hugo)
www.torviewcentre.co.uk Map 200/049604
BB **B** SI D2 TI F4 🚌(Luxulyan)
🄱 🄳 🛏🥾 ! 🥾 See Groups also.

● Mawgan Porth (Newquay)

South West Coast Path

🚌🚲 Trevarrian Lodge, Trevarrian, TR8 4AQ ☎ 01637 860156
www.trevarrianlodge.co.uk Map 200/851661
BB **B** ✕ nearby S3 D3 TI F2 🄱 🄳 🐾🛏🚗! ◆◆

☆ 🚌🚲 **Kernow Trek Lodge**
Trevarrian, TR8 4AQ ☎ 01637 860437 (Tim & Elaine Uff)
www.activityholidayscornwall.co.uk Map 200/850661
BB **C** ✕ nearby T5 F3 Closed Jan-Feb
🄱 🄳 ⊛ 🐾🛏🚗!🥾 Ⓜ ◆◆◆

Kernow Trek Lodge is Cornwall's base camp. Designed for walkers — by walkers.

8 modern comfortable bedrooms, choice of en-suite and non-ensuite. Offering easy access to the SW Coast Path between Newquay and Padstow.

Small hamlet location with village pub. Facilities include drying room, full 16 seat licensed mini-bus service, secure lock-up for kit, decking/BBQ area, range of local walks, weekend and full week guided packages and other activities.

Email: info@activityholidayscornwall.co.uk   RAC 3 sparkling diamonds.

● Mevagissey (St Austell)

South West Coast Path

🚌🚲 The Spa Hotel, Polkirt Hill, PL26 6UY ☎ 01726 842244
(Mr & Mrs Schofield) www.spahotel-cornwall.co.uk Map 204/015443
BB **B** ✕ £15, 6:30-7pm SI D4 T2 F4 Closed Dec-Feb
Ⓥ 🄱 🄳 🐾🛏🥾 ★★

● Morwenstow (Bude)

South West Coast Path

Cornakey Farm, EX23 9SS ☎ 01288 331260 (Monica Heywood)
Map 190/208157 BB **B** ✕ book first £12, 6:30pm DI TI FI Closed Dec
Ⓥ 🄱 🄳 ⊛ 🐾🛏🚗! ◆◆◆

● Mullion (Helston)

South West Coast Path

Campden House, The Commons, TRI2 7HZ ☎ 01326 240365 (Joan Hyde)
Map 203/677194 BB **A/B** ✕ £7.50, 6:30pm S2 D2 TI F2
Ⓥ 🄱 🄳 🐾🛏🥾

Criggan Mill, Mullion Cove, TRI2 7EU ☎ 01326 240496
(Mike & Jackie Bolton) www.crigganmill.co.uk Map 203/667180
BB **B** ✕ book first £9 S4 D4 T4 F4
Ⓥ 🄱 🄳 🐾🛏🥾!🥾 ★★★★★ See SC also.

Trenance Farmhouse, TR12 7HB ☎ 01326 240639
www.trenancefarmholidays.co.uk   Map 203/673185
BB **B**   ✗ nearby   D4 TI   Closed Oct-Feb
🅑 🅓 ⊗ 🐾 🛆 ! 🔥 Ⓜ   ◆◆◆◆

● Newquay

South West Coast Path

Chichester, 14 Bay View Terrace, TR7 2LR ☎ 01637 874216 (S R Harper)
http://freespace.virgin.net/sheila.harper   Map 200/813614
BB **A**   ✗ book first £6, 6:30pm   S2 D2 T2 FI   Closed Dec-Feb
ᴍᴍ(Newquay) Ⓥ 🅑 🅓 🐾 🛆 🔥 Ⓜ   ◆   See Walking Holidays also.

Roma Guest House, 1 Atlantic Road, TR7 1QJ ☎ 01637 875085
(Mrs P Williams)   www.romaguesthouse.co.uk   Map 200/803616
BB **B**   ✗ book first £9, 6pm   SI D2 TI F2   ᴍᴍ(Newquay)
Ⓥ 🅑 🅓 🐾 🛆 !

The Three Tees Hotel, 21 Carminow Way, TR7 3AY ☎ 01637 872055
(Greg & Fiona Dolan)   www.3tees.co.uk   Map 200/823622
BB **B**   ✗ book first £10, 6pm   D4 TI F4   ᴍᴍ(Newquay)
Ⓥ 🅑 🅓 🐾 🛆 🔥   ◆◆◆

Dewolf Guest House, 100 Henver Rd, TR7 3BL ☎ 01637 874746
www.dewolfguesthouse.com   Map 200/828620
BB **B/C**   ✗ book first £9.50, 6pm   SI D3 TI FI   ᴍᴍ(Newquay)
Ⓥ 🅑 🅓 🐾 🛆 🔥

Malmar Hotel, Trenance, Mawgan Porth, TR8 4BA ☎ 01637 860324
(Pippa & James McLuskie)   www.malmarhotel.com   Map 200/849671
BB **B**   ✗ £12, 7-8pm   D9 TI FI   Ⓥ 🅑 🅓 🐾 🛆 🚗 ! 🔥

● Padstow

South West Coast Path & Saints Way

Estuary Views, 8 Treverbyn Road, PL28 8DW ☎ 01841 532551
(Mr W E Champion)   www.smoothhound.co.uk/hotels/estuaryviews
Map 200/921749   BB **B**   ✗ nearby   D2 TI   🅑 🅓 ⊗ 🐾 🛆 ! 🔥

☆ **Trevorrick Farm**
St Issey, PL27 7QH ☎ 01841 540574 (Mr & Mrs M Benwell)
www.trevorrick.co.uk   Map 200/921732
BB **B**   ✗ nearby   D2 TI
🅑 🅓 ⊗ 🛆 !   ◆◆◆

Magnificent location near Padstow. Warm welcome — tea and homemade cake. Pub/restaurant half a mile. Ideal walking/touring base; visiting Eden. Easy footpath access to Camel Trail, Padstow and coast path. Heated swimming pool (seasonal).

● Par

South West Coast Path & Saints Way

No 3 Guesthouse, 3 Tywardreath Highway, PL24 2RW ☎ 01726 816112
(Pat Taylor) http://website.lineone.net/%7Eroyl0/index.htm   Map 200/077556
BB **B** ✗ book first £12.50, 6:30 onwards   SI DI FI   ᴍᴍ(Par)
Ⓥ 🅓 ⊗ 🐾 🛆 ! 🔥

● Pendoggett (Port Isaac)

South West Coast Path

Lane End Farm, PL30 3HH ☎ 01208 880013 (Mrs Linda Monk)
nabmonk@tiscali.co.uk   Map 200/026793   BB **B**   ✗ nearby   SI DI TI
Ⓥ 🅑 🅓 ⊗ 🐾 🛆 🚗 ! Ⓜ   ◆◆◆◆ See SC also.

● Penryn (Falmouth)

South West Coast Path

62 St Thomas Street, TR10 8JP ☎ 01326 374473
(Brian & Penny Ward)   Map 204/786341
BB **A**   ✗ nearby   SI D2 TI FI   Closed Nov-Feb   ᴍᴍ(Penryn) 🅓 🐾 Ⓜ

Sunnyside Bed & Breakfast, Treluswell, Four Cross, TR10 9AN
☎ 01326 379254   (Cathy & Gordon Milton)
www.sunnyside_cornwall.btinternet.co.uk   Map 204/770362
BB **B**   ✗ book first £10   SI DI T2   Ⓥ 🅑 🅓 ⊗ 🐾 🛆 🚗 !

● Penzance

South West Coast Path

Woodstock Guest House, 29 Morrab Road, TR18 4EZ ☎ 01736 369049
(Anne & David Peach)   www.woodstockguesthouse.co.uk   Map 203/472300
BB **B**   ✗ nearby   S3 D3 TI FI   Closed Jan   ᴍᴍ(Penzance)
🅑 ⊗ 🐾 🛆 🚗 ! 🔥 Ⓜ   ◆◆◆

☆ **Torre Vene**
Lescudjack Terrace, TR18 3AE
☎ 01736 364103 (Mrs G Ash)   Map 203/475308
BB **B**   ✗ nearby   S2 D4 T4 F4   ᴍᴍ(Penzance)
🅓 🐾 🛆

Well-appointed guesthouse, delightful views of harbour, Mount's Bay.
Friendly home from home atmosphere.
Ideal overnight stop for Isles of Scilly.
Close to railway, coach stations and coastal paths.
Good home cooking.
A warm welcome awaits you.

☆ **Trewella Guest House**
18 Mennaye Road, TR18 4NG ☎ 01736 363818 (Shan & Dave Glenn)
www.trewella.co.uk   Map 203/469298
BB **B**   ✗ nearby   S2 D4 F2   Closed Nov-Feb   ᴍᴍ(Penzance)
🅑 ⊗ 🛆   ◆◆◆

A warm welcome awaits you at Trewella.
Fully non-smoking, single to triple en-suite rooms.
One mile from main bus/train station, town centre 10 mins walk. Ideal centre for west Cornwall and South West Coast Path.
Discount for 3 or more days.
Email: shan.dave@lineone.net

☆ **Dunedin Hotel**
Alexandra Rd, TR18 4LZ ☎ 01736 362652 (John Bolton)
www.dunedinhotel.co.uk   Map 203/466299
BB **B**   ✗ nearby   SI D5 F2   ᴍᴍ(Penzance)
🅑 🅓 ⊗ 🐾 🛆

A large Victorian house built in 1886, it has 7 tastefully furnished bedrooms, with modern en-suite facilities, TV, radio-alarm, hairdryer and tea/coffee making facilities. Situated on a wide tree-lined avenue leading to the seafront, with its long promenade and sheltered bay.

● Perranporth

South West Coast Path

Chy An Kerensa, Cliff Road, TR6 0DR ☎ 01872 572470 (W Woodcock)
Map 200,203/754543   BB **B**   ✕ nearby   S2 D2 T2 F3
B D 🛏🚗🛁❗🖫 ◆◆◆

☞🛏 Cliffside Hotel, Cliff Rd, TR6 0DR ☎ 01872 573297 (Maureen Burch)
www.cliffsideperranporth.co.uk   Map 200/754544
BB **B**   ✕ book first £10, 6:30-7pm   S3 D5 T1 F2   V B D 🛁🖫

● Polruan (Fowey)

South West Coast Path & Saints Way

Quayside Guest House, The Quay, PL23 1PA ☎ 01726 870377
(Robyn Richley)   quayside-house@tiscali.co.uk   Map 200/125510
BB **B**   ✕ nearby   D3 T1   B D ⊗🛏🛁🚗❗

● Port Isaac

South West Coast Path

☞🛏 Long Cross Hotel & Victorian Garden, Trelights, PL29 3TF
☎ 01208 880243 (D J Crawford) www.longcrosshotel.co.uk Map 200/988795
BB **B**   ✕ £6.75, 6:30-9:30pm   S12 D12 T4 F3
V B D 🛏🛁🛁❗🖫   ◆◆◆

☆ **Anchorage**

The Terrace, PL29 3SG ☎ 01208 880629 (Colin & Maxine Durston)
www.anchorageportisaac.co.uk   Map 200/999807
BB **B**   ✕ book first £10, 7pm   S2 D3 T1 F1   Closed Jan
V B D ⊗🛏🛁❗   ◆◆◆◆

Stunning sea views.
Perfectly situated on the north Cornish
coastal path.
Contact Colin and Maxine Durston

● Porthcurno (Penzance)

South West Coast Path

☞🛏 Sea View House, The Valley, TR19 6JX ☎ 01736 810638 (Susan Davis)
www.seaviewhouseporthcurno.com   Map 203/383227
BB **B**   ✕ book first £13, 5:30-7:30pm   S1 D3 T/D2   Closed Nov-Jan
V B D ⊗🛏🛁🛁❗🖫 Ⓜ

☞🛏 Porthcurno Hotel, The Valley, TR19 6JX ☎ 01736 810119
www.porthcurnohotel.co.uk   Map 203/383227
BB **B**   ✕ book first £22.50, 6-8pm   D/S5 T/S6 F1
V B D 🛏🛁❗🖫   ◆◆◆◆

● Redruth

☞🛏 Tre Vab Yowann, 6 Trevingey Rd, TR15 3DG ☎ 01209 211352
(Margaret Johnson)   www.uk-photos.co.uk/cornwall.htm   Map 203/694425
BB **B**   ✕ book first £10   S1 D1   ᴡᴡ(Redruth)
V B D ⊗🛏🛁🚗❗🖫

● Relubbus (Penzance)

South West Coast Path

☞🛏 Relubbus House, TR20 9EP ☎ 01736 762796 (Chris & Ann Hatton)
www.relubbushouse.co.uk   Map 203/567319
BB **B**   ✕ book first £10, 6-7pm   D2 T2   Closed Jan-Feb
V B D ⊗🛏🛁🚗❗Ⓜ

● Ruan-High-Lanes (Truro)

South West Coast Path

☆ **New Gonitor Farm**

TR2 5LE ☎ 01872 501345
Map 204/905416
BB **B**   ✕ nearby   D1 T1   Closed Dec-Jan
B D ⊗🛏🛁🛁

Stay at our comfortable
farmhouse in the beautiful
Roseland. Wonderful coastal walks
and NT gardens within the local
area. Also, Lost Gardens of
Heligan and Eden Project. En-suite
rooms, traditional farmhouse fare.

● Sennen (Penzance)

South West Coast Path

Treeve Moor House, TR19 7AE ☎ 01736 871284 (Liz Trenary)
www.firstandlastcottages.co.uk   Map 203/353251
BB **B**   ✕ nearby   D1 T1
B D 🛁🚗❗   ◆◆◆◆

● St Agnes

South West Coast Path

Penkerris, Penwinnick Road, TR5 0PA ☎ 01872 552262 (Mrs Gill-Carey)
www.penkerris.co.uk   Map 204/720501
BB **B**   ✕ book first £12.50, 6:30pm   D/S/F4 T/F3
V B D 🛏🛁🖫   ◆◆

● St Austell

South West Coast Path

Spindrift, London Apprentice, PL26 7AR ☎ 01726 69316 (Mrs Mcguffie)
www.spindrift-guesthouse.co.uk   Map 204/007501
BB **B**   ✕ nearby   D1 F2   B ⊗🛁🖫   ◆◆◆ See SC also.

● St Issey (Wadebridge)

South West Coast Path & Saints Way

Manor House Activity & Development Centre, PL27 7QB ☎ 01841 540346
(Lesley Kirk)   www.manoractivitycentre.co.uk   Map 200/927717
BB **B**   ✕ book first £8-£12   T4 F5
V B D ⊗🛏🛁🚗❗ See SC & Groups also.

● St Ives

South West Coast Path

☞🛏 Ren-roy Guest House, 2 Ventnor Terrace, TR26 1DY
☎ 01736 796971 (Mrs M E McPherson)   Map 203/515405
BB **B**   ✕ nearby   S2 D2 T1 F1   ᴡᴡ(St Ives) B D 🛏🚗❗Ⓜ
☞🛏 Ten Steps, Fish St, TR26 1LT ☎ 01736 798222 (Lydia Dean-Barrows)
www.tenstepsbandb.co.uk   Map 203/519408
BB **B**   ✕ nearby   S1 D1 T1 F1   ᴡᴡ(St Ives)
B D ⊗🛏🛁🚗❗   ◆◆◆◆ Veggie breakfasts.

● St Just (Penzance)

South West Coast Path

The Farmhouse, Bollowal, TR19 7NP ☎ 01736 788458 (Mrs Jo Hill)
johanna.hill@btinternet.com   Map 203/359314
BB **A**   ✕ nearby   S1 D1   Closed Jan-Feb   ⊗🛁🚗 See SC also.

⌫⊴ Cobweb Cottage, 6 Botallack Corner, Botallack, TR19 7QG
☎ 01736 786669   (Gill Hanrahan)
gillian_hanrahan@amserve.com   Map 203/369329
BB **A/B** ✕ nearby   DI Ⓓ⊗🐾👆😊 !

The Croft Tregesal, TR19 7PY ☎ 01736 786363 (Mr & Mrs Hicks)
www.croft-tregeseal.com   Map 203/380319
BB **A**   DI T2   Closed Jan-Feb   Ⓑ Ⓓ⊗😊   See SC also.

☆ **Bosavern House**
TR19 7RD   ☎ 01736 788301 (Mrs C Collinson)
www.bosavern.com   Map 203/371305
BB **B**   ✕ nearby   SI D3 T2 F2
Ⓑ Ⓓ⊗🐾👆😊 !   ◆◆◆◆

17th century country house offering centrally heated, comfortable accommodation. Most bedrooms have sea or moorland views; en-suite or private facilities. Lounge with log fire, TV and bar. Drying facilities. Home cooking using local produce. 1/2 mile from the SW Coast Path.

● **St Wenn (Bodmin)**
    Saints Way

Treliver Farm, PL30 5PQ (Jenny Tucker) ☎ 01726 890286
jenny@tucker600.freeserve.co.uk   Map 200/980655   BB **B**   ✕ £15,
until 8:30pm   DI FI   Ⓥ Ⓑ Ⓓ⊗🐾👆😊

☆ **Tregolls Farm**
PL30 5PG   ☎ 01208 812154 (Mrs Marilyn Hawkey)
www.tregollsfarm.co.uk   Map 200/983661
BB **B**   ✕ book first £11.50, 7pm   SI D2 TI
Ⓥ Ⓑ Ⓓ🐾👆😊🚗 !   ◆◆◆◆   See SC also.

Grade II listed Farmhouse with beautiful countryside views from all windows. 3 guest bedrooms. Farm trail links up to Saints Way footpath. Pets corner. Eden, Helligan, Fowey and Padstow all within 25 minutes drive.

● **The Lizard (Helston)**
    South West Coast Path

Trethvas Farm, TR12 7AR ☎ 01326 290720 (Mrs G Rowe)   Map 203/709136
BB **B**   ✕ nearby   DI TI F/DI   Closed Nov-Mar
Ⓑ Ⓓ⊗🐾👆😊 !   ◆◆◆◆

● **Tintagel**
    South West Coast Path

Bossiney House Hotel, PL34 0AX ☎ 01840 770240 (John & Pauline Gibbs)
www.bossineyhouse.co.uk   Map 200/066887
BB **B**   ✕ book first £16/17, 7-9pm   D9 T9 FI   Closed Jan
Ⓥ Ⓑ Ⓓ⊗🐾👆😊🏠 Ⓜ   ★★

Bosayne Guest House, Atlantic Road, PL34 0DE   ☎ 01840 770514
(Sara Hawkins)   www.bosayne.co.uk   Map 200/050890
BB **B/C**   ✕ nearby   S3 D2 TI F2   Ⓑ Ⓓ⊗😊   ◆◆◆

⌫⊴ Sleeps B&B, Geraint, Bossiney Rd, PL34 0AL   ☎ 01840 770399
(Maggie Sleep)   trevor@sleept.fsnet.co.uk   Map 200/062885
BB **B**   ✕ nearby   DI TI   Closed Dec-Jan   Ⓑ Ⓓ🐾👆😊🚗 !

● **Wadebridge**
    Saints Way

⌫⊴ The Paddock, Edmonton, PL27 7JA ☎ 01208 812832 (Sue Russell)
www.paddock-bedandbreakfast.co.uk   Map 200/964727
BB **B**   ✕ book first £7.50, 6-8pm   SI DI TI FI
Ⓥ Ⓑ Ⓓ🐾👆😊🚗 !🏠   ◆◆◆

● **West Looe**
    South West Coast Path

⌫⊴ Schooner Point, 1 Trelawney Terrace, PL13 2AG ☎ 01503 262670
(Paul & Helen Barlow)   www.schoonerpoint.co.uk   Map 201/252536
BB **B**   ✕ nearby   S2 D3 TI F0   Closed Nov   ⋙(Looe)
Ⓥ Ⓑ Ⓓ⊗🐾😊

● **Whitsand Bay**
    South West Coast Path

Fir Cottage, Lower Tregantle, Antony, PL11 3AL
☎ 01752 822626 (Kathy Ridpath)   Map 201/391537
BB **A**   ✕ £7, 6-7pm   SI F3   Ⓥ Ⓓ🐾👆😊🚗 !🏠

● **Zennor (St Ives)**
    South West Coast Path

Trewey Farm, TR26 3DA ☎ 01736 796936 (Mrs N I Mann)   Map 203/45438
BB **B**   ✕ nearby   SI D2 TI F2   Closed Nov-Jan
Ⓥ Ⓓ⊗🐾👆🏠

⌫⊴ Boswednack Manor, TR26 3DD ☎ 01736 794183 (Dr E Gynn)
boswednack-manor@cornwall-county.com   Map 203/442378
BB **B**   ✕ nearby   SI D2 TI FI   Closed Nov-Mar
Ⓥ Ⓑ Ⓓ⊗🐾👆😊 !   See SC also.

DEVON

● **Bampton (Tiverton)**
Rows Farmhouse, EX16 9LD ☎ 01398 331579 (Mr & Mrs H Brooks)
suzannahbrooks@tiscali.co.uk   Map 181/946227
BB **B**   ✕ book first £10   DI TI FI   Ⓥ Ⓑ Ⓓ🐾👆😊 !🏠

● **Barnstaple**
    South West Coast Path & Macmillan Way West

☆ ⌫⊴ **The Yeo Dale Hotel**
Pilton Bridge, EX31 1PG   ☎ 01271 342954
www.yeodalehotel.co.uk   Map 180/556338
BB **A/C**   ✕ nearby   S3 D3 T2 F3   ⋙(Barnstaple)
Ⓑ Ⓓ👆🚗 !   ◆◆◆◆

This Georgian townhouse offers quality accommodation, situated in the historic part of Barnstaple. It is a short walk from the Tarka Trail and just 5 minutes to Barnstaple town centre. A great base to explore the beauty of north Devon.

● **Beer**
    South West Coast Path

⌫⊴ Bay View Guest House, Fore Street, EX12 3EE ☎ 01297 20489
(Mr & Mrs R Oswald)   Map 192/230891
BB **A/B**   ✕ nearby   S2 D4 TI FI   Closed Dec-Mar   Ⓑ Ⓓ🐾👆😊   ◆◆◆

Garlands, Stovar Long Lane, EX12 3EA
☎ 01297 20958 (Ann & Nigel Harding)
www.smoothhound.co.uk/hotels/garlands   Map 192/232895
BB **B**   ✕ nearby   S1 D2 T1 F2   Ⓑ   Ⓓ 🍲 👤 🚲 ! 🏠

● **Belstone (Okehampton)**
Dartmoor
🍴🍲◀ Moorlands House, EX20 1QZ   ☎ 01837 840549
www.moorlands-house.co.uk   Map 191/620935
BB **B**   ✕ nearby   D2 T1   Ⓑ   Ⓓ 🍲 👤 🚲 🏠

● **Bickington (Newton Abbot)**
Dartmoor
Rentor, TQ12 6JW   ☎ 01626 821213 (Mr & Mrs P Warren)
rentor.bnb@talk21.com   Map 191/801721
BB **B**   ✕ nearby   D1 T1   Closed Dec-Feb
Ⓑ   Ⓓ ⊛ 🍲 👤 🚲

● **Bideford**
South West Coast Path
The Mount, Northdown Road, EX39 3LP (Heather & Andrew Laugharne)
☎ 01237 473748   www.themount1.cjb.net   Map 190/449269
BB **B**   ✕ nearby   S2 D3 T1 F1   Ⓑ   Ⓓ 🍲 👤 🚲 ! ◆◆◆◆

☆ 🍲◀ I **Southdown Cottage**
Higher Clovelly, EX39 5SA ☎ 01237 431504 (Mrs Mary McColl)
Map 190/297236
BB **B**   ✕ book first £10, 7pm   S1 D1 T1 F1
Ⓥ   Ⓑ   Ⓓ 🍲 👤 🚲 ! 🏠

We'll make you comfy too! Lovely cosy cottage. Bright attractive rooms with wonderful views. Lifts to/from SW Coast Path, anywhere between Bude & Bideford (further by arrangement), so why not make us your base for a while. Breakfast is our speciality.

🍲◀ Corner House, The Strand, EX39 2ND   ☎ 01237 473722
(Chris & Sally Stone) www.cornerhouseguesthouse.co.uk   Map 190,180/452268
BB **B**   ✕ nearby   S1 D2 T1 F2   Ⓥ   Ⓓ ⊛ 🍲 👤 🏠

● **Braunton**
South West Coast Path
North Cottage, 14 North Street, EX33 1AJ   ☎ 01271 812703
(Mrs Jean Watkins)   north_cottage@hotmail.com   Map 180/485367
BB **B**   ✕ nearby   S2 D1 T1 F1   Ⓑ   Ⓓ 🍲 👤 🚲 ! 🏠 Ⓜ
🍲◀ St Merryn B&B, Higher Park Rd, EX33 2LG   ☎ 01271 813805
(Ros Bradford) www.st-merryn.co.uk   Map 180/496364
BB **B**   ✕ book first £12, 7-7:30pm   S1 D1 T1 F1
Ⓥ   Ⓑ   Ⓓ ⊛ 🍲 👤 🚲 ! 🏠

● **Budleigh Salterton**
South West Coast Path
Ropers Cottage, Ropers Lane, Otterton, EX9 7JF   ☎ 01395 568826 (Mrs Earl)
Map 192/081851   BB **B**   ✕ nearby   S1 T1   Ⓑ   Ⓓ 👤 🏠
🍲◀ Dene Cottage, I Westbourne Terrace, EX9 6BR ☎ 01395 443411
(Mike & Linda Knapton) Map 192/067818
BB **B**   ✕ nearby   D2   Ⓑ   Ⓓ ⊛ 🍲 👤 🏠

● **Chagford (Newton Abbot)**
Dartmoor
Two Moors Way
Cyprian's Cot, 47 New Street, TQ13 8BB   ☎ 01647 432256 (Shelagh Weeden)
www.cyprianscot.co.uk   Map 191/701874
BB **B**   ✕ nearby   D1 T1   Ⓑ   Ⓓ 🍲 👤 🚲 🏠

● **Clovelly (Bideford)**
South West Coast Path

☆ **The New House**
EX39 5TQ   ☎ 01237 431303
www.clovelly.co.uk   Map 190/317248
BB **B**   ✕ £20, 7-8:30pm   D5 T3 F2
Ⓥ 🍲 👤   ★★

The New Inn at Clovelly can honestly claim to be uniquely different. A beautiful location in the heart of this historic fishing village, with the only traffic sounds being footsteps and the occasional donkeys' hoofs on an ancient cobbled street. Open all year round.
Email: newinn@clovelly.co.uk

Boat House Cottage, 148 Sierra Hill, Higher Clovelly, EX39 5ST
☎ 01237 431209 (Mrs Bessie May)   Map 190/310243
BB **B**   ✕ nearby   D1 T1 F1   Ⓓ 🍲 👤 🚲 ! 🏠

● **Colebrooke (Crediton)**
Two Moors Way
The Oyster, EX17 5JQ
☎ 01363 84576 (Pearl Hockridge)   Map 191/770008
BB **B**   ✕ nearby   D2 T1   ⟿(Yeoford) Ⓑ   Ⓓ 🍲 👤 🚲 ! 🏠

● **Colyford (Colyton)**
South West Coast Path

☆ **Horriford Farm**
EX24 6HW   ☎ 01297 552316 (Colin and Valerie Pady)
www.datacottage.com/horriford.htm   Map 192/237922
BB **B**   ✕ book first £12.50, 7pm   S2 D2 T1 F1
Ⓥ   Ⓑ   Ⓓ ⊛ 🍲 👤 🚲 !

16th century character farmhouse set in quiet valley near ford. En-suite double & twin bedrooms & single bedrooms. Log fires in winter. Close to SW Coast Path & East Devon Way. Email:
horriford@datacottage.com

● **Colyton**
🍲◀ Sunnyacre, Rockerhayne Farm, Northleigh, EX24 6DA
☎ 01404 871422   (Mrs Norma Rich)
sunnyacre@tesco.net   Map 192,193/213963
BB **A**   ✕ book first £7, 6:30pm   D1 T1 F1   Closed Dec
Ⓥ   Ⓓ 🍲 👤 🚲 ! 🏠   ◆◆◆

● Combe Martin

Exmoor
South West Coast Path

▣◣ Cobblestones, Wood Lane, EX34 0NE ☎ 01271 882050 (Carol Crawford) www.visitcombemartin.co.uk/cobblestones.htm Map 180/594457
BB **A/B** ✕ nearby D1 F1 Ⓓ ⊛ 🐾🛁🍵! 🏇

▣◣ Mellstock House, Woodlands, EX34 0AR ☎ 01271 882592 (Mary Burbidge) www.mellstockhouse.co.uk Map 180/575473
BB **B/C** ✕ book first £10, 7pm S1 D4 T1 F1
Ⓥ Ⓑ Ⓓ ⊛ 🐾🛁🍵! ◆◆◆◆

▣◣ Hillside, Nutcombe Hill, EX34 0PQ ☎ 01271 882736 (Mrs Dawn Middleton) www.visit-hillside.co.uk Map 180/611462
BB **B** ✕ book first £7-£10, 6:30pm D1 T1
Ⓥ Ⓑ Ⓓ ⊛ 🐾🛁🍵! 🏇

☆ ▣◣ **The Royal Marine Public House Hotel**
Seaside, EX34 0AW ☎ 01271 882470 (M J Lethaby)
www.theroyalmarine.co.uk Map 180/576472
BB **B** ✕ book first £5-£10, 6-10pm D4 T1 F1
Ⓥ Ⓑ Ⓓ 🐾🛁🍵

A warm welcome by the sea awaits you from resident proprietors Pat and Merv. 5 beautiful en-suite rooms with beach views. Award winning licensee for food and service. We specialise in home cooked food. Mini breaks 1, 2, 3, 4 days, mid-week/weekends.

● Dalwood (Axminster)

☆ ▣◣ **Beckford Cottage**
EX13 7HQ ☎ 01404 881641 (Jill Bellamy)
www.beckford-cottage.co.uk Map 192,193/264016
BB **B** ✕ book first £20, 6:30-8pm S2
Ⓥ Ⓑ Ⓓ ⊛ 🐾🛁🚗! ◆◆◆◆ See SC also.

A very comfortable thatched cottage on River Yarty on Channel to Channel Walk. All food home cooked with local produce wherever possible. Good walking in AONB, close to Jurassic Coast. Can collect from Axminster.

● Dartmouth

Dartmoor
South West Coast Path

▣◣ Hill View House, 76 Victoria Road, TQ6 9DZ ☎ 01803 839372 (Suzanne White) www.hillviewdartmouth.co.uk Map 202/872512
BB **C** D3 T2 Closed Jan ⋙(Kingswear)
Ⓑ Ⓓ ⊛ 🛁🚗! ◆◆◆◆Ⓖ

Hillyfields B&B, Townstal Pathfields, TQ6 9HL ☎ 01803 835903 (Maggy & Keith Fielder) Map 202/868514
BB **B** ✕ nearby S1 D1 Ⓑ Ⓓ ⊛ 🐾🛁

● Dawlish

South West Coast Path

▣◣ Sealawn Lodge, Exeter Rd, EX7 0AB ☎ 01626 865998 (Belcher)
Map 192/967771 BB **B** ✕ £12, 6:30pm D1 T1 F1 ⋙(Dawlish)
Ⓥ Ⓓ 🐾🛁🚗!

● East Allington (Totnes)

The Fortescue Arms, TQ9 7RA
☎ 01548 521215 (Samantha Bax & Sandra Prince)
www.fortescue-arms.co.uk Map 202/769485
BB **B** ✕ £8, 6-9pm S1 D4 T2 Ⓥ Ⓑ 🐾🛁🏇

● Exeter

Park View Hotel, 8 Howell Road, EX4 4LG ☎ 01392 271772
www.parkviewexeter.co.uk Map 192/917933
BB **B** ✕ nearby S1 D7 T3 F2 ⋙(Exeter Central)
Ⓑ Ⓓ 🐾🍵 ◆◆◆

● Exmouth

South West Coast Path

Sholton Guest House, 29 Morton Road, EX8 1BA
☎ 01395 277318 (Ann Jones) Map 192/999807
BB **B** ✕ nearby S1 D3 T2 F1 ⋙(Exmouth) Ⓑ Ⓓ ⊛ 🛁

● Hallsands (Kingsbridge)

South West Coast Path

Widget, TQ7 2EX
☎ 01548 511110 (Don & Paula Wolstenholme) Map 202/818385
BB **B** ✕ nearby D2 T1 Ⓑ Ⓓ ⊛ 🛁

● Halwill Junction

☆ ▣◣ **Market House**
EX21 5TN ☎ 01409 221339 (Mrs Caroline Halliwell)
ctandf@aol.com Map 190/447990
BB **B** ✕ £12, 7pm D1 T1
Ⓥ Ⓑ Ⓓ 🐾🛁🚗

An attractive 19th century stone house on the edge of the village with two lovely en-suite rooms; one twin and one double, fabulous views, colour televisions and delicious evening meals can be provided, all within a happy family environment.

● Hartland (Bideford)

South West Coast Path

▣◣ West Titchberry Farm, Hartland Point, EX39 6AU
☎ 01237 441287 (Mrs Y Heard) Map 190/242272
BB **B** ✕ book first £10, 6:30pm D1 T1 F1
Ⓥ Ⓑ Ⓓ ⊛ 🐾🛁🚗!

☆ ▣◣ **Elmscott Farm**
EX39 6ES ☎ 01237 441276 (Mrs Thirza Goaman)
Map 190/231215
BB **B** ✕ book first £12, 6pm D1 T1 F1
Ⓥ Ⓑ Ⓓ ⊛ 🐾🛁🚗! ◆◆◆◆

Comfortable farmhouse, ideally situated on the South West Coast Path. All rooms en-suite or with private facilities. Beautiful coastal scenery.

☆ Gawlish Farm
EX39 6AT ☎ 01237 441320 (Mrs Jill George)
Map 190/256263
BB **B** ✗ book first £10, 6:30pm   DI T2
Ⓥ Ⓑ Ⓓ 🐾 🛁 🚗 ! 📚   ♦♦♦

You will be warmly welcomed to this tastefully furnished farmhouse. Beautifully quiet countryside on route of the South West Coast Path.

● **Hemyock**
Orchard Lea, Culmstock Road, Westown, EX15 3RN
☎ 01823 680057 (Ann & Ray Sworn)
anne@sworns.co.uk   Map 181/119134
BB **B** ✗ book first £6.50, 6-7:30pm   DI T2   Closed Dec
Ⓥ Ⓑ Ⓓ ⊛ 🐾 🛁 🚗 !   ♦♦♦

● **Hexworthy (Princetown)**
Dartmoor
Two Moors Way
The Forest Inn, PL20 6SD ☎ 01364 631211 (James & Irene Glenister)
www.theforestinn.co.uk   Map 191/654725
BB **C** ✗ book first £5-£25, 7-9pm   S2 D5 T3 F2
Ⓥ Ⓑ Ⓓ 🐾 🛁 📚   ♦♦♦♦

● **Hillhead (Brixham)**
South West Coast Path

☆ 🖼◀ Raddicombe Lodge
Kingswear Rd, TQ5 0EX ☎ 01803 882125 (John & Kay Horton)
www.raddicombelodge.co.uk   Map 202/904538
BB **B**   SI D7 T3 F2
Ⓑ Ⓓ ⊛ 🐾 🛁 🚗   ♦♦♦♦

Ideally situated between Brixham & Dartmouth. The lodge offers excellent en-suite accommodation with sea & countryside views only a short distance from beautiful beaches & coves. Ideal for sightseeing, walking or just relaxing in the garden.

● **Hittisleigh (Exeter)**
Two Moors Way
Hill Farm B&B, EX6 6LQ ☎ 01647 24326 (Chris Wood)
www.metafore.com/HillFarmBandB   Map 191/732941
BB **B** ✗ book first £12, 6-8pm   D2 TI
Ⓥ Ⓑ Ⓓ ⊛ 🐾 🚗 ! 📚 Ⓜ

● **Holne (Ashburton)**
Dartmoor
Two Moors Way
Chase Gate Farm, TQ13 7RX ☎ 01364 631261 (Anne & David Higman)
www.chasegatefarm.com   Map 202/716703
BB **B**   D2 TI   Ⓑ Ⓓ 🐾 🛁 🚗 ! 📚

● **Holsworthy**

☆ Leworthy Farmhouse
Pyworthy, EX22 6SJ ☎ 01409 259469 (Mrs Pat Jennings)
www.s-h-systems.co.uk/hotels/leworthy.html
Map 190/322012   BB **B** ✗ nearby   D3 T2 FI
Ⓑ Ⓓ 🐾 🛁 🚗 !   ♦♦♦♦Ⓢ

Charming Georgian farmhouse in quiet backwater.
Beautifully prepared en-suite rooms. Ample fresh milk, teas, biscuits, pretty bone china, fresh flowers, soft carpets and crisp bed linen.
A welcoming home with antiques, objets d'art and extensive collection of books, poetry and glossy magazines. A peaceful guests' lounge with ticking clocks, sparkling china, comfy sofas, old prints and Chinese carpets.
Have a scrumptious full English breakfast with buttery fried potatoes and mushrooms, kippers, delicious local bacon and free-range eggs. Or choose creamy organic porridge, yogurt, dried fruits and nuts, muesli, prunes and fresh fruit salad. Lovely coastal walks and quiet country lanes nearby.

● **Honiton**
🖼◀ Lane End Farm, Broadhembury, EX14 3LU
☎ 01404 841563 (Molly Bennett)
www.farm-holidays.co.uk/cgi/details?sub_ref=908   Map 192,193/109050
BB **B** ✗ book first £12, 6:30pm   TI F2
Ⓥ Ⓑ Ⓓ 🐾 🛁 🚗 ! 📚   ♦♦♦

● **Ilfracombe**
South West Coast Path
🖼◀ The Ilfracombe Carlton Hotel, Runnacleave Road, EX34 8AR
☎ 01271 862446   www.ifracombecarlton.co.uk   Map 180/515477
BB **C** ✗ £15.50, 7-8pm   S8 D20 TI2 F8   Closed Jan-Feb
Ⓥ Ⓑ Ⓓ 🐾 🛁   ★★

🖼◀ The Woodlands, Torrs Park, EX34 8AZ ☎ 01271 863098
(Mark O'Brien) www.thewoodlands-hotel.co.uk   Map 180/511472
BB **B** ✗ nearby   S2 D6 TI FI   Ⓑ Ⓓ ⊛ 🐾 🛁 !   ♦♦♦♦Ⓢ

🖼◀ Norbury House Hotel, Torrs Park, EX34 8AZ ☎ 01271 863888
(Andy Waters) www.norburyhousehotel.co.uk   Map 180/511473
BB **B** ✗ book first £13, 6:30pm   SI D4 F3   Closed Jan
Ⓥ Ⓑ Ⓓ 🐾 🛁 🚗 ! 📚   ♦♦♦♦

🖼◀ Varley House Hotel, EX34 9QW ☎ 01271 863927
www.varleyhouse.co.uk   Map 180/530473
BB **B** ✗ book first £   SI D3 TI F2
Ⓥ Ⓑ Ⓓ 🐾 🛁 ! 📚   ♦♦♦♦

≈⊠◀ The Towers Hotel, Chambercombe Park, EX34 9QN ☎ 01271 862809
(David & Vicki Vernon)　www.thetowers.co.uk　Map 180/530473
BB **B** ✕ £15, 7pm S1 D4 T2 F1
Ⅴ B D ⊛🍴🛁🚗❗🏠 ◆◆◆

● **Ivybridge**
Dartmoor
Two Moors Way
Hillhead Farm, Ugborough, PL21 0HQ ☎ 01752 892674 (Mrs Jane Johns)
www.hillhead-farm.co.uk　Map 202/674564
BB **B** ✕ nearby　D2 T1　Closed Nov-Dec
B D ⊛🍴🛁🚗❗🏠　◆◆◆◆⑤

Blackadon Farm, PL21 0HB　☎ 01752 897034 (Mark Walker)
www.blackadonbarns.co.uk　Map 202/665577
BB **B** ✕ book first £　D5 T5 F1
Ⅴ B D ⊛🍴🛁🚗❗🏠 Ⓜ　See SC & Groups also.

☆ **Kevela**
4 Clare Street, PL21 9DL　☎ 01752 893111 (Ray & May Dunn)
www.may@kevela.co.uk　Map 202/632559
BB **B** ✕ nearby　D2 T1　🚌(Ivybridge)
B D ⊛🍴🛁❗🏠

Ray and May offer you a warm welcome at Kevela, centrally situated in
Ivybridge close to all amenities and with easy access to Dartmoor, the coast and
the historical towns and villages of South Hams.
All rooms en-suite with TV and tea & coffee making facilities.
Full English breakfast.
Pubs and restaurants nearby. Parking.
B&B from £25 per person

● **Knowstone (South Molton)**
Two Moors Way
West Bowden Farm, EX36 4RP ☎ 01398 341224 (Mrs J Bray)
Map 181/833224　BB **B** ✕ book first £11, 6:30pm　S1 D3 T2 F2
Ⅴ B D 🍴🛁❗🏠　◆◆◆

≈⊠◀ Little Oak, EX36 4SA　☎ 01884 881343 (Karen & Graham)
karen@walden7094.fslife.co.uk　Map 181/836212
BB **A** S1 D1　D ⊛🍴🛁🚗❗🏠

● **Loddiswell (Kingsbridge)**
South West Coast Path
≈⊠◀ Blackwell Park, TQ7 4EA　☎ 01548 821230 (Mrs A Kelly)
anne.kelly@tiscali.co.uk　Map 202/714517
BB **B** ✕ £10, 6:30pm　S1 D1 T2 F2　Closed Nov-Mar
Ⅴ B D 🍴🛁🏠

● **Lynmouth**
Exmoor
South West Coast Path & Two Moors Way

☆ **Tregonwell & The Olde Sea-Captain's House**
1 Tors Road, EX35 6ET ☎ 01598 753369 (Mr & Mrs C & J Parker)
www.smoothhound.co.uk/hotels/tregonwl.html　Map 180/727494
BB **A** ✕ nearby　S1 D5 T1 F2　Closed Jan
B D ⊛🍴🛁🚗❗🏠　◆◆◆

Warm welcome guaranteed at the best place for
you Exmoor ramblers. Our elegant award-
winning Victorian riverside guesthouse is
snuggled in wooded valleys, waterfalls, England's
highest clifftops and most enchanting harbour.
Pretty en-suite bedrooms with dramatic views.
Log fires. Garaged parking. Group discounts.

☆ **Glenville House**
2 Tors Road, EX35 6ET　☎ 01598 752202 (Tricia & Alan Francis)
www.glenvillelynmouth.co.uk　Map 180/727494
BB **B** ✕ nearby　S1 D4 T1　Closed Dec-Jan
B D ⊛🍴🛁 Ⓜ　◆◆◆◆

Delightful licensed Victorian house in
idyllic riverside setting. Tastefully
decorated bedrooms and pretty en-suites.
Picturesque harbour and village.
Dramatic Exmoor scenery and spectacular
valley/coastal walks. Peaceful, tranquil,
romantic – a very special place.

☆ **River Lyn View**
26 Watersmeet Road, EX35 6EP ☎ 01598 753501 (Carol Sheppard)
http://members.aol.com/riverlynview　Map 180/725508
BB **B** ✕ nearby　D4 T1　Closed Dec-Jan
B D 🍴🛁🚗❗🏠

River Lyn View offers comfortable B&B.
Rooms are en-suite and overlook the East
Lyn River situated on the edge of Exmoor
near the picturesque harbour in Lynmouth
with its spectacular coastal views. Ideal for
walking holidays. Major credit cards
accepted. Email: riverlynview@aol.com

● **Lynton**
Exmoor
South West Coast Path & Two Moors Way
≈⊠◀ 27 Lee Road, EX35 6BP　☎ 01598 752364 (Lee House)
www.leehouselynton.co.uk　Map 180/717495
BB **B** ✕ book first £15, 7pm　D6 T2 F1
Ⅴ B D ⊛🍴🛁　◆◆◆◆

≈⊠◀ Meadhaven, 12 Crossmead, EX35 6DG ☎ 01598 753288
(Marion Kirk)　Map 180/716493
BB **B** ✕ nearby　S2 D1 T1　D ⊛🍴🛁🛁🏠　◆◆◆

≈⊠◀ 29 Lee Road, EX35 6BS ☎ 01598 753418 (Pat & Trevor Ley)
Map 180/717494　BB **A** ✕ nearby　D1 T1　D 🍴🛁❗🏠

≈⊠◀ Sandrock Hotel, Longmead, EX35 6DH ☎ 01598 753307
(Chris Barnes)　www.sandrockhotel.co.uk　Map 180/715493

BB **B** ✕ £12, 6-8pm   S2 D4 T3 F3
Ⓥ Ⓑ Ⓓ 🍴♨️🚗❗🍵 ★★

☆ **The Denes**
15 Longmead, EX35 6DQ ☎ 01598 753573 (John McGowan)
www.thedenes.com   Map 180/715495
BB **A/B** ✕ book first £12.50, 6:30-8pm   D2 FT/3
Ⓥ Ⓑ Ⓓ ♨️🍴♨️🚗❗ ◆◆◆◆

Glorious place, good food, great value. An ideal base for exploring Exmoor or stop-over for SW Coast Path trekkers. Drying facilities. Car parking. Licensed. Evening meals. En-suites and basic rooms available. From £19-26 pppn. Open all year. Major credit cards accepted.

☆ 🖼 **Meadpool House**
Brendon, EX35 6PS ☎ 01598 741215 (Nigel & Vivienne Wood)
www.whatsonexmoor.co.uk/meadpool   Map 180/771482
BB **A/B** ✕ nearby   D2 TI
Ⓑ Ⓓ ♨️🍴♨️🚗❗

Luxury, smoke-free B&B on East Lyn river. 4 mile walk to Lynmouth via wooded gorge. Upstream to open moor through 'Doone Valley'. Coast Path 2 miles, pub 1 mile. Bedrooms (with TVs) are en-suite or with private bathroom. Lounge. From £20pppn.

☆ **North Cliff Hotel**
North Walk, EX35 6HJ ☎ 01598 752357
www.northcliffhotel.co.uk   Map 180/718497
BB **B** ✕ £15, 6-10pm   S1 D8 T2 F4   Closed Jan
Ⓥ Ⓑ Ⓓ ♨️🍴♨️🚗❗ ★

Family run hotel on South West Coast Path, near Watersmeet, Lorna Doone Valley. All rooms have a view across Lynmouth Bay and are en-suite. Drying room. Restaurant/bar. Car Park. Open all year.

● **Manaton (Newton Abbot)**
Dartmoor
Two Moors Way

☆ 🖼 **Wingstone Farm**
TQ13 9UL ☎ 01647 221215 (Juliette Rich)
www.wingstonefarm.co.uk   Map 191/747811
BB **B** ✕ nearby   S1 D2   Closed Jan
Ⓑ Ⓓ ♨️🍴♨️🚗❗

Comfortable farmhouse on working farm. Stunning views overlooking Bowerman's Nose. Excellent location for peaceful cycling and walking breaks. Experience wildlife closeby. Field access to Moors. Local produce provided. Vegetarians catered for. Dogs and horses welcome. Stabling available.

🖼 Hazelcott B&B, TQ13 9UY ☎ 01647 221405 (Nigel Fisher)
www.dartmoordays.com   Map 191/751822
BB **B** ✕ book first £12.50, 7:30pm   D2 FI
Ⓥ Ⓑ Ⓓ ♨️🍴♨️🚗❗🍵

● **Membury (Axminster)**
🖼 Lea Hill, EX13 7AQ ☎ 01404 881881 (Mrs Susan Avis)
www.leahill.co.uk   Map 193/272018
BB **C** ✕ book first £15, 7:30pm   S2 D2   Ⓑ Ⓓ ♨️🍴♨️🍵

● **Morchard Bishop (Crediton)**
Two Moors Way
Beech Hill Community, EX17 6RF ☎ 01363 877228
http://web.onetel.net.uk/~beechhill   Map 191/782086
BB **A** ✕ book first £5, 7pm   TI F3   Ⓥ Ⓓ ♨️🍴♨️🚗🍵

● **Moretonhampstead (Newton Abbot)**
Dartmoor
Two Moors Way
Great Slon Combe Farm, TQ13 8QF ☎ 01647 440595 (Mrs Trudie Merchant)
www.greatsloncombefarm.co.uk   Map 191/736862
BB **B** ✕ book first £14-£15, 6:30-7pm   D2 TI
Ⓥ Ⓑ Ⓓ ♨️🍴♨️🚗❗🍵 ◆◆◆◆Ⓢ

Little Wooston Farm, TQ13 8QA ☎ 01647 440551 (Jeanne Cuming)
jeannecuming@tesco.net   Map 191/760887
BB **A** ✕ book first £6, 6:30-7pm   S1 D1 F1   ⋘(Newton Abbot)
Ⓥ Ⓓ ♨️🍴♨️🚗🍵 ◆◆◆

☆ **Cookshayes Country Guest House**
33 Court Street, TQ13 8LG ☎ 01647 440374 (Julie Saunders)
www.cookshayes.co.uk   Map 191/751860
BB **B** ✕ book first £14, 6:30pm   S1 D5 TI FI   Closed Dec-Jan
Ⓥ Ⓑ Ⓓ ♨️🍴♨️🍵 ◆◆◆

Beautiful mid-Victorian house set in large gardens on the edge of Dartmoor. Minutes away from village centre. Most rooms en-suite. Email: cooksayes@aol.com

---

● **Murchington (Chagford)**
Dartmoor
Two Moors Way
🖼 St Johns West, TQ13 8HJ ☎ 01647 432468 (Mrs Maureen West)
http://stjohnswest.cjb.net   Map 191/689888
BB **B** ✕ book first £15, 7-8pm   D1 T2   Ⓥ Ⓑ Ⓓ ♨️🍴♨️🚗❗

● **Nadderwater (Exeter)**
🖼 Rowhorne House, EX4 2LQ ☎ 01392 274 675 (Jane Cross)
rowhornehouse@hotmail.com   Map 192/879948
BB **B** ✕ book first £10-£15, 7-9pm   D1 TI   Ⓥ Ⓑ Ⓓ ♨️🍴♨️🚗🍵

● **Newton Abbot (Torquay)**
🖼 Branscombe House B&B, 48 Highweek Village, TQ12 1QQ
☎ 01626 356752 (Miles Opie) www.branscombe-house.co.uk
Map 191/845722   BB **B** ✕ nearby   D2 TI   ⋘(Newton Abbot)
Ⓑ Ⓓ ♨️🍴♨️🚗❗

● Newton Popplford (Sidmouth)

South West Coast Path

☆ **Milestone**
High ST., EX10 0DU ☎ 01395 568267
Map 192/081896
BB **B**   ✗ nearby   S2 D1 T/D1
Ⓑ Ⓓ ⊗ 🖐👜 🚗

Open all year. Royal Society Food Hygiene. Non-smoking. Highly recommended by previous guests. Warm welcome. Saxon village between Budleigh Salterton and Sidmouth. Highest quality. Private home. All comforts. Italian restaurant and good pub 300 yards. Lovely river walks & lanes.

● North Bovey

Dartmoor

Two Moors Way

🖐🍴 Lower Hookner Barn, TQ13 8RS ☎ 01647 221282 (Jenny Pryce-Davies)
lowerhookner@hotmail.com   Map 191/714825
BB **B**   ✗ book first £10, 7:30pm onwards   D1 T1 F1
Ⓥ Ⓑ Ⓓ ⊗ 🖐👜🚗 ! 🐾

● Northam (Bideford)

South West Coast Path

🖐🍴 Tadworthy House, Tadworthy Road, EX39 1JN ☎ 01237 477501
(Jill Drury) rdrury86@yahoo.com   Map 180/445293
BB **B**   ✗ nearby   S1 D1 T1 F1   Ⓑ Ⓓ ⊗ 🖐👜 🚗 ! 🐾

🖐🍴 Riversford Hotel, Limers Lane, EX39 2RG
☎ 01237 474239 (Antony Jarrad) www.riversford.co.uk   Map 180/452281
BB **B**   ✗ £15, 6-9:30pm   S4 D8 T2 F1   Ⓥ Ⓓ 🖐👜 🐾   ★★

● Okehampton

Meadowlea Guest House, 65 Station Road, EX20 1EA
☎ 01837 53200 (Michelle Mossman)   Map 191/588948
BB **B**   ✗ nearby   S2 D1 T3 F1   Ⓑ Ⓓ 👜   ◆◆◆

East Bowerland Farm, EX20 4LZ ☎ 01837 55979 (Ray & Mel Quirks)
www.devonhols.com   Map 191/542929
BB **B**   ✗ nearby   D3 T2 F2   Ⓑ Ⓓ ⊗ 🚗 ! 🐾

Northlake, Stockley, EX20 1QH ☎ 01837 53100 (Pam Jeffrey)
www.northlakedevon.co.uk   Map 191/610953
BB **B**   ✗ book first £8   D2 T1   Ⓥ Ⓑ Ⓓ ⊗ 🖐👜🚗 ! 🐾

● Ottery St Mary

🖐🍴 Fluxton Farm, EX11 1RJ ☎ 01404 812818 (Mrs E A Forth)
Map 192/086934   BB **B**   ✗ nearby   S2 D3 T5 F1
Ⓑ Ⓓ 👜 🐾   ◆◆   Must be cat lovers!

● Plymouth

South West Coast Path

🖐🍴 Old Pier Guest House, 20 Radford Road, West Hoe, PL1 3BY
☎ 01752 268468 (Steve Jones) www.oldpier.co.uk   Map 201/472537
BB **B**   ✗ nearby   S1 D3 T3   🚶(Plymouth)
Ⓑ Ⓓ 🖐👜 ⓜ   ◆◆◆   Veggie breakfasts.

Mount Batten Centre, 70 Lawrence Rd, Mount Batten, PL9 9SJ
☎ 01752 404567   www.mount-batten-centre.com   Map 201/487532
BB **B**   ✗ up to £13, 5-9pm   Ⓥ Ⓑ Ⓓ 🖐

☆ 🖐🍴 **4 Garden Crescent**
West Hoe, PL1 3DA ☎ 01752 250128 (Franca Burge)
francaburge@hotmail.com   Map 201/471537
BB **B**   ✗ nearby   S1 D4 T1 F/T2   Closed Dec   🚶(Plymouth)
Ⓑ Ⓓ 🖐👜

A friendly family run guest house on the South West Coast Path. 5 minutes' walk to the city centre and the historic Barbican. Drying facilities and packed lunches available on request.
Ideal base for exploring Devon and Cornwall.

● Ponsworthy (Newton Abbot)

Dartmoor

Two Moors Way

Old Walls Farm, TQ13 7PN
☎ 01364 631222 (Mrs E Fursdon)   Map 191/701747
BB **B**   S1 D1 T1   Ⓑ Ⓓ 👜 🐾 ! 🐾

● Postbridge (Yelverton)

Dartmoor

Two Moors Way

🖐🍴 Beechwood B&B, PL20 6SY ☎ 01822 880332
(Mrs L Smith, Mrs E Moss) www.beechwoodcottage.com   Map 191/653793
BB **B**   ✗ nearby   S2 D2 T2 F1   Ⓑ 🖐👜 🐾

● Rackenford (Tiverton)

Exmoor

Two Moors Way

🖐🍴 Creacombe Parsonage Farm, Creacombe, EX16 8EL
☎ 01884 881260 (Mrs C Poole) www.creacombe.com   Map 181/820185
BB **B**   ✗ book first £11.50, 6-9pm   T2 F1
Ⓥ Ⓑ Ⓓ ⊗ 🖐👜🚗 ! 🐾

● Sampford Spiney (Yelverton)

Dartmoor

🖐🍴 Withill Farm, PL20 6LN ☎ 01822 853992 (Pam Kitchin)
withillfarm1@aol.com   Map 201/548726
BB **B**   ✗ nearby   D2 T1   Ⓑ Ⓓ 🖐👜🚗 ! 🐾   See SC also.

● Scorriton (Buckfastleigh)

Dartmoor

Two Moors Way

🖐🍴 The Barn, Close Applegarden, TQ11 0JB ☎ 01364 631567
(Pat Dinning) www.thebarndartmoor.com   Map 202/703685
BB **B**   ✗ nearby   D1 T1 F1   Ⓑ Ⓓ ⊗ 🖐👜🚗 ! 🐾

● Seaton

South West Coast Path

🖐🍴 The Baytree, 11 Seafield Rd, EX12 2QS ☎ 01297 24611
(Mrs Hazel Cartwright) seafield11@aol.com   Map 192,193/242900
BB **C**   ✗ nearby   D1 T1 F1   Ⓑ Ⓓ ⊗ 🖐👜 !   ◆◆◆

● Shirwell (Barnstaple)

The Spinney Guest House, EX31 4JR ☎ 01271 850282 (Mrs Janet Pelling)
www.thespinneyshirwell.co.uk   Map 180/590370
BB **B**   ✕ book first £14, 7pm   S1 D2 T1 F1
Ⓥ Ⓑ Ⓓ ☺ ☕ 🏇   ◆◆◆◆Ⓢ

● Sidmouth
South West Coast Path

Canterbury House, Salcombe Road, EX10 8PR ☎ 01395 513373
(Mrs & Mrs M C Penaluna)   cgh@eclipse.co.uk   Map 192/127878
BB **B**   ✕ book first £12, 6pm   S1 D4 T2 F3
Ⓥ Ⓑ Ⓓ ☺ 🐾 ☕ 🏇   ◆◆◆

● Slapton (Kingsbridge)
South West Coast Path

Old Walls, TQ7 2QN ☎ 01548 580516 (V J Mercer)   Map 202/823449
BB **B**   ✕ nearby   S1 D2/F2 T1   Ⓥ Ⓑ Ⓓ ☺ 🐾 ☕ 🚗 ! 🏇 Ⓜ

● South Milton (Kingsbridge)
South West Coast Path

🛏✕ The Old Post Office B&B, TQ7 3JQ ☎ 01548 560235
(Paul & Janice Dennis)   www.oldpostoffice.biz   Map 202/701426
BB **B**   ✕ nearby   S1 T1 F1   Ⓑ Ⓓ ☺ 🐾 🚗 ! 🏇

● South Zeal (Okehampton)
Dartmoor

🛏✕ Cawsandside, Throwleigh Road, EX20 2QD ☎ 01837 840353 (John
Draper)   draperjt@tinyworld.co.uk   Map 191/657914
BB **B**   ✕ book first £12, approx 7:30pm   D1 T2
Ⓥ Ⓑ Ⓓ ☺ 🐾 ☕ 🚗 ! 🏇

☆ Poltimore Guest House

EX20 2PD ☎ 01837 840209 (Ben & Diane Radford)
www.poltimore-southzeal.co.uk   Map 191/652932
BB **B**   ✕ nearby   S1 D3 T2
Ⓑ Ⓓ ☺ 🐾 ☕

Luxurious thatched guest house.
Log fire in own lounge.
Set on the northern edge of Dartmoor
National Park.
Real ale pubs within easy walking
distance. Abundant wildlife and
fantastic walking.

● Teignmouth
South West Coast Path

Brunswick House, 5 Brunswick Street, TQ14 8AE ☎ 01626 774102
(Margrethe & Pete Hockings)   margrethehockings@hotmail.com
Map 192/941727   BB **B**   ✕ nearby   S1 D4 T/F3 F1   ᔐ(Teignmouth)
Ⓑ Ⓓ 🐾 ☕ 🏇

● Tiverton

Bridge Guest House, 23 Angel Hill, EX16 6PE ☎ 01884 252804
www.smoothhound.co.uk/hotels/bridgegh.html   Map 181/953125
BB **B**   ✕ book first £16, 6:30-7pm   S5 D2 T1 F2
Ⓥ Ⓑ Ⓓ 🐾 ☕ 🏇   ◆◆◆

🛏✕ Angel Guest House, 13 St Peter Street, EX16 6NU ☎ 01884 253392
(Tony Evans)   cerimar@eurobell.co.uk   Map 181/954126
BB **B**   ✕ nearby   S1 D3 T1 F2   Ⓑ Ⓓ ☺ 🐾 ☕   ◆◆◆

● Torquay
South West Coast Path

☆ 🛏✕ Meadfoot Bay Hotel

Meadfoot Sea Road, TQ1 2LQ ☎ 01803 294722 (Tracey Tyerman)
www.meadfoot.com   Map 202/926632
BB **B**   ✕ book first £15, 7-8pm   S3 D12 T5 F1   Closed Dec-Jan
ᔐ(Torquay) Ⓥ Ⓑ 🐾 ☕   ◆◆◆◆

Comfortable, friendly hotel close to harbour, beaches and local amenities. Ideal
centre for exploring the South West Coast Path, local walks or touring Torbay
and surrounding area. All rooms en-suite, have colour TV and tea/coffee
making facilities. Email: stay@meadfoot.com

● Wembury (Plymouth)
South West Coast Path

Bay Cottage, 150 Church Road, PL9 0HR ☎ 01752 862559
www.bay-cottage.com   Map 201/519487
BB **B**   ✕ nearby   S1 D2 T2   Closed Dec-Feb
Ⓑ Ⓓ 🐾 ☕ 🏇   ◆◆◆

● West Buckland (Barnstaple)
Macmillan Way West

Huxtable Farm, EX32 0SR ☎ 01598 760254 (Jackie & Antony Payne)
www.huxtablefarm.co.uk   Map 180/665308
BB **B/C**   ✕ book first £20, 7:30pm   D3 T1 F2   Closed Dec-Jan
Ⓥ Ⓑ Ⓓ ☺ 🐾 ☕ 🚗 !   ◆◆◆◆Ⓢ

● Widecombe-in-the-Moor (Newton Abbot)
Dartmoor
Two Moors Way

🛏✕ The Old Rectory, TQ13 7TB ☎ 01364 621231
rachel.belgrave@care4free.net   Map 191/717767
BB **B**   ✕ nearby   D2 T/F1   Closed Nov-Feb
Ⓑ Ⓓ ☺ 🐾 ☕ 🚗 ! 🏇   Veggie breakfasts.

● Woolacombe
South West Coast Path

Clyst House, Rockfield Road, EX34 7DH ☎ 01271 870220 (Ann Braund)
Map 180/455441 BB **B** ✕ book first £11, 6:30pm   S1 D1 T1 F1   Closed Nov-Feb
Ⓓ ☺ 🐾 ☕

☆ Barton-Lea
Beach Rd, EX34 7BT ☎ 01271 870928 (Lynda Vickery)
lynda@bartonlea.fsnet.co.uk   Map 180/460438
BB **B**   ✗ nearby   D1 T1 F1   Closed Dec-Jan
B D 🕸 🍵 👤 🚗 !

Delightful home with sea views. Use of patio garden and BBQ. All rooms en-suite with sea views, hair-dryers, TV, fridges, tea/coffee facilities. 5 mins walk from beach, shops, restaurants and bus stops. 10 min walk from South West Coast Path. Excellent large breakfast menu.

● Yealmpton
South West Coast Path

☆ Kitley House Hotel
Kitley Estate, PL8 2NW ☎ 01752 881555
www.kitleyhousehotel.com   Map 202/559514
BB **C**   ✗ £30, 7-9pm
S1 D9 T2 F7   V   B   D 🍵 👤 ! 🏠   ★★★

Historic Country House set in 600 acres of private estate. Overlooks lake and private woodland. Very quiet with own walks. Dartmoor 15 mins—close to SW Coast Path. Range of bedrooms including suites, full restaurant and lounge service available. Extensive gardens and wildlife around house. Satellite TV and CD. All rooms en-suite with shower. Private car parking.

DORSET

● Abbotsbury (Weymouth)
South West Coast Path & Macmillan Way
Swan Lodge, DT3 4JL ☎ 01305 871249   Map 194/578852
BB **B**   ✗ £7, 6-9:30pm   D3 T2   V   B   D 🍵 🏠   ◆◆◆

● Bournemouth
New Forest
St Michaels Guest House, 42 St Michaels Road, Westcliff, BH2 5DY
☎ 01202 557386 (Mrs E Davies)   www.stmichaelsfriendlyguesthouse.co.uk
Map 195/082910   BB **B**   ✗ £6, 6pm   S1 D2 T2 F1   ⋙(Bournemouth)
V   D 👤 🏠

● Bridport
South West Coast Path & Monarch's Way
Fleet Cottage, 152 West Bay Road, DT6 4AZ ☎ 01308 458698 (Janice
Warburton) janicewarburton@supanet.com   Map 193/465915
BB **B**   ✗ book first £7, 6:30pm   D/S2 T1 F1   V   B   D 🍵 👤 🏠

Green Lane House, Dorchester Road, DT6 4LH ☎ 01308 422619
(Christine Prideaux) greenlanehouse@aol.com   Map 193/483932
BB **B**   ✗ book first £10   S1 D1 T1 F1   V   B   D 🕸 🍵 👤 🚗 🏠

Saxlingham House, West Road, Symondsbury, DT6 6AA ☎ 01308 423629
(Valerie Nicholls) ttp://members.freezone.co.uk/saxlingham/Saxlingham.htm
Map 193/448930   BB **B**   ✗ nearby   D2 T1   Closed Nov-Mar
B   D 👤   See SC also.

🛌🍴 Eypeleaze, 117 West Bay Road, DT6 4EQ ☎ 01308 423363
(Ann Walker) www.eypeleaze.co.uk   Map 193/467912
BB **B**   ✗ nearby   T1   B   D 🕸 🍵 👤 ! 🏠   ◆◆◆◆Ⓢ

☆ Eypes Mouth Country Hotel
Eype, DT6 6AL ☎ 01308 423300 (Kevin & Glenis French)
www.eypesmouthhotel.co.uk   Map 193/448914
BB **C**   ✗ £23, 7-9pm   S2 D12 T3 F1
V   B   D 🍵 🚗 👤 🏠   ★★

The Hotel nestles between the clifftops and downland that form the Heritage Coastline. Close to SW Coast Path, the hotel enjoys stunning seaviews, peace and tranquility, superb food using the best of local produce and offers a high standard of hospitality.

☆ Britmead House
154 West Bay Road, DT6 4EG ☎ 01308 422941
www.britmeadhouse.co.uk   Map 193/465912
BB **C**   ✗ nearby   D4 T2 F2
B   D 🕸 🍵 👤 ! 🏠   ◆◆◆◆

An elegant Edwardian house, situated within walking distance of West Bay harbour and the SW Coast Path, part of the World Heritage Site. We offer comfortable en-suite accommodation with many thoughtful extras. Parking, non-smoking. Dogs welcome by arrangement.

● Cerne Abbas (Dorchester)
Wessex Ridgeway
🛌🍴 Badger Hill, 11 Springfield, DT2 7JZ
☎ 01300 341698 (Patricia Hammett)
badgerhill@amserve.com   Map 194/663014
BB **B**   ✗ nearby   D1 T1   B   D 🕸 🍵 👤 🏠 Ⓜ   ◆◆◆◆

Abbots, 7 Long St, DT2 7JF ☎ 01300 341349 (Robert Lamb)
www.3lambs.com/abbots   Map 194/665011
BB **B**   ✗ nearby   D2 T2   B 🕸 🍵 👤 🚗 🏠

● Chideock (Bridport)
South West Coast Path & Monarch's Way
🛌🍴 Frogmore Farm, DT6 6HT ☎ 01308 456159 (Mrs S Norman)
Map 193/434925   BB **C**   ✗ book first £14, 7pm   D1 T1 F1
V   B   D 🕸 🍵 👤 🚗 ! 🏠

🛌🍴 Rose Cottage, Main Street, DT6 6JQ ☎ 01297 489994
(Sue & Mick Kelson)   www.rosecottage-chideock.co.uk   Map 193/423927
BB **B**   ✗ nearby   D1 T1   Closed Sun-Tues.
B   D 🕸 🍵 👤   ◆◆◆◆

● Dorchester
Jubilee Trail (Dorset)

Cowden House, Fry's Lane, Godmanstone, DT2 7AG ☎ 01300 341377
(Tim Mills) www.cowdenhouse.co.uk Map 194/666970
BB **A** ✗ book first £14.50, 7:30pm D1 T2 F1
V B D 🖤🐾👕🛏 ! 🌙

☆ ▄━◀ **Churchview Guest House**
Winterbourne Abbas, DT2 9LS ☎ 01305 889296
www.churchview.co.uk Map 194/618905
BB **B/C** ✗ £15, 7pm S1 D4 T3 F1
V B D 🐾👕🛏 ! 🌙 ◆◆◆◆ See Groups also.

Our beautiful 17th century guest house set in picturesque countryside makes an ideal rambling base. Period dining room, two lounges, licensed bar. Delicious evening meals. Non-smoking. Groups are our speciality. Call Michael & Jane Deller. Email: stay@churchview.co.uk

● Highcliffe (Christchurch)
▄━◀ Meadow Reach, 56 Smugglers Lane North, Highcliffe-by-Sea, BH23 4NQ
☎ 01425 274887 (Pam & Bob Smith)
www.meadowreach.co.uk Map 195/200939
BB **B** ✗ nearby D1 T1 🚂(Hinton Admiral)
B D 🖤👕🛏

● Ibberton (Blandford Forum)
Wessex Ridgeway
Manor House Farm, DT11 0EN ☎ 01258 817349 (Mrs C Old)
Map 194/788077 BB **B** ✗ nearby D2 T1
B 🖤🐾👕🌙

● Isle Of Portland (Weymouth)
South West Coast Path

☆ ▄━◀ **The Portland Heights Hotel**
DT5 2EN ☎ 01305 821361
www.portlandheights.co.uk Map 194/688729
BB **C** ✗ £20, 7-9pm S32 D30 T31 F5
V B D 🐾👕🛏 ! 🌙 ★★★

Modern friendly hotel with leisure centre and swimming pool. Set on the summit of Portland with spectacular sea and coastal views over Weymouth Bay, Chesil Beach towards Lyme. Central point within World Heritage Coast and South West Coast path.

● Langton Matravers (Swanage)
South West Coast Path
Kamloops, Haycrafts Lane, BH19 3EE ☎ 01929 439193 (Mr D V Joseph)
info@kamloops.co.uk Map 195/983792
BB **B** ✗ nearby D/T3
B D 🖤🐾👕🛏 !

● Lyme Regis
South West Coast Path, Wessex Ridgeway & Monarch's Way

Lucerne, View Road, DT7 3AA ☎ 01297 443752 (Owen Keith Lovell)
http://lymeregis.com/lucerne Map 193/338923
BB **B** S1 D3 T1 B D 🖤🐾👕 ★★★

The Orchard Country Hotel, Rousdon, DT7 3XW ☎ 01297 442972
(Rachel Pike) www.orchardcountryhotel.com Map 193/296916
BB **C** ✗ book first £17.50, 7:15pm S1 D6 T4 Closed Dec-Feb
V B D 🖤👕🛏 ◆◆◆◆

Charnwood Guest House, 21 Woodmead Road, DT7 3AD
☎ 01297 445281 (Wayne & Ann Bradbury)
www.lymeregisaccommodation.com Map 193/339924
BB **B** ✗ nearby S1 D4 T2 F1 B D 🖤👕Ⓜ ◆◆◆◆

▄━◀ Thatch, Uplyme Rd, DT7 3LP ☎ 01297 442212
(Frank & Wendy Rogers) thatchbb@aol.com Map 193/335924
BB **B** ✗ nearby S1 D1 T1 B D 🖤🐾👕🛏🌙 ◆◆◆◆

● Norden (Wareham)
Three Barrows Farm, BH20 5DU ☎ 01929 480797 (Mrs Valerie Bull)
Map 195/938841 BB **B** ✗ nearby D1 T1 F1
B D 🖤🐾👕🛏 ! 🌙

● Piddletrenthide (Dorchester)
Wessex Ridgeway

☆ ▄━◀ **The Poachers Inn**
DT2 7QX ☎ 01300 348358 (Mrs Stephanie Atkinson)
www.thepoachersinn.co.uk Map 194/703002
BB **C** ✗ £8.95, until 9:30pm D15 T4 F1
V B D 🐾👕🛏 ◆◆◆◆

In the heart of the beautiful Piddle valley this family run inn has an excellent choice of seafood, game, pasta and steaks alongside traditional Dorset dishes and homemade sweets. Serving real ales, and extensive wine list. An ideal base for touring Dorset.

● Pimperne (Blandford Forum)
Jubilee Trail (Dorset)
▄━◀ The Old Bakery, Church Road, DT11 8UB ☎ 01258 455173
(John & Joyce Tanner) jjtanners@hotmail.com Map 195/905092
BB **B** ✗ book first £8, 7:30-8pm S1 D/T1 T1 F1
V B D 🖤🐾👕🛏 ! 🌙 ◆◆

● Poole
South West Coast Path
The Laurels, 60 Britannia Road, BH14 8BB ☎ 01202 265861 (Mrs North)
www.thelaurelsbandb.freeservers.com Map 195/033913
BB **B** ✗ nearby S1 D1 T1 F1 🚂(Parkstone) B D 👕

● Portesham (Weymouth)
South West Coast Path & Jubilee Trail (Dorset)
Lavender Cottage, 9 Malthouse Meadow, DT3 4NS ☎ 01305 871924
(Mrs Joan Haine) joanhaine@sagainternet.co.uk Map 194/599856
BB **A** ✗ nearby D1 T1 Closed Nov-Feb D 🖤👕🛏 !

Bridge House, 13 Frys Close, DT3 4LQ ☎ 01305 871685
(Thea Alexander) www.bridgehousebandb.co.uk Map 194/602858
BB **B** ✕ nearby D2 Ⓑ Ⓓ 😊 👙 🚗 🐾 ◆◆◆◆

The Old Fountain,36 Front St, DT3 4ET ☎ 01305 871278 (Ann Martin)
martann981@aol.com Map 194/603860
BB **B** ✕ nearby D1 T1 Ⓓ 😊 🐾 👙 🚗 ! ◆◆◆◆

● **Puddletown (Dorchester)**
Zoar House, DT2 8SR ☎ 01305 848498 (Mrs J Stephens)
Map 194/762942 BB **A** ✕ nearby S1 D1 T1 F1 Ⓑ Ⓓ 😊 🐾 👙 🚗
Ilsington Lawn, DT2 8TE ☎ 01305 848003 (Lauran Church)
www.english-home.biz Map 194/756947
BB **B** ✕ nearby D1 T1 F1 Ⓑ Ⓓ 😊 🐾 👙

● **Seaborough (Beaminster)**
Monarch's Way & Wessex Ridgeway
Seaborough Manor Farm, DT8 3QY ☎ 01308 868272 (Mrs V Barber)
www.seaboroughmanor.co.uk Map 193/431060
BB **B** ✕ book first £12, 6-8pm S1 D2 Ⓥ Ⓑ Ⓓ 🐾 👙 🚗 !

● **Sherborne**
Macmillan Way
Honeycombe View, Lower Clatcombe, DT9 4RH
☎ 01935 814644 (Mrs D Bower) Map 183/637179
BB **B** ✕ nearby T1 Closed Dec 🚶(Sherborne) Ⓑ Ⓓ 😊 🐾

● **Shillingstone (Blandford Forum)**
Wessex Ridgeway
Pennhills Farm, Sandy Lane, Off Lanchards Lane, DT11 0TF ☎ 01258 860491
(Mrs Rosemary Watts) Map 194/819102
BB **B** D/F1 T/S1 Ⓑ Ⓓ 😊 🐾 👙 🚗 ! 🐾 ◆◆◆

● **Shipton Gorge (Bridport)**
South West Coast Path & Monarch's Way
Cairnhill, DT6 4LL ☎ 01308 898203 (Mrs Anne White)
cairnhill@talk21.com Map 193,194/496919
BB **B** ✕ book first £20, 7pm S1 D1 T1 Closed Nov-Feb
Ⓥ Ⓑ Ⓓ 😊 👙 🚗 ! ◆◆◆◆◆Ⓖ

● **Sturminster Newton**
Newton House, DT10 2DQ ☎ 01258 472783 (Margie Fraser)
carolinepass@lineone.net Map 194/783135
BB **B** ✕ nearby S2 D2 T1 Ⓑ Ⓓ 😊 🐾 !
The Homestead, Hole House Lane, DT10 2AA ☎ 01258 471390
(Terry & Carol Townsend) www.townsend.dircon.co.uk Map 194/782128
BB **B** ✕ nearby T1 F1 Ⓑ Ⓓ 😊 🐾 👙 🚗 ! ◆◆◆
See SC also.

● **Swanage**
South West Coast Path
Hermitage Guesthouse, 1 Manor Road, BH19 2BH ☎ 01929 423014
(Susan Pickering) www.hermitage-online.co.uk Map 195/031785
BB **B** ✕ nearby D2 T1 F4 Closed Dec-Feb Ⓓ 😊 👙 🐾 Ⓜ
Sandringham Hotel, 20 Durlston Rd, BH19 2HX
☎ 01929 423076 (Mr & Mrs T Silk)
www.smoothhound.co.uk/hotels/sandringham.html Map 195/033782
BB **B** ✕ book first £15 (groups only), 6:30-7pm S2 D3 T2 F4
Ⓥ Ⓑ Ⓓ 🐾 👙 🚗 ! 🐾 ◆◆◆ See Groups also.

Sandhaven, 5 Ulwell Rd, BH19 1LE ☎ 01929 422322 (Janet Foran)
Map 195/030798 BB **B** ✕ nearby S1 D4 T2 F2 🚶(Swanage-Sr)
Ⓥ Ⓑ Ⓓ 🐾 👙 🐾 ◆◆◆

Perfick Piece, Springfield Road, BH19 1HD ☎ 01929 423178
(Mrs Elaine Hine) www.perfick-piece.co.uk Map 195/028788
BB **A/B** ✕ book first £7.50, 6pm S1 D1 T1 F1
Ⓥ Ⓑ Ⓓ 🐾 👙 ◆◆◆

☆ **The Limes Hotel**
48 Park Road, BH19 2AE ☎ 01929 422664
www.limeshotel.net Map 195/033783
BB **B** ✕ nearby S3 D2 T4 F3 🚶(Swanage)
Ⓑ Ⓓ 🐾 👙 🚗 ! 🐾 ◆◆◆◆

Swanage — just off Coast Path.
Close to town and the beach.
Wonderful for walking.
Car park, bar, laundry.
Open all year for B&B.
Families, groups and pets are welcome.
Email: info@limeshotel.demon.co.uk

● **Sydling St Nicholas (Dorchester)**
Wessex Ridgeway
City Cottage, DT2 9NX ☎ 01300 341300 (Mrs J Wareham) Map 194/632994
BB **B** ✕ nearby S1 D1 Ⓓ 🐾
Magiston Farm, DT2 9NR ☎ 01300 320295 (Mrs Barraclough)
Map 194/637967 BB **B** ✕ book first £12, 7pm S1/2 D1 T3
Ⓥ Ⓑ Ⓓ 🐾 👙 🚗 ◆◆◆

● **Wareham**
Ashcroft, 64 Furzebrook Road, Stoborough, BH20 5AX ☎ 01929 552392
(Mr & Mrs Cake) www.ashcroft-bb.co.uk Map 195/929850
BB **B** ✕ nearby S1 D1 T1 F1 🚶(Wareham)
Ⓑ Ⓓ 😊 🐾 👙 🚗 ◆◆◆◆

Hyde Cottage, Furzebrooke Rd, Stoborough, BH20 5AX
☎ 01929 553344 (D & J Bryer) hydecottbb@yahoo.co.uk Map 195/927853
BB **B** ✕ book first £10, 6:30-7:30pm S1 D1 T1 F2 🚶(Wareham)
Ⓥ Ⓑ Ⓓ 😊 🐾 👙 🚗 ! 🐾 ◆◆◆

Birchfield, 2 Drax Ave, BH20 4DJ ☎ 01929 552462 (Diana Hutton)
jl.hutton@tiscali.co.uk Map 195/922885
BB **B** ✕ nearby S1 D1 T1 Closed Dec-Jan 🚶(Wareham)
Ⓑ Ⓓ 😊 🐾 👙

Worgret Manor Hotel, Worgret Rd, BH20 6AB
☎ 01929 552957 www.worgretmanor.co.uk Map 195/907870
BB **C** ✕ £12-£30, 7-8:30pm S2 D6 T3 F1 🚶(Wareham)
Ⓥ Ⓑ 🐾 👙 🚗 ! 🐾 ★★★

● **West Lulworth (Wareham)**
South West Coast Path
Graybank B&B, Main Road, BH20 5RL
☎ 01929 400256 (Val & Barry Burrill) Map 194/822802
BB **B** ✕ nearby S1 D3 T2 F1 Closed Dec-Jan Ⓓ 🐾 👙 🚗 !

● **Westbourne (Bournemouth)**
The Westbrook Hotel, 64 Alum Chine Rd, BH4 8DZ ☎ 01202 761081
(Peter & Susan) www.westbrookhotel.co.uk Map 195/068911
BB **B** ✕ nearby S1 D4 T2 F2 Closed Dec-Jan 🚶(Bournemouth)
Ⓑ 😊 👙 🐾 Veggie Breakfasts.

● Weymouth
South West Coast Path

🛌◀ Hotel Rembrandt, 12-18 Dorchester Rd, DT4 7JU
☎ 01305 764000 www.hotelrembrandt.co.uk Map 194/679805
BB **C** ✕ £12.50-£14.50, 6:30-9:15pm S14 D29 T24 F8 🚶(Weymouth)
Ⓥ Ⓑ Ⓓ 🐾🛁🧺 ★★★

Kimberley Guest House, 16 Kirtleton Avenue, DT4 7PT
☎ 01305 783333   (Ken & Ann Jones)
Kenneth.Jones@btconnect.com Map 194/679802
BB **A** ✕ book first £7.50, 6pm S2 D6 T1 F2 🚶(Weymouth)
Ⓥ Ⓑ Ⓓ🛁! ◆◆◆

Cunard Guest House, 45/46 Lennox Street, DT4 7HB
☎ 01305 771546   (Mr & Mrs Harris)
www.cunardguesthouse.co.uk Map 194/681798
BB **B** S2 D5 T2 F2 🚶(Weymouth)
Ⓑ Ⓓ🐾🛁🚗🧺Ⓜ ◆◆◆

🛌◀ Harbour Lights Guesthouse, 20 Buxton Rd, DT4 9PJ
☎ 01305 783273 (Mrs Diane Quick)
http://harbourlights-weymouth.co.uk Map 194/672779
BB **B** ✕ nearby S2 D5 T1 F2 Closed Nov-Feb 🚶(Weymouth)
Ⓥ Ⓑ Ⓓ🛁 ◆◆◆ Veggie breakfasts available.

Channel View Guest House, 10 Brunswick Terrace, DT4 7RW
☎ 01305 782527 (Martin & Alison Weller)
leggchannelview@aol.com Map 194/682799
BB **B** ✕ nearby S2 D3 T1 F1 🚶(Weymouth)
Ⓑ Ⓓ🛁! ◆◆◆◆

🛌◀ Greenwood Guest House, 1 Holland Rd, DT4 0AL
☎ 01305 775626 (Angela Monahan)
www.greenwoodguesthouse.co.uk Map 194/674793
BB **B** ✕ nearby D3 T2 F1 🚶(Weymouth)
Ⓑ Ⓓ🐾🛁🚗!🧺

● Winterborne Kingston
Jubilee Trail (Dorset)

🛌◀ West Acres, West Street, DT11 9AT
☎ 01929 471293 (Mr & Mrs Jenkins) Map 194/854976
BB **B** ✕ book first £10, 7:30pm D1 T1 F1
Ⓥ Ⓑ Ⓓ🐾🛁🚗!🧺

GLOUCESTERSHIRE

● Blockley (Moreton-in-Marsh)
Monarch's Way & Heart Of England Way

The Malins, 21 Station Road, GL56 9ED ☎ 01386 700402
www.chippingcampden.co.uk/themalins.htm Map 151/169354
BB **B** ✕ nearby D2 T2
Ⓑ Ⓓ🐾🛁🚗! ◆◆◆◆

For an explanation of the symbols used in
this guide see the Key to Abbreviations and
Symbols on p 7

● Brookthorpe (Gloucester)
Cotswold Way

☆ 🛌◀ **Brookthorpe Lodge**
Stroud Road, GL4 0UQ ☎ 01452 812645 (Robert & Diana Bailey)
www.brookthorpelodge.demon.co.uk Map 162/835128
BB **B** ✕ book first £12.95, until 7pm S3 D2 T3 F2
Ⓥ Ⓑ Ⓓ☺🐾🛁🚗!🧺 ◆◆◆

Elegant Georgian house set in lovely
countryside at the foot of the Cotswold
escarpment between Gloucester & Stroud.
Family run, traditional service and
delicious breakfasts. Excellent walking
country and ideal base for Cotswolds,
Cheltenham and Bath. Good access to M5.

● Cam (Dursley)
Cotswold Way

☆ Foresters
31 Chapel Street, GL11 5NX ☎ 01453 549996 (Mrs Victoria Jennings)
www.foresters-inn.co.uk Map 162/750002
BB **B** ✕ book first £10-14, 6-8:30pm D2 T2 F1 🚶(Cam & Dursley)
Ⓥ Ⓑ Ⓓ☺🐾🛁🚗🧺 ◆◆◆◆
Discounts for 2 nights or more

18th century cosy
former village inn
with pretty walled
garden. Spacious
en-suite beamed
bedrooms and visitor
lounge with open fire
and central heating.
Warm utility room
for drying.

Excellent walking on our doorstep and a wealth of attractions/villages and cities
to visit: Westonbirt, Slimbridge, Bath, Cotswold Way, Berkeley Castle, Gloucester.
Close to Jct 13/14 M5. 10% reduction for 7 nights stay. Dogs welcome by
arrangement. Colour TVs/tea/coffee facilities. 4 poster-beds/2 twins.

● Charlton Kings (Cheltenham)
Cotswold Way

California Farm, Capel Lane, GL54 4HQ ☎ 01242 244746 Map 163/023196
BB **B** ✕ book first £12-£15, 7pm S1 D2 T1
Ⓥ Ⓑ Ⓓ☺🐾🛁🚗!

☆ 🛌◀ Charlton Kings Hotel
London Road, GL52 6UU ☎ 01242 231061
www.charltonkingshotel.co.uk Map 163/977201
BB **C** ✕ £18-£20, 7-9pm S2 D5 T5 F1
Ⓥ Ⓑ Ⓓ🐾🛁 ★★★

Ideally situated on edge of town 1/2 mile from
Cotswold Way. All rooms beautifully refurbished
with bath/shower, most have views of the Cotswold
Hills. Set in an acre of gardens, ample parking.
Restaurant open every night. Conde Nast Johansens
recommended.
Recommendednquiries@charltonkingshotel.co.uk.

22 Ledmore Road, GL53 8RA ☎ 01242 526957 (Geraldine White)
geraldine.white@btinternet.com Map 163/967207
BB **B** nearby S1 D1 T1 (Cheltenham)
B D Ⓜ

Chedworth (Cheltenham)

Monarch's Way & Macmillan Way

The Vicarage, GL54 4AA ☎ 01285 720392 (George & Pattie Mitchell)
canongeorgemitchell@btinternet.com Map 163/052118
BB **A** nearby S1 T1 B D ◆◆◆

Cheltenham

Cotswold Way

St Cloud, 97 Leckhampton Road, GL53 0BZ ☎ 01242 575245 (Ruth Jennings) ruth.jen@virgin.net Map 163/946202
BB **A** nearby S1 D1 T2 F1 (Cheltenham Spa)
D ◆◆◆

Moorend Park Hotel, 11 Moorend Park Rd, GL53 0LA ☎ 01242 224441
www.moorendpark.freeuk.com Map 163/941205
BB **B** nearby S2 D4 T1 F2 (Cheltenham Spa)
B ◆◆◆◆Ⓢ

☆ Cleeve Hill Hotel
Cleeve Hill, GL52 3PR ☎ 01242 672052 (Bob & Georgie Tracey)
www.cleevehillhotel.info Map 163/987269
BB **C** nearby S1 D7 T2
B D ◆◆◆◆◆

Situated in an area of outstanding natural beauty, so views from most bedrooms are spectacular. Direct access to Cotswold Way via Garden Gate.
Private car park.
Strictly non-smoking.

Chipping Campden

Cotswold Way & Heart Of England Way

Volunteer Inn, Lower High Street, GL55 6DY ☎ 01386 840688 (Mrs Sinclair)
www.thevolunteerinn.com Map 151/150392
BB **C** £4.50-£8.50, 7-9pm S1 D3 T2 F1
V B D Ⓜ

Weston Park Farm, Dovers Hill, GL55 6UW ☎ 01386 840835 (Mrs J Whitehouse) www.cotswoldcottages.uk.com Map 151/130390
BB **B** nearby D1 F1 B D ◆◆◆ See SC also.

Lygon Arms Hotel, High Street, GL55 6HB ☎ 01386 840318
www.lygonarms.co.uk Map 151/153394
BB **E** book first £6-£20, 6-10pm D/T5 F2
V B D

The Old Bakehouse, Lower High Street, GL55 6DZ ☎ 01386 840979 (Sarah Drinkwater) oldbakehouse@chippingcampden-cotswolds.co.uk
Map 151/150392 BB **C** nearby D3 T1 F1 B D

Chipping Sodbury

Monarch's Way & Cotswold Way

The Moda Hotel, 1 High St, BS37 6BA ☎ 01454 312135 (Jo Macarthur)
www.modahotel.com Map 172/726822
BB **B** nearby S4 D4 T1 F1 (Yate)
B D ◆◆◆◆

Cirencester

Monarch's Way

☆ Royal Agricultural College
GL7 6JS (Conference Department) ☎ 01285 652531
www.royagcol.ac.uk Map 163/004011
BB **B** book first £18, 7pm S12 T7 (Kemble)
V B D ★★★

Ensuite bedrooms in Britain's oldest agricultural college. Situated 10 minutes walk from bustling market town. Ample parking and close to beautiful walks.
commercial.services@rac.ac.uk

Clearwell (Coleford)

Wye Valley Walk

☆ Tudor Farmhouse Hotel
High Str., GL16 8JS ☎ 01594 833046
www.tudorfarmhousehotel.co.uk Map 162/573080
£20, 7-9pm S6 D12 T2 F2
V B D ★★★

A cosy 13th century stone built hotel with AA Rosette restaurant in the historic and pretty village of Clearwell in the Forest of Dean is the ideal setting for a relaxed or active holiday. Near the Wye Valley Walk and Offa's Dyke with walking also available from the hotel. All rooms en-suite with superior rooms having jacuzzi baths. Drying room and cycle storage available. Pets welcome.

Cleeve Hill (Cheltenham)

Cotswold Way

Heron Haye, Petty Lane, GL52 3PW
☎ 01242 672516 (Edward Saunders)
dick.whittamore@virgin.net Map 163/987273
BB **B** nearby S1 D2 D

Cold Ashton (Bristol)

Cotswold Way

Toghill House Farm, BS30 5RT
☎ 01225 891261 (D Bishop)
www.toghillhousefarm.co.uk Map 172/731724
BB **C** nearby D/S5 T/S3 F/S3
B D ◆◆◆◆

● Coleford
Offa's Dyke & Wye Valley Walk
The Rock, Hillersland, GL16 7NY ☎ 01594 837893 (Mrs Dinah Barrand) www.stayattherock.com Map 162/568144
BB **B** ✗ nearby D2 T2 Closed Nov-Feb
♦♦♦

● Dursley
Cotswold Way
7 Prospect Place, GL11 4JL ☎ 01453 543445 (Mrs Cecilia Boyle)
ceciliaboyle@hotmail.com Map 162/755980
BB **B** ✗ book first £10.50-£12.50, 8pm S1 D1 T1 ⋙(Cam, Dursley)

● English Bicknor (Coleford)
Wye Valley Walk
Dryslade Farm, GL16 7PA ☎ 01594 860259 (Mrs Daphne Gwilliam)
www.drysladefarm.co.uk Map 162/579149
BB **B** ✗ nearby D1 T1 F1 ♦♦♦♦

● Ewen (Cirencester)
Thames Path & Monarch's Way
Brooklands Farm, GL7 6BU ☎ 01285 770 487 (Betty Crew)
Map 163/003975 BB **A** ✗ nearby D2 ⋙(Kemble)
♦♦♦

● Fairford
Thames Path
Kempsford Manor, GL7 4EQ ☎ 01285 810131
http://members.lycos.co.uk/kempsford_manor Map 163/158969
BB **B** ✗ book first £12.50, 7:30-8:30pm S2 D2 F1
♦♦♦

● Gloucester
Cotswold Way
Harescombe Grange, GL4 0UY ☎ 01452 812683 (Messrs Hutton)
Map 162/844105 BB **B** ✗ book first £10, 7:30pm D1 T1

● Guiting Power
Guiting Guest House, GL54 5TZ ☎ 01451 850470 (Barbara Millar)
www.guitingguesthouse.com Map 163/099245
BB **C** ✗ book first £25, 7pm S1 D6 T1 F1 Closed Dec
♦♦♦♦♦Ⓢ

● King's Stanley (Stonehouse)
Cotswold Way
Old Chapel House, Broad Street, GL10 3PN ☎ 01453 826289 (Jean Hanna)
www.geocities.com/bandbinuk Map 162/813033
BB **B** ✗ book first £6 upwards, 6:30-7:30pm S2 D1 T1 F1 Closed Dec
⋙(Stonehouse)

Stantone, Coldwell Lane, Middleyard, GL10 3PR ☎ 01453 822204
(Mrs Louise Walker) rbwstantone@aol.com Map 162/816030
BB **B** ✗ nearby T1 Closed Dec ⋙(Stonehouse)

Vally Views, 12 Orchard Close, Middleyard, GL10 3QA
☎ 01453 827458 (Mrs Pam White) Map 162/819032
BB **B** ✗ book first £5+, 7pm D1 T1 ⋙(Stonehouse)

● Kingscote (Tetbury)
Hunters Hall, GL8 8XZ ☎ 01453 860393 www.oldenglish.co.uk
Map 162/816961 BB **C** ✗ book first £15, 6:30-9:30pm D6 T5 F1

● Lechlade
Thames Path
Leventen House, High St, GL7 3AD ☎ 01367 252592 (Ms Elizabeth Reay)
emreay@aol.com Map 163/212995 BB **B** ✗ nearby S1 D1

● Lechlade-on-Thames
Thames Path
Cambrai Lodge, Oak Street, GL7 3AY
☎ 01367 253173 (Mr John Titchener) Map 163/214998
BB **B** ✗ nearby S2 D3 T2 ♦♦♦♦Ⓢ

● Little Sodbury (Chipping Sodbury)
Cotswold Way
Monarch's Way

☆ New Crosshands Farm
BS37 6RJ ☎ 01454 316366 (Mrs Deborah Snell)
debsnell@tiscali.co.uk Map 172/761826
BB **B** ✗ book first £10-£15, 7:30pm S3 D3 T3 F1

Cotswold stone house set beside Iron Age hill fort with spectacular views over the Severn Vale and beyond. The Cotswold Way runs through the farm land. Quiet rural location, ideal for your stay. 5 mins walk from Monarch's Way. A warm welcome awaits.

● Naunton (Cheltenham)
Mill View Guest House, 2 Mill View, GL54 3AF ☎ 01451 850586
(Patricia Boult) www.millviewguesthousecotswolds.com Map 163/121235
BB **C** ✗ £12.50 D2 T1 ♦♦♦♦

● Newland (Coleford)
Wye Valley Walk
Tan House Farm, GL16 8NQ ☎ 01594 832222 (Peter Chamberlain)
christie.arno3@virgin.net Map 162/552091
BB **B** ✗ nearby S1 D3 T1 ♦♦♦

● North Nibley (Dursley)
Cotswold Way

☆ Nibley House
GL11 6DL ☎ 01453 543108 (Diana A Eley)
john@eley7143.freeserve.co.uk Map 162/737958
BB **B** ✗ nearby D3 T2 F1

Relax — Splendid views — Relax — 2 1/2 acres of garden — Relax — 400 years of history — Relax — Hospitality — Relax — Where to stay on the Cotswold Way — Relax — You've found it.

● Old Sodbury (Bristol)
Monarch's Way & Cotswold Way

Denison Cottage, Combs End, BS37 6SQ ☎ 01454 311510 (Susan Holbrook)
Map 172/754806 BB **B** ✗ nearby TI ⬛ 😊 🐾🛏🚗 ⚡ !

● Painswick (Stroud)
Cotswold Way

🛶⊷ Skyrack, The Highlands, GL6 6SL ☎ 01452 812029 (Wendy Hodgson)
www.painswick.co.uk/skyrack Map 162/868105
BB **B** ✗ nearby S1 D/F1 T/F1
⬛ ⬛ 😊 🐾🛏🚗 ⚡ ! 🏠 ◆◆◆

Orchard House, 4 Court Orchard, GL6 6UU ☎ 01452 813150 (Mrs Barbara
Harley) www.painswick.co.uk Map 162/866095
BB **B** ✗ nearby S0 D1 T1 ⬛ 😊 🐾🛏🚗 ⚡ ! Ⓜ

The Falcon Inn, New Street, GL6 6UN ☎ 01452 814222 (Fiona Johnston)
www.falconinn.com Map 162/866097
BB **C** ✗ book first £9, 7-9:30pm D4 T4 F4
Ⓥ ⬛ ⬛ 🐾🛏🚗 ⚡ ! 🏠 ★★

Cardynham House, The Cross, GL6 6TX ☎ 01452 814006 (John Paterson)
www.cardynham.co.uk Map 162/868098
BB **C** ✗ £24.50, 7pm onwards D6 F3 Ⓥ ⬛ 🛏 ◆◆◆◆

● Pucklechurch (Bristol)
Monarch's Way

🛶⊷ Fern Cottage Country B&B, 188 Shortwood Hill, BS16 9PG
☎ 01179 374966 (Sue James)
www.ferncottagebedandbreakfast.co.uk Map 172/687758
BB **B** ✗ nearby D4 F1 ⬛ ⬛ 😊 🐾🛏🚗 ⚡ !

● Slimbridge
Severn Way

May Cottage, Shepherd's Patch, GL2 7BP
☎ 01453 890820 (Peter & Sue Gibson)
www.smoothhound.co.uk/hotels/maycottage1 Map 162/721044
BB **B** ✗ nearby TI ⬛ ⬛ 😊 🐾

● Southam (Cheltenham)
Cotswold Way

Pigeon House Cottage, next Tithe Barn, Southam Lane, GL52 3NY
☎ 01242 584255 (B J Holden)
barbara.holden@care4free.net Map 163/973255
BB **B** ✗ book first £12 D2 T2 Ⓥ ⬛ ⬛ 😊 🐾🛏🚗 ⚡ !

● St Briavels (Lydney)
Offa's Dyke & Wye Valley Walk

> ☆ **Lindors Country House**
> The Fence, GL15 6RB ☎ 01594 530283
> www.cgholidays.co.uk Map 162/550053
> BB **B** ✗ £12, 6:30pm S3 D9 T13 F1
> Ⓥ ⬛ ⬛ 🐾🛏 ⚡ !
>
> A Christian-based hotel offering fun and fellowship.
> A charming 19th century property in 9 acres of
> gardens. Heated indoor pool, tennis court plus 5 lodges
> for self catering. Ideal for Wye Valley, Offa's Dyke and
> Royal Forest of Dean.
> Email: lindors@cgholidays.co.uk

● Stanton (Broadway)
Cotswold Way

Shenberrow Hill, WR12 7NE ☎ 01386 584468 (Mrs Angela Neilan)
michael.neilan1@btopenworld.com Map 150/071342
BB **B** ✗ nearby D2 T2 F2 ⬛ ⬛ 😊 🐾🛏🚗 ⚡ ! 🏠 ◆◆◆◆

● Stow-on-the-Wold (Cheltenham)
**Heart Of England Way, Monarch's Way &
Macmillan Way**

The Limes, Evesham Road, GL54 1EJ ☎ 01451 830034 (Helen & Graham
Keyte) thelimes@zoom.co.uk Map 163/181264
BB **B** ✗ nearby D3 T1 F1 ⬛ ⬛ 🛏

Corsham Field Farm House, Bledington Road, GL54 1JH
☎ 01451 831750 (Robert Smith)
www.corshamfield.co.uk Map 163/217250
BB **B** ✗ nearby D2 T2 F3 ⬛ ⬛ 🛏 🏠 ◆◆◆

Fifield Cottage, Fosse Lane, GL54 1EH ☎ 01451 831056 (Valerie Keyte)
Map 163/189258 BB **B** ✗ nearby D1 T1 F1 ⬛ ⬛ 😊 🛏 🏠

● Stroud
Cotswold Way

Pretoria Villa, Wells Road, Eastcombe, GL6 7EE
☎ 01452 770435 (Mrs Glynis Solomon)
www.bedandbreakfast-cotswold.co.uk Map 163/891044
BB **B** ✗ book first £16, 7-8:30pm S1 D1 T1
Ⓥ ⬛ ⬛ 😊 🐾🛏🚗 ⚡ ! ◆◆◆◆Ⓢ

> ☆ **The Downfield Hotel**
> 134 Cainscross Road, GL5 4HN ☎ 01453 764496 (Maura & Nigel)
> www.downfieldhotel.co.uk Map 162/841051
> BB **B** ✗ book first £12, 6:30-8:15pm S4 D8 T7 F2 🚌(Stroud)
> Ⓥ ⬛ ⬛ 🐾🛏🚗 ⚡ ! 🏠 ◆◆◆
>
> The Ramblers Rest... for thousands of regulars walking the Cotswold Way!
> Owners Maura and Nigel will make you feel very welcome.
> Comfortable rooms, home cooked food and cosy bar.
> You can easily find us on the A419 west of Stroud and there's plenty of parking.
> Groups are welcome.
> B&B from £22.50

Rusland, Bourne Lane, Brimscombe, GL5 2RQ
☎ 01453 882165 (Freda Watson)
www.charles.freda.freeuk.com Map 162/869025
BB **B** ✗ nearby D1 T1 🚌(Stroud) ⬛ ⬛ 😊 🐾🛏🚗 ⚡

Braemar, Selsey West, GL5 5LG ☎ 01453 826102 (Mrs D Wear)
maurice@wear9.freeserve.co.uk Map 162/828035
BB **B** ✗ book first £10, 7pm S1 D2 🚌(Stroud)
Ⓥ ⬛ 😊 🛏🚗 ⚡ !

🛶⊷ Hillenvale Guest House, The Plain, Whiteshill, GL6 6AB
☎ 01453 753441 (Bob & Sue Baker) www.hillenvale.co.uk
Map 162/840068 BB **B** ✗ nearby D1 T2 🚌(Stroud)
⬛ ⬛ 🛏🚗 ⚡ ! ◆◆◆◆

● Tormarton (Badminton)
Cotswold Way & Monarch's Way

The Compass Inn, GL9 1JB ☎ 01454 218242 www.compass-inn.co.uk
Map 172/760780 BB **C** ✗ £5-£16.95, until 10pm D12 T7 F5
Ⓥ ⬛ ⬛ 🐾🛏🚗 ★★

Chestnut Farm, GL9 1HS ☎ 01454 218563
www.chestnut-farm.co.uk   Map 172/768790
BB **B**   ✕ £10, 8pm   D5 T2   V   B   D ⊛ 🖐 👶 🚗 🐾

Portcullis Inn, GL9 1HZ ☎ 01454 218263   Map 172/767787
BB **B**   ✕ £6.50, 7-9pm   D2 T3 F1   V   B   D 🖐 👶 ! 🐾

● **Uley (Dursley)**
  Cotswold Way

Hodgecombe Farm, GL11 5AN ☎ 01453 860365 (Mrs Catherine Bevan)
www.hodgecombefarm.co.uk   Map 162/790985
BB **B**   ✕ book first £16, 7pm   D2 F0   Closed Nov-Mar
V   B   D ⊛ 🖐 👶 🚗 !   ◆◆◆◆

● **Winchcombe (Cheltenham)**
  Cotswold Way

Gower House, 16 North Street, GL54 5LH
☎ 01242 602616 (Mrs S Simmonds)
gowerhouse16@aol.com   Map 150,163/025284
BB **B**   ✕ nearby   D1 T2   B   D 🖐 👶 ! Ⓜ   ◆◆◆◆

🖼️◀ Cleevely Cottage, Wadfield Farm, Corndean Lane, GL54 5AL
☎ 01242 602059 (Mrs C M Rand)
cleevelybxb@hotmail.com   Map 150/025263
BB **B**   ✕ book first £10, 6:30pm   D1 T1 F1
V   B   D ⊛ 🖐 👶 🚗 ! 🐾   ◆◆◆◆

Mercia, Hailes Street, GL54 5HU ☎ 01242 602251 (Mrs J E Upton)
www.merciaguesthouse.co.uk   Map 150,163/026285
BB **C**   ✕ nearby   D3 T1   B   D ⊛ 🖐 👶 ! 🐾   ◆◆◆◆Ⓢ

1 Stancombe View, GL54 5LE ☎ 01242 603654 (Mrs M Robins)
Map 150,163/023285   BB **A**   ✕ nearby   S1 D1   Closed Dec
B   D ⊛ 🖐 👶 🚗   ◆◆◆   Special diets.

Blair House, 41 Gretton Road, GL54 5EG ☎ 01242 603626
(Mrs S Chisholm)   chissurv@aol.com   Map 150,163/023287
BB **B**   ✕ nearby   S2 D1 T1   B   D ⊛ 🖐 👶   ◆◆◆◆

🖼️◀ Greenhyde, Langley Road, GL54 5QP
☎ 01242 602569 (Dora Wigg)   Map 150, 163/015282
BB **B**   ✕ book first £10, 7pm   D1 T/S1
V   B   D ⊛ 🖐 👶 Ⓜ   ◆◆◆◆

🖼️◀ Glebe Farm, Wood-Stanway, GL54 5PG
☎ 01386 584791 (Ann Flavell-Wood)
www.woodstanway.co.uk   Map 150/065313
BB **B**   ✕ book first £16, 6:30pm   D1 T2   V   B   D 🖐 🐾

Yorklands, 127 Gretton Road, GL54 5EL ☎ 01242 602102 (Wendy Cooke)
Map 150,163/022291   BB **B**   ✕ nearby   D1 T/S1
B   D ⊛ 👶 🚗 Ⓜ

🖼️◀ Wood Stanway Farmhouse, Wood Stanway, GL54 5PG
☎ 01386 584318 (Maggie Green)
www.woodstanwayfarmhouse.co.uk   Map 150/062311
BB **B**   ✕ book first £10, 6-7pm   D1 T1 F1
V   B   D 🖐 👶 🚗 ! 🐾   ◆◆◆

🖼️◀ One Silk Mill Lane, GL54 5HZ ☎ 01242 603952 (Jenny Cheshire)
jenny.cheshire@virgin.net   Map 150,163/026284
BB **B**   ✕ nearby   T2   B   D ⊛ 🖐 👶 🚗 !   ◆◆◆◆

Gaia Cottage, 50 Gloucester St, GL54 5LX
☎ 01242 603495 (Brian & Sally Simmonds)   brian.simmonds@tiscali.co.uk
Map 150,163/022282   BB **B**   ✕ nearby   D1 T1
B   D ⊛ 🖐 👶 ! Ⓜ   ◆◆◆◆

● **Wotton-under-Edge**
  Cotswold Way & Monarch's Way

Wotton Guest House, 31a Long Street, GL12 7BX
☎ 01453 843158   (Mrs Sandra Nixon)
wottongh@aol.com   Map 172,162/757933
BB **B**   ✕ nearby   S1 D3 T2 F1   B   D 🖐 👶 🚗 ! 🐾

Hillesley Mill, Alderley, GL12 7QT
☎ 01453 843258 (Mrs Julie James)   Map 172,162/770905
BB **B**   ✕ nearby   S1 D1 T/F1   B   D 🖐 👶 🚗 ! 🐾   ◆◆◆

● **St Mary's**

☆ **Santa Maria Guest House**
44 Sally Port, TR21 0JE ☎ 01720 422687
Map 203/901104
BB **C**   ✕ book first £13, 6:30pm   S2 D3 T3 F1   Closed Nov-Feb
V   B ⊛ 🖐 👶 !   ◆◆◆◆

"Sample the warmth and friendliness of our hospitality at Santa Maria,
situated in a quiet residential area with panoramic views across Porth Cressa
beach and St Mary's Pool, within minutes of the shops, beaches and quay."
All our rooms are attractively furnished, en-suite, have beverage making
facilities, clock radios and hair dryers. We have rooms to accommodate single,
twin, double and family occupancy.
We have also gained a reputation with our regulars for serving fine food using
fresh produce. Our half board tariff includes English breakfast and four-course
dinner. Vegetarian meals and packed lunches are available if pre-booked. We
have a quiet lounge and a separate residents' bar with a television and video.
Ring today for a brochure or further information.

● **Axbridge**

Waterside, Cheddar Road, BS26 2DP ☎ 01934 743182 (Gillian Aldridge)
gillianaldridge@hotmail.com   Map 182/438545
BB **B**   ✕ book first £10, 7pm   S1 D2 T1   Closed Dec
V   B   D ⊛ 🖐 👶 🐾   ◆◆◆

● **Bath**
  Cotswold Way

Brocks, 32 Brock Street, BA1 2LN ☎ 01225 338374 (Marion Dodd)
www.brocksguesthouse.co.uk   Map 172/746652

BB **C** ✕ nearby   D3 T1 F2   ﹏(Bath Spa)
🄱 🄳 ⊗ ☕ ◆◆◆◆

Flaxley Villa, 9 Newbridge Hill, BA1 3PW
☎ 01225 313237 (M A Cooper)   Map 172/731651
BB **B**   ✕ nearby   S1 D1 T2 F1   ﹏(Bath Spa) 🄱 ☕   ◆◆◆

🚩◀ Marlborough House, 1 Marlborough Lane, BA1 2NQ ☎ 01225 318175
www.marlborough-house.net   Map 172/742651
BB **C**   S7 D7 T1 F2   ﹏(Bath Spa) Ⓥ 🄱 ⊗ 🍵☕ 🚗 🐾 Ⓜ
◆◆◆◆   Vegetarian food only.

St Georges Cottage, Bathampton Lane, BA2 6SJ ☎ 01225 466801 (Joan
Walmsley) www.stgeorgescottagebath.co.uk   Map 172/769660
BB **B**   ✕ nearby   D2 T1   ﹏(Bath Spa)
🄱 ⊗ 🍵☕ 🚗 !   ◆◆◆◆

☆ 🚩◀ **Cranleigh**
159 Newbridge Hill, BA1 3PX   ☎ 01225 310197
www.cranleighguesthouse.com   Map 172/724656
BB **C**   ✕ nearby   D4 T2 F2   ﹏(Bath Spa)
🄱 🄳 ⊗ ☕ 🚗 !   ◆◆◆◆

The Cotswold Way goes close to our door —
this is the perfect spot to begin or end your
walk! Victorian house with beautiful views, 8
en-suite bedrooms and generous breakfasts.
Non-smoking, private car parking.
Email: cranleigh@btinternet.com

☆ 🚩◀ **Number 30 Crescent Gardens**
BA1 2NB (David Greenwood) ☎ 01225 337393
www.numberthirty.com   Map 172/744650
BB **C**   ✕ nearby   S1 D5 T1   ﹏(Bath Spa)
🄱 🄳 ⊗ ☕ Ⓜ   ◆◆◆◆Ⓢ

4 diamond standards of
comfort and housekeeping
in our Victorian house in
Bath city centre. Non-
smoking. Vegetarian
options. All rooms en-suite,
light and airy. No pets.

☆ 🚩◀ **Crescent Guest House**
21 Crescent Gardens, Upper Bristol Rd, BA1 2NA ☎ 01225 425945 (John
& Gilly Deacon) www.crescentbath.co.uk   Map 172/744650
BB **B**   ✕ nearby   S1 D4 T1 F1   ﹏(Bath Spa)
🄱 🄳 ⊗ ☕   ◆◆◆◆Ⓢ

Enjoy a warm welcome at our city centre
Victorian home. Comfort, high standards
of service and cleanliness, and generous
breakfasts (for omnivores and
herbivores) prepared from fresh local
ingredients. 5 mins stroll to the shopping
centre and Bath's many attractions.

● **Batheaston (Bath)**
1 Hill Cottages, Ramscombe Lane, Northend, BA1 8EP ☎ 01225 852769
(Mrs Carole Hughes) www.orchardviewbath.co.uk   Map 172/776688
BB **B**   ✕ nearby   D1 T1   🄳 ⊗ ☕

● **Bathford (Bath)**
Garston Cottage, 28 Ashley Road, BA1 7TT ☎ 01225 852510   (Beverley
Smart)   garstoncot@aol.com   Map 172/792668
BB **B**   ✕ nearby   D2 T/D2 F1   🄱 🄳 ⊗ ☕ 🐾

● **Blagdon**
Monarch's Way

☆ 🚩◀ **Coombe Lodge**
Climes, BS40 7RG ☎ 01761 463355
www.combelodge.co.uk   Map 182,172/496595
BB **B**   ✕ £12, 6:30-8:30pm   S2 D20 T3 F3
Ⓥ 🄱 🄳 ⊗ 🍵☕ !

A Grade II listed country house set in 12
acres of magnificent gardens, in AONB.
The area is dominated by the magnificent
Blagdon Lake and within easy access to
the Mendip Way. 28 bedrooms, some
en-suite, all have hairdryers.
Full English breakfast. Car parking.

● **Bridgwater (Wembdon)**
Macmillan Way West
Cokerhurst Farm, 87 Wembdon Hill, TA6 7QA ☎ 01278 422330
(Mrs D Chappell) www.cokerhurst.clara.net   Map 182/280378
BB **B**   ✕ nearby   D1 T1 F1   ﹏(Bridgewater)
🄱 🄳 ⊗ 🍵🍵☕ 🚗 !   ◆◆◆◆

● **Bristol**
Monarch's Way
Mayfair Lodge, 5 Henleaze Road, Westbury-on-Trym, BS9 4EX
☎ 0117 962 2008 (Mrs A Kitching)
www.smoothhound.co.uk/hotels/mayfairlodge.html
Map 172/573761   BB **B**   ✕ nearby   S5 D2 T2
🄱 ⊗ ☕   ◆◆◆

🚩◀ The Wellsway Inn, Harptree Hill, West Harptree, BS40 6EJ
☎ 01761 221382   Map 182,172/545559
BB **B**   ✕ £8-£12, 6:30-9pm   S1 D2 T1 F1 Ⓥ
🄱 ⊗   ◆◆◆

● **Burnham-on-Sea**
Thizeldo-Vine, 37 Kingsway Rd, TA8 1ET ☎ 01278 782909 (Mrs Janet Keen)
www.thizeldo-vine.co.uk   Map 182/306492
BB **B**   ✕ book first £9.50   S2 D1 T1   ﹏(Highbridge)
🄱 ⊗ 🍵🍵☕ 🚗 !   ◆◆◆◆

● **Charlton Horethorne (Sherborne)**
Monarch's Way & Macmillan Way
Beech Farm, Sigwells, DT9 4LN ☎ 01963 220524 (Susan Stretton)
stretton@beechfarmsigwells.freeserve.co.uk   Map 183/642231
BB **A**   ✕ nearby   S1 D1 T1 F1
🄱 🄳 ⊗ 🚗 🐾 ☕

● **Cheddar**
Constantine, Lower New Road, BS27 3DY
☎ 01934 741339 (Sue & Barry Mitchell) Map 182/450531
BB **B**   ✕ book first £8, 6:30pm   S1 D2 T/D1 F1   Closed Dec
Ⓥ 🄱 🄳 ⊗ 🍵☕   ◆◆◆

Bay Rose House, The Bays, BS27 3QN ☎ 01934 741377 (Andrea & Martin Kay) www.bayrose.co.uk Map 182/463538
BB **B** ✕ book first £12, 7-9pm D1 T1 F1
V B D ◆◆◆

Chew Stoke (Bristol)

Monarch's Way

Orchard House, Bristol Road, BS40 8UB ☎ 01275 333143 (Mrs Ann Hollomon) www.orchardhse.ukgateway.net Map 182, 172/561618
BB **B** ✕ nearby S1 D1 T2 F1 B D ◆◆◆

Churchill (Winscombe)

Mendip Way

The Mendip Gate Guest House, Bristol Rd, BS25 5NL ☎ 01934 852333 (Paul & Sarah Vowles) www.themendipgate.co.uk Map 182,172/451600
BB **B** ✕ book first £8, 8pm S3 D3 T3 F2 V B D

Crewkerne

Monarch's Way

George Hotel and Courtyard Restaurant, Market Square, TA18 7LP ☎ 01460 73650 (Frank E Joyce MHCIMA) www.thegeorgehotelcrewkerne.co.uk Map 193/441098
BB **B/C** ✕ £5-£15, 7-9pm S3 D5 T2 F3 (Crewkerne)
V B D ◆◆◆

Honeydown Farm, Seaborough Hill, TA18 8PL ☎ 01460 72665 (Catherine Bacon) www.honeydown.co.uk Map 193/430072
BB **B** ✕ book first £15, 7pm D2 T1 (Crewkerne)
V B D ◆◆◆◆

Cucklington (Wincanton)

Monarch's Way

Longhill Farm, BA9 9PT ☎ 01747 840234 (John & Wendy Payne) johnandwendypayne@talk21.com Map 183/753277
BB **B** D2 T1 B D

Dulverton

Exmoor

Marsh Bridge Cottage, TA22 9QG ☎ 01398 323197 (Mrs C Nurcombe) Map 181/904288 BB **B** ✕ book first £15.25, 7pm D1 T1 F1
V B D

☆ **Exton House Hotel**
Exton, TA22 9JT ☎ 01643 851365 (Mr & Mrs Glaister) Map 181/926336
BB **B/C** ✕ book first £18.75, 7:30pm S1 D3 T2 F3
V B D Ⓜ ◆◆◆◆Ⓢ See Groups also.

Exmoor Porridge! To sample this renowned breakfast and all our other wonderful food, wines and walks, book a few days with us! Discounts to all individuals or groups. Hotel available for SC or Groups.

Dunster (Minehead)

Exmoor

South West Coast Path & Macmillan Way West

Dollons House, 10-12 Church Street, TA24 6SH ☎ 01643 821880 (Janet & Peter Mott) jmott@onetel.net.uk Map 181/990436
BB **B/C** ✕ nearby D2 T1 (Dunster)
B D Ⓜ ◆◆◆◆◆Ⓢ

☆ **The Yarn Market Hotel**
High Street, TA24 6SF ☎ 01643 821425 (Penny Bale) www.yarnmarkethotel.co.uk Map 181/992437
BB **B** ✕ £20, 5:30-8:30pm S6 D12 T3 F3 (Dunster)
V B D Ⓜ ★★★

Our small hotel provides a friendly atmosphere, home cooking, en-suite single, double 4-poster and family rooms all with colour TV and tea/coffee. Residents' lounge, packed lunches and drying facilities available. Open all year. B&B from £35 (£50 with evening meal). 3 nights £90 (£135). Special offer for walking parties (10-50 people) 3 nights B&B from £80 per person (£120). An ideal centre for exploring Exmoor.
Email: yarnmarket.hotel@virgin.net/ Contact: Penny Bale.

Exebridge

Exmoor

2 Staghound Cottages, TA22 9AZ ☎ 01398 324453 (Penny Richards) www.staghound.co.uk Map 181/930243
BB **B** ✕ nearby S1 D1 T1 B D

Hinton St George

Monarch's Way

Rookwood, West Street, TA17 8SA ☎ 01460 73450 (Mrs B Hudspith) betty.hudspith@virgin.net Map 193/417126
BB **B** ✕ nearby T2 B D ◆◆◆

Holford (Bridgwater)

Macmillan Way West

Forge Cottage, TA5 1RY ☎ 01278 741215 (Mrs Susan Ayshford) Map 181/158413 BB **A** ✕ book first £8, 6-7pm D2 T1
V D

Glenstone Farm, TA5 1RY ☎ 01278 741526 (Mrs V Stone) Map 181/158413 BB **B** ✕ £8, 7-7:30pm S1 D2 T1 F1
V B D

Kilve (Bridgwater)

Macmillan Way West

Kilve Village Stores, TA5 1EA ☎ 01278 741214 (Ian & Jackie Perrior) www.kilvebedandbreakfast.co.uk Map 181/149429
BB **B** ✕ nearby S2 D2 T2 F2 D

Minehead

Exmoor

South West Coast Path & Macmillan Way West

☆ **Lyn Valley Guest House**
3 Tregonwell Road, TA24 5DT ☎ 01643 703748 (Margaret & Julian Hills) www.lynvalleyminehead.co.uk Map 181/973463
BB **B** ✕ nearby S1 D3 T3 F1
V B D ◆◆◆

Comfortable spacious family guest house on quiet residential road. 2 minutes walk from town centre, seafront, restaurants and steam railway.
Close to start of South West Coast Path.

Fernside, The Holloway, TA24 5PB ☎ 01643 707594
(Colin & Maureen Smith) catman.do@btopenworld.com   Map 181/966464
BB **B**   ✕ book first £10, 6-6:30pm   D2 FI
Ⓥ Ⓑ Ⓓ ⊗ 🐾🖐🧺 ◆◆◆

🛏◀ The Parks Guesthouse, 26 The Parks, TA24 8BT ☎ 01643 703547
(Jackie & Richard Trott) www.parksguesthouse.co.uk   Map 181/964462
BB **B**   ✕ nearby   D2 T2 F3   Closed Dec-Jan
Ⓑ Ⓓ ⊗ 🐾🖐🧺🚗!

Higher Rodhuish Farm, TA24 6QL ☎ 01984 640253
(Jennifer & Alan Thomas)   Map 181/011397
BB **A**   ✕ book first £10   D2 TI   Ⓓ 🐾🖐🧺🚗!🥾 ◆◆◆

● **Nether Stowey (Bridgwater)**
Macmillan Way West

🛏◀ The Old Cider House, 25 Castle Street, TA5 1LN ☎ 01278 732228
www.theoldciderhouse.co.uk   Map 181/191397
BB **B**   ✕ book first £12.50, approx 7:30pm   D2 T3
Ⓥ Ⓑ Ⓓ ⊗ 🐾🖐🧺🚗!🥾 Ⓜ ◆◆◆◆

🛏◀ Castle of Comfort Hotel, Dodington, TA5 1LE ☎ 01278 741264
(Carol & Nigel Venner) www.castle-of-comfort.co.uk   Map 181/173399
BB **C**   ✕ book first £28, 7:30-8:30pm   SI D3 TI FI
Ⓥ Ⓑ Ⓓ ⊗ 🐾🖐🧺🚗!🥾 ◆◆◆◆◆Ⓢ

● **North Cadbury**
Macmillan Way & Monarch's Way

🛏◀ Ashlea House, High Street, BA22 7DP ☎ 01963 440891
(Mr & Mrs J Wade) www.ashleahouse.co.uk   Map 183/635274
BB **B**   ✕ book first £12-£14, 7pm   DI TI   Closed Jan-Apr
Ⓥ Ⓑ Ⓓ ⊗ 🐾🖐🧺🚗! ◆◆◆◆Ⓢ

● **North Petherton (Bridgwater)**
Quantock View Guest House, Bridgwater Road, TA6 6PR ☎ 01278 663309
www.quantockview.freeserve.co.uk   Map 182/300341
BB **B**   ✕ book first £10, 6:30-7pm   SI DI TI FI   📶(Bridgwater)
Ⓥ Ⓑ Ⓓ ⊗ 🐾🖐🧺🥾 ◆◆◆

● **Porlock (Minehead)**
Exmoor
South West Coast Path

🛏◀ The Lorna Doone Hotel, High Street, TA24 8PS ☎ 01643 862404
(R G Thornton) lorna@doone99.btconnect.com   Map 181/887469
BB **B**   ✕ book first £14, 6.15-8.30pm   S3 D4 T4 F2
Ⓥ Ⓑ Ⓓ 🐾🖐!🧺 ◆◆◆

Silcombe Farm, Culbone, TA24 8JN ☎ 01643 862248 (Mrs E J Richards)
Map 181/833482   BB **B**   ✕ book first £11, 7.30pm   SI DI T2
Ⓥ Ⓑ Ⓓ ⊗ 🐾🖐🧺🚗!🥾

● **Shipham**
Herongates, Horseleaze Lane, BS25 1UQ ☎ 01934 843280
(Mrs Helen Stickland) herongates@hotmail.com   Map 182/437579
BB **B**   ✕ nearby   DI TI FI   Ⓑ Ⓓ ⊗ 🐾🖐🧺 ◆◆◆◆

● **Street (Glastonbury)**
🛏◀ Old Orchard House, Middle Brooks, BA16 0TU
☎ 01458 442212 (Mrs M Salmon)
old.orchard.house@amserve.com   Map 182/479350
BB **B**   ✕ book first £15, approx 7:30pm   SI D2
Ⓥ Ⓑ Ⓓ ⊗ 🐾🖐🧺 Ⓜ ◆◆◆◆

● **Taunton**
🛏◀ Blorenge House, 57 Staplegrove Road, TA1 1DG ☎ 01823 283005
(Mr & Mrs Painter) www.blorengehouse.co.uk   Map 193/223250
BB **C**   ✕ nearby   S5 D8 T8 F3   📶(Taunton)
Ⓑ Ⓓ 🐾🖐🧺🥾 ◆◆◆◆

● **Tickenham (Nailsea)**

> ☆ 🛏◀ **Elm Tree Cottage**
> Jacklands Bridge, BS21 6SQ ☎ 01275 866484 (Bev Westrup)
> aspecialplacetostay@yahoo.co.uk   Map 171,172/468717
> BB **B**   ✕ book first £10, 7:30pm   SI D2 TI FI   📶(Nailsea)
> Ⓥ Ⓑ Ⓓ ⊗ 🐾🖐🧺🚗!
>
>
> High quality en-suite accommodation set in a conservation area with spectacular rural views. Direct footpath access into adjacent ancient woodland and excellent well marked path network, with access to the Gordano Round. The Mendip Way and Bristol centre only 15 mins by car.

● **Wells**
Monarch's Way

🛏◀ Cadgwith House, Hawkers Lane, BA5 3JH ☎ 01749 677799
(Elspeth Fletcher) fletcherels@yahoo.co.uk   Map 182/559462
BB **B**   SI DI TI FI   Ⓑ Ⓓ ⊗ 🐾🖐🧺🚗🥾 ◆◆◆◆

The Crown At Wells, Market Place, BA5 2RP ☎ 01749 673457
www.crownatwells.co.uk   Map 182,183/550457
BB **C**   ✕ book first £15, 6pm onwards   S2 D7 T4 F2
Ⓥ Ⓑ Ⓓ 🐾🖐 ★★

● **Wheddon Cross**
Exmoor

🛏◀ Exmoor House, TA24 7DU ☎ 01643 841432   www.exmoorhouse.com
Map 181/924388   BB **B**   ✕ book first £18, 7:30pm   D3 TI FI
Closed Dec-Jan   Ⓥ Ⓑ Ⓓ ⊗ 🐾🖐🧺🚗!🥾 ◆◆◆◆◆Ⓢ

● **Williton (Taunton)**
Macmillan Way West

> ☆ 🛏◀ **Hartnells**
> 28 Long Street, TA4 4QU ☎ 01984 634777 (Myra King)
> m.king_hartnells@tiscali.co.uk   Map 181/080412
> BB **B**   ✕ nearby   SI T2
> Ⓑ Ⓓ ⊗ 🐾🖐🧺🚗!🥾 ◆◆◆
>
>
> At the foot of the Quantocks, 'Hartnells' is a non-smoking village cottage within 200 yards of pubs, take-away food and a steam railway. Upstairs & downstairs suites in a welcoming home. Lovely and interesting garden with a malthouse and access to playing fields.

● **Withypool (Minehead)**
Exmoor
Two Moors Way & Macmillan Way West

Hamiltons, TA24 7QP ☎ 01643 831431 (Mrs Ina Gage)   Map 181/846355
BB **B**   ✕ nearby   SI D3 TI   Ⓑ Ⓓ 🐾🖐🧺!🥾

WILTSHIRE

● Ashton Keynes (Swindon)
Thames Path
1 Cove House, SN6 6NS ☎ 01285 861226 (Valerie Threlfall)
roger@covehouse.co.uk Map 173,163/046940
BB **C** ✗ nearby D1 T1 B D ⊗ 🐾🖐🚗 ! 🏠

■►◄ The Firs, High Rd, SN6 6NX ☎ 01285 860169 (Karen Shaw)
http://uk.geocities.com/thefirsbb Map 173,163/045941
BB **B** ✗ nearby S1 D2 B D 🐾🖐🚗 ! 🏠 Ⓜ

● Bradford-upon-Avon
Macmillan Way
■►◄ Bradford Old Windmill, 4 Masons Lane, BA15 1QN
☎ 01225 866842 (Priscilla & Peter Roberts)
www.bradfordoldwindmill.co.uk Map 173/826611
BB **C** ✗ book first £6-£21, 8pm D3 Closed Jan-Feb
▲▲(Bradford-upon-Avon) V B D ⊗ 🐾🖐 ◆◆◆◆◆

● Bremhill (Calne)
Lowbridge Farm, SN11 9HE
☎ 01249 815889 (Elizabeth Sinden) Map 173/987737
BB **B** ✗ £10.50, 7-9pm T1 F1 V D 🐾🖐🚗 ! 🏠

● Castle Eaton
Thames Path

☆ Cornus B&B
School Lane, SN6 6LF ☎ 01285 810202 (Anne Watkis)
annewatkis@yahoo.co.uk Map 163/146956
BB **B** ✗ nearby D2
B D ⊗ 🐾🖐🚗 ! 🏠

Quality accommodation in lovely old village on the Thames, located directly on
the Thames Path route.
5 minutes to village pub offering excellent food/real ales.
Saxon town of Cricklade within walking distance.
Cirencester 10 miles, Cheltenham approximately 30 miles.

● Devizes
Wessex Ridgeway
Rockley, London Road, SN10 2DS ☎ 01380 723209 (Jean & Richard Bull)
www.rockley.org.uk Map 173/003618
BB **B** ✗ nearby S2 D1 T3 F1 B D ⊗ 🐾🖐

■►◄ The Gatehouse, Wick Lane, SN10 5DW
☎ 01380 725283 (Mrs L Stratton)
www.visitdevizes.co.uk Map 173/006605
BB **C/D** ✗ nearby S1 D1 T1 Closed Dec
B D ⊗ 🐾🖐🚗 ! ◆◆◆

● Inglesham (Swindon)
Thames Path
Evergreen, 3 College Farm Cottages, SN6 7QU
☎ 01367 253407 (Mr & Mrs G Blowen)
www.evergreen-cotswolds.co.uk Map 163/204959
BB **B** ✗ nearby S2 D1 B D ⊗ 🐾🖐🚗 !

● Ludwell (Shaftesbury)
Wessex Ridgeway
Birdbush Farm, SP7 9HH ☎ 01747 828252 (Mrs Ann Rossiter)
annrossiter@fsmail.net Map 184/913229
BB **B** ✗ nearby S1 D1 Closed Nov-Mar D ⊗ 🐾🖐🚗

● Malmesbury
■►◄ Mayfield House Hotel, Crudwell, SN16 9EW ☎ 01666 577409
(Chris Marston) www.mayfieldhousehotel.co.uk Map 173,163/954928
BB **C** ✗ £18, 6:30-8:45pm S3 D11 T8 F2
V B D 🐾🖐🚗 ★★ See Groups also.

● Manningford Abbots (Marlborough)
Huntleys Farm, SN9 6HZ ☎ 01672 563663 (Mrs Margot Andrews)
meg@gimpike.fsnet.co.uk Map 173/145593
BB **B** ✗ book first £13.50 D1 T/F1 ▲▲(Pewsey)
V B D ⊗ 🐾🖐🚗 ! 🏠 ★★★

● Marlborough
Wessex Ridgeway

☆ Browns Farm
SN8 4ND ☎ 01672 515129 (Hazel J Crockford)
crockford@farming.co.uk Map 173/198678
BB **B** ✗ nearby D2 T1 F1
B D ⊗ 🐾🖐🏠

Attractive farmhouse set on the
edge of the Savernake Forest.
Large comfortable rooms offering
views over open farmland. Ideal
base for walkers & cyclists. Close
to The Ridgeway, Averbury
and Wansdyke.

● Mere
Monarch's Way
Castleton House, Castle St, BA12 6JE ☎ 01747 860446 (Gail Garbutt)
www.castletonhouse.com Map 183/811323
BB **B** ✗ book first £12.50, 7:30-8:30pm D1 T1 F1
V B D 🐾🖐🚗 ! 🏠 ◆◆◆◆

● Ogbourne St George (Marlborough)
Ridgeway
Foxlynch, Bytham Road, SN8 1TD ☎ 01672 841307 (Mr G H Edwins)
Map 173/190740 BB **B** ✗ nearby F1 B D 🐾🖐🚗 ! 🏠
Bunkroom only.

☆ ■►◄ Parklands Hotel & Restaurant
High Street, SN8 1SL ☎ 01672 841555 (Mark Bentley)
www.parklandshoteluk.co.uk Map 174/200744
BB **C** ✗ book first £10.90, 7-9pm S2 D2 T6
V B D ⊗ 🐾🖐🚗 ! 🏠 ◆◆◆◆

Set in the tiny Wiltshire village of Ogbourne
St George, Parklands Hotel offers
comfortable peaceful accommodation in a
family run hotel conveniently located to the
Ridgeway Path.
To see more details please visit our website

● **Salisbury**

Farthings, 9 Swaynes Close, SP1 3AE ☎ 01722 330749 (Mrs Gill Rodwell)
www.farthingsbandb.co.uk   Map 184/145306
BB **B**   ✕ nearby   S2 D1 T1   ♨(Salisbury) Ⓑ Ⓓ ⊛ ♨   ◆◆◆◆

🚩◄ Hayburn Wyke Guest House, 72 Castle Road, SP1 3RL ☎ 01722 412627
www.hayburnwykeguesthouse.co.uk   Map 184/142309
BB **B/C**   ✕ nearby   D3 T2 F2   ♨(Salisbury) Ⓑ Ⓓ ♨   ◆◆◆

🚩◄ Byways House, 31 Fowler's Rd, SP1 2QP
☎ 01722 328364 (Ann & Peter Arthey)
www.bed-breakfast-stonehenge.co.uk   Map 184/149299
BB **C**   ✕ nearby   S4 D7 T7 F5   ♨(Salisbury) Ⓑ ♨ ♨   ◆◆◆

● **Warminster**

Wessex Ridgeway

Farmers' Hotel, 1 Silver Street, BA12 8PS ☎ 01985 213815
www.farmershotel.yahoo.uk   Map 183/871451
BB **B**   ✕ £9, 6-10pm   S9 D4 T7 F3   ♨(Warminster)
Ⓥ Ⓑ Ⓓ ♨♨ ♨ ♨   ◆

● **West Lavington (Devizes)**

Wessex Ridgeway

Littleton Lodge (A360), Littleton Panell, SN10 4ES ☎ 01380 813131
(May Linton) www.littletonlodge.co.uk   Map 184/997543
BB **C**   ✕ nearby   D2 T1   Ⓑ Ⓓ ⊛ ♨♨ ♨   ◆◆◆◆

● **West Overton (Marlborough)**

Ridgeway & Wessex Ridgeway

Cairncot, SN8 4ER ☎ 01672 861617 (Mrs Rachel Leigh)
www.cairncot.co.uk   Map 173/131680
BB **B**   ✕ nearby   S1 D1   Ⓓ ⊛ ♨♨ ♨ ☞ ! ♨   ◆◆◆

● **Wroughton (Swindon)**

Ridgeway

2 Greens Lane, SN4 0RJ ☎ 01793 813982 (Christine Spooncer)
Map 173/150182   BB **B**   ✕ nearby   D2   Closed Dec
Ⓑ Ⓓ ⊛ ♨♨ ☞ ! ♨

SELF-CATERING

CORNWALL

● **Ashton**

Chycarne Farm Cottages ☎ 01736 762473 (Pauline & Graham Ross)
www.chycarne-farm-cottages.co.uk
£100-£405   Sleeps 1-4. 9 cottages. Closed Nov, Feb, Mar
Beautiful rural location, overlooks Mounts Bay. ⊛ ♨   ★★★

● **Bodmin Moor**

East Rose Farm ☎ 01208 850674 (Mrs V Stansfield) www.eastrose.co.uk
£140-£825   Sleeps 2-6. 7 cottages.
Superb walking, remote, peaceful, near coast. ♨

● **Boscastle**

☎ 01242 238865 (Tony & Enid Pryer)
£145-£315   Sleeps 4. 1 house. Designated parking for two cars. ♨

Bremor Holidays ☎ 01840 230340 (Mrs P A Rogers)
www.north-cornwall.co.uk/client/bremor
£125-£290   Sleeps 2. 1 cottage .
Easy access to coastal footpath. ♨   ★★★

☆ **The Hayloft**
☎ 01840 250218 (Nicola Collings)
www.hayloftbarn.co.uk
£200-£650   Sleeps 2-6. 1 barn conversion.
Sea views. 150yds from coastal path. ⊛   ★★★★★

Beatifully presented 3 bedroom Grade II listed barn conversion, situated in an AONB with stunning sea and countryside views. The Hayloft offers a high standard of accommodation and is ideally located for exploring the north Cornwall coastal paths.

☆ **Venn Down Farmhouse**
☎ 01840 250599 (Diane Bentall)
www.venndownfarmhouse.co.uk
£200-£525   Sleeps 2-4 + cot. 2 apartments.
Kennel only for dogs, max 2. ⊛ ♨   ★★★★

Two luxurious apartments adjacent to 18th century farmhouse standing in 12 acres grounds, finished to a high standard. Tranquil location. Distant sea views. Near Boscastle harbour, Tintagel, Polzeath, Port Isaac. Stunning coastal walks, sandy beaches, Cornish villages, restaurants, pubs and cream teas.

● **Bude**

☆ **Cornwall Holidays 4 All**
☎ 01494 711540 (Sarah Banning)
www.cornwallholidays4all.co.uk
£205-£655   Sleeps 4-5. 3 cottages.
♨   ★★★★

3 cottages within close distance of each other and ideally situated for breathtaking coastal walks with Bude canal and National Trust beaches close by.

Dairy and Campion Cottages are on a small site with breathtaking views. Heated indoor swimming pool, small laundry and wonderful surrounding countryside.

Easterly Cottage is a 400 year old quaint thatched cottage with recently exposed inglenook fireplace. With traditional courtyard garden with seaviews.

Email: sarah@cornwallholidays4all.co.uk

☆ **Flexbury House**
☎ 01600 772918 (Sarah Watkins)
www.flexburyhouse.com
£350-£750   Sleeps 8-10. 1 house.
5 minutes from coast, town, pub. ⊘

Large 4 bed roomed victorian house. Excellent location NT coastal path/beach 4 minutes walk. Bude town centre 10 minutes. Nearest pub, corner shop 5 minutes. Walkers' paradise. Stunning walks from the door. Come home to the smell of your aga-cooked casserole, and soak away your weary legs in our extra deep bath. Drying and laundry facilities. Very well equipped house. Discount for smaller parties out of season.

● **Coverack**

☆ **Heath Farm**
☎ 01326 280521 (Andy & Vicki Goodman)
www.heath-farm-holidays.co.uk
£165-£545   Sleeps 2-7. 4 cottages.
1.5 miles from South West Coast Path. ⊘ 🐾 ★★★★ RA member.

Heath Farm Cottages – 4 star quality accommodation peacefully situated on the Lizard peninsula.

1.5 miles from SW Coast Path. Ideal base for discovering west Cornwall.

Dogs welcome. Cottages superbly renovated and tastefully furnished to provide a home from home.

● **Crackington Haven**
Crackington Manor ☎ 01840 230397   crackington.manor@virgin.net
£115-£390   Sleeps 2-6. 2 flats.   1 min beach, South West Coast Path. 🐾

● **Crantock**
☎ 0845 2265507 (Mrs D M Mills)   www.gw.milco.biz
£200-£1,500   Sleeps 2-9. 3 properties.
SWCP, beach, pubs, shop, 5 minutes. ⊘ 🐾

● **Falmouth**
Little Avalon ☎ 01326 311119 (Joan & Peter McCartney)
www.little-avalon.co.uk
£250-£400   Sleeps 2-4, 1 cottage.
Luxury accommodation, coastal walks, gardens, beaches.
⊘ ᴍᴍ(Falmouth Town) ★★★★

Tregedna Farm Holidays ☎ 01326 250529 (Fran Harris)
www.tregednafarmholidays.co.uk

£105-£280   Sleeps 1-24. 1 barn conversion.
Quiet, peaceful location. Comfortable, spacious accommodation.
⊘ ᴍᴍ(Falmouth-Penmere)   See Hostels also.

☆ **Special Places**
☎ 01872 864400 (Margie Lumby)
www.specialplacescornwall.co.uk
£190-£1,575   Sleeps 2-8. 40 cottages.
Lovely waterside and countryside properties.   ★★★-★★★★★

Self-catering at its best.
Individual waterside and countryside holiday homes with warmth and comfort, in beautiful southern Cornwall

Please phone for a brochure

● **Fowey**
Fowey Harbour Cottages ☎ 01726 832211 (David Hill)
www.foweyharbourcottages.co.uk
£150-£1,000   Sleeps 2-6. 10 cottages & flats.
On Cornish coast path and Saints Way. 🐾 ★★-★★★★

● **Helford**
Helford Cottages ☎ 01326 231666 (Pam Royall)
www.helfordcottages.co.uk
£165-£895   Sleeps 2-9. 12 cottages.
Enchanting creekside cottages on coastal footpath.
⊘ 🐾 ★★★-★★★★

● **Launceston**
East Gate Barn ☎ 01566 782573 (Jill Goodman)
www.eastgatebarn.co.uk
£250-£460   Sleeps 2-4. 1 barn conversion.
Footpath walk-guides to Bodmin Moor. ⊘ ★★★★ RA member

● **Liskeard**
Cutkive Wood Holiday Lodges ☎ 01579 362216 (Andy Lowman)
www.cutkivewood.co.uk
£120-£390   Sleeps 2-6. 6 lodges.
Idyllic rural location, moors, coasts, countryside. 🐾 See Groups also.

● **Looe**

☆ **Wringworthy Holiday Cottages**
☎ 01503 240685 (Kim Spencer)
www.wringworthy.co.uk
£130-£980   Sleeps 2-8 +cots. 8 stone cottages.
Countryside setting, near coast path, moors. ᴍᴍ(Sandplace) 🐾 ★★★★

In 4 acres of valley-top countryside, the perfect walking base for South West Coast Path, Bodmin NT and Cornwall. Our eight spacious stone cottages sleeping 2-8 are heated. Also a games barn, outdoor pool and friendly farm animals. Groups/pets welcome. Short breaks available.

☆ Penvith Cottages
☎ 01483 277894 (Beatrix Windle)
www.penvithcottages.co.uk
£170-£490   Sleeps 4. 2 cottages.
Beautiful rural location, near coast path.   ⊗ ★★★★

Penvith Cottages are situated in lovely open countryside, only a 3 mile drive from the fishing port of Looe, with its traditional inns and restaurants. The South West Coast Path is within easy walking distance.
Email: beatrix@talk21.com

● Mevagissey
Tregonney Hill ☎ 01628 898775 (Sarah Capel-Smith)
cow.view@virgin.net   £180-£390   Sleeps 6. 1 house.
E-mail for pictures and full details.   ⊗

● Mousehole
The Little Net Loft ☎ 020 8220 4538 (Martin King)
www.thelittlenetloft.co.uk   £200-£400   Sleeps 2. 1 converted net loft.
Fully furnished, wood burning stove   ⊗

● Mullion
Criggan Mill ☎ 01326 240496 (Mike & Jackie Bolton) www.crigganmill.co.uk
£160-£715   Sleeps 2-6. 25 timber lodges.
Coastal path 200yds, village 1 mile. 🐾 ★★★★★   See B&B also.

Gweltek ☎ 01326 290443 (Barbara Downing)   www.wetoes.com
£185-£400   Sleeps 6. 1 cottage. SW Coast Path & sea. 🐾

● Newquay
☎ 01637 876104 (Betty Barry) betty.barry@btinternet.com
£115-£350   Sleeps 2-6. 1 apartment.
Convenient for Coastal Paths/Eden Project. ∿(Newquay) ★★

☎ 01637 872654 (Gail Evans-Barry) mebcrofton@aol.com
£100-£270   Sleeps 3. 1 flat. Closed Oct-April
Sea views, coastal walks, outside town. ∿(Newquay) 🐾 RA member

● Padstow
Yellow Sands Cottages ☎ 01637 881548 (Sharon Keast)
www.yellowsands.co.uk £200-£750   Sleeps 1-6. 6 cottages.
Coastal footpath 200 metres, idyllic location. 🐾 ★★★-★★★★

Treginegar ☎ 01275 844741 (Julie Wellen) www.treginegar.com
£250-£1,200   Sleeps 4-10. 1 farmhouse, 7 bungalows.
Rural sea views, spacious, well equipped, tranquil. 🐾

☆ Bosca Brea
☎ 01208 814472 (Mrs Alison Mitchell)
bosca@trevalsa.fsnet.co.uk
£135-£325   Sleeps 1-4. 1 bungalow.
Saints' Way and coastal path nearby. 🐾

Detached bungalow in peaceful hamlet of Tregonce. Views across Little Petherick Creek and towards Padstow from five acre private grounds. Close access to Saints Way, Camel Trail and SW Coast Path. Wadebridge, Padstow, surfing and sandy beaches approx. 5 miles by road.

Manor House Activity & Development Centre ☎ 01841 540346 (Lesley Kirk)
www.manoractivitycentre.co.uk
£850-£2,050   Sleeps 25. 1 manor house.   Grade II listed Georgian manor house.   ⊗   See Groups & B&B also.

● Polperro
West Kellow Farm ☎ 01503 272089 (E M Julian) www.westkellow.co.uk
£150-£550   Sleeps 2-4. 2 cottages.
Quiet peaceful location with panoramic views. ⊗ ★★★★

● Port Isaac
Lane End Farm ☎ 01208 880013 (Mrs Linda Monk) abmonk@tiscali.co.uk
£165-£460   Sleeps 4. 1 bungalow. Beautiful views. Convenient coast path, moors. ⊗ 🐾 ★★★   RA member. See B&B also.

● Rock

☆ Mariners Lettings
☎ 020 7384 9105 (Claire Tordoff)
www.marinersrock.com
£475-£1,045   Sleeps 4-6. 5 houses.
Beautiful views over Camel estuary. 🐾

Luxury fully equipped and beautifully furnished houses; private terraces; wonderful views over Camel estuary; 2 mins from beach; 200yds to Mariners Pub/restaurants; on South West Coast Path. All houses fully equipped including washing machine, bed linen and towels.

● Ruan Minor
Little Gwendreath Holiday Cottages ☎ 01326 290836
littlegwendreath@hotmail.com   £165-£385   Sleeps 1-4. 4 cottages.
Dogs welcome, Coastal Path, idyllic location. 🐾

● Saltash
Crylla Valley Cottages ☎ 01752 851133   www.cryllacottages.co.uk
£160-£768   Sleeps 2-8. 35 cottages.
Close to national parks/coastal walks. 🐾 ★★★★

● St Austell
Spindrift ☎ 01726 69316 (Mrs McGuffie)
www.spindrift-guesthouse.co.uk
£200-£500   Sleeps 2-4. 3 varying types.   Closed Oct-Mar
Between Heligan Gardens and Eden Project. ⊗ 🐾 ★★★ See B&B also.

Magic Hills Lodge ☎ 01726 842583 (David Beadle)
www.cornwall-online.co.uk/magichills
£165-£650   Sleeps 2-6. 3 bungalows. Coastal path on your doorstep. 🐾

● St Ives
St Ives Cottage ☎ 020 8870 3228 (Sue Kibby)
www.btinternet.com/~stives.cottage   £220-£450   Sleeps 4. 1 cottage.
Near Hepworth Museum and Tate Gallery. ⊗ ∿(St Ives) ★★★

● St Just
The Farmhouse ☎ 01736 788458 (Mrs Jo Hill)
johanna.hill@btinternet.com £135-£475   Sleeps 5. 2 cottages.
200 yds SW Coast Path   ⊗ 🐾   See B&B also.

The Croft ☎ 01736 786363 (Mr & Mrs G Hicks)
www.westcornwallcottage.com £220-£500   Sleeps 4-5. I cottage.
Sea views. Parking. Two shower rooms. Ⓧ

● St Neot

☆ **Lower Trengale Holiday Cottages**
☎ 01579 321019 (Brian & Terri Shears)
www.trengale.co.uk
£150-£650   Sleeps 4-6. 3 cottages.
Stunning rural location, suitable all year. 🐾 ★★★★

A wonderful location in the rolling hills of south east Cornwall just off
Bodmin Moor.
All three cottages are rated four star and include log burners and gas
barbecues: great all year round.
Good dogs welcome.
Special rates for couples and short breaks.

● St Teath

Tredarrup ☎ 01208 850994 (Mrs Bailey) www.tredarrup.com
£195-£980   Sleeps 4-6. I barn, I cottage.
Stunning views, near good local walks. Ⓧ

● St Wenn

☆ **Tregolls Farm**
☎ 01208 812154 (Mrs Marilyn Hawkey)
www.tregollsfarm.co.uk
£200-£795   Sleeps 2-8. 4 converted barns.
Clothes drying facilities. Saints Way. ★★★★ See B&B also.

Quality barn conversion in a picturesque
valley overlooking fields of cows and sheep.
Farm trail links up with Saints Way footpath.
Pets corner. Games room. BBQs.
Central heating and log burners.
Only 20 minutes drive from Eden or Padstow.

● The Lizard

Most Southerly House ☎ 01326 290300 (Mr G Sowden)
george@sowden7000fsworld.co.uk
£160-£280   Sleeps 2-3. I clifftop chalet. Closed Nov-Mar
On coastal path, magnificent sea views. Ⓧ

● Zennor

Boswednack Manor ☎ 01736 794183 (Dr E Gynn)
boswednack-manor@cornwall-county.com
£195-£370   Sleeps 4. I cottage.
Walks leaflets, organic garden, sea sunsets. Ⓧ

DEVON

● Aveton Gifford

Marsh Mills ☎ 01548 550549 (Mrs M Newsham) www.marshmills.co.uk
£250-£300   Sleeps 2-3. I cottage annexe.
Own sun terrace, gardens, orchard & parking. Ⓧ 🐾

● **Bampton**
Exmoor

☆ Louise Wilder
☎ 01398 351277
£140-£250
Sleeps 1-6. I mobile home.
Tranquility in the heart of Devon. Ⓧ

Individually situated 2 bedroom mobile
home, set in a tranquil, stream bordered
paddock surrounded by woodland.
Ideally positioned on the southern fringe
of Exmoor for walking, fishing and
exploring Exmoor, Dartmoor, and both
northern and southern coasts.

● **Belstone**
Dartmoor

Coombe Head Farm ☎ 01837 840108 (Jackie Day)
www.coombeheadfarm.co.uk   £195-£350   Sleeps 4 +cot. I cottage.
Superb barn conversion, weekend breaks available. Ⓧ ★★★

● **Chagford**
Dartmoor

☎ 01647 231213 (Mr & Mrs Paget) mpaget@globalnet.co.uk
£130-£230 Sleeps 2. I cottage. Quiet moorland village. Two Moors Way. Ⓧ

● **Chulmleigh**
☎ 01769 581250 (Rodney & Margaret Davies)
http://eggesford-barton.co.uk £506-£1,803   Sleeps 6-10. 3 cottages.
On Tarka Trail. Beautiful forest walks. Ⓧ ⚶(Eggesford) 🐾

● **Combe Martin**
Exmoor

Northcote Manor Farm ☎ 01271 882376 (Pat Bunch)
www.northcotemanorfarm.co.uk
£200-£895   Sleeps 4-6. 5 cottages. Closed Nov
Tranquil location near coast and Exmoor. Ⓧ 🐾 ★★★★

Kentisbury Grange ☎ 01271 883454 (Roy Shindler)
www.kentisburygrange.co.uk
£145-£445 Sleeps 2-6. 4 cabins, 19 caravans. Closed Oct-Mar
Quiet countryside retreat on fringe of Exmoor. Ⓧ 🐾 ★★★★

● **Dunsford**
Dartmoor

☎ 01647 252784 (Mrs Jean May) lesjmay@aol.com
£160-£310 Sleeps 2-4. 2 cottages.
Peaceful farmland, lovely views, woodland walks. Ⓧ

● East Down

☆ Maddox Down
☎ 01271 882641 (Mrs S Lerwill)
www.maddoxdown.co.uk
£230-£650   Sleeps 2-6. 5 cottages.
Fishing lake. Secluded, quiet, panoramic views.

Five character cottages, beautifully furnished and equipped to a very high standard. Games room. Catch-and-release lake, stocked with trout and carp.
3 miles from Combe Martin and coastal path.
2 miles from the edge of Exmoor National Park.

● Hartland

☆ Yapham Cottages
☎ 01237 441916 (Jane Young)
www.yaphamcottages.com
£230-£600   Sleeps 2-4. 3 cottages.
Coastal location, stunning views. Central heating.   ★★★★

3 beautiful 4 star cottages sleeping 2-4. Stunning coastal location Set in landscaped gardens within seven acres of lovely grounds, including woodland walk and wild flower meadow. 1 mile from South West Coast Path.
On the breathtaking and unspoilt Hartland Peninsula, Yapham enjoys complete tranquillity yet is perfect for visiting nearby tourist attractions; Exmoor, Dartmoor, The Eden Project. Our cottages are beautifully furnished including central heating. Excellent home cooked meals and dishes can be provided. Delicious cream tea on arrival, plus chocolates and flowers. Short breaks available.
Email: janeatyapham@onetel.com

● Ivybridge
Dartmoor
Blackadon Farm ☎ 01752 897034 (Mark Walker)
www.blackadonbarns.co.uk
£160-£1,283   Sleeps 2-32. 6 cottages.
Guided walks. Dartmoor Tourist Association inspected.
(Ivybridge)   RA member. See B&B & Groups also.

● Moretonhampstead
Dartmoor

☆ Budleigh Farm
☎ 01647 440835 (Judith Harvey)
www.budleighfarm.co.uk
£140-£480   Sleeps 2-6. 7 varying types.
Heated outdoor swimming pool (summer only).   ★★-★★★★

Climb our hill and admire Dartmoor from the site of an iron-age fort. There's not much left of the fort, but the view is stunning.
Visit historic cities, secret villages, tumbling streams, superb beaches; admire bluebell woods and wildflowers; roam Dartmoor, and sleep soundly after walking the Tors. Short breaks.

● Okehampton
Dartmoor

☆ East Hook Holiday Cottages
☎ 01837 52305 (Mrs M E Stevens)
www.easthook-holiday-cottages.co.uk
£175-£475   Sleeps 2-6. 3 cottages.
Outstanding location, on Tarka Trail/Cycleway 27.   ★★★★

Heart of glorious Devon with beautiful panoramic view of Dartmoor. Set in own grounds, three idyllic country cottages with oak beams and log fire. Wonderful charm and ambience. Comfortable, peaceful and relaxing.

● Sidmouth
Beaufort House ☎ 01628 781901 (Peter Wilton)
www.beaufort.demon.co.uk
£200-£650   Sleeps 8. Regency house.   Closed Nov-Mar
Adjacent beach and on coast path.

☎ 0117 924 3850 (Tracey Wylde) tracey@wyldeia.co.uk
£250-£578   Sleeps 6. 1 cottage.
Newly refurbished 2004. Town centre location.

● Starcross
Regent House ☎ 01626 891947 (Jewel Goss)
www.cottageguide.co.uk/regenthouse
£180-£580   Sleeps 2-6. 3 apartments.
10-15% discount to ramblers, please phone us.
(Starcross) ★★★★

● **Stockland**

☆ **Beckford Cottage**
☎ 01404 881641 (Jill Bellamy)
www.beckford-cottage.co.uk
£275-£550   Sleeps 4. 1 cottage.
Set in beautiful surroundings.   ⊛ 🦽 ★★★★

A very comfortable cottage on River Yarty on Channel to Channel Walk. Set in beautiful tranquil gardens. Good walking in Area of Outstanding Natural Beauty. 7 miles from the sea. 2 bedrooms, 1 double, 1 single. Can collect from station.

● **Tavistock**
Dartmoor
Langstone Manor ☎ 01822 613371 (Jane Kellett)
http://langstone-manor.co.uk £160-£564 Sleeps 2-7. 2 cottages, 2 apartments.
Closed Dec-Feb   Direct access onto Dartmoor. Bar meals.
⊛ 🦽 ★★★★ See Hostels & groups also.

● **Upottery**
Twistgates Farm ☎ 01404 861173 (Mrs Gray) www.twistgatesfarm.co.uk
£180-£480   Sleeps 2-6. 3 cottages.   Closed Oct-Apr
Woodburner, laundry area, meals available. Enchanting.   ⊛ 🦽 ★★★★

● **Walkhampton**
Dartmoor
Withill Farm ☎ 01822 853992 (Mrs P Kitchin) withillfarm@aol.com
£126-£297   Sleeps 2-4. 1 cottage.
Small farm close to open moor. 🦽 See B&B also.

● **Welcombe**
☎ 01793 848482 (Christine Green)
http://welcombe.mysite.wanadoo-members.co.uk
£125-£325 Sleeps 4. 1 bungalow. Peaceful, near coastal walks, beach, inn.⊛

● **Whimple**
Lower Southbrook Farm ☎ 01404 822989 (Angela Lang)
lowersouthbrookfarm@btinternet.com
£165-£396   Sleeps 4-6. 3 cottages.
Comfortable accommodation in delightful rural situation. 🦽 ★★★

● **Widecombe-in-the-Moor**
Dartmoor

☆ **Wooder Manor**
☎ 01364 621391 (Mrs Angela Bell) www.woodermanor.com
£160-£1,000   Sleeps 2-12. 5 varying types.
Beautiful quiet location, with central heating.
🦽 ★★★-★★★★ Access category 2.

Cottages in picturesque valley, surrounded by moors and granite tors. Peaceful location with lovely walks from the doorstep. Clean and well equipped. Central heating. Gardens. Off-road easy parking. Open all year. Good food at 2 local inns. Colour brochure. Groups welcome.

● **Witherage**

☆ **Newhouse Farm Cottages**
☎ 01884 860266 (Mr Keith Jenkins)
www.newhousecottages.com
£198-£1,468   Sleeps 2-10. 8 cottages.
Peaceful location, stunning views. 🦽

Eight beautifully converted well-equipped cosy Grade II listed stone barns, some with wood burning stoves. Choice of accommodation from one bedroom with four-poster bed to our five bedroom barn sleeping ten. Set in 23 acres of peaceful meadows with many enjoyable local walks.

DORSET

● **Abbotsbury**
Gorwell Farm ☎ 01305 871401 (Mrs J M Pengelly) www.gorwellfarm.co.uk
£200-£925   Sleeps 2-8. Cottages.
Coastal path, Macmillan Way. Wheelchair access.
⊛ 🦽 ★★★★-★★★★★★ Access category 2.

☆ **Elworth Farmhouse**
☎ 01305 871693 (Chris Wade)
www.hometown.aol.co.uk/ElworthFarmhouse/Elworth.htm
£300-£750   Sleeps 2-6 +cot. 2 cottages.
Traditional farmhouse cottages by Coast Path. ⊛ ★★★★-★★★★★★

Picturesque oak beamed cottages in farming hamlet close to world heritage coast path. 16th century farmhouse cottage has use of swimming pool, spa and extensive grounds. Poppy's a spacious detached cottage sleeps six. A walkers paradise with footpaths all around.

● **Bridport**
Saxlingham House ☎ 01308 423629 (Valerie Nicholls)
http://members.freezone.co.uk/saxlingham/Saxlingham.htm
£200-£275   Sleeps 4. 1 cottage .   Closed Oct-Feb
Set in beautiful Dorset countryside.   ⊛ 🦽   See B&B also.
Highway Farm ☎ 01308 424321 (Pauline Bale) www.highwayfarm.co.uk
£265-£595   Sleeps 4. 1 cottage.
Ganders, warm, welcoming, fishing, B&B, shortbreaks.   ⊛ ★★★

● **Dorchester**
The Barn ☎ 01305 849344 (Mrs E J Peckover)
stables@epeckover.fsnet.co.uk
£230-£360   Sleeps 2. 1 stable conversion.   Closed Nov-Feb
Central location, Dorset World Heritage Coast. 🦽 ★★★★

● **Litton Cheney**
Glebe Cottage ☎ 01732 884277 (J Jackson) www.dorsetbrambles.com
£195-£475   Sleeps 2-5. 1 cottage.
Idyllic village. Stunning local walks. 🦽 ★★★★

● **Puddletown**
☎ 01305 848003 (Lauran & Nick Church) http://english-home.biz
£225-£475   Sleeps 4-6. 1 cottage.   Private garden. B&B available. ⊛ 🦽

● Sherborne
Uplands ☎ 01935 477043 (Mrs S Brake) ponyexpress@freeuk.com
£180-£420 Sleeps 6. Penthouse flat.
Secluded large balcony. Local footpaths/bridleways.
⊛ ₩(Yeovil Pen Mill) ★★★

● Sturminster Newton
☎ 01258 471390 (Terry & Carol Townsend) www.townsend.dircon.co.uk
£210-£260 Sleeps 4. 1 apartment, 1 lodge.
Picturesque peaceful location. Ideal walking country. ⊛ ★★★ See B&B also.

● Sutton Poyntz

☆ Ebenezer Cottage
☎ 07778 524199 (Cathy Varley)
www.ebenezercottage.co.uk
£305-£675 Sleeps 4 +cot. 1 cottage.
SW Coast Path. World Heritage site. ⊛ ★★★★

Ebenezer Cottage. Charming 4 star ETC three bed terraced cottage on picturesque millstream lane in Sutton Poyntz. Explore the SW Coast Path and savour spectacular views towards the Jurassic coastline in the heart of the World Heritage Site.

● Swanage

☆ California Cottage
☎ 01929 425049 (Karen Delahay) www.californiacottage.co.uk
£475-£1,000 Sleeps 9. 1 barn
Wheelchair accessible, large studio/meetings room.
⊛ 🛏 ★★★★ See Groups also.

California Barn. luxury stone barn on stunning Jurassic Heritage coast. Wheelchair accessible. Pets. Garden and south facing patio with seaviews to Isle of Wight. Access to large studio/meeting room. Arts tuition, archaeological and wildlife tours/talks available. Excellent walking and wildlife.

● Uploders
Tiddlers Cottage ☎ 01308 485478 (Mr Alan Spargo)
www.tiddlerscottage.com £170-£295 Sleeps 2. 1 cottage annexe.
Superb coast and country walking area. ⊛ ★★★

GLOUCESTERSHIRE

● Chipping Campden
Weston Park Farm ☎ 01386 840835 (Mrs J Whitehouse)
http://cotswoldcottages.uk.com
£150-£500 Sleeps 2-5. 1 coach house flat, 2 cottages.
Magnificently situated on Cotswold Way. 🛏 See B&B also.

● Cirencester
Thames Path Cottages ☎ 01285 644416 (Philip Reynolds)
www.thames-path-cottages.co.uk
£390-£655 Sleeps 4-5. 2 cottages. Closed Jan, May-Sept
500 acre estate on Thames Path. 🛏

● Dursley
Little Gables ☎ 01453 543047 (Mrs F A Jones)
lhandfaj32lg@surefish.co.uk £141-£225 Sleeps 4. 1 cottage.
Tranquil village setting near Cotswold Way.
⊛ ₩(Cam & Dursley) ★★★

● Elkstone
The Grannery ☎ 01242 870375 (Mrs Lois Eyre)
www.cottageguide.co.uk/grannery
£180-£300 Sleeps 1-2. Wing of country house. Closed Jan
Comfortable, walker-friendly, maploan, optional extras. ⊛ 🛏

● Soudley
The Wishing Well ☎ 020 8429 3960 (Miriam Catlow)
www.kitchenstudioltd.co.uk/wishingwell
£190-£375 Sleeps 4-5. 1 house. Forest views and walks from doorstep. ⊛

● Stanton

☆ Charity Farm
☎ 01386 584339 (Mrs V Ryland)
www.myrtle-cottage.co.uk/ryland.htm
£195-£480 Sleeps 2-6. 2 cottages. 🛏 ★★★
Idyllic situation near Cotswold Way.

Charming Cotswold stone cottages in picturesque village on the Cotswold Way. Pretty gardens offer 'al fresco' dining. Village pub serves food and Broadway has a selection of pubs and restaurants. Walk the hills or visit National Trust houses and gardens.

● Winchcombe
The Cotswold Retreat ☎ 01242 603124 (Mark Grassick)
www.thecotswoldretreat.co.uk   £150-£400 Sleeps 2-6. 2 cottages.
Great location on Cotswold Way. 🛏 ★★★★

SOMERSET

● Bath

☆ University of Bath
☎ 01225 383926
www.bath.ac.uk/salesandevents
£105.75-£215 Sleeps 1-2000. Campus accommodation.
All meals are available on campus. ⊛ ₩(Bath Spa)

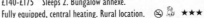

The University of Bath is 1.5 miles from the centre of Bath reached by a regular bus service.
We are on the Bath Skyline Walk and offer all standards of accommodation in vacation time and ensuite accommodation in term time.
Call for further infomation.

● Burrowbridge
Hillview ☎ 01823 698308 (Mrs Ros Griffiths)
£140-£175 Sleeps 2. Bungalow annexe.
Fully equipped, central heating. Rural location. ⊛ 🛏 ★★★

● Cheddar

Sun Holiday Apartments ☎ 01934 842273 (Mrs M M Fieldhouse)
sunholapart@aol.com   £112-£168   Sleeps 3-5. 4 apartments.
Fully equipped with laundry facilities available.   ⊗ 🐾 ★★★

☆ Home Farm

☎ 01934 842078 (Chris & Sue Sanders)
www.homefarmcottages.co.uk
£240-£560   5 cottages. Sleeps 2-5.
⊗ ★★★★

Five beautifully converted stone barns with original beams.
Set in two acres of an AONB, and surrounded by farm and National Trust land.
Many local walks.
All cottages are comfortable warm and fully equipped.

● Exford
Exmoor

Court Farm ☎ 0845 226 7154 (Mr & Mrs Horstmann) www.courtfarm.co.uk
£180-£325   Sleeps 2-5. 3 cottages.
Adjacent to river with private gardens.   🐾 ★★★★

☆ Riscombe Farm

☎ 01643 831480 (Leone & Brian Martin)
www.riscombe.co.uk
£100-£500   Sleeps 2-7. 4 barn-conversion cottages.
See website for current vacancies.   🐾 ★★★★

Relax beside the River Exe in the centre of Exmoor National Park.

Our four charming cottages are converted from stone barns beside an attractive courtyard.

Log fires and exposed beams. Stroll through our woods and riverside meadows.
Laundry room and facilities for drying clothes and boots.

An excellent base for exploring the valleys, moors and the nearby spectacular coast. Pets welcome.

● Ilminster

☎ 01481 253145 (Mrs Barbara Garfield)   garfieldgsy@cwgsy.net
£200-£350   Sleeps 4. 1 cottage.
Set in heart of Blackdown hills.   ⊗ 🐾

● Minehead
Exmoor

Woodcombe Lodge ☎ 01643 702789 (Nicola Hanson)
www.woodcombelodge.co.uk
£120-£1,150   Sleeps 2-12. 6 pine lodges, 2 cottages.
Wonderful views, 2.5 acre gardens.   🐾 ★★★★

● Porlock
Exmoor

☆ The Pack Horse

☎ 01643 862475 (Linda & Brian Garner)
www.thepackhorse.net
£210-£465   Sleeps 2-6. 4 apartments, 1 cottage.
Located in idyllic National Trust village.   🐾 ★★★

Our self-catering apartments and cottage are situated in this unique location alongside the shallow river Aller overlooking the famous Pack Horse Bridge. Enjoy immediate access from our doorstep to the beautiful surrounding countryside, pretty villages, spectacular coast and Exmoor. Open all year. Short breaks. Private parking.

● Simonsbath
Exmoor

Wintershead Farm ☎ 01643 831222 (Jane Styles) www.wintershead.co.uk
£195-£650   Sleeps 2-6. 5 cottages.   Closed Nov-Feb
Ideal base for a walking holiday.   🐾 ★★★★

● Withypool
Exmoor

Newlands House ☎ 01643 831693 (Alex Stokes) flying.flo@virgin.net
£150-£210   Sleeps 2. 1 flat. 2 minutes from Two Moors Way.   ⊗

WILTSHIRE

● Salisbury

Cross Farm ☎ 01722 718293 (Mrs S Kittermaster)
http://visitsalisbury.com-selfcatering   £200-£420.   Sleeps 4-5. 1 cottage.
Ten-acre organically run small holding.   🐾 ★★★

GROUPS

CORNWALL

Cutkive Wood Holiday Lodges (SC) St Ive ☎ 01579 362216
(Andy & Jackie Lowman) www.cutkivewood.co.uk Grid Ref: SX 292676
SC £120-£390   Min 2, max 30. 6 lodges.   Ⓓ ⊗   See SC also

Tamar Outdoor Centre (B&B/SC) Maker Heights, Millbrook ☎ 01752 823623
(Tony Wagner)   www.makerheightscentre.ik.com Grid Ref: 434515 Full board £28,
SC £15pppn   Min 20, max 56. ✕ 🐾 ⊗ ₥(Plymouth) ! 🚗

☆ Tor View Barn & Cottage (SC/B&B)

Corgee Farm, Luxulyan ☎ 01726 850340 (Clare Hugo)
www.torviewcentre.co.uk
BB £24, SC £200-£2,500   Min 4, max 34. 2 barns, 2 cottages .
✕ Ⓑ Ⓓ ! 🚗 ★★★★ See B&B also

Luxury 6 ensuite bedroom barn and 2 bedroom cottage with spa bath. Furnished to your requirements. Families or singles. Minutes from the A30 and the Eden Project. On the Saints Way walking route, overlooking AONB.

☆ Manor House Activity & Development Centre

(B&B/SC) St Issey, Wadebridge ☎ 01841 540346 (Lesley Kirk)
www.manoractivitycentre.co.uk
BB £22.50, SC £850-£2,050 Min 5, max 50. ✕
Ⓑ Ⓓ ⊗ ! 🚗 See B&B & SC also

A beautiful Grade II Listed Georgian Manor House offering exceptionally spacious, comfortable accommodation, for large groups, just 3 miles from Padstow, the coastal path and the Camel Trail. Nine large multi-bedded rooms (some ensuite), fabulous lounge and formal dining room.

DEVON

Dartmoor

Blackadon Farm (B&B/SC) Ivybridge PL21 0HB ☎ 01752 897034 (Mark Walker)
www.blackadonbarns.co.uk Map 202/665517
SC from £160, BB £15-£25 Min 2, max 20. 6 cottages.
✕ 🛏 Ⓑ Ⓓ ⊗ 🚌(Ivybridge) ! See B&B & SC also

Eggesford Barton (SC) Eggesford, Chulmleigh ☎ 01769 581250 (Margaret Davies)
eggesford-barton.co.uk   SC £400-£1,500 Min 6, max 24.
✕ nearby Ⓑ Ⓓ ⊗ 🚌(Eggesford) ! 🚗 See SC also

☆ Royal York & Faulkner Hotel (B&B)

Sidmouth Freephone 0800 220714
www.royalyorkhotel.net
BB £32.50-£48.50 Min 30, max 90. Closed Jan
✕ 🛏 Ⓑ Ⓓ ★★Ⓢ

Beautifully appointed Regency hotel in a superb position on the centre of Sidmouth's elegant esplanade & adjacent to the picturesque town centre.

Family run with a long-standing reputation for hospitality and service, offering all amenities & excellent facilities.

Located on the Jurassic Coast, a World Heritage Site, the area is ideally situated for walking the superb coastal paths and inland walks offering stunning flora, fauna and views. Regular host to Rambling Clubs.

Email: stay@royalyorkhoyel.net

DORSET

Sandringham Hotel (B&B) 20 Durlston Rd, Swanage BH19 2HX
☎ 01929 423076 (Mr & Mrs Silk)
www.smoothhound.co.uk/hotels/sandringham.html Map 195/033782
BB £25-£35 Max 25. Closed mid-July-Aug
✕ 🛏 Ⓑ Ⓓ ! 🚗 See B&B also

☆ Churchview Guesthouse (B&B)

Winterbourne Abbas, Dorchester DT2 9LS ☎ 01305 889296
(Michael & Jane Deller) www.churchview.co.uk Map 194/618905
BB £33-£37 Max 17. ✕ 🛏
Ⓑ Ⓓ ⊗ ! 🚗 ◆◆◆◆ See B&B also

Our beautiful 17th century guest house set in picturesque countryside makes an ideal rambling base. Period dining room, two lounges, licensed bar. Delicious evening meals. Non-smoking. Groups are our speciality. Call Michael & Jane Deller. Email: stay@churchview.co.uk

SOMERSET

Exmoor

Exton House Hotel (B&B/SC) Exton, Dulverton TA22 9JT ☎ 01643 851365
(Martin Glaister) Map 181/926336
BB £38.95-£47, SC £1,400-£2,100 Min 6, max 26.
✕ 🛏 Ⓑ Ⓓ ⊗ ! 🚗 ◆◆◆◆Ⓢ See B&B & SC also

WILTSHIRE

Cotswold Way

☆ Mayfield House Hotel (B&B)

Crudwell, Malmesbury SN16 9EW ☎ 01666 577409 (Mr Chris Marston)
www.mayfieldhousehotel.co.uk Map 173/954928
DBB £36 Min 2, max 46.
✕ 🛏 Ⓑ Ⓓ See B&B also.

Explore the Cotswolds.

Friendly country house hotel in the heart of the Cotswolds.

Excellent restaurant. Fresh food and plenty of it! Proprietor run, 24 lovely bedrooms, regularly used by walking groups. Group rates from £36pppn. Dinner, bed and restaurant

Tel (01666) 577409 Ask for Max or Chris

reception@mayfieldhousehotel.co.uk

www.mayfieldhousehotel.co.uk AA ★★ AA Rosette Award-winning food

For an explanation of the symbols used in this guide see the Key to Abbreviations and Symbols on p 7

HOSTELS, BUNKHOUSES & CAMPSITES

CORNWALL

South West Coast Path

The Old Chapel Zennor Backpackers/Cafe (IH) Zennor, St Ives TR26 3BY
☎ 01736 797219 www.backpackers.co.uk/zennor
Bednight £12 ✕ 🚌 [D] ⊗

Tregedna Farm Holidays (C/IH) Maenporth, Falmouth TR11 5HL ☎ 01326 250529 (Fran Harris) www.tregednafarmholidays.co.uk Grid Ref: SW787304
Bednight £5-£15 ✕nearby 🚆(Falmouth Penmere) [D] ⊗

DEVON

Dartmoor

Two Moors Way

Langstone Manor (C) Moortown, Tavistock, PL19 9JZ
☎ 01822 613371 (Jane Kellett)
www.langstone-manor.co.uk Map 201/528734
Camping £5 Closed Nov-mid-Mar
✕ [B] [D] ★★★★

South West Coast Path

Ocean Backpackers Hostel (IH) 29 St James Place, Ilfracombe EX34 9BJ
☎ 01271 867835 (Chris & Abby Tappenden) www.oceanbackpackers.co.uk
Bednight £8-£12 ✕nearby [B] [D]

DORSET

California Cottage Campsite (OC) Swange
☎ 01929 425049
www.californiacottage.co.uk Grid Ref SY020777
£5 per tent Closed Sept-June ✕nearby See SC also

SOMERSET

Macmillian Way West

Bowdens Crest Caravan & Camping Park (C) Bowdens, Langport TA10 0DD
☎ 01458 250553 www.bowdenscrest.co.uk
Camping £4 ✕ 🚌 [B] ★★★ Caravan suitable for disabled

PUBS & TEAROOMS

CORNWALL

● St Agnes

South West Coast Path

🍸 Driftwood Spars Hotel, Trevannance Cove, Quay Rd, TR5 0RT
☎ 01872 552428 (Gordon & Jill Treleaven)
www.driftwoodspars.com Map 204/721513
✕ [V] 👪 ♫ (Live/Jukebox)
[L] [G] Ⓑ(☺) Ale brewed on premises.

KENT

SOUTH

Undulating hills with expansive sea views, spectacular cliffs and a landscape of historical remains make southern England pleasant walking country.

SOUTHERN KENT DOWNS

Stretching across south Buckinghamshire, the chalk hills and beech woodlands of the Chilterns offer walkers the opportunity to spot rare gentians, and observe the magnificent red kites now successfully re-introduced to the area. Further west, you can find the source of the River Thames and follow the Thames Path all the way to London. The capital can either be circumnavigated by following the London Loop, or criss-crossed using paths giving access to its green spaces, canals and historic attractions.

A member says:

"Nothing beats walking along the South Downs ridge with wind blowing in your face, watching the sea glitter in the sunshine. You can see the Isle of Wight, the North Downs and Windsor Castle from up there. Or notice the changes of seasons while having a drink in a quiet village pub."

Two very different national parks will soon be part of Hampshire's natural heritage: the oak and beech woodlands and wild ponies of the New Forest, and the chalk hills and panoramic seascapes of the South Downs.

The Isle of Wight is often referred to as 'southern England in miniature'. However, unlike the rest of England footpaths outnumber roads, with over 520 miles to choose from within 147 square miles. Downlands hide wild orchids, while coastal walks traverse cliffs and saltmarshes.

Norman castles adorn the South Downs of Sussex, and the heather-clad Ashdown Forest provided A A Milne with inspiration for the Winnie the Pooh stories. The chalky Seven Sisters Hills and the cliffs of Beachy Head, provide gentle coastal walking. To the east the sandstone hills, fields and woods of the High Weald should not be missed.

The North Downs Way follows ancient trackways along chalk ridges, hedgerows and orchards stretching from London to the spectacular white cliffs of Dover. Kent, 'The Garden of England', has a dramatic coast speckled with Roman and Norman defence structures, best explored along the Saxon Shore Way.

Southern England can cater for the ornithologist, horticulturalist or historian in any walker.

PICTURES: THE COUNTRYSIDE AGENCY

Long Distance Paths

Chiltern Way	CHI
Icknield Way	ICK
Isle of Wight Coastal Path	IWC
Macmillan Way	MCM
Midshires Way	MDS
Monarch's Way	MON
North Downs Way	NDN
Ridgeway	RDG
Saxon Shore Way	SXS
Solent Way	SOL
South Downs Way	SDN
Test Way	TST
Thames Path	THM
Wealdway	WLD

Public paths:

34,376km/ 21,348 miles

Mapped access land:

101 square miles (Area 1, South East) 102 square miles (Area 3, Central Southern) to date

Explore

IT'S NOT JUST A WEEKEND THING!

WILDLIFE   COUNTRYSIDE   EVENTS   PLACES TO STAY

☎ 0845 677 0615*
www.leevalleypark.com
*Calls charged at local call rate from a BT land line

Lee
Valley
Park

Open spaces and sporting places

SOUTH
LOCAL RAMBLERS CONTACTS

BERKSHIRE
AREA SECRETARY

Mr Cliff Lambert, Marandella,
1 Lawrence Mead, Kintbury,
Hungerford, RG17 9XT ☎ 01488 608108

GROUP SECRETARIES

Berkshire Walkers Caroline
Mcdonagh, 49 Sharnwood Drive, Calcot,
Reading, Berkshire, RG31 7YD
www.berkshirewalkers.org.uk

East Berkshire Mr Gerald Barnett,
9 Fremantle Road, High Wycombe,
Bucks, HP13 7PQ ☎ 01494 522404
(membs Enq Mrs Welch 01753 662139)
www.eastberksramblers.org

Loddon Valley Mrs J Eves, 4 Carlton
Close, Woodley, Reading, Berks, RG5
4JS ☎ 0118 9690318
(membs Enqs Mrs Curtis 0118 9403158)
www.lvra.org.uk

Mid Berkshire Ms E Cuff, Donkey
Pound Cottage, Beech Hill, Reading,
Berkshire, RG7 2AX ☎ 0118 988 2674
www.mbra.org.uk

Pang Valley Mrs Jean Pitt,
26 Queensway, Caversham Park Village,
Reading, Berks, RG4 6SQ
☎ 0118 947 6017

South East Berks Mr John Moules,
50 Qualitas, Roman Hill, Bracknell,
Berks, RG12 7QG ☎ 01344 421002
http://members.aol.com/seberksra

West Berkshire Mrs J Bowman,
4 Cansfield End, Northcroft Park,
Newbury, Berks, RG14 1XH
☎ 01635 35902

Windsor & District Miss J M Clark,
7 Dyson Close, Windsor, Berkshire,
SL4 3LZ ☎ 01753 866 545

BUCKINGHAMSHIRE & W MIDDLESEX
AREA SECRETARY

Mr D Bradnack, 47 Thame Road,
Haddenham, Aylesbury, Bucks, HP17
8EP ☎ 01844 291069 [before 2100hrs]
www.bucks-wmiddx-ramblers.org.uk

GROUP SECRETARIES

Amersham & District Mrs M Moody,
White Cottage, 93 St Leonard's Road,
Chesham Bois, Amersham, HP6 6DR
☎ 01494 727504

Aylesbury & District Mr G Seymour,
108 Northern Road, Aylesbury,
HP19 9QY ☎ 01296 583562
www.aylesbury-ramblers.me.uk

Chiltern 20s-30s Walking Group
Mr Michael Bailey, 12 Cannon Mill
Avenue, Chesham, Bucks, HP5 1QX
www.chilterns2030s.co.uk

Hillingdon Mrs Sybil Denman,
Chatsworth, 103 Hercies Road,
Hillingdon, Middlesex, UB10 9LU
☎ 01895 234380
www.hillingdonramblers.org.uk

Milton Keynes & District
Mr John West, 45 Blackdown,
Fullers Slade, Milton Keynes, MK11 2AA
☎ 01908 564055
www.mkramblers.freeserve.co.uk

North West London Miss H O Lee,
12b Wellesley Road, Harrow, Middlesex,
HA1 1QN ☎ 020 8863 7628

West London Mr T Berry,
128 Park Lane, South Harrow,
Middlesex, HA2 8NL ☎ 020 8422 3284
www.btinternet.com/~westlondon
groupra

Wycombe District Mr J L Esslemont,
4 Park Farm Way, Lane End, High
Wycombe, Buckinghamshire, HP14 3EG
☎ 01494 881597

HAMPSHIRE
AREA SECRETARY

Mr G Clift, 124 Anmore Road,
Denmead, Waterlooville, PO7 6NZ
☎ 023 92241812
www.geocities.com/perrir_uk/walking/
frames.html

GROUP SECRETARIES

Alton Mrs G M Siddall, Peachings,
South Town Road, Medstead, Alton,
Hampshire, GU34 5ES
☎ 01420 564339

Andover Mr P L & Mrs M Wood,
9 Kingsmead, Anna Valley, Andover,
Hampshire, SP11 7PN ☎ 01264 710 844
www.hants.gov.uk/raag

Eastleigh Mrs P D Beazley,
16 Windover Close, Bitterne,
Southampton, SO19 5JS
☎ 02380 437443
www.hants.org.uk/eastleighramblers

**Hampshire 20s & 30s Walking
Group** Miss R V Lee, Flat 8, 67 Howard
Road, Southampton, SO15 5BG
☎ 023 8033 2069
(membs Enqs 0798 6655660)
www.hants.gov.uk/hantswalk2030

Meon Mrs C Coxwell, 19 New Road,
Fareham, PO16 7SR ☎ 01329 827790
claire.coxwell@talk.co.uk

New Forest Mrs Audrey Wilson,
16 West Road, Dibden Purlieu,
Southampton, SO45 4RJ
☎ 023 8084 6353

North East Hants Mr Brian Austen,
Kappa Crucis, Hillside Road, Farnham,
Surrey, GU9 9DW ☎ 01252 314826

North Hampshire Downs
Mr Mike Taylor, 19 Inkpen Gardens,
Lychpit, Basingstoke, Hants,
RG24 8YQ ☎ 01256 842468

Portsmouth Mrs M G Haly,
95 Winstanley Road, Stamshaw,
Portsmouth, Hants, PO2 8JS
☎ 023 92693874

Romsey Mr T W Radford,
67 Rownhams Lane, North Baddesley,
Southampton, SO52 9HR
☎ 02380 731279
www.romseynet.org.uk/ramblers/
ramblers.htm

South East Hants Mr D Nixon,
27 Brading Avenue, Southsea, Hants,
PO4 9QJ ☎ 023 9273 2649
www.hants.org.uk/sehantsramblers

Southampton Mrs Janet Foskett,
2 Ambleside, Sholing, Southampton,
SO19 8EY ☎ 02380 363177
www.hants.gov.uk/sotonram

Waltham Mrs W E Bassom,
3 Mayfair Court, Botley, Southampton,
SO30 2GT ☎ 01489 784946

Wessex Weekend Walkers
Ms H E Stacey, 18 Langham Close,
North Baddesley, Southampton,
SO52 9NT ☎ 07884 486676
www.wessexweekendwalkers.org.uk

Winchester Mr D Mason, Berkswell,
Rewlands Drive, Winchester, Hants,
SO22 6PA ☎ 01962 883135
www.hants.gov.uk/wramblers

INNER LONDON
AREA SECRETARY

Mr D Purcell, 8 Dryburgh Mansions,
London, SW15 1AJ ☎ 020 8788 1373
www.zoom.ic24.net/inlonarea

GROUP SECRETARIES

Blackheath Ms D O'Toole, 67 Flintmill
Crescent, London, SE3 8LU
☎ 020 8319 8593
http://zoom.ic24.net/bheath

Hammersmith & Wandsworth
Miss K G M Plowman, 52 Felstead Road,
Orpington, Kent, BR6 9AB ☎ (membs
Enqs Ms L Gray 020 8995 5947)

LOCAL RAMBLERS CONTACTS continued

Hampstead Mr K D Jones, Flat 4, 144 Agar Grove, Camden, London, NW1 9TY ☎ 020 7485 2348 Evenings Only www.hampsteadramblers.co.uk

Kensington, Chelsea & Westminster Ms J M Mack, 8n Grove End House, Grove End Road, London, NW8 9HN ☎ 020 7289 0305 (membs Enq Christine 020 7636 5812) http://users.whsmithnet.co.uk/kcw.ramblers

Metropolitan Walkers Please contact main office or visit www.metropolitanwalkers.org.uk

North East London Ms M Mayover, 28 Belle Vue Road, Walthamstow, E17 4DG ☎ 020 8527 0074 http://nelr.co.uk

South Bank Ms J M Robertson, 76 Crawthew Grove, London, SE22 9AB ☎ 020 8516 1171

ISLE OF WIGHT
AREA SECRETARY

Mr Mike Marchant, Merry Meeting, Ryde House Drive, Binstead Road, Ryde, PO33 3NF ☎ 01983 564909

GROUP SECRETARIES

Isle of Wight Mr David Skelsey, Madeira, Hunts Road, St Lawrence, Ventnor, PO38 1XT ☎ 01983 854540

KENT
AREA SECRETARY

Mr Arthur Russ, 7 Barnfield Road, Riverhead, Sevenoaks, Kent, TN13 2AY ☎ 01732 453863 arthurruss@waitrose.com

GROUP SECRETARIES

Ashford (Kent) Miss C M Crowley, 6 East Stour Court, Mabledon Avenue, Ashford, TN24 8BG ☎ 01233 620756 www.Ashford-Ramblers.co.uk

Bromley Mr R A Hutchings, 40 Degema Road, Chislehurst, Kent, BR7 6HW ☎ (Enqs Mrs Whichello 01689 820116)

Canterbury Mr R Cordell, 162 Broadway, Herne Bay, Kent, CT6 8HY ☎ 01227 361 902

Dartford Mr N E Turvey, 84 Park Avenue, Northfleet, Kent, DA11 8DL ☎ 01474 323790

Maidstone Mr P D Royall, 18 Firs Close, Aylesford, Maidstone, Kent, ME20 7LH ☎ 01622 710782 (enqs W Williams 01634 371906) www.maidstoneramblers.org.uk

Medway Mrs D M Ashdown, 94a Hollywood Lane, Wainscott, Rochester, Kent, ME3 8AR

North West Kent Mr Ken Conie, 63 Crofton Avenue, Orpington, Kent, BR6 8DY ☎ 01689 851358

Sevenoaks Mrs S E Penzer, 62 Oakhill Road, Sevenoaks, Kent, TN13 1NT ☎ 01732 461 536

Tonbridge & Malling Miss B Stead, 43 Copse Hill, Leybourne, West Malling, Kent, ME19 5QR

Trailfinders (East Kent) 20s-40s Paul Steed ☎ 01322 387002 steed@highstream.com

Tunbridge Wells Miss M I Coulstock, 29 St Peters Street, Tunbridge Wells, Kent, TN2 4UX ☎ 01892 536715

West Kent Walking Group Mrs J H Rogers, Woodview, Fawkham Green Road, Fawkham, Longfield, Kent, DA3 8NN http://home.freeuk.net/wkwo

White Cliffs Mrs R Hodges, 25 William Avenue, Folkestone, Kent, CT19 5TL ☎ 01303 258022

OXFORDSHIRE
AREA SECRETARY

Mr P Lonergan, 35 Cherwell Close, Abingdon, Oxon, OX14 3TD ☎ 01235 202784 http://ramblers-oxon.org.uk

GROUP SECRETARIES

Bicester & Kidlington Mr Colin Morgan, 11 Spruce Drive, Bicester, OX26 3YE ☎ 01869 369603

Cherwell Mrs Dianna Lathbury, 74 Valley Road, Brackley, Northants, NN13 7DQ ☎ 01280 704320

Didcot & Wallingford Mrs V Tilling, The Cedars, Brookfield Close, Wallingford, OX10 9EQ

Henley & Goring Mrs E Burroughs, 43 Elizabeth Road, Henley-On-Thames, RG9 1RA ☎ 01491 572490 [membs Enq Tony Brown 01491 575500]

Oxford Mrs E M Steane & Mr J Steane, 36 Harpes Road, Summertown, Oxford, OX2 7QL ☎ 01865 552531

Oxon 20s & 30s Walking Group Mr G A Wyatt, 3 Bonar Road, Headington, Oxford, OX3 8RD ☎ 01865 890393 graham@wyatt555j.co.uk

Thame & Wheatley Mrs J E Noyce, 27 Worminghall Road, Ickford, Aylesbury, Bucks, HP18 9JB ☎ 01844 339969

Vale of White Horse Mr P Lonergan, 35 Cherwell Close, Abingdon, Oxon, OX14 3TD % 01235 202784

West Oxfordshire Mr Clive Jones, 49 Harefields, Oxford, OX2 8HG ☎ 01865 514663

SURREY
AREA SECRETARY

Mr G Butler, 1 Leaside Court, Lower Luton Road, Harpenden, Herts, AL5 5BX ☎ 01582 767062

GROUP SECRETARIES

Croydon Mr W Haug, 22 Danvers Way, Caterham, CR3 5FJ ☎ 01883 344 011 www.croydonramblers.org.uk

East Surrey Miss Y A Wood, 65 Mares Field, Chepstow Road, Croydon, Surrey, CR0 5UB ☎ 0208 680 3958 www.eastsurreyramblers.org.uk

Epsom & Ewell Mr D J Newman, 56a Acacia Grove, New Malden, Surrey, KT3 3BU ☎ 0208 949 3471 www.epsomandewellramblers.co.uk

Farnham & District Mrs J A Mcdonald, 57 Heath Lane, Farnham, Surrey, GU9 0PX ☎ 01252 687145

Godalming & Haslemere Mrs S Brewer, Hazeldene, South Munstead Lane, Godalming, Surrey, GU8 4AG ☎ 01483 208357 www.godalmingandhaslemere ramblers.org.uk

Guildford Mr P & Mrs C Hackman, 2 Downside Road, Guildford, GU4 8PH ☎ 01483 573633 ttp://guildfordramblers. mysite.freeserve.com

Kingston Mr M Lake, 87 Porchester Road, Kingston Upon Thames, Surrey, KT1 3PW ☎ 020 8541 3437 (membs Enqs only 020 8546 9692) www.geocities.com/kingstonramblers

Mole Valley Mrs J Kucera, 120 Carlton Road, Reigate, Surrey, RH2 0JF ☎ 01737 765158 (membs Enq Mrs Marles 01372 454012) http://myweb.tiscali.co.uk/ molevalleyramblers

Reigate Mr Glyn Jones, 12 Briars Wood, Horley, Surrey, RH6 9UE ☎ 01293 773198 www.reigateramblers.org.uk

Richmond Mr W Westcott, 47 Capel Gardens, Pinner, Middx, HA5 5RF ☎ 020 8429 0886 (membs Enqs Mrs Sharp 020 8748 0049)

Staines Pat Pratley, 76 Hetherington Rd, Charlton Village, Shepperton, Middlesex, TW17 0SW ☎ 01932 711355 www.stainesramblers.co.uk

Surrey Area Weekend Walkers Mrs C Baron, 6 Moorfield, Mill Road, Holmwood, Dorking, RH5 4NZ www.saww.org.uk

Surrey Heath Mrs C Norris, 11 Warwick Close, Camberley, Surrey, GU15 1ES ☎ 01276 26821

LOCAL RAMBLERS CONTACTS continued

Surrey Under 40s Mr K N & Mrs S J
Harding, 52 Strathcona Avenue,
Bookham, Leatherhead, KT23 4HP
☎ 01372 454 717
www.surreyyoungwalkers.org.uk

Sutton/Wandle Valley Peter Rogers,
8 Claygate Court, All Saints Road,
Sutton, Surrey, SM1 3DB
☎ 020 8641 4339
(membs Enqs 020 8643 2605)
www.suttonandwandlevalley
ramblers.org.uk

Woking & District Mrs A Brown,
Beckdale House, White Hart Lane,
Wood Street Village, Guildford,
Surrey, GU3 3EA http://web.ukonline.
co.uk/wokingramblers

SUSSEX
AREA SECRETARY

Mr Nigel Sloan, Kervesridge, Kerves
Lane, Horsham, West Sussex, RH13 6ES
☎ 01403 258055
(enqs P Brannigan 01243 824135)
www.sussex-ramblers.org.uk

GROUP SECRETARIES

Arun-Adur Miss G M Agate, 136 Abbey
Road, Sompting, Lancing, Sussex,
BN15 0AD ☎ 01903 761352

Beachy Head Miss M O'brien,
Southease, Folkington Lane, Folkington,
Polegate, BN26 5SA
☎ 01323 482068

Brighton & Hove Mrs F M Leenders,
14 Middle Road, Brighton, BN1 6SR
☎ 01273 501233
http://homepage.ntlworld.com/
marcbowden/rambler/index.html

Crawley & North Sussex Miss S M
Darby, 14 Chevening Close, Broadfield,
Crawley, RH11 9QU
☎ 01293 533242

Heathfield & District Mrs R Brown,
Chant House, Eridge Lane, Rotherfield,
Nr Crowborough, Sussex, TN6 3JU
☎ 0189 285 2153

High Weald Walkers Mr N Singer,
Croft Lodge, Bayhall Road, Tunbridge
Wells, Kent, TN2 4TP

☎ 01892 523821
www.highwealdwalkers.org.uk

Horsham & Billingshurst
Mrs Brenda Miles, 22 Little Comptons,
Horsham, West Sussex, RH13 5UW
☎ 01403 242916
www.sussex-ramblers.org.uk/
horsham/horsham.htm

Mid Sussex Mrs Celia Parrott,
27 Dale Avenue, Hassocks, West Sussex,
BN6 8LP ☎ 01273 843715

Rother Mr L E Pringle, The Stacks,
Sandrock Hill, Crowhurst, Battle,
TN33 9AT ☎ 01424 830170
www.rotherramblers.org.uk

South West Sussex
Mrs Anne Parker, 11 Palmers Field
Avenue, Chichester, West Sussex,
PO19 6YE ☎ 01243 536080

Sussex Young Walkers
Mrs Sue Jackson, 11 Clayton Drive,
Burgess Hill, West Sussex, RH15 9HH
☎ 01444 235 540
www.sussexyoungwalkers.fsnet.co.uk

LOCAL RAMBLERS PUBLICATIONS

Avon Valley Path
55km/34-mile route from Salisbury to
Christchurch.
*£3.50 + 44p p&p from 9 Pine Close,
Dibden Purlieu, Southampton SO45 4AT.
Cheques payable to Ramblers Association
New Forest Group.*

**The Chairman's Walk around the
perimeter of West Berkshire**
edited by Geoff Vince,
ISBN 1 901184 59 5. A series of 25
linear walks, each of about 7km/4 miles,
grouped in 10 sections and completing a
158km/98-mile circuit.
*£7 + £1 p&p from West Berks Ramblers,
38 Kipling Close, Thatcham RG18 3AY
Cheques to West Berks Ramblers [11/03].*

Four Stations Way
18.5km/11 mile route via stations from
Godalming to Haslemere.
*£1.50 + 25p p&p from Kate Colley, 6 Hill
Court, Haslemere GU27 2BD. Cheques to
Godalming and Haslemere RA Group.*

King's Way
by Pat Miles, ISBN 0 86146 093 X (Meon
Group). A 72km/45-mile walk from
Portchester to Winchester.
*£3.25 + £1 p&p from 19 New Road,
Fareham PO16 7SR. Cheques to Ramblers
Association Meon Group.*

Maidstone Circular Walk Part Two
a set of six walk cards describing half of a
circular route around Maidstone. *£1.80 +
50p p&p from Little Preston Lodge,
Coldharbour Lane, Aylesford ME20 7NS.
Cheques to Ramblers' Association –
Maidstone Group.*

More Than the New Forest
by New Forest Ramblers, ISBN 1 901184
75 7. Recollections of Group members
from the early days in 1969 to the present.
£2.95 + 45p p&p
More Walks Around the New Forest
17 walks between 5km/3 miles and
13km/8 miles covering the whole of the
proposed National Park. *£3.50 + 44p p&p
Both from 9 Pine Close, Dibden Purlieu,
Southampton SO45 4AT. Cheques payable
to Ramblers Association New Forest Group.*

**Rambling for Pleasure Footpath
maps for East Berkshire:**
Cookham & District: 50p, Hurley &
District: 50p, Windsor & The Great Park
ISBN 1 874258 10 4. 50p
*Plus 30p p&p per map from East Berks
Ramblers' Association Publications, PO Box
1357, Maidenhead SL6 7FP. Cheques to
East Berks RA Publications.*
**Rambling for Pleasure Guides
Along the Thames**
5th edition, ISBN 1 874258 09 0.

24 walks of 3km/2 miles to 9.5km/6 miles.
£2.95
Around Reading – 1st Series,
ISBN 1 874258 12 0 and 2nd Series,
ISBN 1 974258 16 3. Two books each of
24 easy country walks of 5km/3 miles to
16km/10 miles. *£2.95 each.*
In East Berkshire ISBN 1 874258 15 5.
24 mainly flat walks of 5km/3 miles to
12km/7.5 miles around Maidenhead,
Wokingham, Bracknell and Ascot, including
6 from stations. *£2.95*
Kennet Valley & Watership Down
ISBN 1 874258 13 9. 24 walks of
4km/2.5 miles and 11km/7 miles exploring
the hidden countryside between Reading,
Newbury and Basingstoke. *£2.95*
Thames Valley and Chilterns
ISBN 1 874258 07 4. 24 varied walks of
5km/3 miles to 19km/12 miles between
Windsor and Abingdon, mainly linear
walks returning by public transport,
*£2.95 + 50p p&p per guide from East
Berks RA Publications, PO Box 1357,
Maidenhead SL6 7FP. Cheques to East
Berks RA Publications.*

**Rural Rambles from the villages
around Alton**
by Alton and District RA. 10 circular walks
from 9.5km/6 miles to 16km/10 miles
starting from villages.
£3.50 from Green Bank, Wilsons Road,

Headley Down, Bordon GU35 8JG. Cheques to Alton and District Ramblers.

Rural Walks around Richmond

by Ramblers' Association Richmond Group. 21 walks of between 3km/2 miles and 24km/15 miles, many with various short options, in a London borough rich in green space. Eight walks have details of wheelchair-accessible sections, including one route that is accessible throughout. *£1.80 + 45p p&p from 59 Gerard Road, London SW13 9QH. Cheques to Margaret Sharp.*

Sussex Diamond Way Midhurst – Heathfield

96km/60 mile walk across the county. *Free + £1 p&p.*

Walks to Interesting Places in Sussex & Kent

(Heathfield Ramblers), ISBN 0 900613 99 8. 21 walks from 4km/2.5 miles to 16km/10 miles across easy terrain, including some linear walks returning on preserved railways. *£3.50.*

Walks in the Weald

revised 2nd edition. 36 walks from 5km/3 miles to 16km/10 miles (average 10km) across varied terrain. *£3.50.*
All from Cobbetts, Burnt Oak Road, High Hurstwood, Uckfield TN22 4AE. Cheques to Heathfield and District RA Group.

Three Castles Path

ISBN 1 874258 08 2. A 96km/60-mile route from Windsor to Winchester with six circular walks.
£2.95 + 50p p&p from East Berks RA Publications, PO Box 1357, Maidenhead SL6 7FP. Cheques to East Berks RA Publications

Walks From Alton

10 walks from 6km/3.75 miles to 14km/8.75 miles through typical Hampshire landscapes, all starting in the town. *£3.50 from Green Bank, Wilsons Road, Headley Down, Bordon GU35 8JG. Cheques to Alton and District Ramblers.*

Walks in South Bucks by West London Ramblers

17 short walks. *£1.50 from 128 Park Lane, Harrow HA2 8NL. Cheques to West London Group Ramblers' Association.*

Walking the Wessex Heights

Detailed maps and route descriptions for a 123km/77-mile route and 14 circular walks. *£2.50 + 44p SAE as More Walks Around the New Forest above.*

12 Walks in and Around Winchester

Moderate-level walks varying from 3km/2 miles to 14.5km/9 miles. *£1.50 + 50p*

p&p from Underhill House, Beech Copse, Winchester SO22 5NR. Cheques to Winchester Ramblers.

12 Favourite Walks on the Isle of Wight
12 More Favourite Walks on the Isle of Wight
12 Walks from Towns on the Isle of Wight

Walks of between 5km/3 miles and 14.5km/9 miles, with simple maps and route descriptions. *All £2 + 40p p&p each from Dibs, Main Road, Rookley, Ventnor PO38 3NQ. Cheques to Mrs Joan Deacon.*

21 Walks for the 21st Century

walks on the Berkshire/Wiltshire border of between 8km/5 miles and 14.5km/9 miles. *£6 + £1 p&p from West Berks Ramblers, 38 Kipling Close, Thatcham RG18 3AY. Cheques to West Berks Ramblers.*

Twenty-five Favourite Walks in West Surrey & Sussex

by Godalming and Haslemere Ramblers, revised edition, ISBN 1 901184 63 3. Variety of circular walks offering both short and long options between 5.5km/3.5 miles and 25.5km/16 miles. *£4.95 + 50p p&p from Elstead Maps. Cheques to Elstead Maps.*

millets stores in this region

ALDERSHOT	1/2 Wellington Centre GU11 1DB
ANDOVER	29 High Street SP10 1LJ
ASHFORD	Unit 24 Park Mall TN24 8RY
AYLESBURY	13 Market Square HP20 2PZ
BANBURY	9 High Street OX16 8DZ
BASINGSTOKE	11/12 Potters Walk RG21 7GQ
BEXLEYHEATH	119 The Broadway DA6 7HF
BICESTER	26/27 Crown Walk OX26 6HY
BOGNOR REGIS	38 London Road PO21 1PZ
BOURNEMOUTH	39 Old Christchurch Road BH1 1DS
BRACKNELL	58 The Broadway RG12 1AR
BRIGHTON	153 Western Road BN1 2DA
BROMLEY	65 High Street BR1 1JY
BURGESS HILL	Unit 77, Church Walk, The Martlets RH15 9BQ
CAMBERLEY	33 High Street GU15 3RB
CANTERBURY	47 Burgate CT1 4BH
CHESHAM	35 High Street HP5 1BW
CHICHESTER	4 South Street PO19 1EH
CHISWICK	167 Chiswick High Road W4 2DR
CRAWLEY	22 Haslett Avenue RH10 1HS
CROYDON	52 High Street CR0 1YB
DORKING	5 South Street RH4 2DY
EAST GRINSTEAD	23 London Road RH19 1AL
EASTBOURNE	146/148 Terminus Road BN21 3AN
ELTHAM	122 Eltham High Road SE9 1BJ
ENFIELD	21 Palace Gardens EN2 6SN
EPSOM	17 High Street KT19 8DD
FAREHAM	80/82 Osborne Mall, Hampshire PO16 0PW
FARNBOROUGH	Unit 5/7 The Mead GU14 7RT
FARNHAM	2/3 West Street, Surrey GU9 7DN
FLEET	158 Fleet Road GU13 8BE
GUILDFORD	21 Friary Street GU1 4GH
HASTINGS	12/13 York Building, Wellington Place TN34 1NN
HAYWARDS HEATH	98 South Road RH16 4LJ
HIGH WYCOMBE	4/5 Church Street HP11 2DE
HORSHAM	18 West Street RH12 1TV

HOUNSLOW	156 High Street TW3 1LR
KENSINGTON	176 Kensington High Street W8 7RG
KINGSTON	3/5 Thames Street KT1 1PH
LEWISHAM	205 Lewisham High Street SE13 6LY
LONDON	176 Kensington High Street W8 7RG
LYMINGTON	52 High Street SO41 9AG
MAIDSTONE	70 Week Street ME14 1QT
NEWBURY	68/69 Northbrook Street RG13 1AE
NEWPORT (Isle of Wight)	21 St James Square PO30 1UX
ORPINGTON	178 High Street BR6 0JW
OXFORD	42/43 Queen Street OX1 1ET
PETERSFIELD	8 Rams Walk GU32 3JA
PORTSMOUTH	213/215 Commercial Road PO1 4BJ
PUTNEY	98 High Street SW15 1RB
RAMSGATE	8 Queen Street CT11 9DR
READING	4/5 St Mary's Butts RG1 2LN
REDHILL	29 High Street RH1 1RD
RICHMOND	36/37 The Quadrant TW9 1BP
RINGWOOD	7 The Furlong Centre BH24 1AT
ROMFORD	42/44 South Street RM1 1RB
SITTINGBOURNE	119 High Street ME10 4AQ
SLOUGH	186/188 High Street SL1 1JS
SOUTHAMPTON	104 East Street SO14 3HH
SOUTHSEA	5 Palmurston Road PO5 3QQ
St. ALBANS	19/21 French Row AL3 5DZ
STAINES	111A High Street TW18 4PQ
SUTTON	86 High Street SM1 1JG
SWINDON	Sub Unit 4 The Parade SN1 1BA
TONBRIDGE	70 High Street TN9 1SD
TUNBRIDGE WELLS	3/7 Camden Road TN1 2PS
WIMBLEDON	34 The Broadway SW19 0BB
WINCHESTER	149 High Street SO23 9AY
WINDSOR	42 Peascod Street SL4 1DE
WITNEY	Unit 18A, Woolgate OX28 6AP
WOKING	31 Commercial Road GU21 1XR
WOKINGHAM	37 Peach Street RG4 0IXJ
WORTHING	95 Montague Street BN11 3BN

BED & BREAKFAST

BERKSHIRE

● Hungerford
🚶🚲🚗 Alderborne, 33 Bourne Vale, RGI7 0LL ☎ 01488 683228
www.honeybone.co.uk   Map 174/333682
BB **B**   ✕ nearby   S2 T2   ᴀᴡ(Hungerford)
🅱 🅳 ⊛ 🍵☕ ☕ ! Ⓜ   ◆◆◆◆

● Hurley (Maidenhead)
Thames Path, London Loop & Chiltern Way
Hurley Bed and Breakfast, The Old Farm House, High St, SL6 5NB
☎ 01628 825446 (Mrs Katie Gear)
www.hurleybedandbreakfast.co.uk   Map 175/825839
BB **B**   ✕ nearby   D3 T2   🅱 ⊛ ☕

● Inkpen (Hungerford)
Test Way
The Swan Inn, RGI7 9DX ☎ 01488 668326 (Mary Harris)
www.theswaninn-organics.co.uk   Map 174/358644
BB **C**   ✕ £8, 7-9:30pm   S1 D4 T3 F2   ᴀᴡ(Kintbury)
Ⓥ 🅱 🅳 🍵☕   ◆◆◆◆

● Maidenhead
Thames Path
🚶🚲🚗 Sheephouse Manor Guest House, Sheephouse Road, SL6 8HJ
☎ 01628 776902 (Mrs C J Street)
www.sheephousemanor.co.uk   Map 175/898831
BB **C**   S2 DI TI   ᴀᴡ(Maidenhead)   🅱 🅳 ⊛ 🍵☕ ☕ ! 🚲   ◆◆◆

● Windsor
Thames Path
🚶🚲🚗 The Laurells, 22 Dedworth Road, SL4 5AY
☎ 01753 855821 (Mrs Joyce)   Map 175,176/952765
BB **B**   ✕ nearby   S1 T2   ᴀᴡ(Central & Riverside)   🅱 🅳 ⊛ 🍵☕

BUCKINGHAMSHIRE

● Amersham
Chiltern Way
🚶🚲🚗 Cherry Trees, 51 Longfield Drive, HP6 5HE
☎ 01494 729321   (Angelica Schweiger)
www.cherrytrees-bandb.co.uk   Map 165,176/962982
BB **B**   ✕ nearby   S1 DI   ᴀᴡ(Amersham)   🅱 🅳 ⊛ ☕   ◆◆◆◆

● Bledlow
Ridgeway, Chiltern Way & Midshires Way
Cross Lanes Cottage, West Lane, HP27 9PF ☎ 01844 345339 (Ron Coulter)
www.crosslanes.net   Map 165/773024
BB **C**   ✕ nearby   D2 TI   Closed Dec   ᴀᴡ(Princes Risborough)
🅱 🅳 ⊛ 🍵☕ 🚗   ◆◆◆◆⑤

● Chesham
Chiltern Way
49 Lowndes Avenue, HP5 2HH ☎ 01494 792647 (Mrs P Orme)
pageormelowndes@tiscali.co.uk   Map 165/957021
BB **B**   ✕ nearby   S1 TI   ᴀᴡ(Chesham)   🅳 ⊛ ☕ 🚗 🚲   ◆◆◆

● Coleshill (Amersham)
Chiltern Way
Pond Cottage, Village Rd, HP7 0LH ☎ 01494 728177
(Hilary & Tony Wayland)   pondcott@msn.com   Map 165/947950
BB **C**   ✕ nearby   S1 D2 TI   🅱 🅳 ⊛ 🍵☕ ! ◆◆◆◆

● Edlesborough (Dunstable)
Ridgeway, Icknield Way & Chiltern Way
Ridgeway End, 5 Ivinghoe Way, LU6 2EL ☎ 01525 220405 (Mr & Mrs Lloyd)
www.ridgewayend.co.uk   Map 165/974183
BB **B**   ✕ nearby   S1 DI TI FI   🅱 🅳 ⊛ 🍵☕ 🚗 !

● Great Kingshill (High Wycombe)
Hatches Farm, Hatches Lane, HP15 6DS ☎ 01494 713125 (Mrs M A Davies)
Map 165/873980   BB **B**   ✕ nearby   DI TI   🅳 ⊛ 🚗   ◆◆

● High Wycombe
Chiltern Way
🚶🚲🚗 South Fields, Cadmore End, HP14 3PJ ☎ 01494 881976
(Judith Crichton) www.crichtonville.freeserve.co.uk   Map 175/783926
BB **B**   ✕ nearby   S2 DI TI   Ⓥ 🅱 🅳 ⊛ 🍵☕ ☕ 🚗 !   ◆◆◆

● Little Hampden (Great Missenden)
Chiltern Way, Ridgeway & London Loop
🚶🚲🚗 The Rising Sun, HP16 9PS ☎ 01494 488393
www.rising-sun.demon.co.uk   Map 165/859037
BB **C**   ✕ £15, 7-9pm   D3 T2   Ⓥ 🅱 🅳 ⊛ 🍵☕ 🚲

● Marlow
Thames Path & Chiltern Way
Merrie Hollow, Seymour Court Hill, Marlow Road, SL7 3DE
☎ 01628 485663 (Mr & Mrs B Wells)   Map 175/837889
BB **B**   ✕ book first £12, 7-8pm   DI TI   ᴀᴡ(Marlow)
Ⓥ 🅳 ⊛ 🍵☕ 🚗 🚲   ◆◆◆

Acha Pani, Bovingdon Green, SL7 2JL
☎ 01628 483435 (Mrs Mary Cowling)
mary@achapani.freeserve.co.uk   Map 175/834869
BB **A**   ✕ book first £8   S1 DI TI   ᴀᴡ(Marlow)
Ⓥ 🅱 🅳 🍵☕ 🚗 🚲   ◆◆◆

● Saunderton (High Wycombe)
Ridgeway, Chiltern Way & Midshires Way
Hunters Gate, Deanfield, HP14 4JR ☎ 01494 481718 (Mrs Anne Dykes)
www.huntersgatebandb.co.uk   Map 165/809975
BB **B**   ✕ nearby   D2 TI   ᴀᴡ(Saunderton)
🅱 🅳 🍵☕ 🚗 ! 🚲 Ⓜ   ◆◆◆

● St Leonards (Tring)
Chiltern Way & Ridgeway
Field Cottage, HP23 6NS ☎ 01494 837602 (Mike & Sue Jepson)
www.smoothhound.co.uk/hotels/field.html   Map 165/900062
BB **B**   ✕ nearby   S1 DI TI   🅱 🅳 ⊛ ☕   ◆◆◆◆⑤

● Wendover (Aylesbury)
Ridgeway & Chiltern Way
26 Chiltern Road, HP22 6DB ☎ 01296 622351 (Mrs E C Condie)
Map 165/865082   BB **A**   ✕ nearby   S1 T/FI   ᴀᴡ(Wendover)
🅳 ⊛ ☕ 🚲 Ⓜ   ◆

● **West Wycombe (High Wycombe)**

Chiltern Way

The Swan Inn, HP14 3AE ☎ 01494 527031   Map 175/829945
BB **B** ✕ nearby SI D2 TI FI ∰(Saunderton)

EAST SUSSEX

● **Alfriston**

South Downs Way & Wealdway

Riverdale House, Seaford Road, BN26 5TR ☎ 01323 871038
www.riverdalehouse.co.uk Map 199/516024
BB **C** ✕ nearby D3 T2 FI ∰(Berwick)
Ⓑ Ⓓ ⊛ 🐾🗆 ♦♦♦♦

Dacres, BN26 5TP ☎ 01323 870447 (Mrs Patsy Embry) Map 199/518028
BB **B** ✕ nearby TI ∰(Alfriston) Ⓑ Ⓓ ⊛ 🗆 !

5 The Broadway, BN26 5XL ☎ 01323 870145 (Mrs Janet Dingley)
janetandbrian@dingley5635.freeserve.co.uk Map 199/516030
BB **B** ✕ nearby SI DI TI Ⓑ Ⓓ ⊛ 🐾🗆 🚗 !

● **Beddingham (Lewes)**

South Downs Way

🚶🛏 Kington Cottage, Itford Farm, BN8 6JS ☎ 01273 858431
(Mrs Debbie Brickell) www.kingtoncottage.co.uk Map 198/433054
BB **B** ✕ nearby SI D2 ∰(Y) Ⓓ ⊛ 🐾🗆 🚗 🐾 Bicycle lock-up.

● **Blackboys (Uckfield)**

Wealdway

Rangers Cottage, Terminus Rd, TN22 5LX ☎ 01825 890463
(David & Elizabeth Brown) leighton1@evemail.net Map 199/518207
BB **B/C** ✕ nearby DI TI Ⓑ Ⓓ 🐾🗆 🚗 ♦♦♦♦

● **Chiddingly (Lewes)**

Wealdway

🚶🛏 Hale Farm House, BN8 6HQ ☎ 01825 872619 (David & Sue
Burrough) www.halefarmhouse.co.uk Map 199/555145
BB **B** ✕ book first £7.50, 6-8pm T2 FI
Ⓥ Ⓑ Ⓓ ⊛ 🐾🗆 🚗 🐾 ♦♦♦♦

● **Colemans Hatch (Hartfield)**

Wealdway

Gospel Oak, TN7 4ER ☎ 01342 823840 (Mrs L Hawker)
lindah@thehatch.freeserve.co.uk Map 187/447327
BB **B** ✕ book first £14, 8pm DI TI
Ⓥ Ⓑ Ⓓ ⊛ 🐾🗆 🚗 !🗆 Ⓜ ♦♦♦

● **Danehill (Haywards Heath)**

Green Acres, Horsted Lane, RH17 7HP
☎ 01825 790863 (Mrs J M Jennings) Map 187,198/397278
BB **A** ✕ book first £7, 6-8:30pm DI TI Closed Dec
Ⓥ Ⓑ Ⓓ ⊛ 🐾🗆 🚗 Ⓜ

● **East Dean (Eastbourne)**

South Downs*

South Downs Way & Wealdway

🚶🛏 The Welkin, 2 The Link, BN20 0LB ☎ 01323 423384
(Mrs Phyll Workman) phyll.workman@tesco.net Map 199/560989
BB **B** ✕ book first £10 SI TI
Ⓥ Ⓑ Ⓓ ⊛ 🐾🗆 🚗

● **Eastbourne**

South Downs Way & Wealdway

Ambleside Hotel, 24 Elms Avenue, BN21 3DN
☎ 01323 724991 (J Pattenden)
www.SmoothHound.co.uk/hotels/ambleside.html Map 199/616989
BB **A** S2 D6 T6 ∰(Eastbourne) Ⓑ Ⓓ 🗆 🐾

Brayscroft Hotel, 13 South Cliff Avenue, BN20 7AH ☎ 01323 647005
www.brayscrofthotel.co.uk Map 199/609980
BB **B** ✕ book first £14, 6pm SI D3 T2 ∰(Eastbourne)
Ⓥ Ⓑ ✕ ⊛ 🐾🗆 🐾 ♦♦♦♦Ⓢ

Southcroft, 15 South Cliff Ave, BN20 7AH ☎ 01323 729071 (Andrew
Johnson) southcroft@eastbourne34.freeserve.co.uk Map 199/609980
BB **B** ✕ £12, 6pm D3 T2 ∰(Eastbourne)
Ⓥ Ⓑ Ⓓ ⊛ 🐾🗆 🚗 ! ♦♦♦♦

☆ 🚶🛏 **The Atlanta Hotel**
10 Royal Parade, BN22 7AR ☎ 01323 730486 (Jason Osbourne)
www.hotelatlanta.co.uk Map 199/619993
BB **B** ✕ book first £9, 6pm D4 T3 F2 Closed Jan ∰(Eastbourne)
Ⓥ Ⓑ 🐾🗆 🐾 ♦♦♦

RAC 3 diamonds.
Licensed Hotel.
The Atlanta Hotel boasts a friendly atmospshere
and staff.
It is ideally situated on the seafront.
Convenient for South Downs Way.

● **Fairlight (Rye)**

Stream House, Pett Level Rd, TN35 4ED ☎ 01424 814916 (Sandra Lewis)
www.stream-house.co.uk Map 199/876126
BB **B** D2 Closed Dec-Jan
Ⓑ Ⓓ ⊛ 🗆 🐾 ♦♦♦♦♦ Veggie breakfasts.

● **Fairwarp (Uckfield)**

Wealdway

Broom Cottage, Browns Brook, TN22 3BY ☎ 01825 712942 (Jane Rattray)
Map 198/472272 BB **B** ✕ nearby DI TI
Ⓑ Ⓓ ⊛ 🐾🗆 🐾 ♦♦♦♦

● **Groombridge (Tunbridge Wells)**

Wealdway

🚶🛏 Ventura, The Ridge, Withyam Road, TN3 9QU
☎ 01892 864711 (Brenda Horner) Map 188/521369
BB **B** ✕ book first £10, 6:30-7pm SI D/FI TI
Ⓥ Ⓑ Ⓓ 🐾🗆 🚗 🐾

● **Hailsham**

Wealdway

🚶🛏 Longleys Farm Cottage, Harebeating Lane, BN27 1ER ☎ 01323 841227
(David & Jill Hook) Map 199/598105 BB **B** ✕ nearby DI TI FI
Ⓑ Ⓓ ⊛ 🐾🗆 🚗 🐾 ♦♦♦

● **Hastings**

🚶🛏 Grand Hotel, Grand Parade, St Leonards, TN38 0DD
☎ 01424 428510 (Peter Mann) Map 199/802089
BB **B** ✕ book first £10, 5-7pm S3 D9 T7 F4 ∰(Warrior Square)
Ⓥ Ⓑ Ⓓ ⊛ 🐾🗆 🚗 ! ♦♦♦

● **Heathfield**

Spicers Bed and Breakfast, 21 Spicers Cottages, Cade Street, TN21 9BS
☎ 01435 866363 (Graham & Valerie Gumbrell)
www.spicersbb.co.uk Map 199/605212
BB **B** ✕ book first £12-£15, 6-8pm   S1 D1 T1
Ⓥ Ⓑ Ⓓ ⊛ 🐾🛏🚗! 🌿   ◆◆◆◆

● **Horam (Heathfield)**

Wealdway

▪️🍴◀ Oak Mead Nursery, Cowden Hall Lane, TN21 9ED
☎ 01435 812962 (Mrs Barbara Curtis) Map 199/592171
BB **B** ✕ nearby S1 D1 T1   Closed Dec-Feb   Ⓑ Ⓓ ⊛ 🐾🛏🚗
▪️🍴◀ Wimbles Farm, Foords Lane, Vines Cross, TN21 9HA ☎ 01435 812342
(Mrs S Ramsay-Smith) www.wimblesfarm.com Map 199/599167
BB **B** ✕ nearby S1 D2 T1 F1
Ⓑ Ⓓ ⊛ 🐾🛏! 🌿   ◆◆◆

● **Kingston (Lewes)**

South Downs Way

Settlands, Wellgreen Lane, BN7 3NP   ☎ 01273 472295 (Mrs Diana Artlett)
diana-a@solutions-inc.co.uk   Map 198/398082
BB **B/C** ✕ nearby D1 T1 ▲▲▲(Lewes)
Ⓓ ⊛ 🐾🛏🚗! ◆◆◆◆Ⓢ

Bethel, Kingston Ridge, BN7 3JX   ☎ 01273 478658 (Tim & Nancy Lear)
www.lewes-area-bed-and-breakfast.com/bethel Map 198/387085
BB **B/C** ✕ nearby D1 T2 ▲▲▲(Lewes)
Ⓑ Ⓓ ⊛ 🐾🛏🚗!

● **Lewes**

South Downs*

South Downs Way

B&B Number 6, Gundreda Rd, BN7 1PX   ☎ 01273 472106 (Jackie Lucas)
www.stayinlewes.co.uk   Map 198/406105
BB **B** ✕ nearby D2 T1 ▲▲▲(Lewes)
Ⓑ Ⓓ ⊛ 🐾🛏🚗! ◆◆◆◆
▪️🍴◀ Knowle View, 24 Mill Rd, BN7 2RU   ☎ 01273 477477 (Diana Gunnell)
www.knowleview.co.uk   Map 198/422111
BB **B/C** ✕ book first £15, 7pm D2 T1 F1 ▲▲▲(Lewes)
Ⓥ Ⓑ Ⓓ ⊛ 🐾🛏🚗! Ⓜ   ◆◆◆◆

● **Mayfield**

April Cottage Guest House and Tearoom, West Street, TN20 6BA
☎ 01435 872160 (Miss B Powner) Map 188,199/585269
BB **B** ✕ nearby S1 D/S1 T/S1 Ⓑ Ⓓ 🐾🌿

● **Newhaven**

South Downs*

South Downs Way

▪️🍴◀ Newhaven Lodge, 12 Brighton Rd, BN9 9NB   ☎ 01273 513736
(Jan Cameron) NewhavenLodge@aol.com Map 198/442013
BB **B** ✕ nearby S2 D1 T1 F3 ▲▲▲(Newhaven) Ⓑ 🐾🛏! 🌿   ◆◆◆

● **Nutley (Uckfield)**

Wealdway

▪️🍴◀ West Meadows B&B, Bell Lane, TN22 3RD
☎ 01825 712434 (Alex Everett) Map 187,198/409253
BB **B** ✕ nearby D2 T1
Ⓑ Ⓓ ⊛ 🐾🛏🚗! 🌿   ◆◆◆◆Ⓢ

● **Rye**

Saxon Shore Way

Little Saltcote, 22 Military Rd, TN31 7NY   ☎ 01797 223210
(Barbara & Denys Martin) littlesaltcote.rye@virgin.net Map 189/923212
BB **B** ✕ nearby D2 F3 ▲▲▲(Rye) Ⓑ Ⓓ ⊛ 🐾🛏🚗! 🌿   ◆◆◆

Culpeppers, 15 Love Lane, TN31 7NE   ☎ 01797 224411
www.culpeppers-rye.co.uk Map 189/918209
BB **B** ✕ book first £, 6-6:30pm   S2 T1   Closed Dec   ▲▲▲(Rye)
Ⓥ Ⓑ Ⓓ ⊛ 🐾🛏🚗! 🌿   ◆◆◆◆Ⓢ

▪️🍴◀ The Old Vicarage, Rye Harbour, TN31 7TT   ☎ 01797 222088 (Jonathan
Bosher) jonathan@oldvicarageryeharbour.fsnet.co.uk Map 189/941190
BB **B** ✕ nearby D1 T1 ▲▲▲(Rye) Ⓓ 🐾🛏🚗 🌿   ★★★

☆ **Jeake's House**

Mermaid Street, TN31 7ET ☎ 01797 222828 (Mrs J Hadfield)
www.jeakeshouse.com   Map 189/919203
BB **C** ✕ nearby S1 D7 T1 F2 ▲▲▲(Rye)
Ⓑ Ⓓ 🛏🌿   ◆◆◆◆◆Ⓢ

Dating from 1534, this listed building stands in Rye's medieval town centre.

Breakfast is served in the elegant galleried hall and features traditional, vegetarian, devilled kidneys and fish dishes. Stylishly restored bedrooms combine luxury and modern amenities.

After rambling the Romney Marshes you can relax in the book-lined bar with a drink. Bike hire nearby. Private car park.

Flackley Ash Hotel

Peasmarsh, TN31 6YH ☎ 01797 230651
www.flackleyashhotel.co.uk Map 199,189/881233
BB **C** ✕ £22.50, 7-9:30pm   D23 T18 F4
Ⓥ Ⓑ Ⓓ 🐾🛏! 🌿   ★★★

Warm and friendly Georgian country house hotel set in 5 acres of beautiful grounds. Bedrooms individually furnished in the style of a traditional country house. Award winning candlelit restaurant with fine wines & fresh local fish. Leisure centre with indoor pool, spa, sauna, steam and beauty treatments. Wonderful country and seaside walks. Discover medieval Rye, the beautiful Bodiam and Sissinghurst castles.

● Streat

South Downs*

South Downs Way

North Acres, BN6 8RX ☎ 01273 890278 (Mrs Valerie Eastwood)
www.northacres-streat.co.uk Map 198/353154
BB **B** S2 DI TI ⚹(Plumpton) Ⓓ ⊛ 🐾 ♨ 🚗 !

● Wilmington (Polegate)

South Downs Way & Wealdway

🚩 Crossways Hotel, BN26 5SG ☎ 01323 482455 (David Stott)
www.crosswayshotel.co.uk Map 199/547048
BB **C** ✕ book first £32.95, 7:30-8:30pm S2 D3 T2
Closed Jan ⚹(Polegate) Ⓥ Ⓑ Ⓓ🐾♨! ◆◆◆◆◆

HAMPSHIRE

● Alton

St Swithun's Way

🚩 The Manor House, Holybourne, GU34 4HD ☎ 01420 541321
(Clare Whately) clare@whately.net Map 186/734411
BB **B** ✕ nearby T2 ⚹(Alton) Ⓓ ⊛ 🐾 ♨ 🚗 ! 🐾 ◆◆◆◆

● Ashurst (Southampton)

New Forest

Test Way

🚩 The Barn Vegetarian Guest House, 112 Lyndhurst Rd, SO40 7AY
☎ 023 8029 2531 (Richard Barnett)
www.veggiebarn.net Map 196/338105
BB **B** ✕ £14, 6:30pm DI TI ⚹(Ashurst)
Ⓥ Ⓑ Ⓓ ⊛ ♨ 🚗 Exclusively veggie/vegan

● Boldre (Brockenhurst)

New Forest

Solent Way

🚩 Hilden B&B, Southampton Road, SO41 8PT
☎ 01590 623682 (Mrs A Arnold-Brown)
www.newforestbandb-hilden.co.uk Map 196/307989
BB **B** ✕ nearby D/F3 ⚹(Brockenhurst) Ⓑ Ⓓ ♨ 🚗 !

● Broughton (Stockbridge)

Monarch's Way & Test Way

Kings, Salisbury Road, SO20 8BY ☎ 01794 301458 (Ann Heather)
Map 185/301331 BB **A/B** ✕ book first £7.50-£10 SI TI
Ⓥ Ⓑ Ⓓ 🐾 ♨ 🚗

● Buriton (Petersfield)

South Downs*

South Downs Way

Nursted Farm, GU31 5RW ☎ 01730 264278 (Mrs M Bray)
Map 197/754214 BB **B** ✕ nearby T3 FI Closed Mar-Apr ⚹(Petersfield)
Ⓑ Ⓓ ⊛ 🐾 🚗

● Burley (Ringwood)

New Forest

Holmans, Bisterne Close, BH24 4AZ ☎ 01425 402307 (Robin & Mary Ford)
Map 195/229025 BB **C** ✕ nearby D2 TI
Ⓑ Ⓓ ⊛ ♨ 🚗 ! 🐾 ◆◆◆◆Ⓢ

Wayside Cottage, 27 Garden Rd, BH24 4EA ☎ 01425 403414 (Janet West)
www.wayside-cottage.co.uk Map 195/209030
BB **B** ✕ book first £15, 7:30pm D3 T2 FI Ⓥ Ⓑ Ⓓ ⊛

● Cadnam

New Forest

Walnut Cottage B&B, Old Romsey Rd, SO40 2NP
☎ 02380 812275 (Marian Chitty) Map 196/293137
BB **B/C** ✕ nearby DI T2 Ⓑ Ⓓ ⊛ ♨ ◆◆◆◆

● Cheriton (Alresford)

South Downs Way

Brandy Lea, SO24 0QQ ☎ 01962 771534 (Margaret Hoskings)
Map 185/581283 BB **B** SI TI Ⓑ Ⓓ ♨ 🚗 🐾

● Dibden Purlieu (Southampton)

New Forest

Solent Way

Ashdene Guest House, Beaulieu Rd, SO45 4PT
☎ 02380 846073 (Mrs Diana Norman)
www.ashdenehouse.co.uk Map 196/411060
BB **B** ✕ nearby S3 T4 FI Ⓑ Ⓓ 🐾 ♨ 🐾 ◆◆◆

● Dummer (Basingstoke)

☆ 🚩 **Oakdown Farm**
RG23 7LR ☎ 01256 397218 (Mrs E Hutton)
Map 185/587472
BB **B** ✕ nearby DI T2 ⊛ 🐾 ♨ 🚗 ! 🐾 Ⓜ ◆◆◆

Wayfarers Walk 200 metres.
North of Junction 7 M3. Secluded position. Evening meal locally. Lifts available. Car parking.

● East Meon (Petersfield)

South Downs Way

Dunvegan Cottage, Frogmore Lane, GU32 1QJ
☎ 01730 823213 (Jenny d'Amato)
www.dunvegan.btinternet.co.uk Map 185/688217
BB **B** ✕ nearby D2 T3 FI
Ⓑ Ⓓ ⊛ 🐾 ♨ 🚗 ! 🐾 ◆◆◆◆

● Fordingbridge (Alderholt)

New Forest

Alderholt Mill, Sandleheath Road, SP6 1PU ☎ 01425 653130
(Mr & Mrs R Harte) www.alderholtmill.co.uk Map 195/119143
BB **B** ✕ book first £15, 7-8:30pm SI D3 TI
Ⓥ Ⓑ Ⓓ ⊛ 🐾 ♨ 🚗 ! 🐾 ◆◆◆◆ See SC also.

● Freefolk (Whitchurch)

🚩 The Old Rectory, RG28 7NW ☎ 01256 895408 (Sue Etridge)
Map 185/487487 BB **B** ✕ nearby DI TI FI ⚹(Whitchurch)
Ⓑ Ⓓ 🐾 ♨ 🚗 ! 🐾

● **Hambledon (Waterlooville)**

Monarch's Way

Mornington House, Speltham Hill, PO7 4RU (Mr & Mrs Lutyens)
☎ 023 9263 2704　Map 196/644149
BB **B**　✕ nearby　T2　⬚🐾♨🍵🚗🐴

● **Highclere (Newbury)**

Westridge (Open Centre), Star Lane- off A 345, RG20 9PJ
☎ 01635 253322　Map 174/436604
BB **A**　✕ nearby　T2　⬚♨　Booking ahead essential.

● **Hordle (Lymington)**

Solent Way

Miranda, Vaggs Lane, SO41 0FP　☎ 01425 621561 (Shirley Davis)
Map 195/264964　BB **B**　✕ book first £16　S1 D2 T1　🚶(New Milton)
Ⓥ B ⬚ 🐾♨🍵🚗🐴!🏠 ◆◆◆◆

● **Ibthorpe (Andover)**

Test Way

Staggs Cottage, Windmill Hill, Hurstbourne Tarrant, SP11 0BP
☎ 01264 736235 (Mr & Mrs Norton)
staggscottage@aol.com　Map 185/374536
BB **B**　✕ book first £9, 6-9pm　D1 T2　Ⓥ ⬚ 🐾♨🍵🚗🐴 Ⓜ ◆◆◆

● **Lymington**

New Forest

Solent Way

The Anchorage, Kings Farm, Everton Rd, Hordle, SO41 0HD
☎ 01425 622375 (Jean & Ken Aitken)
http://theanchorage.mysite.wanadoo-members.co.uk　Map 195/277950
BB **B**　✕ nearby　S1 T1　🚶(Sway) B ⬚ ⊛🐾♨🚗 Ⓜ

Durlston House, Gosport St, SO41 9EG　☎ 01590 677364 (Jenny Ridgway) www.durlstonhouse.co.uk　Map 196/325959
BB **B**　✕ nearby　S6 T1 F/T3　🚶(Lymington Town)
B ⬚ ⊛ 🐾♨🍵🚗🐴!🏠 ◆◆◆◆

● **Lyndhurst**

New Forest

Stable End, Emery Down, SO43 7FJ　☎ 023 8028 2504
(William & Mary Dibben)　dibbenfam@aol.com　Map 196/290089
BB **B**　✕ nearby　D1 T1　🚶(Ashurst)
B ⬚ ⊛♨🍵🚗! ◆◆◆◆

Whitemoor House Hotel, Southampton Road, SO43 7BU
☎ 023 8028 2186 (Sue Scregg)　www.whitemoorhotel.co.uk
Map 196/308085　BB **C**　✕ nearby　D3 T3 F2　🚶(Ashurst)
Ⓥ B ⬚ 🐾♨🍵🚗 ◆◆◆◆

☆ **Rufus Guest House**

Southampton Rd, SO43 7BQ　☎ 02380 282930 (Paul & Alma Carter)
www.rufushousehotel.co.uk　Map 196/304082
BB **B**　✕ book first £12, 6-8pm　S1 D9 T1 F2
Ⓥ B ⬚ ⊛🐾♨🍵🏠

Delightful Victorian house set in beautiful gardens. Superb location, close to village and opposite open forest. Relaxed, friendly atmosphere offering outstanding accommodation at affordable prices. Extensive knowledge of local walks and attractions. Complementary flasks of tea/coffee. Extended stay discounts.

☆ **Ormonde House Hotel**

Southampton Road, SO43 7BT　☎ 02380 282806 (Paul Ames)
www.ormondehouse.co.uk　Map 196/305083
BB **B/C**　✕ book first £15-£19, 6:30-8pm　S1 D17 T4 F1　🚶(Ashurst)
Ⓥ B ⬚ 🐾♨🍵🏠 ★★

Perfect base for walking; Ormonde House Hotel and Pinewood Cottage lie opposite the open forest, within walking distance of Lyndhurst village. Furnished to a high standard the hotel has 19 pretty en-suite bedrooms with colour TV and hairdryers. Pinewood Cottage Suites are self-contained, fully serviced and have full kitchens with washing machines, dryers and dishwashers. Pets are welcome. Privately owned and renowned for its excellent home cuisine. Discounts for midweek 3 & 4 day breaks and for parties of min. 6 out of season. Email: enquiries@ormondehouse.co.uk

The Penny Farthing Hotel & Cottages, Romsey Road, SO43 7AA
☎ 023 8028 4422　www.pennyfarthinghotel.co.uk　Map 196/298082
BB **C**　✕ nearby　S3 D12 T3 F2　B ⬚ ♨🍵 ◆◆◆◆　See SC also.

● **New Milton**

New Forest

St Ursula, 30 Hobart Road, BH25 6EG　☎ 01425 613515 (Mr & Mrs M Pearce)
Map 195/239947　BB **B**　✕ nearby　S2 D1 T2 F1　🚶(New Milton)
B ⬚ ⊛🐾♨🍵🚗🐴!🏠 ◆◆◆◆　Access Category 3.

● **Petersfield**

South Downs*

South Downs Way

Heath Farmhouse, GU31 4HU　☎ 01730 264709 (Mrs P Scurfield)
www.heathfarmhouse.co.uk　Map 197/757224
BB **B**　D1 T1 F1　🚶(Petersfield) B ⬚ ⊛🐾♨🍵🚗🐴!🏠 ◆◆◆

1 The Spain, Sheep St, GU32 3JZ　☎ 01730 263261 (Jennifer Tarver)
allantarver@ntlworld.com　Map 197/748232
BB **B**　✕ nearby　S1 D2 T1　🚶(Petersfield)
B ⬚ ⊛🐾♨🍵🏠 ◆◆◆◆

Copper Beeches, Torberry Farm, Hurst, GU31 5RG　☎ 01730 826662
(Mrs Janet Chew)　www.visitsussex.org/copperbeeches　Map 197/768200
BB **B**　✕ book first £7.50, 7-9pm　D1 F1
Ⓥ B ⬚ ⊛🐾♨🍵🚗🐴!🏠 ◆◆◆

☆ **Border Cottage**

4 Heath Rd, GU31 4DU　☎ 01730 263179 (Mrs Laura Lawrence)
www.bordercottage.co.uk　Map 197/749232
BB **B**✕ nearby　D1 T1　🚶(Petersfield) B ⬚ ⊛🐾♨🍵🚗🐴 ◆◆◆

16th century character cottage in centre of attractive historic town of Petersfield. Short walk from railway station. Large pretty bedroom (twin or double bed-extra folding bed on request) with comfortable sitting area. TV and private bathroom. En-suite planned 2005.

● Pilley (Lymington)
New Forest
Solent Way
🏷◀ Kenilworth House, SO41 5QG
☎ 01590 676720 (Keith and Jenny Pritchard)
www.newforest.demon.co.uk/Kenilworth.htm   Map 196/327982
BB **B**   ✕ nearby   D2 TI   Closed Jan   ⋘(Lymington)
Ⓑ Ⓓ ⊛ 🐾🚸🛏🚗🍴🛁

● Ringwood
Fraser House, Salisbury Road, Blashford, BH24 3PB
☎ 01425 473958 (Mrs M Burt)   www.fraserhouse.net   Map 195/149068
BB **B**   D4 T2   Ⓓ ⊛ 🐾🛏🛁   ◆◆◆◆

● Romsey
Monarch's Way & Test Way
Roselea, Hamdown Crescent, East Wellow, SO51 6BJ
☎ 01794 323262 (Penny Cossburn)   www.roselea.info   Map 185/306189
BB **B**   ✕ book first £15.50, 7:30pm   DI TI
Ⓥ Ⓑ Ⓓ ⊛ 🐾🛏🚗🛁   ◆◆◆◆

Berties, 80 The Hundred, SO51 8BX   ☎ 01794 830708
www.berties.co.uk   Map 185/354211
BB **C**   ✕ £11.05, 6:30-10pm   S2 D5 T2 FI   ⋘(Romsey) Ⓥ Ⓑ

● Selborne (Alton)
South Downs*
🏷◀ Thatched Barn House, Grange Farm, Gracious Street, GU34 3JG
☎ 01420 511007 (Mrs Judy Thompstone)
www.bobt.dircon.co.uk   Map 186/738339
BB **B**   ✕ nearby   DI TI   Ⓑ Ⓓ ⊛ 🐾🚗🍴🛁   ◆◆◆◆

● Stockbridge
Monarch's Way & Test Way
Carbery Guest House, Salisbury Hill, SO20 6EZ   ☎ 01264 810771
Map 185/350351   BB **B**   ✕ book first £15, 7pm   S4 D4 T2 FI
Ⓥ Ⓑ Ⓓ 🐾🛁   ◆◆◆

● Stroud
South Downs Way
🏷◀ Journeys End, Chapel Lane, Ebley, GL5 4TD   ☎ 01453 752099
(Jane Fletcher)   www.cotswold-way.co.uk/journeysend   Map 162/827048
BB **B**   ✕ £12.50, 7-9pm   DI TI   ⋘(Stroud)
Ⓥ Ⓑ Ⓓ ⊛ 🐾🛁🚗🍴

● Sway (Lymington)
New Forest
Squirrels, Broadmead, off Silver Street, SO41 6DH   ☎ 01590 683163
(Ken & Jean Kilford)   www.squirrelsbandb.co.uk   Map 196/957288
BB **B**   ✕ nearby   SI DI TI FI   Closed Jan   ⋘(Sway)
Ⓑ ⊛ 🐾🛁🛁   ◆◆◆

● Winchester
South Downs*
Monarch's Way & South Downs Way
The Farrells, 5 Ranelagh Road, SO23 9TA   ☎ 01962 869555
therosie@talk21.com   Map 185/475285
BB **B**   ✕ nearby   SI DI TI FI   ⋘(Winchester)
Ⓑ Ⓓ ⊛ 🛁Ⓜ   ◆◆◆

Shawlands, 46 Kilham Lane, SO22 5QD   ☎ 01962 861166
(Mrs Kathy Pollock)   kathy@pollshaw.u-net.com   Map 185/456288
BB **B**   ✕ nearby   D2 T2 FI   ⋘(Winchester)
Ⓑ Ⓓ ⊛ 🛁   ◆◆◆◆

🏷◀ St Margaret's, 3 St Michael's Road, SO23 9JE   ☎ 01962 861450
(Mrs Brigid Brett)   www.winchesterbandb.com   Map 185/479290
BB **B**   ✕ nearby   S2 DI TI   ⋘(Winchester) Ⓓ ⊛ 🛁   ◆◆◆

🏷◀ 5 Compton Road, SO23 9SL   ☎ 01962 869199 (Gillian Davies)
vicb@csma-netlink.co.uk   Map 185/476291
BB **B**   ✕ nearby   T2 FI   ⋘(Winchester)
Ⓓ ⊛ 🐾🛁🛏🚗🍴Ⓜ   ◆◆◆

Brookside, Back St, St Cross, SO23 9SB   ☎ 01962 854820 (Jane Harding)
www.brookside-stcross.co.uk   Map 185/477279
BB **B**   ✕ nearby   DI TI   ⋘(Winchester) Ⓑ   Ⓓ ⊛ 🐾🛁🚗🍴

ISLE OF WIGHT

● Bembridge
Isle Of Wight Coastal Path
🏷◀ Sea Change, 22 Beachfield Road, PO35 5TN
☎ 01983 875558 (Vi & Richard Beet)
www.wightonline.co.uk/accommodation/bandb/seachange.html
Map 196/654875   BB **B/C**   ✕ nearby   D2 TI   Closed Nov-Feb
Ⓑ 🐾🛁🍴   ◆◆◆◆Ⓢ

🏷◀ Redruth Cottage, Manna Rd, PO35 5UX   ☎ 01983 875205
(Shirley Cotton)   www.red-ruth.co.uk   Map 196/644879
BB **B**   ✕ nearby   DI   Closed Dec-Mar   Ⓑ   Ⓓ ⊛ 🐾🛁🛁

Windmill Inn, I Steyne Rd, PO35 5UH   ☎ 01983 872875
(Graham & Liz Miles)   www.windmill-inn.com   Map 196/648877
BB **C**   ✕ £15, 6:30-9:30pm   DII T3 F2
Ⓥ Ⓑ 🐾🛁🚗🍴   ★★★

● Bonchurch (Ventnor)
Isle Of Wight Coastal Path

☆ **The Lake Hotel**
Shore Road, PO38 IRF   ☎ 01983 852613
www.lakehotel.co.uk   Map 196/572778
BB **B**   ✕ £10, 6:30-7pm S2 D8 T6 F4   Closed Dec-Jan   ⋘(Shanklin)
Ⓥ Ⓑ Ⓓ 🐾🛁🛁   ◆◆◆◆

Visiting beautiful Bonchurch? Then we can offer comfortable double/twin
en-suite accommodation in charming country house hotel in beautiful two
acre garden. Residential bar and private car park. Run by the same family for
over 40 years. First class food and service assured. AA/RAC recommended.
Special 4 night break including car ferry, dinner and breakfast £175 incl.

Brighstone

Isle Of Wight Coastal Path

Buddlebrook Guest House, Moortown Lane, PO30 4AN ☎ 01983 740381
www.buddlebrookguesthouse.co.uk   Map 196/426832
BB **B**   ✕ nearby   D2 T1
🏠 🅓 ⊗ ♨ 🚗 ✱ !

Chale

Isle Of Wight Coastal Path

Cortina, Gotten Lane, PO38 2HQ   ☎ 01983 551292 (Mrs E L Whittington)
Map 196/487791   BB **B**   ✕ nearby   D1 T1   Closed Dec
🅓 ⊗ 🚗 ✱ !   Veggie breakfasts.

▰▰ Butterfly Paragliding, Sunacre, The Terrace, PO38 2HL
☎ 01983 731611 (Miranda Botha) www.paraglide.uk.com
Map 196/484774   BB **B**   ✕ nearby   T2 F1
🅓 ⊗ 🐾 !   Organic & vegetarian food.

Cowes

Isle Of Wight Coastal Path

Caledon Guest House, 59 Mill Hill Road, PO31 7EG   ☎ 01983 293599
Map 196/495956   BB **A**   ✕ nearby   S2 D1 T1 F2   🅓 ♨ 🎱

Freshwater

Isle Of Wight Coastal Path

The Traidcraft Shop, 119 School Green Road, PO40 9AZ   ☎ 01983 752451
(Mr & Mrs C Murphy)   Map 196/340870
BB **B**   ✕ nearby   D1 T1   Closed Dec   🅓 ♨ ! Ⓜ   ◆◆

Rookley

Sundowner B&B, Niton Rd, PO38 3NX   ☎ 01983 721350
(Pauline & Peter Wade) www.sundowner.iowight.com   Map 196/508835
BB **B**   ✕ nearby   D2 T/F1   🅓 🅓 ⊗ 🐾 ♨ 🎱

Ryde

Isle Of Wight Coastal Path

Rowantrees, 63 Spencer Road, PO33 3AF   ☎ 01983 568081
Map 196/585926   BB **B**   ✕ nearby   S2 D/F1 F1   ⋙(Ryde Esplanade)
🅓 ⊗ 🚗 ✱ ! Ⓜ

▰▰ Sea View, 8 Dover Street, PO33 2AQ   ☎ 01983 810976 (Diana Davies)
seaviewbandbinryde@hotmail.com   Map 196/595926
BB **B**   ✕ nearby   D1 T1   ⋙(Ryde Esplanade)
⊗ 🐾 ♨ !   ◆◆◆

**ARE YOU A MEMBER
OF THE RAMBLERS' ASSOCIATION?**

Help us to preserve our right to walk in
our beautiful countryside
Use the form on p 11 for membership at a
reduced rate

Sandown

Isle Of Wight Coastal Path

▰▰ Heathfield House, 52 Melville St, PO36 8LF   ☎ 01983 400002
www.heathfieldhousehotel.com   Map 196/595841
BB **B**   ✕ nearby   S3 D2 T1 F2   ⋙(Sandown) 🏠   🅓 ⊗ 🐾 ♨   ◆◆◆

Shalfleet (Newport)

Isle Of Wight Coastal Path

Hebberdens, Yarmouth Road, PO30 4NB   ☎ 01983 531364 (Mrs Ridler-Lee)
www.hebberdens.com   Map 196/430890
BB **B**   ✕ nearby   D1 T1 F1   🏠   🅓 🐾 ♨ 🚗 ! 🎱

Shanklin

Isle Of Wight Coastal Path

Atholl Court, 1 Atherley Road, PO37 7AT   ☎ 01983 862414 (Louise Bond)
www.atholl-court.co.uk   Map 196/582818
BB **B**   ✕ nearby   S3 D2 T3   ⋙(Shanklin) 🏠 🐾 ♨ 🚗   ◆◆◆

☆ **Somerton Lodge Hotel**
43 Victoria Ave, PO37 6LT   ☎ 01983 862710 (Mike Lawrence)
www.somertonlodge.com   Map 196/576811
BB **B**   ✕ £10, 6:30-7:30pm   S2 D6 T6 F4   Ⓥ 🏠   🅓 🐾 ♨ 🚗 !

The Somerton Lodge is a beautiful Victorian hotel set within the idyllic
backdrop of a leafy tree lined avenue. The hotel is situated just a few hundred
yards from Shanklin Old Village and The Chine.

The Isle of Wight is an all season walkers' paradise with over 500 miles of well
maintained footpaths winding through fields and forests, most of which is
designated as an area of outstanding natural beauty.

All rooms have en-suite showers, colour TVs, hospitality trays and hairdryers.
Non-smoking dining room and dry lounge. Large comfortable bar. Large car
park at rear.

Hambledon Hotel, 11 Queens Road, PO37 6AW   ☎ 01983 862403
(Bill Grindley) www.step-by-step.co.uk   Map 196/584814
BB **B**   ✕ book first £11, 6:30-7pm   S1 D5 T2 F2   Closed Dec ⋙(Shanklin)
Ⓥ 🏠 🅓 ⊗ 🐾 ♨ 🚗 ! Ⓜ   ◆◆◆◆   See Walking Holidays also.

The Edgecliffe Hotel, Clarence Gardens, PO37 6HA   ☎ 01983 866199
(Mick & Dru Webster) www.wightonline.co.uk/edgecliffehotel Map 196/585820
BB **B**   ✕ book first £10.95, 6:30pm   S2 D3 T2 F3   ⋙(Shanklin)
Ⓥ 🏠 🅓 ⊗ 🐾 ♨   ◆◆◆◆

☆ The Roseglen Hotel
12 Palmerston Rd, PO37 6AS ☎ 01983 863164 (Angela Lawrence)
www.roseglen.co.uk   Map 196/583814
BB **B**   ✕ £35, 6pm   S4 D3 T6 Fl   ⋙(Shanklin)
Ⓥ Ⓑ Ⓓ 🍵☕🚗❗   ◆◆◆◆   See Groups also.

A warm welcome awaits you at the Roseglen, an attractive Victorian Hotel located in picturesque Shanklin.

Situated just a few hundred yards from Shanklin Chine, old village, town centre and the cliff lift to the esplanade, the Roseglen is the perfect place for any holiday. Our 14 rooms are light and airy, a well stocked bar, comfortable lounge and beautiful dining room renowned for its excellent food.

The Hotel offers a Door to Door collection service as well as offering a drop off and collection service for ramblers throughout your stay ensuring that you are left to enjoy the 500 miles of well maintained footpaths throughout the Island.

● Totland Bay
Isle Of Wight Coastal Path
Littledene Lodge, Granville Road, PO39 0AX
☎ 01983 752411   (Trevor & Judy Barnes)
littledenehotel@aol.com   Map 196/326871
BB **B**   ✕ book first £12-£14, 6-7pm   S1 D2 T1 F3
Ⓥ Ⓑ Ⓓ 🍵☕🚗❗🖩   ◆◆◆

● Ventnor
Isle Of Wight Coastal Path
⋙☀◀ St Andrew's Hotel, Belgrave Rd, PO38 1JH   ☎ 01983 852680
www.standrewsventnor.com   Map 196/559774
BB **A**   ✕ book first £14, 6pm (Mon-Thurs)   D5 T3 F2
Ⓥ Ⓑ Ⓓ ⊛🚗

☆ Hillside Hotel
151 Mitchell Avenue, PO38 1DR   ☎ 01983 852271
hillside-hotel@btconnect.com   Map 196/565779
BB **B**   ✕ book first £15, 7:30pm onwards   S2 D7 T2 Fl
Ⓥ Ⓑ Ⓓ 🍵☕🚗❗🖩   ★★

Simply delightful in summer and a comfortable retreat in winter. Built circa 1789, Hillside is Ventnor's oldest and only thatched hotel. Set in two acres of grounds, at the foot of St Boniface Downs, with sea views. All bedrooms en-suite with TV. Licensed bar. Extensive choice of breakfast & evening menu. Dogs welcome.

⋙☀◀ Hill House, 22 Spring Hill, PO38 1PF ☎ 01983 854581
(Barbara Roscoe) HillhouseVentnor@aol.com   Map 196/565777
BB **B**   ✕ nearby   S1 D1 T1 Fl   Closed Jan
Ⓑ Ⓓ ⊛🍵☕🚗❗

● Yarmouth
Isle Of Wight Coastal Path
⋙☀◀ Wavells B&B & Bike Hire, The Square, PO41 0NP   ☎ 01983 760738
www.yarmouthiw.fsworld.co.uk   Map 196/355896
BB **B**   ✕ nearby   S1 D3 T1 Fl   Ⓑ Ⓓ ⊛☕❗Ⓜ
No children under 8.

KENT

● Aldington (Ashford)
Saxon Shore Way
Hogben Farm, Church Lane, TN25 7EH   ☎ 01233 720219 (Mrs Ros Martin)
rosalind.martin@tesco.net   Map 189,179/077371
BB **B**   ✕ book first £15-£17.50, 6:30-8pm   D1 T2
Ⓥ Ⓑ Ⓓ ⊛🍵☕🚗❗🖩   ◆◆◆◆

● Bilsington (Ashford)
Saxon Shore Way
Willow Farm, Stone Cross, TN25 7JJ ☎ 01233 721700 (Mrs Hopper)
www.willowfarmenterprises.co.uk   Map 189/028366
BB **B**   ✕ book first £8   S1 D1 T1 Fl
Ⓥ Ⓓ 🍵🚗❗   ◆◆◆

● Brenchley (Tonbridge)

☆ ⋙☀◀ Hononton Cottage
Palmers Green Lane, TN12 7BJ ☎ 01892 722483 (Simon Marston)
marston.brenchley@tinyworld.co.uk   Map 188/687417
BB **B**   ✕ nearby   D1 T1   Closed Jan-Mar   ⋙(Paddock Wood)
Ⓑ Ⓓ ⊛🍵☕🚗❗🖩

Picturesque 16th century listed farmhouse sympathetically modernised with wealth of exposed beams on a quiet lane in Kent orchards. Ideal base for walkers with High Weald Landscape Trail passing the door. Full English breakfast with local produce where possible.

● Canterbury
North Downs Way
⋙☀◀ Little Courtney, 5 Whitstable Rd, St Dunstans, CT2 8DG
☎ 01227 454207 (John Mercer) littlecourtneyca@aol.com
Map 179/142584   BB **B**   S1 T2   ⋙(Canterbury West)
Ⓓ 🍵☕❗🖩

● Charing (Ashford)
North Downs Way
23 The Moat, TN27 0JH   ☎ 01233 713141 (Mrs Margaret Micklewright)
m.micklewright@btinternet.com   Map 189/955492
BB **B**   ✕ nearby   T1   Closed Nov-Mar   ⋙(Charing)
Ⓑ Ⓓ ⊛☕Ⓜ

● Chartham (Canterbury)
North Downs Way
The Barn Oast, Nicklefarm, CT4 7PF ☎ 01227 731255 (Mrs Mary Arnold)
www.thebarnoast.co.uk   Map 179/092561
BB **B**   ✕ nearby   D1 T1 F1   ⚐(Chartham) Ⓑ Ⓓ ⊗ 🚲👜🚗

● Chilham (Canterbury)
North Downs Way
🏃⛺ Folly House, CT4 8DU ☎ 01227 738669 (Elisabeth Dyke)
www.follyhouse.co.uk   Map 179, 189/070536
BB **B**   ✕ book first £12, 7pm   S1 D2 T1 F1   ⚐(Chilham)
Ⓥ Ⓑ Ⓓ 🚲👜🚗!🌲   ◆◆◆◆

● Cranbrook
The Hollies, Old Angley Road, TN17 2PN ☎ 01580 713106
(Mrs D M Waddoup)   digs@waddoup.freeserve.co.uk   Map 188/775367
BB **B**   ✕ book first £10, 7pm   S1 T1 F1   ⚐(Staplehurst)
Ⓑ Ⓓ ⊗ 🚲👜🚗 🌲

● Deal
Saxon Shore Way
🏃⛺ Ilex Cottage, Temple Way, Worth, CT14 0DA ☎ 01304 617026
(Mrs Stobie)   www.ilexcottage.com   Map 179/335560
BB **B**   ✕ nearby   D1 T1 F1   ⚐(Sandwich)
Ⓑ Ⓓ ⊗ 🚲👜🚗!🌲   ◆◆◆◆

🏃⛺ Sparrow Court, Chalk Hill Road, Kingsdown, CT14 8DP
☎ 01304 389253 (Hon Mrs E G Maude)
www.farm-stay-kent.co.uk/popups/sparrowcourt.html   Map 179/374481
BB **B**   ✕ nearby   D1 T1   ⚐(Deal)
Ⓑ Ⓓ 🚲👜🚗!🌲   ◆◆◆◆

● Dover
North Downs Way & Saxon Shore Way
🏃⛺ Amanda Guest House, 4 Harold Street, CT16 1SF ☎ 01304 201711
www.amandaguesthouse.homestead.com   Map 179/320418
BB **A/B**   ✕ nearby   D1 T1 F1   ⚐(Dover Priory) Ⓓ ⊗   ◆◆

Bleriot's, 47 Park Avenue, CT16 1HE ☎ 01304 211394   (M J Casey)
www.bleriots.net   Map 179/316422
BB **B**   ✕ nearby   S1 D3 T2 F2   ⚐(Dover Priory) Ⓑ 👜   ◆◆◆

● Dymchurch (Romney Marsh)
Waterside Guest House, 15 Hythe Road, TN29 0LN ☎ 01303 872253
www.watersideguesthouse.co.uk   Map 189/105298
BB **B**   ✕ £5, 5:30-8pm   D2 T2 F1
Ⓥ Ⓓ ⊗ 🚲👜   ◆◆◆◆

● Etchinghill (Folkestone)
North Downs Way & Saxon Shore Way
One Step Beyond, Westfield Lane, CT18 8BT ☎ 01303 862637
(John & Jenny Holden)   johnosb@rdplus.net   Map 189,179/166394
BB **B**   ✕ book first £10   S1 D1   Ⓥ Ⓑ Ⓓ ⊗ 🚲👜🚗!

● Folkestone
North Downs Way & Saxon Shore Way
🏃⛺ Wycliffe Hotel, 63 Bouverie Road West, CT20 2RN
(Mike & Kate Sapsford) ☎ 01303 252186
www.wycliffehotel.com   Map 189,179/219357

BB **B**   ✕ book first £14, 6:30pm   S2 D5 T4 F2   ⚐(Folkestone Central)
Ⓥ Ⓑ Ⓓ 🚲👜🚗!🌲

🏃⛺ Harbourside Hotel, 12-14 Wear Bay Rd, CT19 6AT (Ray & Joy)
☎ 01303 256528   www.harboursidehotel.com   Map 189,179/236364
BB **C** ✕ book first £16   S3 D9 T3 F2   ⚐(Folkestone Central)
Ⓥ Ⓑ Ⓓ ⊗ 🚲👜🚗!   ◆◆◆◆◆Ⓖ

● Gillingham
Mayfield Guest House, 34 Kingswood Road, ME7 1DZ
☎ 01634 852606 (A Z Sumner)   Map 178/776685
BB **B**   ✕ nearby   S4 D2 T2 F2   Closed Dec   ⚐(Gillingham)
Ⓑ👜   ◆◆

● Harrietsham (Maidstone)
North Downs Way
🏃⛺ Homestay, 14 Chippendayle Drive, ME17 1AD ☎ 01622 858698
(Mrs Barbara Beveridge)   www.kent-homestay.info   Map 189/870527
BB **B**   ✕ nearby   T2   ⚐(Harrietsham)
Ⓑ Ⓓ ⊗ 🚲👜🚗   ◆◆◆◆

● Lyminge (Folkestone)
North Downs Way & Saxon Shore Way
🏃⛺ Southfields, Farthing Common, CT18 8DH ☎ 01303 862391
(B M Wadie)   Map 189/138404
BB **B**   ✕ book first £10, approx 7:30pm   T2   Closed Nov-Mar
Ⓥ Ⓑ Ⓓ ⊗ 🚲👜🚗!

● Otford (Sevenoaks)
North Downs Way
9 Warham Road, TN14 5PF ☎ 01959 523596 (Mrs Patricia Smith)
Map 188/526590   BB **B**   ✕ nearby   S1 D1 T1   ⚐(Otford)
Ⓓ ⊗ 🚲👜🚗🌲   ◆◆

● Rochester
North Downs Way & Saxon Shore Way
255 High Street, ME1 1HQ ☎ 01634 842737 (Mrs E Thomas)
thomasbandb@btinternet.com   Map 178/748681
BB **A**   ✕ nearby   D1 T1 F1   ⚐(Rochester)
Ⓑ Ⓓ 🚲👜 👜

🏃⛺ St Martin, 104 Borstal Road, ME1 3BD ☎ 01634 848192
(Mrs H Colvin)   icolvin@stmartin.freeserve.co.uk   Map 178/736673
BB **A**   ✕ book first £8   D1 T2   Closed Dec   ⚐(Rochester)
Ⓥ Ⓓ 🚲👜🚗!🌲 Ⓜ   ◆◆◆

● Sandwich
Saxon Shore Way
Le Trayas, Poulders Road, CT13 0BB ☎ 01304 611056 (Mrs R A Pettican)
www.letrayas.co.uk   Map 179/322576
BB **B**   ✕ nearby   D1 T2   ⚐(Sandwich)
Ⓑ Ⓓ ⊗ 🚲👜🚗!

● Shepherdswell (Dover)
North Downs Way
🏃⛺ Sunshine Cottage, The Green, Mill Lane, CT15 7LQ ☎ 01304 831359
(B & L Popple)   www.sunshine-cottage.co.uk   Map 179/261478
BB **B**   ✕ nearby   D/S4 T/S1 F1   ⚐(Shepherdswell)
Ⓑ Ⓓ ⊗ 🚲👜🚗   ◆◆◆◆Ⓢ

● Stelling Minnis (Canterbury)

Great Field Farm, Misling Lane, CT4 6DE ☎ 01227 709223
(Mrs L Castle) www.great-field-farm.co.uk   Map 189,179/134452
BB **B**   ✕ nearby   D2 TI FI
▣ ▣ ⊗ 🐾🛁🚗❗ ◆◆◆◆Ⓢ

● Tenterden

Old Burren, 25 Ashford Rd, TN30 6LL ☎ 01580 764442 (Gill Pooley)
www.oldburren.co.uk   Map 189/886337
BB **B**   ✕ nearby   D2
▣ ▣ ⊗ 🐾🛁🧺 ◆◆◆◆

● Wye (Ashford)

North Downs Way

Selsfield, Oxtenturn Road, TN25 5AZ ☎ 01233 812133 (Joan & John Morris)
morij@tesco.net   Map 189,179/052457
BB **B**   ✕ nearby   SI DI TI   ᗤᗤ(Wye)
▣ ⊗ 🐾🛁

LONDON

● Brentford

Thames Path

Primrose House, 56 Boston Gardens, TW8 9LP ☎ 020 8568 5573
(Garrie & Constance Williams) www.primrosehouse.com   Map 176/164786
BB **C**   ✕ nearby   D2 TI   ᗤᗤ(Brentford)
▣ ⊗ 🛁🚗🧺 ◆◆◆◆

● Central London

Thames Path

St Athan's Hotel, 20 Tavistock Place, WCIH 9RE ☎ 020 7837 9140
www.stathanshotel.com   Map 176,177/300823
BB **C**   ✕ nearby   SI6 D20 TI0 F8   ᗤᗤ(Euston) ▣ ▣ 🧺 ◆

☆ Lincoln House Hotel
33 Gloucester Place, WIU 8HY ☎ 020 7486 7630
www.lincoln-house-hotel.co.uk   Map 176/279814
BB **B/C**   ✕ nearby   S6 D6 T4 F7   ᗤᗤ(Paddington) ▣ 🛁

Built in the days of King George III,
this hotel offers Georgian charm and
character. En-suite rooms with
modern comforts. Competitively
priced. Located in London's West End,
next to Oxford Street shopping,
Theatreland and nightlife.
Ideal for business and leisure.

☆ Cardiff Hotel
5-9 Norfolk Square, W2 1RU ☎ 020 7723 3513 (Debbie & Andrew Davies)
www.cardiff-hotel.com   Map 176/268812
BB **C**   ✕ nearby   S25 D22 T9 F5   ᗤᗤ(Paddington)
▣ 🛁 ◆◆◆

15 minutes from Heathrow Airport
by express train, the Cardiff Hotel
overlooks a quiet garden square just
2 minutes walk form Paddington
station. Rooms have a TV, phone,
hairdryer and tea making facilities.
Hearty English breakfast included.

● Greenwich

Thames Path

Blackheath B&B, 41 Eastcombe Ave, SE7 7JD
☎ 020 8305 0621   (Anthony Mayne)
www.blackheathbedandbreakfast.co.uk   Map 177/405776
BB **B**   ✕ nearby   S3 T3 F2   ᗤᗤ(Westcombe Park)
▣ ▣ ⊗ 🛁🚗❗🧺

● Hammersmith

Thames Path

91 Langthorne St, SW6 6JU ☎ 020 7381 0198 (Brigid Richardson)
www.londonthameswalk.co.uk   Map 176/236770
BB **B/C**   ✕ nearby   DI TI/DI   ᗤᗤ(Hammersmith)
▣ ▣ ⊗ 🧺 ◆◆◆

● Richmond-upon-Thames

London Loop & Thames Path

Ivy Cottage, Upper Ham Road, Ham Common, TW10 5LA
☎ 020 8940 8601 (David Taylor) www.dbta.freeserve.co.uk   Map 176/178717
BB **B**   ✕ nearby   SI DI T2 FI
▣ ▣ 🐾🛁🚗❗🧺 ◆◆◆

● Twickenham

Thames Path & London Loop

33 Arlington Road, St Margarets, TWI 2AZ ☎ 020 8287 7492
(David & Silvia Kogan) www.33arlingtonroad.co.uk   Map 176/170744
BB **C**   ✕ nearby   SI DI   ᗤᗤ(St Margarets)
▣ 🛁Ⓜ ◆◆◆◆

● Wimbledon

London Loop & Thames Path

Beggars Roost, 6 Augustus Road, SWI9 6LN ☎ 020 8788 9438
(Mrs Pamela O'Neill)   Map 176/246732
BB **B**   ✕ book first £10, 6:30pm   SI T4   ᗤᗤ(Southfields)
Ⓥ ▣ ⊗ 🛁

OXFORDSHIRE

● Binfield Heath (Henley-on-Thames)

Thames Path & Chiltern Way

Teapot Cottage, Shiplake Row, RG9 4DR ☎ 01189 470263
(Clare Jevons)   www.teapot-cottage.co.uk   Map 175/752784
BB **C**   ✕ nearby   D/T2   ᗤᗤ(Shiplake)
▣ ▣ ⊗ 🐾🛁🚗

● Burford

☆ The Inn For All Seasons
The Barringtons, OX18 4TN ☎ 01451 844324 (Matthew R Sharp)
www.innforallseasons.com   Map 163/204120
BB **C**   ✕ £16, 6:30-9:30pm   S5 D5 T5 F2
Ⓥ ▣ ▣ 🛁🚗❗🧺 ★★★

16th century family run Cotswold inn in the
Windrush Valley with many local historic walks.
10 en-suite rooms, a well stocked cellar and a
kitchen famous for its use of local produce. An
ideal place for small groups. Drying rooms and
ample secure parking. Small enough to care,
large enough to be professional.

● **Chipping Norton**
▬◄ I Lower Barns, Salford, OX7 5YP
☎ 01608 643276 (Mrs Barnard)   Map 163/287279
BB **A**   TI   Ⓑ   Ⓓ ⊛ ♨ ● ▲ ! 🐾

● **Faringdon**
  Thames Path
▬◄ Sudbury House Hotel, London Street, SN7 8AA
☎ 01367 241272 (Andrew Ibbotson)
www.sudburyhouse.co.uk   Map 164/294954
BB **C**   ✕ £23.50, 7-9:30pm   D39 T10 F2
Ⓥ   Ⓑ   Ⓓ 🐾 ♨ ● ▲ ! 🐾 Ⓜ   ★★★

● **Goring-on-Thames (Reading)**
  Ridgeway, Thames Path & Chiltern Way
▬◄ Northview House, Farm Rd, RG8 0AA   ☎ 01491 872184
(I Sheppard)   hi@goring-on-thames.freeserve.co.uk   Map 175/603808
BB **B**   ✕ nearby   D2 TI   ⇝(Goring)   Ⓓ ⊛ 🐾 ♨ ▲ ! 🐾 Ⓜ

● **Henley-on-Thames**
  Thames Path & Chiltern Way
▬◄ Lenwade, 3 Western Road, RG9 IJL   ☎ 01491 573468 (Mrs J Williams)
www.w3b-ink.com/lenwade   Map 175/760817
BB **B**   ✕ nearby   D2 TI   ⇝(Henley-on-Thames)
Ⓑ   Ⓓ ⊛ 🐾 ♨   ◆◆◆◆◆

● **Leafield (Burford)**

☆ ▬◄ **Potters Hill Farm**
OX29 9QB (Mrs K Stanley) ☎ 01993 878018
potterabout@freenet.co.uk   Map 164/300148
BB **B**   D2 TI   Ⓑ   Ⓓ ⊛ 🐾 ♨ ▲ !   ◆◆◆◆

Sympathetically converted former coachhouse, adjacent to main house, set in 15 acres of peaceful, mature parkland, at the heart of our 770 acre mixed family farm. Friendly, comfortable atmosphere, with lots of tourist information and help available.

● **Long Hanborough (Witney)**
▬◄ Wynford House, 79 Main Rd, OX29 8JX   ☎ 01993 881402 (Carol Ellis)
www.accommodation.uk.net/wynford.htm   Map 164/424142
BB **B**   ✕ nearby   DI TI FI   ⇝(Hanborough)   Ⓑ   Ⓓ ⊛ 🐾 ♨ !

● **Moulsford-on-Thames (Wallingford)**
  Thames Path, Ridgeway & Chiltern Way
White House, OX10 9JD   ☎ 01491 651397 (Mrs Maria Watsham)
www.stayatwhitehouse.co.uk   Map 174/591837
BB **C**   ✕ book first £25   SI DI TI
Ⓥ   Ⓑ   Ⓓ ⊛ 🐾 ♨ ▲ !   ◆◆◆◆Ⓢ

● **North Moreton (Didcot)**
  Thames Path
▬◄ North Moreton House, OX11 9AT   ☎ 01235 813283 (Katie Miles)
www.northmoretonhouse.co.uk   Map 174/561894
BB **C**   ✕ nearby   SI DI T2   Ⓑ   Ⓓ ⊛ 🐾 ♨ ▲ ! 🐾   ◆◆◆◆◆Ⓢ

● **North Stoke (Wallingford)**
  Ridgeway & Chiltern Way
Footpath Cottage, The Street, OX10 6BJ
☎ 01491 839763 (Mrs Tanner)   Map 175/610863
BB **B**   ✕ book first £12   SI D2   Ⓥ   Ⓑ ⊛ 🐾 ♨ ● ▲ 🐾

● **Oxford**
  Thames Path
Acorn Guest House, 260/262 Iffley Road, OX4 ISE   ☎ 01865 247998
(Nest Lewis)   acorn_gh_oxford@freezone.co.uk   Map 164/527049
BB **B**   ✕ nearby   S4 D4 T2 F2   Ⓑ   Ⓓ ⊛ ●   ◆◆◆

River Hotel, 17 Botley Road, OX2 0AA   ☎ 01865 243475
www.riverhotel.co.uk   Map 164/503062
BB **C**   ✕ nearby   S4 D9 T2 F/D/T5   ⇝(Oxford)
Ⓑ   Ⓓ ⊛ 🐾 ♨ ●   ◆◆◆

● **Pishill (Henley-on-Thames)**
  Chiltern Way
▬◄ Bank Farm, RG9 6HS   ☎ 01491 638601 (Mrs E Lakey)
e.f.lakey@btinternet.com   Map 175/713898
BB **B**   ✕ nearby   D2 TI   Ⓓ ⊛ 🐾 ♨ ▲ ! 🐾   ◆◆

● **Shillingford (Wallingford)**
  Thames Path
▬◄ The Kingfisher Inn, 27 Henley Road, OX10 7EL   ☎ 01865 858595
(Alexis or Mayumi) www.kingfisher-inn.co.uk   Map 174,164/595928
BB **C**   ✕ £10, 7:30-9:30pm   D5 TI
Ⓥ   Ⓑ   Ⓓ ⊛ 🐾 ♨ ▲ !   ◆◆◆◆

● **Swyncombe (Henley-on-Thames)**
  Ridgeway & Chiltern Way
▬◄ Pathways, Cookley Green, RG9 6EN
☎ 01491 641631(Mrs Ismayne Peters)
ismayne.peters@tesco.net   Map 175/695901
BB **B**   ✕ book first £9, 7-8pm   DI T2
Ⓥ   Ⓑ   Ⓓ ⊛ 🐾 ♨ ● ▲ !

● **Tackley (Kidlington)**
▬◄ 55 Nethercote Road, OX5 3AT   ☎ 01869 331255 (June Collier)
www.colliersbnb.com   Map 164/482206
BB **B**   ✕ nearby   DI TI   ⇝(Tackley)
Ⓑ   Ⓓ ⊛ 🐾 ♨ ● ▲ ! 🐾   ◆◆◆

● **Wallingford**
  Thames Path, Ridgeway & Chiltern Way
Little Gables, 166 Crowmarsh Hill, OX10 8BG
☎ 01491 837834 (Jill & Tony Reeves)
www.stayingaway.com   Map 175/627887
BB **B**   ✕ nearby   SI D/S2 T/S3 F/S2   ⇝(Cholsey)
Ⓑ   Ⓓ ⊛ 🐾 ♨ ▲ !   ◆◆◆◆ Veggie breakfasts available.

● **Wantage**
  Ridgeway
Lockinge Kiln Farm, The Ridgeway, Chain Hill, OX12 8PA
☎ 01235 763308 (Mrs Stella Cowan)
www.lockingekiln.co.uk   Map 174/423833
BB **B**   ✕ book first £10, 7pm   DI T2   Closed Jan-Feb
Ⓥ   Ⓓ ⊛ 🐾 ♨ !

● **Watlington (Wallingford)**
Ridgeway & Chiltern Way
Cedar Lodge, Howe Rd, OX49 5ER ☎ 01491 613770 (Mrs Linda Vancke)
hbaw@abbottms.force9.co.uk   Map 175/694932
BB **B**   ✗ nearby   D1   B   D   ⊗ 🍳 ♨ 🚗 ! 🔊

● **Woodstock (Witney)**

☆ **Gorselands Hall**
Boddington Lane, OX29 6PU (Mr & Mrs N Hamilton)
☎ 01993 882292   www.gorselandshall.com   Map 164/399135
BB **B/C** ✗ nearby   D4 T1 F1   ₥(Hanborough)
B   D ⊗ ♨ 🔊   ◆◆◆◆Ⓢ

Lovely old Cotswold stone country house with oak beams and flagstone floors in delightful rural setting. Large secluded garden. Good walking country. Ideal for Blenheim Palace, the Cotswolds and Oxford. All rooms en-suite. Lounge with snooker table. Winter discounts. Fax: 01993 883629

● **Wootton (Woodstock)**
8 Manor Court, OX20 1EU ☎ 01993 811186 (Mrs Nancy Fletcher)
Map 164/438199   BB **B**   ✗ nearby   S1 D1   Closed Dec
B   D ⊗ 🍳 ♨ 🚗

SURREY

● **Bowlhead Green (Godalming)**
Heath Hall Farm, GU8 6NW ☎ 01428 682808 (Mrs Susanna Langdale)
www.heathhallfarm.co.uk   Map 186/918388
BB **B** ✗ book first £12 S1 D1 T1 F1 Ⓥ B   D ⊗ 🍳 ♨ 🚗 🔊 ◆◆◆

● **Cranleigh**
The White Hart, Ewhurst Road, GU6 7AE ☎ 01483 268647
pasilver@netcomuk.co.uk   Map 187/060390
BB **D/E**   ✗ £5-£10, 6-9pm S2 D7 T3 F2   Ⓥ   B   D 🍳 ♨ 🔊

● **Dorking**
North Downs Way
🔊 5 Rose Hill, RH4 2EG ☎ 01306 883127 (Margaret Walton)
www.altourism.com/uk/walt.html   Map 187/166491
BB **B**   ✗ book first £16, 7:30pm onwards S1 D2 T1 F1   ₥(Dorking North)
Ⓥ   D 🍳 ♨ ! 🔊

Fairdene Guest House, Moores Road, RH4 2BG ☎ 01306 888337
(Clive Richardson)   zoe.richardson@ntlworld.com   Map 187/169496
BB **C** ✗ nearby D2 T2 F2 ₥(Dorking) B   D ⊗ 🍳 ♨ 🚗 ! 🔊 ◆◆◆

☆ **Hindover**
21 St Pauls Rd West, RH4 2HT ☎ 01306 742306 (Susan Aitchison)
www.hindover.co.uk   Map 187/164488
BB **B**   ✗ book first £12.50, 6-8:30pm S1 D1 T1 F1   ₥(Dorking)
Ⓥ   D ⊗ 🍳 ♨ 🚗 !

Large Edwardian house with comfortable, spacious rooms. All rooms have armchairs, TV, irons & hairdryers. Conveniently situated for the North Downs Way, Polsden Lacy & numerous walks in the Surrey hills. Close to good pubs and restaurants. hindover@aol.com

● **Forest Green (Dorking)**
Bridgham Cottage, Horsham Rd, RH5 5PP ☎ 01306 621044 (Max Taylor)
http://mysite.freeserve.com/bridcott   Map 187/123400
BB **B**   ✗ nearby S1 D1 T1
B   D ⊗ 🍳 ♨ 🚗 🔊   ◆◆◆◆

● **Gatwick (Horley)**

☆ **The Turret Guest House**
48 Massetts Road, RH6 7DS ☎ 01293 782490
www.theturret.com   Map 187/286426
BB **C**   ✗ nearby S2 D3 T2 F3   ₥(Horley)
B   ⊗ 🍳 ♨ Ⓜ   ◆◆◆   Veggie breakfasts.

RA member's very comfortable Victorian house B&B. All rooms en-suite, with TV, tea/coffee facilities. Full English or continental breakfast. Airport transport (1.5 miles) and holiday parking available. Walking distance to pubs and restaurants. Email: info@theturret.com

● **Guildford**
North Downs Way
25 Scholars Walk, Ridgemount, GU2 7TR ☎ 01483 531351
Map 186/988498   BB **C**   ✗ nearby   S2   ₥(Guildford) ⊗ ♨

🔊 Highfield House, 18 Harvey Rd, GU1 3SG ☎ 01483 534946
(Mike & Jo Anning) Map 186/001494
BB **B**   ✗ nearby   D1 T1   ₥(Guildford) B   D ⊗ ♨ Ⓜ

● **Horley**
The Lawn Guest House, 30 Massetts Rd, RH6 7DF ☎ 01293 775751
(Adrian Grinsted) www.lawnguesthouse.co.uk   Map 187/283428
BB **A**   ✗ nearby D3 T3 F6   ₥(Horley)
B   D ⊗ ♨ 🔊   ◆◆◆◆Ⓢ

● **Merstham**
North Downs Way
Boors Green Farmhouse, Harps Oak Lane, RH1 3AN ☎ 07968 239234
(Rosemary & Richard) www.boorsgreenfarmhouse.co.uk Map 187/284546
BB **B**   ✗ book first £7.50, 6:30-7:30pm S1 D1 T1   ₥(Merstham)
Ⓥ   B   D ⊗ 🍳 ♨ 🚗 !

● **Oxted**
North Downs Way
🔊 Pinehurst Grange Guesthouse, East Hill (A25), RH8 9AE
☎ 01883 716413 (Laurie Rodgers)
laurie.rodgers@ntlworld.com   Map 187/392525
BB **B**   ✗ nearby   S1 D1 T1   ₥(Oxted) D ⊗ 🍳 ♨

Meads, 23 Granville Road, RH8 0BX ☎ 01883 730115 (Helen Holgate)
holgate@meads9.fsnet.co.uk   Map 187/399530
BB **B**   ✗ nearby S0 D2 T1   ₥(Oxted)
B   D ⊗ 🍳 ♨ 🚗 !   ◆◆◆◆

● **Shalford (Guildford)**
North Downs Way
🔊 The Laurels, 23 Dagden Road, GU4 8DD ☎ 01483 565753
(Mrs M J Deeks) Map 186/000475
BB **B**   ✗ book first £8, 7-8pm   D1 T1   ₥(Shalford)
Ⓥ   B   D ⊗ 🍳 ♨ 🚗 ! 🔊 Ⓜ   ◆◆◆

WEST SUSSEX

● Amberley (Arundel)
South Downs*
South Downs Way & Monarch's Way

◆ Woodybanks Cottage, Crossgates, BN18 9NR (Mr & Mrs G Hardy)
☎ 01798 831295   www.woodybanks.co.uk   Map 197/041136
BB **B**   ✗ nearby   D1 T1   ⋙(Amberley)
Ⓓ ⊛ 🐾🍵🍴🚗   ◆◆◆◆   Some disabled facilities.

14 Crossgates, BN18 9NS   ☎ 01798 831683 (Mrs Valerie Figg) Map 197/040134
BB **B**   ✗ nearby   T1 F1   ⋙(Amberley)   Ⓑ   Ⓓ🐾🍵🍴🚗!🏠

● Arundel
South Downs Way & Monarch's Way

Arden Guest House, 4 Queen's Lane, BN18 9JN
☎ 01903 882544   Map 197/019068
BB **B**   ✗ nearby   D5 T3   ⋙(Arundel) Ⓑ ⊛🍵   ◆◆◆

◆ Dellfield, 9 Dalloway Road, BN18 9HJ   ☎ 01903 882253
(Mrs J M Carter)   jane@heron-electric.com   Map 197/006064
BB **B**   ✗ nearby   S1 T1   Closed Dec   ⋙(Arundel)
Ⓑ Ⓓ⊛🐾🍵🍴Ⓜ

● Burgess Hill
◆ The Homestead, Homestead Lane, Valebridge Road, RH15 0RQ
☎ 01444 246899 (Sue & Mike Mundy) www.burgess-hill.co.uk
Map 198/323208   BB **B**   ✗ nearby   S1 D1 T2 F1   ⋙(Wivelsfield)
Ⓑ Ⓓ⊛🐾🍵🍴🚗   ◆◆◆◆

● Bury (Pulborough)
South Downs Way & Monarch's Way

◆ Harkaway, 8 Houghton Lane, RH20 1PD   ☎ 01798 831843
(Mrs Carol Clarke)   www.harkaway.org.uk   Map 197/012130
BB **B**   ✗ nearby   S2 D1 T1   ⋙(Amberley)
Ⓑ Ⓓ⊛🐾🍵🍴!

◆ Arun House, RH20 1NT   ☎ 01798 831736 (Jan & Chris Briggs)
www.arunhousesussex.co.uk   Map 197/010137
BB **B**   ✗ book first £10, 6:30-8:30pm   S1 D1 T1 F1   ⋙(Amberley)
Ⓥ Ⓓ⊛🐾🍵🍴🚗!🏠   ◆◆◆

● Charlton (Chichester)
South Downs*
Monarch's Way & South Downs Way

☆ **Woodstock House Hotel**
PO18 0HU   ☎ 01243 811666 (Aidan F Nugent)
www.woodstockhousehotel.co.uk   Map 197/889129
BB **C**   ✗ nearby   S2 D6 T4 F1   Ⓑ Ⓓ⊛🚗!🏠   ◆◆◆◆

Situated in magnificent South Downs just 1 mile from South Downs Way. Converted from an old farmhouse our licensed B&B hotel has 13 en-suite bedrooms with all modern amenities. Our local inn for dinner is just 1 minute's walk.

● Chichester
South Downs*

Old Chapel Forge, Lagness, PO20 1LR
☎ 01243 264380 (Sandra Barnes-Keywood)
www.smoothhound.co.uk/hotels/oldchapelforge   Map 197/907004
BB **B**   ✗ book first £10-£15, 6-8pm   D2 T2 F1   ⋙(Chichester)
Ⓥ Ⓑ Ⓓ⊛🐾🍵🍴!🏠   ◆◆◆◆

● Clayton (Hassocks)
South Downs*
South Downs Way

Dower Cottage, Underhill Lane, BN6 9PL   ☎ 01273 843363(Mrs C Bailey)
www.dowercottage.co.uk   Map 198/309136
BB **B**   ✗ nearby   S1 D2 T1 F2   ⋙(Hassocks)
Ⓑ   Ⓓ⊛🐾🍴!🏠   See Groups also.

● Cocking (Midhurst)
South Downs*
South Downs Way

Downsfold, Bell Lane, GU29 0HU   ☎ 01730 814376 (Malcolm & Janet Hunt)
www.downsfold.co.uk   Map 197/876176
BB **B**   ✗ nearby   D1 T1   Ⓓ⊛🐾🚗

● Ditchling (Hassocks)
South Downs*
South Downs Way

South Cottage, 2 The Drove, BN6 8TR   ☎ 01273 846636   Map 198/326153
BB **B**   ✗ nearby   D2 T1   ⋙(Hassocks)
Ⓓ⊛🐾🍵🚗🏠

● East Grinstead
◆ Cranston House, Cranston Road, RH19 3HW   ☎ 01342 323609
www.cranstonhouse.co.uk   Map 187/397385
BB **C**   ✗ book first £6 (snacks), 7-8pm   S2 D2 T5 F1   ⋙(East Grinstead)
Ⓥ Ⓑ Ⓓ⊛🐾🍵   ◆◆◆◆

● Fontwell (Arundel)
Monarch's Way

◆ Woodacre, Arundel Road, BN18 0QP   ☎ 01243 814301 (Vicki Richards)
www.woodacre.co.uk   Map 197/960068
BB **B**   ✗ nearby   D1 T2 F1   ⋙(Y)
Ⓑ Ⓓ⊛🐾🍵🚗🏠   ◆◆◆◆

● Fulking (Henfield)
South Downs*
South Downs Way & Monarch's Way

Knole House, Clappers Lane, BN5 9NH   ☎ 01273 857387 (Jill Bremer)
www.knolehouse.co.uk   Map 198/249124
BB **B/C**   ✗ book first £15, 7-8pm   S1 D/T1
Ⓥ   Ⓑ   Ⓓ⊛🐾🍵🚗!

● Gatwick (Crawley)
April Cottage, 10 Langley Lane, Ifield Green, RH11 0NA
☎ 01293 546222   (Brian & Liz Pedlow)
www.aprilcottageguesthouse.co.uk   Map 187/253379
BB **C**   ✗ nearby   D1 T2 F1   ⋙(Ifield)
Ⓑ ⊛🐾🍵!   ◆◆◆◆   Guide dogs welcome.

● **Graffham (Petworth)**
South Downs Way

Brook Barn, GU28 0PU ☎ 01798 867356 (Mr & Mrs S A Jollands)
brookbarn@hotmail.com   Map 197/929180
BB **C**   ✗ nearby D1 B D 🐕🛁🚗 ◆◆◆◆◆⑤

● **Heyshott (Midhurst)**
South Downs*
South Downs Way

Little Hoyle, Hoyle Lane, GU29 0DX ☎ 01798 867359
(Robert & Judith Ralph) www.smoothound.com/littlehoyle   Map 197/906187
BB **B**   D1 B D ⊛🐕🛁🚗 ◆◆◆◆

● **Pulborough**

🍴🍺🛏 Hurston Warren, Golf Club Lane, RH20 2EN   ☎ 01798 875831
(Kate & John Glazier) Kjglazier@aol.com   Map 197/070166
BB **B**   D1 T2 ∧∧(Pulborough) B D ⊛🐕🛁🚗!🌟 ◆◆◆

● **South Harting (Petersfield)**
South Downs*
South Downs Way

Torberry Cottage, Torberry Farm, GU31 5RG ☎ 01730 826883
(Mrs Maggie Barker) www.visitsussex.org/torberrycottage   Map 197/767200
BB **B**   D1 T1 B D ⊛🐕🛁🚗! ◆◆◆◆

● **Steyning**
Monarch's Way & South Downs Way

5 Coxham Lane, BN44 3LG ☎ 01903 812286 (Mrs J Morrow) Map 198/176116
BB **A**   ✗ nearby S1 T2   Closed Oct-Mar B D 🛁🚗!

🍴🍺🛏 Springwells Hotel, 9 High Street, BN44 3GG ☎ 01903 812446
www.springwells.co.uk   Map 198/177112
BB **C**   ✗ nearby S2 D3 T4 F1
B D 🐕🛁🚗!🌟 ◆◆◆◆

🍴🍺🛏 Fircroft, Kings Barn Villas, BN44 3FH ☎ 01903 816109 (Mary Hope)
www.bedandbreakfaststeyning.co.uk   Map 198/182111
BB **B**   ✗ nearby S2 T2 D ⊛🐕🛁🚗!

Buncton Manor Farm, Steyning Rd, Wiston, BN44 3DD ☎ 01903 812736
(Nancy Rowland) www.bunctonmanor.supanet.com   Map 198/148138
BB **B**   ✗ book first £14, 7:30pm   D1 T1   V D ⊛🐕🛁!

Northfield Cottage, Kings Barn Lane, BN44 3YR ☎ 01903 815862
(Jennifer Shanahan) mob.club@virgin.net   Map 198/188123
BB **B**   ✗ book first £5, 6-8pm   D1 T1   B D ⊛🐕🛁🚗!🌟

● **Thakeham**

White House, Storrington Rd, RH20 3EQ ☎ 01798 812029
(Mrs Lindy Walby)   jameswalby@hotmail.com   Map 198/102167
BB **B**   ✗ book first £10, 7:30pm   S1 T1   V D ⊛🐕🛁🚗

● **Washington (Pulborough)**
South Downs Way & Monarch's Way

Long Island, School Lane, RH20 4AP ☎ 01903 892237 (Barry & Mary Sturgess)
bandb@longisland.freeserve.co.uk   Map 198/120129
BB **B**   ✗ nearby D1 T1 F1   D ⊛🐕🛁🌟

🍴🍺🛏 Holt House, The Holt, RH20 4AW ☎ 01903 893542 (Anne Simmonds)
annesimmonds_holthouse@yahoo.co.uk   Map 198/121128
BB **B**   ✗ nearby   S1 D1 T1
B D ⊛🐕🛁🚗!🌟 ◆◆◆

● **Worthing**

🍴🍺🛏 Manor Guest House, 100 Broadwater Rd, BN14 8AN ☎ 01903 236028
(Sandy Colbourne) www.manorworthing.com   Map 198/147040
BB **B**   ✗ £7, 6-8pm   S1 D2 T1 F2   ∧∧(Worthing)
V B D ⊛🐕🛁🚗!🌟 ◆◆◆

SELF-CATERING

EAST SUSSEX

● **Battle**

Crowhurst Park ☎ 01424 773344 (Juliet Moth) www.crowhurstpark.co.uk
£250-£880   Sleeps 4-6. 54 pine lodges. Closed Jan-Feb
Indoor pool, bar, restaurant, shop, bikes. ∧∧(Battle) ★★★★★

● **Rye**

Bramley Cottages ☎ 07815 734665 (Lahra Benn)
www.bramleycottages.co.uk £325-£575   Sleeps 4-6. 2 cottages.
Linen, electricity and heating included.   ⊛

☆ **Cadborough Farm**
☎ 01797 225426 (Jane Apperly)
www.cadborough.co.uk
£165-£395   Sleeps 2. 5 cottages.
Newly converted. Full GCH. Linen included.   ⊛ ∧∧(Rye) 🌟 ★★★★

5 newly converted individual farm cottages
providing luxurious and spacious accommodation
for two people. Located 1 mile from Rye with
direct access to 1066 Country Walk. Full gas c/h.
Linen and towels included. No smoking. One
small well behaved dog welcome. Email:
info@cadborough.co.uk Fax: 01797 224097

HAMPSHIRE

● **East Meon**
South Downs*

Church Farm House ☎ 01730 823256 (Christopher Moor)
www.gardenchalet.co.uk   £80-£160   Sleeps 2. 1 chalet.
Beautiful village, near South Downs Way.

● **Fordingbridge**
New Forest

Alderholt Mill ☎ 01425 653130 (Sandra Harte) www.alderholtmill.co.uk
£220-£520   Sleeps 2-6. 3 flats.
Working water mill conversion. Rural setting.
⊛ 🌟 ★★★ See B&B also.

● **Lymington**
New Forest

The Old Exchange ☎ 01590 679228 (Sarah Alborino)
www.newforest.demon.co.uk/OldExchange.htm
£300-£600   Sleeps 2-7. 1 apartment.
Central village location. Walking, riding. Beaches.
⊛ ∧∧(Sway) ★★★

● Lyndhurst
New Forest
Penny Farthing Hotel & Cottages ☎ 023 802 84422 (Mike)
www.pennyfarthinghotel.co.uk   £525-£950   Sleeps 4-8. 5 varying types.
Quality inspected properties in village centre.   ⊛ ★★★★ See B&B also.

● Medstead
The Barn ☎ 01420 562682 (Sarah Darch) www.barfordfarmhouse.com
£250-£325 Sleeps 2-4. 1 cottage. B&B available.   ⊛ 🏠 ★★★

● Romsey
1 Thatched Cottage ☎ 01794 340460 (Mrs R J Crane)
£177-£305 Sleeps 5. 1 cottage.
Bed linen supplied. Thatched roof. Picturesque.   〰(Romsey) 🏠

● Sway
New Forest
☎ 01590 682049 (Mrs Helen Beale)
£160-£380 Sleeps 2-6. 1 cottage, 2 flats.
Comfortable accommodation in excellent walking area. 〰(Sway) 🏠 ★★★

● Winchester
South Downs*
☎ 01962 777887 (Mrs Barbara Crabbe) crabbesleg@aol.com
£200 Sleeps 3. 1 appartment. On Pilgrims Way. Pub half mile.   ⊛ 🏠

ISLE OF WIGHT

● Bonchurch
☎ 01798 872433 (Mrs J M Burstow)   £250-£550   Sleeps 5+. 1 flat.
Peaceful seafront location on coastal path.   ⊛ 🏠

● Kingston
☆ Island Cottage Holidays
☎ 01929 480080 (Honor Vass)
www.islandcottageholidays.com
£145-£1,225   Sleeps 1-12. 60 cottages   🏠 ★★★-★★★★★

Charming individual cottages in lovely rural and coastal surroundings. Close to the coastal paths & the extensive trails that cross the Island. £145-£1,225pw. Low season, short breaks £91-£395. Dogs welcome.

OXFORDSHIRE

● Woodstock
The Lodge (Marianne Robottom) www.oxfordshirecottage.co.uk
£220-£260 Sleeps 2. 1 cottage. Converted small stable. Wetroom (no bath). ⊛

SURREY

● Farnham
Tilford Woods ☎ 01252 792199 (Malcolm Sutcliffe) www.tilfordwoods.co.uk
£385-£700 Sleeps 2-6. 33 lodges.
Luxury lodges in rural setting. ⊛ 🏠 ★★★★

● Holmbury St Mary
☎ 01306 730210 (Gill Hill)   £220-£380   Sleeps 2-4. 2 units.
Converted farm buildings on Greensand Way   🏠 ★★★ Access Category 1.

WEST SUSSEX

● Arundel
South Downs*
Mill Lane House ☎ 01243 814440 (Jan Fuente) www.mill-lane-house.co.uk
£280-£420 Sleeps 4. 2 flats. In NT village. Views to coast. ⊛ 🏠 ★★★

● Chichester
South Downs*
Yew Tree House ☎ 023 9263 1248 (Mr J Buchanan)
d.buchanan@btinternet.com   £165-£270   Sleeps 2. 1 flat.
Ideal for walking South Downs.   ⊛ 🏠 ★★★

● Henfield
South Downs*

☆ New Hall
☎ 01273 492546 (Mrs M W Carreck)
£180-£345 Sleeps 4-5. 1 cottage, 1 flat.
On footpath close to South Downs.   🏠 ★★★

Self-contained flat and 17th century cottage in two wings of manor house, set in three and a half acres of mature gardens, surrounded by farmland and footpaths. Half a mile from river Adur and Downslink long distance footpath. Two and a half miles from the South Downs Way.

● Singleton
South Downs*
☎ 01243 783852 (Alan Stanley) AStanleyChi@hotmail.com
£240-£600 Sleeps 6. 1 cottage.
Many footpaths, cycle routes, near pubs.   ⊛

GROUPS

HAMPSHIRE

South Downs*

☆ The Wessex Centre (B&B)
Sparsholt College, Sparsholt, Winchester SO21 2NF
☎01962 797259 (Sue Reeves)
www.thewessexcentre.co.uk   Map 85/423319
Min 8, max 250 ✗ 🐾 B D 〰(Winchester) ★★Ⓢ

Agricultural college offering comfortable ensuite bedrooms, good food, sports facilities and friendly atmosphere, within 400 acre working farm. Ideal base for exploring the South Downs Way, Clarendon Wat & Test Way. Please book in advance. Groups of 10 or more.
Open March April, August & September.

Wetherdown Hostel (B&B/SC), The Sustainability Centre, Droxford Rd, GU32 1HR
☎01730 823549 www.earthworks-trust.com Map 197/676190
BB £20 Min 8, max 30 ✕ 🐾 D ⊗ See Hostels also.

ISLE OF WIGHT

Isle of Wight Coastal Path

☆ **The Roseglen Hotel** (B&B)
12 Palmerston Rd, Shanklin, PO37 6AS
☎01983 863164 (Angela Lawrence) www.roseglen.co.uk
BB £25 Min 8, max 28
✕ 🐾 B D ⋙(Shanklin) ⚘ ⬌ ◆◆◆◆ See B&B also

A warm welcome awaits you at the Roseglen, an attractive Victorian hotel located in picturesque Shanklin.

Situated just a few hundred yards from Shanklin Chine, old village, town centre and the cliff lift to the esplanade, the Roseglen is the perfect place for any holiday. Our 14 rooms are light and airy, a well stocked bar, comfortable lounge and beautiful dining room renowned for its excellent food.

The Hotel offers a Door to Door collection service as well as offering a drop off and collection service for ramblers throughout your stay ensuring that you are left to enjoy the 500 miles of well maintained footpaths throughout the Island.

WEST SUSSEX

South Downs*
South Downs Way

Dower Cottage (B&B/SC) Underhill Lane, Clayton, Hassocks BN6 9PL
☎ 01273 843363 (Mrs C Bailey) www.dowercottage.co.uk Map 198/309136
BB £30, SC £350 1 cottage, 1 bunkhouse. Min 2, max 6.
✕ 🐾 B D ⊗ ⚘ ⋙(Hassocks) See B&B also.

HOSTELS, BUNKHOUSES & CAMPSITES

BERKSHIRE

Thames Path

Hurley Riverside Park (C) Park Office, Hurley, Maidenhead SL6 5NE
☎ 01628 823501 www.hurleyriversidepark.co.uk
£8-£15 per tent Closed Nov-Feb ★★★★ Disabled facilities

HAMPSHIRE

South Downs*

Wetherdown Hostel (C/IH), The Sustainability Centre, Droxford Rd, GU32 1HR
☎01730 823549 www.earthworks-trust.com Map 197/676190
B&B £20 ✕ 🐾 D ⊗ See Groups also

WEST SUSSEX

South Downs*
South Downs Way

Washington Caravan & Camping Park (C) London Rd, Washington, RH20 4AJ
☎01903 892869 (Max F Edlin) www.washcamp.com
Camping £6 ✕ nearby 🐾 D ⋙ (Worthing) ★★★★
Wheelchair access and toilet

PUBS & TEAROOMS

BUCKINGHAMSHIRE

● **Great Hampden (Great Missenden)**
Ⓨ Hampden Arms, Great Missenden, HP16 9RQ
☎ 01494 488255 (Louise Lucas)
louise@thehampden.fsnet.co.uk Map 165/846015
✕ Ⓥ ♨ Ⓖ ⊗ Ⓑ(L)

HAMPSHIRE

● **Binsted (Alston)**
South Downs*
Ⓨ The Cedars, The Street, Binsted, GU34 4PB
☎ 01420 22112 (Mick and Tina Chant) Map 186/773411
⋙(Bentley) ✕ Ⓥ ♨ Ⓛ Ⓖ ⊗ Ⓑ(☺)

Wherever Swarovski is,
nature becomes
more fascinating.
Swarovski Pocket 8x20 B

www.swarovskioptik.com

Pocket 8x20

**Perfect for all outdoor activities,
ideal for the theatre,
or as a second binocular:**
Swarovski Pocket Binoculars fit into any
pocket and provide a truly great viewing
experience. They have the world's most
complex optical system for compact
binoculars, as well as the patented
SWAROBRIGHT® prism coating for
optimum colour fidelity across the entire
light spectrum. Individually adjustable,
removable, twist-up eyecups enable an
extremely large visual field - even for
spectacle wearers.

SWAROVSKI
OPTIK

Swarovski U.K. LTD. • Perrywood Business Park • Salfords, Surrey RH1 5JQ • Tel. 01737-856812 • Fax 01737-856815

KENT

● Tonbridge
Wealdway

> ⓉThe Plough Inn
> Leigh Rd, Leigh, TN11 9AJ ☎ 01732 832149 (Alex Barnard)
> http://Theploughatleigh.co.uk Map 188/567468
> ⋙(Leigh) ✕ Ⓥ ⋔ ♫ (Recorded)
> Ⓛ Ⓖ Ⓑ(L) Children's play area.
>
>
> Close to several 'Wealden Walks' our 16th century
> pub offers home-made food from bar snacks to
> banquets, and a selection of real ales.
> We welcome families with our large gardens and
> children's playground. Large car park available
> for 'round trips'.

● Westerham
North Downs Way
ⓉThe Fox & Hounds, Toys Hill, TN16 1QG ☎ 01732 750328
(Tony Hickmott) hickmott1@hotmail.com Map 188/469515
✕ Ⓥ ⋔ ♫ (Live/Recorded) Ⓛ Ⓖ ⊛ Ⓑ(☺) Disabled toilets.

SURREY

● Tilford
ⓉThe Barley Mow, GU10 2BU ☎ 01252 792205 (Charles Barton)
www.thebarleymowtilford.com Map 186/872434
⋙(Farnham) ✕ Ⓥ ⋔ Ⓛ Ⓖ ⊛ Ⓑ(☺) Function room

EAST SUSSEX

● Ditchling
South Downs Way
ⓉThe White Horse, West Street, Ditchling, BN6 8TS ☎ 01273 842006
(Ian & Mary Turner) Map 198/325151
⋙(Hassocks) ✕ Ⓥ ⋔ ♫ (Live)
Ⓛ Ⓖ Ⓑ(☺)

● Falmer (North Brighton)
South Downs*
South Downs Way
ⓉSwan Inn, Middle Street, Falmer, BN1 9PP
☎ 01273 681842 (John Woodruff) Map 198/354090
⋙(Falmer) ✕ Ⓥ ⋔
Ⓛ Ⓖ ⊛ Ⓑ(L) Real ale.

WEST SUSSEX

● Graffham (Petworth)
South Downs Way
ⓉThe Foresters Arms, Graffham, Petworth, GU28 0QA
☎ 01798 867202 (Lloyd Pocock)
Map 197/978215 ✕ Ⓥ ⋔
Ⓛ Ⓖ ⊛ Ⓑ(☺) ⌐

● Selham (Petworth)
South Downs Way
ⓉThe Three Moles, Selham, GU28 0PN ☎ 01798 861303 (Val Wingate)
www.thethreemoles.co.uk Map 197/934206
⋔ Ⓛ Ⓖ Ⓑ(☺) Bring your own sandwiches.

EAST

The region's ancient historical monuments and nature reserves spread out from the North Norfolk Heritage Coast, through the criss-crossed dikes and fens of Cambridgeshire, across the heathland and chalk valleys of Suffolk and down into the windswept marshlands and ancient woodlands of Essex.

WWW.BRITAINONVIEW.COM/ROD EDWARDS
CLEY-NEXT-THE-SEA, NORFOLK

Although much of the region is flat, in Bedfordshire the rolling hills of the Dunstable Downs offer splendid views of the steep escarpments of the Chiltern Hills. In neighbouring Hertfordshire the National Trust's Ashridge Estate on the Chilterns Ridge provides excellent walks through leafy woods and over chalk downland.

The Thames Estuary and Essex coast, accessible by lengthy sea wall paths, lead you to wildlife sanctuaries, marshes and creeks, dotted with coves and inlets with a history of smuggling and Saxon invasions.

Our members say:

"Lots of agricultural farmland and more rolling areas too are easily accessible by lots of well-maintained footpaths."

"The wildlife and bird watching opportunities are the perfect way to enhance a stroll in England's most pleasant of lands."

The Suffolk Heritage Coast too is easily accessible along the Suffolk Coast and Heaths Path, whilst the Dedham Vale Area of Outstanding Natural Beauty on the Essex and Suffolk borders is Constable Country, so called because the area features in many of the artist's paintings.

Further north, the untamed heathland of the Brecks on the Norfolk and Suffolk borders is pleasingly desolate. The famous Broads come complete with windmills and abundant birdlife. The picturesque North Norfolk coastline stretches for 43 miles, linked by the Peddars Way and Norfolk Coast Path.

To the west you can follow the old sea bank along the Wash to King's Lynn, an historic port on the river Great Ouse. This heavily canalised area provides gentle walking amongst the fens, rivers and an abundance water-life and wildfowl.

Cambridgeshire offers the walker idyllic scenery, from the hills of the 'Little Cotswolds' to the flat expanses of man-made fens where the open vistas provide breathtaking sunsets to admire at the end of a day's walking.

Long Distance Paths

Chiltern Way	CHI
Essex Way	ESX
Icknield Way	ICK
London Loop	LNL
Nene Way	NEN
Peddars Way & Norfolk Coast Path	PNC
Ridgeway	RDG
Suffolk Coast & Heaths Path	SCH

Public paths:

25,240km/ 15,674 miles

THE RIVER CAM, SAFFRON WALDEN, ESSEX

EAST
LOCAL RAMBLERS CONTACTS

BEDFORDSHIRE
AREA SECRETARY
Mr Nick Tims, 19 Honeygate, Luton, Beds, LU2 7EP ☎ 01582 737 724

GROUP SECRETARIES
Ivel Valley Mrs R Bryce, 7 Wood Close, Biddenham, Bedford, MK40 4QG ☎ 01234 272898
www.ivelvalleywalkers.org.uk
Lea & Icknield Miss S H Lewis, 21 Simpson Close, Leagrave, Luton, LU4 9TP ☎ 01582 847273
Leighton Buzzard Mr J & Mrs C Duxbury, 8 Carlton Grove, Leighton Buzzard, Beds, LU7 3BR ☎ 01525 383595
http://jduxbury.users.btopenworld.com
North Bedfordshire Mrs L J Tongue & Mr D Tongue, 25 Field Cottage Road, Eaton Socon, St Neots, Cambs, PE19 8HA ☎ 01480 350345
Ouse Valley Mrs W J Bleaney, 10 Barnes Road, Wootton, Bedford, MK43 9FB ☎ 01234 764 670
www.dawson98.freeserve.co.uk

CAMBRIDGESHIRE & PETERBOROUGH
AREA SECRETARY
Miss J Cartwright, 8 Willoughby Avenue, Market Deeping, Peterborough, PE6 8JE ☎ 01778 344831
http://web.ukonline.co.uk/ cambs.ramblers

GROUP SECRETARIES
Cambridge Ms J Tuffnell, 62 Beche Road, Cambridge, CB5 8HU ☎ 01223 362881
Cambridge 20s & 30s Walking Group Mr M Bingham, Flat 4.5, The Old Mill, London Road, St Ives, PE27 5EY ☎ 01480 352733
www.walkcambridge.org
East Cambridgeshire Mrs Sue Summerside, Mow Fen Hall, 4a Silt Road, Littleport, Ely, Cambs, CB6 1QD ☎ 01353 861435
Fenland Mrs S L Ledger, 18 Alexandra Road, Wisbech, Cambs, PE13 1HS ☎ 01945 587135
Huntingdonshire Mr William Thompson, 2 Bankers Walk, Ramsey, Huntingdon, Cambs, PE26 1EG ☎ 01487 812022

Peterborough Mr P Bennett, 93 Woodhurst Road, Stanground, Peterborough, Cambs, PE2 8PQ ☎ 01733 553828
Peterborough Younger Walkers Miss K L Hornsby, 11 Albany Walk, Peterborough, PE2 9JN ☎ 01733 557381
http://web.ukonline.co.uk/cambs.ramblers/pbg_20-30_info.htm

ESSEX
AREA SECRETARY
A Vincent-Jones, Flat 14, Nelmes Court, Hornchurch, Essex, RM11 2QL ☎ 01708 473253

GROUP SECRETARIES
Basildon Greenway Mr D J Tucker, 5 Mount Close, Wickford, Essex, SS11 8HF ☎ 01268 734932 [membs Enq: 01375 670464]
Brentwood Mr R V Carpenter, 43 Arnolds Avenue, Shenfield, Brentwood, Essex, CM13 1ET ☎ 01277 220781
roy.v.carpenter@btinternet.co.uk
www.brentwoodramblers.co.uk
Chelmer & Blackwater Mr B Liddle, 159 Hullbridge Road, South Woodham Ferrers, Essex, CM3 5LN ☎ 01245 323279
Colchester Mrs L K Sherman, 29 Chaplin Road, East Bergholt, Suffolk, CO7 6SR ☎ 01206 298930
www.colchester-ramblers.ccom.co.uk
East Essex Friends Mr J King, 2a Park Road, Burnham-on-Crouch, Essex, CM0 8ER ☎ 01621 783031
Essex Friends Mrs Dee Dealtrey, The Old Counting House, 46 Wantz Road, Maldon, Essex, CM9 5DE ☎ 01621 858662
Essex Young Ramblers A Vincent-Jones, Flat 14, Nelmes Court, Hornchurch, Essex, RM11 2QL ☎ 01708 473253
Havering & East London Mr Ken Richards, 26 Arundel Road, Harold Wood, Romford, Essex, RM3 0RT ☎ 01708 375559
http://uk.geocities.com/helramblers
Lea Valley Friends Mrs M Brown, 11 Harford Road, London, E4 7NQ ☎ 020 8529 1602
Maldon & Dengie Hundred Mr Jim Mcwhirr, 18 Blacksmith Lane,

Wickham Bishops, Witham, Essex, CM8 3NR ☎ 01621 891055
www.maldondengieramblers.org.uk
North West Essex Mr David Harvey, 18 Clydesdale Road, Braintree, Essex, CM7 2NX
Redbridge Mrs Wendy Rogers, 4 Kershaw Close, Hornchurch, Essex, RM11 1SW ☎ 01708 456771
Rochford & Castle Point C Parr, 33 Tylney Avenue, Rochford, Essex, SS4 1QP ☎ 01702 547297
www.btinternet.com/~bta.wga/ rochford-ramblers
South East Essex Mrs Paula Hayes, 29 Keswick Close, Rayleigh, Essex, SS6 8LG ☎ 01268 772668
www.e-cox.fsnet.co.uk
Stort Valley Mr Chris Abbott, 68 Glebelands, Harlow, Essex, CM20 2PB ☎ 01279 305 725
www.geocities.com/stortvalleywalkers
Tendring District Mrs Ann Jones, Wayside, Hall Road, Great Bromley, Colchester, Essex, CO7 7TS
www.tendringramblers.co.uk
Thurrock Mr S G Dyball, 29 Bishops Road, Corringham, Stanford Le Hope, Essex, SS17 7HB ☎ 01375 676442
Uttlesford Mrs A Corke, Roston House, Dunmow Road, Thaxted, Essex, CM6 2LU ☎ 01371 830 654
West Essex Mr P B Spence, 6 Oak Glen, Hornchurch, Essex, RM11 2NS ☎ 01708 702095

HERTFORDSHIRE & NORTH MIDDLESEX
AREA SECRETARY
Mr D S Allard, 8 Chilcourt, Royston, Herts, SG8 9DD ☎ 01763 242677
www.herts-northmiddlesex-ramblers.org.uk

GROUP SECRETARIES
Dacorum Mr N T Jones, 47 Cedar Walk, Hemel Hempstead, Herts, HP3 9ED ☎ 01442 211794
www.dacorumramblers.com
East Hertfordshire Miss P A Hemmings, 16 Smiths Green, Debden, Saffron Walden, CB11 3LP
Finchley & Hornsey Mrs J Haynes, 33 Links Road, Cricklewood, London, NW2 7LE ☎ (membs Enqs Mrs V Mallindine 020 8883 8190)

LOCAL RAMBLERS CONTACTS continued

North Hertfordshire Mr R T Jarvis, 17 Moormead Close, Hitchin, Herts, SG5 2BA ☎ 01462 422837

North London & South Herts Mr M Noon, 100 Wynchgate, London, N14 6RN ☎ 020 8886 0348 (membs Enqs 020 8449 7982)

Royston Ms S Allison, 3 Tannery Close, Royston, Hertfordshire, SG8 5DH ☎ 01763 243504

Watford & Three Rivers Mrs V M Buckley, 4 Firbank Drive, Watford, Herts, WD19 4EL ☎ 01923 222591

NORFOLK
AREA SECRETARY
Miss E Martin, 111 Belvoir Street, Norwich, Norfolk, NR2 3AZ ☎ 01603 612644
http://homepage.ntlworld.com/bcmoore/NorfolkRA

GROUP SECRETARIES
Fakenham Mrs A Easton, Pear Tree Cottage, The Street, Little Snoring, Fakenham, Norfolk, NR21 0AJ ☎ 01328 878872

Great Yarmouth Mrs P A Sharrock, Aldebaran, The Street, West Somerton, Norfolk, NR29 4EA ☎ 01493 393671

King's Lynn Mr J Keenan, 15 Gaskell Way, King's Lynn, Norfolk, PE30 3SD ☎ 01553 674262

Mid-Norfolk Mrs Carol Jackson, Mandola, Mill Street, Elsing, Dereham, Norfolk, NR20 3EJ ☎ 01362 637752

Norwich Mr D J Goddard, 49 Lindford Drive, Eaton, Norwich, Norfolk, NR4 6LR

Sheringham & District Mr Don Davenport, 'Malbank', 20 Newhaven Close, Cromer, Norfolk, NR27 0BD ☎ 01263 514955

Southern Norfolk Mr G H Head, Jubilee Villa, 8 Friarscroft Lane, Wymondham, Norfolk, NR18 0AT

Wensum Mr Tony Smith, 3 Priors Drive, Old Catton, Norwich, NR6 7LJ ☎ 01603 423085

SUFFOLK
AREA SECRETARY
Mr P Snelling, 12 Market Place, Lavenham, Suffolk, CO10 9QZ ☎ 01787 248 079

GROUP SECRETARIES
Alde Valley Miss M B Perry, 16 Chapel Road, Saxmundham, Suffolk, IP17 1BG ☎ 01728 604712

Bury St Edmunds Mrs J M Bolwell, 42 Cloverfields, Sandpit Lane, Thurston, Bury St. Edmunds, Suffolk, IP31 3TJ http://myweb.tiscali.co.uk/burystedmundsra

Ipswich & District Mr John Laycock, 8 Church Lane, Henley, Ipswich, Suffolk, IP6 0RQ ☎ 01473 831236 www.ipswichramblers.co.uk

Newmarket & District Mrs C C Lee, Corner Cottage, Sharps Lane, Horringer, Bury St Edmunds, IP29 5PW ☎ 01284 735971 www.newmarketramblers.co.uk

Stour Walking Group Miss L Ward, Two Rose Cottage, 46 Head Street, Halstead, CO9 2BX ☎ 01787 479761 www.stourwalkinggroup.co.uk

Stowmarket Mrs B Peart, 8 Elmsett Close, Stowmarket, Suffolk, IP14 2NU ☎ 01449 675315 www.stowmarketramblers.org.uk

Sudbury Mrs I Kay, 6 Chaplin Walk, Great Cornard, Sudbury, Suffolk, CO10 0YT ☎ 01787 370019 www.sudburyra.freeserve.co.uk

Waveney Lionel Hardy, 24 Meadow Gardens, Beccles, Suffolk, NR34 9PA ☎ 01502 716253

LOCAL RAMBLERS PUBLICATIONS

Angles Way
edited by Sheila Smith, ISBN 1 901184 49 8. 125km/78mile route following the Waveney Valley along the Norfolk/Suffolk border, and completing the circuit of the Peddars Way National Trail and Weavers Way. £2.70 + 30p p&p.
Iceni Way
edited by Sheila Smith, ISBN 1 901184 64 1 (new edition, 2004): 134.5km/84-mile route from Knettishall Heath in Breckland to the coast at Hunstanton along the Little and Great Ouse Valleys. (New this year) £2.70 + 30p p&p.
Walking the Peddars Way & Norfolk Coast Path with Weavers Way
edited by Ian Mitchell, ISBN 1 901184 71 4. Concise guide covering a total distance of 239km/149miles. the National Trail. £2.70 + 30p p&p
Norfolk Heritage Walks
by Allan Jones, ISBN 1 901184 55 2: 16 circular walks of between 6.5km/4 miles and 19km/12 miles, mostly below 16km/10 miles. £2.10 + 40p p&p.

All from Caldcleugh, Cake Street, Old Buckenham, Attleborough NR17 1RU; post free if three or more guides are ordered together. Cheques to Ramblers' Association Norfolk Area.

Camuplodunum
by Colchester Ramblers. 40km/25 miles around Colchester via Great Horkesley and Mersea Road. No printed guide but a full route description, updated in 2004, is available on Colchester Ramblers website. (New this year)

Cornard and Beyond
by Laurie Burroughs, ISBN 1 901194 65 X (Sudbury Ramblers). 4 short easy walks of 6.5km/4 miles or less through the countryside around Cornard.
Glemsford and Beyond
by Lesley Pilbrow (Sudbury Ramblers). A4 route cards with three walks of 6.5km/4 miles to 9.5km/6 miles, all starting at Glemsford's 15th century church. (New this year).
Both £1.20 + 50p p&p each from 6

Chaplin Walk, Great Cornard, Sudbury CO10 0YT. Cheques to Sudbury and District Ramblers.

East Suffolk Line Walks: Station to Station Ipswich to Lowestoft
by Roger Wolfe, ISBN 0 9547865 0 5. 11 walks linking the stations along the East Suffolk Line, ranging from a short stroll beside a tidal estuary (2.5km/1.5 miles) to a lengthy field path and woodland walk (16km/10 miles). Jointly published by the East Suffolk Travellers Association, Suffolk Ramblers and Railfuture. (New this year)
£2 from East Suffolk Travellers Association, 15 Clapham Road South, Lowestoft NR32 1RQ, or downloadable at www.eastsuffolklinewalks.co.uk.

Guide to the Fen Rivers Way
Describes this 80km/50-mile route, part of E2, from Cambridge to Ongar Hill, with some circular walks of 6.5km/4 miles to 13km/8 miles linked to the main route.

Walks in East Cambridgeshire
ISBN 0 9522518 0 9: circular lowland walks from 9.5km/6 miles to 19km/12 miles.

Walks in South Cambridgeshire
ISBN 0 9522518 3 3: circular lowland walks from 8km/5 miles to 19km/12 miles.

Walks on the South Cambridgeshire Borders
ISBN 0 9522518 2 5: 20 easy to moderate walks of from 8km/5 miles to 19km/12 miles.
All £4.50 each including p&p from 52 Maids Causeway, Cambridge CB5 8DD. Cheques to Cambridge Group of the Ramblers' Association.

Leighton Buzzard Millenium Walks
(Leighton Buzzard Group). Ten tried and tested walks.
Free + first class stamp from 8 Carlton Grove, Leighton Buzzard LU7 3BR.

Nelson's Heritage Walks
by Allan Jones (King's Lynn Ramblers). 16 walks with based on people, places or events associated with Lord Nelson to mark his bicentenary (forthcoming January 2005). (New this year)
£2.70 + 40p p&p.

West Norfolk Walkaway - 2
by Ian Smith (King's Lynn Ramblers), ISBN 1 901184 55 2. 16 easy circular walks between 7km/4.5 miles and 19.5km/12 miles, in the area of the Peddar's Way between Kings Lynn and Fakenham. *£2.10 + 40p p&p.*

Both from 42 Elvington, Springwood, King's Lynn PE30 4TA. Cheques to Ramblers' Association.

The Ramblers Millennium Walk
37km/23 mile walk around Southend-on-Sea and district.
£1 + A5 SAE from Lisa Jolley, Southend Borough Council Leisure Services Department, Civic Centre, Victoria Avenue, Southend-on-Sea SS2 6ER. Cheques to Southend Borough Council.

15 Walks in South East Essex
for all the Family ISBN 0 900613 97 1

Walk in Norfolk

Norfolk is perfect for walking. Whether you prefer refreshing sea breezes or leafy countryside you will find a great choice of walks to suit you.
To plan your route go to
www. visitnorfolk .co.uk

17 More Walks in and around South East Essex
ISBN 1 901184 17X

Short Walks in the area of Southend-on-Sea
ISBN 1 901184 50 1
Walks of 6.5km/4 miles to 14.5km/9 miles. *£2.25 each including postage from 29 Keswick Close, Rayleigh SS6 8LG. Cheques to S E Essex Group RA.*

Rural Rambles Round Beccles
(Waveney Ramblers) 12 walks, 5.5km/3.5 miles to 13km/8 miles

Rural Rambles Round Lowestoft
(Waveney Ramblers) 11 walks, 6.5km/4 miles to 16km/10 miles

Rural Rambles Round Southwold
(Waveney Ramblers) 12 walks, 8km/5 miles to 13km/8 miles
All £1.80 + 35p p&p each, as Waveney Way above.

Ten Walks in North Herts
by North Hertfordshire Ramblers, ISBN 0 900613 90 4. Ten walks of 9.5km/6 miles, each a personal favourite of one of the Group.
£2.50 from 21 Bedford Road, Hitchin SG5 2TP. Cheques to North Herts Ramblers Group.

Waveney Way (Waveney Ramblers). 115km/72 mile circular walk from Lowestoft. £2.10 + 35p p&p from 1 Church Close, Redenhall, Harleston IP20 9QS. Cheques to Ramblers Association.

stores in this region

BASILDON	21A Town Square SS1 41BA	HEMEL HEMPSTEAD	221 The Marlowes HP1 1WR
BEDFORD	"3 West Arcade, Church Street" MK40 1LQ	HERTFORD	18 Fore Street SG14 1BZ
BIGGLESWADE	2 Market Square SG18 8AP	HITCHIN	26 Market Place SG5 1DT
BISHOP STORTFORD	26 South Street CM23 3AT	HUNTINGDON	Unit 5 St Germain Walk PE29 3FG
BRAINTREE	86/88 High Street CM7 1JP	ILFORD	154 High Road IG1 1LL
BRENTWOOD	7 Chapel High CM14 4RY	IPSWICH	14/16 Carr Street IP4 1EJ
BURY ST EDMUNDS	2 Buttermarket IP33 1DB	LEIGHTON BUZZARD	47 High Street LU7 1DN
CAMBRIDGE	26 St Andrews Street CB2 3AX	LUTON	Unit 125 Arndale Centre LU1 2ND
CHELMSFORD	34 High Chelmer CM1 1XR	NORWICH	9/11 St Stephens Street NR1 3QN
COLCHESTER	17/18 High Street CO1 1DB	PETERBOROUGH	47 Bridge Street PE1 1HA
DUNSTABLE	14 Nicholas Way LU6 1TD	SAFFRON WALDEN	37/39 King Street CB10 1EU
ELY	26 Market Place CB7 4NT	SOUTHEND	4/19 York Road
GRAVESEND	Unit 4 Anglesea Centre DA11 0AU	SUDBURY	14 North Street CO10 1RB
GREAT YARMOUTH	20/21 Market Place NR30 1LY	WATFORD	Unit A8 The Harlequin Centre WD1 2TB
HARLOW	5 Eastgate CM20 1HP	WELWYN GARDEN CITY	41 Wigmores North AL8 6PG
HAVERHILL	17 High Street CB9 8AD	WEST THURROCK	Unit 338 Lakeside RM20 2ZH

BED & BREAKFAST

BEDFORDSHIRE

● **Dunstable**
Icknield Way & Chiltern Way
Cherish End B&B, 21 Barton Avenue, LU5 4DF
☎ 01582 606266 (Gill & Dave Gravestock)
www.smoothhound.co.uk/hotels/cherishend.html Map 166/028215
BB **C** ✗ nearby T3 ⬚Ⓑ ⊛ 🐾☕ 👜 ◆◆◆◆Ⓢ

● **Luton**
Icknield Way
▪️🛏️◀ 4 Friars Way, Farley Hill, LU1 5PR ☎ 01582 724086 (T & J Wilson)
jeanandtom70@hotmail.com Map 166/077203
BB **B** ✗ book first £6 S1 D3 T1 F1 ⋘(Luton Midland Road)
Ⓥ ⬚Ⓑ ⬚Ⓓ 🐾☕ 👜 🛁

● **Ravensden (Bedford)**
Tree-Garth, Church End, MK44 2RP ☎ 01234 771745 (Sue & Bruce
Edwards) treegarth@ukonline.co.uk Map 153/079547
BB **B** ✗ nearby S1 D1 T1 ⬚Ⓓ ⊛ 🐾☕ 👜 🚗 ◆◆◆◆

CAMBRIDGESHIRE

● **Caldecote (Cambridge)**

> ☆ **Avondale**
> 35 Highfield Road, CB3 7NX
> ☎ 01954 210746 (Margaret & George Baigent)
> avondalecambs@amserve.com Map 154/358590
> BB **C** D1 T1 F1 ⬚Ⓑ ⬚Ⓓ ⊛ ☕ 🛁
>
> Small exclusive bungalow, offering friendly accommodation.
> Situated in a peaceful village location surrounded by wooded areas, and
> interlaced with bridle paths and long country walkways.
> Television and tea/coffee making facilities.
> Weekly rates.

● **Cambridge**
145 Gwydir Street, CB1 2LJ ☎ 01223 356615 (Mrs M Sanders)
www.thegwydirhouse.co.uk/index.php Map 154/462579
BB **B** ✗ nearby T1 ⋘(Cambridge) ⬚Ⓓ ⊛ 🐾☕ 👜 🚗 !
Dykelands Guest House, 157 Mowbray Road, CB1 7SP
☎ 01223 244300 (Alison Tweddell) www.dykelands.com Map 154/471561
BB **B** ✗ nearby S1 D3 T2 F3 ⋘(Cambridge) ⬚Ⓑ ⬚Ⓓ ⊛ ☕ 🛁 ◆◆◆

● **Ely**
Jane's B&B, 82 Broad St, CB7 4BE ☎ 01353 667609 www.janes-bnb.co.uk
Map 143/542798 BB **B** ✗ nearby S1 D1 T1 ⋘(Ely)
⬚Ⓑ ⬚Ⓓ 🐾☕ 👜 🚗 !
Jane's B&B, 82 Broad St, CB7 4AE ☎ 01353 667609 (Jane Hull)
Map 143/545803 BB **B** ✗ book first, 8-12pm D1 T1 ⋘(Ely)
⬚Ⓑ ⬚Ⓓ 🐾☕ 👜 🚗 !

● **Great Shelford (Cambridge)**
Norfolk House, 2 Tunwells Lane, CB2 5LJ
☎ 01223 840287 (Mrs Janet Diver) Map 154/463521
BB **B** ✗ nearby D1 T2 ⋘(Great Shelford) ⬚Ⓑ ⬚Ⓓ ⊛ ☕

● **Great Wilbraham (Cambridge)**
The Sycamore House, 56 High Street, CB1 5JD ☎ 01223 880751
(B W & E A Canning) www.thesycamorehouse.co.uk Map 154/549572
BB **B** ✗ nearby S1 D2 ⋘(Cambridge)
⬚Ⓑ ⬚Ⓓ ⊛ 🐾☕ 🚗 🛁 Ⓜ ◆◆◆◆
▪️🛏️◀ Rose Bungalow, 68 High St, CB1 5JD ☎ 01223 882385
(Mr & Mrs Bagstaff) rose.bungalow@btinternet.com Map 154/549572
BB **B** ✗ nearby S1 T1 ⬚Ⓑ ⬚Ⓓ ⊛ 🐾☕ 👜 🚗 ! ◆◆◆◆

● **Kirtling (Newmarket)**

> ☆ **Hill Farm**
> CB8 9HQ ☎ 01638 730253 (Mrs Ann Bailey)
> Map 154/682583
> BB **B** ✗ nearby S1 D1 T1
> ⬚Ⓑ ⬚Ⓓ 🐾☕ 🚗 🛁 ◆◆◆
>
>
>
> Picturesque 400 year old farmhouse with super views of rural Strudland. Tea/coffee facilities, CH, en-suites available. Log fires, TV lounge, games room. Excellent home cooking with choice of menu. Special diets by arrangement. Licensed. Fire certificate. Access at all times. £30 single, £55 double.

● **Welney (Wisbech)**
Stockyard Farm B&B, Wisbech Rd, PE14 9RQ
☎ 01354 610433 (Mrs C Bennett) Map 143/528944
BB **B** ✗ nearby D1 T1 ⬚Ⓓ ⊛ 🐾☕ 👜 🛁 Veggie breakfasts

ESSEX

● **Bradfield (Manningtree)**
Essex Way

> ☆ **Emsworth House**
> Ship Hill, CO11 2UP ☎ 01255 870860 (Penny Linton)
> www.emsworthhouse.co.uk Map 168,169/142310
> BB **C** ✗ book first £19, until 8pm S3 D2 T1 F1
> Ⓥ ⬚Ⓑ ⬚Ⓓ ⊛ 🐾☕ 👜 🚗 !
>
>
>
> Stunning view of the river and the countryside on the Essex Way. Comfort and hospitality are my speciality.
>
> Email:
> emsworthhouse@hotmail.com

● **Colchester**
Essex Way
Scheregate Hotel, 36 Osborne Street, CO2 7DB ☎ 01206 573034 (J Powell)
Map 168/996250 BB **B** ✗ nearby S15 D6 T8 F1 ⋘(Colchester)
⬚Ⓑ ⬚Ⓓ 🛁 ◆◆

● **Great Chesterford (Saffron Walden)**
Icknield Way
Mill House, CB10 1NS ☎ 01799 530493 (Mrs Christine King)
Map 154/504431 BB **A** ✗ nearby S1 D4 T1 ⋘(Gt Chesterford)
⬚Ⓓ ⊛ 🐾☕ 🚗 🛁

● Ramsey (Harwich)
Essex Way
Woodview Cottage, Wrabness Road, CO12 5ND ☎ 01255 886413
(Anne Cohen) www.woodview-cottage.co.uk Map 168,169/191310
BB **B** ✗ book first £3.50 (light supper) SI DI FI ⋙(Wrabness)
Ⓥ Ⓑ Ⓓ ⊛ 🐾 ⚲ 🚗 🏕 ◆◆◆◆Ⓢ

HERTFORDSHIRE

● Tring
Ridgeway & Chiltern Way
Rangers Cottage, Tring Park, Wigginton, HP23 6EB ☎ 01442 890155
(Sally Dawson) www.rangerscottage.com Map 165/936102
BB **C** ✗ nearby D2 TI ⋙(Tring) Ⓑ Ⓓ ⊛ 🐾 ⚲ 🚗 ◆◆◆◆

NORFOLK

● Aldborough
Weavers Way
Butterfly Cottage, The Green, NR11 7AA ☎ 01263 768198
(Mrs Janet Davison) www.butterflycottage.com Map 133/184343
BB **B** ✗ nearby SI DI TI FI Ⓑ Ⓓ 🐾 ⚲ 🚗 ! 🏕 ◆◆◆

● Aylsham (Norwich)
Weavers Way

☆ ⬒🍴◀ **The Old Pump House**
2 Holman Road, NR11 6BY ☎ 01263 733789
www.smoothhound.co.uk/hotels/oldpumphouse.html Map 133,134/190269
BB **B** ✗ book first £20, 6.30pm SI D3 TI FI
Ⓥ Ⓑ Ⓓ ⊛ 🐾 ⚲ 🏕 ◆◆◆◆Ⓢ

18th century family home by thatched pump near marketplace, convenient for Weavers Way. Centrally located heated rooms (4 en-suite) with TV and hot drinks. Hearty breakfasts in pine-shuttered sitting room overlooking peaceful garden. Evening meals Oct-April by arrangement. Non-smoking.

● Brancaster (King's Lynn)
Peddars Way & Norfolk Coast Path
The Ship, Main Rd, PE31 8AP ☎ 01485 210333
www.shipinnbrancaster.co.uk Map 132/774438
BB **B** ✗ £7.50, 7-9pm D3 TI FI Ⓥ Ⓑ ⊛ 🐾 ⚲ ! ★★★

● Burgh Castle (Great Yarmouth)
Weavers Way & Angles Way
Church Farm, Church Rd, NR31 9QG ☎ 01493 780251
enquiries@churchfarm.uk.net Map 134/478050
BB **B** ✗ £8, 6:30-9:30pm D/T/F6 Ⓥ Ⓑ Ⓓ 🐾 ⚲ 🚗 ! ◆◆◆

● Catfield (Great Yarmouth)
The Broads
Weavers Way
Grebe Cottage, New Road, NR29 5BQ ☎ 01692 584179 (Mrs Jill Wickens)
jill@wickens61.freeserve.co.uk Map 133,134/388218
BB **A/B** ✗ nearby D2 TI Ⓑ ⊛ ⚲ 🚗 🏕

● Cromer
Peddars Way & Norfolk Coast Path, Weavers Way

☆ **The White Cottage**
9 Cliff Drive, NR27 0AW ☎ 01263 512728 (Mrs J Boocock)
www.whitecottagecromer.co.uk Map 133/224419
BB **B** ✗ nearby D2 TI ⋙(Cromer)
Ⓑ Ⓓ ⊛ 🐾 ⚲ ⬩ ◆◆◆◆

Enviably located B&B on the peaceful coastal path. Superb views, TVs, hospitality trays, radios, in exceptionally decorated rooms. Off road parking. Delicious breakfast with local produce, homemade bread and marmalade. Sorry no children, pets or smoking. Visit our website for more information.

● Great Cressingham
Peddars Way & Norfolk Coast Path
The Vines, IP25 6NL ☎ 01760 756303 (Mike & Vanessa Woolnough)
www.thevines.fsbusiness.co.uk Map 144/850016
BB **B** ✗ nearby D2 TI FI
Ⓑ Ⓓ ⊛ 🐾 ⚲ 🚗 ! 🏕 ◆◆◆◆

● Hickling (Norwich)
Weavers Way
Black Horse Cottage, The Green, NR12 0YA ☎ 01692 598691 (Yvonne Pugh)
www.blackhorsecottage.com Map 134/410234
BB **B** ✗ nearby SI D2 Ⓓ ⊛ 🐾 ⚲ 🚗 ! ◆◆◆◆

● Holme-next-the-Sea (Hunstanton)
Peddars Way & Norfolk Coast Path
Seagate House, 60 Beach Rd, PE36 6LG ☎ 01485 525510
(Mrs Norma Hasler) dshinholme@aol.com Map 132/698435
BB **C** ✗ nearby D2 TI Ⓑ Ⓓ ⊛ ⚲ ! ◆◆◆◆

● Hunstanton
Peddars Way & Norfolk Coast Path
⬒🍴◀ The Gables, 28 Austin Street, PE36 6AW ☎ 01485 532514
(Mrs Barbara Bamfield) www.thegableshunstanton.co.uk Map 132/674411
BB **B** ✗ book first £13.99, 6:30pm D2 T2 F3
Ⓥ Ⓑ Ⓓ ⊛ 🐾 ⚲ Ⓜ ◆◆◆◆ Discounts for groups.

● Little Cressingham (Thetford)
Peddars Way & Norfolk Coast Path

☆ **Sycamore House B&B**
IP25 6NE ☎ 01953 881887 (Mr J Wittridge)
Map 144/872001
BB **BC** ✗ nearby S2 D2 TI
Ⓑ Ⓓ 🐾 ⚲ 🚗 !

Sycamore House is a large country home in a tranquil village. Close to Thetford Forest, which is host to many activities to suit people of all ages. It is situated on The Peddars Way and near the historic market towns of Watton, Swaffham and Thetford.

● Morston (Holt)
Peddars Way & Norfolk Coast Path
Scaldbeck Cottage, Stiffkey Rd, NR25 7BJ
☎ 01263 740144 (E Hamond)
eandnhamond@dialstart.net   Map 133/004440
BB **A**   ✕ nearby D1 T1 Closed Dec-Jan   ▣ ☺ ♨

● Neatishead (Norwich)
The Broads
▃◖◄ Regency Guest House, The Street, NR12 8AD
☎ 01692 630233 (Sue Wrigley)
www.norfolkbroads.com/regency   Map 133,134/340210
BB **B**   ✕ book first D1 T1 F1   ▣ ▣ 🐾♨!🌣 ◆◆◆◆

▃◖◄ Allens Farmhouse, School Lane, NR12 8BU
☎ 01692 630080 (Jeremy Smerdon)
alensfarmhouse@clara.co.uk   Map 133, 134/343200
BB **BC**   ✕ nearby D2 T1 ⚑(Wroxham)
▣ ▣ 🐾🚗♨!🌣 ◆◆◆◆

● North Pickenham (Swaffham)
Peddars Way & Norfolk Coast Path
▃◖◄ Riverside House, Meadow Lane, PE37 8LE
☎ 01760 440219 (Mrs B J Norris)
jeannorris@tiscali.co.uk   Map 144/865065
BB **B**   ✕ nearby D1 T2 F1   ▣ 🐾🚗♨!🌣

● North Walsham
Weavers Way

☆ ▃◖◄ **Green Ridges**
104 Cromer Road, NR28 0HE   ☎ 01692 402448 (Yvonne Mitchell)
www.greenridges.com   Map 133/272307
BB **B**   ✕ book first £14.99, 5:30-8:30pm D1 T1 F1
⚑(North Walsham) ▣ ▣ ▣ ☺ 🐾♨🌣 ◆◆◆◆

Offering superior en-suite accommodation for the discerning traveller and delicious home cooked home grown produce. Conveniently situated within walking distance of town centre. "Comfort and quality at a price you'll like".

● Norwich
The Old Rectory, Crostwick, NR12 7BG   ☎ 01603 738513 (Mrs D Solomon)
info@oldrectorycrostwick.com   Map 133,134/256159
BB **C**   ✕ book first £13.50, 6:30-8:30pm S1 D5 T5 F2
▣ ▣ ▣ 🐾♨🌣 ★★

▃◖◄ Foxhole Farm, Windy Lane, Foxhole, Saxlingham Thorpe, NR15 1UG
☎ 01508 499226 (John & Pauline Spear)
foxholefarm@hotmail.com   Map 134/218971
BB **B**   ✕ book first £12 D1 T1   ▣ ▣ ▣ ☺ 🐾♨ ◆◆◆◆

● Salthouse (Holt)
Peddars Way & Norfolk Coast Path
Cumfus Bottom, Purdy Street, NR25 7XA   ☎ 01263 741118
Map 133/073437 BB **B**   ✕ nearby D2 T1   ▣ ▣ 🐾♨!🌣

● Sedgeford (Hunstanton)
Peddars Way & Norfolk Coast Path
Park View, PE36 5LU   ☎ 01485 571352 (Mrs J Frost)   Map 132/711366
BB **A**   ✕ book first £8 S1 D1 T1 Closed Dec-Feb
▣ ▣ ▣ 🐾♨🚗♨!🌣

● Sheringham
Peddars Way & Norfolk Coast Path
Wykeham Guest House, Morley Road North, NR26 8JB
☎ 01263 823818 (Mrs E Meakin) Map 133/158427
BB **B**   ✕ nearby S1 D1 T1 Closed Nov-Mar ⚑(Sheringham)
▣ ▣ ☺ 🐾♨🚗♨!🌣

▃◖◄ Oakleigh, 31 Morris Street, NR26 8JY   ☎ 01263 824993
(Mrs Diana North) dnorthoak@hotmail.com   Map 133/157434
BB **B**   ✕ book first £10, 6:30pm S1 D1 Closed Nov-Mar ⚑(Sheringham)
▣ ▣ ▣ ☺ 🐾♨🌣

▃◖◄ Elmwood, 6 The Rise, NR26 8QA   ☎ 01263 825454
Map 133/160426 BB **B**   ✕ nearby D1 T1 ⚑(Sheringham)
▣ ▣ ☺ 🚗♨!🌣 Ⓜ

☆ **The Beaumaris Hotel**
15 South St, NR26 8LL   ☎ 01263 822370 (Alan & Hilary Stevens)
www.thebeaumarishotel.co.uk Map 133/155431
BB **C**   ✕ £18.50, 7-8:30pm S5 D/T16 Closed Jan-Feb
⚑(Sheringham) ▣ ▣ ▣ 🐾♨🚗♨!🌣 ★★

Owned by the same family since 1947 with a reputation for personal service and excellent English cuisine. Five minutes walk from Norfolk Coast Path. National Trust properties and bird watching at Cley close by.

☆ ▃◖◄ **Bay Leaf Guest House**
10 St Peters Rd, NR26 8QY   ☎ 01263 823779 (Graham & Ros)
bayleafgh@aol.com   Map 133/156431
BB **C**   ✕ £3-£5 (bar snacks), 4-9pm D3 T2 F2 ⚑(Sheringham)
▣ ▣ ☺ 🐾♨🌣 ◆◆◆◆

The Bayleaf is a charming Victorian guest house. Ideal for ramblers, bird watchers and steam railway enthusiasts. One minute walk to town centre, sea front and steam railway. All rooms en-suite with licensed colour TV and drinks tray.

● Taverham (Norwich)
▃◖◄ Foxwood Guest House, Fakenham Road, NR8 6HR   ☎ 01603 868474
www.foxwoodhouse.co.uk   Map 133/154152
BB **B**   ✕ book first £10, 6:30pm D1 T2   ▣ ▣ ▣ ☺ 🐾♨🚗♨!

● Thompson (Thetford)
Peddars Way & Norfolk Coast Path
College Farm, IP24 1QG   ☎ 01953 483318 (Lavender Garnier)
collegefarm@amserve.net   Map 144/933966
BB **B**   ✕ nearby D2 T1   ▣ ▣ 🐾♨🚗

Thatched House, Mill Rd, IP24 1PH ☎ 01953 483577 (Brenda Mills)
thatchedhouse@amserve.com   Map 144/919967
BB **B** ✗ nearby D1 T2 Ⓥ Ⓑ Ⓓ ⊛ 🐾 🛏 🚗 ! 🏇 Ⓜ

● **Titchwell (King's Lynn)**
   Peddars Way & Norfolk Coast Path

☆ 🍴⊪ **Briarfields**
Main Street, PE31 8BB ☎ 01485 210742
www.norfolkhotels.co.uk   Map 132/757438
BB **C** ✗ £12.50, 6:30-9pm   D10 T7 F4
Ⓥ Ⓑ Ⓓ ⊛ 🐾 🛏 🏇 ★★

A renovated barn complex with sea views next to the RSPB reserve in Titchwell, a perfect centre for exploring the north Norfolk coast, Sandringham and Peddars Way. All rooms en-suite. Discounts for large parties. Traditional home cooked food with local seafood and game. A warm atmosphere guaranteed.

● **Trunch**
   Weavers Way
The Manor House, Brewery Rd, NR28 0PU ☎ 01263 721015
www.manorhousetrunch.co.uk   Map 133/283349
BB **B** ✗ nearby S1 D2 T1 ∿(Gunton) Ⓑ Ⓓ ⊛ 🐾 🛏 🚗 ! 🏇

● **Watton (Thetford)**
   Peddars Way & Norfolk Coast Path
🍴⊪ The Hare & Barrel Hotel, 80 Brandon Road, IP25 6LB
☎ 01953 882752   (M Raven)
www.hare-and-barrel-hotel-norfolk.co.uk   Map 144/906007
BB **C** ✗ book first £8, 6.30-9pm S6 D4 T7 F1 Ⓥ Ⓑ 🐾 🛏 Ⓜ

● **Wells-next-the-Sea**
   Peddars Way & Norfolk Coast Path
Meadowside, Two Furlong Hill, NR23 1HQ ☎ 01328 710470 (C & L Shayes)
Map 132/913433   BB **B** ✗ nearby D1 T1 Ⓑ Ⓓ 🛏
The Old Custom House, East Quay, NR23 1LD
☎ 01328 711463 (Madeline Rainsford)
www.eastquay.co.uk   Map 132/919437
BB **C** ✗ nearby D2 T1 Ⓑ Ⓓ ⊛ 🛏 🏇 ◆◆◆
🍴⊪ The Old Shop, 4 Burnt St, NR23 1HR ☎ 01328 863711
jennshaw@netbreeze.co.uk   Map 132/917431
BB **B** ✗ nearby D1 T1 Ⓓ ⊛ 🐾 🛏 🚗 ! 🏇

● **West Rudham (King's Lynn)**
   Peddars Way & Norfolk Coast Path
🍴⊪ Oyster House, Lynn Rd, PE31 8RW
☎ 01485 528327 (Mrs Veronica Prentis)
www.oysterhouse.co.uk   Map 132/814280
BB **B** ✗ nearby D2 T1 Ⓑ Ⓓ ⊛ 🛏 ◆◆◆◆

● **Weybourne**
   Peddars Way & Norfolk Coast Path
Sedgemoor, Sheringham Road, NR25 7EY ☎ 01263 588533   Map 133/113429
BB **A** ✗ nearby D2 ∿(Weybourne) Ⓓ 🛏 🚗 🏇

SUFFOLK

● **Beccles**
   The Broads
   Angles Way & Weavers Way
Catherine House, 2 Ringsfield Road, NR34 9PQ
☎ 01502 716428   (Mr & Mrs W T Renilson) Map 156/418897
BB **B** ✗ nearby D3 ∿(Beccles) Ⓥ Ⓑ Ⓓ ⊛ 🐾 🛏 ◆◆◆◆

● **Blaxhall (Woodbridge)**
🍴⊪ The Ship Inn, IP12 2DY ☎ 01728 688316
www.shipinnblaxhall.co.uk   Map 156/367570
BB **C** ✗ book first £8.50, 7-9pm   T4
Ⓥ Ⓑ Ⓓ ⊛ 🐾 🛏 🚗 🏇 ◆◆

● **Brandon**
🍴⊪ Riverside Lodge, 78 High St, IP27 0AU ☎ 01842 811236   (Mrs C Arnold)
Map 144/783867   BB **B** ✗ nearby S1 D1 T1 F1 ∿(Brandon)
Ⓑ Ⓓ ⊛ 🛏 🏇

● **Bures (Sudbury)**
🍴⊪ Queens House, Church Square, CO8 5AB
☎ 01787 227760 (Roger Arnold) www.queens-house.com   Map 155/908341
BB **C** ✗ book first £12 D3 T2 F1 ∿(Bures)
Ⓥ Ⓑ Ⓓ ⊛ 🐾 🛏 🚗 ! 🏇 ◆◆◆◆

● **Bury St Edmunds**
Rose Cottage & Laurels Stables, Horringer-cum-Ickworth, IP29 5SN
☎ 01284 735281   Map 155/825613
BB **B** ✗ nearby D1 T2 ∿(Bury St Edmunds)
Ⓑ Ⓓ 🐾 🛏 🏇   Access Category 1.

🍴⊪ Oak Cottage, 54 Guildhall Street, IP33 1QF
☎ 01284 762745 (Sheila Keeley) sheekee@talk21.com   Map 155/852638
BB **B** ✗ book first £15 S1 D1 T1 F1 ∿(Bury St Edmunds)
Ⓥ Ⓑ Ⓓ ⊛ 🐾 🛏 🏇 Ⓜ

● **East Bergholt (Colchester)**
   Essex Way & Suffolk Coast & Heaths Path
Rosemary, Rectory Hill, CO7 6TH ☎ 01206 298241 (Mrs Natalie Finch)
Map 155,169/073344   BB **B** ✗ nearby S1 T3 ∿(Manningtree)
Ⓓ ⊛ 🐾 🛏 🚗 🏇 ◆◆◆

● **Elmswell (Bury St Edmunds)**
Kiln Farm, Kiln Lane, IP30 9QR ☎ 01359 240442 (Mrs Macarage)
Map 155/981628   BB **B** ✗ £6, 6:30pm S3 D5 T2 F2 ∿(Elmswell)
Ⓥ Ⓑ Ⓓ ⊛ 🐾 🛏 🏇 ★★★

● **Framlingham (Woodbridge)**
Shimmens Pightle, Dennington Road, IP13 9JT
☎ 01728 724036 (Brian & Phyllis Collett) Map 156/277643
BB **B** ✗ nearby S1 D1 T1 F1 Closed Nov-Mar Ⓓ ⊛ 🛏 ◆◆◆

● **Framsden (Stowmarket)**
Greggle Cottage, Ashfield Rd, IP14 6LP
☎ 01728 860226 (Jim & Phil Welland)
wellands@ukgateway.net   Map 156/194609
BB **B** S1 D1 T/D1 Ⓑ ⊛ 🐾 🛏 🚗 ! 🏇

● **Lavenham (Sudbury)**
Brett Farm, The Common, CO10 9PG ☎ 01787 248533 (Mrs M Hussey)
www.brettfarm.com Map 155/923491 BB **B** D2 T1 ⋘(Sudbury)
🅱 Ⓓ ⊛ 🐾 ♨ 🚗 ! ◆◆◆◆

● **Lowestoft**
  **Angles Way, Weavers Way, Suffolk Coast
  & Heaths Path**
The Albany Hotel, 400 London Road South, NR33 0BQ ☎ 01502 574394
(Mr Geoff Ward) http://albanyhotel-lowestoft.co.uk Map 134/541914
BB **B** ✗ book first £8.50, 6-7:30pm S2 D2 T/D2 F1 ⋘(Lowestoft)
Ⓥ 🅱 Ⓓ 🐾 ♨ 🛁 ⚄ ◆◆◆◆

● **Newmarket**
  Icknield Way
Sandhurst, 14 Cardigan Street, CB8 8HZ ☎ 01638 667483 (Mrs Linda
Crighton) crighton@rousnewmarket.freeserve.co.uk Map 154/644630
BB **B** ✗ nearby S1 D1 T2 ⋘(Y) Ⓓ ⊛ 🐾 ♨ 🛁 ◆◆◆

● **Polstead**
Polstead Lodge, Mill St, CO6 5AD ☎ 01206 262196
(Mrs M Howard) www.polsteadlodge.com Map 155/989375
BB **B** ✗ book first S2 D2 T1 F1
Ⓥ 🅱 Ⓓ ⊛ 🐾 ♨ 🚗 ! ◆◆◆◆

● **Reydon (Southwold)**
  Suffolk Coast & Heaths Path
49 Halesworth Road, IP18 6NR ☎ 01502 725075 (Miss E A Webb)
Map 156/498770 BB **B** ✗ nearby D2 T1 🅱 Ⓓ ⊛ 🐾 ♨ 🚗 ! 🛁

● **Saxmundham**
🍴 Georgian Guest House, 6 North Entrance, IP17 1AY
☎ 01728 603337 www.thegeorgian-house.com Map 156/385634
BB **C** ✗ book first £18, 7-8pm D4 T1 F2 ⋘(Saxmundham)
Ⓥ 🅱 Ⓓ ⊛ 🐾 ♨ 🛁 ! ◆◆◆◆◆Ⓢ

● **Sudbourne (Woodbridge)**
Long Meadows, Gorse Lane, IP12 2BD ☎ 01394 450269 (Mrs A Wood)
Map 156/412532 BB **B** ✗ book first £10, 7:30pm S1 D1 T1
Ⓥ 🅱 Ⓓ ⊛ 🐾 ♨ 🚗 ! 🛁 ◆◆◆

● **Thorpeness (Leiston)**
  Suffolk Coast & Heaths Path
🍴 Dolphin Inn, IP16 4NA ☎ 01728 454994 www.thorpenessdolphin.com
Map 156/472598 BB **B** ✗ book first £6.50+, 7-9pm T/D3
Ⓥ 🅱 Ⓓ 🐾 ♨ 🚗 ! ★★★

● **Wenhaston (Halesworth)**
🍴 Rowan House, Hall Road, IP19 9HF ☎ 01502 478407
(Mrs Patricia Kemsley) rowanhouse@freeuk.com Map 156/427749
BB **B** ✗ book first £12, 7:30pm D1 T1
Ⓥ 🅱 Ⓓ 🐾 ♨ 🚗 ! 🛁 ◆◆◆◆

● **Westleton (Saxmundham)**
  Suffolk Coast & Heaths Path
21 Grange View, IP17 3EJ ☎ 01728 648481 (Mrs Molly Catchpole)
mm@catchmoy.fsnet.co.uk Map 156/438689
BB **B** ✗ nearby D1 Ⓓ 🐾 ♨ 🚗 ! Ⓜ

● **Woodbridge**

┌───┐
☆ **French's Farm**
Debach, IP13 6BZ ☎ 01473 277126 (Maggie Jennings)
www.treadsuffolk.co.uk/ffbbmain.htm Map 156/243552
BB **B** ✗ book first £8 D1 T1 F1
Ⓥ 🅱 Ⓓ ⊛ 🐾 ♨ 🚗 ! Ⓜ See Walking Holidays also.

Beautiful 16th century former farmhouse,
Grade II listed. Guest lounge, log fires,
homemade breads and preserves.
Grounds with large ponds. Access:
Woodbridge, Dunwich, Framlingham,
Heritage Coast. Friendly, welcoming hosts.
Email: maggie@treadsuffolk.co.uk
└───┘

Oxfam B&B Scheme, Deben Lodge, Melton Rd, IP12 1NH
☎ 01394 382740 (Rosemary Schlee)
(33 separate hosts) Map 169/278498
BB **B** ✗ nearby S2 D1 T1 ⋘(Woodbridge)
Ⓓ ⊛ 🛁 🏫 ★★ 1/3 profits to Oxfam.

SELF-CATERING

NORFOLK

● **Castle Acre**
☎ 01534 727480 (Mrs A C C Swindell) www.castleacre.org
£175-£350 Sleeps 6. 1 cottage.
Delightful village on Peddars Way. 🏫 ★★★

● **Cley-next-the-Sea**

┌───┐
☆ **Archway Cottage**
☎ 01992 511303 (Mrs V Jackson)
£200-£480 Sleeps 2-7. 1 cottage.
Character cottage, comfortable and well-equipped.
⊛ 🏫 ★★★

Archway Cottage, Cley-next-the-Sea.

Comfortable and well-equipped
character cottage – sleeps 7.

Another cottage in Wells-next-the-Sea.

VisitBritain 3 stars
└───┘

● **Cromer**
☎ 01263 512412 (John Graveling)
http://thegrovecromer.co.uk
£145-£545 Sleeps 2-6. 6 cottages.
Cottages in 3 acre grounds. ⊛ ⋘(Cromer) 🏫 ★★★

● **Dereham**
Moor Farm Stable Cottages ☎ 01362 688523 (Mr P Davis)
www.moorfarmstablecottages.co.uk
£190-£570 Sleeps 3-8. 12 varying types.
365 acres woodland; ideal for ramblers 🏫 ★★★

● **Lyng**

☆ **Collin Green Cottages**
☎ 01603 880158   (Mrs K Thomas)
thomaslyng@supanet.com
£225-£375   Sleeps 6. 2 cottages.   Footpaths from the door. Beautiful
countryside.   Closed Oct-Feb   RA member ★★★

Semi detached cottages with their own
gardens. Situated in central Norfolk close
to Marriots Way and within driving
distance of Peddars Way, Norfolk Coast
Path and Weavers Way. Shop, pub and
garage in Lyng (one and a half miles) in
picturesque Wensum Valley.

● **Salthouse**
The Dun Cow Public House ☎ 01263 740467 (Antony Groom)
www.theduncow-salthouse.co.uk £280 Sleeps 2 + cot. 2 flats.
Peaceful break on north Norfolk coast.   ★★★

● **Wells-next-the-Sea**
☎ 020 7485 0573 (Ms Lesley Whitby) l.whitby@ucl.ac.uk
£250-£320 Sleeps 2. 1 cottage.
Traditional flint cottage by saltmarshes. ⊛ ★★★

SUFFOLK

● **Aldeburgh**
☎ 01986 798609   (Lesley Valentine) j.r.valentine@btinternet.com
£200-£385 Sleeps 3. 1 flat.
Refurbished ground floor flat. Comfortable, warm. ⊛ ★★★★

Easton Farm Park ☎ 01728 746475 (Philippa Storey)
www.eastonfarmpark.co.uk £401-£785 Sleeps 7. 1 cottage.
Seaside location. ⊛

● **Beccles**
   The Broads
Bluebell Cottages ☎ 01502 712325 (Mrs Vera Thirtle)
www.bluebellcottages.com
£150-£500 Sleeps 2-11. 1 cottage, 1 studio.
Lockable storage. Rural site. Families welcome. ⊛ ★★★

● **Ipswich**
☎ 01206 825410 (Lin Pettican) lcpettican@aol.com
£240-£350 Sleeps 1-4. Victorian cottage.
Shotley Peninsula walking, National Trust land. ⊛

GROUPS

NORFOLK

Norfolk Coast Path

Deepdale Granary Group Hostel (SC) Burnham Deepdale
☎ 01485 210256 www.deepdalefarm.co.uk Map 132/804441
Max 18 nearby B D ⊛ ★★★ See Hostels also.

HOSTELS, BUNKHOUSES & CAMPSITES

NORFOLK

Norfolk Coast Path

Deepdale Backpackers and Camping (C/IH) Burnham Deepdale
☎ 01485 210256 www.deepdalefarm.co.uk Map 132/803443
Bednight £10.50 nearby B D ⊛ ★★★★
See Groups also.

PUBS & TEAROOMS

ESSEX

● **Abridge**
Crowther Nurseries, Ongar Road, RM4 1AA
☎ 01708 688479 (Ken & Vivienne)
www.gardeningwithken.com Map 177,167/483969
V ⊛ B(☺) Retail nursery & clematis specialist

● **Colne Engaine (Colchester)**
   Essex Way
Five Bells, Mill Lane, Colne Engaine, CO6 2HY
☎ 01787 224166 (Darran Lingley)
www.fivebells.net Map 168/851303
V L G ⊛ B(L)

● **Little Baddow (Chelmsford)**
The Rodney, North Hill, Little Baddon, CM3 4TQ
☎ 01245 222385 (Lynne Smeeton)
therodney@barstewards.com Map 167/779079
V ♪ (Recorded) G B(L)

● **Little Horkesley (Colchester)**
   Essex Way
The Beehive, Little Horkesley, CO6 4DH
☎ 01206 579879 (Hazel or Erica)
ericafirmin@aol.com Map 168/960321
V G B(L)

● **Purleigh (Chelmsford)**
The Bell, The Street, CM3 6QJ
☎ 01621 828348 (Barry & Julie Mott) Map 168/841019
V L G B(L) No children under 14 yrs

SUFFOLK

● **Snape**
Snape Maltings, Snape, IP17 1SR
☎ 01728 688303 (Dawn Hannan)
www.snapemaltings.co.uk Map 156/392574
V ♪ (Recorded) L G Real ale.

EAST MIDLANDS

BRITAINONVIEW/MARTIN BRENT

UPPER DERWENT VALLEY, DERBY

The East Midlands is full of variety. Seamless views over the Lincolnshire Wolds, the summits and moorlands of the Peak District National Park, legendary Sherwood Forest, and the Precambrian rocks of Charnwood Forest can all be taken in along nearly 20,000 kms of public paths.

The Viking Way traverses the Lincolnshire Wolds; a chalky landscape with open hill-tops, prehistoric settlements, Roman vestiges and the 'Rambler's Church' at Walesby. It continues south along the Lincolnshire Edge, a limestone escarpment from where the distinctive triple towers of Lincoln Cathedral can be seen. Further east, the Macmillan Way passes Norman castles, sandstone villages and terminates at the Wash near the sand dunes, salt marshes and freshwater habitats of Gibraltar Point.

Nottinghamshire's Trent River valley coils past Newark Castle, the Vale of Belvoir and nature reserves. The Robin Hood Way traces the folk-hero's steps through the ancient oaks of Sherwood Forest, visiting the Dukeries' parklands along the way.

Continuing west, the dramatic gritstone of Derbyshire's Dark Peak extends through brooding peat and moorland, contrasting with the lush limestone hills and forested dales of the White Peak. Many Peakland towns and villages still decorate their wells, a tradition known as 'well-dressing', originally in thanksgiving for deliverance from the plague.

600-million-year-old volcanic rocks distinguish Leicestershire's Charnwood Forest, the slate of which typifies the area's architecture. Its roaming deer, bracken-covered fields and the walks and views from the imposing Beacon Hill Park, the site of a Bronze Age fort, are priceless. Rutland, Britain's smallest county, boasts Rutland Water, western Europe's largest artificial lake and the finishing point of the Viking Way.

The green rolling hills, and the abundance of canals, rivers and lakes in Northamptonshire, are easily reached from London and provide a pleasant gateway to the region.

A member says:

"The richness of the landscape, the glorious views and the variety of historical attractions make this one of the best walking destinations in the country."

Long Distance Paths

Macmillan Way	MCM
Midshires Way	MDS
Nene Way	NEN
Pennine Bridleway	PNB
Pennine Way	PNN
Robin Hoods Way	RHD
Staffordshire Way	SFS
Trans Pennine Way	TPW
Viking Way	VIK

Public paths:

19,780km/ 12,283 miles

LINCOLN FENS

EAST MIDLANDS
LOCAL RAMBLERS CONTACTS

DERBYSHIRE
AREA SECRETARY
Mr John Hayes, The Old Rectory,
Old Brampton, Chesterfield, Derbyshire,
S42 7JG ☎ 01246 569260

GROUP SECRETARIES
Amber Valley Mrs M A Siddons,
Overdene, Ridgeway Lane, Nether
Heage, Nr Belper, Derbyshire, DE56 2JT
www.ambervalleyramblers.org.uk

Derby & S Derbyshire Mrs P Vaughan,
'Greenways', 13 Evans Avenue,
Allestree, Derbys, DE22 2EL
☎ 01332 558552
www.derbyramblers.org.uk

Derbyshire Dales Mrs Karen
Jenkinson, 6 Wolds Rise, Matlock,
Derbyshire, DE4 3HH ☎ 01629 582053
www.derbyshiredalesramblers.org.uk

Derbyshire Family Rambling
Mrs Julie Osborne,
☎ 01332 841975/554756
www.derbyshirefamilyrambling.org.uk

Erewash District Tony Beardsley,
14 York Avenue, Sandiacre, Nottingham,
NG10 5HB ☎ 0115 917 0082

LEICESTERSHIRE & RUTLAND
AREA SECRETARY
Mrs E Sandeman, 39 Maple Way,
Earl Shilton, Leicestershire, LE9 7HW
☎ 01455 848166
http://uk.geocities.com/ramblingjohn/
Leics.html

GROUP SECRETARIES
Coalville Ms S Marlow, 47 Edward St,
Anstey, Leicester, LE7 7DQ
☎ 0116 236 5789
www.trig222.f9.co.uk/coalvilleramblers

Hinckley Mrs B Elliston, 20 Surrey
Close, Burbage, Hinckley, Leics,
LE10 2NY ☎ 01455 238881
www.hinckleyramblers.cjb.net

Leicester Mr R Phipps, 21 Piers Rd,
Glenfield, Leicester, LE3 8PB
☎ 0116 233 2613
http://leicesterramblers.co.uk

**Leicestershire & Rutland Walking
Group** Andrew Hann, 119 Beatrice
Road, Leicester, LE3 9FJ
☎ 0116 224 6171www.lrwg.org.uk

Loughborough & District Mrs J Noon,
8 Ribble Drive, Barrow-Upon-Soar,

Loughborough, Leics, LE12 8LJ
☎ 01509 414519
http://uk.geocities.com/ramblingjohn/
Loughborough.html

Lutterworth Mrs Y Coulson,
12 Elmhirst Road, Lutterworth,
Leicestershire, LE17 4QB
☎ 01455 552265

Melton Mowbray Mr Richard Angrave,
12 Charnwood Ave, Asfordby, Melton
Mowbray, Leics, LE14 3YG
☎ 01664 812771
www.meltonra.org.uk

Rutland Joy Coleman, 6 Shannon Way,
Oakham, Rutland, Leics, LE15 6SY
☎ 01572 755813
www.rutland-ramblers.co.uk

LINCOLNSHIRE
AREA SECRETARY
Mr S W Parker, 129 Broughton Gardens,
Brant Road, Lincoln, LN5 8SR
☎ 01522 534655
www.lincscountyramblers.co.uk

GROUP SECRETARIES
Boston Mrs Sheila Pratt, Capri,
Whitehouse Lane, Fishtoft, Boston,
PE21 0BH ☎ 01205 369835
http://homepage.ntlworld.com/
colinj.smith/bostonwalks1.htm

Gainsborough Mr M A Clapham,
69 Beckett Avenue, Gainsborough,
Lincolnshire, DN21 1EJ
☎ 01427 615871
www.lincscountyramblers.co.uk

Grantham Mr P Walden, 1 Drift Hill,
Redmile, Notts, NG13 0GH
☎ 01949 844019
www.granthamramblers.co.uk

Grimsby & Louth Mrs S C Lundie,
2 Carlton Close, Cleethorpes,
DN35 0NP ☎ 01472 816157
http://uk.geocities.com/tjrambler

Horncastle Mr G Vessey, 51Elm
Crescent, Burgh Le Marsh, Skegness,
PE24 5EG ☎ 01754 810049
http://homepage.ntlworld.com/
colinj.smith/hcastlewalks1.htm

Lincoln Mrs Miriam Smith, 2 Belgravia
Close, Forest Park, Lincoln, LN6 0QJ
☎ 01522 682479

Lincolnshire Walking Group Mr S W
Parker, 129 Broughton Gardens, Brant
Road, Lincoln, LN5 8SR ☎ 01522
534655 www.lincswalkinggroup.org.uk

Scunthorpe Mrs V Bowser, 4 Orchid
Rise, Church Lane, Scunthorpe,
DN15 7AB ☎ 01724 336757
http://homepage.ntlworld.com/
colinj.smith/scunthorpeWalks1.htm

Skegness Mr A Malcolm, 9 Winston
Drive, Skegness, Lincs, PE25 2RE
☎ 01754 899 878
www.skegnessramblers.
gothere.uk.com

Sleaford Mr Dave Houghton,
19 Eastgate, Heckington, Sleaford, Lincs,
NG34 9RB ☎ 01529 461220
http://homepage.ntlworld.com/
colinj.smith/Sleafordwalks1.htm

Spalding Mrs W A Hicks, 2 Jubilee
Close, Spalding, Lincolnshire, PE11 1YD
☎ 01775 725531
www.spaldingramblers.org.uk

Stamford Mrs F Jacklin, 15 Perth Road,
Stamford, Lincs, PE9 2TX
☎ 01780 752736
http://homepage.ntlworld.com/
colinj.smith/StamfordWalks1.htm

NORTHAMPTONSHIRE
AREA SECRETARY
Mr B G Davies (acting), 12 Loire Close,
New Duston, Northampton, NN5 6SE
☎ 01604 591214
http://mysite.freeserve.com/
northantsramblers

GROUP SECRETARIES
Daventry Mrs P A Robinson,
7 Cotswold Close, Daventry,
Northants, NN11 5SP

Kettering Miss E M Wildman,
36 Skeffington Close, Geddington,
Northants, NN14 1BA
http://kra-g.org

Northampton Ms K A Lucas,
74 Osmund Drive, Goldings,
Northampton, NN3 8XB
www.northamptonra.org.uk

Northants 20s & 30s Walking
Miss Kate Butlin, 10 Haresmoor Drive,
Towcester, NN12 6HB
☎ 01327 352543
http://mysite.wanadoo-members.co.uk/
northants20s30s/index.html

Wellingborough & District
Mrs Pamela Barrett, 132 Wellingborough
Road, Earls Barton, Northampton,
NN6 0JS ☎ 01604 812556
www.wellingboroughramblers.org.uk

NOTTINGHAMSHIRE

AREA SECRETARY

Mr Rod Fillingham, 1 Albany Close,
Arnold, Nottingham, NG5 6JP
☎ 0115 9204066)
www.nottsarearamblers.co.uk

GROUP SECRETARIES

Broxtowe Dr A H Brittain, 23 Banks
Road, Toton, Nottingham, NG9 6HE
☎ 0115 9720 258

Collingham Mrs L J Piper, 92 High
Street, Collingham, Newark,
NG23 7NG ☎ 01636 892795

Dukeries Mr A Gamble,
35 Greenwood Crescent, Boughton,
Newark, Notts, NG22 9HX
☎ 01623 861376

Gedling Mrs J M Fillingham, 1 Albany
Close, Arnold, Nottingham, NG5 6JP
☎ 0115 9204066
www.innotts.co.uk/ramblers

Hucknall Miss J Bramford, 30 Ockerby
Street, Bulwell, Nottingham, NG6 9GA
☎ 0115 911 0044

**Mansfield & Sherwood Walking
Group** Mr A Radford, 6 Robey Close,
Forest Town, Mansfield, NG19 0DY
☎ 01623 427934
www.mansfield-ramblers.co.uk

Newark Mrs C Grant, 16 Elizabeth
Road, Newark, Notts, NG24 4NP
☎ 01636 681994
www.newarkramblers.co.uk

Nottingham Mrs E M Collison,
13 Overdale Road, Basford,
Nottingham, NG6 0LR
☎ 0115 970 8796

Notts Derby Walking Group
Sarah Mathews, 44 The Downs,
Silverdale, Nottingham, NG11 7DY
☎ 0115 914 5653 www.ndwg.co.uk

Notts Weekend Walkers Kevin
Matthews, 44 The Downs, Silverdale,

Nottingham, NG11 7DY
☎ 0115 914 5653

Ravenshead Allan Rogers, 63 Quarry
Road, Ravenshead, Nottingham,
NG15 9AP ☎ 01623 797321

Retford Mrs J Anson, Townrows Farm,
High Street, Elkesley, Notts, DN22 8AJ
☎ 01777 838 763

Rushcliffe Mr R Parrey, 61 West Leake
Road, Kingston On Soar, Notts,
NG11 0DN ☎ 0115 9830730
www.theburks.org/ramblers

Southwell Ms M Macdonald, 64 Bullpit
Road, Balderton, Newark, Nottingham,
NG24 3LY ☎ 01636 677395

Vale of Belvoir Mrs L Pitt,
4 Rockingham Grove, Bingham,
Nottingham, NG13 8RY
☎ 01949 876146

Worksop Ms S J Mcguire, 44 Sandy
Lane, Worksop, Notts, S80 1SW
☎ 01909 500278

LOCAL RAMBLERS PUBLICATIONS

Country Walks in Kesteven
by N S P Mitchell (new for 2002).
30 circular walks, many with shorter
options, from 2.5km/1.5 miles to
14.5km/9 miles, within a 24km/15-mile
radius of Grantham.
*£3.50 post free from Tweedsdale, Aviary
Close, Grantham NG31 9LF. Cheques to
Grantham Ramblers.*

Danelaw Way
by Brett Collier. A 100km/60-mile walk
between Lincoln and Stamford.
Forthcoming 2005 (see Lindsey Loop
below).

**Gingerbread Way A Grantham
Perimeter Country Walk**
(Grantham Group). 40km/25 mile
challenging circuit developed to celebrate
the Ramblers' Association Golden Jubilee in

1985. The name of the path refers to the
gingerbread biscuit, a Grantham speciality.
*Booklet with route description and OS 1:50
000 map, £1.20 post free from Tweedsdale,
Aviary Close, Grantham NG31 9LF.
Cheques to Grantham Ramblers.*

Lindsey Loop
by Brett Collier, ISBN 1 901184 13 7
(2nd edition). 154km/96 miles through the
Lincolnshire Wolds AONB between
Market Rasen and Louth, in eight stages.
(New this year) £5.95 + 70p p&p.
Plogsland Round
by Brett Collier, ISBN 1 901184 41 2.
A 75km/47 mile circular walk around
Lincoln. £5.50 + 60p p&p.
*Both from B Collier, 208 Nettleham Road,
Lincoln LN2 4DH. Cheques to B Collier.*
Lindsey Loop sew-on badge also
available from same source, £1.50 + p&p.

Towers Way
by Alan Nash, Janet Nash and Tony
Broad. A meandering 160km/
100-mile route linking 40 churches
between Barton Upon Humber and
Lincoln Cathedral, as an alternative to
the Viking Way.
*Route description available from
39 Fiskerton Road, Reepham,
Lincoln LN3 4EF.*

**Walks Through Derbyshire's
Gateway**
Favourite walks of the Bolsover Ramblers'
Association Group in their own backyard.
Five leaflets, each describing a single
circular walk of between 6.5km/4 miles
and 13km/8 miles.
*Leaflets free from local outlets or send an
SAE to 34 Lime Tree Avenue, Glapwell,
Chesterfield S44 5LE.*

millets THE OUTDOORS STORE **stores in this region**

BAKEWELL	Unit 3 Rutland Square DE45 1BZ
BOSTON	16 Market Street PE21 6EH
BUXTON	53/55 Spring Gardens SK17 6BJ
DERBY	1 East Street DE1 2AU
GRIMSBY	22 Baxtergate, Freshney Place DN31 1QL
LEICESTER	121/123 Granby Street LE1 6FD
LINCOLN	321/322 High Street LN5 7DW
LOUGHBOROUGH	4 Market Street LE11 3EP
LOWESTOFT	71 London Road North NR32 1LS
MANSFIELD	48 Westgate NG18 1RR
NEWARK	25 Middlegate NG24 1AL
NORTHAMPTON	24 Market Square NN1 2DX
NOTTINGHAM	12 Exchange Walk NG1 2NX
SCUNTHORPE	116 High Street DN15 6HB
STAMFORD	63 High Street PE9 2LA

BED & BREAKFAST

DERBYSHIRE

● Alsop-en-le-Dale (Ashbourne)
Peak District
Dove Top Farm, Coldeaton, DE6 1QR ☎ 01335 310472 (Mrs Ann Wainwright)
www.dovetopfarm.co.uk   Map 119/147566
BB **B**   ✕ book first £10   D1 F1   Closed Nov-Mar
Ⓥ Ⓑ Ⓓ ⊛ 🐾 ♨ 🚗 ⛳

● Ashbourne
Mercaston Hall, Mercaston, DE6 3BL ☎ 01335 360263
(Angus & Vicki Haddon)   www.mercastonhall.com   Map 119, 128/279419
BB **B**   D1 T2   Ⓑ Ⓓ ⊛ 🐾 ♨ 🚗 ⛳   ◆◆◆

☆ ▨◀ Holly Meadow Farm
Bradley, DE6 1PN ☎ 01335 370261 (Babette Lawton)
www.hollymeadowbandb.freeserve.co.uk   Map 128,119/229454
BB **B/C**   ✕ nearby   D2
Ⓑ Ⓓ ⊛ 🐾 🚗 ! ⛳   ◆◆◆◆Ⓢ

Wake to birdsongs! Quietly located on 260 acre farm. Superb views. Spacious double rooms with high degree comfort. Delicious breakfasts include homemade conserves and local produce. Stroll along wildlife conservation trail. Near Ashbourne, Dovedale, Carsington Water and Chatsworth.

▨◀ Compton House, 27-31 Compton, DE6 1BX ☎ 01335 343100
(Jane Maher)   www.comptonhouse.co.uk   Map 128,119/180464
BB **B**   ✕ book first £15, 7pm   D3 T1 F1
Ⓥ ⊛ 🐾 ♨ 🚗 ! ⛳   ◆◆◆◆

Mona Villas B&B, Church Lane, Middle Mayfield, DE6 2JS ☎ 01335 343773
www.mona-villas.fsnet.co.uk   Map 128,119/149448
BB **B**   ✕ nearby   D2 T1   Ⓑ Ⓓ ⊛ 🐾 ♨ 🚗 ⛳   ◆◆◆

● Bakewell
Peak District
Mandale House, Haddon Grove Farm, nr Over Haddon, DE45 1JF
☎ 01629 812416 (Mrs J Finney)   www.mandalehouse.co.uk
Map 119/184664   BB **B**   D2 T1   Closed Dec-Jan
Ⓑ Ⓓ ⊛ 🐾 ♨ 🚗 !   ◆◆◆◆

▨◀ 1 Glebe Croft, Monyash Rd, DE45 1FG ☎ 01629 810013 (Mrs P Green)
www.glebecroft-bakewell.co.uk   Map 119/215684
BB **B**   ✕ book first £10, 6:30-8pm   D2 T1
Ⓥ Ⓑ Ⓓ ⊛ 🐾 ♨ 🚗 ! Ⓜ   ◆◆◆◆   Special diets catered for

▨◀ Holly Cottage, By Pilsley Post Office, Bun Alley, Pilsley, DE45 1UH
☎ 01246 582245 (Julie & Phil Rodgers)
www.hollycottagebandb.co.uk   Map 119/241709
BB **B**   ✕ nearby   D1 T1   Ⓑ Ⓓ ⊛ 🐾 ♨ 🚗 !   ◆◆◆◆

● Bamford (Hope Valley)
Peak District
The White House, S33 0BG ☎ 01433 651487 (Fiona Middleton)
Map 110/200818   BB **B**   ✕ nearby   S2 D2 T1   ⋙(Bamford)
Ⓓ 🐾 ♨ 🚗 ⛳   ◆◆◆

☆ Pioneer House
Station Road, S33 0BN ☎ 01433 650638 (Janet Treacher)
www.pioneerhouse.co.uk   Map 110/207825
BB **A**   ✕ nearby   D2 T1   ⋙(Bamford)
Ⓑ Ⓓ ⊛ 🐾 ♨ 🚗 ⊛ Ⓜ   ◆◆◆◆

Begin your day with a hearty breakfast, and return and relax in the traditional style and comfort of your spacious en-suite room.
Our delightfully furnished period home is the ideal base for exploring the Peak District and the Derbyshire Dales.
For more information, call Janet Treacher, visit our website or email us.
Email: pioneerhouse@yahoo.co.uk

● Belper
Midshires Way
Woodlands B&B, Sawmills, DE56 2JQ ☎ 01773 856178 (Gill & David Hirst)
dhirst316@aol.com   Map 119/364522
BB **B**   ✕ book first £5, 7-8pm   D1 T1 F1   ⋙(Ambergate)
Ⓥ Ⓑ Ⓓ ⊛ 🐾 ♨ ⛳

● Biggin-By-Hartington (Buxton)
Peak District

☆ ▨◀ Biggin Hall Hotel
SK17 0DH ☎ 01298 84451
www.bigginhall.co.uk   Map 119/153594
BB **C**   ✕ book first £15.50, 7pm   S1 D8 T8 F3
Ⓥ Ⓑ Ⓓ ⊛ 🐾 ♨ ⛳   ★★

Small 17th century Old Hall, 1,000ft up in the Peak District National Park, close to Dovedale, in peaceful open countryside with beautiful uncrowded footpaths and bridleways. Baths ensuite, log fires, warmth, comfort, quiet, and fresh home cooked dinner. Licensed.
Telephone for a free brochure or Fax: 01298 84681
Email: enquiries@bigginhall.co.uk

● Birch Vale (Hayfield)
Midshires Way & Pennine Bridleway

☆ ▨◀ Sycamore Inn
Sycamore Rd, SK22 1AB ☎ 01663 747568
www.sycamoreinn.co.uk   Map 110/013869
BB **C**   ✕ £7-£12, until 9pm   S6 D6 T3 F2   ⋙(New Mills Central)
Ⓥ Ⓑ Ⓓ 🐾 ♨ ! ⛳   ◆◆◆◆

Sycamore Inn has stone walls and oak beams that speak of a tradition of hospitality. Beautiful views across the valley, with Kinder Scout nearby. The menu is varied and the food homecooked. Bar and restaurant are open all day.

● **Bradwell (Hope Valley)**
Peak District

Eden Tree House, S33 9JT ☎ 01433 621448 (Marion Allcroft)
Map 110/174818 BB **A** ✗ nearby D1 T2 ⋘(Hope) ⊗ 🐾 🖐

● **Buxton**
Peak District
Midshires Way

The Old Manse, 6 Clifton Road, Silverlands, SK17 6QL
☎ 01298 25638 (T W & P A Cotton)
www.oldmanse.co.uk Map 119/063734
BB **B** ✗ book first £11, 6:30pm S1 D4 T2 F2 ⋘(Buxton)
Ⓥ Ⓑ Ⓓ 🐾 🖐 ◆◆◆

Abbey Guest House, 43 South Ave, SK17 6NQ ☎ 01298 26419
aghbuxton@aol.com Map 119/059732
BB **A** ✗ nearby T1 F1 ⋘(Buxton) Ⓓ 🖐 🍴 ◆◆◆

Linden Lodge, 31 Temple Rd, SK17 9BA ☎ 01298 27591 (Mrs Eileen Blane)
www.lindentreelodge.co.uk Map 119/052727
BB **B** ✗ nearby D1 T1 ⋘(Buxton) Ⓑ Ⓓ ⊗ 🐾 🖐 ◆◆◆◆

☆ **Devonshire Lodge Guest House**
2 Manchester Road, SK17 6SB ☎ 01298 71487 (Mrs S Pritchard)
www.devonshirelodgeguesthouse.co.uk Map 119/055738
BB **B** D2 T1 ⋘(Buxton)
Ⓑ Ⓓ ⊗ 🖐 ◆◆◆◆Ⓢ

Set in the elegant town of Buxton, in the heart of the English Peak District,
Devonshire Lodge is a friendly, family-run guest house offering quality
accommodation. This fine Victorian house is just three minutes walk from the
Opera House, Pavilion Gardens and the town centre.

● **Calver (Hope Valley)**
Peak District

Pear Tree Cottage, Main Street, S32 3XR
☎ 01433 631243 (Dianne Payne) Map 119/238745
BB **B** ✗ book first £10, 6-7:30pm S2 D1 ⋘(Grindleford)
Ⓥ Ⓑ Ⓓ ⊗ 🐾 🖐 🍴

▪🛏 Valley View, Smithy Knoll Road, S32 3XW ☎ 01433 631407 (Sue Stone)
www.a-place-2-stay.co.uk Map 119/243745
BB **B** ✗ nearby D2 T2 F1
Ⓥ Ⓑ Ⓓ ⊗ 🐾 🖐 🚗 🍴 ◆◆◆◆

▪🛏 Bridge End, Dukes Drive, Curbar, S32 3YP
☎ 01433 630226 (Catherine Hunt)
hunt@g3fwb.wanadoo.co.uk Map 119/247744
BB **B** ✗ nearby T1 ⋘(Grindleford) Ⓑ Ⓓ ⊗ 🐾 🖐 🚗 🍴 🖐

● **Castleton (Hope Valley)**
Peak District
Pennine Way & Pennine Bridleway

☆ **Rambler's Rest**
Mill Bridge, S33 8WR ☎ 01433 620125 (Mary Gillott)
www.ramblersrest-castleton.co.uk Map 110/150831
BB **B** ✗ nearby S2 D5 T2 F1 ⋘(Hope)
Ⓑ Ⓓ 🐾 🖐 🍴 ◆◆◆

A 17th century guesthouse in the picturesque
village of Castleton. The house is pleasant
and olde worlde with 5 bedrooms, 3 en-suite.
All have central heating, colour TV and tea
making facilities. Own car park.

Cryer House, S33 8WG ☎ 01433 620244 (Mr & Mrs T Skelton)
fleeskel@aol.com Map 110/149829
BB **B** ✗ nearby D2 ⋘(Hope)
Ⓑ Ⓓ 🐾 🖐

▪🛏 Dunscar Farm, S33 8WA ☎ 01433 620483 (Janet Glennerster)
www.dunscarfarm.co.uk Map 110/143835
BB **B** ✗ nearby D3 T2 ⋘(Hope)
Ⓑ Ⓓ ⊗ 🖐 🚗 🍴 ◆◆◆◆

Bargate Cottage, Market Place, S33 8WQ ☎ 01433 620201 (Fiona Saxon)
www.bargatecottage.co.uk Map 110/150827
BB **B/C** ✗ nearby D2 T1 ⋘(Hope)
Ⓑ Ⓓ ⊗ 🐾 🖐 🚗 🍴 ◆◆◆ Guide dogs welcome.

☆ ▪🛏 **Losehill Hall**
Peak District National Park Centre, S33 8WB ☎ 01433 620373
www.losehill.org.uk Map 110/153838
BB **B** ✗ book first £16, 6pm S23 D1 T16 F1 ⋘(Hope)
Ⓥ Ⓑ Ⓓ 🖐 ◆◆◆

Set in 27 acres of beautiful parkland
in the heart of the Peak District,
Losehill Hall offers stunning scenery,
a relaxed environment and friendly
staff. Close to the Pennine Way and
Limestone Way. We also offer Walking
and Navigation Skills holidays.

☆ ▪🛏 **Ye Olde Cheshire Cheese Farm**
How Lane, S33 8WJ ☎ 01433 620330 (Ken Slack)
www.cheshirecheeseinn.co.uk Map 110/152830
BB **B** ✗ £10, until 8:30pm S1 D11 T1 ⋘(Hope)
Ⓥ Ⓑ Ⓓ 🐾 🖐 🚗 🍴 ★★★★

This delightful 17th century free-house is situated in the heart of the Peak
District and is an ideal base for walkers and climbers. All bedrooms are
ensuite. A 'Village Fayre' menu is available all day, all dishes home-cooked
in the traditional manner; there is also a selection of daily specials.
All credit cards accepted. Special golf packages.
Email: kslack@btconnect.com

● Chelmorton (Buxton)
Peak District
Midshires Way

☆ **Ditch House**
SK17 9SG ☎ 01298 85719 (Trish Simmonds)
info@ditchhouse.co.uk   Map 119/107697
BB **B**   ✕ nearby   D2 T1
B D 🏷 🐾 🛏 🛁 🚗 ! ◆◆◆◆⑤

Comfortable and spacious en-suite rooms in restored 18th century house with glorious views. Good walking area, near Limestone Way, new Pennine Bridleway and cycle tracks. Convenient for Buxton, Bakewell and Chatsworth. Christmas walking breaks available.

● Chesterfield
Trans Pennine Trail
🐾📧 Anis Louise Guest House, 34 Clarence Rd, S40 1LN
☎ 01246 235412 (Ian & Katia)
www.anislouise.co.uk   Map 119/378712
BB **B**   ✕ book first £5, until 9pm   S1 D1 T2 F1   ⋘(Chesterfield)
V B D 🏷 🐾 🛏 🛁 🚗 ! ◆◆◆

● Crich
Midshires Way
Clovelly Guest House, Roe's Lane, DE4 5DH
☎ 01773 852295 (Janice Lester)   Map 119/352545
BB **B**   ✕ book first £6, 6pm   S1 D2   ⋘(Y)
V D 🏷 🐾 🛏 🛁 🚗 ! ◆◆

● Crich Carr (Whatstandwell)
Peak District
Midshires Way
🐾📧 Riverdale, Middle Lane, DE4 5EG
☎ 01773 853905 (Mrs V A Durbridge)
riverdale@clara.co.uk   Map 119/336542
BB **B**   ✕ £10, 7pm   D2 T1   ⋘(Whatstandwell)
V B D 🐾 🛏 🛁 🚗 🏔 Ⓜ   ◆◆◆◆

● Edale (Hope Valley)
Peak District
Pennine Way
Brookfield, S33 7ZL ☎ 01433 670227 (J E Chapman)   Map 110/113847
BB **B**   ✕ nearby   D1 T1   Closed Nov-Mar   ⋘(Edale)
D 🏷 🐾 🛏 🛁   ◆◆◆

🐾📧 Mam Tor House, S33 7ZA   ☎ 01433 670253 (Caroline Jackson)
www.mantorhouse.co.uk   Map 110/123858
BB **A/B**   T2 F1   ⋘(Edale) D 🏷 🐾 🛏 🏔   ◆◆◆

● Eyam (Hope Valley)
Peak District
White Peak Way
Crown Cottage, Main Road, S32 5QW ☎ 01433 630858 (Angela Driver)
www.crown-cottage.co.uk   Map 119/215766
BB **B**   ✕ nearby   D2 T2   Closed Jan-Feb   ⋘(Grindleford)
B D 🏷 🐾 🛏 🛁 🚗 ! 🏔   ◆◆◆◆

● Fenny Bentley (Ashbourne)
Peak District
White Peak Way
Millfields Bed & Breakfast, DE6 1LA ☎ 01335 350454 (Mrs Susan Drabble)
www.millfieldsbandb.co.uk   Map 119/177493
BB **B**   ✕ nearby   D2 T1   B D 🏷 🐾 🛁 🚗 ! ◆◆◆

🐾📧 Cairn Grove, Ashes Lane, DE6 1LD ☎ 01335 350538
(Mrs Thelma Wheeldon)   www.cairngrove.co.uk   Map 119/173501
BB **B**   ✕ nearby   D2 T1   B D 🏷 🐾 🛏 🛁 🚗 ! 🏔   ◆◆◆◆

● Foolow
Peak District

☆ 🐾📧 **Housley Cottage**
Housley, S32 5QB ☎ 01433 631505 (Kevin Tighe)
http://housley.mysite.wanadoo-members.co.uk   Map 119/194759
BB **B**   ✕ nearby   D3 T3 F1   Closed Nov-Jan
B D 🏷 🐾 🛏 🛁 🚗 ! ◆◆◆◆

A 16th century farm cottage set in open countryside with views from all rooms over rolling fields. Within 10 minutes walk of the pretty village of Foolow and the Bull's Head Inn. Public footpaths pass by our garden gate leading to Millers Dale, Monsal head, Chatsworth House and the plague village of Eyam.

● Glossop
Peak District
Pennine Way & Trans Pennine Trail
🐾📧 Birds Nest Cottage, 40 Primrose Lane, SK13 8EW
☎ 01457 853478 (Sandra Newman)
birds@nest49.freeserve.co.uk   Map 110/025939
BB **A**   ✕ nearby   S2 T3 F1   ⋘(Glossop)
D 🏷 🐾 🛏 🛁 🏔   Mini kitchen for guests. Veggie breakfasts.

● Grangemill (Matlock)
Peak District
Midshires Way & Pennine Bridleway
Avondale Farm, DE4 4HT ☎ 01629 650820 (Louise Wragg)
www.avondalefarm.co.uk   Map 119/244577
BB **B**   ✕ nearby   T1   B D 🏷 🛁 🚗 ! 🏔   ◆◆◆◆⑤

● Hartington (Buxton)
Peak District
Midshires Way & Pennine Bridleway
Bank House, Market Place, SK17 0AL ☎ 01298 84465 (Mrs H Harrison)
Map 119/128604   BB **B**   ✕ book first £10-£13, 6:30pm   S1 D1 T1 F2
V B D 🏷 🐾 🛏 🛁 🚗 ! ◆◆◆

● Hathersage (Hope Valley)
Peak District
Sladen Cottage, Castleton Road, S32 1EH ☎ 01433 650104 (Mrs Julie Colley)
www.sladencottage.co.uk   Map 110/227814
BB **C**   ✕ book first £10, 7.30pm   D3 T3 F1   ᴡᴡ(Hathersage)
Ⓥ Ⓑ Ⓓ ⊛ 🐾🦮👜🚗❗ ◆◆◆◆

☆ Cannon Croft
Cannonfields, S32 1AG ☎ 01433 650005 (Mrs Sandra Oates)
www.cannoncroft.fsbusiness.co.uk   Map 110/226815
BB **B**   ✕ nearby   D3 T2 F1   ᴡᴡ(Hathersage)
Ⓑ Ⓓ ⊛ 🐾👜 ◆◆◆◆Ⓖ   Veggie breakfasts.

Stunning panoramic views. Famous for our hospitality and breakfast, try Sundancer eggs or porridge with whiskey for example! Standard of cleanliness is exceptional as is the friendliness and caring attention provided throughout your stay, in keeping with our Gold Award status.
Off road and private parking. All rooms en-suite.
Recommended by Holiday Which?, Country Walking and Food & Travel magazines. ETC 4 diamonds Gold Award, new this year AA 4 RED diamonds.

☆ Polly's B&B
Moorview Cottage, Cannonfields, S32 1AG
☎ 01433 650110 (Polly Fisher) Map 110/225815
BB **B**   ✕ nearby   D2 T1   ᴡᴡ(Hathersage)
Ⓑ Ⓓ ⊛ 🐾🦮👜❗ ◆◆◆◆

The Cottage nestles in a quiet location with stunning views of the surrounding countryside. A warm welcome awaits you at Moorview, where a varied and imaginative breakfast menu is offered (including our famous Mumbled Eggs). The rooms are furnished to a high standard with many thoughtful extras.

● Hulland (Ashbourne)
🛌🍴 October Cottage, DE6 3EP ☎ 01335 372801 (Mike & Pauline Severn)
Map 128,119/249466   BB **B**   ✕ nearby   S1 D1 T1
Ⓑ Ⓓ ⊛ 🐾🦮🚗❗

● Ilam (Ashbourne)
Peak District
🛌🍴 Throwley Hall Farm, DE6 2BB ☎ 01538 308202 (Mrs M A Richardson)
www.throwleyhallfarm.co.uk   Map 119/110526   BB **B**   D2 T1 F1   Closed Dec
Ⓑ Ⓓ ⊛ 🦮👜🚗❗🐾 ◆◆◆◆   See SC also.

● Matlock
Peak District
Riverbank House, Derwent Avenue, DE4 3LX ☎ 01629 582593
bookings@riverbankhouse.co.uk   Map 119/299599
BB **B**   ✕ nearby   D3 T1 F2   ᴡᴡ(Matlock)
Ⓑ Ⓓ ⊛ 🐾🦮Ⓜ ◆◆◆◆

☆ Glendon
Knowleston Place, DE4 3BU ☎ 01629 584732 (Mrs S Elliott)
Map 119/301598
BB **B**   ✕ nearby   D2 T2 F1   ᴡᴡ(Matlock)
Ⓑ Ⓓ ⊛ 🐾🦮 ◆◆◆◆

This Grade II listed building by the river and park is on the Heritage Way. It is conveniently situated near the town centre and bus/rail stations. Comfortable, well equipped accommodation in a relaxed atmosphere. Large private car park.

☆ Woodside
Stanton Lees, DE4 2LQ ☎ 01629 734320 (Mrs K M Potter)
www.stantonlees.freeserve.co.uk   Map 119/254633
BB **B**   ✕ book first   D2 T1
Ⓑ Ⓓ ⊛ 🐾🦮 ◆◆◆◆

When visiting the Peak District enjoy a friendly welcoming B&B in a rural Peakland village with panoramic views. Ideal for walking, sightseeing, birdwatching. En-suite bedroom, TV, hospitality tray. Non-smoking. Chatsworth, Bakewell, Matlock 4 1/2miles.
derwentkk@potter8378.freeserve.co.uk

● Matlock Bath (Matlock)
Peak District
🛌🍴 The Firs, 180 Dale Road, DE4 3PS
☎ 01629 582426 (Bernhard Trotman)
bernhard@thefirs180.demon.co.uk   Map 119/295594
BB **B**   ✕ nearby   D1 T/D2   ᴡᴡ(Matlock Bath)
Ⓑ Ⓓ ⊛ 🐾🦮❗👜 ◆◆◆

● Middleton-by-Youlgreave (Bakewell)
Peak District
Midshires Way
🛌🍴 Castle Farm, DE45 1LS
☎ 01629 636746 (Mrs G F Butterworth)
Map 119/192631   BB **B**   ✕ nearby   D1 F1
Ⓑ Ⓓ ⊛ 🐾🦮🦮 ◆◆◆◆

● Monsal Head (Bakewell)
Peak District

☆ Castle Cliffe
DE45 1NL ☎ 01629 640258 (Mrs J Mantell)
www.castle-cliffe.com   Map 119/185716
BB **B**   ✕ nearby   D2 T2 F2
Ⓑ Ⓓ ⊛ 🐾🦮❗🦮 ◆◆◆◆

Stunning position overlooking the beautiful Monsal Dale. Noted for its friendly atmosphere, hearty breakfasts and exceptional views. Drinks in the garden or around an open log fire in winter. Choice of dinner venues within an easy stroll. Suitable for groups.

● **Monyash (Bakewell)**

Peak District

Midshires Way

Rowson House Farm, DE45 1JH ☎ 01629 813521 (Garry Mycock)
www.rowsonhousefarm.com   Map 119/151664
BB **B**   ✗ nearby   D/T/F4   B D ⊗ 🐾🛏 ♿ ! 🏇

● **Parwich (Ashbourne)**

Peak District

Flaxdale House, DE6 1QA ☎ 01335 390252 (Michael & Gill Radcliffe)
www.flaxdale.demon.co.uk   Map 119/188544
BB **C**   D1 T1   B D ⊗ 🐾♿   ◆◆◆◆⑤

● **Risley**

Midshires Way

Braeside Guest House, 113 Derby Rd, DE72 3SS ☎ 01159 395885
www.braesideguesthouse.co.uk   Map 129/457357
BB **C**   ✗ nearby   D3 T1   B D ⊗ 🐾♿   ◆◆◆◆

● **Rowsley (Matlock)**

Peak District

🚐🍴 Eastfield, Chatsworth Road, DE4 2EH ☎ 01629 734427
www.east-field.co.uk   Map 119/260662
BB **A**   ✗ nearby   D1 T2   D 🐾♿ 🚗 ! Ⓜ

● **Thorpe (Ashbourne)**

Peak District

The Old Orchard, Stoney Lane, DE6 2AW ☎ 01335 350410 (Mrs B Challinor)
www.theoldorchardguesthouse.co.uk   Map 119/157503
BB **B**   ✗ nearby   D2   Closed Nov-Feb   B   D ⊗ 🐾♿ 🚗 ! 🏇 ◆◆◆

Jasmine Cottage, DE6 2AW ☎ 01335 350465 (Liz Round) Map 119/155502
BB **B**   ✗ £12.50, 7pm   D1 T1   B D ⊗ 🐾♿ 🚗

☆ 🚐🍴 **Hillcrest House**
Dovedale, DE6 2AW ☎ 01335 350436 (Margaret Sutton)
hillcresthouse@freenet.co.uk   Map 119/152505
BB **B**   ✗ nearby   S1 D4 T1 F1
V B D ⊗ 🐾♿ 🚗 !   ◆◆◆◆

Start your day with a full English breakfast and finish off with a nightcap in our lounge. Plenty of off road car parking. All king-size beds and four-posters. En-suite, TV, tea/coffee making facilities, radio alarm and hairdryer.

● **Tideswell (Buxton)**

Peak District

Rockingham Lodge, Market Square, SK17 8LQ ☎ 01298 871684 (Nick
Brelsford)   www.peaksaccommodation.co.uk   Map 119/151758
BB **B**   ✗ nearby   D1 T2   B D ⊗ 🐾 🚗 ! Ⓜ   See SC also.

● **Whaley Bridge (High Peak)**

Midshires Way & Pennine Bridleway

Springbank Guest House, 3 Reservoir Rd, SK23 7BL ☎ 01663 732819
(Margot Graham) www.whaleyspringbank.co.uk   Map 110/010814
BB **B**   ✗ book first £8, 7pm   D2 T3 F1   🚌(Whaley Bridge)
V B D ⊗ 🐾♿ 🚗 !   ◆◆◆◆

● **Youlgreave (Bakewell)**

Peak District

Pennine Bridleway & Midshires Way

The Old Bakery, Church Street, DE45 1UR ☎ 01629 636887 (Anne Croasdell)
www.cressbrook.co.uk/youlgve/oldbakery   Map 119/210643
BB **B**   ✗ nearby   D2 T2   B D ⊗ 🐾♿ !   ◆◆◆

The Farmyard Inn, Main St, DE45 1UW ☎ 01629 636221 (Joanne Healey)
sjghealy@aol.com   Map 119/208641
BB **B**   ✗ £7, 7-9pm   D2 T1 F1   V   B D 🐾♿ !   ◆◆◆

LEICESTERSHIRE

● **Great Dalby (Melton Mowbray)**

Midshires Way

Dairy Farm, 8 Burrough End, LE14 2EW ☎ 01664 562783 (Mrs L Parker)
dairyfarm@tesco.net   Map 129/744141
BB **B**   ✗ nearby   D2 T1   B D 🐾♿ 🚗 ! 🏇   ◆◆◆

● **Hugglescote**

☆ **Church View**
3 St John's Close, LE67 2FY ☎ 01530 812356
Map 129/417127
BB **A**   ✗ book first £5.50, 7pm   S2 D1
V B ⊗ 🐾♿

Former YHA warden welcomes you to her family home, situated in the heart of the National Forest.
Places of interest close by include Battlefields of Bosworth and Calke Abbey.
TV lounge. Non-smoking.
Packed lunches and evening meals available on request.
£12.50- £14.00pppn

● **Loughborough**

Peachnook Guest House, 154 Ashby Road, LE11 3AG ☎ 01509 264390
(Valerie Wood) www.smoothhound.co.uk/hotels/peachno-html
Map 129/529196   BB **B**   ✗ nearby   S1 D1 T1 F2   🚌(East Midlands)
B 🐾♿   ◆◆   Special diets catered for.

● **Market Harborough**

The Wrongs, Sibbertoft, LE16 9UJ ☎ 01858 880886 (Mrs M J Hart)
www.brookmeadow.co.uk   Map 141/666829
BB **B**   ✗ nearby   S1 D1   D ⊗ 🐾♿ 🚗 🏇   See SC also.

● **Upper Broughton (Melton Mowbray)**

Midshires Way

Sulney Fields, Colonel's Lane, LE14 3BD
☎ 01664 822204 (Hilary Collinson)
hillyc@talk21.com   Map 129/683262
BB **B**   ✗ nearby   S1 D2 T2   B D ♿ 🚗 🏇

LINCOLNSHIRE

● **Alford**

The Windmill Family & Commercial Hotel, Market pLace, LN13 9EB
☎ 01507 463377 (Keith Briggs)
www.alfordwindmillhotel.co.uk   Map 122/454760
BB **C**   ✗ £15, 7-8:30pm   S1 D4 T2 F3   V   B 🐾♿ 🏇

● **Barnetby (South Humberside)**

Viking Way

Holcombe House, Victoria Road, DN38 6JR
☎ 07850 764002 (Mrs Angela Vora)
www.holcombeguesthouse.co.uk   Map 112/059097
BB **A/B**   ✗ book first £5, 6-8pm   S4 D1 T2 F2   ⅏(Barnetby)
Ⓥ Ⓑ Ⓓ ⊛ ♨ 🐾   ◆◆◆◆

● **Barton-upon-Humber**

**Viking Way, Trans Pennine Trail &
Yorkshire Wolds Way**

☆ ⌂◀ **Reeds Hotel**
Westfield Lakes, Farings Rd, DN18 5RG   ☎ 01652 632313
www.reedshotel.co.uk   Map 106,112,107/009229
BB **C**   ✗ £6+, until 10pm   S3 D15 T10 F2   ⅏(Barton-upon-Humber)
Ⓥ Ⓑ Ⓓ ⊛ 🐾♨ ☕   ★★★

Luxury hotel with outstanding views of freshwater lakes, reed beds, the Humber
Bridge, estuary and surrounding wildlife. Luxury en-suite rooms with modern
facilities, full laundry and drying service. Light snacks, bar meals and full four
course meals are available daily, with packed lunches available if required.

Ideally situated for daily walks along the estuary banks or for those walking
the Viking Way or Yorkshire Wolds Way National Trail.

Member of the Yorkshire Tourist Board's Walkers Welcome Scheme.
Discount available for group bookings and week-end breaks.

Please call to enquire.
Email: info@reedshotel.co.uk

● **Cranwell (Sleaford)**

Viking Way

⌂◀ Byards Leap Cottage, NG34 8EY
☎ 01400 261537 (Anne Wood)   Map 130/011498
BB **B**   ✗ book first £10, 6:30pm onwards   D1 T1
Ⓥ Ⓓ ⊛ 🐾☕ 🚗   ◆◆◆ Special diets. Guide dogs welcome.

● **Goxhill (Barrow-upon-Humber)**

⌂◀ Kings Well, Howe Lane, DN19 7HU
☎ 01469 532471 (Mr & Mrs R McDonald)
www.springald.com/kingswell   Map 107,113/101213
BB **A**   ✗ book first £5-£10, 6-8pm   S1 D1 T1 F1   ⅏(Goxhill)
Ⓥ Ⓑ Ⓓ ⊛ 🐾☕ 🚗 ! 🍴   ◆◆◆

● **Lincoln**

Viking Way

Old Rectory Guest House, 19 Newport, LN1 3DQ   ☎ 01522 514774
(Tony Downes)   Map 121/975722
BB **B**   ✗ nearby   S1 D3 T1 F1   ⅏(Lincoln) Ⓑ   Ⓓ ⊛ ☕   ◆◆◆

☆ **Edward King House**
The Old Palace, Minster Yard, LN2 1PU   ☎ 01522 528778
www.ekhs.org.uk   Map 121/976718
BB **B**   S5 T11 F1   ⅏(Lincoln)
⊛ 🐾♨☕   ◆◆

A peaceful location in uphill
Lincoln next to the Bishop's
Palace. Close to cathedral and
castle. Enjoy magnificent views
from our beautiful garden.

● **Louth**

The Old Rectory, Muckton, LN11 8NU   ☎ 01507 480608 (Francis Warr)
www.louth-bedandbreakfast.co.uk   Map 122/374814
BB **B**   ✗ nearby   D2 T1   Ⓑ   Ⓓ ⊛ 🐾☕ 🚗 🍴

● **Market Rasen**

Viking Way

Waveney Cottage Guest House, Willingham Road, LN8 3DN
☎ 01673 843236 (Mrs J Bridger)
www.waveneycottage.co.uk   Map 121,113/111890
BB **B**   ✗ book first £8.50, 6pm   D/F1 T2   ⅏(Market Rasen)
Ⓥ Ⓑ Ⓓ ⊛ 🐾☕ 🚗   ◆◆◆◆

● **North Somercotes (Louth)**

Pigeon Cottage, Conisholme Road, LN11 7PS   ☎ 01507 359063
www.llalincs.co.uk   Map 113/413965
BB **B**   ✗ nearby   D1 T2 F2   Ⓑ   Ⓓ 🐾☕ 🚗 🍴   ◆◆◆

● **Ruskington (Sleaford)**

Sunnyside Farm, Leasingham Lane, NG34 9AH
☎ 01526 833010 (Daphne Luke)
www.sunnysidefarm.co.uk   Map 121/074502
BB **B**   ✗ nearby   D1 T1   ⅏(Ruskington)
Ⓑ Ⓓ 🐾☕ 🚗 🍴   ◆◆◆

● **Stamford**

Macmillan Way

⌂◀ Birch House, 4 Lonsdale Road, PE9 2RW
☎ 01780 754876 (Mrs Julie Headland)
birchhouse@hotmail.com   Map 141/015067
BB **B**   ✗ nearby   S2 D1 T1   ⅏(Stamford)
Ⓑ Ⓓ ⊛ ☕ 🚗   ◆◆◆

● **Wainfleet (Skegness)**

⌂◀ Willow Farm, Thorpe Fendykes, PE24 4QH   ☎ 01754 830316
www.willowfarmholidays.co.uk   Map 122/452611
BB **B**   ✗ £5, 6-9pm   D1 T1   ⅏(Thorpe Culvert)
Ⓥ Ⓑ Ⓓ 🐾☕ 🚗 ! 🍴

● **Walesby (Market Rasen)**
Viking Way

◄━◄ Blaven, Walesby Hill, LN8 3UW ☎ 01673 838352 (Jacqy Braithwaite)
www.blavenhouse.co.uk   Map 113/135924
BB **B**   D2 TI   B   D ⊗ 🍴🛏🚗🏠   ◆◆◆◆◆

● **Wigtoft (Boston)**

☆ ◄━◄ **Asperton Cottage**
Asperton Road, PE20 2PJ ☎ 01205 460570
nickdr@tiscali.co.uk   Map 131/262387
BB **A**   ✕ book first £10, 6:30pm   TI
V   B   D 🍴🛏🚗

Quiet, rural, fenland cottage with all amenities close by. Superior ground floor, en-suite accommodation with air conditioned, under-floor heated sun lounge for guests' sole use. Ideal short breaks all year: golf, birdwatching, fishing, walking and the coast.

● **Woodhall Spa**
Viking Way

Claremont Guest House, 9/11 Witham Road, LN10 6RW ☎ 01526 352000
(Claire Brennan) www.woodhall-spa-guesthouse-bedandbreakfast.co.uk
Map 122/191630   BB **A/B**   ✕ nearby   S3 D2 TI F5
B   D ⊗ 🍴🛏🏠   ◆◆

● **Wrawby (Brigg)**
Viking Way

◄━◄ Wish-u-Well Guest House, Brigg Road, DN20 8RH ☎ 01652 652301
(Mrs J Jobson) www.wishuwellguesthouse.com   Map 112/017085
BB **B**   S2 D2 T2 FI   ➿(Brigg Town) B   D ⊗ 🍴🛏   ◆◆◆

NORTHAMPTONSHIRE

● **Braunston (Daventry)**
The Old Castle, London Road, NN11 7HB ☎ 01788 890887
Map 152/533660   BB **B**   ✕ nearby   S3 D2 TI FI   B   D 🛏🏠

● **Cranford St Andrew (Kettering)**
Dairy Farm, NN14 4AQ ☎ 01536 330273 (Audrey E Clarke)   Map 141/923773
BB **B**   ✕ book first £15-£17, 7pm   D2 T2 FI   ➿(Kettering)
V   B   D ⊗ 🍴🛏🏠   ◆◆◆◆Ⓢ

● **Middleton (Market Harborough)**
Valley View, 3 Camsdale Walk, LE16 8YR
☎ 01536 770874 (Kathleen Randle) Map 141/840898
BB **B**   ✕ nearby   DI TI   D ⊗ 🍴🛏   ◆◆◆

● **Nether Heyford (Northampton)**
Nene Way & Midshires Way

◄━◄ Heyford B&B, 27 Church Street, NN7 3LH ☎ 01327 340872
(Pam Clements) http://heyfordguesthouse.co.uk   Map 152/659586
BB **B**   ✕ nearby   SI T3   B   D 🍴🛏🚗 !   ◆◆

● **Sibbertoft (Market Harborough)**
The Wrongs, LE16 9UJ ☎ 01858 880886 (Mrs M J Hart)
www.brookmeadow.co.uk   Map 141/666829
BB **B**   ✕ nearby   SI DI   D ⊗ 🍴🛏🚗🏠   See SC also.

NOTTINGHAMSHIRE

● **Farnsfield (Newark)**
Robin Hood Way

Grange Cottage B&B, Main Street, NG22 8EA ☎ 01623 882259
(Mrs J Kitchin) www.grange-cottage.co.uk   Map 120/649565
BB **B**   ✕ nearby   T3   B   D ⊗ 🍴🛏🚗🏠   ◆◆◆

● **Fiskerton (Southwell)**
Robin Hood Way

◄━◄ The Three Firs B&B, 21 Marlock Close, NG25 0UB ☎ 01636 830060
(Christine & Peter Jakeman) www.threefirs.co.uk   Map 120/734512
BB **B**   ✕ nearby   S2 DI   Closed Dec-Jan   ➿(Fiskerton)
B   D ⊗ 🍴🛏🚗 !

● **Laxton (Newark)**
Manor Farm, Moorhouse Road, NG22 0NU
☎ 01777 870417 (Mrs Pat Haigh)   Map 120/724666
BB **B**   ✕ nearby   DI F2   D 🍴🛏🏠   ◆◆◆

● **Mansfield**
◄━◄ Bridleways Guest House, Newlands Rd, Forest Town, NG19 0HU
☎ 01623 635725 (Gillian & Michael Rand) www.stayatbridleways.co.uk
Map 120/579624   BB **B**   ✕ nearby   S5 D2 T2   B   ⊗ 🛏

● **South Scarle (Newark)**
Greystones Guest Accommodation, Main St, NG23 7JH ☎ 01636 893969
www.greystonesguests.co.uk   Map 121/847638
BB **B**   ✕ book first £12-£15, 7:30pm   D2 TI   ➿(Collingham)
V   B   D ⊗ 🍴🛏🚗 !

RUTLAND

● **Barrowden (Oakham)**
The Spinneys, 31 Wakerley Road, LE15 8EP ☎ 01572 747455
(Valerie & John Hennessy) www.barrowden.plus.com   Map 141/950002
BB **B**   ✕ book first £6, 6:30-7:30pm   SI DI TI FI   Closed Dec
V   B   D ⊗ 🍴🛏🚗   Facilties for disabled.

High House, Wakerley Rd, LE15 8EP ☎ 01572 747354 (Mrs P Dawson)
www.highhouse.net   Map 141/949002
BB **B**   ✕ book first £15, 6-7:30pm   D2 T2   Closed Dec-Jan
B   D ⊗ 🍴🛏🚗 !

● **Belton-in-Rutland (Oakham)**
Macmillan Way

☆ ◄━◄ **The Old Rectory**
LE15 9LE ☎ 01572 717279
bb@iepuk.com   Map 141/814010
BB **B**   ✕ nearby   SI D2 T3 FI
B   D ⊗ 🛏🚗 !🏠   ◆◆◆   See SC also.

Macmillan Way, Leicestershire Round, Rutland Water, Barnsdale gardens. Comfortable B&B accommodation in conservation village. Pub 200 yards. SC also available.

● Oakham
Macmillan Way & Viking Way
🚶◄ The Old Wisteria Hotel, 4 Catmose Street, LE15 6HW
☎ 01572 722844 (Emad Saleeb) www.wisteriahotel.co.uk Map 141/862086
BB **C** ✕ From £12.50, 7-9pm   S7 TD/18   ∿(Oakham)
Ⓥ Ⓑ Ⓓ 🐾🐾🍵🍷 ★★★ See Groups also.

● Uppingham
🚶◄ Meadow Sweet Lodge, South View, LE15 9TU
☎ 01572 822504   Map 141/867995
BB **B** ✕ nearby SI TI Ⓑ Ⓓ 🐾🐾🍵🚗!🍷

SELF-CATERING

DERBYSHIRE

● Alstonefield
Peak District
River Dales ☎ 0161 4328916 (Alan & Delia Exley)
www.riverdales.co.uk £170-£280   Sleeps 4. I house.
Village location. Private garden. Pubs nearby. 🐾

● Ashbourne
Peak District
Throwley Hall Farm ☎ 01538 308202 (Mrs Muriel Richardson)
throwley@btinternet.com   £300-£1,000
Sleeps 7-12. 2 farmhouses, I cottage. Open fires. Spacious farmhouse, well
equipped. 🐾 ★★★-★★★★   See B&B also.

Windlehill Farm ☎ 01283 732377 (Keith & Joan Lennard)
www.windlehill.btinternet.co.uk   £120-£420 Sleeps 2-6. I apt, I cottage.
Beamed barns on small organic farm. 🐾🐾 ★★★★

Willow Bank ☎ 01335 343308 (Mary Vaughan) www.kniveton.net
£275-£350   Sleeps 4. I flat.   Beautiful situation, luxurious
accommodation, wonderful walking. 🐾 ★★★★

☆ Sandybrook Country Park
Pinelodge Holidays Ltd ☎ 01335 300000
www.pinelodgeholidays.co.uk/sandybrook.ihtml
£260-£950 Sleeps 2-8. 41 pine lodges. Pinelodges sleep 2-8
Indoor swimming pool. 🐾 ★★★-★★★★ See Matlock also.

Luxurious pinelodges with glorious views, excellent base for Peak District.

Children's adventure playground, soft play and indoor pool. Woodland walk.

The Coach House bar and restaurant serves an extensive menu and takeaways.

The luxurious Pinelodges have satellite television and video recorders.
Fully fitted kitchens and a range of appliances. Each has a verandah with garden
furniture. All linen is included. Weeks and short breaks available year round.
Email: enquiries@pinelodges.co.uk

☆ Offcote Grange Cottage Holidays
☎ 01335 344795 (Pat Walker)
www.offcotegrange.com
£705-£1,500 Sleeps 10-14 +cots. 2 cottages.
Oak beams, log fires, beautiful gardens. 🐾 ★★★★★

Hillside Croft and Billy's Bothy

Two large, luxurious 5 bedroom historic detached character cottages, fully
restored to an exceptional standard within peaceful rural locations and
beautiful scenery.

Close to Carsington Water, Chatsworth House and the Peak District.

Each with separate lounge and dining rooms, exceptional farmhouse kitchens,
quality bath/shower rooms.

Availability of small conference facilities and gymnasium.

Patios with furniture and BBQ in own gardens, private parking.

Excellent walking area, central Derbyshire, ideal base for all attractions.

● Ashford-in-the-Water
Peak District
I, Sunny Lea ☎ 01629 815285 (Mrs D Furness)
£220-£395   Sleeps 4. I cottage.
Beamed cottage, high standard, owner maintained. 🐾 ★★★★

● Belper
☎ 01773 853086 (Jan Wickham)
www.country-holidays.co.uk.propertynet17118
£163-£307   Sleeps 4-5. I cottage.
Spectacular views of working Heage windmill.
∿(Ambergate) 🐾 ★★★

● Buxton
Peak District
Northfield Farm ☎ 01298 22543 (Liz Andrews)
www.northfieldfarm.co.uk   £90-£465   Sleeps 2-9. 4 barn conversions.
Excellent walking & riding. Facilities for groups. 🐾 ★★★

☎ 01298 813444 (Noel & Rita Pollard) www.holidayapartments.org
£250-£380   Sleeps 4. I cottage.
Wonderful views, idyllic hideaway.
🐾 ∿(Chapel-en-le-Frith) ★★★★★

● Chapel-en-le-Frith
Peak District
Saffi House ☎ 01298 812441 (Carole Coe) www.saffihouse.co.uk
£375-£800   Sleeps 8 +cot. I cottage.
Spacious 3 storey, all modern amenities.   ∿(Chapel-en-le-Frith)

● Chinley
Peak District
☎ 01663 750566 (Pam Broadhurst) www.cotebank.co.uk
£230-£600   Sleeps 2-6. 2 cottages.
Footpaths from the door. 🐾 ★★★★

● Curbar
Peak District

Curbar Cottages ☎ 01433 631885 (Mr & Mrs Pierce)
http://curbarcottages.com £165-£275   Sleeps 2-6. 2 cottages.
Newly renovated. Can let as one. 🛏 ★★★

● Edale
Peak District

☆ **Upper Holt Cottage**
☎ 01433 670420   (Richard Code)
www.upperholtcottage.com
£350-£490 Sleeps 4. I cottage.
Open fire, stunning views. 🚫 ᴡᴡ(Edale) ★★★★

This charming 17th century cottage has stunning views across the Edale Valley to Kinder Scout.
Excellent base for walkers, with footpaths in all directions from the cottage set in 20 acres of meadow and woodland.
With open wood-burning fire.
Email: upperholtcottage@uku.co.uk

● Eyam
Peak District

☆ **Sheen Cottage**
☎ 01270 874979 (Janice Mills)
www.sheencottage.co.uk
£190-£350   Sleeps I-4. I cottage.
Open fire, beams, warm and cosy. 🚫

Lovely Grade II listed cottage. Modernised to high standards while maintaining character and charm. Clean, warm and welcoming. Excellent base for exploring White Peak. Adjoins quiet pub serving good food. Includes heating, electricity, coal, logs and bed linen. Email: janice@sheencottage.co.uk

☆ **Dalehead Court Country Cottages**
☎ 01433 620214 (Mrs Dorothy Neary)
£185-£485   Sleeps 2-6. 3 cottages.
Unique village square setting, private parking.
★★★★-★★★★★★ See Hope also.

A fine house, a delightful 17th century barn and cosy cottage overlooking Derbyshire's most historic village square. Exceptional decor and furnishings; walled courtyard garden and private parking. Village inn, shops 2 mins. Breaks from £115. Phone for a brochure.

● Glossop
Peak District

Moorfield Lodge ☎ 01457 869709 (Glenn Toole)
www.moorfieldlodge.co.uk
£150-£330   Sleeps 2-6. I cottage, I flat.
Pennine Way I 1/2 miles. Extensive grounds. ᴡᴡ(Glossop) 🛏

● Hartington
Peak District

☎ 01298 84447 (Mrs Frances Skemp) www.cotterillfarm.co.uk
£200-£900   Sleeps 2-6. 6 cottages.
Footpaths, nature reserve on our doorstep. 🚫 ★★★★   RA member.

● Hope
Peak District

☎ 01433 620640 (Mrs Gill Elliott) www.farfield.gemsoft.co.uk
£225-£525   Sleeps 2-7. 3 cottages.
Spacious, well-equipped accommodation in scenic location.
ᴡᴡ(Hope) ★★★★

☆ **Peak District Holiday Cottages**
☎ 01433 620214 (Mrs Dorothy Neary)
www.peakdistrictholidaycottages.com
£170-£380   Sleeps 2-6. 3 cottages.
Delightful riverside setting bordering Hope village.
ᴡᴡ(Hope) 🛏   ★★★★ See Eyam also.

Hope – Riverside setting.
Award-winning conversion of three beamed farm barns into delightful self-catering cottages. River and hill walks abound: train/buses nearby for walk and ride-back options. Conveniently located near village amenities. Breaks from £110   Phone for a brochure or Email: laneside@lineone.net

● Hope Valley
Peak District

Peak Farm Holidays ☎ 01433 620635 (Mrs Angela Kellie)
www.peakfarmholidays.co.uk
£250-£425   Sleeps 4-6. 3 cottages.   Tennis court, gardens, farm walks, fishing. 🚫 ᴡᴡ(Bamford) 🛏 ★★★★

● Matlock
Peak District

☆ **Darwin Forest Country Park**
Pinelodge Holidays LTD ☎ 01629 732428
www.pinelodgeholidays.co.uk/darwin_forest.ihtml
£260-£950 Sleeps 2-8. 85 pine lodges.   Pinelodges sleep 2-8, indoor swimming pool. 🛏   ★★★-★★★★★ See Ashbourne also.

Set in 44 acres of stunning woodland, excellent base for exploring Peak District. Tennis courts, children's play areas, and indoor pool.

The Forester's Inn serves an extensive menu and takeaways. Handy shop and wine store.
The luxurious Pinelodges have satellite television and video recorders.
Fully fitted kitchens and a range of appliances. Each has a verandah with garden furniture. All linen is included. Weeks and short breaks available year round.
Email: enquiries@pinelodgeholidays.co.uk

Rosebank Cottage ☎ 0114 2652315 (Mrs J Putland)
JPO14e9272@blueyonder.co.uk £215-£370 Sleeps 4-5. 18th century cottage.
Original features, aga, parking. Delightful surroundings. ⊗

● Parwich
Peak District

Croft Cottage ☎ 01335 390440 (Saskia or Terry Tallis)
www.croftcottage.co.uk £192-£348 Sleeps 3 + cot. 1 cottage.
Cosy 18th century cottage. Quiet village location. ⊗ 🐾 ★★★★

● Tideswell
Peak District

Rockingham Lodge ☎ 01298 871684 (Nick Brelsford)
www.peaksaccommodation.co.uk
£175-£420 Sleeps 4-6. 1 cottage. RA member ⊗ See B&B also.

● Wirksworth

☆ ☎ 01623 465437 (Andy & Pat Colclough)
patandandycole@ntlworld.com
£200-£360 Sleeps 2-4. 1 cottage.
Conservation village. Distant views.
⊗ ★★★★

Beautiful detached country cottage in Brassington village.
Cosy log fire and vaulted ceiling with oak beams create a truly
relaxing atmosphere.
Village pubs 50 and 150 yards away. Lovely walks and
Carsington Reservoir closeby.
Chatsworth, Dovedale, Matlock, Bath Spa all within close proximity.

LEICESTERSHIRE

● Market Harborough
Brookmeadow ☎ 01858 880886 (Mary & Jasper Hart)
www.brookmeadow.co.uk £160-£450 Sleeps 3-6. 3 chalets.
Peaceful lakeside setting, camping. 🐾 ★★★-★★★★ See B&B also.

NORTHAMPTONSHIRE

● Sibbertoft
Brookmeadow ☎ 01858 880886 (Mary & Jasper Hart)
www.brookmeadow.co.uk £160-£450 Sleeps 3-6. 3 chalets.
Peaceful lakeside setting, camping. 🐾 ★★★-★★★★ See B&B also.

NOTTINGHAMSHIRE

● Edwinstowe
Crow Hollow ☎ 01636 677847 (Mrs Helen Proctor)
www.crowhollow.co.uk £250-£350 Sleeps 2-6. 1 cottage.
Beautiful location, Robin Hood's Sherwood Forest. 🐾 ★★★

RUTLAND

● Belton-in-Rutland
The Old Rectory ☎ 01572 717279 (Richard & Vanessa Peach)
bb@iepuk.com £150-£295 Sleeps 2-5. 1 apartment.
On Macmillan Way and Leicestershire Round. ⊗ 🐾 See B&B also.

● Caldecott

☆ Wisteria Cottage
☎ 01536 771357 (Mel Hudson)
www.rutland-cottages.co.uk
£185-£450 Sleeps 2-8. 1 cottage.
Restaurants and pub nearby. Dogs welcome. 🐾 ★★★

A charming stone-built
cottage in the historic
county of Rutland,
overlooking Rockingham
Castle and the rolling hills
of the Welland valley. An
ideal location for walkers,
with Rutland Heritage
trails and the Jurassic Way
nearby.

Eyebrook trout fishery and Rutland Water are within easy reach, for cycling,
fishing and bird watching.
Wisteria Cottage can be used as one or, divided into two dwellings, offering
high quality accommodation, gardens and secure parking

enquiries@rutland-cottages.co.uk

● Uppingham
Wardley House ☎ 01572 717671 (Ann Kanter) http://wardleyhouse.com
£270-£425 Sleeps 2-6. 2 properties.
Outstanding views. Direct access to footpath. ⊗ ★★★★

GROUPS

DERBYSHIRE

Peak District

The Glenorchy Centre (SC) United Reformed Church
Coldwell Street, Wirksworth, DE4 4FB ☎ 01629 824323 (Mrs E M Butlin)
www.glenorchycentre.org.uk Map SK287541
SC £990 Max 30 Closed Dec-Feb ✗ nearby Ⓓ ᴧᴧ(Cromford)

Peak District
Midshires Way

New Buildings Farm (SC) Ashleyhay, Wirksworth, Matlock DE4 4AH
☎ 01629 823191 (Ned Wiltshire & Jo Stanistreet)
www.newbuildingsfarm.co.uk Map 119/296518
SC £180-£420 1 cottage Min 2, max 6 Ⓓ See Hostels also

RUTLAND

The Old Wisteria Hotel (B&B) 4 Catmose St, Oakham, Rutland, LE15 6HW
☎ 01572 722844 www.wisteriahotel.co.uk Map 141/862086
DBB £47.50 Min 15, max 45 ✕ 🐾
B D ⓢ ₩(Oakham) ★★★ See B&B also

HOSTELS, BUNKHOUSES & CAMPSITES

DERBYSHIRE

Peak District
Midshires Way

New Buildings Farm (SC) Ashleyhay, Wirksworth, Matlock DE4 4AH
☎ 01629 823191 (Ned Wiltshire & Jo Stanistreet)
www.newbuildingsfarm.co.uk Map 119/296518
Bednight £10 (min £80) D See Groups also

Please mention **walk BRITAIN**
when booking your accommodation

WEST MIDLANDS

The importance of the West Midlands in the industrial revolution and its proximity to Wales make it an intriguing region for walkers. Birmingham's canals and the industrial archaeology in Shropshire contrast with the green hills of the southern counties.

WORCESTERSHIRE WAY

The Staffordshire Way follows the northerly moorlands, towered by the rugged Roaches hills, down to the steep wooded valleys and small fields of the Churnet Valley. It continues across Cannock Chase's open downland and forest, to the sandstone ridge of Kinver Edge. From here you can see the Fauld crater, the result of an underground RAF ammunitions dump accidentally exploding in 1944. An interesting urban alternative would be a walk through Stoke-on-Trent's six towns, affectionately known as 'the Potteries'.

A member says:

"Birmingham's 100 miles of canals outnumber those of Venice. Towpaths weave through interesting archaeological and industrial sites, and even extend to walks under the enormous 'spaghetti junction'".

The Shropshire Hills are the most rugged part of this region, where mountainous Wales spills over the border into England. The Shropshire Way passes the World Heritage Site of Ironbridge Gorge, and provides splendid views of Long Mynd, the isolated Wrekin Hill and of buzzards circling the rocky Stiperstones.

Possibly the region's most picturesque walk follows Herefordshire's Wye Valley through the market town of Ross-on-Wye and across Symonds Yat Gorge, a dramatic wooded limestone outcrop and home to the peregrine falcon.

Britain's longest riverside walk, the Severn Way, cuts through the centre of Worcestershire, across the Malvern Hills, renowned for their grassy slopes and mistletoe, and through ancient Hollybush Wood before disappearing into the Welsh hills. To the northeast lies the red sandstone of the Severn plain and the beginning of the Monarch's Way, a long trail that traces Charles II's flight towards France following his defeat at the Battle of Worcester. The Way continues south and joins the intimate valley walk along Warwickshire's River Avon, leading walkers to Shakespeare's Stratford-upon-Avon, in the heart of the Vale of Evesham.

Long Distance Paths

Cotswold Way	CWD
Heart of England	HOE
Macmillan Way	MCM
Monarch's Way	MON
Offa's Dyke Path	OFD
Sandstone Trail	SAN
Severn Way	SVN
Shropshire Way	SHS
Staffordshire Way	SFS
Wye Valley Walk	WVL

Public paths:

21,308km / 13,232 miles

LUDLOW, SHROPSHIRE

WEST MIDLANDS
LOCAL RAMBLERS CONTACTS

HEREFORDSHIRE
AREA SECRETARY
Mr Phil Long, 5 Gillow Cottages,
St. Owens Cross, Hereford, HR2 8LE
☎ 01989 730697

GROUP SECRETARIES
Hereford Mr A W Lee, 61 Bredon
Grove, Malvern, Worcs, WR14 3JS
☎ 01684 575044

Herefordshire Hikers Mr J Lappage,
Pengarth, New Street, Ledbury,
Herefordshire, HR8 2EE
www.geocities.com/
herefordshirehikers

Leadon Vale Mrs I C Gibson, 41 Jubilee
Close, Ledbury, Herefordshire,
HR8 2XA ☎ 01531 635139

Mortimer Mrs P A Bickerton,
35 Mortimer Drive, Orleton, Ludlow,
Shropshire, SY8 4JW
☎ 01568 780827

Ross-on-Wye Mr Sam Phillips, Thelsam,
Chapel Road, Ross-On-Wye,
Herefordshire, HR9 5PR
☎ 01989 563874

SHROPSHIRE
AREA SECRETARY
Mrs Marion Law, 3 Mead Way, Shifnal,
Shropshire, TF11 9QB
☎ 01952 462855)
marionlaw@rapid.ial.co.uk
www.shropshireramblers.org.uk

GROUP SECRETARIES
Broseley & Wenlock Mr R Ryder,
29 Coneybury View, Broseley,
TF12 5AX ☎ 01952 883479

Market Drayton Mrs H J Morris,
10 Golf Links Lane, Wellington, Telford,
TF1 2DS

Oswestry Mrs A Parker, 11 St Johns
Hill, Ellesmere, Shropshire, SY12 0EY
☎ 01691 623026

Shrewsbury & Mid-Shropshire
Mrs Chris Cluley, Birches Farm, Clun,
Craven Arms, Shropshire, SY7 8NL
☎ 01588 640243
roy@birchesfarm.freeserve.co.uk

South Shropshire Dr P Johnson,
Pedlars Rest, Elsich Court, Seifton,
Ludlow, Shropshire, SY8 2DL

Telford & East Shropshire
Mrs L E M Norton, 7 Aston Court
Mews, Shifnal, Shropshire, TF11 8TP

STAFFORDSHIRE
AREA SECRETARY
Geoff Budd, 28 Cricketers Close,
Burton-On-Trent, DE15 9EH
☎ 01283 561535
http://homepages.tesco.net/~staffsra

GROUP SECRETARIES
Biddulph Mr N Oakden, Dukes Well,
Cloudside, Congleton, Cheshire,
CW12 3QG ☎ 01260 226617
www.biddulphra.freeuk.com

Bilston Mrs J Tyler, 50 Wellington Place,
Wednesfield, Willenhall, West Midlands,
WV13 3AB ☎ 01902 633849
www.bilstonramblers.org.uk

Chase & District Mr Phil Chalmers,
16 Peakes Road, Rugeley, WS15 2LY
☎ 01889 583793

East Staffordshire Mrs Jane King,
39 Faraday Avenue, Stretton,
Burton On Trent, Staffs, DE13 0FX
☎ 01283 543483

Leek Mrs Shirley Lunt, 17 Rennie
Crescent, Cheddleton, Leek, ST13 7HD
☎ 01538 360907 www.raleek.co.uk

Lichfield Mrs A Thompson,
1 Blythe Close, Burntwood, WS7 9JJ
☎ 01543 672180

Mid Staffordshire Mrs S A Benn,
11 Porlock Avenue, Stafford, Staffs,
ST17 0HS ☎ 01785 603646
www.midstaffs-ra.freeserve.co.uk

Sandwell Christine D'agostino,
13 Park Crescent, West Bromwich,
B71 4AJ ☎ 0121 525 8955
www.sandwellramblers.org.uk

Staffordshire Walking Group
Mr P Patrick, 65 Stoney Lane, Cauldon,
Stoke on Trent, ST10 3EP
☎ 01782 760136
www.staffs-walkers.org.uk

Stoke/Newcastle Mr Graham Evans,
65 Pacific Road, Trentham, Stoke on
Trent, ST4 8RS ☎ 01782 642872
[membs Enqs 01782 846838]
http://hyperhelp.co.uk/ra/index.htm

Stone Mrs P M Conlong, Langdales,
108 Newcastle Road, Stone, ST15 8LG
☎ 01785 812410 ww.stoneramblers.com

Stourbridge Mrs Joan Crowe,
29 Stennels Avenue, Halesowen, West
Midlands, B62 8QJ ☎ 0121 422 1698

Walsall Mrs Alice Harrison,
30 Clarendon Place, Pelsall, Walsall,
WS3 4NL ☎ 01922 683411

Wolverhampton Mrs Christine Ellitts,
The Flat, Chillington Hall, Codsall Wood,
Wolverhampton, WV8 1RE
☎ 01902 851660

WARWICKSHIRE
AREA SECRETARY
Mr Michael Bird, 16 Melford Hall Road,
Solihull, West Midlands, B91 2ES
☎ 0121 705 1118
www.warwickshire.freeserve.co.uk

GROUP SECRETARIES
Bear Group Steven Bick,
11 Normandy Close,
Hampton Magna, Warwick,
Warwickshire, CV35 8UB
☎ 01926 400842
stephen@sbick.wanadoo.co.uk

Castle Bromwich Mr R Kitchen,
89 Sandhurst Avenue, Hodge Hill,
Birmingham, B36 8EH ☎ 0845 4583848
www.iccastlebromwichramblers.co.uk

City of Birmingham Ms C D Dittrich,
10 Peel Walk, Harborne,
Birmingham, B17 8SR
www.bhamramblers.btinternet.com

Coventry Estelle Rollins,
140 Hawkes Mill Lane, Allesley,
Coventry, West Midlands, CV5 9FN
☎ 02476 403862
http://members.aol.com/coventryra

Mid Warwickshire Mrs S M Coates,
40 Windy Arbour, Kenilworth,
Warwickshire, CV8 2AS
☎ 01926 855123
www.midwarksramblers.org

Rugby Mrs F Debonnaire,
5 Hobley Close, Bilton,
Rugby, Warks, CV22 7PU
☎ 01788 815484
http://uk.geocities.com/
rugbyramblers

Solihull Mrs S M Woolley,
36 Alderwood Place, Princes Way,
Solihull, West Midlands, B91 3HX
☎ 0121 7055753

South Birmingham
Mrs C Stefaniak, 12 Henlow Road,
Birmingham, B14 5DT ☎ 0121 680 3853
www.icsbramblers.co.uk

Southam Mr C Haywood,
44 Pendicke Street, Southam,
Warks, CV47 1PF ☎ 01926 812820
http://members.aol.com/southamra/
southam.htm

164

LOCAL RAMBLERS CONTACTS continued

Stratford upon Avon
Mrs E M Leavesley, 16 Icknield Row,
Alcester, Warwicks, B49 5EW
☎ 01789 764798
www.stratforramblers.com

Sutton Coldfield
Please contact our main office or visit
www.suttoncoldfieldramblers.co.uk

West Midlands Walking Group
Mr J Pizzey, 4 Lutley Drive, Pedmore,
Stourbridge, DY9 0YQ
☎ 01384 827735
www.wmwg.fsnet.co.uk

WORCESTERSHIRE
AREA SECRETARY
Mr R A Hemmings, 25 Whinfield Road,
Worcester, WR3 7HF ☎ 01905 451142

GROUP SECRETARIES
Bromsgrove Mrs J Deakin, 106
Salwarpe Road, Charford, Bromsgrove,
Worcs, B60 3HS ☎ 01527 875385

Evesham Ms D K Harwood [acting],
12 Queen's Rd, Evesham, WR11 4JN
www.communigate.co.uk/
worcs/ramblersevesham

Redditch Mr S Lund, 32 Dobbs Mill
Close, Selly Park, Birmingham, B29 7NQ
☎ 0121 471 4159

Worcester Mrs P Mayo,
197 Bilford Road, Worcester,
WR3 8HL ☎ 01905 453087

Worcester 20s & 30s
Mrs E & Mr J Baker, 19 St Peters
Crescent, Droitwich, WR9 8QD

Wyre Forest Hugh Buttress,
132 Elan Avenue, Stourport On Severn,
DY13 8LR ☎ 01299 878 181
www.wyreforest.50megs.com

LOCAL RAMBLERS PUBLICATIONS

Birmingham Greenway
by Fred Willits, ISBN 1 869922 40 9.
From the southern to the northern
boundary of Birmingham using footpaths,
riversides and towpaths.
*£4.95 + £1 p&p from Meridian Books, 40
Hadzor Road, Oldbury B68 9LA*

Bromsgrove Ramblers
30 mile circular walk in the countryside
around Bromsgrove. 48km/30-mile circuit
around Bromsgrove from Wychbold
via Chaddesley Corbett and Alvechurch,
devised to celebrate the 30th anniversary of
the local Ramblers Group. (New this year).
*£1.50 from 13 Victoria Road, Bromsgrove
B61 0DW. Cheques to Ramblers'
Association Bromsgrove Group.*

**Leisure Walks from Worcester
Bridge** by Worcester Ramblers,
ISBN 1 901184 34 X. A selection of walks
suitable for all the family of between
5km/3 miles and 11km/7 miles all starting
from Worcester Bridge, including maps,
illustrations, historical notes and a city walk
visiting the cathedral.
*£2.95 + 50p p&p from M Palmer, 2 Witley
Road, Holt Heath, Worcester WR6 6LX.
Cheques to Worcester Ramblers'
Association.*

Our Favourite Herefordshire Walks
(Hereford Group), ISBN 0 9511995 9 5.
12 easy to moderate walks of between 6.5
km/4 miles to 19 km/12 miles, scattered
around the county.
*£3.95 post free from Book Secretary,
Gawsworth, Kingsland, Leominster HR6 9RU.
Cheques to Hereford Group of the Ramblers'
Association.*

Our Favourite Walks
12 walks of between 11km/7 miles and
22.5km/14 miles, mainly in Staffordshire but
venturing into Derbyshire and Shropshire.
*£2.95 + 35p p&p, contact main office or see
www.ramblers.org.uk for the latest details.*

**Ramblers Guide to the Shropshire
Way** by Shropshire Ramblers,
ISBN 1 946679 44 4. (New this year)
MU Publishers £6.99 + p&p.

Walks Around Stone
(Stone Ramblers). 12 walks each from
Westridge Post and from Downs Banks,
between 1.5km/1 mile and 11km/7 miles
with route descriptions, maps and guidance
on healthy walking in plastic cover. *£3 +
50p p&p from 1 Vanity Close, Oulton, Stone
ST15 8TZ. Cheques to Ramblers' Association
Stone Group.*

Walks Around Stourbridge A range of
easy walks between 6km/4 miles and
12km/8 miles.
*£4.50 inc p&p from Mrs J Crowe (Secretary),
29 Stennels Avenue, Halesowen B62 8QJ.
Cheques payable to Ramblers' Association –
Stourbridge Group.*

Walks in the Vale of Evesham
2nd edition: 12 walks, all reasonably easy, of
between 2.5km/1.5 miles and 11.5km/7.25
miles, in and around Evesham.
*£3 + A5 SAE from 12 Queens Road,
Evesham WR11 4JN. Cheques to Ramblers'
Association Vale of Evesham Group.*

Warwick District Walks
*£2 post free from Mr P Heelis, 7 Almond
Grove, Warwick CV34 5TB. Cheques to Mid-
Warwickshire Ramblers' Association.*

Waterside Walks in the Midlands
by Birmingham Ramblers, ISBN 1 869922
09 3. 22 walks by brooks, streams, pools,
rivers and canals. *£4.95 + £1 p&p.*
**More Waterside Walks in the
Midlands** by Birmingham Ramblers, ISBN
1 869922 31 X. A second collection of
Midlands walks. *£5.95 + £1 p&p.
Both from Meridian Books as Birmingham
Greenway above.*

 stores in this region

BIRMINGHAM	35 Union Street B2 4SR
BURTON ON TRENT	12 St Modwens Walk DE14 1HL
COVENTRY	19 Smithford Way CV1 1FY
DUDLEY	205/206 High Street DY1 1PB
EVESHAM	33 Bridge Street WR11 4SQ
HANLEY	10/12 Upper Market Square ST1 1NS
HEREFORD	12/14 Eign Gate HR4 0AB
KIDDERMINSTER	21 The Bull Ring DY10 2AZ
LEAMINGTON SPA	23/31 The Parade CV32 4BC
LEEK	34 Derby Street ST13 5AB
LICHFIELD	19 Tamworth Street WS13 6JP

MERRY HILL	11 Merry Hill, Brierley Hill DY5 !QX
NEWCASTLE U LYME	53 High Street ST5 1PN
NUNEATON	14/15 Abbey Gate Centre CV11 4HL
REDDITCH	12 Kingfisher Walk B97 4EY
RUGBY	14/15 Market Place CV21 3DU
SOLIHULL	50 Drury Lane B91 3BG
STAFFORD	13 Gaolgate Street ST16 2BQ
SUTTON COLDFIELD	56 The Parade B72 1DS
TELFORD	207 Dean Street TF34BT
WALSALL	9 The Bridge, West Midlands WS1 1LR
WOLVERHAMPTON	2 Wulfrun Centre WV1 3HF
WORCESTER	7/8 The Shambles WR1 2RF

BED & BREAKFAST

BIRMINGHAM & THE BLACK COUNTRY

● **Hampton In Arden (Solihull)**
Heart Of England Way
▪◄ The Cottage, Kenilworth Road, B92 0LW ☎ 01675 442323 (Roger)
www.smoothhound.co.uk/hotels/cottage.html   Map 139/224792
BB **B** ✕ nearby S4 D4 T2 F2 ﹉(Hampton In Arden) Ⓑ Ⓓ ⬡ ⬠ 🖰 ⬡ ◆◆◆

● **Solihull**
Heart Of England Way
▪◄ Ivy House, Warwick Road, Heronfield Knowle, B93 0EB ☎ 01564 770247
(Mr & Mrs J Townsend) www.smoothhound.co.uk/hotels/ivyguest.html
Map 139/194750 BB **B** ✕ nearby S3 D2 T2 F1 ﹉(Dorridge)
Ⓑ ⊛ ⬠ 🖰 ◆◆◆

HEREFORDSHIRE

● **Brockhampton (Hereford)**
Wye Valley Walk
Ladyridge Farm Guest House, HR1 4SE ☎ 01989 740220 (Carol Grant)
carolgrant@ladyridgefarm.fsworld.co.uk   Map 149/592320
BB **B** ✕ book first £10, 7-9pm S1 D2 T1
Ⓥ Ⓑ Ⓓ ⊛ 🐾🖰 ⬠ ⬡ ! 🖰 ◆◆◆◆

● **Collington (Bromyard)**
The Granary, Church House Farm, HR7 4NA ☎ 01885 410345 (Margaret Maiden)
Map 149,138/655600 BB **B** ✕ £13+, 6-9pm D1 T4 Ⓥ Ⓑ Ⓓ 🐾🖰 ⬡

● **Dilwyn**
Conifers, 6 Orchard Close, HR4 8HQ ☎ 01544 318125 (Miss N J Perry)
Map 148,149/416539 BB **B** ✕ book first £12, 7pm S1 D1 Closed Jan
Ⓥ Ⓓ ⊛ 🐾🖰 ⬠ ! 🖰

● **Eaton Bishop (Hereford)**

☆ **The Ancient Camp Inn**
Ruckhall, HR2 9QX ☎ 01981 250449 (Kathryn Mackintosh)
www.theancientcampinn.co.uk Map 161,149/449393
BB **C** ✕ book first £, 7-9pm D4 T1
Ⓥ Ⓑ Ⓓ ⊛ 🐾🖰 ⬠

Hideaway country inn on the banks of the River Wye between Hay on Wye and Hereford. Landrover transport available to Wye and Golden Valleys, Three Castles and Black Mountains. Family run, excellent food (AA Rosette restaurant), fantastic river views.

● **Fownhope (Hereford)**
Wye Valley Walk
Pippins, Capler Lane, HR1 4PJ ☎ 01432 860677 (Ann Corby) Map 149/581340
BB **B** ✕ nearby T2 Ⓑ Ⓓ ⊛ 🐾🖰 ⬠ !

● **Goodrich (Ross-on-Wye)**
Wye Valley Walk
▪◄ Jolly's Of Goodrich, HR9 6HX ☎ 01600 890352 www.jollysofgoodrich.co.uk
Map 162/574194 BB **B** ✕ nearby D1 T1 Ⓑ ⊛ 🐾🖰

● **Hereford**
Wye Valley Walk
▪◄ The New Priory Hotel, Stretton Sugwas, HR4 7AR ☎ 01432 760264
www.newprioryhotel.co.uk Map 161,148,149/465429
BB **B** ✕ £5-£15, 6:30-9:00pm S2 D4 T1 F1
Ⓥ Ⓑ Ⓓ 🐾🖰 ⬠ ⬡ ! 🖰

● **Hoarwithy (Hereford)**
Wye Valley Walk
▪◄ The Old Mill, HR2 6QH ☎ 01432 840602 (Carol Probert)
www.theoldmillhoarwithy.co.uk Map 149/545293
BB **B** ✕ book first £14-£17, 7pm S1 D4 T2
Ⓥ Ⓑ Ⓓ 🐾🖰 ⬠ ! 🖰 ◆◆◆◆Ⓢ

● **Kington**
Offa's Dyke
▪◄ Burton Hotel, Mill Street, HR5 3BQ ☎ 01544 230323
www.hotelherefordshire.co.uk Map 148/296565
BB **C** ✕ £7.70-£20, 7:30pm onwards S2 D6 T5 F3
Ⓥ Ⓑ Ⓓ 🐾🖰 ! 🖰 ★★★

Church House, Church Road, HR5 3AG ☎ 01544 230534 (Mr & Mrs Darwin)
www.churchhousekington.co.uk Map 148/291567
BB **B** ✕ nearby D1 T1 Ⓓ ⊛ 🐾🖰 ! 🖰

Southbourne, Newton Lane, HR5 3NF
☎ 01544 231706 (Geoff & Patsy Cooper)
geoff_patsy@btopenworld.com Map 148/290570
BB **A** ✕ book first £10, 7pm S1 D2 T2
Ⓥ Ⓓ ⊛ 🐾🖰 ⬠ ! Green Tourism Award

▪◄ The Beacon, Bradnor Hill, HR5 3RE ☎ 01544 230182 (Robert Pritchard)
www.thetopbeacon.co.uk Map 148/292576
BB **B** ✕ book first £6, 6-8pm S1 T2 Ⓑ Ⓓ ⊛ 🐾🖰 ⬠ !

● **Leominster**
Ladymeadow Farm, Luston, HR6 0AS ☎ 01568 780262 (Mrs J Ruell)
www.ladymeadowfarm.co.uk Map 148/483645
BB **B** ✕ nearby S1 D1 T1 F1 Closed Nov-Feb
Ⓑ ⊛ ⬠ ◆◆◆◆

● **Much Birch (Hereford)**

☆ ▪◄ **Pilgrim Hotel**
Ross Road, HR2 8HJ ☎ 01981 540742
www.pilgrimhotel.co.uk Map 149/498310
BB **C** ✕ £20, 7-9pm S4 D12 T4 F2
Ⓥ Ⓑ Ⓓ 🐾🖰 ⬠ ⬡ ! 🖰 ★★★

Beautiful country house hotel set in four acres of parkland, in sleepy village of Much Birch. A wonderful base for a walking holiday, convenient for the Wye Valley Walk. Cosy beamed bar and award winning restaurant. Country breaks: B&B from £38 pp.

● **Much Marcle (Ledbury)**
Wye Valley Walk
▪◄ New House Farm, HR8 2PH ☎ 01531 660604 (Anne Jordan)
Map 149/640320 BB **A** ✕ book first £12.50 D1 T1
Ⓥ Ⓑ Ⓓ 🐾🖰 ⬠ ! ◆◆◆

● Ross-on-Wye
Wye Valley Walk
Sunnymount Hotel, Ryefield Road, HR9 5LU
☎ 01989 563880 (Denise & Bob Robertson)
sunnymount@tinyworld.co.uk   Map 162/606242
BB **B**   ✗ £12.50, 6pm   S1 D4 T2   Ⓥ Ⓑ Ⓓ 🐾 👶 🛏   ◆◆◆◆

Radcliffe Guest House, HR9 7BS   ☎ 01989 563895 (Mrs Sue Wall)
www.radcliffeguesthouse.co.uk   Map 162/597242
BB **C**   ✗ nearby   S1 D2 T2 F1   Ⓑ Ⓓ 🐾 👶 🛏 !   ◆◆◆

●🚃 The Hill House, Howle Hill, HR9 5ST   ☎ 01989 562033 (Duncan or Alex)
www.thehowlinghillhouse.com   Map 162/599207
BB **B**   ✗ book first £7+   D2 F1
Ⓥ Ⓑ Ⓓ 🐾 👶 🛏 ! 🌐 Ⓜ   ◆◆◆

● Stoke Lacy
☆ Dovecote Barn
HR7 4HJ   ☎ 01432 820968 (Judy Young)
www.dovecotebarn.co.uk   Map 149/619494
BB **B**   ✗ book first £18.50   D1 T1
Ⓥ Ⓑ Ⓓ ⊛ 🐾 👶 🛏 ! 🌐

A warm welcome awaits at this 17th century barn, on the edge of the village in a beautiful conservation area. Locally sourced organic food, lavish breakfasts and dinners, or free lifts to excellent pubs nearby. Between Malvern Hills & Black Mountains/Brecon.

● Weobley
●🚃 Mellington House, Broad St, HR4 8SA   ☎ 01544 318537
mellingtonhouse@weobley.freeserve.co.uk   Map 148,149/402516
BB **B**   ✗ nearby   D1 T1 F1   Ⓑ Ⓓ ⊛ 🐾 👶 🛏 ! 🌐

SHROPSHIRE

● Abdon (Craven Arms)
Shropshire Way
Earnstrey Hill House, SY7 9HU   ☎ 01746 712579 (Mrs Jill Scurfield)
Map 137/587873   BB **B**   ✗ book first £18.50   D1 T2
Ⓥ Ⓑ Ⓓ ⊛ 🐾 👶 🛏 !   ◆◆◆◆

● Bayston Hill (Shrewsbury)
Shropshire Way
Lythwood Hall B&B, 2 Lythwood Hall, Lythwood, SY3 0AD
☎ 07074 874747 (Julia Bottomley) lythwoodhall@amserve.net   Map 126/470085
BB **B**   ✗ £12, 6-8pm   S2 D1 T1   〰(Shrewsbury)
Ⓥ Ⓓ ⊛ 🐾 👶 🛏 🌐   ◆◆◆

● Bishop's Castle
Shropshire Way
●🚃 The Old Brick Guesthouse, 7 Church Street, SY9 5AA
☎ 01588 638471 (Norm & Rosie Reid) www.oldbrick.co.uk   Map 137/323885
BB **B**   ✗ nearby   D3 T1 F1   Ⓑ Ⓓ 🐾 👶 🛏 🌐

●🚃 Boars Head Hotel, Church Street, SY9 5AE   ☎ 01588 638521
www.boarsheadhotel.co.uk   Map 137/322884
BB **C**   ✗ £8.50, 6:30-9:30pm   D1 T2 F1
Ⓥ Ⓑ Ⓓ 🐾 👶 🛏 ! 🌐   ◆◆◆

Old Time, 29 High Street, SY9 5BE   ☎ 01588 638467 (Jane Carroll)
www.oldtime.co.uk   Map 137/323888
BB **B**   ✗ nearby   D2 T1   Ⓑ Ⓓ 🐾 👶 🛏 ! 🌐   ◆◆◆

Claremont, Bull Lane, SY9 5BW   ☎ 01588 638170 (Mrs Audrey Price)
www.priceclaremont.co.uk   Map 137/324889
BB **B**   ✗ nearby   D1 T2   Ⓑ Ⓓ ⊛ 🐾 👶 🛏 ! 🌐

●🚃 The Porch House, 33/35 High Street, SY9 5BE   ☎ 01588 638854 (Gill Lucas)
www.theporchhouse.com   Map 137/323888
BB **B**   ✗ nearby   D2   Ⓑ Ⓓ ⊛ 🐾 👶 🛏 !   See SC also

● Broseley
●🚃 Orchard House, 40 King Street, TF12 5NA   ☎ 01952 882684 (Diane Kaiser)
Map 127/671022   BB **B**   ✗ nearby   D1 T1 F1
Ⓑ Ⓓ 🐾 👶 🛏   ◆◆◆

● Bucknell
●🚃 Ash Leys, SY7 0AL   ☎ 01547 530546   (A & G Jenkinson)
scenesetters@btinternet.com   Map 148,137/349740
BB **A**   ✗ nearby   T1   〰(Bucknell)   Ⓑ Ⓓ 🐾 👶 🛏 ! 🌐

The Willows B&B, SY7 0AA   ☎ 01547 530201 (Mr Klaus Steffes)
www.willows-bucknell.co.uk   Map 148,137/355739
BB **B**   ✗ nearby   D3 T1 F1   〰(Bucknell)
Ⓑ Ⓓ ⊛ 🐾 👶   ◆◆◆◆Ⓦ   Veggie breakfasts.

● Church Stretton
Shropshire Way
Dalesford, Carding Mill Valley, SY6 6JF   ☎ 01694 723228 (Mrs C Blount)
Map 137/448943   BB **B**   ✗ book first £7   D1 F1   〰(Church Stretton)
Ⓥ Ⓑ Ⓓ 🐾 👶 🛏 ! 🌐

●🚃 Belvedere Guest House, Burway Road, SY6 6DP   ☎ 01694 722232
www.belvedereguesthouse.co.uk   Map 137/451941
BB **B**   ✗ nearby   D2 T4 F1   〰(Church Stretton)
Ⓑ Ⓓ ⊛ 🐾 👶 🛏 🌐   ◆◆◆◆

☆ Brereton's Farm
Woolston, SY6 6QD   ☎ 01694 781201 (Joanna Brereton)
www.breretonsfarm.co.uk   Map 137/424871
BB **B**   D1 T1   Closed Dec-Feb
Ⓑ Ⓓ ⊛ 🐾 👶 🛏   ◆◆◆◆   See SC also.

Victorian farmhouse on working farm with spacious en-suite rooms offering spectacular views, peace and tranquillity in abundance! Long Mynd and Stiperstones nearby, as are Ludlow, Iron Bridge and Powis Castle. Perfect base for south Shropshire holiday.

☆ 🚃 Brookfields Guest House
Watling Street North, SY6 7AR   ☎ 01694 722314 (Angie & Paul Bradley)
www.smoothhound.co.uk/hotels/brookfieldsgh.html   Map 137,138/459937
BB **B**   ✗ book first £16, 6:30-7:30pm   S1 D2 T1 F1   〰(Church Stretton)
Ⓥ Ⓑ Ⓓ ⊛ 🐾 👶 🛏 !   ◆◆◆◆

Large comfortable Edwardian house and grounds, ample parking. Stroll to town and train station. Luxury en-suite bedrooms. Ideal base for walkers and tourers. Great views of Long Mynd. Licensed. Non-smoking. Drying room. Special rates for weekly or party bookings.

Sayang House, Hope Bowdler, SY6 7DD ☎ 01694 723981 (Patrick & Madeline Egan) www.sayanghouse.com　Map 137,138/476924
BB **B**　✕ book first £15, 6:30pm onwards　D3 T1 F/D2　ᴧᴧᴧ(Church Stretton)
Ⓥ Ⓑ Ⓓ 🐾🍴♿🚗❗🏔　◆◆◆◆

Old Rectory House, Burway Road, SY6 6DW ☎ 01694 724462　(Mike Smith)
info@oldrectoryhouse.co.uk　Map 137/452938
BB **C**　✕ book first £10, 7:30pm　D2 T1　ᴧᴧᴧ(Church Stretton)
Ⓥ Ⓑ Ⓓ ⊛🐾🍴🚗　◆◆◆◆

Jinlye, Castle Hill, All Stretton, SY6 6JP ☎ 01694 723243 (Mrs J Tory)
www.jinlye.co.uk　Map 137,138/456959
BB **B**　✕ nearby　D4 T4　ᴧᴧᴧ(Church Stretton)
Ⓑ Ⓓ ⊛🐾🍴♿　◆◆◆◆◆Ⓒ　Disabled facilities available

🚲⊣ Ragdon Manor, Ragdon, SY6 7EZ ☎ 01694 781389 (Wendy Clark)
www.ragdonmanorbandb.co.uk　Map 137,138/455915
BB **B**　D1 T1　ᴧᴧᴧ(Church Stretton) Ⓑ　Ⓓ🐾🍴♿🚗🏔　◆◆◆◆

☆ **The Longmynd Hotel**
Cunnery Road, SY6 6AG ☎ 01694 722244
www.longmynd.co.uk　Map 137/449935
BB **C**　✕ £18.95, 6:45-9pm　S6 D23 T12 F9　ᴧᴧᴧ(Church Stretton)
Ⓥ Ⓑ Ⓓ🐾🍴♿🏔　★★★　See Groups also.

Breathtaking views, fine restaurant and bar facilities. Ideal location for walking the Shropshire Way and touring the area. Special interest packages and many amenities (incl. sauna, heated pool, golf, croquet) available.
Email: info@longmynd.co.uk

☆ **Malt House Farm**
Lower Wood, SY6 6LF ☎ 01694 751379　(Lyn Bloor)
Map 137,138/466974
BB **B**　✕ book first £15, 7pm　D2 T1　Closed Dec
Ⓥ Ⓑ Ⓓ ⊛🐾♿　◆◆◆

'The Malthouse' is a century old working farm situated on the lower slopes of The Long Mynd Hills AONB. Peace, quiet and stunning scenery. Excellent walking from our door. Many places of interest to visit. Half an hour drive from Ludlow, Shrewsbury and Ironbridge Gorge.
All rooms en-suite, colour television, hairdryers and beverage tray. Comfortable guest lounge. Home cooked dinners available in the beamed dining room. Fully licensed. Warm welcome. Regret: no children or pets.

● **Cleobury Mortimer (Kidderminster)**
Cox's Barn, Bagginswood, DY14 8LS ☎ 01746 718415 (Dinah M Thompson)
www.southshropshire.org.uk/coxsbarn　Map 138/682805
BB **B**　✕ book first £8-£12, 6:30-8:30pm　D3
Ⓥ Ⓑ Ⓓ ⊛🐾🍴🚗🏔　◆◆◆◆

● **Clun**
Shropshire Way
Clun Farm House, High Street, SY7 8JB ☎ 01588 640432
(Anthony & Sue Whitfield) www.clunfarmhouse.co.uk　Map 137/302808
BB **B**　✕ book first £15-£18　S2 D/F1 T/D1 F1
Ⓥ Ⓑ Ⓓ ⊛🐾🍴♿❗🏔

☆ 🚲⊣ **Crown House**
Church Street, SY7 8JW ☎ 01588 640780 (Reg Maund & Judy Bailey)
Map 137/300805
BB **B**　✕ nearby　S1 D1 T1
Ⓑ Ⓓ ⊛🐾🍴♿❗🏔Ⓜ　◆◆◆◆　Veggie breakfasts.

Walking the Shropshire Way or Offa's Dyke? If you visit Clun, visit us! We welcome muddy boots, wet anoraks and happy people. We have superb accommodation in self-contained annexe. Lifts and luggage transfers by arrangement.

🚲⊣ Glebelands, 25 Knighton Road, SY7 8JH ☎ 01588 640442
(John & Judy Adamson) tourism@clun25.freeserve.co.uk　Map 137/299805
BB **B**　✕ nearby　T2　Closed Jan-March
Ⓑ Ⓓ ⊛🐾🍴♿❗　◆◆◆

The White Horse Inn, The Square, SY7 8JA ☎ 01588 640305
www.whi-clun.co.uk　Map 137/300808
BB **B**　✕ £10, 6:30-8:30pm　F2　Ⓥ Ⓑ Ⓓ🐾♿❗🏔　★★★

● **Craven Arms (Newcastle-on-Clun)**
Shropshire Way

☆ 🚲⊣ **Hopton House B&B**
Hopton Heath, SY7 0QD ☎ 01547 530885 (Karen Thorne)
www.shropshirebreakfast.co.uk　Map 148,137/381773
BB **C**　✕ book first £20, 7pm　D1 F1　ᴧᴧᴧ(Hopton Heath)
Ⓑ Ⓓ ⊛🐾🍴♿❗　◆◆◆◆ⓈⓌ

A very comfortable and welcoming converted barn with stunning views, located in the beautiful Clun Valley. With many lovely local walks and just one minute walk to the very scenic Heart of Wales railway line, allowing access to many circular walks in Wales, including Offa's Dyke at Knighton. Both bedrooms are en-suite with TV and drink making facilities, one king size and the other triple or super king size. Full English breakfast and evening meal.

● Ellesmere
Hordley Hall, Hordley, SY12 9BB ☎ 01691 622772 (Mrs Hazel Rodenhurst)
Map 126/381308 BB **B** ✗ book first £12-£14, 6-7pm S1 D2 T1
Ⓥ Ⓑ Ⓓ ⊗ 🐾🚗🚲 ◆◆◆

● Gobowen (Oswestry)
Clevelands, Station Road, SY11 3JS ☎ 01691 661359 (Miss O Powell)
Map 126/302334 BB **A** ✗ nearby S2 D1 �ココ(Gobowen) ⊗ 🐾

● High Ercall (Telford)
Shropshire Way
■⟺◀ The Mill House, Shrewsbury Road, TF6 6BE ☎ 01952 770394 (Judy Yates)
www.ercallmill.co.uk Map 126/584163
BB **B** ✗ nearby D1 T1 F1 Ⓑ Ⓓ ⊗ 🐾🚗🚲! 🐾 ◆◆◆◆

● Ironbridge
Shropshire Way & Monarch's Way
■⟺◀ Post Office House, 6 The Square, TF8 7AQ ☎ 01952 433201 (Janet Hunter)
www.pohouse-ironbridge.fsnet.co.uk Map 127/673034
BB **C** ✗ nearby D1 T1 F1 Ⓑ Ⓓ🐾🚲! 🐾 ◆◆◆

● Knowbury (Ludlow)
Shropshire Way
Stonybrook, Hope Bagot Lane, SY8 3LT ☎ 01584 890570 (Sally Thompson)
www.stonybrook-ludlow.co.uk Map 137,138/581747
BB **B** ✗ nearby D2 ⊗ 🚲🚗 ◆◆◆◆

● Little Stretton (Church Stretton)
Shropshire Way

☆ ■⟺◀ **Conrad House**
6 Ludlow Rd, SY6 6RF ☎ 01694 720197 (Joan Cole)
www.conradguesthouse.co.uk Map 137/443915
BB **B** ✗ nearby D1 T1 �ココ(Church Stretton)
Ⓑ Ⓓ ⊗ 🐾🚲! 🐾

A warm friendly house situated on the edge of the village set amidst the Shropshire Hills. Walking along the Long Mynd Hills begins outside our doorstep! Good food and ale at the village pub, just a two minute walk away. Ludlow is 20 minutes.

● Ludlow
Shropshire Way

☆ **Cecil Guest House**
Sheet Road, SY8 1LR ☎ 01584 872442 (Ron Green)
Map 137,138/525742
BB **B/C** ✗ book first £18, 6:30pm S2 D2 T4 F1 �ココ(Ludlow)
Ⓥ Ⓑ Ⓓ🐾🚗🚲! 🐾 ◆◆◆

Comfortable guesthouse offering relaxed atmosphere, freshly cooked food & spotlessly clean surroundings. 9 bedrooms (7 en-suite), with CH & TV. Residents bar and lounge. Smoking only in bar. Off-street parking. Double/ twin ensuite £28-£31pp (dual occupancy) £38-£41 (single) Standard single £22. Fax/Tel: 01584 872442

■⟺◀ The Mount Guest House, 61 Gravel Hill, SY8 1QS ☎ 01584 874084
(Mandy Callender) rooms@themountludlow.co.uk Map 137,138/515751
BB **B** ✗ nearby S1 D3 T1 ⟺ᴍ(Ludlow)
Ⓑ Ⓓ ⊗ 🐾🚗🚲! 🐾 Ⓜ ◆◆◆

● Melverley (Oswestry)
Severn Way
■⟺◀ Church House, SY10 8PJ ☎ 01691 682754 (Jane Sprackling)
www.members.aol.com/melverley Map 126/332166
BB **B** ✗ nearby D2 T1 Ⓓ ⊗ 🐾🚗🚲 🐾 ◆◆◆◆

● Myddle (Shrewsbury)
■⟺◀ Oakfields, Baschurch Road, SY4 3RX ☎ 01939 290823 (Mrs Gwen Frost)
Map 126/465235 BB **A** ✗ nearby D1 T1 F1 ⟺ᴍ(Yorton)
Ⓓ ⊗ 🐾🚲🐾 ◆◆◆

● Newcastle-on-Clun (Craven Arms)
Shropshire Way & Offa's Dyke
■⟺◀ The Quarry House, Church Rd, SY7 8QJ ☎ 01588 640774 (Michelle Evans)
www.quarry-house.com Map 137/255827
BB **B** ✗ £11.50, 6-9pm D1 T/S/F1 Ⓥ Ⓑ Ⓓ ⊗ 🐾🚗🚲!

● Norbury (Bishop's Castle)
Shropshire Way
Shuttocks Wood, SY9 5EA ☎ 01588 650433 (Ann Williams)
www.smoothhound.co.uk/hotels/shuttock.html Map 137/367924
BB **B** ✗ book first £12.50, 6:30-7pm D2 T2
Ⓥ Ⓑ Ⓓ ⊗ 🐾🚲🚗! ◆◆◆◆

● Oswestry
Offa's Dyke
B.J's, 87 Llwyn Rd, SY11 1EW ☎ 01691 650205 (Barbara Williams)
barbara@williams87.fsnet.co.uk Map 126/294303
BB **A** ✗ nearby D1 T1 Ⓓ🐾🚗🚲 ◆◆◆

● Shrewsbury
Shropshire Way
Lucroft Hotel, Castlegates, SY1 2AD
☎ 01743 362421 (Pia Widen & John Brookes)
www.lucrofthotel.co.uk Map 126/492128
BB **B** ✗ nearby S4 D4 T3 F1 ⟺ᴍ(Shrewsbury) Ⓑ 🚲

☆ ■⟺◀ **Sydney House Hotel**
Coton Crescent, Coton Hill, SY1 2LJ ☎ 01743 354681
www.sydneyhousehotel.co.uk Map 126/490135
BB **B** ✗ nearby S2 D3 T1 F1 ⟺ᴍ(Shrewsbury)
Ⓑ Ⓓ🐾🚗🚲 🐾 ◆◆◆

Within 10 minutes' walk of town centre and train/bus stations. All en-suite rooms. Private car park. Walkers' special needs happily catered for. Residents' bar. £25-30 per person. Major credit cards accepted.

■⟺◀ Abbey Court House, 134 Abbey Foregate, SY2 6AU ☎ 01743 364416
(Mrs V.A Macleod) www.abbeycourt.biz Map 126/503122
BB **B** ✗ nearby S2 D3 T4 F1 ⟺ᴍ(Shrewsbury) Ⓑ 🐾🚲 ◆◆◆◆

● **Trefonen (Oswestry)**
The Pentre, SY10 9EE ☎ 01691 653952 (Helen & Stephen Gilbert)
www.thepentre.com   Map 126/238260
BB **B**   ✕ book first £14, 7:30pm   T1 F2
Ⓥ Ⓑ Ⓓ ⊛ 🛏♿🚗! 🐾   ◆◆◆◆

● **Wem (Shrewsbury)**
   Shropshire Way
Forncet, Soulton Road, SY4 5HR   ☎ 01939 232996 (Mrs Anne James)
Map 126/521292   BB **B**   ✕ nearby   S1 D1 T1   ⋙(Wem)
Ⓓ ⊛ 🐾 🚗

☆ 🛏◄ **Fairview Country B&B**
Paddolgreen, SY4 5QZ ☎ 01939 232302 (Mike Harris)
www.fairviewcountry.co.uk   Map 126/507320
BB **B**   D2   Closed Jan-Feb   ⋙(Wem)
Ⓑ Ⓓ ⊛ 🛏♿🚗!🐾

Situated two miles north of Wem, in a
truly rural setting, Fairview Country
offers the ideal northern stopover for
walking the Shropshire Way and a base
for investigating the ancient north
Shropshire Mosses and Meres with their
intriguing myths and legends.

● **Whixall (Whitchurch)**
   Shropshire Way
Roden View, Dobson's Bridge, SY13 2QL   ☎ 01948 710320 (Jean James)
www.roden-view.co.uk   Map 126/493343
BB **B**   ✕ £10, 6-8:30pm   D1 T2 F1
Ⓥ Ⓑ Ⓓ ⊛ 🛏♿🚗 🐾   ◆◆◆◆

STAFFORDSHIRE

● **Cannock Wood**
   Heart Of England Way
Tuktawa, Uplands Close, WS15 4RH ☎ 01543 684805 (John & Avril Green)
tuktawa@hotmail.com   Map 128/046124
BB **A**   ✕ nearby   S1 D1 T1 F1   Ⓑ   Ⓓ ⊛ 🛏♿

● **Cheadle (Stoke-on-Trent)**
   Staffordshire Way
The Old Convent, Bank Street, ST10 1NR ☎ 01538 756356 (David & Kate Scorey)
Map 119/008432   BB **A**   ✕ nearby   D2 T1   Ⓓ ⊛ 🛏♿🚗 🐾

● **Cheddleton (Leek)**
   Staffordshire Way
🛏◄ Prospect House Guest House, 334 Cheadle Road, ST13 7BW ☎ 0870 7564155
(Rolf & Jackie Griffiths) www.prospecthouseleek.co.uk   Map 118/967506
BB **B**   ✕ book first £14   S1 D1 T1 F2   Ⓥ Ⓑ 🛏♿🚗!🐾   ◆◆◆◆

● **Endon (Stoke-on-Trent)**
   Staffordshire Way
Hollinhurst Farm, Park Lane, ST9 9JB ☎ 01782 502633 (Mr J.Ball)
www.smoothhound.co.uk/hotels/hollinhurst.html   Map 118/942531
BB **B**   D2 T1 F1   Ⓑ ⊛ 🛏♿🚗!🐾   ◆◆◆

● **Greendale (Oakamoor)**
   Staffordshire Way
🛏◄ The Old Furnace, ST10 3AP ☎ 01538 703331
www.oldfurnace.co.uk   Map 128,119/041435
BB **B**   ✕ book first £7.50   S2 D2 T1
Ⓥ   Ⓓ ⊛ 🐾 🚗!   See SC also.

● **Grindon (Leek)**
   Peak District

☆ **Summerhill Farm**
ST13 7TT ☎ 01538 304264 (Mrs P Simpson)
www.summerhillfarm.co.uk   Map 119/083534
BB **B**   ✕ book first £12, 6:30-7pm   D2 T/D1 F1
Ⓥ Ⓑ Ⓓ ⊛ 🛏♿🚗 🐾   ◆◆◆◆

Tastefully furnished, en-suite facilities,
tea/coffee, colour TV. Amid rolling
countryside overlooking the Dove and
Manifold Valleys. "Wonderful for Walkers".
Ideally situated for Buxton, Chatsworth
House, Potteries & Alton Towers. Email:
info@summerhillfarm.co.uk

Horton (Leek)
   Staffordshire Way
Croft Meadows Farm, ST13 8QE ☎ 01782 513039   (Mrs Irene Harrison)
Map 118/921577   BB **A**   ✕ book first £10   S3 D1 T1
Ⓥ Ⓑ Ⓓ ⊛ 🛏♿🚗!Ⓜ

● **Lichfield (Farewell)**
   Heart Of England Way
Little Pipe Farm, Chorley, WS13 8BS (Mrs E Clewley) ☎ 01543 683066
Map 128/078105   BB **B**   ✕ nearby   S1 D1 T1 F1   Ⓓ 🐾 🚗   ◆◆◆

● **Longnor**
   Midshires Way & Pennine Bridleway

☆ 🛏◄ **Spring Cottage B&B**
Leek Rd, SK17 0PA (Garry & Noeleen Roe)
☎ 01298 83101   garry.roe1@btopenworld.com   Map 119/088649
BB **B**   ✕ nearby   D2   Ⓑ   Ⓓ ⊛ 🛏♿🚗!

We offer first-rate accommodation
situated on the edge of the picturesque
village of Longnor. We are perfectly
located to explore the upper reaches of
the Dove and Manifold valleys. Our
hearty walkers' breakfasts are always
prepared with quality local produce.

● **Waterhouses (Stoke-on-Trent)**
   Peak District
Leehouse Farm, Leek Road, ST10 3HW ☎ 01538 308439 (Josie Little)
Map 119/081503   BB **B**   D2 T1
Ⓑ   Ⓓ ⊛ 🛏♿🚗!   ◆◆◆◆Ⓢ

WARWICKSHIRE

● Bidford-on-Avon

Heart Of England Way

▪◄ Fosbroke House, 4 High Street, B50 4BU ☎ 01789 772327 (M Swift)
www.smoothhound.co.uk/hotels/fosbroke.html   Map 150/101519
BB **B**   ✗ nearby   DI TI FI   B D ⊗ ☺   ◆◆◆◆

● Kenilworth

Banner Hill Farmhouse Accommodation, Rouncil Lane, CV8 1NN
☎ 01926 852850 (Mrs Patricia Snelson) Map 140/268708
BB **B**   ✗ book first £8.50   S2 D2 T4 F2   V   B   D   ☺ 🚗 ! ♨

● Long Marston (Stratford-upon-Avon)

Heart Of England Way

Church Farm, CV37 8RH ☎ 01789 720275 (Mrs Taylor)
www.churchfarmhouse.co.uk   Map 151/153484
BB **B**   ✗ nearby   DI T/FI F/DI   B D ⊗ ☺ 🚗 ♨   ◆◆◆◆

● Shustoke (Coleshill, Birmingham)

Heart Of England Way

Priory Farmhouse, B46 2AZ ☎ 01675 481550 (Mrs Margaret Manley)
Map 139/220900   BB **B**   ✗ nearby   S2 D2 TI FI   B D ☺ 🚗 ♨

● Stratford-upon-Avon

Heart Of England Way

▪◄ The Hunter's Moon Guesthouse, 150 Alcester Road, CV37 9DR
☎ 01789 292888 (Rosemary & David Austin) www.huntersmoonguesthouse.com
Map 151/186552   BB **B**   ✗ nearby   S2 D2 T2 FI   ⚌(Stratford-upon-Avon)
B D ☺   ◆◆◆

☆ ▪◄ **Parkfield Guest House**
3 Broad Walk, CV37 6HS ☎ 01789 293313 (Jo & Roger Pettitt)
www.parkfieldbandb.co.uk   Map 151/197546
BB **B**   ✗ nearby   SI D3 T2 FI   ⚌(Stratford-upon-Avon)
B D ⊗ ☺   ◆◆◆

Attractive Victorian house in quiet location, five mins' walk to town centre and Royal Shakespeare Theatre, one min from Greenway leading to Heart of England Way. Most rooms en-suite, with colour TV. Full English or vegetarian breakfast. Brochure on request. Large private car park. Non-smoking.
Email: parkfield@btinternet.com

● Warwick

▪◄ Chesterfields, 84 Emscote Rd, CV34 5QJ ☎ 01926 774864 (Mr William John Chapman) jchapman@chesterfields.freeserve.co.uk   Map 151/296655
BB **B**   ✗ nearby   S2 D2 TI F2   ⚌(Warwick)
B D ☺ 🚗 !   ◆◆◆

WORCESTERSHIRE

● Ashton-under-Hill (Evesham)

▪◄ Holloway Farm House, WR11 7SN ☎ 01386 881910 (M Sanger-Davies)
www.hollowayfarmhouse.btinternet.co.uk   Map 150/998382
BB **B**   ✗ nearby   T2 FI   B D ☺ 🚗 ! ♨

● Bewdley

Severn Way

Bank House, 14 Lower Park, DY12 2DP ☎ 01299 402652 (Fleur Nightingale)
http://bewdley-accommodation.co.uk   Map 138/789754
BB **B**   ✗ nearby   S2 DI TI   D ⊗ 🚗 ♨   ◆◆◆

▪◄ Tarn, Longbank, DY12 2QT ☎ 01299 402243 (Mrs Topsy Beves)
www.tuckedup.com   Map 138/764749
BB **B**   ✗ nearby   S2 T2   Closed Dec-Jan   D ⊗ 🚗 🚗 ! ♨

Severn Valley Guest House, 240 Westbourne St, DY12 1BS ☎ 01299 402192
(Linda & Julian) www.severnvalleyguesthouse.co.uk   Map 138/790754
BB **B**   ✗ nearby   S2 D2 T2 F2   B 🚗 ☺ ♨

● Broadway

Cotswold Way

Southwold House, Station Road, WR12 7DE ☎ 01386 853681
www.broadway-southwold.co.uk   Map 150/091378
BB **B**   ✗ nearby   SI D4 T2 FI   B D ⊗ 🚗 ☺ ♨   ◆◆◆◆⑤

Old Station House, Station Drive, WR12 7DF ☎ 01386 852659
www.broadway-cotswolds.co.uk/oldstationhouse.html   Map 150/090380
BB **B**   ✗ nearby   SI D2 T2 FI   B D ⊗ 🚗 ! ♨   ◆◆◆◆⑤

▪◄ Pathlow House, 82 High Street, WR12 7AJ ☎ 01386 853444 (Adrian Green)
www.pathlowguesthouse.co.uk   Map 150/101376
BB **B**   ✗ £10, 6:30-7:30pm   D5 T3 F2   V   B   D ⊗ 🚗 ♨   ◆◆◆

Brook House, Station Road, WR12 7DE ☎ 01386 852313 (Mrs Marianne Thomas)
brookhouse.broadway@virgin.net   Map 150/090379
BB **B**   ✗ nearby   SI D2 TI FI   B D ☺ ! ♨

▪◄ The Driffold Guest House, Murcot Turn, WR12 7HT ☎ 01386 830825
(Barbara & Mike Reohorn) www.cotswoldsguesthouse.co.uk   Map 150/073405
BB **B**   ✗ nearby   SI DI TI   B D ⊗ 🚗 ☺ 🚗 ! ♨   ★★★

● Evesham

▪◄ Anglers View B&B, 88-90 Albert Rd, WR11 4LA ☎ 01386 442141
(Sarah Tomkotowicz) Map 150/033441
BB **B**   ✗ nearby   S2 DI T3 F2   ⚌(Evesham)
D ⊗ 🚗 🚗 ! ♨   Veggie breakfasts.

● Great Malvern

Severn Way

Croft Guest House, Bransford, WR6 5JD ☎ 01886 832227 (Mrs Ann Porter)
www.croftguesthouse.com   Map 150/795524
BB **B**   ✗ book first £10-£12.50, 7-7:30pm   D4 T/FI
B D 🚗 ☺ ♨   ◆◆◆

Bredon House Hotel, 34 Worcester Road, WR14 4AA ☎ 01684 566990
(Sue Reeves) www.bredonhousehotel.co.uk   Map 150/775463
BB **C**   ✗ book first £   S2 D4 T2 FI   ⚌(Great Malvern) V   B   D 🚗 ☺
🚗 ! ♨   ◆◆◆◆

☆ **Abbey Hotel**
Abbey Road, WR14 3ET ☎ 01684 892332
www.sarova.co.uk/sarova/hotelcollection/abbey   Map 150/775458
BB **C**   ✗ £21.50, 7-9:30pm   S10 D47 T37 F9   ⚌(Great Malvern)
V   B 🚗 ☺ ♨ Ⓜ   ★★★

Sarova Hotels: "Individual venues for individual people". 103 bedrooms. Foot of the Malvern Hills. Brecon Beacons nearby. Near Vale of Evesham. Group accommodation available.
Email: abbey@sarova.co.uk

☆ **Sidney House**
40 Worcester Road, WR14 4AA ☎ 01684 574994
www.sidneyhouse.co.uk   Map 150/775463
BB **B/C** ✕ nearby   S1 D4 T2 F1   ⋙(Great Malvern)
Ⓑ Ⓓ 🐾🛁🌣   ◆◆◆

Run by walkers for walkers!
Grade II listed building. Extensive views, 150 yards from town centre, even less from hills. Tea/coffee facilities, clock alarm radios, hairdryers, Malvern water and colour TV in all rooms. Private facilities. Car park. Licensed.
B&B from £22. AA 3 stars commended.
Email: info@sidneyhouse.co.uk

● **Hartlebury**
Monarch's Way

☆ ⋙ **Garden Cottages**
Crossway Green, DY13 9SL ☎ 01299 250626 (P Terry)
www.gardencottages.co.uk   Map 138/844685
BB **B** ✕ book first £15   S1 D1 T2   ⋙(Hartlebury)
Ⓥ Ⓑ Ⓓ ⊗🐾🛁🚗⛽!🌣   ◆◆◆◆

Traditional oak beamed cottage. All rooms en-suite, colour TV, hospitality tray, hairdryers, irons. Heart of Worcestershire. Close to M5.
Single £35 pppn.
Double £60 per room/night.

● **Malvern Wells**
⋙ Chestnut Hill, Oaklands, Green Lane, WR14 4HU ☎ 01684 564648
pat@chestnut55.freeserve.co.uk   Map 150/776422
BB **B**   S1 D3 T1   Closed Jan-Feb   ⋙(Great Malvern)
Ⓑ Ⓓ ⊗🐾🛁   ◆◆◆

● **Ombersley (Droitwich)**
Severn Way
⋙ Tytchney Gables, Boreley, WR9 0HZ ☎ 01905 620185 (Margaret Peters)
Map 138, 150/825658   BB **B**   S3 D1 T1 F1 Ⓑ   Ⓓ ⊗🐾🛁🚗!🌣

● **Pershore**
⋙ Jofran House, 31 Cherry Orchard, WR10 1EL ☎ 01386 555653
www.jofranhouse.co.uk   Map 150/948462
BB **B** ✕ nearby   S1 D1 T1   ⋙(Pershore) Ⓑ   Ⓓ ⊗🐾🛁

● **Worcester**
Monarch's Way
⋙ University College Worcester, Henwick Grove, WR2 6AJ
☎ 01905 855369   (Deborah Naylor) www.worc.ac.uk   Map 150/834554
BB **B** ✕ book first £7.50, 6pm   S332   Closed Sept   ⋙(Worcester Foregate)
Ⓥ Ⓑ Ⓓ ⊗🐾🛁   See SC & Groups also

Please mention **walk BRITAIN**
when booking your accommodation

SELF-CATERING

HEREFORDSHIRE

● **Kington**
Crossing Cottage ☎ 01625 582550 (N Passey) www.crossingcottage.info
£192-£352 Sleeps 6. 1 cottage. Rural riverside cottage. Offa's Dyke path. ⊗ 🐾

● **Ross-on-Wye**
Main Oaks ☎ 01531 650448 (Mrs P Unwin) www.mainoaks.co.uk
£200-£750 Sleeps 2-7. 6 farm cottages. Beside River Wye, short breaks available.
🐾 ★★★-★★★★

Wye Valley Walk

The Old Mill ☎ 01432 840602 (Carol Probert) www.theoldmillhoarwithy.co.uk
£150-£275 Sleeps 4. 1 cottage. Black and white cottage. ⊗ 🐾 ★★★

● **St Weonards**

☆ **Treago Castle Cottages**
☎ 01981 580208 (Sir Richard & Lady Mynors)
fiona.mynors@cmail.co.uk
£336-£1,596 Sleeps 4+2-10. 3 cottages.
Heated indoor pool. Some cottages interconnect. ⊗ 🐾

The Looseboxes (sleeps 10) Hollyhock House (7+3) The Coach House (4+2)
Comfortably converted from the stable building in the grounds of 15th century Treago Castle. Suit families or large groups, with The Coach House connecting with both The Looseboxes and Hollyhock House.
All have beamed sitting rooms with woodburners, dishwashers and fridge/freezers. Cots and highchairs. Laundry facilities. Storage heaters. Electricity by meter reading. The Looseboxes includes 34ft sitting room with grand piano. 35ft indoor heated pool. Quiet rural situation, with arboretum and vineyard (wines available). Good village shop and bus half a mile. 7 castles locally!
Midway between Black Mountain and Forest of Dean. Close to Wye Valley and Three Castles Walks.

● **Whitbourne**
Dial House ☎ 01886 821534 (Mrs Anne Evans)
a.evans@candaevans.fsnet.co.uk
£330-£595 Sleeps 11 +cot. 19th century farmhouse. Spacious, personally maintained, 5 bedrooms. Fishing. ⊗ 🐾 ★★★

SHROPSHIRE

● All Stretton

☆ **Overbatch House**
☎ 01694 723511 (Chris Cotter)
www.churchstretton.co.uk/acpottery.htm
£225-£300 Sleeps 2-4. 1 cottage. Wood-burning stove. Central heating
utility. ⊗ ♨(Church Stretton)

Eco-friendly converted pottery on side of
Long Mynd. Solar heated water in summer.
Excellent base for walking/cycling the
Shropshire Hills. Double bedroom (converts
to twin). En-suite shower room. Double sofa
bed in living room.
Email: chrisjcotter@yahoo.co.uk

● Bishop's Castle

Maureen Thuraisingham ☎ 01588 638560
maureen@thuraisingham.freeserve.co.uk £185-£275. Sleeps 2-4. 1 cottage.
Open views, garden, log stove, spacious. ♨ ★★★

Annette Bedford ☎ 01588 620770 www.bordercottages.co.uk
£199-£539 Sleeps 2-5. 1 cottage, 1 flat. Relaxing and picturesque country house
setting. ⊗ ♨ ★★★★★

☆ **The Byre**
☎ 01743 891412 (Yvonne and John Hart)
yj.hart@virgin.net
£140-£240 Sleeps 2. 1 studio.
Garden, patio, glorious countryside. ⊗

Luxurious, detached studio nestling in the
heart of the tranquil Shropshire Hills on small
farm. Panoramic views of the Stiperstones
Hills. Long Mynd, Kerry Ridgeway, Offa's Dyke
and Shropshire Way nearby. Walks from door.
AONB. Drop off/pick up available. Email:
yj.hart@virgin.net

☆ **The Porch House**
☎ 01588 638854 (Gill Lucas)
www.theporchhouse.com
£160-£330 Sleeps 2-4. 2 apartments.
Historic Elizabethan town centre house. ⊗ ★★★ See B&B also.

Two recently converted apartments each
with central heating, open fires and
retaining many original features. Off road
parking and cycle store. Real ale pubs and
good choice of restaurants within a short
walk. Close to Long Mynd, Stiperstones and
Offa's Dyke.

● Church Stretton

Lower Barn ☎ 01694 781427 (Mrs Carol Morris)
£140-160 Sleeps 2. 1 cottage. Map 137/423872, near Longmynd/Wenlock Edge. ♨

Poole House ☎ 0151 722 8050 (Carolyn Yates)
http://virtual-shropshire.co.uk/pool £265-£400 Sleeps 4-5. 1 cottage.
Peaceful location, lovely walks, pub nearby. ⊗

☆ **Brereton's Farm**
☎ 01694 781201 (Joanna Brereton)
www.breretonsfarm.co.uk
£270 Sleeps 4. 1 annexe conversion. Closed Feb
Peaceful location. Lovely views. Working farm. ⊗ ♨ ★★★ See B&B also.

Perhaps not the prettiest place you will have stayed at, but this converted
garage/annexe offers excellent comfortable accommodation with twin and double
en-suite rooms and an extensive garden to relax and enjoy extensive views.
Ideal base for enjoying the delights of south Shropshire – Ludlow, Long Mynd,
Ironbridge etc. Email: info@breretonsfarm.co.uk. See Bed & Breakfast also.

☆ **Caradoc Cottage**
☎ 01694 751488 (Wendy Lewis)
www.churchstrettoncottages.co.uk £200-£300 Sleeps 4. 1 cottage.
Superb walking. Woodburner. Short breaks available.
♨(Church Stretton) ★★★★

A central location for exploring beautiful
Shropshire. Adjoins owner's family home
nestling between Stretton Hills. Church Stretton
2 3/4 miles away. Excellent bird watching,
walking from the door. Fully equipped, exposed
beams, wood burner for cosy winter breaks.
Relaxing garden immaculately kept.

● Craven Arms

Hesterworth ☎ 01588 660487 (Roger & Sheila Davies) www.hesterworth.co.uk
£123-£426 Sleeps 2-8. 11 cottages & flats.
Beautiful area, caring owners, short breaks. ♨(Broome) ♨ ★★-★★★

● Knighton

☆ **Black Hall**
☎ 01547 528909 (Andrew or Sharon)
wwwblackhallfarm.com
£270-£695 Sleeps 2-6. 6 cottages.
Log fire, exposed beams, stunning scenery. ⊗

Six luxury Canadian Round Log cottages –
unique to the UK. Situated on a secluded site
just in south Shropshire. Spacious 1-3
bedrooms, some with four poster beds and hot
tubs, woodburners and many other original
features. Ideal for total relaxation or to explore
the surrounding area. Offa's Dyke 1/2 miles.

● **Ludlow**

Goosefoot Barn ☎ 01584 861326 (Mrs S Loft) www.goosefootbarn.co.uk
£190-£425 Sleeps 2-6. 4 cottages.
Tranquil setting. Games room. Short breaks. ⊗ 🛏 ★★★★

☆ **Sutton Court Farm**
☎ 01584 861305 (Jane Cronin)
www.suttoncourtfarm.co.uk
£200-£500 Sleeps 2-6. 6 cottages
Cream teas, evening meals by arrangement. 🛏 ★★★★

Six special cottages set around a peaceful, rural, courtyard in the Corvedale. Walk from the door or explore further afield in the beautiful south Shropshire countryside. Enjoy a cream tea or evening meal on your return (by prior arrangement).

Mocktree Barns ☎ 01547 540441 (Clive & Cynthia Prior)
www.mocktreeholidays.co.uk £195-£375 Sleeps 1-6. 5 cottages.
Country walking from door. Transport available. ⊗ 🛏 ★★★

Mrs Jean Mellings ☎ 01584 873315 www.mellings.freeserve.co.uk
£370-£750 Sleeps 6 + cot. 1 cottage
Cottage, village location, garden. Near Ludlow. ⊗ 🛏 ★★★★★

● **Stiperstones**

☆ **Ovenpipe Cottage**
☎ 01743 791401 (Mrs Penelope Thornton)
www.ovenpipecottage.com
£100-£195 Sleeps 2+1 + cot . 1 cottage.
Breathtaking scenery. Shop and inn nearby. 🛏 ★★★

Attractively restored well-equipped barn at the edge of Stiperstones Nature Reserve.
This peaceful area offers excellent walking and breathtaking views over Shropshire and Welsh Borderland. Long Mynd and Offa's Dyke within easy reach.
Email: tankervillelodge@supernet.com

STAFFORDSHIRE

● **Calton**
  Peak District

☆ **Field Head Farmhouse Holidays**
☎ 01538 308352 (Janet Hudson)
www.field-head.co.uk
£565-£1,195 Sleeps 11-14. 1 farmhouse.
Groups welcome, Sky TV, spa bath. ⊗ 🛏 ★★★★

Grade II listed farmhouse, 5 bedrooms, 2 bathrooms, spa bath/shower room. Well equipped, secluded location set in beautiful surroundings close to Dovedale and the Manifold Valley. Open all year, short breaks, bargain mid-week breaks.
info@field-head.co.uk

● **Hollington**

The Raddle Inn ☎ 01889 507278 (Peter Wilkinson) www.logcabin.co.uk
£250-£350 Sleeps 6 . 6 log cabins. Log cabins in woods with views.
⊗ 🛏 ★★★

● **Oakamoor**

☆ **The Old Furnace**
☎ 01538 703331 (Annette Baxter) www.oldfurnace.co.uk
£30-£40 per day Sleeps 1-3. 1 annexe.
Transport available. Adjoins Staffordshire Way
⊗ 🛏 ★★★ See B&B also.

Comprising three single beds in two rooms, The Annexe is situated beside a trickling stream in beautiful Dimmingsdale. Superb walking all round; Staffordshire Way and National Trust Nature Reserve both 400 yards. Short breaks available all year. EQM Environment Award.

WARWICKSHIRE

● **Aston Cantlow**

☆ **Cantlow Cottage**
☎ 01789 488513 (Mr & Mrs John & Jane Nickless)
www.stratford-upon-avon.co.uk/cantlow.html
£230-£330 Sleeps 3. 1 cottage. Excellent walking in Shakespeare country.
⊗ ᴍᴍ (Wooton Wawen) ★★★

A charming mid-terrace Victorian cottage. One double, one single bedroom, lounge/dining room, woodburner, television, kitchen, electric cooker, dishwasher, microwave and fridge. Utility, washing machine, tumble dryer. Downstairs bathroom. Garden. Parking. Linen, towels, heating and lighting included. Excellent walking.

WORCESTERSHIRE

● **Broadway**

☆ **Yew Tree Cottage**
☎ 01527 63389 (Mrs Lynskey)
www.broadwaycottages.com
£245-£725 Sleeps 4-8. 1 cottage, 1 apt.
Beautiful village location in conservation area. ⊗ 🛏

Yew Tree Cottage is a traditional Cotswold stone cottage overlooking the village green and duck pond in Willersey. Beautifully decorated 3 bedrooms, lounge, dining room. Newly fitted kitchen and bathroom. Lovely gardens. The Huntings is a large 2 bedroom apartment in the very heart of the Broadway.

● **Clifton-on-Teme**

Lion Cottage ☎ 01886 812577 (Janet Lawrence)
£160-£290 Sleeps 4-5. 1 cottage. Next to 12th century village pub. 🛏

● **Great Malvern**

Rosehill Cottage ☎ 01684 561074 (Mrs Gwyn Sloan) sloaniain@hotmail.com
£185-£210   Sleeps 2. I detached studio.
Situated in Malvern Hills, stunning views. ⊗ 🛁 ★★★

● **West Malvern**

Greenbank ☎ 01684 567328 (Mr D G Matthew)
matthews.greenbank@virgin.net   £140-£205   Sleeps 2-4. I flat.
Conservatory, drying room; near Worcestershire Way.
⋙(Colwall) 🛁 ★★★

● **Worcester**

University College Worcester ☎ 01905 855300 (Deborah Naylor) www.worc.ac.uk
£78-£105   Sleeps 6-7. 54 flats.   Easy access to Malvern Hills/Worcester.
Closed Mid-Sept-mid-June ⊗ ⋙(Worcester Forgate)
See B&B also.

GROUPS

HEREFORDSHIRE

Wye Valley Walk

Llangarron (SC) nr Ross-on-Wye ☎ 01600 750333 (Angela Farr)
www.farrcottages.co.uk
SC £150-£700   4 cottages   Min 2, max 30   Ⓓ

☆ **The Talbot Hotel** (B&B)
Leominster, HR6 8EP   ☎ 01568 616347
www.smoothhound.co.uk/hotels/talbot2.html
BB £29-£30   Min 10, max 42 ✂ 🐾
Ⓑ Ⓓ ⚑ ⋙(Leominster) ★★★

Originally a 15th century coaching house sympathetically updated with en-suite
bedrooms. Ideal location for ramblers visiting Herefordshire. Designated Black
and White trail through picturesque villages and beautiful countryside. Special
rates offered for Ramblers Group block bookings.
For enquiries and brochure telephone 01568 616347
www.smoothhound.co.uk/hotels/talbot2.html
talbot@bestwestern.co.uk

SHROPSHIRE

☆ **Longmynd Hotel** (B&B)
Cunnery Rd, Church Stretton ☎ 01694 722244 (Rowena Jones)
www.longmynd.co.uk Map 137/449935
BB £42 Min 20, max 100 ⋙(Church Stretton) ✂ 🐾
Ⓑ Ⓓ See B&B also

Breathtaking views, fine restaurant and
bar facilities. Ideal location for walking
the Shropshire hills and touring the
area. Special interest packages and
many amenities (incl. sauna, heated
pool, golf, croquet) available.
Email: info@longmynd.co.uk

HOSTELS, BUNKHOUSES & CAMPSITES

HEREFORDSHIRE

Heart Of England Way

Berrow House Camping/Bunkhouse (C/B/IH/OC) Hollybush, Ledbury HR8 IET
☎ 01531 635845 www.berrowhouse.co.uk Map 150/763368
Bednight £7 ⊗

PUBS & TEAROOMS

WARWICKSHIRE

● **Henley in Arden (Solihull)**

Heart Of England Way

☕ Henley Ice Cream Ltd, 152 High Street, B95 5BT
☎ 01564 795172 (Cindy Brittan) www.henleyicecream.co.uk Map 151/150655
⋙(Henley In Arden) ✂ Ⓥ ♨ ⊗ Ⓑ(L)

NORTH WEST

Sprawling urban conurbations in Greater Manchester and Merseyside, and the industrial heritage of salt production and textile manufacturing on the Cheshire and Lancashire plains, share the North West region with the rolling Pennines and two great national parks.

Open moorland close to Manchester and neighbouring Rochdale on the edge of the Pennines provides spectacular views of river valleys, meadows and woodland to the south and west.

THE PEAK DISTRICT

Ideal walking country is plentiful in Cheshire, with 2,000 miles of public footpaths serving the lowlands and pastures of the East Cheshire plains, seen best from the sandstone upthrust of Alderley Edge. East Cheshire takes the walker into open hill country as the plains rise towards the gritstone foothills of the Pennines.

A member says:

"The majesty of the Lakeland Peaks, especially when washed white with snow, will take your breath away."

The landscape of Lancashire is similarly divided. There are low sandy beaches and salt marshes on the western coastal plain including the resorts of Morecambe and Blackpool.

Eastwards the open, windswept moors of the south and west Pennines invite walkers to explore the Ribble Valley and the Forest of Bowland.

Perhaps the most popular destination in the North West for walkers and visitors alike is the Lake District, offering rigorous fellwalking and England's highest peak, Scafell Pike (978m), although a gentle stroll around the serene lakes or through bluebell-carpeted woods offers ample opportunity to appreciate the dramatic landscape.

The rest of Cumbria is not to be missed; the wooded river valley of the Eden Way beneath the Pennines cannot fail to impress with its panoramic views of the Howgills and the Lakeland mountains.

In the west, the grassy dunes and stretches of beach on the Solway Coast are excellent not only for discovering the wildlife and nature, but also offer a tantalising taste of Scotland across the Solway Firth.

Long Distance Paths

Coast to Coast Walk..................C2C
Cumbria Way...........................CMB
Dales Way.................................DLS
Hadrian's Wall Path.................HNW
Midshires Way ....MDS
Pennine Bridleway ....PNB
Pennine Way............................PNN
Ribble Way ....RIB
Sandstone Trail........................SAN
Staffordshire Way.....................SFS
Teesdale Way...........................TSD
Trans Pennine Way...................TPW

Public paths:

21,318km / 13,239 miles

Mapped access land:

400 square miles (Area 2, Lower North West) to date

GRITSTONE TRAIL, CHESHIRE

NORTH WEST
LOCAL RAMBLERS CONTACTS

MANCHESTER & HIGH PEAK
AREA SECRETARY
Please contact our main office or visit www.manchester-ramblers.org.uk

GROUP SECRETARIES
Bolton Mr B Wise,
27 Grange Park Road, Bromley Cross, Bolton, Lancs, BL7 9YA
☎ 01204 592786
http://homepage.ntlworld.com/boltonramblers

Bury Mrs M Smith, 87 Bankhouse Road, Bury, Lancashire, BL8 1DY
☎ 0161 764 8598
http://website.lineone.net/~philip-oliver

Mad Walkers (Manchester & District) David Lacey,
18 Hyde Grove, Sale, M33 7TE
www.madwalkers.org.uk

New Mills Mr Allan Minchin,
1 Diglands Avenue, New Mills, Stockport, Cheshire, SK22 4JD
☎ 01663 743983
www.nmramblers.freeserve.co.uk

Oldham Janet Hewitt,
2 Hillside Avenue, Carrbrook, Stalybridge, Cheshire, SK15 3NE
☎ 01457 834769
www.stephenslater.freeserve.co.uk/oldham.htm

Rochdale Mrs S Blatcher, 5 Enfield Close, Rochdale, Lancashire, OL11 5RT
☎ 01706 641041
www.stephenslater.freeserve.co.uk/rochdale.htm

Stockport Mrs L Sangster,
98 Mile End Lane, Great Moor, Stockport, SK2 6BP ☎ 0161 4838774
www.stockportramblers.org.uk

Wigan & District Mr P Taylor,
11 Corfe Close, Aspull, Wigan, Lancs, WN2 1UW ☎ 01942 832938
www.cms.livjm.ac.uk/wiganramblers

MERSEYSIDE & WEST CHESHIRE
AREA SECRETARY
Miss G F Thayer, 53 Bramwell Avenue, Prenton, Wirral, CH43 0RQ
☎ 0151 608 9472

GROUP SECRETARIES
Cestrian (Chester) Ms F Parsons,
32 Wetherby Way, Little Sutton, South Wirral, CH66 4NY
☎ 0151 3391178

Liverpool Mrs M Hems, 19 Moorcroft Road, Liverpool, L18 9UG
☎ 07980 856101
www.liverpoolramblers.co.uk

Merseyside 20s-30s Walkers
Ms B Roche, 212 Pilch Lane, Liverpool, L14 0JQ ☎ 07880 535 221
www.fillyaboots.org.uk

Southport Mr D Wall, 22 Dunbar Crescent, Southport, Merseyside, PR8 3AB ☎ 01704 579924

St Helens Mrs C Walsh, 13 Owen Street, Toll Bar, St Helens, WA10 3DW
☎ 01744 601608

Wirral Mr A Wall, 35 Mount Avenue, Bebington, Wirral, CH63 5QY
☎ 0151 608 0586

LAKE DISTRICT
AREA SECRETARY
Peter Jones, 44 High Fellside, Kendal, LA9 4JG ☎ 01539 723705)
www.ralakedistrict.ukf.net

GROUP SECRETARIES
Carlisle Miss A M Cole, 101 Etterby Lea Crescent, Stanwix, Carlisle, Cumbria, CA3 9JR ☎ 01228 546544
www.ralakedistrict.ukf.net

Furness Mrs P Leverton,
6 Churchill Drive, Millom, Cumbria, LA18 5DD ☎ 01229 772217
www.ralakedistrict.ukf.net

Grange over Sands Mrs Wendy Bowen, Hollyhow, Hazelrigg Lane, Newby Bridge, Ulverston, Cumbria, LA12 8NY ☎ 015395 31785
www.ralakedistrict.ukf.net

Kendal Mr Lester Mather,
5 Airethwaite, Kendal, Cumbria, LA9 4SP ☎ 01539 731788)
www.ralakedistrict.ukf.net

Lancaster Dr Brian Jones,
116 North Road, Carnforth, Lancs, LA5 9LX ☎ 01524 732305
www.ralakedistrict.ukf.net

Penrith Mr Jim Burns, Hawkshead, 3 Asby Hall Mews, Great Asby, Appleby-In-Westmorland, CA16 6EN
☎ 017683 52264
www.ralakedistrict.ukf.net

Summit Good Mr Paul Strzoda,
8 Highcroft Drive, Allithwaite, Grange-over-Sands, LA11 7QL ☎ 015395 33523
www.lakedistrictwalkers.co.uk

West Cumbria Mr David Woodhead, Cropple How, Birkby, Ravenglass, Cumbria, CA18 1RT ☎ 01229 717270
www.ralakedistrict.ukf.net

MID LANCASHIRE
AREA SECRETARY
Mr D Kelly, 4 Buttermere Close, Bamber Bridge, Preston, Lancs, PR5 4RT ☎ 01772 312027
www.lancashire-ramblers.org.uk

GROUP SECRETARIES
Chorley Mrs J Tudor Williams, Oaklands, 5 The Bowers, Chorley, Lancs, PR7 3LA
www.lancashire-ramblers.org.uk/chorley

Fylde Mr D J Stokes, 7 Cedar Close, Newton With Scales, Kirkham, Lancs, PR4 3TZ ☎ 01772 671134
www.lancashire-ramblers.org.uk/fylde

Garstang & District Mrs C Stenning, 20 Meadowcroft Avenue, Catterall, Garstang, Lancs, PR3 1ZH
☎ 01995 601478

Lancashire Walking Group
Mr P Roberts, ☎ 07812 555668
www.lypwc.org.uk

Preston Mr A Manzie, 3 Ruthin Court, Dunbar Road, Ingol, Preston, Lancs, PR2 3YE ☎ 01772 736467
www.prestonra.co.uk

South Ribble Mr B A Kershaw,
2 Moss Way, New Longton, Preston, Lancs, PR4 4ZQ

West Lancashire Mr W G Wright,
49 Riverview, Tarleton, Preston, Lancs, PR4 6ED ☎ 01772 812034
www.wiechers.freeserve.co.uk/ramblers/wlramble.htm

NORTH EAST LANCASHIRE
AREA SECRETARY
Mrs S Baxendale, 101 Blackburn Road, Clayton-Le Moors, Accrington, Lancs, BB5 5JT ☎ 01254 235049

GROUP SECRETARIES
Blackburn & Darwen Miss M G Brindle, 103 School Lane, Guide, Blackburn, BB1 2LW ☎ 01254 671269

Burnley & Pendle Mrs M Broadley, 18 Station Road, Padiham, Lancashire, BB12 8EB ☎ 01282 778 153
http://bpramblersassn.mysite.freeserve.com

Clitheroe Mr B Brown, 2 Chorlton Terrace, Barrow, Whalley, Clitheroe, Lancs, BB7 9AR ☎ 01254 822851

Hyndburn Mr P J Bedson, 8 Mill Street, Church, Accrington, Lancs, BB5 4EJ ☎ 01254 399559
www.hyndburnramblers.co.uk

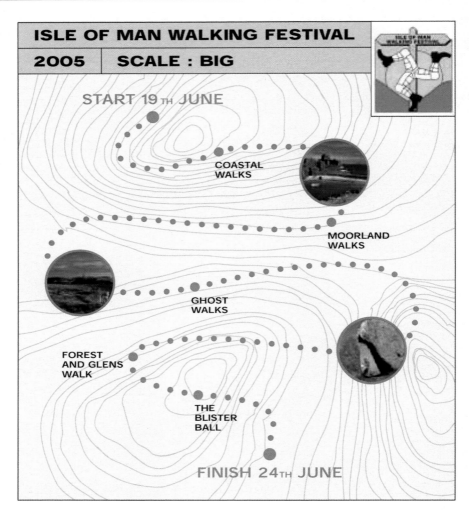

ISLE OF MAN WALKING FESTIVAL

2005 | SCALE : BIG

START 19TH JUNE

COASTAL WALKS

MOORLAND WALKS

GHOST WALKS

FOREST AND GLENS WALK

THE BLISTER BALL

FINISH 24TH JUNE

Whether you're an ambler or a rambler, there's so much more to the Isle of the Man when you explore it on foot. The landscape is endlessly varied, the wildlife and the history uniquely compelling and the lifestyle perfectly relaxing.

Six-night festival packages include return travel, accommodation, walks and social events and start from just £282*.

* Based on two sharing

To book, call 01624 66 11 77 or visit our website at www.isleofmanwalking.com quoting WF01.

Isle OF man

VisitIsleofMan.com

Rossendale Mr P G Aizlewood, Lynwood, 265 Haslingden Old Road, Rossendale, BB4 8RR ☎ 01706 215085 www.waidew.btinternet.co.uk

SOUTH & EAST CHESHIRE
GROUP SECRETARIES

Congleton Mrs J Rishworth, 54 Bailey Crescent, Congleton, Cheshire, CW12 2EW ☎ 01260 271869

East Cheshire Mr Ian Mabon, `Highwinds', 15 Churchfields, Bowdon, Altrincham, Cheshire, WA14 3PL ☎ 0161 928 3437 [fax Also]

South Cheshire Mr P Callery, 45 Broughton Lane, Wistaston, Crewe, CW2 8JR ☎ 01270 568714 www.ramblerssouthcheshire.org.uk

NORTH & MID CHESHIRE
AREA SECRETARY

Mrs D Armitage, Birchtree Bungalow, Red Lane, Appleton, Warrington, WA4 5AB ☎ 01925 268540 http://nmc-ramblers.org.uk

GROUP SECRETARIES

Halton Mr Phil Williams, 21 Castner Ave, Weston Point, Runcorn, WA7 4EG http://nmc-ramblers.org.uk/halton1.htm

North & Mid Cheshire Under 40 Mr A Williams, 39 Acton Avenue, Appleton, Warrington, WA4 5PS www.cheshirewalkers.freeserve.co.uk

Vale Royal and Knutsford Mrs D Armitage, Birchtree Bungalow, Red Lane, Appleton, Warrington, WA4 5AB

Warrington Mr M & Mrs B Elebert, Yellow Lodge, Park Lane, Higher Walton, Warrington, WA4 5LW

LOCAL RAMBLERS PUBLICATIONS

Cown Edge Way (Manchester Area): 32km/20-mile walk in six sections from Hazel Grove, Stockport to Gee Cross, Woodley. £1 from 31 Wyverne Road, Manchester M21 0ZW. Cheques to Ramblers' Association Manchester Area.

The Cumbria Way by John Trevelyan, ISBN 1 855681 97 8 (Lake District Ramblers/Dalesman). Concise guide to this popular 112kmk/70-mile route from Ulverston to Carlisle. £2.99 post free from Lakeing, Grasmere, Ambleside LA22 9RW, cheques to Lake District Ramblers' Association.

Round Preston Walk by Preston Ramblers. 37km/23-mile walk around Preston. £1.80 post free from 3 Ruthin Court, Dunbar Road, Ingol, Preston PR2 3YE. Cheques to Ramblers' Association Preston Group.

Rambles Around Oldham by Oldham Ramblers. 20 easy walks of between 6.5km/4 miles and 16km/10 miles, all connecting with bus services. £3.50 + 50p p&p from A Forster, 682 Ripponden Road, Oldham OL4 2LP. Cheques to Oldham Ramblers Book Account.

Ten Walks around Preston by Preston Ramblers. Walks of 6.5km/4

miles to 11km/7 miles, one in each of Preston's parishes, on separate A4 sheets in a plastic wallet. £2.30 post free from 3 Ruthin Court, Dunbar Road, Ingol, Preston PR2 3YE. Cheques to Ramblers' Association Preston Group.

25 Favourite Walks in the Ribble Valley by Clitheroe Ramblers, ISBN 1 901184 72 2. 25 walks from 6.5km/4 miles to 9.5km/6. £5.99 from 1 Albany Drive, Salesbury, Blackburn BB1 9EH. Cheques to The Ramblers' Association Clitheroe Group Social Account. (New this year)

Walks Around Carlisle & North Cumbria ISBN 0 9521458 0 4 (Carlisle Ramblers). 17 fairly easy walks of between 8km/5 miles and 14.5km/9 miles in the lowland countryside around Carlisle. £3.50 post free to members+ 50p p&p to non-members from 24 Currock Mount, Carlisle CA2 4RF. Cheques to Carlisle Ramblers.

Walks Around Heywood by S Jackson and D M Williams (Rochdale Ramblers). 20 easy to moderate walks of 5km/3 miles to 10km/6 miles in Heywood and surrounding area. £3 + 50p p&p from 152 Higher Lomax Lane, Heywood OL10 4SJ. Cheques to Ramblers' Association Rochdale Group.

Walks from the Limestone Link New edition, 2003. 17 easy walks of between 2km/1.5 miles and 16km/10 miles in the beautiful limestone area north of Lancaster, and the 19km/12-mile Limestone Link path.

Walks in the Lune Valley 14 walks of between 4km/2.5 miles and 24km/15 miles, and the Lune Walk, 37km up the north bank of the river and 38.5km/24 miles down the south bank.

Walks in North West Lancashire 15 easy walks of between 6.5km/4 miles and 14.5km/9 miles in the areas surrounding the rivers Lune, Keer and Wyre and parts of Silverdale and Arnside and Forest of Bowland AONBs. All £2.95 + 45p p&p each from 116 North Road, Carnforth LA5 9LX. Cheques to Ramblers' Association Lancaster Group.

Walks in the Kendal Area Book 1, 3rd edition, ISBN 0 904350 40 1. 18 low level walks within 16km/10 miles of Kendal.

Walks in the Kendal Area Book 3, 2nd Edition, ISBN 0 904350 37 1: mostly lower level walks of between 6.5km/4 miles and 24km/15 miles within 16km/10 miles of Kendal. Each £2.95 post free from Mrs M Adams, 6 Riverbank Road, Kendal LA9 5JS. Cheques payable to Ramblers Kendal Group.

millets stores in this region

ALTRINCHAM		101 George Street WA14 1RN
AMBLESIDE	Unit 12 Market Cross Shopping Centre LA22 9BT	
BIRKENHEAD		32/34 Borough Pavement CH41 2XX
BLACKPOOL		22 Church Street FY1 1EW
BOLTON		53/55 Victoria Square BL1 1RY
BURNLEY		64/66 St James Square BB11 1NH
CARLISLE		59 English Street CA3 8JU
CHESTER		15/17 Northgate CH1 1HA
CREWE		7 Queensway CW1 2HH
KENDAL		26/28 Highgate LA9 4SX
KESWICK		85/87 Main Street, Cumbria CA12 5DT
LANCASTER		7 Cheapside LA1 1LY
LEIGH	Unit 33 Spinning Gate Centre, Ellesmere St WN7 4PG	
LIVERPOOL		15 Ranelagh Street L1 1JW
MACCLESFIELD		45 Mill St SK11 6NE
MANCHESTER		Unit 49 Arndale Centre M4 2HU
PRESTON		28 Market Place PR1 2AR
SOUTHPORT		4/8 Tulketh Street, Merseyside PR8 1AQ
St. HELENS		2/4 Cotham Street WA10 1SQ
STOCKPORT		29/31 Princes Street SK1 1SU
WARRINGTON	28 Golden Square Shopping Centre WA1 1QE	
WIGAN		24/26 Market Street WN1 1HX
ISLE OF MAN		13 The Strand Shopping Centre IM1 2ER

BED & BREAKFAST

CHESHIRE

● **Altrincham**
   Trans Pennine Trail
▪️🛏️◀ Oasis Hotel, 46-48 Barrington Road, WA14 1HN ☎ 0161 928 4523
www.oasishotel.co.uk   Map 109/769885
BB **B** ✕ £10, 5:30-10:30pm   S10 D11 T9 F3   ⋙(Altrincham)
Ⓥ Ⓑ Ⓓ 🐾☕👤 ★★

● **Church Minshull (Crewe)**
Higher Elms Farm, Cross Lane, Minshull Vernon, CW1 4RG
☎ 01270 522252   (Mrs A M Charlesworth)
http://members.aol.com/tomsworld/higherelmsfarmhomepage.html
Map 118/669607   BB **B**   ✕ nearby   S1 D1 T1 F1
Ⓑ Ⓓ☺🐾☕🚗🏠 ♦♦♦

● **Congleton**
   Staffordshire Way
▪️🛏️◀ Yew Tree Farm, North Rode, CW12 2PF   ☎ 01260 223569
(Mrs Sheila Kidd) www.yewtreebb.co.uk   Map 118/890665
BB **B** ✕ book first £14, 6:30pm   D1 F1
Ⓥ Ⓑ Ⓓ☺🐾☕🚗 ♦♦♦♦

● **Macclesfield**
▪️🛏️◀ Ryles Arms, Hollin Lane, Higher Sutton, SK11 0NN
☎ 01260 252244 (Ian Brown) www.rylesarms.com   Map 118/939695
BB **C** ✕ £15, 6:30-9:30pm   D3 T1 F1 Ⓥ Ⓑ Ⓓ☺🐾☕👤! ♦♦♦♦

● **Manley (Frodsham)**
   Sandstone Trail
Rangeway Bank Farm, WA6 9EF   ☎ 01928 740236 (Jane Challoner)
Map 117/517717   BB **B** ✕ book first £10   D1 T1 F1   ⋙(Mouldsworth)
Ⓥ Ⓑ Ⓓ☺🐾☕🚗!🏠

● **Nantwich**
▪️🛏️◀ Downstream, 44 Marsh Lane, CW5 5LH ☎ 01270 625125
(Nancy Cleave) www.downstream.me.uk   Map 118/644519
BB **B**   ✕ nearby   F1   ⋙(Nantwich) Ⓑ Ⓓ☺🐾☕Ⓜ

Oakland House, Blakelow, CW5 7ET   ☎ 01270 567134
(Sandra & Malcolm Groom)   Map 118/689513
BB **B**   ✕ nearby   S1 D8   ⋙(Nantwich)
Ⓑ Ⓓ☺🐾☕🚗!🏠 ♦♦♦♦♦

● **Northwich**
Ash House Farm, Chapel Lane, Acton Bridge, CW8 3QS ☎ 01606 852717
(Mrs S M Schofield) www.ashhousefarm.co.uk   Map 117/587755
BB **B**   S1 D1 T1 F1   ⋙(Acton Bridge) Ⓑ Ⓓ🐾☕🚗   ♦♦♦♦

Manor Farm, Cliff Road, Acton Bridge, Weaverham, CW8 3QP ☎ 01606 853181
(Mrs Terri Campbell) terri.mac.manorfarm@care4free.net Map 117/587767
BB **B** ✕ nearby   S1 D1 T1   ⋙(Acton Bridge)
Ⓑ Ⓓ☺🐾☕🚗!🏠 ♦♦♦♦

● **Oakmere (Northwich)**
▪️🛏️◀ Springfield, Chester Rd, CW8 2HB ☎ 01606 882538
(Mark & Julie Newns) mark.newns@dsl.pipex.com Map 117/570692
BB **B** ✕ nearby   S2 D1 T1 F1   ⋙(Delamere) Ⓑ Ⓓ☺🐾☕🏠

● **Romiley (Stockport)**
Upper Watermeetings Barn, Watermeetings Lane, SK6 4HJ ☎ 01614 270220
www.watermeetingsbarn.com   Map 109/954905
BB **B** ✕ nearby   S1 D1 T1 F1   ⋙(Romiley) Ⓑ Ⓓ🐾☕🚗🏠

● **Siddington (Macclesfield)**
▪️🛏️◀ The Golden Cross Farm, SK11 9JP
☎ 01260 224358 (Hazel Rush)   Map 118/848707
BB **B** ✕ nearby   S2 D2   Ⓑ Ⓓ☺👤🚗 ♦♦♦

● **Spurstow (Tarporley)**
   Sandstone Trail
Haycroft Farm, Peckforton Hall Lane, CW6 9TF ☎ 01829 260389
(Richard Spencer) www.haycroftfarm.co.uk   Map 117/554573
BB **B** ✕ nearby   S2 D2 T2 F1   Ⓓ☺🐾☕🚗!🏠   See Groups also.

● **Willaston (South Wirral)**
Pollards Inn, Village Sq, CH64 2TU ☎ 0151 3274615
www.liverpool-wirral.com   Map 117/329776
BB **B**   ✕ book first £, 7-9pm   D4   ⋙(Hooton)
Ⓥ Ⓑ Ⓓ🐾☕   Bar food available during day

● **Wincle (Macclesfield)**
   Peak District
Hill Top Farm, SK11 0QH   ☎ 01260 227257 (Mrs Susan Brocklehurst)
brocklehurst@mcs.co.uk   Map 118/965661
BB **B**   ✕ book first £11, 6-6:30pm   D1 T2   Closed Dec-Feb
Ⓥ Ⓑ Ⓓ☺🐾☕🚗🏠 ♦♦♦♦

● **Wybunbury (Nantwich)**

☆ ▪️🛏️◀ **Lea Farm**
Wrinehill Road, CW5 7NS ☎ 01270 841429 (Mrs Jean E Callwood)
contactus@leafarm.co.uk   Map 118/716489
BB **B**   ✕ book first £7, 7pm   D1 T1 F1
Ⓥ Ⓑ Ⓓ☺🐾☕🚗🏠 ♦♦♦

Charming farmhouse set in landscaped gardens where peacocks roam. 150 acres of peaceful family farm. Delightful bedrooms. All amenities, some en-suite rooms. Snooker/pool table. Fishing available.

CUMBRIA

● **Allonby (Maryport)**
Bowscale Farm, CA15 6RB ☎ 0777 304 7591 (Brenda Wilson)
Map 85/102431   BB **B**   ✕ nearby   S1 D2 T1 F1
Ⓑ Ⓓ🚗!   See SC & Groups also.

● **Alston**
   Pennine Way
▪️🛏️◀ Greycroft, Middle Park, The Raise, CA9 3AR
☎ 01434 381383 (Mrs P M Dent) www.greycroft.co.uk   Map 86/706463
BB **B**   ✕ nearby   S1 D1 T/F1   Ⓑ Ⓓ☺🐾☕🚗! ♦♦♦♦Ⓢ

High Field, Bruntley Meadows, CA9 3UX ☎ 01434 382182
(Mrs Celia Pattison) cath@cybermoor.org.uk   Map 87/720461
BB **A**   ✕ £8, 7-9pm   S1 D1 T1 F1   Ⓥ Ⓑ Ⓓ☺🐾☕
Remedial massages available

The Cumberland Hotel, Townfoot, CA9 3HX ☎ 01434 381875
(Helen & Guy Harmer) www.cumberlandalston.co.uk Map 86,87/717464
BB **B** ✗ £7.50+, 6:30-9pm D2 T2 FI Ⓥ Ⓑ Ⓓ 🛏️🍴♨️

● **Ambleside**
Lake District
Coast To Coast Walk & Cumbria Way
Brantfell, Rothay Road, LA22 0EE ☎ 015394 32239/34124
(Chris & Jane Amos) www.brantfell.co.uk Map 90/374043
BB **B/C** ✗ nearby SI D6 T2 F2 Ⓑ Ⓓ 🛏️🍴♨️ ◆◆◆◆

☆ **The Old Vicarage**
Vicarage Road, LA22 9DH ☎ 015394 33364
www.oldvicarageambleside.co.uk Map 90/373044
BB **C** ✗ nearby S2 D8 T2 F2
Ⓑ Ⓓ 🛏️🍴♨️ ◆◆◆◆

Quality Bed & Breakfast accommodation. Quiet central location. Own car park. Pets welcome. All bedrooms have TV, hairdryer, alarm clock radio, video, mini fridge, kettle, CH, private bath/shower and WC. Indoor heated pool, sauna & hot-tub. Email: the.old.vicarage@kencomp.net

☆ **Croyden House**
Church Street, LA22 0BU ☎ 015394 32209 (Sylvia & John Drinkall)
www.croydenhouseambleside.co.uk Map 90/376043
BB **B** ✗ nearby S3 D6 T4 F2
Ⓑ Ⓓ 🛏️🍴♨️

A guest house centrally situated on a quiet street 2 minutes walk from the main bus stop and centre of Ambleside. Offering a friendly welcome, generous home cooked breakfasts, comfortable rooms with TV, tea/coffee making facilities and private car park.

☆ **Smallwood House Hotel**
Compston Road, LA22 9DJ ☎ 015394 32330
www.smallwoodhotel.co.uk Map 90/375044
BB **B** ✗ £18, 6:30-7:30pm S2 D4 T3 F3
Ⓥ Ⓑ Ⓓ 🛏️🍴♨️ ◆◆◆◆ See Groups also.

We pride ourselves on a quality, friendly service in the traditional way.

Dinners and packed lunches. Drying facilities. Group discounts. Winter breaks. Leave your cars in our car park and walk from here.

Please telephone Anthony or Christine Harrison for a full brochure & tariff.

enq@smallwoodhotel.co.uk

Norwood House, Church Street, LA22 0BT ☎ 015394 33349
(Mr & Mrs K Morgan) www.norwoodhouse.net Map 90/375043
BB **B** ✗ nearby S2 D4 T2 F2 Ⓑ Ⓓ 🛏️🍴♨️ ◆◆◆◆

Lyndale Guest House, Lake Road, LA22 0DN ☎ 015394 34244
(Alison Harwood) www.lyndale-guesthouse.co.uk Map 90/377036
BB **B** ✗ nearby S2 D2 T2 F2 Ⓑ Ⓓ 🛏️🍴♨️ ◆◆◆

☆ **Nab Cottage**
Rydal, LA22 9SD ☎ 015394 35311 (Liz & Tim Melling)
www.rydalwater.com Map 90/355064
BB **B** book first £15, 7pm SI D2 T2 F2 Closed Jul-Sept 🚶(Windermere)
Ⓥ Ⓑ Ⓓ 🛏️🍴♨️ ◆◆◆

A Grade II listed 16th century cottage overlooking Rydal Water. Once home of Thomas de Quincey and Hartley Coleridge. Superb walks in every direction. Delicious home cooked food. Informal atmosphere. Email: tim@nabcottage.com

☆ **Broadview Guest House**
Low Fold, Lake Road, LA22 0DN ☎ 015394 32431 (Alan & Sue Clarke)
www.broadview-guesthouse.co.uk Map 90/377036
✗ nearby D3 TI F2
Ⓑ Ⓓ 🛏️🍴♨️ ◆◆◆

Comfortable non-smoking B&B in Ambleside, short stroll from village & Lake Windermere at Waterhead. Always a warm welcome & a hearty breakfast. Packed lunches, morning weather reports & drying facilities. Walks start from our front door. Special breaks available all year.

☆ **Stepping Stones**
Under Loughrigg, LA22 9LN ☎ 015394 33552 (Amanda Rowley)
www.steppingstonesambleside.com Map 90/366055
BB **B** ✗ nearby D3 TI
Ⓑ Ⓓ 🛏️🍴♨️ ◆◆◆◆ See SC also.

Lakeland stone Victorian house, set in outstanding location with spectacular views over river, stepping stones and fells. Beautifully appointed, spacious bedrooms with period furnishings. Walks from door. Landscaped gardens with ample private parking.

● **Appleby-in-Westmorland**
☆ **Limnerslease**
Bongate, CA16 6UE ☎ 017683 51578 (Mrs Kathleen Coward)
http://mysite.freeserve.com/limnerslease Map 91/689200
BB **B** ✗ nearby D2 TI Closed Dec 🚶(Appleby)
Ⓓ 🛏️🍴♨️

"Limnerslease" is a charming guest house situated in the historic picturesque market town of Appleby-in-Westmorland. You are assured a warm welcome and clean, comfortable accommodation. 5 mins walk from town centre and 10 mins walk from the famous Carlisle to Settle line.

☆ 🍴◄ **Bongate House**
CA16 6UE ☎ 017683 51245 (Anne & Malcolm Dayson)
www.bongatehouse.co.uk   Map 91/689200
BB **B**   ✕ nearby   S1 D3 T2 F2   Closed Nov-Feb   ⋙(Appleby)
Ⓥ Ⓑ Ⓓ 🐾🍵🛏🚗❗🎿 ◆◆◆◆

Attractive comfortable Georgian guesthouse in acre of garden. 8 bedrooms, 5 en-suite all with CH, TV & beverage facilities. Hearty breakfasts & lovely walks. Lakes, Pennines & Eden Valley. Groups welcome. Selection of eating places close at hand. information@bongatehouse.co.uk

● **Arnside**
Willowfield Hotel, The Promenade, LA5 0AD   ☎ 01524 761354
(Janet & Ian Kerr) www.willowfield.uk.com   Map 97/456788
BB **B**   ✕ book first £14.50, 7pm   S2 D3 T4 F2   ⋙(Arnside)
Ⓥ Ⓑ Ⓓ ⊛ 🐾🛏🚗❗ ◆◆◆◆

Stonegate, Promenade, LA5 0AA ☎ 01524 762560 (Kate Moore)
kmoore@beeb.net   Map 97/455786
BB **B**   ✕ nearby   S2 D2 T1   ⋙(Arnside) Ⓑ Ⓓ ⊛ 🐾🛏🚗🎿

● **Bampton (Penrith)**
   Lake District
   Coast To Coast Walk

☆ **Mardale Inn**
CA10 2RQ ☎ 01931 713244 (Neil & Katherine Stocks)
www.mardaleinn.co.uk   Map 90/514181
BB **B**   ✕ £8, 6-8pm   D3 T3
Ⓥ Ⓑ ⊛ 🐾🛏🚗🎿

Welcoming 18th century inn with en-suite accommodation, near Haweswater. Entirely non-smoking. Wooden beams, open fire, real ale & homemade food using local produce. Tranquil location in beautiful countryside, by Coast to Coast route. Email: info@mardaleinn.co.uk

● **Bampton Grange (Penrith)**
   Lake District
   Coast To Coast Walk
Crown & Mitre Hotel, CA10 2QR ☎ 01931 713225
www.freewebs.com/crownmitre   Map 90/520179
BB **B** ✕ £5.25-£7.90, 6-9:30pm   S2 D1 T1 F2   Ⓥ Ⓑ Ⓓ 🐾🛏🚗❗🎿

● **Boot (Eskdale)**
   Lake District
The Post Office, Dale View, CA19 1TG ☎ 019467 23236 (John & Leigh Gray)
www.booteskdale.co.uk   Map 89,90/176010
BB **B**   ✕ nearby   S1 D2 T1   ⋙(Dalegarth) Ⓓ 🐾🛏

● **Borrowdale (Keswick)**
   Lake District
   Coast To Coast Walk & Cumbria Way
6 Chapel Howe, Stonethwaite, CA12 5XG ☎ 017687 77649
(Christine J Edmondson) rcj.edmondson@aol.com   Map 89, 90/260139
BB **B**   ✕ nearby   D2 T1   Closed Dec   Ⓓ 🐾🛏🎿

🍴◄ Royal Oak Hotel, CA12 5XB   ☎ 017687 77214
www.royaloakhotel.co.uk   Map 90/259148
BB **C**   ✕ £10, 7pm   S2 D5 T2 F6   Ⓥ Ⓑ Ⓓ 🐾🛏🚗❗🎿 ★

● **Bowness-on-Solway**
   Hadrian's Wall
Kings Arms, CA7 5AF   ☎ 016973 51426
www.kingsarms.fsnet.co.uk   Map 85/222627
BB **B**   ✕ £5.50, 6-9pm   T2 F2   Ⓥ Ⓓ 🐾🛏🎿

● **Bowness-on-Windermere (Windermere)**
   Lake District
   Dales Way

☆ **Lingwood**
Birkett Hill, LA23 3EZ ☎ 015394 44680 (Mr R I Atkinson)
www.lingwood-guesthouse.co.uk   Map 96,97/402963
BB **B**   ✕ nearby   D3 T1 F2   ⋙(Windermere)
Ⓑ Ⓓ ⊛🛏 ◆◆◆◆

A modern family run guest house in a quiet location but within 400 yards of Lake Windermere. A 10 minute walk from the end of the Dales Way and free off road parking whilst you walk it!

☆ 🍴◄ **Virginia Cottage**
Kendal Rd, LA23 3EJ ☎ 01539 444891 (David Clarke)
www.virginia-cottage.co.uk   Map 96,97/403967
BB **B**   ✕ nearby   S1 D11   ⋙(Windermere)
Ⓑ Ⓓ 🐾🛏🎿

Virginia Cottage is located in the heart of Bowness only 150 yards from Lake Windermere. Shops, restaurants and pubs are even closer. Quality accommodation comprising 4 poster beds, complimentary sherry, TV/Video & CD player. Free parking & leisure facilities. Pets welcome.

● **Brampton**
   Hadrian's Wall
New Mills House, CA8 2QS ☎ 016977 3376 (Janet Boon)
www.newmillshouse.co.uk   Map 86/549617
BB **B**   ✕ book first £12.50+, 7:30-8pm   D1 T1   ⋙(Brampton)
Ⓥ Ⓑ Ⓓ ⊛🐾🛏❗🎿 ◆◆◆

● **Brough (Kirkby Stephen)**
🍴◄ The Castle Hotel, Main St, CA17 4AX ☎ 01768 341252 (Tracey Letaief)
zakaradog@hotmail.com   Map 91/794146
BB **B**   ✕ £6.95, 6-8:30pm   S3 D6 T3 F2
Ⓥ Ⓑ Ⓓ 🐾🚗❗

● **Broughton-in-Furness**
   Lake District
Middlesyke, Church Street, LA20 6ER ☎ 01229 716549 (David & Sarah Hartley)
Map 96/208876   BB **B**   ✕ nearby   D2   ⋙(Foxfield)
Ⓑ Ⓓ ⊛🐾🛏❗🎿 Ⓜ ◆◆◆◆Ⓢ

The Black Cock Inn, Princes St, LA20 6HQ ☎ 01229 716529
(Alex & Dale Jarvis) www.theblackcockinncumbria.co.uk Map 96/212874
BB **B** ✕ £7.99, 5:30-9:30pm D3 FI ⋘(Foxfield)
Ⓥ Ⓑ Ⓓ 🐾 ⛄ 🚗 ! 🛏 ◆◆◆◆

● **Caldbeck (Wigton)**
   Lake District
   Cumbria Way

☆ ⋙ **The Briars**
Friar Row, CA7 8DS ☎ 016974 78633 (Dorothy H Coulthard)
Map 90/325399
BB **B** ✕ nearby SI DI TI
Ⓑ Ⓓ ⊛ ⛄ ◆◆◆

Situated in Caldbeck village, overlooking Caldbeck Fells. Ideal for touring Lake District, Scottish Borders and Roman Wall. We are right on the Cumbrian Way route. Near Reivers cycle route. Tea-making facilities. Rooms en-suite with TV. 2 mins walk to village inn.

☆ **Swaledale Watch**
Whelpo, CA7 8HQ ☎ 016974 78409 (Mr & Mrs Savage)
www.swaledale-watch.co.uk Map 90/309396
BB **B** ✕ nearby D2 TI FI
Ⓑ Ⓓ ⊛ 🐾 ⛄ 🚗 ! ◆◆◆◆Ⓢ

Enjoy comfort, beautiful surroundings and peaceful countryside on our farm. Central for touring or walking the northern fells. Lifts to and from Caldbeck village available. A warm welcome awaits you. Ideal for the Cumbria Way. All rooms have private facilities.

● **Carlisle**
   Hadrian's Wall, Cumbria Way & Pennine Way

Angus Hotel & Almonds Bistro, 14 Scotland Road, Stanwix, CA3 9DG
☎ 01228 523546 www.angus-hotel.co.uk Map 85/400571
BB **C** ✕ £18, 6-9pm S3 D3 T4 F4 ⋘(Carlisle)
Ⓥ Ⓑ Ⓓ 🐾 ⛄ ! 🛏 ◆◆◆◆
Free packed lunch for **walk BRITAIN** readers!

Craighead, 6 Hartington Place, CA1 IHL
☎ 01228 596767 (Mrs Pam Smith) Map 85/406559
BB **B** ✕ nearby SI D2 TI FI ⋘(Carlisle)
Ⓑ Ⓓ ⊛ 🐾 ⛄ ! 🛏 ◆◆◆

⋙ 'Dalroc', 411 Warwick Road, CA1 2RZ ☎ 01228 542805 (Mrs M Irving)
www.dalroc.co.uk Map 85/421559
BB **A** ✕ nearby SI DI TI ⋘(Carlisle) Ⓓ 🐾 ⛄ 🚗 ! ★★★

Number Thirty One, 31 Howard Place, CA1 IHR ☎ 01228 597080
(Prue Irving) www.number31.freeservers.com Map 85/407559
BB **B/C** ✕ book first £20, 6-9pm D/S2 TI ⋘(Carlisle)
Ⓥ Ⓑ Ⓓ ⊛ 🐾 ⛄ ! ◆◆◆◆◆◆Ⓖ

⋙ Knockupworth Hall, Burgh Road, CA2 7RF ☎ 01228 523531
(Patricia Dixon) www.knockupworthdi.co.uk Map 85/370566
BB **B** ✕ book first £10+, 7pm D2 T2 FI Closed Dec ⋘(Carlisle)
Ⓥ Ⓑ Ⓓ ⊛ 🐾 ⛄ 🚗 !

Abberley House, 33 Victoria Place, CA1 IHP ☎ 01228 521645
www.abberleyhouse.co.uk Map 85/406561
BB **B** ✕ nearby S3 D2 T2 FI ⋘(Carlisle) Ⓑ Ⓓ ⊛ ⛄ ! ◆◆◆◆

⋙ Marlborough House, Marlborough Gardens, Stanwix, CA3 9NW
☎ 01228 512174 (Ian McKenzie Brown) www.marlborough-housebb.co.uk
Map 85/399570 BB **B** ✕ nearby SI D3 T3 F3 ⋘(Carlisle)
Ⓑ Ⓓ ⊛ 🐾 ⛄ ! 🛏 ◆◆◆

⋙ Cambro House, 173 Warwick Rd, CA1 ILP ☎ 01228 543094
(David & Alice) davidcambro@aol.com Map 85/412559
BB **B** ✕ nearby D2 TI ⋘(Carlisle) Ⓑ Ⓓ ⊛ 🐾 ⛄ ! ◆◆◆◆

● **Cartmel (Grange-over-Sands)**
Bank Court Cottage, The Square, LA11 6QB
☎ 015395 36593 (Mrs P C Lawson) Map 96,97/378787
BB **B** ✕ nearby SI DI ⋘(Grange) Ⓓ ⊛ 🐾 ⛄ 🛏 ◆◆◆

● **Coniston**
   Lake District
   Cumbria Way

☆ **Beech Tree House**
Yewdale Road, LA21 8DX ☎ 015394 41717
Map 96/302976
BB **B** ✕ nearby D6 T2
Ⓥ Ⓑ Ⓓ ⊛ 🐾 ⛄ 🚗 ◆◆◆◆

Charming 18th century house with attractive gardens situated 150m from the village centre and all amenities. Ideally situated for a walking holiday or overnight stay on the Cumbria Way. Good drying facilities, ample parking. B&B from £21. Ensuites available.

☆ ⋙ **Thwaite Cottage**
Waterhead, LA21 8AJ ☎ 015394 41367 (Marguerite & Graham Aldridge)
www.thwaitcot.freeserve.co.uk Map 96/311977
BB **B** ✕ nearby D2 TI
Ⓑ Ⓓ ⊛ 🐾 ⛄ ◆◆◆◆

A beautiful 17th century cottage in a peaceful wooded garden, close to village and lake. Central heating, log fires, beamed ceilings. Bathrooms, private or en-suite. Off road parking. Non-smoking.

Lakeland House Guest House, Coffee & Eating Hse, Tilberthwaite Ave, LA21 8ED
☎ 015394 41303 www.lakelandhouse.com Map 96,97/304976
BB **B** SI D3 TI F5 Ⓑ Ⓓ ⊛ 🐾 ⛄ ! 🛏 ◆◆◆

Waverley, Lake Road, LA21 8EW ☎ 015394 41127 (Jenny Graham)
Map 96,97/302974 BB **A** ✕ nearby SI DI TI FI Ⓓ ⊛ 🐾 🛏

Crown Hotel, LA21 8ED ☎ 015394 41243
www.crown-hotel-coniston.com Map 96, 97/304976
BB **B** ✕ £10, until 9pm D6 T4 F2 Ⓥ Ⓑ Ⓓ ⊛ 🐾 ⛄ ◆◆◆◆

Orchard Cottage, 18 Yewdale Road, LA21 8DU ☎ 015394 41319
(Jean Johnson) www.conistonholidays.com Map 96,97/302976
BB **B** ✕ nearby D2 TI Ⓑ Ⓓ ⊛ 🐾 ⛄ 🚗 ! Ⓜ ◆◆◆◆

☆ ⌾◀ **Wilson Arms**
Torver, LA21 8BB ☎ 015394 41237 (Frances Mayvers)
Map 96,97/283941
BB **B** ✕ book first £, 6:30-9pm SI D4 TI F2
Ⓥ Ⓑ ⊛ 🍴♨ ⛽ ! ▓ ◆◆◆

Comfortable rooms with en-suite facilities, TV and tea/coffee making facilities. Good walking area, within easy reach of Coniston Water and the Central Lakes.

☆ ⌾◀ **Wheelgate Country Guest House**
Little Arrow, LA21 8AU ☎ 015394 41418 (Steve & Linda Abbott)
www.wheelgate.co.uk Map 96,97/290950
BB **C** ✕ nearby S2 D3 TI
Ⓑ Ⓓ ⊛ 🍴♨ ⛽ ◆◆◆◆◆ See SC also.

17th century farmhouse with beamed ceilings, spacious en-suite bedrooms and cosy bar. Excellent breakfasts cater for all tastes. Ideally situated for access to central Lakes, with superb local walks to suit all ages and abilities.

☆ ⌾◀ **Yew Tree Farm**
LA21 8DP ☎ 01539 441433 (Caroline Watson)
www.yewtree-farm.com Map 96,97/319998
BB **B** D2 T2 FI
Ⓑ Ⓓ ⊛ 🍴 ! ▓ See SC also.

In the beautiful Yew Dale Valley this picturesque farmhouse once owned by Beatrix Potter is one of the Lake District's most photographed farms. Surrounded by superb walking to suit all, we offer a special experience in this historic farmhouse. Original oak features throughout, cosy guest lounge with real fire, unlimited tea, coffee and biscuits. Hearty breakfasts in the dining room furnished by Beatrix Potter herself. A very warm welcome awaits you.

● Cowgill (Dent)
Yorkshire Dales
Dales Way
River View, Lea Yeat, LA10 5RF ☎ 015396 25592 (Mr & Mrs Playfoot)
www.dedicate.co.uk./river_view Map 98/761869
BB **B** ✕ book first £15, 7pm DI TI ⋙(Dent)
Ⓥ Ⓑ Ⓓ ⊛ 🍴⛽ !

● Dent (Sedbergh)
Yorkshire Dales
Dales Way
⌾◀ Rash House, Dent Foot, LA10 5SU ☎ 015396 20113 (Mrs A E Hunter)
annehunter21@msn.com Map 98/667897
BB **A** ✕ book first £10, 6.30pm DI FI Ⓥ Ⓓ 🍴♨⛽ ! ▓

Garda View Guest House, Main Street, LA10 5QL ☎ 015396 25209
(Rita Smith) rita@gardaview.co.uk Map 98/705870
BB **B** ✕ nearby SI D2 TI Ⓑ Ⓓ ⊛ 🍴♨

⌾◀ Whernside Manor, LA10 5RE ☎ 015396 25213 (Louise Johnson)
www.whernsidemanor.com Map 98/725858
BB **B** ✕ book first £16, 6:30pm SI DI TI Closed Dec-Jan ⋙(Dent)
Ⓥ Ⓓ ⊛ 🍴♨⛽ ! Ⓜ ◆◆◆◆

Stone Close, Main Street, LA10 5QL (Heather Pleasance) ☎ 015396 25231
www.dentdale.com Map 98/705869 BB **B** ✕ book first £12.50, until
5:30pm SI DI T/FI Ⓥ Ⓓ ⊛ 🍴♨⛽ Ⓜ ◆◆◆

● Dufton (Appleby)
Pennine Way & Teesdale Way
Ghyll View, CA16 6DB ☎ 017683 51855 (Mrs M Hullock) Map 91/691250
BB **B** ✕ nearby, 7pm S2 DI T2 Closed Dec-Jan Ⓑ Ⓓ 🍴

⌾◀ Coney Garth, CA16 6DA ☎ 017683 52582 (Mrs J T Foster)
www.coneygarth.co.uk Map 91/685257
BB **B** ✕ book first £10, 7-7:30pm DI TI FI
Ⓥ Ⓑ Ⓓ ⊛ 🍴♨⛽ !

● Eamont Bridge (Penrith)
River View, 6 Lowther Glen, CA10 2BP ☎ 01768 864405 (Mrs C O'Neil)
http://river-view.co.uk Map 90/524285
BB **B** ✕ nearby S2 D2 T2 Closed Dec ⋙(Penrith)
Ⓑ Ⓓ 🍴♨⛽

● Ennerdale Bridge (Cleator)
Lake District
Coast To Coast Walk
Low Cock How, Kinniside, CA23 3AQ ☎ 01946 861354 (Mrs D Bradley)
www.walk-rest-ride.co.uk Map 89/056144
BB **C** ✕ book first £10 SI T2 FI Ⓥ Ⓓ 🍴♨⛽ ▓

● Eskdale Green
Lake District
⌾◀ The Ferns, CA19 1UA ☎ 019467 23217 (John & Jenny Prestwood)
www.eskdalebreaks.co.uk Map 89/142000
BB **B** ✕ nearby D2 TI ⋙(Eskdale Green) Ⓑ Ⓓ ⊛ 🍴♨⛽ !

● Garrigill (Alston)
Pennine Way
⌾◀ Ivy House, CA9 3DU ☎ 01434 382501 (Ms Laurie Taft)
www.bedandbreakfastcumbria.co.uk Map 86,87/744414
BB **B** ✕ nearby S3 D2 T3 F2 Ⓑ Ⓓ ⊛ 🍴♨⛽ ! ▓

● Gilsland (Brampton)
Hadrian's Wall & Pennine Way
⌾◀ The Hill on the Wall, CA8 7DA ☎ 016977 47214 (Mrs Elaine Packer)
www.hadrians-wallbedandbreakfast.com Map 86/624668
BB **C** ✕ book first £15, 7-7:30pm DI T2
Ⓥ Ⓑ Ⓓ ⊛ 🍴♨ ◆◆◆◆Ⓢ

Glenridding (Penrith)
Lake District
Coast To Coast Walk

☆ ▰◂ **Moss Crag Guest House**
CA11 0PA ☎ 017684 82500 (Mr Mark Hook)
www.mosscrag.co.uk   Map 90/385170
BB **C**   ✗ book first £18, 6:30-9pm   D4 T2
Ⓥ Ⓑ Ⓓ ⊛ ⏴⏴ ⏶ ⌂   ◆◆◆

Overlooking Glenriddingbeck and Dodd.
Step out the door to a walker's paradise, or sail on the lake and come back for morning coffee, light lunch or afternoon tea.

Fax: 017684 82500
Email: info@mosscrag.co.uk

Grange-over-Sands
▰◂ Corner Beech Guest House, I Methven Terr, Kents Bank Rd, LA11 7DP
☎ 015395 33088 (Ian Wright) www.cornerbeech.co.uk   Map 96,97/402772
BB **C**   ✗ book first £15, 6:30pm   D3 T1 F1   Closed Dec-Jan
▰(Grange-over-Sands) Ⓥ Ⓑ Ⓓ ⊛ ⏴⏴ ⏶ ⌂ !   ◆◆◆◆

Grasmere (Ambleside)
Lake District
Coast To Coast Walk & Cumbria Way
Silver Lea Guest House, Easedale Rd, LA22 9QE ☎ 015394 35657
(Dorothy Walker) www.silverlea.co.uk   Map 90/335079
BB **C**   ✗ book first £10, 6:30pm   D2 T2   Closed Dec-Feb
Ⓥ Ⓑ Ⓓ ⊛ ⏴⏴ ⏶   ◆◆◆◆

Oak Lodge, Easedale Rd, LA22 9QJ ☎ 015394 35527 (Mrs Alison Dixon)
www.oaklodge-grasmere.co.uk   Map 90/331081
BB **B**   ✗ nearby   D2 T1   Ⓑ Ⓓ ⊛ ⏴⏴ ⏶

▰◂ Thistle Grasmere, Keswick Rd, LA22 9PR ☎ 0870 3339135
www.grasmerethistle.co.uk   Map 90/341068
BB **B/C**   ✗ £19.95, 7-9pm   S17 D22 T27 F6
Ⓥ Ⓑ Ⓓ ⏴⏴ ⏶ ⌂   ★★★

☆ **Dunmail House**
Keswick Road, LA22 9RE ☎ 015394 35256 (Trevor & Lesley Bulcock)
www.dunmailhouse.com   Map 90/339084
BB **B**   ✗ nearby   S1 D3 T1 F0
Ⓑ Ⓓ ⏴⏴ ⏶   ◆◆◆◆

A traditional stone house with a friendly family atmosphere. Beautiful views from all rooms and the spacious gardens. Convenient for lake and village. Non-smoking. Car park.
enquiries@dunmailhouse.freeserve.co.uk

Grayrigg (Kendal)
Dales Way
Punchbowl House, LA8 9BU ☎ 01539 824345 (Mrs D Johnson)
www.punchbowlhouse.co.uk   Map 97/580972
BB **B**   ✗ book first £15, 7:30pm   D2 T1   Closed Jan-Feb
Ⓥ Ⓑ Ⓓ ⊛ ⏴⏴ ⏶   ◆◆◆◆Ⓢ

Great Corby (Carlisle)
Hadrian's Wall
▰◂ Riverside B&B, Brocklewath House, Randlaw Lane, CA4 8NL
☎ 01228 562370 (Mrs Jan Rhodes) www.riverside-stay.co.uk Map 86/487518
BB **B**   ✗ book first £12, 6-7pm   S1 T1
Ⓥ Ⓓ ⊛ ⏴⏴ ⏶ ⌂ ! ⌂   ◆◆◆◆

Helton (Penrith)
Lake District
▰◂ Beckfoot Country House, Guest Accommodation, CA10 2QB
☎ 01931 713241 (Mrs Lesley White) www.beckfoot.co.uk   Map 90/500210
BB **C**   ✗ nearby   S1 D3 T2 F1   Closed Jan
Ⓥ Ⓑ Ⓓ ⏴⏴ ⏶ ⌂ ⌂   ◆◆◆◆

Hesket Newmarket (Caldbeck)
Lake District
Cumbria Way
Newlands Grange, CA7 8HP ☎ 016974 78676 (Mrs Dorothy Studholme)
studholme_newlands@hotmail.com   Map 90/350394
BB **B**   ✗ book first £9.50, 6:30pm   S1 D1 T1 F2
Ⓑ Ⓓ ⊛ ⏴⏴ ⏶ ⌂ ! ⌂   See SC also.

Ings (Kendal)
Lake District
Dales Way

☆ **Meadowcroft Guesthouse**
LA8 9PY ☎ 01539 821171 (R Keen)
www.meadowcroft-guesthouse.com   Map 97/446986
BB **B**   ✗ nearby   S1 D4 T1 F4   ▰(Windermere)
Ⓑ Ⓓ ⊛ ⏴⏴ ⏶ ⌂ ⌂

Meadowcroft is for visitors who seek a rural location in a small hamlet at the gateway to England's most beautiful national park — the Lake District.

Ings is just 2 miles from Kendal. Meadowcroft overlooks hills and fells in an area of outstanding natural beauty and provides a superb base from which to explore Lakeland. Meadowcroft is just 12 miles from junction 36 of the M6 — it is ideal for a comfortable break on the long journey north or south.

Kendal
Lake District
Dales Way
▰◂ Hillside Bed & Breakfast, 4 Beast Banks, LA9 4JW
☎ 01539 722836 (Mrs Joanne Buchanan)
www.hillside-kendal.co.uk   Map 97/513925
BB **B**   ✗ nearby   S3 D3 T1   ▰(Oxenholme)
Ⓑ Ⓓ ⊛ ⏶   ◆◆◆

☆ ▨◣ The Glen

Oxenholme, LA9 7RF ☎ 01539 726386 (Chris Green)
www.smoothhound.co.uk/hotels/glen2.html Map 97/534900
BB **B** ✕ book first £15, 6-6:30pm S1 D3 T1 F2 ⟱(Oxenholme)
Ⓥ Ⓑ Ⓓ ⊛ ⬛⬛⬛ ⬛ ! ⬛ ◆◆◆◆

We are situated in a quiet location on the outskirts of Kendal under 'The Helm', where there is a local walk & viewpoint of the Lakeland Mountains, but within short walk of country pub and restauarnt. Ideal for touring the Lakes & Yorkshire Dales.

Sundial House, 51 Milnthorpe Road, LA9 5QG ☎ 01539 724468
(Sue & Graeme Richardson) sundialgh@aol.com Map 97/516916
BB **B** ✕ book first £10-£15 S2 D2 T2 F/D/T1 ⟱(Oxenholme)
Ⓥ Ⓑ Ⓓ ⬛⬛⬛ ⬛

Bridge House, 65 Castle Street, LA9 7AD
☎ 01539 722041 (Sheila Brindley)
www.bridgehouse-kendal.co.uk Map 97/521930
BB **B** ✕ nearby S1 D1 T1 ⟱(Kendal) Ⓑ Ⓓ ⊛ ⬛⬛ ⬛ ⬛

● Kentmere (Kendal)
Lake District

Maggs Howe, LA8 9JP ☎ 01539 821689 (Mrs Christine Hevey)
www.smoothhound.co.uk/hotels/maggs Map 90/462041
BB **B** ✕ book first £11, 7pm S1 D1 T1 F1
Ⓥ Ⓑ Ⓓ ⬛⬛⬛ ⬛ ! ⬛

● Keswick
Lake District
Cumbria Way

☆ ▨◣ Richmond House

39 Eskin Street, CA12 4DG ☎ 017687 73965
www.richmond-house.net Map 89,90/270232
BB **B** ✕ book first £14, 7pm D3 T1
Ⓥ Ⓑ Ⓓ ⊛ ⬛⬛ ⬛ ◆◆◆

Lakeland stone guesthouse.
Ideal for walking, climbing, trekking. All rooms en suite.
Menu choice before all meals.
Separate TV and bar lounges—ornate alpine bar.
Non-smoking, drying room.
Big enough to cater for walking parties.

☆ Tarn Hows

3-5 Eskin Street, CA12 4DH ☎ 017687 73217
www.tarnhows.co.uk Map 89, 90/268233
BB **B** ✕ book first £13 (groups only), 6:30pm S2 D5 T1
Ⓥ Ⓑ Ⓓ ⊛ ⬛⬛ ⬛ ⬛ ◆◆◆◆

Traditional Victorian residence pleasantly situated in a quiet location, Tarn Hows is only a few minutes walk from the town centre, with easy access to the lake and the surrounding fells. Private car park. Non-smoking. Drying facilities.

▨◣ Seven Oaks Guest House, 7 Acorn Street, CA12 4EA ☎ 017687 72088
(L Furniss & C Firth) www.sevenoaks-keswick.co.uk Map 89,90/269232
BB **B/C** ✕ nearby S1 D4 T2 F1 Ⓑ Ⓓ ⊛ ⬛⬛ ⬛ ⬛ ! ◆◆◆

Melbreak House, 29 Church Street, CA12 4DX ☎ 017687 73398
(John, Jen & Carol Hardman) www.melbreakhouse.co.uk Map 89,90/269232
BB **B** ✕ nearby D7 T3 Ⓑ Ⓓ ⊛ ⬛⬛ ⬛ ⬛ ◆◆◆

Anworth House, Vegetarian B&B, 27 Eskin Street, CA12 4DQ ☎ 01768 772923
(Miss Garland & Mr Love) www.anworthhouse.co.uk Map 89,90/270232
BB **B** ✕ book first £10, 7pm D4 T1 Ⓥ Ⓑ Ⓓ ⊛ ⬛⬛ Ⓜ ◆◆◆

☆ Hedgehog Hill

18 Blencathra Street, CA12 4HP ☎ 017687 74386 (Nel & Keith Nicholls)
www.hedgehoghill.co.uk Map 89,90/269233
BB **B** ✕ nearby S2 D3 T1
Ⓑ Ⓓ ⊛ ⬛⬛ ⬛ ◆◆◆

Wet clothes and boots are welcome in our friendly Victorian guesthouse near town centre, fells and lake. Freshly prepared breakfasts with choice.
Packed lunches available.
Flasks filled for free.
All rooms with colour TV, tea/coffee making facilities.
Most rooms en-suite.
Central heating.
Mountain views.
Motorcycle parking.
Non-smoking.
Credit cards accepted.
rambler@hedgehoghill.co.uk

☆ ▨◣ Glencoe Guest House

21 Helvellyn, CA12 4EN ☎ 017687 71016 (Teresa Segasby)
www.glencoeguesthouse.co.uk Map 89,90/269233
BB **B** ✕ nearby S1 D3 T2
Ⓑ Ⓓ ⊛ ⬛⬛ ⬛ ⬛ ! ◆◆◆◆

Victorian home offering high quality accommodation & services. A warm welcome assured. Quiet, en-suite rooms. Excellent Breakfasts. Keswick centre 5 mins. Drying room, cycle storage, weather reports, maps & books. Ideal for walking, cycling or touring. Email: ramblers@glencoeguesthouse.co.uk

☆ Greystones

Ambleside Road, CA12 4DP ☎ 017687 73108 (Robert & Janet Jones)
www.greystones.tv Map 89/268232
BB **B** ✕ nearby S1 D5 T2 Closed Nov-Dec
Ⓑ Ⓓ ⊛ ⬛ ◆◆◆◆

Tranquil location with excellent fell views. Short walk to the market square and Lake Derwentwater. Eight delightful en-suite rooms, each with TV and hot drinks tray. Aga cooked breakfasts. Drying and storage facilities. ETC Highly Commended. Non-smoking. Parking.

Grassmoor Guest House, 10 Blencathra Street, CA12 4HP
☎ 017687 74008 (Mike Hirst/ Maureen Shirvell)
www.grassmoor-keswick.co.uk   Map 89,90/269233
BB **B**   ✗ nearby   D/T2 F/D/T2   V B D ⊗ 🚗 ⅃ ⚑ ! M
♦♦♦♦ⓦ   Laundry facilities & internet access.

☆ Cumbria House
1 Derwentwater Place, Ambleside Road, CA12 4DR   ☎ 017687 73171
(Barry & Cathy Colam) www.cumbriahouse.co.uk   Map 89,90/268232
BB **B**   ✗ book first £14 (groups only), 6:45pm
S3 D2 T3 F1   Closed Dec-Jan
V B D 🚗 ⅃ ⚑ M   ♦♦♦♦   Discounts for car-free guests.

We can't guarantee the weather — but at least we have an efficient drying room and provide a local weather forecast twice a day.

Freshly cooked breakfast using local produce with plenty of choice, home made rolls, marmalade & jams, plus Fairtrade teas, coffees & fruit juice.

Comfortable lounge with library of walking books.

At the UK's first Green Globe Benchmarked and Climate-neutral guest house, be assured your stay will be as environmentally sustainable as possible. We'll even give discounts to car-free guests.

Advice on walks freely given or Pace the Peaks with Cathy & Kim

See walking hollidays also

☆ Badgers Wood

30 Stanger Street, CA12 5JU   ☎ 017687 72621 (Anne Paylor)
www.badgers-wood.co.uk   Map 89,90/265235
BB **B**   ✗ nearby   S2 D4 T1   Closed Jan
B D ⊗ ⅃   ♦♦♦♦

A friendly welcome awaits you at this delightful Victorian terraced house situated in a quiet elevated position just a 2 minute walk from the heart of town, with its shops, restaurants and bus station.

All our comfortable, attractive rooms are en-suite, furnished to a high standard with colour TVs and tea/coffee making facilities and have views of the surrounding fells.

For our guests' comfort we are totally non-smoking.

Honister House, 1 Borrowdale Road, CA12 5DD   ☎ 017687 73181
(Sue Harrison) www.honisterhouse.co.uk   Map 89/267233
BB **B**   ✗ nearby   D3 T2 F2   B D ⊗ 🚗 ⅃   ♦♦♦♦
Vegetarian society approved

Clarence House, 14 Eskin St, CA12 4DQ   ☎ 017687 73186
(Jenny & Pat Stokes) www.clarencehousekeswick.co.uk   Map 89,90/269232
BB **B**   ✗ nearby   D4 T1 F3   B D ⊗ 🚗 ⅃ 🚗 ⚘   ♦♦♦♦

Lakemere Guest House, 13 Leonard ST., CA12 4EL   ☎ 01768 772772
(Les & Julie Stevens) www.lakemere.co.uk   Map 89,90/269233
BB **B**   ✗ nearby   S1 D2 T1 F1   B D ⊗ 🚗 ⅃ !

☆ Hazeldene Hotel
The Heads, CA12 5ER   ☎ 01768 772106
www.hazeldene-hotel.co.uk   Map 89,90/264232
BB **B**   ✗ nearby   S1 D10 T4 F2
B D ⊗ 🚗 ⅃ ⚘   ♦♦♦♦

At Hazeldene Hotel our aim is simple: to provide our guests with exceptional quality and value accommodation in an outstanding location.

Large en-suite bedrooms, excellent food and a relaxed and peaceful atmosphere combine to make Hazeldene a perfect holiday haven.

Email: info@hazeldene-hotel.co.uk

☆ Hawcliffe House
30 Eskin Street, CA12 4DG   ☎ 017687 73250 (Diane & Ian McConnell)
www.hawcliffehouse.co.uk   Map 89,90/270232
BB **B**   ✗ nearby   D3 T2 F1
B D ⊗ 🚗 ⅃

Small, family run guest house.
Warm welcome assured.
Non-smoking.
Packed lunches available on request.
Short walk from town centre.

Call Diane for more information.

☆ The Paddock Guest House
Wordsworth Street, CA12 4HU   ☎ 017687 72510 (Val & Alan Hewer)
www.thepaddock.info   Map 89,90/270235
BB **B**   ✗ nearby   D4 T1 F1
B D ⊗ 🚗 ⅃   ♦♦♦♦

A warm welcome awaits you at the Paddock, a delightful residence dated mid 18th century. Close to the town centre and lake.
En-suite rooms with all facilities.
Non-smoking. Parking. Own keys.
RAC 4 Sparkling Diamond Award.

☆ High Hill Farm
High Hill, CA12 5NY ☎ 017687 74793 (Lillian and Keith Davies)
lillankei@btinternet.com   Map 89/262238
BB **B** ✕ nearby D2 T1
🅱 🅳 ⊗ 🐾 ♨ Ⓜ

Former farmhouse, 5 mins level walk
to town centre. B&B for non-smokers
in 3 en-suite rooms with tea/coffee &
beautiful views. Parking. Special
breaks of 3 days plus — except bunk
houses. Excellent centre for walking.

☆ ▰◀ Appletrees
The Heads, CA12 5ER ☎ 017687 80400 (John or Sue)
www.appletreeskeswick.com Map 89,90/264232
BB **B** ✕ nearby S1 D5 T1
🅱 🅳 ⊗ 🐾 ♨

Victorian house overlooking Hope Park and Lake.
Two mins walk to town centre, theatre and bus
station. En-suite rooms. Colour TV (teletext).
Tea/coffee making facilities. Excellent breakfasts.
Drying room and secure cycle storage. Limited
private parking. Non-smoking.
Email: john@armstrong2001.fsnet.co.uk

☆ Littlefield
32 Eskin Street, CA12 4DG ☎ 017687 72949 (Maureen Hardy)
www.keswick98.fsnet.co.uk Map 89,90/270233
BB **B** ✕ nearby S1 D3 T1
🅱 🅳 ⊗ 🐾 ♨

A warm welcome assured by Ali and
Maureen. Comfortable guest lounge.
Drying facilities.
Packed lunches. Conveniently situated for
the town, lake and theatre.
Many walks possible from the door.
Private parking.

☆ ▰◀ Greystoke House
9 Leonard St, CA12 4EL ☎ 01768 772603
www.greystokeguesthouse.co.uk Map 89,90/269233
BB **B** ✕ book first £10, 6:30pm S2 D4 T1
Ⓥ 🅱 🅳 ⊗ 🐾 ♨ 🚗 ! Ⓜ

Typical Victorian lakeland town house.
Ideal base for walking, cycling and
touring. In a quiet location within a
few minutes walk of town, lake and
fells. Friendly relaxed atmosphere.
Providing good hearty breakfasts.
Safe cycle storage and drying room.

☆ ▰◀ Rivendell Guest House
23 Helvellyn St, CA12 4EN ☎ 01768 773822 (Pat & Linda Dent & June Muse)
www.rivendellguesthouse.com Map 89,90/269233
BB **B** ✕ nearby S2 D6 T4 F2
🅱 🅳 ⊗ 🐾 ! ♨ Ⓜ

A warm and friendly welcome awaits you at our lovely Victorian home run by
RA members. Set in a quiet location close to the town centre and Fitz park with
plenty of unrestricted parking. Most rooms en-suite. Drying facilities.
Pets welcome (by prior arragement). Anything from single to groups of 15.
Lots of local knowledge, with map and walks to suit all levels.

Email: info@rivendellguesthouse.com

☆ Cragside Guest House
39 Blencathra St, CA12 4HX ☎ 01768 773344 (Wayne & Alison Binks)
http://cragside-keswick.mysite.wanadoo-members.co.uk
Map 89,90/271234 BB **B** ✕ nearby D2 F2
🅱 🅳 ⊗ 🐾 ♨ 🐾 ◆◆◆ Veggie breakfasts.

Alison and Wayne invite you to stay
at our friendly Victorian home, with
stunning views of the local fells. We
are close to Keswick town centre and
on the Cumbria Way.
Family rooms can sleep four adults
in single beds.

● Kirkby Stephen

Coast To Coast Walk
Lockholme, 48 South Road, CA17 4SN ☎ 017683 71321 (Mrs M E Graham)
www.lockholme.co.uk Map 91/772079
BB **B** ✕ nearby S1 D1 T1 F1 ᎲᎲᎲ(Kirkby Stephen)
🅱 🅳 ⊗ 🐾 ♨ 🚗 ! Ⓜ
Fletcher House, Fletcher Hill, CA17 4QQ ☎ 017683 71013
(Mr & Mrs S Bamford) www.fletcherhousecumbria.co.uk Map 91/774086
BB **B** ✕ nearby S1 D2 T1 F1 ᎲᎲᎲ(Kirkby Stephen)
🅱 🅳 ⊗ 🐾 ♨ 🚗 Veggie breakfasts.
The Manor House, Mellbecks, CA17 4AB ☎ 017683 72757 (Jean Leeson)
www.manorhouse.netfirms.com Map 91/777085
BB **B** ✕ nearby D2 F1 ᎲᎲᎲ(Kirkby Stephen) 🅱 🅳 ⊗ 🐾 ♨ 🚗 🐾

☆ Redmayne House
Silver Street, CA17 4RB ☎ 017683 71441(Mrs C J Prime)
Map 91/774088
BB **B** ✕ nearby S1 D1 T1 F1 ᎲᎲᎲ(Kirkby Stephen)
🅳 ⊗ 🐾 ♨ 🐾

A spacious and attractive Georgian home
set in a large garden.

Home made bread and preserves, walkers'
breakfasts, private sitting room, parking.

● Langdale (Ambleseide)
Lake District
Coast to Coast Walk & Cumbria Way

☆ **New Dungeon Ghyll Hotel**
LA22 9JX ☎ 015394 37213
www.dungeon-ghyll.com Map 89,90/295064
BB **C** ✗ £20-£25, 7-8:30pm DI3 T6 FI
Ⓥ Ⓑ Ⓓ ⊛ 🐾🏠☂🍴🎒 ★★

Set amidst the splendour of Lakeland's most dramatic fells. Situated at the foot of the Langdale Pikes in the heart of the Langdale Valley.

After a day's walking relax in the peace and tranquility of England's most spectacular scenery where service is never compromised. It is possible to take a different fell walk every day of the week from our front door. Great bargain breaks all year.

Fax: 01539 437666
Email: enquiries@dungeon-ghyll.com

● Levens (Kendal)
Lake District
Birslack Grange Country Guest House, Hutton Lane, LA8 8PA
☎ 01539 560989 (Jean Carrington-Birch)
www.birslackgrange.co.uk Map 97/486866
BB **B** ✗ nearby S2 D2 T2 FI Closed Dec-Jan
Ⓑ Ⓓ ⊛ 🐾🏠🚗🍴🎒

● Lindale (Grange-over-Sands)
Lake District
🐾 Greenacres Guest House, LA11 6LP
☎ 015395 34578 (Barbara Pettit)
greenacres_lindale@hotmail.com Map 96,97/419804
BB **B** ✗ nearby D2 TI FI 🚌(Grange-over-Sands)
Ⓥ Ⓑ Ⓓ ⊛ 🐾🏠☂🚗🍴 ◆◆◆◆Ⓢ

● Long Marton (Appleby-in-Westmorland)
Pennine Way & Teesdale Way
Broom House, CA16 6JP ☎ 017683 61318 (Mrs Sandra Bland)
http://broomhouseappleby.co.uk Map 91/666238
BB **B** ✗ book first £ SI DI F/TI Closed Dec-Jan
Ⓥ Ⓑ Ⓓ ⊛ 🐾🏠🚗 ◆◆◆◆

● Low Crosby (Carlisle)
Hadrian's Wall & Cumbria Way
Madgwick, Green Lane, CA6 4QN ☎ 01228 573283 (M J Plane)
www.madgwickonwall.co.uk Map 85/445593
BB **B** ✗ nearby SI TI Closed Nov-Feb Ⓓ ⊛ 🐾🏠☂🍴

● Lowick Green (Ulverston)
Lake District
Cumbria Way
🐾 Garth Row, LA12 8EB ☎ 01229 885633 (Jenny Wickens)
www.garthrow.co.uk Map 96,97/289856
BB **B** ✗ nearby D/SI F/S/TI Ⓓ ⊛ 🐾🏠☂Ⓜ ◆◆◆

● Motherby (Penrith)

☆ 🐾 **Motherby House**
CA11 0RJ ☎ 017684 83368 (Jacquie Freeborn)
www.motherbyhouse.co.uk Map 90/429285
BB **B** ✗ book first £13.50, 7pm F4
Ⓥ Ⓑ Ⓓ ⊛ 🐾🏠 See SC also.

18th century warm and friendly guest house with beamed lounge and log fires. Drying facilities. Packed lunches and flask filling. Excellent 3 course meal for healthy outdoor appetites. Near Ullswater Helve, Ilyn and Blencathra. Small groups & muddy boots welcome.

● Near Sawrey (Hawkshead)
Lake District
Dales Way
Little Ees Wyke, LA22 0JZ ☎ 015394 36335 (Mrs Margaret Lambert)
www.near-sawrey.com Map 96,97/366957
BB **B** ✗ book first £12, 6:30pm DI T2 Ⓥ Ⓑ Ⓓ ⊛ 🐾🏠☂🏛

● Newlands (Keswick)
Lake District
Cumbria Way
Birkrigg, Newlands Valley, CA12 5TS ☎ 017687 78278 (Mrs M Beaty)
Map 89,90/214194 BB **B** ✗ nearby SI D2 F/TI Closed Dec-Feb
Ⓓ ⊛ 🐾 ◆◆◆ See SC also.

● Patterdale (Penrith)
Lake District
Coast To Coast Walk

☆ **Grisedale Lodge**
Grisedale Bridge, CA11 0PJ ☎ 017684 82084 (Mrs Joan B Martin)
www.grisedalelodge.co.uk Map 90/391162
BB **B** ✗ nearby D2 T2
Ⓑ Ⓓ ⊛ 🐾🏠☂🏛 See SC also.

Situated in quite location next to Lake Ullswater, this ideal base for the Helvelyn and High Street ranges offers a comfortable, spacious, clean cottage feel, cosy open fire character beams and spectacular views of the surrounding fells.
Email: enquiries@grisedalelodge.co.uk

Fellside, Hartsop, CA11 0NZ ☎ 017684 82532 (Mrs Anne-Marie Knight)
Map 90/408132 BB **B** ✗ nearby T2 Ⓓ 🛏️ 🍵 ♨️ Ⓜ️

�.🍴◀ Brotherswater Inn & Sykeside Camping Park, Brotherswater, CA11 0NZ
☎ 017684 82239 www.sykeside.co.uk Map 90/407130
BB **B** ✗ £10, 5:30-9:30pm D6 T8 Ⓥ Ⓑ Ⓓ 🛏️ 🍵 ♨️ Ⓜ️

☆ **Old Water View**
CA11 0NW ☎ 017684 82175
www.oldwaterview.co.uk Map 90/398158
BB **B** ✗ nearby D4 T2 F2
Ⓑ Ⓓ 🕸️ 🛏️ 🍵

Elegant and welcoming, this Bed & Breakfast is beautifully situated on the banks of Goldrill Beck. Guests are welcome to enjoy the guest lounge and garden at any time during their stay. Telephone for a brochure or view the website. Credit cards accepted.

● **Penrith**
🚂🍴◀ 27 Sandgate, CA11 7TJ
☎ 01768 865057 (Mrs V Bardgett) Map 90/516302
BB **A** ✗ nearby D1 F1 �(Penrith) Ⓑ Ⓓ 🛏️ 🍵 🚗 ♨️

● **Portinscale (Keswick)**
   Lake District
   Cumbria Way
Skiddaw Croft, CA12 5RD ☎ 017687 72321 (Janette Taylor)
janette@croft343.wanadoo.co.uk Map 89,90/254236
BB **B** ✗ nearby S2 D2 T1 F1 Ⓑ Ⓓ 🛏️ 🍵 ♨️ Ⓜ️

🚂🍴◀ The Mount Guest House, CA12 5RD ☎ 017687 73970
(Lindsay & Ann Ferguson) www.mountferguson.co.uk Map 89/252236
BB **B** ✗ nearby S1 D1 T1 F1 Ⓑ Ⓓ 🕸️ 🛏️ 🍵 ♨️

● **Ravenglass**
   Lake District

☆ 🚂🍴◀ **Rose Garth**
Main Street, CA18 1SQ ☎ 01229 717275
www.rosegarth1.fsnet.co.uk Map 96/084964
BB **B** ✗ nearby S1 D3 T1 F1 🚍(Ravenglass)
Ⓑ Ⓓ 🛏️ 🍵 ♨️

Overlooking village green and estuary. All rooms en-suite, CH and tea making facilities. Near Eskdale and Wasdale. BR station in village. Walks: Cumbrian Coastal Way, Cumberland Way, Furness Way, Lakeland to Lindisfarne and Ravenglass to Scarborough routes.

🚂🍴◀ Muncaster Country Guest House, Muncaster, CA18 1RD
☎ 01229 717693 (Ron & Jan Stringer)
ronandjan@muncastercountryguesthouse.com Map 96/099968
BB **B** ✗ book first £15 S2 D4 T1 F1 🚍(Ravenglass)
Ⓑ Ⓓ 🕸️ 🛏️ 🍵 🚗 ! ◆◆◆

● **Ravenstonedale (Kirkby Stephen)**
   Coast To Coast Walk

🚂🍴◀ The Kings Head Hotel, CA17 4NH ☎ 015396 23284 (Mr Gary J Kirby)
www.kings-head.net Map 91/740032
BB **B** ✗ £6-£14, 6-9:30pm S1 D2 T1 F1
Ⓥ Ⓑ Ⓓ 🛏️ 🍵 🚗 ! 🐾 Ⓜ️ ◆◆◆

● **Rosthwaite (Borrowdale)**
   Lake District
   Coast To Coast Walk & Cumbria Way

☆ 🚂🍴◀ **Scafell Hotel**
CA12 5XB ☎ 017687 77208
www.scafell.co.uk Map 89/259149
BB **C** ✗ £21, 7-8:15pm S3 D7 T12 F2
Ⓥ Ⓑ Ⓓ 🛏️ 🍵 ♨️ Ⓜ️ ★★

A former coaching inn situated in the heart of the Borrowdale Valley, adjacent to the Allerdale Ramble, Cumbria Way, Lakeland Way and Coast to Coast footpaths.

24 en-suite rooms. Renowned for its fine food, bars and friendly service. This hotel, through its superb location, is frequented by walkers of all ages and abilities. Special breaks available.

Fax: 017687 77280
Email: info@scafell.co.uk

● **Sedbergh**
   Yorkshire Dales
   Dales Way
Holmecroft, Station Road, LA10 5DW
☎ 015396 20754 (Mrs S Sharrocks)
www.holmecroftbandb.co.uk Map 97/650919
BB **B** ✗ nearby D2 T1 Ⓓ 🕸️ 🛏️ 🚗 ! ◆◆◆

🚂🍴◀ Wellbright Cottage, 15 Back Lane, LA10 5AQ
☎ 015396 20251 (Miss M Thurlby)
antique.thurlby@amserve.net Map 97/659921
BB **B** ✗ nearby D1 T1
Ⓓ 🕸️ 🛏️ 🍵 🚗 ! 🐾 ◆◆

 Yew Tree Cottage, 35 Loftus Hill, LA10 5SQ
☎ 015396 21600 (Mrs Anne Jones)
www.sedbergh.org.uk Map 97/658917
BB **B** ✗ nearby DI TI ▢ ☺ 🐾 🛁 ! 🍳 ◆◆◆

☆  **St Mark's**
Cautley, LA10 5LZ ☎ 015396 20287 (Mrs Barbara Manwaring)
www.saintmarks.uk.com Map 98/690944
BB **B** ✗ book first £10.50, 7-7:30pm SI T3 FI
Ⓥ ▢ Ⓓ ☺ 🐾 🛁 🚗 ! 🍳 ◆◆◆◆

Treat yourself to the tranquility
of the Howgill Fells and western
Dales. Outstanding setting,
national park, comfortable
en-suite rooms, Grade II listed,
open fires, home cooking. Also
course: embroidery and quilting.

Bridge House, Brigflatts, LA10 5HN ☎ 015396 21820 (Joyce Cox)
bridgehousebb@free.uk.com Map 97/640911
BB **B** ✗ book first £13, 7pm DI TI
Ⓥ ▢ 🐾 🛁 🚗 ◆◆◆◆ Special diets catered for.

Brantrigg, Winfield Rd, LA10 5AZ ☎ 015396 21455 (Linda Hopkins)
brantrigg@btinternet.com Map 97/658923
BB **B** ✗ nearby TI ▢ Ⓓ ☺ 🐾 🛁 🚗

● Slaggyford (Alston)
Pennine Way
 Yew Tree Chapel, CA8 7NH ☎ 01434 382525 (David & Mary Livesey)
www.yewtreechapel.co.uk Map 86,87/677525
BB **B** ✗ book first £14, 7pm DI T3
Ⓥ ▢ Ⓓ ☺ 🐾 🛁 🚗 ! 🍳 ◆◆◆

● St Bees
Coast To Coast Walk
Stonehouse Farm, Main Street, CA27 0DE
☎ 01946 822224 (Carole Smith) www.stonehousefarm.net Map 89/971119
BB **B** ✗ nearby SI D3 T2 F3 ﹏(St Bees)
▢ Ⓓ 🐾 🛁 🚗 ! 🍳 ◆◆◆

I Tomlin House, Beach Road, CA27 0EN
☎ 01946 822284 (Mr & Mrs Whitehead)
id.whitehead@which.net Map 89/963118
BB **B** ✗ nearby DI T2 FI ﹏(St Bees) ▢ Ⓓ ☺ 🐾 🛁 🚗 🍳

● Staveley (Kendal)
Lake District
Dales Way
Stock Bridge Farm, LA8 9LP ☎ 01539 821580 (Mrs Betty Fishwick)
Map 97/475977 BB **B** ✗ nearby SI D4 FI Closed Nov-Feb
﹏(Staveley) ▢ ☺ 🐾 ! 🍳

 Ramblers Cottage, I School Lane, LA8 9NU ☎ 01539 822120
(Mrs Craven) www.ramblers-cottage.co.uk Map 97/469984
BB **B** ✗ nearby DI TI ﹏(Staveley)
▢ Ⓓ 🐾 🛁 🚗 ! 🍳

● Talkin (Brampton)

☆  **High Close**
CA8 ILD ☎ 01697 746125 (Jane Johnson)
www.smoothhound.co.uk/hotels/highclose.html Map 86/558573
BB **B** ✗ book first £ SI D/T2 ﹏(Brampton)
Ⓥ ▢ Ⓑ Ⓓ ☺ 🐾 🛁 🚗 ! 🍳

Attractive 19th century former farmhouse
situated above village of Talkin in AONB.
Comfortable accommodation, large
garden and stunning views. Ideal base
for a relaxing holiday or walking
Hadrian's Wall, Pennine Way, Lake
District and Eden Valley.

● Threkheld (Kewsick)
Lake District
Cumbria Way

☆ **Scales Farm Country Guest House**
CA12 4SY ☎ 01768 779660 (Alan & Angela Jameison)
www.scalesfarm.com Map 90/341268
BB **B** ✗ nearby D3 T2 FI
▢ Ⓓ ☺ 🐾 🛁 🚗 🍳 ◆◆◆◆

Stunning views and a warm welcome
await you at this 17th century fells
farmhouse sensitively modernised to
provide accommodation of the
highest standard. The farm is on the
lower slopes of Blencathra, with a
Lakeland inn next door.

● Ulpha (Broughton-in-Furness)
Lake District
Oakbank, Ulpha, Duddon Valley, LA20 6DZ ☎ 01229 716393
(Ray & Susan Batten) susan@soakbank.freeserve.co.uk Map 96/201938
BB **B** ✗ book first £10, 7pm DI T2 Ⓥ ▢ 🐾 🛁 🚗 🍳 ◆◆◆

● Ulverston
Lake District
Cumbria Way
Rock House, I Alexander Road, LA12 0DE ☎ 01229 586879
(Ian and Linda Peters) www.rock-house.info Map 96,97/287779
BB **B** ✗ nearby SI F/D/T3 ﹏(Ulverston) ▢ Ⓓ ☺ 🐾 🛁 🚗 !
The Walkers Hostel, Oubas Hill, LA12 7LB ☎ 01229 585588 (Jean Povey)
www.walkershostel.co.uk Map 96,97/296787
BB **A** ✗ book first £8, 7pm SI D3 T3 F4 Closed Nov-Dec ﹏(Ulverston)
Ⓥ ▢ 🐾 🛁 🚗 ! Ⓜ
Dyker Bank, 2 Springfield Road, LA12 0DS ☎ 01229 582423 (M H Abbott)
Map 96,97/284779 BB **B** ✗ nearby SI TI FI ﹏(Ulverston)
▢ Ⓑ ☺ 🐾 🛁 🍳 Ⓜ
Low Hall, Kirkby-in-Furness, LA17 7TR ☎ 01229 889220 (Paul J Pye)
www.low-hall.co.uk Map 96/232812
BB **B** ✗ nearby DI TI FI Closed Dec-Jan ﹏(Kirkby-in-Furness)
▢ Ⓓ ☺ 🐾 🛁 🚗 🍳 ◆◆◆

St Mary's Mount, Belmont, LA12 7HD ☎ 01229 583372
(Marlon Bobbett) www.stmarysmount.co.uk Map 96,97/290788
BB **B** ✗ book first £15, 2:30-9pm S1 D2 T1 ⟶(Ulverston)
Ⓥ Ⓑ Ⓓ ⊛ 🐾♨ 🍴 ！

● **Warcop (Appleby-in-Westmorland)**

☆ ⟶ **The Coach House**
Eden Gate, CA16 6PL ☎ 01768 341955 (Mr & Mrs Hider)
www.coachhouse-in-eden.co.uk Map 91/745152
BB **B** ✗ book first £10 D1 T1
Ⓥ Ⓑ Ⓓ ⊛ 🐾♨ 🍴 🦴 Ⓜ

A warm welcome from like minded walkers. Our Grade II listed coach house contains a pocket history of Lady Anne Clifford and overlooks the River Eden. Centrally located for lakes, Lady Anne's Way, the Eden Way and the Coast to Coast Walk.

● **Wasdale Head (Gosforth)**
Lake District
Coast To Coast Walk & Cumbria Way
Burnthwaite Farm, Seascale, CA20 1EX ☎ 019467 26242 (Mrs Gillian Race)
burnthwaite123@aol.com Map 89/193091
BB **B** ✗ nearby S1 D2 T4 Ⓑ Ⓓ 🐾♨🦴 See SC also.

● **Watermillock (Ullswater)**
Lake District

☆ ⟶ **Land Ends Country Lodge**
CA11 0NB ☎ 017684 86438 (Barbara Holmes)
www.landends.co.uk Map 90/433245
BB **C** ✗ nearby S2 D3 T2 F1 Closed Dec-Feb
Ⓑ Ⓓ 🐾♨ Ⓜ ◆◆◆ See SC also.

Peaceful setting in 25 acres with 2 lakes and lovely courtyard with flowers, pots and fishpond. Red squirrels, ducks, moorhens, owls and fabulous birdlife live in the grounds. Ullswater 1.3 miles. Rooms are light, clean and airy. Great breakfasts.

● **Windermere**
Lake District
Dales Way

☆ ⟶ **Holly Lodge**
6 College Road, LA23 1BX ☎ 015394 43873
(Anne & Barry Mott) http://hollylodge20.co.uk Map 96,97/411985
BB **B** ✗ nearby S1 D3 T1 F4 ⟶(Windermere)
Ⓑ Ⓓ ⊛ 🐾♨🦴 ◆◆◆

Quietly situated in the village of Windermere, close to shops, restaurants, buses and trains.
Family run. Friendly atmosphere.
Good English breakfast.
Tel/Fax: 015394 43873, Mob: 07774 967805
e-mail: anneandbarry@hollylodge6.fsnet.co.uk

☆ **Lynwood**
Broad Street, LA23 2AB ☎ 015394 42550 (Mrs F Holcroft)
www.lynwood-guest-house.co.uk Map 96,97/413982
BB **B** ✗ nearby S1 D4 T1 F3 ⟶(Windermere)
Ⓑ Ⓓ ⊛ 🐾♨🦴 ◆◆◆◆

Relax in our elegant Victorian house in the heart of Windermere. Each bedroom is individually furnished and smoke-free with en-suite shower and w/c, colour TV, hairdryer and beverages. Convenient for bus and train stations and close to parking. From £30 per night for a double room with reductions for families.

LANCASHIRE

● **Burnley**
Pennine Bridleway
Rosehill House Hotel, Rosehill Ave, BB11 2PW ☎ 01282 453931
www.rosehillhousehotel.co.uk Map 103/834315
BB **C** ✗ £8+, 7-9:30pm S9 D21 T4 F4 ⟶(Burnley)
Ⓥ Ⓑ Ⓓ 🐾♨🦴 🍴 ★★★

● **Chipping (Clitheroe)**

☆ ⟶ **Rakefoot Farm**
Thornley Rd, Chaigley, BB7 3LY ☎ 01995 61332 (Mrs Pat Gifford)
www.rakefootfarm.co.uk Map 103/663416
BB **B** ✗ book first £15, 5-7pm S1 D/S4 T/S2 F3
Ⓥ Ⓑ Ⓓ 🐾♨🦴 ◆◆◆◆ See SC also

17th century farmhouse and traditional stone barn on family farm. Original features, woodburners, home cooked meals/convenient restaurants, laundry, en-suite and ground floor available. Longridge Fell/Forest of Bowland/ AONB/ panoramic views. Transport available.

● **Clitheroe**
Ribble Way
Lower Standen Farm, Whalley Road, BB7 1PP
☎ 01200 424176 (Mr & Mrs R E Berry)
owerstanden@yahoo.co.uk Map 103/739400
BB **B** ✗ nearby D2 T1 ⟶(Clitheroe)
Ⓑ Ⓓ ⊛ 🐾♨ 🍴🦴 ◆◆◆

☆ ⟶ **Foxhill Barn**
Howgill Lane, Gisburn, BB7 4JL
☎ 01200 415906 (Janet & Peter Moorhouse)
www.foxhillbarn.co.uk Map 103/843467
BB **B** T3 F1 Ⓓ ⊛ 🐾♨🦴 ◆◆◆◆

A newly converted barn with beautiful panoramic views close to the Lancashire/Yorkshire border. Many scenic walks traversing the farm. Ribble Way and Pendle nearby. Unwind afterwards with a jacuzzi, or in our homely guest lounge with wood burner and oak beams.

🏠 Selborne House, Back Commons, Kirkmoor Rd, BB7 2DX
☎ 01200 423571 (Judith V Barnes)
www.selbornehouse.co.uk   Map 103/738420
BB **B**   ✗ nearby   S4 D4 TI FI   🚶(Clitheroe)
Ⓑ Ⓓ ⊛ 🍴🛏🚲 ! 🔥   ◆◆◆◆

● **Colne**
🏠 Old Laithe B&B, Hill Lane, BB8 7EF ☎ 01282 866257
www.oldlaithe.co.uk   Map 103/911409
BB **A**   ✗ nearby   DI TI FI   🚶(Colne)
Ⓑ Ⓓ ⊛ 🍴🛏 ! 🔥

☆ 🏠 **Wickets**
148 Keighley Road, BB8 0PJ ☎ 01282 862002 (Mrs Etherington)
wickets@colne148.fsnet.co.uk   Map 103/897402
BB **B**   ✗ nearby   DI TI   Closed Jan-Feb   🚶(Colne)
Ⓑ Ⓓ ⊛ 🍴🛏   ◆◆◆◆

Spacious Edwardian family home providing quality accommodation in attractive & comfortable en-suite rooms. All the local amenities of the town yet close to open countryside, lovely walks & breathtaking views. Pick up a bargain in the Mill shops.

● **Eccleston (Chorley)**

☆ 🏠 **Parr Hall Farm**
Parr Lane, PR7 5SL ☎ 01257 451917 (Mike & Kate Motley)
parrhall@talk21.com   Map 108/519174
BB **B**   ✗ nearby   SI D9 T3 F2
Ⓑ Ⓓ ⊛ 🍴🛏🚲 !   ◆◆◆◆

Charming property with mature gardens peacefully located in the countryside, a few miles from the M6. Built in 1721, it has been renovated, providing comfortable guest rooms with en-suite facilities, TV & hospitality trays. With many attractions nearby, it is a good stopover from Scotland & the Lake District.

● **Grindleton (Clitheroe)**
  Ribble Way
🏠 Herris's Farm, Smalden Lane, BB7 4RX ☎ 01200 440725
(Vivien & Mark Leslie) www.herrisesfarm.co.uk   Map 103/760474
BB **B**   ✗ nearby   DI TI   Ⓑ Ⓓ ⊛ 🛏🚲

● **Oldham**
Temple Bar Farm, Wallhill Rd, Dobcross, Saddleworth, OL3 5BH
☎ 01457 870099 (Christine Howarth)
www.templebarfarm.co.uk   Map 109/982066
BB **B**   ✗ nearby   D2 TI   🚶(Saddleworth)
Ⓑ Ⓓ ⊛ 🍴🛏🚲🔥   ◆◆◆◆

● **Scorton (Preston)**

☆ **The Priory Hotel**
PR3 1AU ☎ 01524 791255
www.theprioryscorton.co.uk   Map 102/502488
BB **B**   ✗ £8.50, 9am-9pm   SI D6 TI FI
Ⓥ Ⓑ Ⓓ 🍴🛏   ◆◆◆◆

An attractive family run small hotel on the fringes of the Trough of Bowland, in the lovely village of Scorton. Serving local produce and real ale. On the Wyre Way, 15 minutes from Lancashire Coastal Path, 40 minutes from the Lakes.

● **Silverdale (Carnforth)**
🏠 Spring Bank House, 19 Stankelt Rd, LA5 0TA ☎ 01524 702693
(Mrs Nancy Bond) www.springbankhousesilverdale.co.uk   Map 97/463749
BB **B**   ✗ nearby   SI DI T2 FI   🚶(Silverdale) Ⓑ Ⓓ ⊛ 🍴🛏🚲 Ⓜ

● **Southport**
  Trans Pennine Trail
🏠 Bay Tree House, No.1 Irving St, Marine Gate, PR9 0HD
☎ 01704 510555   www.baytreehousesouthport.co.uk   Map 108/339180
BB **C**   ✗ book first £16, 7pm   D4 T2   Closed Jan   🚶(Southport)
Ⓥ Ⓑ Ⓓ ⊛ 🍴🛏 ! 🔥

● **Wycoller (Colne)**
🏠 Parson Lee Farm, BB8 8SU ☎ 01282 864747 (Pat Hodgson)
www.parsonleefarm.co.uk   Map 103/937385
BB **B**   ✗ book first £9, 6:30-8pm   DI TI FI
Ⓥ Ⓑ Ⓓ 🍴🛏🚲 ! 🔥   ◆◆◆

SELF-CATERING

CHESHIRE

● **Macclesfield**
Acorn Cottages ☎ 01260 223388 (Susan Bullock)
www.acorncottages-england.co.uk   £220-£300   Sleeps 4-5. 2 cottages.
Oak beams, stone floors, undulating scenery.   ⊛   ★★★★

CUMBRIA

● **Allonby**
Bowscale Farm ☎ 01900 881228 (Mrs Brenda Wilson) www.crookhurst.com
£140-£850   Sleeps 2-14. Half a farm house.
Private, spacious, easy for Lake District   ★★★★   See B&B & Groups also.

● **Ambleside**
  Lake District
Ramsteads ☎ 015394 36583 (Gareth Evans)   www.ramsteads.co.uk
£165-£395   Sleeps 4-6. 7 lodges.   Closed Dec-Feb
Secluded woodland setting in central Lakeland.   ★-★★

For an explanation of the symbols used in this guide
see the Key to Abbreviations and Symbols on p 7

☆ Wheelwrights
☎ 015394 37635 (Mervyn Bass)
www.wheelwrights.com
£195-£2,300   Sleeps 2-14 . 70 properties.
Escape to the beauty of the lakes.   🛁 ★★-★★★★★

For over a quarter of a century, we have been letting some of the best cottages in the Lake District, all of which are set in stunning scenery.

Based in Elterwater, in the heart of magnificent Great Langdale, we are surrounded by the beauty of the mountains and the lakes and would like to share it with you!

Whether you are just wanting a romantic short break for two or a really good family holiday, do give us a call to discuss your options.

As a small company, we pride ourselves on our personal service and ability to find the right cottage for all occasions.

☆ Grove Cottages
☎ 015394 33074 (Peter & Zorika Thompson)
www.grovecottages.com
£235-£595   Sleeps 2-6. 4 cottages.
Superior cottages, centre of the Lakes.   ⊗   ★★★★-★★★★★

4 beautiful, traditional cottages set in our 200 acres of Stockghyll Valley. Magnificent views to Coniston Old Man and The Langdales but only 1½ miles from Ambleside shops and restaurants. Wonderful walks from your doorstep and a warm personal welcome.

☆ Rydal Holiday Lettings
☎ 015394 31043 (Neil Rowley) www.steppingstonesambleside.com
£220-£399   Sleeps 2-4. 4 flats.
Lovely apartments in idylic riverside setting.
⊗ 🛁 ★★★★   See B&B also.

Superbly situated apartments, furnished and equipped to high, clean standard with video and CD player. Large landscaped gardens with BBQ area and spectacular views. Ample private parking. Private water supply.

☎ 015394 32326 (P F Quarmby)
£130-£200   Sleeps 4. 1 flat.   Closed Nov-Feb
Opens onto garden. Private parking.   ⊗ 🛁

The Haven   ☎ 015394 32441 (Fiona Sparrow)
www.havengreen.fsbusiness.co.uk   £225-£340   Sleeps 4. 3 cottages.
Close to shops and amenities.   🛁

● Appleby
☎ 01704 892175 (Honor Thornhill)   www.cottagebreak.co.uk
£130-£300   Sleeps 7-9. 1 cottage.   Listed building.   ⋙(Appleby) 🛁

● Bassenthwaite
Lake District
Brook House Cottages   ☎ 017687 76393 (Alison Trafford)
www.holidaycottageslakedistrict.co.uk
£100-£750   Sleeps 2-20. 3 cottages, 1 studio.
Village cottages & B&B by stream/farm.   🛁

Irton House Farm   ☎ 017687 76380 (Mrs J Almond)
www.irtonhousefarm.com
£295-£695   Sleeps 2-6. 5 apartments, 1 caravan.
Superb views. Table tennis, snooker/pool.   ⊗ 🛁 ★★★★

● Bowness-on-Windermere
Lake District
☎ 0151 228 5799 (Mr & Mrs E Jones) eejay@btinternet.com
£120-£260   Sleeps 2-3. 1 flat.
Lake views, central situation, well-equipped.   ⊗

☆ Mrs J Kay
☎ 01925 755612
£205-£340   Sleeps 4. 1 flat.   Closed Nov-March
Modern, central, lake view, private parking.
⊗ ⋙(Windermere)

2 bedroom flat. Very attractively furnished. Central situation near shops, restaurants and places of interest. Lake view. Private parking. No dogs or children under 10. No smoking.

● Brampton
Low Luckens Organic Resource Centre   ☎ 016977 48331
www.lowluckensfarm.co.uk
£375   Sleeps 9. 1 property.
Organic Farm, excellent walking, cycling, wildlife.   ⊗ 🛁

● Caldbeck
Lake District
Monkhouse Hill   ☎ 016974 76254 (Jennifer or Andy Collard)
www.monkhousehill.co.uk
£290-£2,025   Sleeps 2-14. 9 cottages.
Award-winning. Rural setting. Evening meals.   🛁 ★★★★-★★★★★

Newlands Grange   ☎ 016974 78676 (Mrs Dorothy Studholme)
studholme_newlands@hotmail.com
£100-£140   Sleeps 6. 1 caravan.
On working farm, lovely views.   ⊗   See B&B also.

● **Cockermouth**
Lake District

Wood Farm Cottages ☎ 01900 829533 (Mrs A Cooley)
www.woodfarmcottages.com £260-£440 Sleeps 6. 2 cottages.
Rural accommodation, peaceful setting. OS ref.119263

● **Coniston**
Lake District

☆ **Coniston Country Cottages**
☎ 015394 41114 (Steve, Linda or Sharon) www.conistoncottages.co.uk
£200-£650 Sleeps 2-6. 16 cottages.
Quality cottages in superb surroundings
★★★-★★★★ See B&B also

Cosy Lakeland cottages in superb surroundings. Tastefully furnished and well-equipped. Easy access to central Lakes, with local walking to suit all ages and abilities. Most cottages have free use of a nearby leisure club.

☆ **The Coppermines**
☎ 015394 41765 (Mr Philip Johnston)
www.coppermines.co.uk
£195-£4,500 Sleeps 2-30. 60+ cottages.
Lovely cottages in stunning mountain scenery. ★★-★★★★★

The Lakes:
Coniston – Hawkshead – Sawrey – Windermere – Woodland – Broughton – The Duddon Valley – Grasmere

The Dales:
Garsdale

Over 60 unique Lakeland and Dales cottages and group accommodation of quality and character sleeping 2-30 in stunning lake & mountain scenery. Weeks & short breaks for couples families & groups

Also visit www.lakescottages.info & www.conistonslate.com
The Estate Office, The Bridge, Coniston, Cumbria. LA21 8HJ

☆ **Herdwick View**
☎ 015394 41433 (Caroline Watson)
www.yewtree-farm.com
£225-£310 Sleeps 5. 1 cottage
See B&B also.

Herdwick View self catering cottage.
Part of Yew Tree Farm formerly owned by Beatrix Potter, this cosy bungalow has stunning views of Holme Fell and Wetherlam.
Surrounded by superb walking from the door to suit all, ample parking, croft area adjacent, short breaks available.

Barn House ☎ 015394 41477 (Mrs G Coward)
£180-£320 Sleeps 3-4. 2 cottages.
Quiet, garden, parking. Village facilities nearby.

● **Eskdale**
Lake District

☎ 01732 459168 (Mrs J Holland)
£350-£650 Sleeps 8. 1 farmhouse.
17th century farmhouse, elevated position, stunning views.
RA member

● **Gamblesby**
Church Villa ☎ 01768 881682 (Patricia Clowes)
www.gogamblesby.co.uk
£165-£395 Sleeps 2-6. 1 barn conversion, 2 cottages.
Tranquil, picturesque village. Views, gardens.
★★★-★★★★ See Helton also.

● **Glenridding**
Lake District

☆ **Lower Grisedale Lodge**
☎ 017684 82084 (Mrs J B Martin) www.grisedalelodge.co.uk
£200-£405 Sleeps 2-5. 1 ground floor apt .
Beamed, spacious cottage feel, open fire.
★★★★ See B&B also.

Situated in quite location next to Lake Ullswater, this deal base for the Helvelyn and High Street ranges offers a comfortable, spacious, clean cottage feel, cosy open fire character beams and spectacular views of the surrounding fells.
Email: enquiries@grisedalelodge.co.uk

● **Grange-over-Sands**
☎ 01253 813682 (Lynn Branson)
£180 Sleeps 2. 1 cottage.
Close to amenities and recreational paths.
(Grange-over-Sands)

● **Grasmere**
Lake District

☆ **Broadrayne Farm**
☎ 015394 35055 (Mrs Jo Dennison Drake)
www.grasmere-accommodation.co.uk £245-£565 Sleeps 2-5. 3 cottages.
Dramatic views, quiet location, colour brochure.
★★★★ See Hostels & Groups also.

Broadrayne Farm is at the heart of the Lake District. Superb traditional cottages. Quiet location.Open fires, C/H & parking. Dogs welcome. Dramatic views. Classic Lakeland walks from front door. Brochure. Sauna and drying room on site. Resident owners.
Email: jo@grasmere-accommodation.co.uk

● **Greystoke**

☆ Motherby House
☎ 017684 83368 (Mrs Jacquie Freeborn)
www.motherbyhouse.co.uk
£175-£235   Sleeps 4-6. I cottage.
Converted coach house.   See B&B also.

18th century warm and friendly guest house with beamed lounge and log fires. Drying facilities. Packed lunches and flask filling. Excellent 3 course meal for healthy outdoor appetites. Near Ullswater Helve, Ilyn and Blencathra. Small groups & muddy boots welcome.

● **Hawkshead**
Lake District

Broomriggs ☎ 015394 36280 (Mrs Haddow)   www.broomriggs.co.uk
£150-£340   Sleeps 3-4 . I cottage.
Ideal for walking. Quiet, pleasant views.   ★★★ See Sawrey also.

☆ High Dale Park Barn
☎ 01229 860226 (Mr P Brown)
www.lakesweddingmusic.com/accomm
£195-£670   Sleeps 2-6. 17th century barn.   ★★★
Quiet valley, superb position, many walks.   ★★★

Idyllic setting in Grizedale Forest. Charming 17th century barn conversion. Two units, let together or separately. Totally non-smoking. Off road parking. Fully fitted, well equipped kitchens.

Popular catering service available. Owner managed. Trout-fishing nearby. Secure undercover cycle storage. High Dale Park Barn is a recently converted 17th century barn that nestles in a small, peaceful valley within Grizedale Forest – Lakeland's largest forest area. Woodland walks literally seconds away. Email: peter@lakesweddingmusic.com

● **Helton**
Lake District

Church Villa ☎ 01768 881682 (Mark Cowell) www.gogamblesby.co.uk
£185-£465   Sleeps 2-5. 2 cottages.
Beautiful views, log fire, garden.   ★★★★ See Gamblesby also.

● **Keswick**
Lake District

Birkrigg ☎ 017687 78278 (Mrs Beaty)
£170-£320   Sleeps 1-4. I cottage.   Closed Jan
Pleasantly, peacefully situated, wonderful mountainous view.
★★★ See B&B also.

☎ 01992 463183 (Mrs Smith)
£90-£320   Sleeps 2-8. 2 flats.   Near bus station and Lake Derwentwater.

Hope Cottages ☎ 01900 85226 (Christine M England)
www.hope-farm-holiday-cottages.co.uk
£220-£420. Sleeps 3-4. 2 cottages.   Closed Nov-Feb
Quiet and comfortable, lovely views/walks.   ★★★

☆ Derwent House Holidays
☎ 01889 505678 (Mary & Oliver Bull)
www.dhholidays-lakes.com
£105-£365   Sleeps 2-6. I cottage, 3 flats.
Central heating & parking.   ★★★

Traditional stone Lakeland building now four comfortable well-equipped self-catering holiday suites at Portinscale village on Derwentwater, I mile from Keswick. Central heating and linen included. Parking. Open all year. Short breaks. Prices £95 to £345. Some reductions for two people only.

☆ Brigham Farm
☎ 017687 79666 (N Green) www.keswickholidays.co.uk
£135-£350   Sleeps 2-4. 6 apartments.
Lovely garden. Ample parking. Owner maintained.   ★★★★
See The Studio (below) also.

Quietly situated 5 mins walk from town centre, former farmhouse converted to six spacious self-contained apartments. Handsomely furnished and well equipped, gas-fired CH, with garden and plenty of parking space. Carefully owner maintained. Email: selfcatering@keswickholidays.co.uk

☆ The Studio
☎ 017687 79666 (N Green) www.keswickholidays.co.uk
£135-£310   Sleeps 2-4. Apartments.
Tasteful barn conversion with stunning views.   ★★★★
See Brigham Farm (above) also.

Tasteful barn conversion in the lovely Vale of St Johns. Well equipped, handsomely furnished with beautiful views. Five miles from Keswick. Personally maintained. selfcatering@keswickholidays.co.uk

☆ Croft House Holidays
☎ 017687 73693 (Mrs Jan Boniface) www.crofthouselakes.co.uk
£220-£695   Sleeps 2-8. 4 cottages.
Stunning, panoramic views. Peaceful rural setting.
★★★★ RA member

Outstanding lake and mountain views. Cottage and ground floor apartment in a Victorian country house and two other cottages – all in Applethwaite, just one mile from Keswick. Open all year, short breaks.

Keswick Cottages ☎ 01900 822993 (Lynn Rimmer)
www.keswickcottages.co.uk   £170-£950   Sleeps 2-10. 35 varying types.
High quality, warm, clean, cosy properties.   ⊗ 🐾 ★★★-★★★★

☎ 016973 23067 (Sara & David)   www.cottageretreat.co.uk
£200-£400   Sleeps 2-3 + cot. I cottage.
Beautiful countryside retreat, chill and relax.   ⊗

● Morland
Rose Cottage ☎ 01977 681372 (Trevor & Tracey Robinson)
www.coast-country.info   £390-£780   Sleeps 4-6. I house.
Superbly equipped, beautiful location near Ullswater.   ⊗   ★★★★
See Robin Hoods Bay and Staithes also.

● Patterdale
Lake District

☆ Patterdale Hall Estate
☎ 017684 82308 (Sue Kay)
www.patterdalehallestate.com
£148-£475   Sleeps 2-6. 17 varying types.
Private 300 acre estate below Helvellyn.   ⊗ 🐾 ★★-★★★

Between Helvellyn and the picturesque shores of Ullswater, the private 300-acre Estate offers a range of 17 self-catering properties in an idyllic and relaxing setting with stunning views.

With its own foreshore, woodland and gardens it is perfect for peaceful leisurely holidays and is an ideal starting point for many great Lakeland walks. The Estate's central location makes it a perfect base from which to explore the entire Lake District.

● Penrith
Howscales ☎ 01768 898666 (Mrs E Webster)
www.howscales.co.uk
£195-£450   Sleeps 2-4. 5 cottages.
Set in open, tranquil countryside.   ⊗ ᴀᴀᴀ(Lazonby) 🐾 ★★★★

● Pooley Bridge
Lake District
Swarthbeck Farm ☎ 017684 86432 (W H Parkin)
www.farm-holidays.co.uk
£195-£1298   Sleeps 6-14. 5 cottages.
Public rights of way nearby.   🐾 ★★★

● Ravenstonedale
Lake District
Antlesgarth Lodges ☎ 0113 2323273 (Mick Franks)
www.lodgebreaks.co.uk
£150-£500   Sleeps 6 + cot. 3 pine lodges.
A place for country-lovers.   🐾 ★★★

● Sawrey
Lake District
Broomriggs ☎ 015394 36280 (Mrs J Haddow) www.broomriggs.co.uk
£150-£470   Sleeps 2-6. Cottages & apartments.
Magnificent mountain/lake views, boats.   ⊗ 🐾 ★★★-★★★★★
See Hawkshead also.

● Silverdale
☎ 0114 2338619 (Dot McGahan) dotmcgahan@aol.com
£150-£300   Sleeps 2-5. I cottage.   Closed Feb
AONB/nature reserve location, lake views.   ⊗ ᴀᴀᴀ(Silverdale)   RA member.

● Ulverston
Lake District
St Mary's Mount ☎ 01229 583372 (Marion Bobbett) www.stmarysmount.co.uk
£450-£550   Sleeps 4 + 2. I converted stable.
Lovely views. Peaceful location. Large garden.   ⊗ ᴀᴀᴀ(Ulverston)

● Wasdale Head
Lake District
Burnthwaite Farm ☎ 01946 726242 (Gillian Race) burnthwaite123@aol.com
£300-£450   Sleeps 4. I cottage. Main route to Scafell Pike.   🐾

● Watermillock
Lake District

☆ Land Ends
☎ 017684 86438 (Barbara Holmes)
www.landends.co.uk
£250-£530   Sleeps 2-5. 4 log cabins.
Peaceful 25 acre grounds, 2 ponds.   🐾 ★★★ See B&B also.

For real countrylovers! Peaceful fellside setting in 25 acres with 2 lakes. Red Squirrels, ducks, moorhens, owls and fabulous birdlife on your doorstep. Lake Ullswater only 1.3 miles. Dramatic scenery and superb walks close by! Warm and cosy interiors.

LANCASHIRE

● Chipping
Outlane Head Cottage ☎ 01995 61160 (Mrs J Porter)
joanporter@ukonline.co.uk   £160-£210   Sleeps 2. I coach house.
Superb fell views, excellent walking. Woodburner.   ⊗ 🐾 ★★★★

☆ Rakefoot Farm
☎ 01995 61332 (Mrs Pat Gifford)   www.rakefootfarm.co.uk
£95-£560   Sleeps 2-22. 4 cottages in barn conversion.
Woodburners, meals, laundry, CH, panoramic views.
🐾 ★★★-★★★★ See B&B also.

Past winner of North West Tourist Board Silver Award. Traditional stone barn conversion. Family farm in the Forest of Bowland. Most bedrooms en-suite, some groundfloor. Original features with comforts of modern living. Gardens, games room, meals service.

Thornley Hall Farm ☎ 01995 61243 (Mrs Gill Airey) www.thornleyhall.co.uk
£260-£280 Sleeps 6. I house.
Spacious farmhouse, panoramic views. Listed building. ⊗ ★★★

● **Clitheroe**
Crimpton Cottages ☎ 01200 448278 (Mrs Elsie Miller)
www.crimptoncottages.co.uk
£100-£290 Sleeps 2-4. 3 cottages.
Cottages of character. Forest of Bowland. 🐾 ★★★★

● **Longridge Fell**
Rams clough ☎ 01995 61476 (Ness & Oliver Starkey) loudview@v21.me.uk
£220-£635 Sleeps 4-10 + 2 cots. 2 cottages.
AONB with panoramic views. Laundry/CH. 🐾

GROUPS

CUMBRIA

Lake District

☆ **Smallwood House Hotel** (B&B)
Compston Rd, Ambleside LA22 9DJ ☎ 015394 32330
(Christine & Anthony Harrison) www.smallwoodhotel.co.uk
B £33 Min 10, max 24
✖ B D 🐾 ◆◆◆◆ See B&B also

We pride ourselves on a quality, friendly service in the traditional way.

Dinners & packed lunches .
Drying facilities.
Group discounts.
Winter breaks.
Leave your cars in our car park & walk from here.

Please telephone Anthony or Christine Harrison for a full brochure & tariff
enq@smallwoodhotel.co.uk

Birdoswald Roman Fort (B&B/SC) Gilsland, Brampton CA8 7DD
☎ 016977 47602 http://birdoswaldromanfort.org
BB £21 Min 10, max 39 ✖ 🐾 D ⊗ ★★★★

Brathay Exploration Group (SC) Brathay Hall, Ambleside LA22 0HP
☎ 015394 33942 www.brathayexploration.org.uk Map 90/366028
SC £197.29-£440.51 I lodge Max 32 ✖ D ⊗

Lake District

Catbells Camping Barn (SC) Newlands
☎ 017687 72645 (Mrs Ann Grave) Map 90/243208
Bednight £5 Min I, max 12 D ⊗ ! 🚗

Crookhurst Farm (B&B/SC) Bowscale, Allonby, Maryport CA15 6RB
☎ 0777 304 7591 (Brenda Wilson) www.crookhurst.com
BB £22, SC £850 ✖ nearby B D ! 🚗 ★★★★ See B&B & SC also

Lake District
Coast to Coast Path

Grasmere Independent Hostel (SC), Broadrayne Farm Grasmere LA22 9RU
☎015394 35055 (Mr Bev Dennison) www.grasmerehostel.co.uk Grid Ref: 336094
Bednight £14.50, SC £275-£350 Min I, max 24
✖ nearby 🐾 B D ⊗ ! ★★★★ See Hostels & SC also

HOSTELS, BUNKHOUSES & CAMPSITES

CUMBRIA

Yorkshire Dales

Catholes Farm (B) Sedbergh ☎ 015396 20334 (Mrs Jean Handley)
Grid Ref: SD653908 Bednight £7 Closed Dec-Feb D

Lake District

Causeway Foot Camping Barn (CB/BB) Causeway Foot Farm, Naddle, Keswick
☎ 017687 72290 (Greg Nicholson)
www.causewayfoot.co.uk Map 89/295219
Bednight £4 D

Lake District
Coast to Coast Path

☆ **Grasmere Independent Hostel** (IH)
Broadryne Farm Grasmere LA22 9RU ☎ 015394 35055 (Mr Bev Dennison)
www.grasmerehostel.co.uk Grid Ref: 336094
Bednight 14.50 ✖ nearby 🐾
B D ⊗ ★★★★ Hostel See Groups & SC also

Quiet, clean and friendly. Ensuite bedrooms. Sleeps 24. Beds made up. Superb S/C kitchens, dining, drying rooms, laundry, sauna, full C/H, parking. Fantastic walks from door. Individuals to whole hostel group hire welcome. Colour brochure. Hostel is behind farmhouse
bev@grasmere-accommodation.co.uk

PUBS & TEAROOMS

CHESHIRE

● **Kelsall** (Tarporley)
Sandstone Trail
☕ Summertrees Tearoom, Tirley Lane, CW6 0PF
☎ 01829 751145 (Mrs B Bates)
bbbates@tesco.net Map 117/539673
〰(Delamere) ✖ V 🚻 G ⊗ B(☺)

WHETHER YOU'RE TAKING A CHALLENGING HIKE OR A CASUAL STROLL, SCOTLAND IS A BREATHTAKING EXPERIENCE.

Loch Garry, Highlands

Wherever you're walking in Scotland the views will inspire you. It might be a gentle stroll along a magnificent coastline. Perhaps a challenging hike up a Munro for unforgettable panoramas. Or simply a wander along a forest trail, spotting Scotland's diverse wildlife in its natural habitat. So come and see this awe-inspiring country as it was meant to be seen, on foot. And visitscotland.com/walking would be a great place to start from.

Live it. Visit Scotland.
visitscotland.com 0845 22 55 121
The No.1 booking and information service for Scotland.

CUMBRIA

● Chapel Stile (Ambleside)
Lake District
Cumbria Way

⌂ **Brambles Cafe**
Langdale Loop, LA22 9JE
☎ 015394 37500 (Mrs S Rodway)
Map 90/321053
✗ Ⓥ ⊗ Ⓑ(☺)

Open all year, 9:30-4:30 (winter), 9-5:30 (summer), closed 2 weeks mid-Jan. Brambles Cafe is situated on the first floor of Langdale Coop at the back with great views of the fells. We serve delicious breakfasts, lunches, cakes and soup, all made to a high standard on the premises.

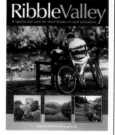

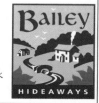

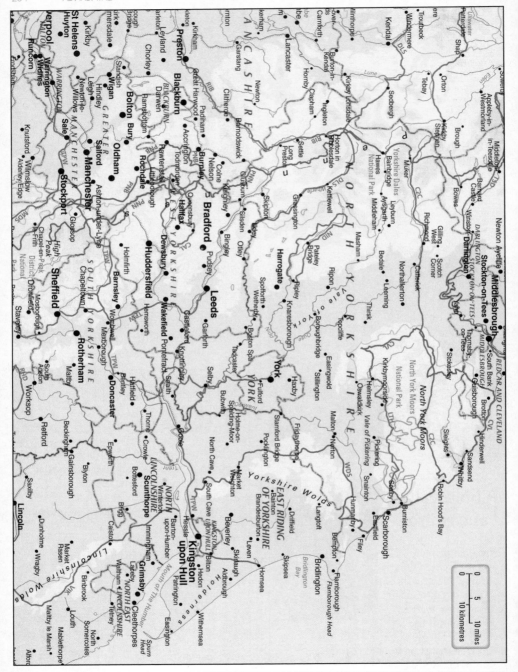

YORKSHIRE

Yorkshire has something to offer even the most experienced walker. From stunning views of the eastern Heritage Coast cliffs to the Pennines and Yorkshire Dales in the west, from the moors in the north to the industrial archaeology and wooded valleys in the south.

The North York Moors National Park alone has over 1,400 miles of paths and tracks to choose from, including the famous Cleveland Way and the ancient Hambleton Drove Road.

BRIAN R HILL (WWW.YORKSHIREIMAGES.COM)
FOUNTAINS ABBEY

To the north of the Moors lie the valleys of the North Pennines, offering the chance to follow the River Tees as it passes Barnard Castle and flows on past meadows and over waterfalls before reaching its outlet on the north-east coast at Middlesborough.

Moving west, the Yorkshire Dales, notable for their dramatic limestone formations, lead-mining heritage and distinctive drystone walls, were created by glacial erosion over millions of years. More recently human settlers shaped the Dales, from the monks who first created cheese in Wensleydale to the castles and hunting forests of Norman settlers.

A member says:

"The region has a little bit of something for everybody. Nothing much has been altered, most things have been left reasonably untouched – the more you look, the more you find."

Following the Pennines south along the border with Lancashire and the Peak District leads to the West Riding, where following gritstone moors and deep wooded valleys you arrive in the lush Vale of York via Bradford, Harrogate and Leeds. Two well-known long distance footpaths, the Pennine Way and the Dales Way, serve this area.

Heading back towards the coast through the broad expanse of East Yorkshire and Derwent, the Yorkshire Wolds Way follows a chalk escarpment for 76 miles from the Humber Bridge up to Filey.

So whether you seek an invigorating hike across rugged, remote moorland or a gentle stroll around the historical and cultural heritage of one of its bustling cities, Yorkshire offers one of the most varied selections of walking terrain in Britain.

Long Distance Paths

Cleveland Way CVL
Dales Way.................................DLS
Nidderdale Way ....NID
Pennine Bridleway ....PNB
Pennine Way ....PNN
Ribble Way ....RIB

Public paths:

20,808km/12,922 miles

Mapped access land:

 91 square miles (Area 2, Lower North West) to date

MALHAM, YORKSHIRE DALES

YORKSHIRE
LOCAL RAMBLERS CONTACTS

EAST YORKSHIRE & DERWENT
AREA SECRETARY

Mr M Dixon, 8 Horseman Avenue, Copmanthorpe, York, YO23 3UF
☎ 01904 706850 Mob: 0775 2089011

GROUP SECRETARIES

Beverley Mr J Roach, Hollins, The Park, Swanland, HU14 3LU ☎ 01482 632117

Driffield Mr J R Jefferson, Delamere, 2 Spellowgate, Driffield, YO25 5BB
☎ 01377 252412

East Yorks Get Your Boots On
Miss N Sydenham, 23 Ash Street, York, YO26 4UR ☎ 07980 828741 (Fiona)
www.gybo.org.uk

Goole & Howden Chris Bush, 23 Albemarle Road, York, YO23 1EW ☎ 01904 612401
chris.bush@whsmithnet.co.uk

Hull & Holderness Mrs Sue Ripley, 17 Clifford Avenue, Hull, HU8 0LU
☎ 01482 708026
www.hullramblers.org.uk

Pocklington Mrs K Brooks, 59 Springfield Road, Pocklington, York, YO42 2UY ☎ 01759 307453
www.pocklingtonramblers.org.uk

Ryedale John Williams, The Old School, Howsham, York, YO60 7PH
☎ 01653 618 583
www.ryedaleramblers.org.uk

Scarborough & District
Mrs Elizabeth Jackson, 18 Chantry Meadow, Kilham, Driffield YO25 4RB ☎ 01262 420102

York Miss V Silberberg, 41 North Parade, Bootham, York, YO30 7AB ☎ 01904 628134
www.communigate.co.uk/york/yorkramblers2

NORTH YORKS & SOUTH DURHAM
AREA SECRETARY

Mr D G Lawrenson, Smithy Cottage, Hunton, Bedale, North Yorkshire, DL8 1QB ☎ 01677 450422
www.bigwig.net/nysd_ramblers

GROUP SECRETARIES

Barnard Castle Mr T Fenton, Garden House, Westholme, Winston, Darlington, Co Durham, DL2 3QL
☎ 01325 730895
http://uk.geocities.com/barney_ramblers

Cleveland Mr A Patterson, 141 Castle Road, Redcar, TS10 2NF
☎ 01642 474864

Crook & Weardale Mrs K Berry, 11 Wood Square, Bishop Auckland, Co Durham, DL14 6QQ ☎ 01388 608979
http://members.aol.com/crookramblers

Darlington Mr Bryan Spark, 3 Thirlmere Grove, West Auckland, Bishop Auckland, Co Durham, DL14 9LW ☎ 01388 834213

NYSD 20s & 30s Walking Miss J M Bird, Middle Garth, Stainton, Barnard Castle, DL12 8RD ☎ 01833 637756

Northallerton Mr M F Kent, 131 Valley Road, Northallerton, North Yorkshire, DL6 1SN ☎ 01609 777618

Richmondshire Mrs V Darwin, 4 Sycamore Avenue, Richmond, North Yorks, DL10 4BN ☎ 01748 822 845

SOUTH YORKS & NE DERBYSHIRE
AREA SECRETARY

See www.ramblers.org.uk or contact our main office for current details
www.syned-ramblers.org.uk

GROUP SECRETARIES

Barnsley & Penistone
Miss D S Mouncey, 17 Orchard Close, Mapplewell, Barnsley, South Yorkshire, S75 6HX ☎ 01226 386102

Bolsover District Mrs J Lee, 193 Langwith Road, Bolsover, Chesterfield, S44 6LU ☎ 07817 419250

Chesterfield & North East Derbyshire Mr A Hunt, 17a Loads Road, Holymoorside, Chesterfield, Derbyshire, S42 7ET

Dearne Valley Mrs Pauline Gibbons, 6 Ruskin Avenue, Mexborough, South Yorkshire, S64 0AU

Doncaster Mrs M Thompson, 31 Broom Hill Drive, Cantley 6, Doncaster, South Yorkshire, DN4 6QZ ☎ 01302 371093
www.geocities.com/donramblers

Rotherham Metro District
Mrs A Balding, 2 Calcot Green, Swinton, Mexbrough, South Yorks, S64 8SY

Sheffield Mrs Pat Peters, 751 Gleadless Road, S12 2QD ☎ 0114 239 8505
www.sheffield.ramblers.care4free.net

Sheffield 20s & 30s Miss C Scholes, 114 St Anthony Road, Sheffield, S10 1SG ☎ 0114 2682870
www.sheffieldwalkinggroup.org.uk

WEST RIDING
AREA SECRETARY

Gwendoline Goddard, Spring Bank, Hebden Bridge, West Yorks, HX7 7AA
☎ 01422 842558
www.ramblerswestriding.org.uk

GROUP SECRETARIES

Bradford Mr M J Pitt, Fairbank, Beck Lane, Bingley, BD16 4DN
☎ 01274 563426

Calderdale Mrs D F Hall, 11 School Close, Ripponden, Halifax, Yorks, HX6 4HP ☎ 01422 823440

Castleford & Pontefract Mrs J A Hartley, 2 Moorleigh Close, Kippax, Leeds, LS25 7PB ☎ 0113 286 6737

Craven Ms D Lindsay, 15 Sycamore Croft, Beeston, Leeds, LS11 6BB
☎ 0113 2776110

Dewsbury Mr E I Shaw, 15 Rectory Lane, Emley, Nr Huddersfield, HD8 9RR ☎ 01924 848364

Harrogate Mrs M J Clack, 40 Woodlands Grove, Harrogate, North Yorkshire, HG2 7BG ☎ 01423 884481
www.willouby.demon.co.uk/ramblers association/harrogategroup.htm

Huddersfield Mr J M Lieberg, 11 Woodroyd Avenue, Honley, Huddersfield, West Yorks, HD9 6LG
☎ 01484 662866

Keighley Mr Jeff Maud, 50 Cliffe Lane South, Baildon, Bradford, West Yorkshire, BD17 5LB ☎ 01274 597718

Leeds Ms J B Morton, 6 Lawns Green, New Farnley, Leeds, West Yorkshire, LS12 5RR ☎ 0113 279 0229
www.leedsramblers.org.uk

Leeds & Bradford 20s & 30s
Mr R Hoskin, 13 Methley Drive, Leeds, LS7 3NE ☎ 0113 262 1478
www.takeahike.org.uk

Lower Wharfedale Mrs P Atkins, Coppywood, Curly Hill, Ilkley, LS29 0BA ☎ 01943 609081

Ripon Mr A G Clothier, 49 Boroughbridge Road, Knaresborough, HG5 0ND ☎ 01423 865412

Wakefield Ms J Douglas, 19 Clifton Avenue, Stanley, Wakefield, West Yorkshire, WF3 4HB ☎ 01924 820732

Wetherby & District Mrs Pauline Clarke, 7 Raby Walk, Wetherby, W Yorks, LS22 6SA ☎ 01937 583378

LOCAL RAMBLERS PUBLICATIONS

Airedale Way
by Douglas Cossar, ISBN 0 900613 95 5:
an 80km/50-mile riverside walk from Leeds
to Malham Tarn in the Dales.
£4.50 + £1 p&p from 11 Woodroyd
Avenue, Honley, Holmfirth HD9 6LG.
Cheques to West Riding Rambler's
Association.

Brontë Way
by Marje Wilson, ISBN 1 901185 05 6.
A 69km/43-mile walk from Oakwell Hall,
Birstall to Gawthorpe Hall, Padiham.
£4.50 + £1 p&p as Airedale Way above;
cheques to West Riding Rambler's
Association.

Chalkland Way
by Ray Wallis. 66km/40-mile circular walk
through the chalk hills of the Yorkshire
Wolds from Pocklington.
Colour leaflet, free + A5 SAE to R Wallis,
75 Ancaster Avenue, Kingston upon Hull
HU5 4QR.

Dales Way Handbook
edited by West Riding Rambler's
Association. An annually updated guide to
accommodation and transport along the
path between Ilkley and Windermere.
£1.50 + £1 p&p as Airedale Way above;
cheques to West Riding Rambler's
Association.

Danum Trail
Walks linking villages and towns in
Doncaster borough, creating a
80km/50-mile walk.
£1.30 from 31 Broom Hill Drive, Doncaster
DN4 6QZ. Cheques to Ramblers' Association
Doncaster Group.

Harrogate Dales Way Link
32km/20 miles from Valley Gardens,
Harrogate to Bolton Abbey, linking to the
Dales Way.
A5 leaflet, 30p + SAE. Sew-on badge
available on completion, £1.50+SAE.

Harrogate Ringway
(Harrogate Ramblers). 33.5km/21 miles.
A5 leaflet, 30p + SAE. Sew-on badge
available on completion, £1.50 + SAE. Both
from 20 Pannal Ash Grove, Harrogate HG2
0HZ. Cheques to Harrogate Group
Rambler's Association.

Kirklees Way
Circular walk around Huddersfield and
Dewsbury. £2.70 + £1 p&p as Airedale
Way above; cheques to West Riding
Rambler's Association.

Knaresborough Round
32km/20 mile circular walk round this
ancient town, in two stages with bus
connections.
A5 leaflet, 30p + SAE, as Harrogate Dales
Way above. Sew-on badge available on
completion, £1.50.

Minster Way
by Ray Wallis (Hull Rambler's
Association). An 83km/50-mile signed walk
established in 1980 between the Minsters
of Beverley and York.
£4 + 55p p&p from 75 Ancaster Avenue,
Hull HU5 4QR. Cheques payable to R
Wallis. Badge and accommodation list
available from same source.

Penistone Line Trail
Sheffield to Huddersfield by the
Penistone Line Partnership, supported by
South Yorkshire and North Derbyshire
Ramblers. 95km/60 miles. £4.95 + 55p
(or £2.95 + 55p p&p for RA or Partnership
members) from PLP, St Johns Community
Centre, Church Street, Penistone S36 9AR.
Cheques to Penistone Line Partnership.

Rambles Around Ripon
by Ripon Ramblers: 15 countryside walks
2km/1.5 miles to 20km/13 miles.
£3.60 + 70p p&p.

Ripon Rowel Walk
by Les Taylor. 80km/50 mile cicular route
from Ripon Cathedral via Masham.
£4.95 + 70p p&p from 49 Boroughbridge
Road, Knaresborough HG5 0ND. Cheques
to The Ripon Rowel and Rambles Around
Ripon, repectively. Order both books for £8
+ 70p p&p

Rotherham Ring Route
(Rotherham Metro). An 80km/50-mile
circular walk.
£2 + £1 p&p from Rotherham Visitor
Centre, 40 Bridge Gate, Rotherham
S60 1PQ ☎ 01709 835904. Cheques to
Rotherham TIC. Badges and completion
cards from same source.

Sheffield Country Walk
3rd edition by Sheffield Ramblers'
Association and Sheffield City Council.
87km/54.5 mile. £3.95 + 55p p&p from
Ramblers' Association Sheffield Group,
33 Durvale Court, Sheffield S17 3PT.
Cheques to Ramblers' Association
Sheffield Group.

Yorkshire Wolds Way
Accommodation Guide
(E Yorks & Derwent Area).
95p + SAE from Mrs S M Smith,
65 Ormonde Avenue, Kingston upon Hull
HU6 7LT.

SHORTER WALKS

Car-Free Countryside Walks
accessible from York
by Patsy Pendegrass, ISBN 1 904446 04 03
(East Yorkshire and Derwent Ramblers).
15 walks from stations or bus stops, all
8km/5 miles to 19.5km/12 miles.
£4.99 + 50p p&p from Quacks Books,
7 Grape Lane, York YO1 7HU. Cheques to P
M Pendegrass. All profits to Ramblers'
Association. (New this year)

All the following from 11 Woodroyd
Avenue, Honley, Holmfirth HD9 6LG.
Cheques to West Riding Ramblers.

Country Walks in Mirfield,
Emley, Thornhill and Denby Dale
by Douglas Cossar and John Lieberg,
ISBN 1 901184 30 7. 11 circular walks
of between 6km/3.75 miles and 12km/
7.5 miles. £4.75 + £1 p&p.

Kiddiwalks Currently out of print,
new edition in preparation.

More Walks in and around Kirklees
15 varied, hand-illustrated walks in
Huddersfield/Holmfirth area by
Huddersfield Ramblers. £2.40 + £1 p&p.

Ramblers' Bradford Volume 1
by Douglas Cossar, ISBN 1 901184 22
6. 20 circular walks 3km/2 miles to
16km/10 miles. £4.95 + £1p&p.

Ramblers' Leeds Volume 1
East of Leeds
by Douglas Cossar, ISBN 1 901184 23
4. 25 mostly circular walks, 5.5km/3.5
miles to 18.5km/11.5 miles, accessible
by public transport. £4.95 + £1 p&p.

Ramblers' Leeds Volume 2
West of Leeds
by Douglas Cossar, ISBN 1 901184 24
2. 24 mainly circular walks, 4km/2.5
miles to 14.5km/9 miles, accessible by
public transport. £5.95 + £1 p&p.

Ramblers' Wakefield
by Douglas Cossar, ISBN 0 900613 96 3.
42 mostly circular walks of 5km/3 miles
to 17km/10.5 miles. £5.50 + £1 p&p.

Walks in and around Kirklees
12 varied, hand-illustrated walks in the
Huddersfield/Holmfirth area planned by
Huddersfield Ramblers. £2.40 + £1 p&p.

BED & BREAKFAST

EAST YORKSHIRE

● **Beverley**

⌐◄ I Woodlands, HU17 8BT ☎ 01482 862752 (Sarah King)
www.number-one-bedandbreakfast-beverley.co.uk   Map 106,107/029395
BB **B**   ✗ book first £12, 7pm   SI DI T2   ⋘(Beverley)
Ⓥ Ⓑ Ⓓ◉🍴🏠♨🚲! ◆◆◆

⌐◄ 5 Hurn View, Norfolk St, HU17 7DP ☎ 01482 880521
www.hurnview.co.uk   Map 106,107/025400
BB **B**   ✗ nearby   SI DI TI   ⋘(Beverley)
Ⓑ Ⓓ◉🍴🏠♨🚲!🏛 ★★★

● **Bridlington**

☆ **Rosebery House**
I Belle View, Tennyson Avenue, YO15 2ET ☎ 01262 670336
(Helen Gallagher) www.roseburyhouse.biz   Map 101/186671
BB **B**   ✗ nearby   D3 TI F3   ⋘(Bridlington)
Ⓑ Ⓓ🏠♨🏛 ◆◆◆◆   Veggie breakfasts.

A Grade II listed Georgian house with a long garden and sea view. Amenities close by. Ideal for walking and touring. Near Flamborough Head and Bempton Bird Reserve. High standard of comfort and friendliness. All rooms en-suite, CH, TV, tea/coffee facilities. Some parking. Vegetarians/vegans welcome, packed lunches available.

● **Goole**
   Trans Pennine Trail
The Briarcroft Hotel, 49-51 Clifton Gardens, DN14 6AR ☎ 01405 763024
www.briarcrofthotel.co.uk   Map 105,106,112/739241
BB **B**   ✗ nearby   S5 D5 T6 FI   ⋘(Goole Town)
Ⓑ Ⓓ🍴♨ ◆◆◆

● **Huggate**
The Wolds Inn, Driffield Road, YO42 IYH ☎ 01377 288217 (John & Jane
Leaver) huggate@woldsinn.freeserve.co.uk   Map 106/882550
BB **B**   ✗ £9, 7-9:30pm   S3 D2 TI   Ⓥ Ⓑ🍴♨ ◆◆◆

● **Hull**
   Trans Pennine Trail
⌐◄ Roseberry House, 86 Marlborough Ave, HU5 3JT
☎ 01482 445256 (Tim Pritchard)
www.smoothhound.co.uk/hotels/conway.html   Map 107/079300
BB **A/B**   ✗ nearby   S2 D3 T2 F2   ⋘(Hull Paragon)
Ⓑ Ⓓ♨ ◆◆◆◆

● **Londesborough (York)**
   Yorkshire Wolds Way
Towthorpe Grange, YO43 3LB ☎ 01430 873814 (Mrs P Rowlands)
towthorpegrange@hotmail.com   Map 106/869437
BB **A**   ✗ book first £10   D/S2 T/SI   Ⓥ Ⓓ🍴♨🏛 ◆◆

● **Millington (York)**
   Yorkshire Wolds Way
⌐◄ Laburnum Cottage, YO42 ITX ☎ 01759 303055 (Mrs Maureen Dykes)
roger&maureen@labcott.fslife.co.uk   Map 106/830517
BB **B**   ✗ book first £9, 7pm   TI FI   Closed Nov-Feb
Ⓥ Ⓑ Ⓓ◉🍴♨🚲!🏛 ◆◆◆

● **North Ferriby**
   Trans Pennine Trail & Yorkshire Wolds Way
B&B at 103, 103 Ferriby High Road, HU14 3LA ☎ 01482 633637
(Margaret Simpson) www.bnb103.co.uk   Map 106/999260
BB **B**   ✗ book first £3-£5, 5-8pm   SI DI TI FI
Ⓥ Ⓑ Ⓓ◉🍴♨🏛 ◆◆◆

● **South Cave (Brough)**
   Yorkshire Wolds Way
⌐◄ Rudstone Walk Country Accommodation, HU15 2AH ☎ 01430 422230
(Laura & Charlie Greenwood)   www.rudstone-walk.co.uk   Map 106/917342
BB **C**   ✗ book first £18.75, 7:30pm onwards   S2 D5 T7 F2
Ⓥ Ⓑ Ⓓ🍴♨🚲!🏛 ◆◆◆◆   See SC also.

NORTH YORKSHIRE

● **Ainthorpe (Whitby)**
   North York Moors
   Coast To Coast Walk
⌐◄ Rowantree Farm, Fryup Rd, YO21 2LE ☎ 01287 660396 (Mrs L Tindall)
krbsatindall@aol.com   Map 94/704073
BB **B**   ✗ book first £10   TI FI   Closed Jan-Feb   ⋘(Danby)
Ⓥ Ⓑ Ⓓ◉🍴♨ ◆◆◆

● **Ampleforth**
   North York Moors
Shallowdale House, West End, YO62 4DY ☎ 01439 788325 (P Gill)
www.shallowdalehouse.co.uk   Map 100/579786
BB **C**   ✗ book first £29.50, 7:30pm   DI T/D2
Ⓥ Ⓑ Ⓓ◉♨! ◆◆◆◆◆ⓖ

● **Askrigg (Leyburn)**
   Yorkshire Dales
Syke's House, DL8 3HT ☎ 01969 650535 (Mr & Mrs B Bowe)   Map 98/947910
BB **B**   ✗ book first £11, 7pm   DI TI FI
Ⓥ Ⓓ🍴♨🚲!🏛   See SC also.
Milton House, DL8 3HJ ☎ 01969 650217 (Mrs B Percival)   Map 98/948910
BB **B**   ✗ nearby   DI TI
Ⓑ Ⓓ◉🍴♨ ◆◆◆◆   Private parking
⌐◄ Whitfield Helm, DL8 3JF ☎ 01969 650565 (Mrs Kate Empsall)
www.askrigg-cottages.co.uk   Map 98/934916
BB **B**   DI TI   Ⓑ Ⓓ◉🍴♨🚲!🏛 ◆◆◆◆
Thornsgill House, Moor Rd, DL8 3HH ☎ 01969 650617 (Miss Wendy Turner)
www.thornsgill.co.uk   Map 98/949912
BB **B**   ✗ nearby   SI DI TI   Ⓑ Ⓓ◉🍴♨🚲! ◆◆◆◆

● Aysgarth (Leyburn)
Yorkshire Dales

☆ **Stow House Hotel**
Aysgarth Falls, DL8 3SR ☎ 01969 663635
www.stowhouse.co.uk   Map 98/014883
BB **C**   ✕ book first £18.50, 7:30pm   D5 T4
Ⓥ Ⓑ Ⓓ 🐾 ♨ ! 🐿   ◆◆◆◆

Family run former Victorian vicarage with magnificent views near Aysgarth
Falls. Superb walks from the door. En-suite rooms, comfortable lounge and cosy
bar. The house overlooks Wensleydale and Bishopdale and stands in 2 acres of
garden with tennis and croquet lawns.
Email: info@stowhouse.co.uk

● Buckden (Skipton)
Yorkshire Dales
Dales Way

🍳 Romany Cottage, BD23 5JA
☎ 01756 760365 (Tim & Gwen Berry)
www.thedalesway.co.uk/romanycottage   Map 98/942772
BB **B**   ✕ nearby   S1 D1 T2   Ⓓ ⊗ 🐾 ♨ 🚗 ! 🐿

West Winds Cottage, BD23 5JA
☎ 01756 760883 (Lynn Thornborrow)
thornborrow@westwindscottage.fsnet.co.uk   Map 98/942772
BB **B**   ✕ nearby   D2 T1   Ⓓ ⊗ 🐾 ♨

Birks View, BD23 5JA ☎ 01756 760873 (Mrs A Huck)
Map 98/943772   BB **B**   ✕ nearby   D1 T1
Ⓓ ⊗ 🐾 ♨

● Burnsall (Skipton)
Yorkshire Dales
Dales Way

☆ **Burnsall Manor House Hotel**
BD23 6BW ☎ 01756 720231 (Mr J E Lodge)
www.manorhouseuk.co.uk   Map 98/032614
BB **B**   ✕ book first £10, 7-8pm   D5 T3
Ⓥ Ⓑ Ⓓ 🐾 ♨ ! 🐿   ◆◆◆

A small private hotel on the bank
of the River Wharfe, in the
Yorkshire Dales National Park,
with the Dales Way at the foot of
the garden.
Mid-week 4 nights for 3 offer.
Email: joe@manorhouseuk.co.uk

● Castleton (Whitby)
North York Moors

🍳 Greystones, 30 High Street, YO21 2DA ☎ 01287 660744
(Mrs Della Wedgwood)   thewedgwoods@aol.com   Map 94/684079
BB **A**   ✕ nearby   D3   ♒(Castleton Moor)
Ⓑ Ⓓ ⊗ 🐾 ♨ 🚗 !   ◆◆◆

● Catterick Village (Richmond)
Coast To Coast Walk

Rose Cottage Guest House, 26 High Street, DL10 7LJ
☎ 01748 811164 (Carol Archer)   Map 99/249979
BB **B**   ✕ book first £12, 6:30pm   S1 D1 T2
Ⓥ Ⓑ 🐾 ♨ 🐿 Ⓜ   ◆◆◆

● Clapham
Yorkshire Dales

☆ **Moor View**
Cold Cotes, LA2 8JA ☎ 01524 242085 (Jenny & Gary Woodhead)
www.moorviewingleton.co.uk   Map 98/707706
BB **B**   ✕ book first £12, 6pm   D2   ♒(Clapham)
Ⓥ Ⓑ Ⓓ ⊗ 🐾 ♨

Moorview is conveniently situated just off the A65 between Clapham and
Ingleton at the foot of Ingleborough and enjoys 360-degree views of the fells &
moorland. This area is unsurpassed walking country with the "Three Peaks" on
the doorstep. Also the Pennine Way, Dales Way and Ribble Way close by.
Other interesting geological sites nearby are The White Scar Show Cave, Norber
Erratics and the famous Ingleton Waterfalls Walk.

● Clay Bank Top (Bilsdale)
North York Moors
Coast To Coast Walk

Maltkiln House, Urra, Chopgate, TS9 7HZ ☎ 01642 778216
(Wendy & Gerry Broad)   www.maltkiln.co.uk   Map 93/571019
BB **A**   ✕ £9.50, 7pm   D1 T2   Ⓥ Ⓑ Ⓓ ⊗ 🐾 ♨ !

● Cloughton (Scarborough)
Cleveland Way & Link Through the Tabular Hills Walk

☆ **Cober Hill**
YO13 0AR ☎ 01723 870310
www.coberhill.co.uk
Map 101/010948   BB **B**   ✗ £10, 6:30-7pm   S22 D6 T26 F10
Ⓥ Ⓑ Ⓓ ⊛ 🛏️ 🍴 🖐️ 🚗 🏠

The perfect location for the Cleveland Way & surrounding areas, Cober Hill promises you a warm welcome and pleasant surroundings, with excellent facilities & superb hospiatlity. 63 en-suite bedrooms, six comfortable lounges and two drying rooms. Open all year.

● Cowling (Skipton)
Pennine Way

🛏️ Woodland House, 2 Woodland Street, BD22 0BS ☎ 01535 637886
(Mrs Susan Black)   www.woodland-house.co.uk   Map 103/973432
BB **B**   ✗ nearby   D1 T1   Closed Dec
Ⓑ Ⓓ ⊛ 🛏️ 🖐️ 🚗 ! Ⓜ   ◆◆◆◆

● East Marton (Skipton)
Pennine Way

Sawley House, BD23 3LP ☎ 01282 843207 (Joan Pilling)
jon@pilling16.fsnet.co.uk   Map 103/909515
BB **B**   ✗ nearby   D1 T2   ⋙(Gargrave) Ⓓ 🛏️ 🖐️ !

● Ebberston (Scarborough)
Givendale Head Farm, YO13 9PU ☎ 01723 859383 (Sue Gwilliam)
www.givendaleheadfarm.co.uk   Map 94,101/894875
BB **B**   ✗ book first £15, 7pm   D2 T1
Ⓥ Ⓑ Ⓓ ⊛ 🛏️ 🚗   ◆◆◆◆

● Egton Bridge
North York Moors

☆ 🛏️ **Broom House**
Broom House Lane, YO21 1XD ☎ 01947 895279 (Mr & Mrs D White)
www.egton-bridge.co.uk   Map 94/796054
BB **B**   ✗ book first £(groups only), 7pm   S1 D/T4 F2   ⋙(Egton Bridge)
Ⓥ Ⓑ Ⓓ ⊛ 🛏️ 🖐️ 🚗 !   ◆◆◆◆Ⓢ   See SC also.

An excellent place to stay. Comfortable en-suite rooms and an idyllic setting with views of the Esk valley. En-route Coast to Coast and Esk Valley Walks. Local pubs serving good meals within easy walking distance. In house evening meals for large parties.
Email: mw@broom-house.co.uk

● Faceby (Middlesbrough)
North York Moors
Cleveland Way & Coast To Coast Walk

Four Wynds B&B, Whorl Hill, TS9 7BZ
☎ 01642 701315 (Sue Barnfather)   Map 93/487033
BB **B**   ✗ book first £9, 5-7pm   D1 T1 F1 Ⓥ Ⓑ Ⓓ 🛏️ 🖐️ 🚗 ! ◆◆◆

● Filey
Yorkshire Wolds Way & Cleveland Way

Seafield Hotel, 9/11 Rutland Street, YO14 9JA ☎ 01723 513715
seafieldhotel@btopenworld.com   Map 101/117804
BB **B**   ✗ book first £9, 6pm   S3 D4 T2 F5   ⋙(Filey)
Ⓥ Ⓑ Ⓓ 🛏️ 🖐️   ◆◆◆

Wrangham House Hotel, Stonegate, Hunmanby, YO14 0NS
☎ 01723 891333   (Mervyn Poulter)
www.wranghamhouse.co.uk   Map 101/098775
BB **C**   ✗ book first £16-£19.50, 7-9:30pm   S1 D9 T1 F1   ⋙(Humanby)
Ⓥ Ⓑ Ⓓ 🛏️ 🖐️ 🚗   ★★

🛏️ Gables Guest House, Rutland St, YO14 9JB
☎ 01723 514750 (Kim & Linda Wood)
www.thegablesfiley.co.uk   Map 101/116804
BB **B**   ✗ book first £12.50   D/S2 T/D/F2 F1   ⋙(Filey)
Ⓥ Ⓑ Ⓓ ⊛ 🛏️ 🖐️ 🚗   ◆◆◆◆

🛏️ The Fairway, 11 Valley Road, Primrose Valley, YO14 9QX
☎ 01723 512174 (Mrs Ruth Milner)   Map 101/118784
BB **B**   ✗ nearby   S1 D1 F1   ⋙(Filey and Hunmanby)
Ⓑ Ⓓ ⊛ 🛏️ 🚗 !

● Fylingthorpe (Robin Hood's Bay)
North York Moors
Coast To Coast Walk & Cleveland Way

🛏️ Lincoln House, Thorpe Lane, YO22 4TH
☎ 01947 880766 (John & Olwen Lumsden)
Lincoln-House@amserve.com   Map 94/945052
BB **A**   ✗ book first £6.50   S1 D2 F1   Closed Nov-Feb
Ⓥ Ⓓ ⊛ 🛏️ 🚗 !

Middlethorpe, Sledgate Farm, YO22 4QB ☎ 01947 880690
(Mrs Wendy Williamson)   www.middlethorpe.co.uk   Map 94/933045
BB **B**   ✗ nearby   D2   Ⓑ Ⓓ 🛏️ 🚗

● Ganton (Scarborough)
Yorkshire Wolds Way

Cherry Tree Cottage, 23 Main Street, YO12 4NR
☎ 01944 710507 (Mrs Iris Hallaways)
www.gantonholidays.co.uk   Map 101/988776
BB **B**   ✗ nearby   S1 T1 F1   Closed Dec-Feb
Ⓓ ⊛ 🛏️ 🖐️ ! Ⓜ   ◆◆◆   See SC also.

● Giggleswick (Settle)
Yorkshire Dales
Ribble Way

☆ 🛏️ **Harts Head Hotel**
Belle Hill, BD24 0BA ☎ 01729 822086
www.hartsheadhotel.co.uk   Map 98/812640
BB **B**   ✗ book first £7.50, 5:30-9pm   S2 D5 T2 F1   ⋙(Settle)
Ⓥ Ⓑ Ⓓ 🛏️ 🖐️ !   ◆◆◆◆

Significantly refurbished country inn offering 10 en-suite bedrooms, superb food (30 main courses), listed in CAMRA Good Beer Guide 2002 & 2003. Emphasis on quality & service. Great base for exploring the Dales. Special rate for 3 night stay from £49 pp including breakfast.

● Glaisdale (Whitby)
North York Moors
Coast To Coast Walk

☆ **Red House Farm**
YO21 2PZ ☎ 01947 897242 (Tom or Sandra Spashett)
www.redhousefarm.net   Map 94/771049
BB **B**   ✗ nearby   S1 D2 T1 F1   ᴙᴙ(Glaisdale)
Ⓑ Ⓓ ⊛ 🍵🛏 See SC also.

Listed Georgian farmhouse featured in Houses of the North Yorkshire Moors. Completely refurbished to the highest standards & retaining all original features. All bedrooms en-suite, with CH, TV & tea making facilities. Wonderful walking country. Coast to Coast Walk 400 yds from house.

● Glasshouses (Harrogate)
🛶 Arran House, 3 Glencoe Terrace, HG3 5DU ☎ 01423 712785
(Lynda Coates) suite4two@hotmail.com   Map 99/175647
BB **B**   ✗ nearby   D1 T1 F1   Closed Dec-Feb
Ⓑ Ⓓ ⊛ 🍵🛏 🚗 ! 🛁

● Grassington (Skipton)
Yorkshire Dales
Dales Way
Springroyd House, 8a Station Road, BD23 5NQ ☎ 01756 752473
(Mrs P Robertshaw) www.springroydhouse.co.uk   Map 98/001639
BB **B**   ✗ nearby   D1 T/D2   Ⓑ Ⓓ ⊛ 🍵🛏🛁   ◆◆◆

🛶 Scar Lodge, 13 Hardy Grange, BD23 5AJ
☎ 01756 753388 (Valerie Emmerson) Map 98/003639
BB **B**   ✗ nearby   D2   Ⓑ Ⓓ ⊛ 🍵🛏🚗 ! 🛁

☆ 🛶 **Mayfield**
Low Mill Lane, BD23 5BX ☎ 01756 753052 (Mrs Trewartha)
www.mayfieldgrassington.co.uk   Map 98/007633
BB **B**   ✗ nearby   S1 D2 T1 F1
Ⓑ Ⓓ ⊛ 🍵🛏 🚗 ! 🛁

On the Dales Way beside the river, a quiet B&B just 10 minutes from the village centre. Beautiful setting with open views over the hills and fields. Very comfortable rooms and a warm welcome await you.
Email: suzanneatmayfield@talk21.com

☆ **Foresters Arms**
Main Street, BD23 5AA ☎ 01756 752349 (R M Richardson)
Map 98/003642
BB **B**   ✗ £8.50, 6-8:30pm   D4 T1 F2
Ⓥ Ⓑ 🍵🛏🛁   ◆◆◆

Once an old coaching inn, the Foresters Arms offers a warm and friendly atmosphere serving traditional ales and home-cooked food, lunchtime and evenings.

B&B from £ 30 pppn.

● Great Ayton
North York Moors
Crossways, 116 Newton Road, TS9 6DL ☎ 01642 724351
(Miss Sue Drennan) susieds@crossways26.fsnet.co.uk   Map 93/563115
BB **B**   ✗ nearby   S2 D1 T1   ᴙᴙ(Great Ayton)
Ⓑ Ⓓ ⊛ 🍵🛏🚗 !   ◆◆◆◆

● Guisborough
Cleveland Way
The Three Fiddles Public House, 34 Westgate, TS14 6BA
☎ 01287 632417 (Jill Henderson) Map 94/613160
BB **A**   ✗ book first £5   D1 T3 F1   Ⓥ Ⓓ 🍵🛏🚗 !   ★★

● Gunnerside (Richmond)
Yorkshire Dales
Coast To Coast Walk & Pennine Way
Oxnop Hall, DL11 6JJ ☎ 01748 886253 (Mrs A I Porter) Map 98/931973
BB **A/B**   ✗ nearby   S1 D2 T2   Closed Nov-Feb
Ⓥ Ⓑ 🍵🛏   ◆◆◆◆

● Harrogate
Yorkshire Dales
Barker's Guest House, 204 Kings Road, HG1 5JG ☎ 01423 568494
(Mrs E Barker) eebarkeruk@yahoo.co.uk   Map 104/304563
BB **B** ✗ nearby   S1 D1 F/T/D1   ᴙᴙ(Harrogate) Ⓑ Ⓓ ⊛ 🍵🛏   ◆◆◆

🛶 Amadeus Hotel, 115 Franklin Road, HG1 5EN ☎ 01423 505151
(Janet Frankland) www.acartha.com/amadeushotel   Map 104/303560
BB **B/C**   ✗ nearby   S4 D3 T4   ᴙᴙ(Harrogate)
Ⓑ Ⓓ ⊛ 🍵🛏 ! Ⓜ   ◆◆◆◆

● Hawes (Wensleydale)
Yorkshire Dales
Pennine Way

☆ **Dalesview**
East Marry, Gayle, DL8 3RZ ☎ 01969 667397 (Mrs S McGregor)
Map 98/871893
BB **B**   ✗ nearby   D1 T1   Closed Dec-Feb
Ⓑ Ⓓ ⊛ 🍵🛏

A modern comfortable bungalow situated in the picturesque village of Gayle, 1/2 mile from the small market town of Hawes. 100m from Pennine Way. Lovely views, quiet location, an ideal centre for touring, cycling & walking in the Yorkshire Dales.

☆ **Thorney Mire House**
Appersett, DL8 3LU ☎ 01969 667159 (Mrs S Turner)
www.thorneymire.yorks.net   Map 98/852899
BB **B**   S1 D2   Closed Nov-Feb
Ⓑ Ⓓ ⊛ 🍵🛏 🚗 Ⓜ   ◆◆◆◆

Recommended in the Which? Bed & Breakfast Guide. A warm welcome awaits you at our traditional Dales house, surrounded by woods, fells & meadows, a place to unwind. Excellent walking, ideal for bird watchers. Off road parking.

Ebor Guest House, Burtersett Road, DL8 3NT ☎ 01969 667337
(Mrs Gwen Clark) gwen@eborhouse.freeserve.co.uk   Map 98/876897
BB **B**   ✕ nearby   D2 TI   B   D   ❖❖❖

White Hart Inn, Main Street, DL8 3QL ☎ 01969 667259 (Diane Horner)
www.whiteharthawes.co.uk   Map 98/875897
BB **B**   ✕ £8.50, 7-8:30pm   SI D4 T2   V   D   ❖❖❖

☆ Cocketts Hotel & Restaurant
Market Place, DL8 3RD ☎ 01969 667312 (Bob & Lesley Barber)
www.cocketts.co.uk   Map 98/871898
BB **B/C**   ✕ £14.95, 7-8:30pm   D6 TI F/TI   Closed Jan
V   B   D   ❖❖❖❖

A warm welcome awaits you at our 17th century stone built hotel in the centre of Hawes. Ideal for small walking groups, with our restaurant serving Table d'Hote and A La Carte meals and a small residents bar.

● Hawnby (Helmsley)
North York Moors

☆ The Hawnby Hotel
Hilltop, YO62 5QS ☎ 01439 798202 (Dave Young)
www.hawnbyhotel.co.uk   Map 100/542898
BB **B**   ✕ book first £8, 7-10pm   D6 T3
V   B   D   ❖❖❖❖

Situated in an unspoilt village in the heart of the North Yorkshire Moors National Park. An ideal spot for a walking holiday. Group bookings available.

● Hebden (Skipton)
Yorkshire Dales
Dales Way

Court Croft, Church Lane, BD23 5DX
☎ 01756 753406 (Mrs Philippa Kitching) Map 98/026630
BB **B**   ✕ nearby   T2   D   ❖❖❖   Tea garden.

● Helmsley
North York Moors
Cleveland Way

Carlton Grange, YO62 5HH
☎ 01439 770259 (Mrs Ann Kirby)   Map 100,94/615879
BB **A**   ✕ book first £3 (light supper)   SI DI   Closed Nov-Feb
V   D   ❖!

● Hirst Courtney (Selby)
Trans Pennine Trail

☆ Royal Oak Inn
Main St, YO8 8QT ☎ 01757 270633 (Steven Whitley)
www.royaloakinn-hotel.co.uk   Map 105/611245
BB **B**   ✕ £6, 6pm onwards   S2 D2 T6 FI
V   B   ❖❖❖

Traditional family run country pub on the Trans Pennine Trail. 7 miles from Selby with large medieval abbey. 30 minutes drive to the historic city of York. Large camping and caravanning field. Extensive menu with midweek specials.

● Ingleby Cross (Northallerton)
North York Moors
Coast To Coast Walk

Park House, DL6 3PE ☎ 01609 882571 www.coast-to-coast.org.uk
Map 99/453995   BB **A**   ✕ nearby   S2 F3   D   ❖❖

● Ingleton (Carnforth)
Yorkshire Dales

Ingleborough View Guest House, Main Street, LA6 3HH ☎ 015242 41523
(Mrs Sue King)   www.ingleboroughview.com   Map 98/695732
BB **B**   ✕ nearby   D3 T2 FI   B   D   ❖❖❖

Newbutts Farm, High Bentham, LA2 7AN
☎ 015242 41238 (Jean Newhouse)   Map 98/696695
BB **B**   ✕ book first £12.50, 6-7pm   S2 D2 T2 F2   Closed Dec
V   B   D   ❖❖❖

☆ The Dales Guest House
Main Street, LA6 3HH ☎ 015242 41401 (Penny & Paul Weaire)
dalesgh@hotmail.com   Map 98/692727
BB **B**   ✕ book first £12, 6:30pm   SI D3 TI
V   B   D   M   ❖❖❖

A friendly welcome, cosy en-suite rooms with lovely views & excellent home cooking will make your stay one to remember.
The perfect base for exploring the Dales, Lakes and the Forest of Bowland.
For details of bargain breaks & a brochure call Penny or Paul.

☆ Riverside Lodge
24 Main Street, LA6 3HJ ☎ 015242 41359 (Andrew Foley)
www.riversideingleton.co.uk   Map 98/691727
BB **C**   ✕ book first £15   D/T7   ❖❖❖❖

Beautiful riverside location, rooms with views of Ingleborough or wooded riverbank. Nearby waterfalls walk, 2 ground floor rooms, all rooms en-suite, large lounge, open fire, T.V. Snooker table, sauna, licensed, conservatory dining room, private car park.

The Station Inn, Ribblehead, LA6 3AS ☎ 015242 41274
www.thestationinn.net Map 98/779799
BB **B** ✕ £5, 6:30-8:30pm SI D3 TI FI ⚌(Ribblehead)
Ⓥ Ⓑ Ⓓ 🐾☕♨🚗🛄Ⓜ ◆◆◆ See Hostels also.

● **Keld (Richmond)**
　Yorkshire Dales
　Pennine Way & Coast To Coast Walk

☆ **Butt House**
DL11 6LJ ☎ 01748 886374(Ernest & Doreen Whitehead)
butthouse@supanet.com Map 91/893009
BB **B** ✕ book first £12, 7:30pm SI D2 TI FI Closed Oct-Feb
Ⓥ Ⓑ Ⓓ ⊛ 🐾☕♨

Country house Bed and Breakfast on Coast to Coast Walk, Pennine Way, Herriot Way & Swale Way. Also available: the original Coast to Coast Accommodation Guide (2005 edition due out 3rd January 2005). Price £3 to cover cost & postage.

● **Kettlewell (Skipton)**
　Yorkshire Dales
　Dales Way
Lynburn, BD23 5RF ☎ 01756 760803 (Lorna Thornborrow)
lorna@lthornborrow.fsnet.co.uk Map 98/970720
BB **B** ✕ nearby DI TI Ⓓ 🐾♨ ◆◆◆

🐾☕ Greta House, Middle Lane, BD23 5QX ☎ 01756 760268 (Sue Light)
www.gretahouse.com Map 98/969723
BB **B** ✕ nearby D2 TI Ⓑ Ⓓ ⊛ 🐾♨

● **Kilburn (York)**
　North York Moors
　Cleveland Way
🐾☕ Church Farm, YO61 4AH ☎ 01347 868318 (Mrs C Thompson)
churchfarmkilburn@yahoo.co.uk Map 100/516796
BB **B** ✕ book first £9, 6-8pm DI FI Ⓥ Ⓑ Ⓓ 🐾☕♨🚗♨ ◆◆

● **Kildale (Whitby)**
　North York Moors
　Cleveland Way
Bankside Cottage, YO21 2RT
☎ 01642 723259 (Mrs Ann Addison) Map 94/603100
BB **B** ✕ book first £12, 7pm DI TI FI ⚌(Kildale) Ⓥ Ⓓ ⊛ 🐾

● **Kirkby Malham (Skipton)**
　Pennine Way
Victoria Inn, BD23 4BS ☎ 01729 830499 Map 98/894609
BB **C** ✕ £6.50, 6-8:30pm D3 TI Ⓥ Ⓑ 🐾☕♨

● **Kirkbymoorside (York)**
　North York Moors
　Link Through the Tabular Hills Walk
Mount Pleasant, Rudland, Fadmoor, YO62 7JJ ☎ 01751 431579
(Mary Clarke) www.mountpleasantbedandbreakfast.co.uk Map 100/657917
BB **B** ✕ book first £6.50, 6:30-8pm TI FI Ⓥ Ⓓ 🐾♨🚗 ◆◆◆

● **Leyburn**
The Haven, Market Place, DL8 5BJ ☎ 01969 623814 (Paula & David Burke)
www.havenguesthouse.co.uk Map 99/111904
BB **B** ✕ nearby D4 F2 Ⓑ Ⓓ ⊛ 🐾♨🚗! ◆◆◆◆

● **Long Preston (Skipton)**
　Yorkshire Dales
　Ribble Way
The Barn, 8 Main St, BD23 4ND
☎ 01729 840426 (Mrs Elaine Fleming) Map 103/834581
BB **B** ✕ nearby D2 ⚌(Long Preston) Ⓑ Ⓓ ⊛ 🐾☕♨🚗!

● **Malham (Skipton)**
　Yorkshire Dales
　Pennine Way

☆ 🐾☕ **River House Hotel**
BD23 4DA ☎ 01729 830315
www.riverhousehotel.co.uk Map 98/901628
BB **C** ✕ book first £15, 7-8pm SI D6 T2 FI
Ⓥ Ⓑ Ⓓ ⊛ 🐾☕♨! ◆◆◆◆

A Victorian country house hotel, originally built in 1664, offering superb breakfasts & evening meals. Centrally located in this beautiful Dales village amidst stunning scenery, with the Pennine Way running just past the front door. A warm welcome awaits you on your arrival.

☆ 🐾☕ **Beck Hall Guest House**
BD23 4DJ ☎ 01729 830332 (Simon Maufe)
www.beckhallmalham.com Map 98/898631
BB **B** ✕ £7.50, 7-9pm SI D6 T3 FI
Ⓥ Ⓑ Ⓓ 🐾☕♨!♨ ◆◆◆

A friendly family welcome to all at 18th century Beck Hall. 3 nights price of 2 Nov-Feb midweek. Located on Pennine Way and Dales Way. Riverside location. Special diets catered for. Meals until 6pm or 2 pubs 100 yards away. Internet PC. Group discounts.

● **Malton**
　Yorkshire Wolds Way

☆ **Old Station Farm**
High St, Amotherby, YO17 6TL ☎ 01653 693683 (Heather Hailstone)
www.oldstationfarm.co.uk Map 100/749735
BB **C** ✕ book first £20, 7pm D2 TI FI Closed Dec-Jan
Ⓥ Ⓑ Ⓓ ⊛ 🐾☕♨ ◆◆◆◆Ⓖ

Old Station Farm is an award winning Georgian farmhouse. 4 miles from Castle Howard. En-suite bedrooms. Ideally located for walking enthusiasts. Close to Howardian Hills and North Yorkshire Moors.

Suddaby's Crown Hotel, Wheelgate, YO17 7HP ☎ 01653 692038
(R N Suddaby) www.suddabys.co.uk   Map 100/788718
BB **B**   ✕ nearby   D1 T4 F3   ▰(Malton) Ⓑ Ⓓ ☎ ♿

● **Masham (Ripon)**
Bank Villa Guest House, HG4 4DB ☎ 01765 689605
www.bankvilla.com   Map 99/224810
BB **C**   ✕ book first £15, 7:30pm   D3 T2 F1
Ⓥ Ⓑ Ⓓ ⊛ ☎♿ ➔ !   ◆◆◆◆

● **Newby Wiske (Northallerton)**
▰◀ Well House, DL7 9EX
☎ 01609 772253 (Mrs Judith Smith)   Map 99/368875
BB **B**   ✕ book first £8, 6-7pm   D2
Ⓑ Ⓓ ⊛ ☎♿☎ ➔ !   ◆◆◆◆

● **Northallerton**
Coast To Coast Walk
▰◀ Alverton Guest House, 26 South Parade, DL7 8SG ☎ 01609 776207
(Mrs M Longley) www.alvertonguesthouse.com   Map 99/367934
BB **B**   ✕ nearby   S3 D2 T1 F1   ▰(Northallerton)
Ⓑ Ⓓ ☎♿☎ ➔   ◆◆◆

● **Osmotherley (Northallerton)**
North York Moors
Cleveland Way & Coast To Coast Walk
Stonehaven, Thimbleby, DL6 3PY ☎ 01609 883689 (Margaret Shepherd)
stonehaven@tiscali.co.uk   Map 99/449954
BB **B**   ✕ book first £6, 6:30pm   D1 T1
Ⓥ Ⓑ Ⓓ ☎♿☎ ➔ Ⓜ   ◆◆◆

The Walking Shop, 4 West End, DL6 3AA
☎ 01609 883818 (Mr Chris Gaunt)
www.coast2coast.co.uk/osmotherleywalkingshop   Map 99/456973
BB **B**   ✕ nearby   S1 D1 T2   Ⓓ ⊛ ☎♿☎   ◆◆◆

● **Pateley Bridge (Harrogate)**
Roslyn Hotel, 9 King Street, HG3 5AT ☎ 01423 711374
www.roslynhotel.co.uk   Map 99/157656
BB **C**   ✕ nearby   D2 T2 F2   Ⓑ Ⓓ♿ ➔   ◆◆◆

☆ **Harefield Hall Hotel**
Ripon Rd, HG3 5QE ☎ 08451 662507 (Carl, Tina, Roger Blancken)
www.harefieldhallhotel.co.uk   Map 99/162650
BB **C**   ✕ £25.95, 6:30-9:30pm   S6 D8 T6 F4
Ⓥ Ⓑ Ⓓ ☎♿ ➔ ! ♨

Located in 28 acres of woodland and alongside the River Nidd. An ideal base to explore the surrounding AONBs and also the nearby attractions of Brimham Rocks, Mother Shiptons Cave and Stump Cross Caverns. All rooms en-suite.

● **Pickering**
North York Moors
103 Westgate, YO18 8BB ☎ 01751 472500 (Mrs R Metcalf)
Map 100/793840   BB **B**   ✕ nearby   D2 T1

☆ **Vivers Mill**
Mill Lane, YO18 8DJ ☎ 01751 473640
www.viversmill.com   Map 100/796835
BB **B**   ✕ nearby   D5 T2 F1   ▰(Pickering)
Ⓑ ⊛ ♿☎   ◆◆◆

Ancient watermill set in peaceful surroundings. Working waterwheel and milling machinery retained. Original millstone centrepiece of large comfortable lounge. Ideal for NYM, moors, coast, York. Non-smoking.

☆ **The Old Manse Guest House**
Middleton Road, YO18 8AL (Mr & Mrs C Gardner)
☎ 01751 476484   www.oldmansepickering.co.uk   Map 100/792841
BB **B**   ✕ book first £15.75, 7pm   D7 T2 F1   ▰(Pickering)
Ⓥ Ⓑ Ⓓ ⊛ ☎♿☎   ◆◆◆◆

The Old Manse has ten en-suite bedrooms, large on-site car park and is located four minutes walk from North York Moors Steam Railway and the town centre. Dinner is available every night. Superb walks nearby.

☆ ▰◀ **Bramwood Guest House**
19 Hallgarth, YO18 7AW (Marilyn Bamforth)
☎ 01751 474066   www.bramwoodguesthouse.co.uk   Map 100/800840
BB **B**   ✕ book first £17.50, 6:30pm   S2 D4 T1 F1   ▰(Pickering)
Ⓥ Ⓑ Ⓓ ⊛ ☎♿ ➔ ! Ⓜ   ◆◆◆◆Ⓢ   See SC also

Elegant Georgian Grade II listed building in quiet location close to town centre. All rooms are en-suite with TV & generous hospitality trays. Hearty breakfasts. Lounge with log fire & TV. Private parking. Charming walled garden. Steam railway nearby.

● **Reeth (Richmond)**
Yorkshire Dales
Coast To Coast Walk
▰◀ Springfield House, Quaker Close , DL11 6UY ☎ 01748 884634
(Mrs Denise Guy) denise@guy426.fsnet.co.uk   Map 98/039993
BB **B**   ✕ nearby   D1 T1   Ⓑ Ⓓ ⊛ ☎♿ ➔   ◆◆◆◆
Free refreshments on arrival

For an explanation of the symbols used in this guide see the
Key to Abbreviations and Symbols on p 7

The Buck Hotel, DL11 6SW ☎ 01748 884210
www.buckhotel.co.uk   Map 98/038993
BB **C** ✗ £9, 6-9pm   S1 D6 T2 F1   Ⓥ Ⓑ Ⓓ 🐾🛁❗✿   ◆◆◆◆

Arkle House, Mill Lane, DL11 6SJ ☎ 01748 884815
www.arklehouse.com   Map 98/040994
BB **B** ✗ nearby   D1 F1   Ⓑ Ⓓ ⊗ 🐾🛁❗ ◆◆◆◆

Walpardoe, Anvil Square, DL11 6TE ☎ 01748 884626 (Ann Bain)
www.coast2coast.co.uk   Map 98/038992
BB **A** ✗ nearby   S1 T1   Closed Nov-Jan   Ⓓ 🐾🛁

Hillary House, 4 Hillary Terrace, DL11 6TG
☎ 01748 884171   (Clive Blodwell)
hillaryreeth@aol.com   Map 98/039994
BB **A** ✗ nearby   D1 T1   Ⓓ ⊗ 🐾🛁

Elder Peak, Arkengarthdale Road, DL11 6QX ☎ 01748 884770
(Mrs M E Peacock)   Map 98/036999
BB **A** ✗ nearby   D1 T1   Closed Nov-Mar   🐾🛁🚗   ◆◆◆

● **Richmond**
  North York Moors
  Coast To Coast Walk

West End Guest House & Cottages, 45 Reeth Road, DL10 4EX
☎ 01748 824783 (K & T Teeley) www.stayatwestend.com   Map 92/161011
BB **B** ✗ nearby   S1 D3 T1   Closed Dec-Jan
Ⓑ Ⓓ ⊗ 🐾🛁🚗❗ ◆◆◆◆ See SC also.

☆ **Willance House Guest House**
24 Frenchgate, DL10 7AG ☎ 01748 824467 (Thelma Jackson)
www.willancehouse.com   Map 92/174012
BB **B** ✗ nearby   S1 D1 T1 F1
Ⓑ Ⓓ ⊗ 🐾🛁🚗🎿 ◆◆◆◆

Willance House, once the home of Robert
Willance the first alderman of Richmond, is
the oldest in Richmond dating back to 1660.
Set on a wide cobbled street just 2 mins walk
from the market place. All rooms are en-suite
with TV. Comfortable lounge for our guests.

The Old Brewery Guest House, 29 The Green, DL10 4RG
☎ 01748 822460   www.oldbreweryguesthouse.com   Map 92/168006
BB **B** ✗ nearby   S1 D3 T2   Ⓑ Ⓓ ⊗ 🐾🛁❗🎿   ◆◆◆◆

● **Ripon**
Bishopton Grove House, HG4 2QL
☎ 01765 600888 (Susi Wimpress)
wimpress@bronco.co.uk   Map 99/301711
BB **B** ✗ nearby   D1 T1 F1   Ⓑ Ⓓ 🐾🛁🎿   ◆◆◆

● **Robin Hood's Bay (Whitby)**
  North York Moors
  Cleveland Way & Coast To Coast Walk
South View, Sledgates, Fylingthorpe, YO22 4TZ
☎ 01947 880025 (Mrs Reynolds)   Map 94/940048
BB **B** ✗ nearby   D2   🐾🛁

The Villa, Station Rd, YO22 4RA ☎ 01947 881043 (Jane Saxton)
www.thevillarhb.co.uk   Map 94/952054
BB **C** ✗ nearby   S2 D2 T1   ⚐(Whitby) Ⓓ 🐾🛁❗

● **Rosedale Abbey (Pickering)**
  North York Moors

☆ **Sevenford House**
Thorgill, YO18 8SE ☎ 01751 417283 (Mrs Linda Sugars)
www.sevenford.com   Map 100,94/724949
BB **B** ✗ nearby   D1 T1 F1
Ⓑ Ⓓ ⊗ 🐾🛁🚗❗ ◆◆◆◆Ⓢ

Originally a
vicarage, built from
the stones of
Rosedale Abbey,
Sevenford House
stands in 4 acres of
lovely gardens in the
heart of the beautiful
Yorkshire Moors
National Park.

The tastefully furnished bedrooms offer wonderful views of valley and moorland
& overlook Rosedale. There is a relaxing guests' lounge with open fire & shelves
full of books. An excellent base for exploring the region with over 500 square
miles of open moorland, with ruined abbeys, Roman roads and a steam railway.
Children welcome. Non-smoking.
Email: sevenford@aol.com

● **Runswick Bay (Saltburn-by-the-Sea)**
  North York Moors
  Cleveland Way

☆ **The Firs**
26 Hinderwell Lane, TS13 5HR ☎ 01947 840433
www.the-firs.co.uk   Map 94/791168
BB **B** ✗ book first £16.50, 6-9pm   S1 D4 T2 F4   Closed Jan-Feb
Ⓥ Ⓑ Ⓓ 🐾🛁🎿 ◆◆◆◆ See Groups also

Situated at the top of the bank in
the beautiful scenic coastal village
of Runswick Bay. An ideal base for
moors and coast, on the edge of
the North Yorkshire Moors NP,
Cleveland Way and Coast to Coast
paths, 5 minutes from the beach.

● **Saltburn-by-the-Sea (Middlesbrough)**
  Cleveland Way
The Rose Garden, 20 Hilda Place, TS12 1BP ☎ 01287 622947
(Rose Thacker)   www.therosegarden.co.uk   Map 94/661212
BB **B** ✗ nearby   D/T2 T1   Closed Jan   ⚐(Saltburn)
Ⓑ Ⓓ ⊗ 🐾🛁🚗   ◆◆◆◆

● **Scarborough**
  Cleveland Way & Link Through the Tabular
  Hills Walk
Brincliffe Edge Private Hotel, 105 Queens Parade, YO12 7HY ☎ 01723 364834
www.brincliffeedgehotel.co.uk   Map 101/039895
BB **B** ✗ nearby   S2 D5 F3   Closed Dec-Jan   ⚐(Scarborough)
Ⓑ Ⓓ 🐾🛁 ◆◆◆

☆ 🛰◀ **Gordon Hotel**
24 Ryndleside, YO12 6AD ☎ 01723 362177 (Lawrence & Christine Watson)
www.gordonhotel.co.uk Map 101/032891
BB **B** ✗ £8, 6pm S1 D5 T2 F2 ⚍(Scarborough)
Ⓥ Ⓑ Ⓓ ⊛🐾☕🛏🚗❗ ◆◆◆◆

The Gordon Hotel is a 10 bedroom detached and licensed establishment in a beautiful situation peacefully overlooking Peasholm Glen & Park.

Our delightful bar offers a good selection of drinks where you can end the day relaxing with the many friends you are sure to make.
The English Tourism Council have rated The Gordon Hotel as 4 diamonds, so whether you are staying for bed and breakfast or half board we can offer the highest standards and excellent value for money.
Email: sales@gordonhotel.co.uk

🛰◀ Russell Hotel, 22 Ryndleside, YO12 6AD
☎ 01723 365453 www.russellhotel.net Map 101/033893
BB **B** ✗ book first £10, 5:45pm S1 D3 T2 F3 ⚍(Scarborough)
Ⓥ Ⓑ Ⓓ 🐾☕🛏🚗❗🏍 ◆◆◆◆

🛰◀ Princess Court Guest House, 11 Princess Royal Terrace, YO11 2RP
☎ 01723 501922 (Pam & Irvin Randerson)
www.princesscourt.co.uk Map 101/041875
BB **B** ✗ book first £9, 6pm S2 D2 T1 F2 ⚍(Scarborough)
Ⓥ Ⓑ Ⓓ 🐾☕🛏 ◆◆◆

Brontes Guest House, 135 Columbus Ravine, YO12 7QZ
☎ 01723 362934 Map 101/037892
BB **A** ✗ £5, 7pm S1 D2 T2 F2 ⚍(Scarborough)
Ⓥ Ⓑ Ⓓ 🐾☕🛏❗

DAVID BELL

● Settle
Yorkshire Dales
Ribble Way & Pennine Way

☆ **Low Skibeden Farmhouse**
Harrogate Rd, BD23 6AB ☎ 01756 793849 (Mrs Simpson)
www.yorkshirenet.co.uk/accgde/lowskibeden
Map 104/012524 BB **B** D2 T1 F3 ⚍(Skipton)
Ⓑ Ⓓ ⊛🐾☕🛏 ◆◆◆◆

16th century farmhouse. Quiet country location set in private grounds. Beautiful views, garden and parking. Offering home from home comforts and little luxuries in guests' lounge. Close to many AONBs. 2 mins by car to the market town of Skipton.

☆ **Whitefriars Country Guest House**
Church Street, BD24 9JD ☎ 01729 823753
www.whitefriars-settle.co.uk Map 98/819637
BB **B** ✗ nearby S1 D3 T2 F3 ⚍(Settle)
Ⓥ Ⓑ Ⓓ ⊛🐾☕🛏❗ ◆◆◆◆

Delightful 17th century family home, standing in secluded gardens in the heart of the market town of Settle. Ideal for walking, cycling and touring: Yorkshire Dales National Park, The Three Peaks and Settle-Carlisle Railway. Recommended by WHICH? Good B&B Guide.

Liverpool House Guest House, Chapel Square, BD24 9HR
☎ 01729 822247 (Greta & Robert Duerden) Map 98/822635
BB **B** ✗ nearby S2 D3 T2 ⚍(Settle)
Ⓑ Ⓓ ⊛🐾☕🚗 ◆◆◆◆

● Skelton (Saltburn-by-the-Sea)
Cleveland Way
🛰◀ Westerland's Guest House, 27 East Parade, TS12 2BJ
☎ 01287 650690 (B Bull) Map 94/655185
BB **A** ✗ book first £6, 6:30-7pm S2 D3 F1
Ⓥ Ⓑ Ⓓ ⊛🐾☕🛏🚗❗🏍 ◆◆◆◆

● Skipton
Yorkshire Dales

☆ **Golden Lion Hotel**
Duke Street, BD24 9DU ☎ 01729 822203
www.yorkshirenet.co.uk/stayat/goldenlion
Map 98/819635 BB **B** ✗ book first £8.75, 6-10pm D8 T2 F2
⚍(Settle) Ⓥ Ⓑ Ⓓ 🐾☕🏍 ◆◆◆◆

17th century coaching inn with log fires, in Settle's bustling market place. Prime centre for exploring the Yorkshire Dales, Three Peaks and five minutes walk from Settle — Carlisle Railway. Groups welcome.

● Sleights (Whitby)
North York Moors
Coast To Coast Walk

☆ Ryedale House
156 Coach Road, Sleight, YO22 5EQ
☎ 01947 810534 (Pat Beale) Map 94/866070
BB **B** ✗ nearby S2 D2 Closed Nov-Mar
Ⓑ Ⓓ ⊗ 🍵♨ ◆◆◆◆

Welcoming home at foot of the moors in National Park 4 miles from Whitby. Magnificent scenery, superb walking, picturesque harbours, cliffs, beaches, scenic railways— it's all here!

Beautifully appointed rooms, private facilities, many extras. Guest lounge, extensive breakfast menu served with panoramic views, facing large landscaped gardens. Local inn and fish restaurant just a short walk. Minimum booking 2 nights. Regret no pets/children. B&B £23-27. Exclusive to non-smokers

---

● Staithes (Saltburn-by-the-Sea)
North York Moors
Cleveland Way

Brooklyn, Brown's Terrace, TS13 5BG
☎ 01947 841396 (Margaret Heald)
mheald@tesco.net Map 94/782187
BB **B** ✗ nearby D2 T1 Ⓓ 🐴♨🍵🚗! 🔦 ◆◆◆

● Summerbridge (Harrogate)
🍴 Dalriada, Cabin Lane, Dacre Banks, HG3 4EE
☎ 01423 780512 (Mrs J E Smith) Map 99/196621
BB **B** ✗ nearby S1 D1 T1 Ⓑ Ⓓ ⊗ 🐴♨🚗 ◆◆◆

● Sutton Bank (Thirsk)
North York Moors
Cleveland Way

High House Farm, YO7 2HJ
☎ 01845 597557 (Mrs K M Hope) Map 100/514834
BB **B** ✗ book first £10, 6pm S1 D1 T1 F1
Ⓥ Ⓓ 🐴♨🚗! ◆◆◆

Cote Faw, YO7 2EZ ☎ 01845 597363 (Mrs J Jeffray)
Map 100/522829
BB **A** ✗ nearby S1 D1 T1 Ⓓ 🐴 ◆◆

● Thwaite (Richmond)
North York Moors
Pennine Way

Kearton Country Hotel, DL11 6DR ☎ 01748 886277 (I & J Danton)
www.keartoncountryhotel.co.uk Map 98/892982
BB **B** ✗ book first £6, 6:30-7pm S1 D3 T7 F2
Ⓥ Ⓑ Ⓓ 🍵♨ ◆◆◆

● Westhouse (Ingleton)
Yorkshire Dales

☆ 🍴 Hazelwood Barn
LA6 3PF ☎ 01524 242111
(Mrs Christine Lawson) Map 98/675726
BB **B** ✗ nearby D1 T2 Closed Dec-Jan
Ⓑ Ⓓ ⊗ 🐴♨🍵🚗!

A warm welcome awaits you in a converted dales barn 1/2 mile from Ingleton, where hot drinks & home baking are served in visitors lounge each evening at 9pm. Peaceful, beautiful views. Ideally situated for walking or touring the Dales and Lakes.

● Whitby
North York Moors
Cleveland Way & Coast To Coast Walk

Ashford Guest House, 8 Royal Crescent, YO21 3EJ
☎ 01947 602138 (Janice & Donna Hillier)
www.ashfordguesthouse.co.uk Map 94/894113
BB **B** ✗ nearby D5 T1 F3 🚍(Whitby) Ⓑ Ⓓ ⊗ ♨ ◆◆◆

🍴 Prospect Villa, 13 Prospect Hill, YO21 1QE
☎ 01947 603118 (J & C Gledhill)
chris@prospectvilla.freeserve.co.uk Map 94/894105
BB **B** ✗ nearby S2 D2 T1 F2 🚍(Whitby) Ⓑ Ⓓ ⊗ 🐴♨ ◆◆◆

Storrbeck Guest House, 9 Crescent Avenue, YO21 3ED ☎ 01947 605468
www.storrbeck.fsnet.co.uk Map 94/894110
BB **B** ✗ nearby S5 D5 🚍(Whitby)
Ⓑ Ⓓ ⊗ 🐴♨ ◆◆◆◆Ⓢ

☆ Rosewood
3 Ocean Rd, YO21 3HY ☎ 01947 820534
Map 94/890113
BB **B** ✗ nearby D2 🚍(Whitby)
Ⓥ Ⓑ Ⓓ ⊗ 🐴♨ ◆◆◆◆Ⓢ

Quiet B&B, 4 Diamonds Silver Award. Large double en-suite rooms, bath and showers, hospitality trays and fridges. Residents' own lounge with coal fire, TV and video. Tea and sandwiches on arrival.

£25 pppn. Open all year round.

☆ 🍴 Saxonville Hotel
Ladysmith Ave, YO21 3HX ☎ 01947 602631 (Richard Newton)
www.saxonville.co.uk Map 94/891113
BB **C** ✗ £11, 7-8:30pm S4 D8 T9 F2 Closed Dec-Jan 🚍(Whitby)
Ⓥ Ⓑ Ⓓ 🐴🍵 ★★★ See Groups also

Family run, the Saxonville Hotel is found just a few minutes stroll from the narrow streets and winding alleyways of Whitby's historic town centre. Whitby is the gateway to the North Yorkshire Moors, and well situated for the Cleveland Way and Coast to Coast walks.

Kimberley House Hotel, 7 Havelock Place, YO21 3ER ☎ 01947 604125
(Julie & Steve Walton) www.kimberleyhousehotel.co.uk   Map 94/896112
BB **B**   ✗ nearby   S1 D5 T2 F2   Closed Jan   ᴧᴧᴧ(Whitby)
Ⓥ Ⓑ Ⓓ ⊛ 🐾 🛆 ♦♦♦♦

● **Wigglesworth (Skipton)**
Ribble Way
Cowper Cottage, BD23 4RP ☎ 01729 840598 (Marion Howard)
www.yorkshirenet.co.uk/stayat/cowper   Map 103/810569
BB **B**   ✗ nearby   D1 T1   Ⓑ Ⓓ ⊛ 🐾 🛆 🛆 ⬤ !   ♦♦♦♦

SOUTH YORKSHIRE

● **Doncaster**
10 Saxton Avenue, DN4 7AX ☎ 01302 535578 (Mrs A Gibbs)
johnrichard.gibbs@virgin.net   Map 111/602020
BB **B**   ✗ book first £10, 7:30pm   S2 D2 T2   ᴧᴧᴧ(Doncaster)
Ⓥ Ⓑ Ⓓ ⊛ 🐾 🛆 🛆 ! Ⓜ

● **Elsecar (Barnsley)**
Trans Pennine Trail
Old Bank House, 82 Fitzwilliam ST, S74 8EZ ☎ 01226 747960 (Ron Foster)
www.webcare.co.uk/obh   Map 110,111/384999
BB **B**   ✗ nearby   T1 F1   ᴧᴧᴧ(Elsecar)   🛆 ! 🐾   ♦♦♦

WEST YORKSHIRE

● **Greetland (Halifax)**
Calderdale Way
Crawstone Knowl Farm, Rochdale Road, Upper Greetland, HX4 8PX
☎ 01422 370470 (Mrs Sylvia Shackleton)   Map 104/081213
BB **B**   ✗ nearby   S1 D1 T1 F1   ᴧᴧᴧ(Sowerby Bridge)
Ⓑ Ⓓ ⊛ 🐾 🛆 🛆 ! 🐾   ♦♦♦

● **Haworth**
Pennine Way
Apothecary Guest House, 86 Main Street, BD22 8DP ☎ 01535 643642
(Mr N J Sisley) http://theapothecaryguesthouse.co.uk   Map 104/030372
BB **B**   ✗ nearby   S1 D3 T2 F1   ᴧᴧᴧ(Haworth)
Ⓑ Ⓓ ⊛ 🐾 🛆   ♦♦♦

● **Hebden Bridge**
Pennine Way, Calderdale Way & Pennine Bridleway
Myrtle Grove, Old Lees Road, HX7 8HL ☎ 01422 846078
(Mrs M J Audsley) www.myrtlegrove.btinternet.co.uk   Map 103/994278
BB **B**   ✗ nearby   D1 F1   ᴧᴧᴧ(Hebden Bridge)
Ⓑ Ⓓ 🐾 🛆 🛆 ! 🐾 Ⓜ   ♦♦♦♦   See SC also. Vegetarian/Vegan
Mytholm House, Mytholm Bank, HX7 6DL ☎ 01422 847493
(Brenda & Jim Botten) www.mytholmhouse.co.uk   Map 103/983274
BB **B**   ✗ book first £12   S1 D/T2   ᴧᴧᴧ(Hebden Bridge)
Ⓥ Ⓑ Ⓓ ⊛ 🐾 🛆 🛆 Ⓜ   ♦♦♦♦Ⓢ

● **Holmfirth (Huddersfield)**
Uppergate Farm, Hepworth, HD9 1TG ☎ 01484 681369
(Mrs Alison Booth) www.uppergatefarm.co.uk   Map 110/162068
BB **B**   ✗ book first £10, 7-9pm   T2 F1
Ⓥ Ⓑ Ⓓ ⊛ 🐾 🛆 🛆 !   ♦♦♦♦

● **Kirkburton (Huddersfield)**
The Woodman Inn, Thunderbridge, HD8 0PX ☎ 01484 605778
www.woodman-inn.co.uk   Map 110/189115
BB **C**   ✗ £10, until 9:30pm   S2 D9 T1   Ⓥ Ⓑ Ⓓ 🐾 🛆   ♦♦♦♦

● **Marsden (Huddersfield)**
Pennine Way
Throstle Nest Cottage, 3 Old Mount Road, HD7 6DU ☎ 01484 846371
(Ms Joan Hayes) www.throstle-nest.co.uk   Map 110/045115
BB **B**   ✗ nearby   T1 F1   ᴧᴧᴧ(Marsden)
Ⓓ ⊛ 🐾 🛆 🛆 ! Ⓜ   ♦♦♦♦   Veggie breakfasts

● **Stanbury (Keighley)**
Pennine Way

☆ **Ponden House**
BD22 0HR ☎ 01535 644154 (Mrs Taylor)
www.pondenhouse.co.uk   Map 103/992371
BB **B**   ✗ book first £14, 7pm   D1 T1 F1
Ⓥ Ⓑ Ⓓ 🐾 🛆 🐾 Ⓜ   ♦♦♦♦

"Brontë Country"

Relax in a tranquil historic setting.
Enjoy panoramic views over reservoir and
moors, log fires, imaginative home cooking
and warm hospitality.

Call Brenda Taylor for a brochure.

● **Todmorden**
Pennine Way & Calderdale Way
Highstones Guest House, Rochdale Road, Walsden, OL14 6TY
☎ 01706 816534 (Heather Pegg)   Map 103/939208
BB **A**   ✗ book first £10, 7-7:30pm   S1 D2   ᴧᴧᴧ(Walsden)
Ⓥ Ⓑ Ⓓ ⊛ 🐾 🐾   ♦♦♦
Cross Farm, Mankinholes, OL14 6HB
☎ 01706 813481 (Lesley Parkinson)   Map 103/960239
BB **B**   ✗ nearby   D/S2 T/S2 F1   ᴧᴧᴧ(Todmorden)
Ⓑ Ⓓ ⊛ 🐾 🛆 🛆 !   ♦♦♦♦

SELF-CATERING

EAST YORKSHIRE

● **Grindale**

☆ **Smithy Cottage**
☎ 01262 602367 (Mrs Charlotte Davey)
www.smithycottage.moonfruit.com
£250-£380 Sleeps 1-4 + cot. 1 cottage.
Inglenook fireplace. Four-poster bed. Aga cooker.   ⊛ 🐾   ★★★★

Set in quiet farming village. Ideal base for
Wolds, Moors, Yorkshire Coast four miles.
Single story detached cottage boasts
central heating, double glazing, Inglenook
with wood burner. Fully equipped country
kitchen with Aga. Four-poster bed. Private
parking and garden.

● South Cave

Rudstone Walk Farm ☎ 01430 422230 (Mrs Laura Greenwood)
www.rudstone-walk.co.uk
£230-£525   Sleeps 1-6. 6 apartments.
Superb views. Near Yorkshire Wolds Way. 🐾 ★★★★ See B&B also.

NORTH YORKSHIRE

● Askrigg
Yorkshire Dales

Syke's House ☎ 01969 650535 (Mrs B Bowe)
£250   Sleeps 4. 1 cottage.
Lounge with open fire. 🐾 See B&B also.
Elm Hill Cottage ☎ 01969 624252 (Peter & Liz Haythornthwaite)
www.elmhillholidaycottages.co.uk
£175-£400   Sleeps 4-6. 2 cottages.
High quality, central heating, private parking. 🚭 ★★★

● Aysgarth Falls
Yorkshire Dales

☆ Meadowcroft
☎ 01792 280068 (M C Mason)
mcmason@globalnet.co.uk
£172-£316   Sleeps 5. 1 cottage.
Wensleydale, unspoiled village in National Park. 🚭 🐾 ★★★

Wensleydale. Unspoilt village with pub and shop. Modern comfortable conversion of large traditional Dales barn in heart of National Park. Network of footpaths directly from cottage – a walker's pardise. Lovely views. Secure off-street parking and private paddock.

● Egton Bridge
North York Moors

☆ Broom Cottage
☎ 01947 895279 (M White)
www.egton-bridge.co.uk
£220-£610   Sleeps 4. 2 cottages.
🚭 ⚓(Egton Bridge) ★★★★ See B&B also.

Broom Cottage and Riverside Cottage, Egton Bridge. North Yorkshire Moors National Park. 4 star cosy cottages well equipped to a high standard. Quiet village setting with superb views. For a virtual tour visit our website. For further details and a brochure please phone or Email: mw@broom-house.co.uk

● Ganton

☎ 01944 710507 (Mrs Iris Hallaways)
www.gantonholidays.co.uk
£200-£250   Sleeps 3. 1 flat.   Closed Dec-Feb
Quiet. Close to Yorkshire Wolds Way, Moors.
🐾 See B&B also.

● Glaisdale
North York Moors

Red House Farm ☎ 01947 897242 (T J Spashett) www.redhousefarm.net
£200-£567   Sleeps 2-4. 2 cottages, 1 studio flat.
Award winning, listed barn conversions. ⚓(Glaisdale) 🐾 See B&B also.

● Grassington
Yorkshire Dales

☎ 01253 404726 (Ann Wadsworth)
£125-£260   Sleeps 2-4. 1 apartment.
Large, comfortable accommodation, overlooking village square. 🐾 ★★★
See Skipton also.

☆ Jerry & Ben's Holiday Cottages
☎ 01756 752369 (Judith Joy)
www.yorkshirenet.co.uk/stayat/jerryandbens
£134-£425   Sleeps 2-9. 7 cottages & flats.
Family run business for 33 years. 🐾

7 properties, Hebden Gill near Grassington, Yorkshire Dales National Park.
Open all year, sleep 2-9, £134- £425.
Brochure available: Mrs J Joy, Jerry and Ben's, Hebden, Skipton, N. Yorks BD23 5DL. Fax: 753370 Email: dawjoy@aol.com
Family run business for 33 years

● Grosmont
North York Moors

Ormonde House ☎ 01636 815570 (Mrs Miriam Duffy)
www.esk.org.uk
£275-£400   Sleeps 8. 1 cottage.
Stunning location, fantastic walks, coast, luxury. 🚭 ⚓(Grosmont) 🐾

● Hawes
Yorkshire Dales

Mile House Farm ☎ 01969 667481 (Anne Fawcett)
www.wensleydale.uk.com
£175-£650   Sleeps 2-7. 4 cottages.
Lovely character old dales stone cottages. 🚭 🐾 ★★★★

☎ 01959 523071 (Steve Birkin)   sbirkin@tinyworld.co.uk
£130-£280   Sleeps 6. 1 cottage.
Idyllic. Walking biking. Secure storage. Telephone 🚭 🐾

● Helmsley
North York Moors

Summerfield Farm ☎ 01439 748238 (Isabelle Rickatson)
£110-£250   Sleeps 6. 1 cottage.
Garden, open fire, winter short breaks. 🐾

● Ingleton
Yorkshire Dales

Hollin Tree Cottage ☎ 0151 7241067 (Paul Davenport)
www.hollintreecottage-ingleton.co.uk   £160-£260   Sleeps 4. 1 cottage.
Village location, waterfall walks. Three Peaks. ☺

● Kirkbymoorside
North York Moors

☎ 01751 417588 (Mrs A M Wilson)
£150-£210   Sleeps 3. 1 cottage. Good walking country, in national park. 🏠

● Leyburn

Dales View Hoiday Homes ☎ 01969 623707/622808 (Mr Chilton)
www.daleshols.co.uk   £140-£305   Sleeps 3-4. 3 cottages, 3 apts.
Secluded courtyard off marketplace. ⚊(Leyburn) 🏠 ★★★-★★★★

☆ Throstlenest Cottages
☎ 01969 623694 (Tricia Smith)
www.throstlenestcottages.co.uk
£170-£380   Sleeps 1-6. 6 cottages.
Glorious view, rural, town half mile. ⚊(Leyburn) ★★★   RA member

Six cosy, comfortable, well-equipped cottages converted from stone barns. All have a glorious panoramic view over Wensleydale and the high fells of Coverdale. Rural, yet town centre only half a mile. Sorry — no pets.

● Masham

☆ Dales View Cottages
☎ 01765 688820 (Hartley Moyes)
hrmoyes@aol.com
£250-£450   Sleeps 2-4. 2 cottages.
Stunning views. Located on village green. ☺ ★★★★

Two recently renovated Grade II listed barn conversions.

Set around picturesque village green of Fearby, with stunning rear views. Masham only 1.5 miles.

With splendid retained features, exposed oak beams, hand-made limestone fireplaces and luxury fitted bathrooms, and high quality kitchens. Excellent location for Wensleydale, Nidderdale and the much loved but little visited Colsterdale. Four reservoirs within 10 miles, Ripon Rowel walk 0.5 miles.

● Newton-upon-Rawcliffe
North York Moors

Manor Farm ☎ 01751 472601 (Elizabeth Kirk)
www.members.aol.com/manorfarmnewton
£195-£450   Sleeps 2-8. 3 cottages.
Character and comfort after splendid walks! 🏠 ★★★★

● Pickering
North York Moors

Cliff House Cottage Holidays ☎ 01723 859440 (Simon Morris)
www.cliffhouse-cottageholidays.co.uk
£225-£945   Sleeps 2-6.   6 cottages, 2 apt.
Indoor heated swimming pool. ★★★★

Let's Holiday ☎ 01751 475396 (John Wicks)
www.letsholiday.com
£255-£720   Sleeps 2-6. 1 cottage, 2 apts.
Indoor heated pool, jacuzzi and sauna   ☺ 🏠 ★★★★

Black Bull Caravan Park ☎ 01751 472528
http://blackbullpark.co.uk
£230-£330   Sleeps 6. 4 static caravans.   Closed Nov-Feb
Low season short breaks a possibility.   ☺ 🏠 See Hostels also.

☎ 07739 040358 (Paula Foster)
www.yorkshire-cottage.com
£185-£400   Sleeps 4. 1 cottage.
Cosy cottage, open fire, original beams.   ☺ 🏠

☆ Keld Head Farm Cottages
☎ 01751 473974 (Penny & Julian Fearn) www.keldheadcottages.com
£173-£964   Sleeps 2-8. 9 cottages.
Off peak discounts, couples, senior citizens ☺   ★★★★
See Groups also. Access category 3.

In open countryside on the edge of Pickering and the York Moors a picturesque group of stone cottages with beamed ceilings, stone fireplaces. Furnished with emphasis on comfort, some rooms with four-poster beds. Large gardens with garden house, play and barbecue area.

☎ 01751 473446 (Marilyn Bamforth)
www.bramwoodguesthouse.co.uk
£195-£450   Sleeps 2-4. 2 cottages.
Tastefully converted stables, Grade II listed.   ☺ ⚊(Pickering) ★★★★
RA member. See B&B also.

● Richmond
North York Moors

West End Guest House & Garden Cottages ☎ 01748 824783 (Trevor Teeley)
www.stayatwestend.com
£214-£356   Sleeps 4. 4 cottages.
Beautifully equipped, ideal for the Dales.   🏠   See B&B also.

● Robin Hood's Bay
North York Moors

Lingers Hill Farm ☎ 01947 880608 (Mrs F Harland)
£180-£325   Sleeps 2-4. 1 cottage.
Cosy character cottage. Lovely views. 🏠 ★★★

Grange Farm ☎ 01947 881080 (Denise Hooning)
www.grangefarm.net
£680-£1,700   Sleeps 14. 1 farmhouse.
Excellent base to explore Coast & Moors.   ☺   ★★★★

Rose Cottage ☎ 01977 681372 (Trevor & Tracey Robinson)
www.coast-country.info   £230-£350   Sleeps 2-4. 2 cottages.
Open fires, cosy and well equipped.   ☺   See Staithes & Morland also.

● Scarborough
North York Moors

☆ Wrea Head View
Anne Carlton ☎ 01484 659946
Sleeps 4 £240-£320 Closed Oct-Feb
Central heating and double glazing 1 bungalow

Spacious 2 bed bungalows, rural aspect. Central for walking in National Park and coastal paths. Many local attractions. Large conservatory and garden with table and seating giving extensive views to castle and sea. Parking in drive for 2 cars. Brochure.

● Settle
Yorkshire Dales

Selside Farm ☎ 01729 860367 (Mrs S E Lambert)
www.yorkshirenet.co.uk/stayat/selsidefarm
£160-£400 Sleeps 2-6. 1 cottage, 1 barn conversion.
Centre Three Peaks. Selside. Electric included. ★★★-★★★★

● Skipton
Yorkshire Dales

☎ 01253 404726 (Ann Wadsworth)
£145-£295 Sleeps 2-5. 1 house.
Panoramic moorland views, close Skipton centre.
(Skipton) ★★★ See Grassington also.

☎ 01756 795024 (Shelly Green) www.thistledo.co.uk
£163-£284 Sleeps 2. 1 cottage.
Peaceful and convenient location in Skipton. (Skipton)

● Staithes
North York Moors

Rose Cottage ☎ 01977 681372 (Trevor & Tracey Robinson)
www.coast-country.info
£360-£630 Sleeps 4-7. 1 cottage.
Stunning sea views, very well equipped
See Robin Hood's Bay & Morland also.

● Whitby
North York Moors

☆ Aislaby Lodge Cottages
☎ 01947 811822 (Mrs S Riddolls)
www.aislabylodgecottages.co.uk
£190-£600 Sleeps 2-21 4 farmhouse cottages
Stunning views, quiet location. (Ruswarp) ★★★-★★★★

Traditional stone cottages with stunning views over Esk Valley. 4 miles from Whitby and coastal villages. Ideal base for North Yorkshire Moors and coast. Excellent facilities, including laundry and drying room. Quiet location, ample parking.

Swallow Cottages ☎ 01947 603790 (Jill & Brian McNeil)
www.swallowcottages.co.uk £120-£505 Sleeps 2-7. 4 cottages.
Supervised by owners. (Whitby) ★★★★

The Crows Nest ☎ 01642 492144 (Mr E Tayler) www.crowsnestwhitby.co.uk
£145-£600 Sleeps 4-11. 1 house, 1 apartment.
Spacious 5 bedroom house. Apartment, panoramic views.
(Whitby) ★★★

WEST YORKSHIRE

● Hebden Bridge
Myrtle Grove ☎ 01422 846078 (Mr J A Holcroft)
www.myrtlegrove.btinternet.co.uk £230-£390 Sleeps 4. 1 cottage.
Secluded scenic historic stone weavers cottage.
(Hebden Bridge) ★★★ RA member. See B&B also.

Robin Hood Cottage ☎ 07977 459913 (Liz Woznicki)
www.robinhoodcottage.co.uk £150-£240 Sleeps 3. 1 cottage.
Cosy beams, real fire, weekends available.

GROUPS

NORTH YORKSHIRE

☆ Cober Hill (B&B)
Newlands Rd, Cloughton, Scarborough YO13 0AR
☎ 01723 870310 • www.coberhill.co.uk • Map/Grid Ref: 101/010948
BB £26 • Max 130 •
B D • See B&B also

Based six miles north of Scarborough on the edge of the North Yorkshire Moors and Heritage Coast, Cober Hill is an ideal location from which to enjoy walks along the Cleveland Way National Trail and surrounding areas.

Open all year, offering first class facilities to rambling groups, with a choice of 63 en-suite bedrooms, residents' lounges, high standards of hospitality, appetising packed lunches, drying room facilities and a minibus.

Email: enquiries@coberhill.co.uk

Yorkshire Dales

The Confluence Centre (SC) Northcote, Kilnsey, Skipton, BD23 5PT
☎ 01756 753525 (Tim Illingworth) www.the.confluencecentre.co.uk
SC £1,200 Min 18 D

North Yorkshire Moors

The Firs (B&B) 26 Hinderwell Lane, Runswick Bay, Nr Whitby TS13 5HR
☎ 01947 840433 (Mandy Shackleton) www.the-firs.co.uk Map 94/791168
BB £30 Min 2, max 24 Closed Nov-Feb
B D ◆◆◆◆ See B&B also

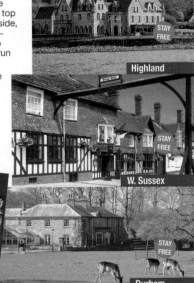

☆ **Saxonville Hotel** (B&B)
Ladysmith Ave, Whitby, YO21 3HX
☎ 01947 602631   www.saxonville.co.uk   Map 94/892114
DBB £55.50   Min 20, max 42   Closed Dec-Jan, July-Aug
✗ 🍴 Ⓑ Ⓓ ⊗ ⋙(Whitby) ★★★Ⓢ See B&B also

Family run, the Saxonville Hotel is found just a few minutes stroll from the narrow streets and winding alleyways of Whitby's historic town centre. Whitby is the gateway to the North Yorkshire Moors, and well situated for the Cleveland Way and Coast to Coast walks.

Keld Head Farm Cottages (SC) Pickering
☎ 01751 473974 (Penny & Julian Fearn) www.Keldheadcottages.com
SC £173-£946   9 cottages Min 2, max 44
✗ nearby 🍴 Ⓑ ★★★★ See SC also

Pincroft (SC) Ingleton ☎ 015242 41462   www.pine-croft.co.uk
Grid Ref: 699719   SC £1,680   Max 48   ✗ nearby ⊗ Ⓓ

HOSTELS, BUNKHOUSES & CAMPSITES

North Yorkshire Moors

Black Bull Caravan Park (C) Malton Rd, Pickering, YO18 8EA
☎ 01751 472528   http://blackbullpark.co.uk   Map 100/802815
Camping £5   Closed Nov-Feb ✗ ⊗ See SC also

The Royal Oak Inn (C) Main St, Hirst Courtney, Selby
☎ 01757 270633 (Steven Whitley)
www.royaloakinn-hotel.co.uk Map 105/611245
✗ 🍴 Ⓑ ◆◆◆ See B&B also

Yorkshire Dales
Dales Way

Skirfare Bridge Dales Barn (IH/BB) Kilnsey
☎ 01756 761028 (Mrs J L Foster)
www.skirfaredalesbarn.co.uk Map 98/971689
Bednight £8 ✗ nearby Ⓓ ⊗

Yorkshire Dales
Dales Way & Pennine Way

The Station Inn (B), Ribblehead, Ingleton ☎ 015242 41274
www.thestationinn.net   Map 98/764792
Bednight £8 ✗ 🍴 Ⓓ ⋙(Ribblehead) ◆◆◆
See B&B also

North Yorkshire Moors
Cleveland Way & Coast to Coast

Whitby Backpackers At Harbour Grange (IH) Spital Bridge,
Whitby YO22 4EF ☎ 01947 600817
www.whitbybackpackers.co.uk Map 94/901104
Bednight £10 ✗ nearby 🍴 ⊗ Ⓓ ⋙(Whitby)

Trans Pennine Trail

Greensprings Touring Park (C) Rockley Abbey Farm, Rockley Lane,
Worsbrough, Barnsley S75 3DS
☎ 01226 288298 (Mr R Hodgson)   Map 110/330020
Camping £4.50   Closed Nov-Mar   ✗ nearby

PUBS & TEAROOMS

● **Horton-in-Ribblesdale (Settle)**
Yorkshire Dales
⊤ The Golden Lion Hotel, Horton-in-Ribblesdale, BD24 0HB
☎ 01729 860206 (Michael Johnson)
www.goldenlionhotel.co.uk   Map 98/809721
⋙(Horton-in-Ribblesdale) ✗ Ⓥ 🏠 ♪ (Recorded)
Ⓛ Ⓖ Ⓑ(☺) ⤴

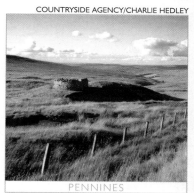

PENNINES

Northumberland is the largest county in the North East and includes over 60 miles of coast overlooked by majestic castles and windswept dunes studded with isolated coves.

Bordering Scotland to the north lie the Cheviot Hills, a spectacular walking destination of upland moors and grasslands dotted with ancient fortified dwellings and hillforts, remnants of past violent struggles to settle the land.

In the centre of the county the dramatic sandstone escarpments of the Simonside Hills and open hill walking of Upper Coquetdale contrast with the flatter plains and river valleys of Rothbury. To the west the Tyne Walk follows the great river from the High Pennines through wooded valleys and on to the coast of urban Tyneside.

A member says:

"To me there is always a sense of excitement when walking in the Cheviots. Be warned though, they can be very boggy underfoot."

Hadrian's Wall runs along Whin Sill ridge and through the Northumberland National Park offering views over Kielder Forest and far into the Cumbrian Hills in the west.

The 3,337 kilometres of paths in the neighbouring county of Durham include an 18-kilometre waymarked coastal footpath from Seaham to Crimdon, as well as trails through the National Nature Reserve at Castle Eden Dene; a sanctuary of the native red squirrel and the rare bird's nest orchid.

Sandwiched between Northumberland and Durham, Tyne and Wear has its share of walking attractions: roam along miles of sandy beaches or follow the nearby Derwent Valley Railway Path, with excellent views of the surrounding countryside from the 175-foot high Hownsgill Viaduct.

South of Durham, Redcar and Cleveland is sprinkled with forests, valleys and woodland, including the steep and sometimes treacherous East Cleveland valley. From Godfalter Hill in Flatts Lane Woodland Country Park you can see right across the Tees valley to the Durham Hills and the Hartlepool coast in the north, whilst the Guisborough Forest offers a tantalising taste of the neighbouring North York Moors.

Long Distance Paths

Cleveland Way CVL
Hadrian's Wall Path ....HNW
Pennine Way ....PNN
St Cuthbert's Way ....STC
Teesdale Way ....TSD

Public paths:

9,156km/ 5,686 miles

DURHAM COAST

COUNTRYSIDE AGENCY/CHARLIE HEDLEY

NORTH EAST
LOCAL RAMBLERS CONTACTS

NORTHUMBRIA
AREA SECRETARY
Mrs J P Taylor, 2 The Poplars, Gosforth,
Newcastle Upon Tyne, NE3 4AE
☎ 0191 285 3482
http://northern.ra-area.org.uk

GROUP SECRETARIES
Alnwick Mr C Whitney, The Haven,
Boulmer, Alnwick, Northumberland,
NE66 3BW ☎ 01665 577420

Berwick Mr John Bamford,
112 Main Street, Spittal,
Berwick On Tweed, TD15 1RD
☎ 01289 302559

Chester le Street Mr Brian Stout,
37 Kirkstone Drive, Carrville,
Durham City, DH1 1AH
☎ 0191 3864089

Derwentside Mrs J D Thomas,
48 Alderside Crescent, Lanchester,
Durham, DH7 0PZ
☎ 01207 520568
joycedthomas@hotmail.com

Durham City Mr C Ludman,
5 Church Street, Durham, DH1 3DG
☎ 0191 386 6886

Gateshead Mrs Hilary Clark,
15 Shibdon Park View, Blaydon,
Tyne & Wear, NE21 5HA
☎ 0191 4134 3643

Hexham Mrs R Blaylock,
10 Quatre Bras, Hexham,
Northumberland,
NE46 3JY ☎ 01434 604639

Morpeth Miss M Siggens,
17 Kingswell, Carlisle Lea,
Morpeth, Northumberland,
NE61 2TY ☎ 01670 518031

Northumbria Family Walking
Mrs E Smith, 18 Bath Terrace,
Newcastle Upon Tyne, NE3 1UH
☎ 0191 2132102

Northumbria Walking
Mrs A Johnstone, 27 Regents Park,
Wallsend, NE28 8UE

Ponteland Mr Colin Braithwaite,
105 Western Way, Ponteland,
Newcastle Upon Tyne, NE20 9LY
☎ 01661 822929

Sunderland Mrs P Jackson,
73 Houghton Road,
Hetton-Le-Hole,
Houghton Le Spring, DH5 9PQ
☎ 0191 526 0434

Tyneside Mrs Pennie Porter,
4 Angerton Gardens, Fenham,
Newcastle Upon Tyne, NE5 2JB

**For Local Ramblers Contacts in East
Yorkshire & Derwent, see Yorkshire**

NORTH YORKS & SOUTH DURHAM
AREA SECRETARY
Mr D G Lawrenson, Smithy Cottage,
Hunton, Bedale, DL8 1QB
☎ 01677 450422
www.bigwig.net/nysd_ramblers

GROUP SECRETARIES
Barnard Castle Mr T Fenton,
Garden House, Westholme, Winston,
Darlington, Co Durham, DL2 3QL
☎ 01325 730895
http://uk.geocities.com/
barney_ramblers

Cleveland Mr A Patterson,
141 Castle Road, Redcar, TS10 2NF
☎ 01642 474864

Crook & Weardale Mrs K Berry,
11 Wood Square, Bishop Auckland,
Co Durham, DL14 6QQ
☎ 01388 608979
http://members.aol.com/
crookramblers

Darlington Mr Bryan Spark,
3 Thirlmere Grove,
West Auckland, Bishop Auckland,
Co Durham, DL14 9LW
☎ 01388 834213
www.bigwig.net/darlington.ramblers

Darlington Hills & Dales
Mr David Lawrenson, Smithy Cottage,
Hunton, Bedale,
North Yorkshire, DL8 1QB
☎ 01677 450422

Northallerton Mr M F Kent,
131 Valley Road, Northallerton,
North Yorkshire, DL6 1SN
☎ 01609 777618
http://web.onetel.net.uk/
~murraykent

Richmondshire Mrs V Darwin,
4 Sycamore Avenue, Richmond,
North Yorkshire, DL10 4BN
☎ 01748 822 845

LOCAL RAMBLERS PUBLICATIONS

Berwick Walks
by Arthur Wood, ISBN 0 9545331 0 0.
A beautifully hand-drawn and calligraphed
pocket book with 24 town, coastal,
countryside and riverside walks within a
19km/12-mile radius of Berwick upon
Tweed, many of them shorter walks.
*£4.95 + 50p p&p from Berwick
Ramblers, 5 Quay Walls, Berwick upon
Tweed TD15 1HB. Cheques to Ramblers'
Association.*

**Walking the Tyne: 25 walks from
mouth to source**
by J B Jonas, ISBN 1 901184 56 0
(Northumbria Area). A route along all
133km/83 miles of this great river,
divided into 25 linked, mainly circular
walks of 8km/5 miles to 14.5km/
9 miles, with suggestions for lunch
stops, time estimates, public transport
details, and notes on stiles, terrain and
places of interest.
*£4.50 + £1 p&p from 8 Beaufront
Avenue, Hexham NE46 1JD. Cheques to
The Ramblers' Association.*

 stores in this region

| NEWCASTLE UPON TYNE 121/125 Grainger Street NE1 5AE | DARLINGTON | 5/7 East Row DL1 5PZ |
| BISHOP AUCKLAND 63/65 Newgate Street DL14 7EW | GATESHEAD | 31 The Galleria NE11 9YP |

BED & BREAKFAST

DURHAM

● **Castleside (Consett)**

☆ 🍴 **Bee Cottage Farmhouse**
DH8 9HW ☎ 01207 508224 (Melita & David Turner)
www.smoothhound.co.uk/hotels/beecottage.html   Map 87/070453
BB **B**   ✖ book first £16.50, 7pm   S1 D2 T2 F4
Ⓥ Ⓑ Ⓓ ⊛ 🐾🐟🔥 ◆◆◆◆

On edge of Durham Dales with walking/cycling from our carpark. Ideal base for Durham, Beamish, Newcastle, Hadrian's Wall. Stunning views, relaxing. Licensed. Dinner available. Good, clean accommodation. All rooms en-suite, with TV and tea tray. Warm welcome guaranteed.

● **Cowshill (Wearhead)**

Low Cornriggs Farmhouse, DL13 1AQ ☎ 01388 537600 (Janet Elliott)
www.alstonandkillhoperidingcentre.co.uk   Map 86,87/845413
BB **B**   ✖ book first £14, 6.30pm   D2 T1
Ⓥ Ⓑ Ⓓ ⊛ 🐾🐟☕ ◆◆◆◆

● **Durham**

Hillrise Guest House, 13 Durham Road West, Bowburn, DH6 5AU
☎ 0191 377 0302 (George Webster)   www.hill-rise.com   Map 93/306376
BB **B**   ✖ nearby   S1 D2 T2 F1   Ⓑ Ⓓ ⊛ ☕ ◆◆◆◆

● **Forest-in-Teesdale**
   Pennine Way & Teesdale Way

The Dale, DL12 0EL ☎ 01833 622303(Mrs Jean Bonnett) Map 91/869298
BB **A**   ✖ book first £10, 7pm   D1 F1   Closed Dec-Feb   Ⓥ 🐾🚗 🔥

● **Middleton-in-Teesdale (Barnard Castle)**
   Pennine Way & Teesdale Way

Brunswick House, 55 Market Place, DL12 0QH
☎ 01833 640393 (Andrew & Sheila Milnes)
www.brunswickhouse.net   Map 91,92/946255
BB **B**   ✖ book first £17.50, 7:30pm   D3 T2
Ⓥ Ⓑ Ⓓ ⊛ 🐾🐟☕ ◆◆◆◆

Belvedere House, 54 Market Place, DL12 0QA ☎ 01833 640884
(Mrs J A Finn)   www.thecoachhouse.net   Map 91,92/947254
BB **B**   ✖ nearby   D2 T1   Ⓑ ⊛ 🐾🐟🔥 ◆◆◆◆

Wemmergill Hall Farm, Lunedale, DL12 0PA
☎ 01833 640379 (Irene Stoddart)
www.wemmergill-farm.co.uk   Map 91,92/901218
BB **B**   ✖ book first £10, 6:30pm   S/D1 T/F1
Ⓥ Ⓑ Ⓓ ⊛ 🐾🐟🚗 ◆◆◆◆   See SC also

🍴 Lonton South Farm, DL12 0PL
☎ 01833 640 409 (Mrs Irene Watson)
Map 91,92/954245
BB **A/B**   ✖ nearby   S1 D1 T1   Closed Dec-Jan
Ⓓ ⊛ 🐾🐟🔥 ◆◆◆

🍴 The Teesdale Hotel, Market Place, DL12 0QG ☎ 01833 640264
(Mr J Falconer)   Map 91,92/947255
BB **B**   ✖ £7.50, 7-9pm   S2 D4 T3   Ⓥ Ⓑ Ⓓ 🐾🐟🔥

● **Piercebridge (Darlington)**
   Teesdale Way

🍴 The Bridge House, DL2 3SG ☎ 01325 374727
elizabeth.formstone@btinternet.com   Map 93/210156
BB **B**   ✖ nearby   D1 T1 F1   Ⓑ Ⓓ ⊛ 🐾🐟🚗 🔥 ◆◆◆◆

● **Rookhope (Bishop Auckland)**

☆ 🍴 **The Rookhope Inn**
DL13 2BG ☎ 01388 517215 (Chris Jones)
www.rookhope.com   Map 87/938428
BB **B**   ✖ £6, 7pm   T4 F1
Ⓥ Ⓑ Ⓓ ⊛ 🐟🔥 ! 🐾   See Groups also.

This is upper Weardale in the north Pennines, secluded 300 year old village inn offering en-suite accommodation, good food and cask ales. Groups of up to 12 welcome. Drying facilities, maps and excellent walking venues. B&B: £25 / DB&B: £33

● **Stanhope**

🍴 Redlodge Guest House, 2 Market Place, DL13 2UN
☎ 01388 527851   www.redlodgegh.co.uk   Map 92/996391
BB **B**   ✖ nearby   S1 T2 F1   Ⓓ ⊛ 🐾🔥

🍴 The Queens Head, 89 Front St, DL13 2UB   ☎ 01388 528160
(Mr Graeme McKellar) queenshead_stanhope@yahoo.co.uk
Map 92/998390   BB **B**   ✖ £5, 7-9pm   T4   Ⓥ Ⓑ Ⓓ 🐾🐟 !

Belle Vue Farm Cottages, Hall Rd, Weardale, DL13 2EZ ☎ 01388 526225
(Mr & Mrs Lazenby) Map 87/981402
BB **B**   D4 T1   Closed Nov-Mar   Ⓑ ⊛ 🐟

NORTHUMBERLAND

● **Bamburgh**

Broome, 22 Ingram Road, NE69 7BT   ☎ 01668 214287 (Mary Dixon)
mdixon4394@aol.com   Map 75/180347
BB **B**   ✖ book first £20, 7:30-8pm   D1 T1   Ⓥ Ⓓ ⊛ 🐟 ◆◆◆◆

☆ **The Sunningdale**
21/23 Lucker Rd, NE69 7BS ☎ 01668 214334
www.sunningdale-hotel.com   Map 75/178347
BB **C**   ✖ £14, 7pm   S2 D8 T3 F5   Closed Dec-Jan
Ⓥ Ⓑ Ⓓ 🐾🐟🚗 ! 🐾 ◆◆◆

Comfortable family run hotel in the beautiful village of Bamburgh. Perfectly situated to enjoy walking on the unspoilt coastline, the Cheviot Hill range, and the many castles and nature reserves the area boasts. Log fire. Superb evening meals. Licensed bar/lounge.

● **Bardon Mill (Hexham)**
   Northumberland National Park
   Pennine Way & Hadrian's Wall

Twice Brewed Inn, Military Rd, NE47 7AN ☎ 01434 344534 (Brian Keen)
www.twicebrewedinn.co.uk   Map 86,87/753669
BB **B**   ✖ £6.50, 6-8:30pm   S3 D4 T6 F1   Closed Jan   🚌(Bardon Mill)
Ⓥ Ⓑ 🐾🐟 ◆◆◆

● **Beal (Berwick-upon-Tweed)**
St Cuthbert's Way

☆ ▰ **Brockmill Farmhouse**
TD15 2PB ☎ 01289 381283
www.lindisfarne.org.uk/brock-mill-farmhouse   Map 75/060436
BB **B** ✗ nearby   S1 D1 T1 F1
D ⊗ ♨ 🛏 🚗 🐾   ◆◆◆

Brockmill Farmhouse is peacefully situated 1 1/2 miles from the A1 on the road to Holy Island. The St Cuthbert's Way is just 1 1/2 miles away.

Ideally situated for touring and exploring north Northumberland and Borders. A warm welcome awaits in superbly furnished quality rooms with TV, tea making facilities, vanity units and 2 seater settees. Pick-ups available for ramblers. Evening meals nearby. Full English or vegetarian breakfasts.

● **Belford**
The Farmhouse Guest House, 24 West Street, NE70 7QE ☎ 01668 213083
(Mrs Anne Murdoch) www.thefarmhouseguesthousebelford.co.uk Map 75/107339
BB **B** ✗ nearby   D2 F/T1   B D ⊗ ♨   ◆◆◆◆

● **Bellingham (Hexham)**
Northumberland National Park
Pennine Way
Lyndale Guest House, Riverside Walk, NE48 2AW ☎ 01434 220361
(Ken & Joy Gaskin) www.lyndaleguesthouse.co.uk Map 80/839833
BB **B** ✗ nearby   S1 D2 T1 F1
B D 🐾 🛏 🚗 !   ◆◆◆◆   Veggie breakfasts.

● **Berwick-upon-Tweed**
▰ Orkney Guest House, 37 Woolmarket, TD15 1DH ☎ 01289 331710
(Helen Rutherford) orkneyguesthouse@yahoo.co.uk Map 75/000528
BB **B** ✗ nearby   D2 T2 F1   ▰(Berwick-upon-Tweed)
B D 🐾 🐾   ◆◆

● **Corbridge**
Hadrian's Wall

☆ ▰ **Dyvels Hotel**
Station Rd, NE45 5AY ☎ 01434 633633
bdoddsy@aol.com   Map 87/989636
BB **B** ✗ £6, 7-9pm   S6 D3 T3 F1   ▰(Corbridge)
V B D 🐾 🚗 ! 🛏

Cosy, friendly atmosphere. Fully stocked bar, offering a good selection of cask ales, lagers and fine wines. Separate restaurant, serving a full English breakfast and excellent home-cooked food. Beer garden. All rooms tastefully decorated and furnished and equipped with TV and beverage tray.

▰ The Hayes, Newcastle Rd, NE45 5LP ☎ 01434 632010
(Mrs M J Matthews) www.hayes-corbridge.co.uk Map 87/996643
BB **B/C** ✗ nearby   S1 T1 F2   ▰(Corbridge)
B D ⊗ 🐾 🛏 🚗 !   ◆◆◆

● **Fenwick (Berwick-upon-Tweed)**
St Cuthbert's Way
▰ The Manor House, TD15 2PQ ☎ 01289 381016 (Christine Humphrey)
www.manorhousefenwick.co.uk Map 75/066401
BB **B** ✗ book first £15   S1 D1 T1 F1   V B D ⊗ 🐾 🛏 🚗 !

● **Ford (Berwick-upon-Tweed)**
▰ The Estate House, TD15 2PX ☎ 01890 820668 (Liz Wood)
www.theestatehouse.co.uk Map 74,75/946373
BB **B** ✗ book first £12.50-£16, 7pm   D2 T1
V B D ⊗ 🐾 🛏   ◆◆◆◆ Ⓢ

● **Greenhead (Brampton)**
Northumberland National Park
Hadrian's Wall & Pennine Way
10 Blenkinsopp Terrace, Bankfoot, CA8 7JN ☎ 016977 47429
(Robin & Jean Fuller) robingfuller@yahoo.co.uk Map 86/663645
BB **B** ✗ book first £8-£12   S1 D1 T/F1   V B D ⊗ 🐾 🛏 🚗 ! Ⓜ

● **Haltwhistle**
Northumberland National Park
Pennine Way & Hadrian's Wall
▰ Hall Meadows, Main Street, NE49 0AZ ☎ 01434 321021
(Mrs Heather Humes) Map 86,87/708641
BB **B** ✗ nearby   S1 D1 T1   ▰(Haltwhistle) B D 🐾 🚗   ◆◆◆◆
▰ Burnhead Bed & Breakfast, NE49 9PJ ☎ 01434 320841 (Terry Burke)
www.burnheadbedandbreakfast.co.uk Map 86,87/716669
BB **B** ✗ nearby   T2   ▰(Haltwhistle) B D ⊗ 🐾 🛏 🚗 !

☆ ▰ **Broomshaw Hill Farm**
Willia Road, NE49 9NP ☎ 01434 320866 (Mrs J Brown)
www.broomshaw.co.uk Map 86/707653
BB **B**   D2 T1   Closed Dec-Feb   ▰(Haltwhistle)
B D 🐾 🛏 🚗 !   ◆◆◆◆◆ Ⓖ

An 18th century farmhouse enlarged and modernised to the highest standards. The house is quietly situated on the conjunction of footpath and bridleway leading to Hadrian's Wall. Easy access to major Roman sites, town and Hadrian's Wall. Warm welcome assured.

☆ ▰ **Doors Cottage B&B**
Shield Hill, NE49 9NW ☎ 01434 322556 (Lesley Lewis)
www.doorscottage.co.uk Map 86,87/712649
BB **B** ✗ nearby   D1 T1   ▰(Haltwhistle)
D ⊗ 🐾 🛏 🚗 !   ◆◆◆

Mid 19th century former farmhouse, centrally situated at Cawfields, and overlooking the Hadrian's Wall national path. Ideal for visits to housesteads, Vindolanda and Roman museum. Warm, friendly service where you can relax after the day's walking. Local inn 400 yards.

● Heddon-on-the-Wall

Hadrian's Wall

Rambler's Repose, 8 Killie Brigs, NE15 0DD ☎ 01661 852419
(Mrs PA Millward)   Map 88/130665
BB **B**   ✗ nearby   D1 T1   ⊗ ☺ ! Veggie breakfasts.

● Once Brewed (Bardon Mill)

Northumberland National Park

Pennine Way & Hadrian's Wall

☆ ▸⊲ **Gibbs Hill Farm**
NE47 7AP   ☎ 01434 344030 (Mrs Valerie Gibson)
www.gibbshillfarm.co.uk   Map 86,87/750691
BB **B**   ✗ book first £14, 7pm   D1 T4
Ⓥ Ⓑ Ⓓ ⊗ 🍴☕☺🚗! 🖼   ◆◆◆◆   See Hostels also.

17 century working farm on Hadrian's Wall. Comfortable en-suite rooms, spectacular views. Traditional farmhouse cooking using all local ingredients. Walking, birdwatching from hide on Greenlee Lough Nature Reserve, stables, trout fishing. Central for Roman sites/Pennine Cycleways.

● Rothbury

Northumberland National Park

▸⊲ Well Strand, NE65 7UD
☎ 01669 620794 (Helen & David Edes)   Map 81/056016
BB **A**   ✗ nearby   S1 D1 T1   Ⓓ ⊗ 🚗! 🖼

☆ **Katerina's Guest House**
High Street, NE65 7TQ   ☎ 01669 620691 (Cathryn Mills)
www.katerinasguesthouse.co.uk   Map 81/055017
BB **C**   ✗ £14.50, 7-8:30pm   D3
Ⓥ Ⓑ Ⓓ ⊗ 🍴☕☺🚗   ◆◆◆◆Ⓖ

Luxurious fourposter bedrooms in lovely Rothbury village, next to all amenities — ideal location for hills, coast, castles, Hadrian's Wall and Scottish Borders. Wide and varied breakfast menus, plus optional licensed evening meal. Non-smoking walkers' paradise!

● Stannersburn (Kielder Water)

Northumberland National Park

☆ **The Pheasant Inn**
NE48 1DD   ☎ 01434 240382
www.thepheasantinn.com   Map 80/721866
BB **C**   ✗ £7.95-£15, 7-9pm   D4 T/S3 F1
Ⓥ Ⓑ 🍴☕☺ 🖼   ◆◆◆◆Ⓢ

380 yr old, traditional family run country inn bursting with character and charm, beamed ceiling, open fires. Bar lunches and evening meals available daily. Excellent area for walking and cycling in and around Kielder Water and Forest.

● Twice Brewed (Haltwhistle)

Northumberland National Park

Hadrian's Wall & Pennine Way

Saughy Rigg Farm, NE49 9PT ☎ 01434 344120 (Kath Dowle)
www.saughyrigg.co.uk   Map 86,87/755675
BB **B**   ✗ book first £12.50, 7-9pm   S1 D2 T2 F1
Ⓥ Ⓑ Ⓓ 🍴☕☺🚗! 🖼   ◆◆◆◆

● Wark (Hexham)

Northumberland National Park

Pennine Way

☆ ▸⊲ **Battlesteads Hotel**
NE48 3LS ☎ 01434 230209 (Bob Rowland)
www.battlesteads-hotel.co.uk   Map 87/860770
BB **C**   ✗ £3.50-£15, 6:30-9:30pm   S1 D4 T7 F2
Ⓥ Ⓑ Ⓓ 🍴☕☺🚗! 🖼   ★★   Wheelchair access.

A converted 17th century farmhouse which has been carefully modernised to provide comfortable and friendly surroundings while retaining olde worlde charm. A fine place for relaxation with a cosy open fire in the lounge in winter. All rooms en-suite with TV, ironing facilities and hairdryers. Large car parks and rear garden. We boast an excellent reputation for our food and Sunday lunch, cooked to order. The attractive dining room provides an intimate setting for enjoying a Table d'Hote dinner. Vegetarians are catered for with prior notice.
Email: info@Battlesteads-Hotel.co.uk

● Warkworth (Morpeth)

Bide a While, 4 Beal Croft, NE65 0XL
☎ 01665 711753 (Mrs D Graham)   Map 81/249053
BB **B**   ✗ nearby   D1 T1 F1
Ⓑ Ⓓ ☕ 🖼

● West Woodburn (Hexham)

Pennine Way

▸⊲ Yellow House Farm, NE48 2SB
☎ 01434 270070 (Avril A Walton)
www.yellowhousebandb.co.uk   Map 80/898870
BB **B**   ✗ nearby   D1 T1 F1
Ⓑ Ⓓ ⊗ 🍴☕☺🚗! 🖼   ◆◆◆◆

● Wooler
Northumberland National Park
St Cuthbert's Way

☆ ✉ **Winton House**
39 Glendale Road, NE71 6DL ☎ 01668 281362 (Terry & Veronica Gilbert)
www.wintonhousebandb.co.uk   Map 75/991283
BB **B**   ✗ nearby   D2 T1   Closed Dec-Feb
B D ⊗ ⛿ 🕭 ⚘ 🚗   ◆◆◆

Charming Edwardian house with spacious, comfortable rooms. Situated on a quiet road close to village centre just 250m from St Cuthbert's Way. Much praised breakfasts, using local produce. Walkers very welcome.

☆ ✉ **Tilldale House**
34/40 High Street, NE71 6BG ☎ 01668 281450 (Julia Devenport)
tilldalehouse@freezone.co.uk   Map 75/990281
BB **B**   ✗ nearby   D3 T3
B D ⊗ ⛿ 🕭 ⚘ 🍴 🔔   ◆◆◆◆   Special diets catered for.

Our stone built 17th century home offers spacious comfortable en-suite bedrooms. An ideal base for walking, cycling, fishing, golf or riding. Located off the main road, 150 yards from the St Cuthberts Way Walk. Further details on request.

TYNE & WEAR

● Newcastle-upon-Tyne
Hadrian's Wall
The Barn B&B, East Wallhouses, Military Rd, NE18 0LL
☎ 01434 672649 (Brenda Walton)
www.smoothhound.co.uk/hotels/thebarn1.html   Map 87/047683
BB **B**   ✗ nearby   D1 T2   Closed Dec   B D ⊗ ⛿ 🕭 🔔

☆ ✉ **Clifton House Hotel**
46 Clifton Rd, NE4 6XH
☎ 0191 2730407 (Mrs Caterina Love)   Map 88/226639
BB **B/C**   ✗ book first £16, 8-9pm   S3 D2 T2 F3   ⚊⚊(Newcastle)
V B D ⛿ ⚘ 🚗 ⚘ 🕭   ◆◆◆

Excellent base for touring Northumberland, within easy reach of Hadrian's Wall and market towns of Hexham and Morpeth. Northumberland's coastline remains unspoiled and boasts many places of real interest. Easy access to historic Durham with famous cathedral and beautiful surrounding countryside.

● Whitley Bay
Northumberland National Park
Hadrian's Wall
✉ Windsor Hotel, South Parade, NE26 2RF ☎ 0191 251 8888
www.windsorhotel-uk.com   Map 88/357722   BB **C**   ✗ £12, 6-10pm   S2
D33 T34   ⚊⚊(Whitley Bay)   V B D ⛿ ⚘ 🚗   ★★★

SELF-CATERING

DURHAM

● **Barnard Castle**

☆ **East Briscoe Farm**
☎ 01833 650087 (Emma Wilson)
www.eastbriscoe.co.uk
£120-£455   Sleeps 2-6. 6 cottages.
Beautiful countryside, superb area for walking. 🕭   ★★★★

By high Pennine moorland and traditional farm meadows, East Briscoe is a 14 acre riverside estate offering a superb base for walkers. The cottages are decorated in a comfortable style, to a high standard, and are well equipped. Pets welcome in three cottages. One wheelchair accessible. Winner of Northumbria self-catering of the year and a County Durham Environment Award. Linen, towels and heating included.

● **Middleton-in-Teesdale**
Wemmergill Hall Farm ☎ 01833 640379 (Irene Stoddart)
www.wemmergill-farm.co.uk   £180-£450   Sleeps 6-7. 1 house.
Near Pennine Way and Teesdale Way.   ✗ ★★★★   See B&B also.

● **Wolsingham**
Bradley Burn Farm ☎ 01388 527285 (Judith Stephenson)
www.bradleyburn.co.uk   £160-£375   Sleeps 2-5. 4 cottages.
Short breaks. Working farm. Caravan park. 🕭   ★★★

☎ 01388 527538 (Mrs M Gardiner)
£130-£233   Sleeps 4. 2 terraced cottages.
Cosy cottages, excellent scenic walking area. 🕭   ★★★

NORTHUMBERLAND

● **Alwinton**
Northumberland National Park
Barrowburn ☎ 01669 621176 (Mrs Tait)   www.barrowburn.com
£280   Sleeps 4-6. 1 cottage.
Gas lighting, open fire, stunning location. 🕭

● **Embleton**
Doxford Farm ☎ 01665 579348 (Sarah Shell)
www.doxfordfarmcottages.com   £150-£550   Sleeps 2-7. 7 cottages.
Working farm on beautiful country estate. 🕭

● **Hexham**
Moorgair ☎ 01434 673473 (Mrs Vicki Ridley)   www.moorgair.co.uk
£180-£330   Sleeps 4-5 + cot. 1 cottage.
Great countryside, great cottage, great holiday!   ⊗ ★★★★

● **Norham**

☆ **The Boathouse**
☎ 020 7584 8996 (Emma Crabtree)
www.crabtreeandcrabtree.com/boathouse
£480-£950   Sleeps 9. I house.
Stunning views, riverfront setting, private fishing. 🏠 ★★★

Delightful, period house in quiet, secluded position on banks of River Tweed, fi mile from historic village of Norham.
Spacious accommodation for 9 people.
Extensive walks run from the house and only 8 miles to coast and Berwickshire Coastal Path.

● **Wooler**

Northumberland National Park
☎ 01668 216077 (Mrs Jean Davidson)   http://westnewtonestate.com
£195-£380   Sleeps 4. 2 cottages.
Beautiful stone cottages in Cheviot foothills. 🚭 🏠 ★★★

GROUPS

DURHAM

☆ **The Rookhope Inn** (B&B)
Rookhope, Weardale DL13 2BG   ☎ 01388 517215 (Chris Jones)
www.rookhope.com Map 87/939428
BB £25, DBB £32 ✕ 🐾
B D See B&B also

Traditional village located in upper Weardale in an area of outstanding natural beauty. Excellent walking country, comfortable ensuite accommodation, good traditional food, real ales, log fires and drying facilities, well behaved dogs are welcome.

HOSTELS, BUNKHOUSES & CAMPSITES

NORTHUMBERLAND

Northumberland National Park
Hadrian's Wall & Pennine Way

☆ **Gibbs Hill Bunkhouse** (B/IH)
Once Brewed, Bardon Mill, Hexham NE47 7AP
☎ 01434 344030 (Mrs Valerie Gibson)
www.gibbshillfarm.co.uk Map 86,87/750691
Bednight £12 🐾 B D See B&B also.

New bunkhouse sleeps up to 20 people. En-suite showers, spacious cooking facilities, comfortable lounge. Ideal for families, weekly room rates, short breaks and special weekly rates for groups. Some evening meals available on-site. Pennine Bridleway – new stables on site.

HADRIAN'S WALL COUNTRY
IS WALKING COUNTRY

COME AND DISCOVER ITS WIDE OPEN SPACES

Want to know more?
For a free Holiday Guide call the brochureline on **01434 652364**.
To walk the Hadrian's Wall Path call **01434 322002**.

www.hadrianswallcountry.org

NEATH, WEST GLAMORGAN

WALES

Walking in Wales is a truly unique experience. The long coastline bordering the Irish Sea to the west and Offa's Dyke snaking down England's border to the east, embrace a country of cultural and linguistic diversity. Wales offers coastal paths for sea-lovers and a heartland bristling with hills and mountains.

Wales is also blessed with three peaks: to the north is Snowdon/Yr Wyddfa the highest peak in England and Wales, mid-Wales has Cadair Idris (though some would argue that Plynlimon/Pumlumon is mid-Wales' peak) and Pen y Fan in the Brecon Beacons National Park. Each can provide the focus for a great day out.

WWW.BRITAINONVIEW.COM

PEMBROKE CASTLE

The Brecon Beacons offer up waterfalls and caves and some of the best hill-walking in southern Britain. The Black Mountains provide gentler walking with spectacular views across rolling hills and valleys. There's also plenty of history on offer from the remains of Roman occupation to the legacy of the industrial revolution.

A member says:

"To go up into the Black Mountains after a hard week at work can give you a real sense of isolation from the world – it's great to just go up there and chill."

South Wales' rolling grasslands and extensive beaches helped the Gower peninsula become Britain's first designated Area of Outstanding Natural Beauty in 1956.

Moving westwards, Pembrokeshire gives Britain its only coastal national park and home to the 186-mile long Pembrokeshire Coast Path. From the narrow cliff-top paths walkers can expect to see seals, porpoises and perhaps even dolphins in the Atlantic facing sea. The northern section of the Park includes the Preseli Hills, where the blocks for Stonehenge were quarried, and the Cardigan Bay coastline dotted with beautiful fishing villages.

The Isle of Anglesey, to the north of Snowdonia National Park, is another AONB with Neolithic and Bronze Age sites. The 125-mile Isle of Anglesey Coastal Path winds around the Island and an extensive network of paths criss-cross the flat-topped ridges and shallow valleys giving walkers ample opportunity to explore inland.

It is expected that there will be up to 1,158 square miles of access land available to walkers in May 2005 – together with Forestry Commission land dedicated for public access (386 square miles), this means walkers will have the legal right to roam on 20 percent of the land in Wales.

Long Distance Paths

Cambrian Way	CAM
Clwydian Way	CLW
Glyndwr's Way	GLN
Isle of Anglesey Coastal Path	ANC
Offa's Dyke Path	OFD
Pembrokeshire Coast Path	PSC
Severn Way	SVN
Usk Valley Walk	USK
Valeways Millennium Heritage Trail	VMH

Public paths:

33,211km/ 20,637 miles

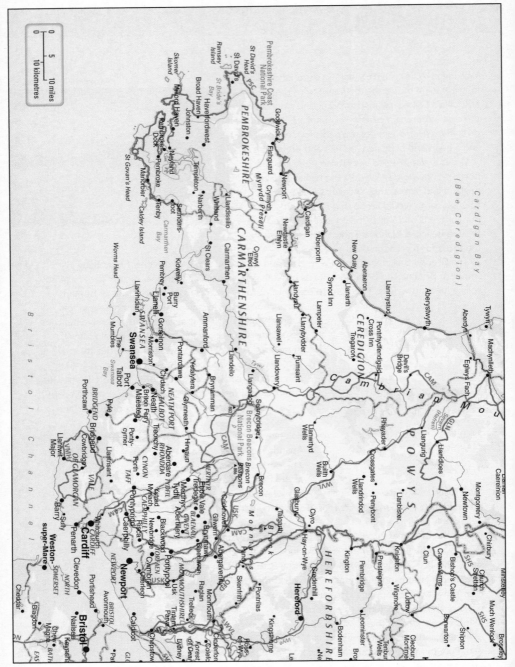

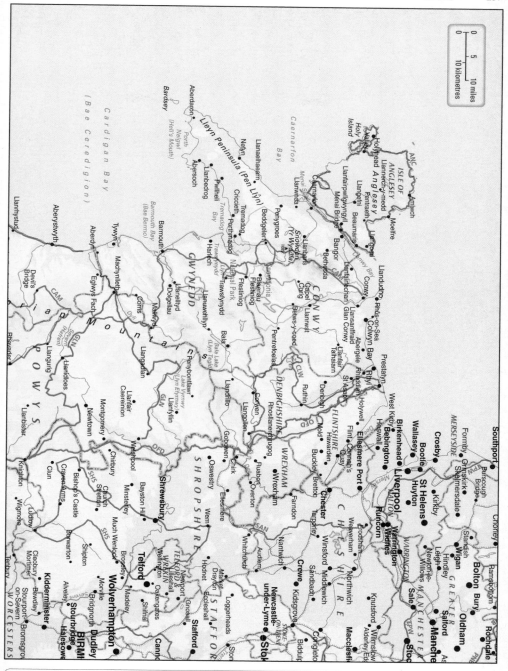

CEREDIGION
CARDIGAN BAY

From spectacular walks along Ceredigion coastal paths, through lush
green river valleys to the heathered uplands and forests of the Cambrian Mountains -
the panoply of walking opportunities on offer is hard to better.

WALES
LOCAL RAMBLERS CONTACTS

DYFED
AREA SECRETARY
Vacant

GROUP SECRETARIES
Aberystwyth Mrs S A Kinghorn,
16 Bryn Glas, Llanbadarn, Aberystwyth,
Dyfed, SY23 3QR ☎ 01970 624965
http://users.aber.ac.uk/dib/AberRamblers

Cardigan & District Mrs K Gill,
Abersylltyn, Cwm Cou, Newcastle
Emlyn, Dyfed, SA38 9PN
☎ 01239 710858

Carmarthen & District Mr David
Bush, 31 Eldergrove, Llangunnor,
Carmarthenshire, Dyfed, SA31 2LQ
☎ 01267 230994
http://mysite.freeserve.com/beauchamp

Dinefwr Mr David Foot, Ty Isaf, Taliaris,
Llandeilo, SA19 7DE ☎ 01550 777623
http://mysite.freeserve.com/beauchamp/
index.html

Lampeter Mr D G Hughes & Ms J
Mcdowall, Ddol Brenin, Ffarmers,
Llanwrda, SA19 8PZ ☎ 01558 650339
www.lampeterwalkers.org.uk

Llanelli Mr Norman Jones,
44 Brynmor Road, Llanelli, Carms,
SA15 2TG ☎ 01554 774970

Pembrokeshire Ms C M Morris,
24 St Lawrence Close, Hakin, Milford
Haven, Dyfed, SA73 3NE
☎ 01646 697 543

GLAMORGAN
AREA SECRETARY
Mr J E Thomas, 7 Parc Afon, Porth,
Mid Glamorgan, CF40 1JF
☎ 01443 681082

WEST GLAMORGAN

WWW.BRITAINONVIEW.COM

GROUP SECRETARIES
Bridgend & District Mr John Sanders,
3 Bryn Rhedyn, Pencoed Bridgend,
CF35 6TL ☎ 01656 861835
http://freespace.virgin.net/alex.marshall/
ramblers.htm

Cardiff Ms Diane Davies,
9 Cyncoed Rise, Cyncoed, Cardiff,
CF23 6SF ☎ 029 2075 2464
www.btinternet.com/~cardiff.ramblers

Cynon Valley Mr Allan Harrison,
8 Stuart Street, Aberdare,
Mid Glamorgan, CF44 7LY
☎ 01685 881824
http://freespace.virgin.net/alex.marshall/
cynon.htm

Maesteg Mr R Hart-Jones,
Llys Hen Lanciau, Llangynwyd, Maesteg,
CF34 9SB ☎ 01656 736347

Merthyr Valley Mr A J Richards,
8 St Davids Close, Penpedairheol,
Hengoed, Mid Glamorgan, CF82 8BL
☎ 01443 833719

Neath Port Talbot
Mr D A Davies & Ms Y Humphreys,
2 Cwrt Coed Parc, Maesteg, CF34 9DG
☎ 01656 733021

Penarth & District Mrs L Davies,
3 Barrians Way, Barry,
CF62 8JG ☎ 01446 407595
http://freespace.virgin.net/
alex.marshall/penarth.htm

Taff Ely Mr J T Roszkowski,
18 Parc Y Coed, Creigiau, Nr Cardiff,
CF15 9LX ☎ 02920 891455
www.apyule.demon.co.uk/taffely.htm

Tiger Bay Ramblers
Mrs C Haythornthwaite,
64 Mynachdy Road, Cardiff,
CF14 3EA ☎ 029 20610098
www.btinternet.com/~tigerbayramblers

Vale of Glamorgan Mr I D Fraser,
44 Millfield Drive, Cowbridge,
CF71 7BR ☎ 01446 774706
http://freespace.virgin.net/alex.marshall/
Vale.htm

West Glamorgan Zetta Flew,
8 Meadow Croft, Southgate, Swansea,
SA3 2DF ☎ 01792 232060
http://homepage.ntlworld.com/
alex.thomas

GREATER GWENT
AREA SECRETARY
Mr Mike Williams, 7 Cwm Sor Close,
New Inn, Pontypool, NP4 0NN
☎ 01495 753040   www.ra-gga.co.uk

GROUP SECRETARIES
Gelligaer Mrs D Price, 26 Tyn Y Coed,
Ystrad Mynach, Caerphilly, CF82 7DD
☎ 01443 813220

Islwyn Ms M Thomas & Ms A Thomas,
15 Carlton Terrace, Cross Keys,
Newport, NP11 7BU ☎ 01495 273057

Lower Wye Mr Ron Gladwin,
3 St Thomas Road, Monmouth,
NP25 5SA ☎ 01600 713726
www.lowerwyeramblers.co.uk

North Gwent Mr A Nicholas,
31 Windsor Road, Brynmawr, Blaenau
Gwent, NP23 4HE ☎ 01495 311088

Pontypool Mrs Barbara Whitticase,
Glantawell, Llanfihangel Talyllyn, Brecon,
Powys, LD3 7TH ☎ 01874 658386
www.pontypool-ramblers.co.uk

South Gwent Mr K Phillips,
39 Penylan Close, Bassaleg, Newport,
NP10 8NW ☎ 01633 894172
http://myweb.tiscali.co.uk/ra.sgr

NORTH WALES
AREA SECRETARY
Mr Ron Williams, 11 Fron Las, Holywell,
Clwyd, CH8 7HX ☎ 01352 715723

GROUP SECRETARIES
Bangor-Bethesda Miss A G Penketh,
2 Sychnant View, Old Mill Road,
Penmaenmawr, Gwynedd, LL34 6TN
☎ 01492 622887

Berwyn Mr J A & Mrs S Kay,
Erw Fain, Llantysilio, Llangollen,
Clwyd, LL20 8BU ☎ 01978 861793

Caernarfon/Dwyfor Ms E Watkin,
Ty N Lon, Bethel, Caernarfon,
Gwynedd, LL55 1UW ☎ 01248 671243

Clwydian Mr E Ankers,
14 Bron Yr Eglwys, Mynydd Isa, Mold,
Clwyd, CH7 6YQ ☎ 01352 754659

Conwy Valley Mr F R Parry, 2 Derwen
Avenue, Rhos On Sea, Colwyn Bay,
LL28 4SP ☎ 01492 547967

Deeside Mr Jim Irvine, 30 St Davids
Drive, Connahs Quay, Flintshire,
CH5 4SR ☎ 01244 818577
www.deesideramblers.org.uk

Eryri 20.30 Delyth Roberts, Tre Wen,
Groeslon, Waunfawr, Caernarfon,
LL55 4EZ ☎ 01286 650295
www.walk20.30.btinternet.co.uk

Meirionnydd Mrs S A Higdon,
38 Branksome Esteate, Ffordd Pentre
Mynach, Barmouth, Gwynedd,
LL42 1EN ☎ 01341 280732

LOCAL RAMBLERS CONTACTS continued

Vale of Clwyd
Mr M R Wilkinson,
49 Victoria Road West, Prestatyn,
Denbighshire, LL19 7AA
☎ 01745 888137
www.voc-ramblers.org.uk

Walking On Wales
Dr F Lloyd-Williams, Plas Wern, Waen,
St Asaph, LL17 0DY
☎ 07702 955344
www.walkersonwales.fsnet.co.uk

Wrexham Mr Paul Davies,
5 Glyndwr Road, Wrexham, LL12 7TR
☎ 01978 362253

Ynys Mon Mr S Hughes,
Glyn Pentraeth Road,
Menai Bridge, Anglesey,
Gwynedd, LL59 5HU
☎ 01248 712315
http://members.aol.com/dnfwhite/
ynysmongroup.htm

POWYS
AREA SECRETARY
Mr K M Jones, 1 Heyope Road,
Knucklas, LD7 1PT
☎ 01547 520 266
www.powysramblers.org.uk

GROUP SECRETARIES
4 Wells Miss M Emery, Little Nant,
Bettws, Hundred House, Llandrindod
Wells, LD1 5RP ☎ 01982 570366
www.fourwells.freeuk.com

Brecon Mr H Hoare, 3 Erw Bant,
Llangynidr, Crickhowell, Powys,
NP8 1LX ☎ 01874 730509

East Radnor Mr K M Jones,
1 Heyope Road, Knucklas, LD7 1PT
☎ 01547 520 266

Welshpool Mrs Lynda Dabinett,
Pentre Isaf, Llangyniew, Welshpool,
Powys, SY21 0JT ☎ 01938 810069

LOCAL RAMBLERS PUBLICATIONS

**Cardigan Centre for Walkers –
Aberteifi Canolfan Cerddwyr**
by Cardigan and District Ramblers. 11
graded walks of between 5km/3 miles and
16km/10 miles. Bilingual Welsh/English.
£5.50 + 50p p&p from G Torr, Parc-y-
Pratt, Cardigan SA43 3DR. Cheques to
Cardigan and District Ramblers.

Clwydian Way
by David Hollett, ISBN 1 901184 36 6.
Circular route around Denbighshire,
including details of 12 short circular walks.
£5.95 + £1.55 p&p from PO Box 139,
Llanfairpwllgwyngyll LL61 6WR. Cheques to
The Ramblers' Association North Wales Area.

Lampeter Walks – Llwybrau Llanbed
by Lampeter RA, ISBN 1 901184 58 7.
16 walks 2.5km/1.5 miles to 13km/8
miles, with route maps and
accommodation listings. Bilingual
Welsh/English.
£4.95 + £1 p&p from Lampeter Bookshop,
21 Bridge Street, Lampeter SA48 7AA.
Cheques to Lampeter Ramblers.

Lower Wye Rambles
edited by Allan Thomas and Gill
Nettleship. 16 walks between Chepstow

and Monmouth, 4-14km/2.5-9 miles.
£3.75 from 1 Mounton Close, Chepstow
NP16 5EG. Cheques to Lower Wye Group
RA. (New this year)

The Pioneer Ramblers 1850-1940
by David Hollett, ISBN 1 901184 54 4.
The history of walking is full of vivid
incidents and striking characters,
many of them captured in this new
book. Thus George Allen, who walked a
thousand miles to advance vegetarianism,
shares a cover with Lawrence Chubb,
the severely conservative first secretary
of the Open Spaces Society, and the
young communists who trespassed on
Kinder Scout in 1932 jostle with
Victorian mountaineers and natural
history enthusiasts. The pictures are a
delight. (Ann Holt)
North Wales Ramblers, £8.95 + £1 p&p
from 69 Wethersfield Road, Prenton CH43
9YF. Cheques to North Wales Area RA.

Walking Around Gower
4th edition by Albert White,
ISBN 0 951878 01 8 (West Glamorgan
Ramblers): 10 circular walks of between
8km/5 miles and 21km/13 miles around the
Gower peninsula.

**Walking Around Northern Gower
and the Swansea Valley**
by Peter Beck and Peter J Thomas, based
on an original work by Albert White, ISBN
0 951878 11 5. 10 circular walks that can
be split into 25 shorter circuits, giving
options of between 8km/5 miles and
21km/13 miles.
Both £7.50 each post free from Peter Beck,
24 Hazelmere Road, Sketty, Swansea SA2
0SN. Cheques to The Ramblers' Association.

Walks you will enjoy
pack of 18 walks in east Radnorshire and
northwest Herefordshire on laminated
pocket-sized cards.
£4.50 (£3.75 to RA members) from East
Radnor Publications, 1 Heyope Road,
Knucklas LD7 1PT. Cheques to East Radnor
Publications.

Valeways Millennium Heritage Trail
by B Palmer and G Woodnam (Vale of
Glamorgan). Fascinating 99km/62-mile
circular walk, developed by a partnership
of the RA, Vale of Glamorgan Council and
other organisations.
£6.99 + £1.50 p&p from Valeways, Unit 7
BCEC, Skomer Road, Barry CF62 9DA.
Cheques to Valeways.

millets stores in this region

ABERGAVENNY	Unit 3 Cibi Walk NP7 5AJ	LLANDUDNO	67 Mostyn Street LL30 2NN
ABERYSTWYTH	3 Great Darkgate Street SY23 1DE	LLANELLI	42 Stepney Street SA15 3YA
BRECON	31/32 High Street LD3 7AN	MONMOUTH	21 Monnow Street NP25 3EF
BRIDGEND	Brackla Street Centre CF31 1EB	NEATH	1/3 Green Street SA11 1DN
CARDIFF	109/111 Queen Street CF1 4BH	NEWPORT (GWENT)	3 Llanarth Street, Gwent NP20 1HS
CARMARTHEN	1 Red Street SA31 1QL	PONTYPRIDD	80 Taff Street CF37 4SD
CWMBRAN	14 Monmouth Walk NP44 1PE	RHYL	60/62 High Street LL18 1ET
HAVERFORDWEST	25 Bridge Street SA61 2AZ	SWANSEA	234 High Street SA1 1NZ
		WREXHAM	24 Queen Street LL11 1AL

BED & BREAKFAST

ANGLESEY

● Cemaes
Isle of Anglesey Coastal Path

Tredolphin Guest House, Cemaes Bay, LL67 0ET
☎ 01407 710388 (Frances & Bill O'Donnell) Map 114/370935
BB **B** ✕ book first £8.25, 6pm S1 D2 T2 F2
Ⅴ Ⓑ Ⓓ ⬤🍵🚗🛁 ★★★ Guide dogs welcome.

● Rhoscolyn (Holyhead)
Isle of Anglesey Coastal Path

Glan Towyn, LL65 2NJ ☎ 01407 860380 (Carol Gough)
www.glantowyn-rhoscolyn.co.uk Map 114/272752
BB **B** ✕ nearby S1 D2 T1 Closed Dec-Jan Ⓑ ⬤🍵🚗🛁! ★★★

● Valley (Holyhead)
Isle of Anglesey Coastal Path

Ty Mawr, LL65 3HH ☎ 01407 740235 (Mrs Anne Lloyd)
www.angleseybedandbreakfast.co.uk Map 114/296784
BB **B** ✕ nearby S1 D2 T1 Closed Dec-Jan ♨(Valley)
Ⓓ ⬤🍵🚗!🛁 ★★★

CARMARTHENSHIRE

● Abergorlech (Llanfynydd)
Faraway School B&B, Clawddowen School House, SA32 7TN
☎ 01558 685389 (Sheila & Cliff) www.faraway-school.co.uk Map 146/579307
BB **B** ✕ book first £8, 6-8pm D1 T1 F1 Ⅴ Ⓑ Ⓓ ⬤🍵🚗!

● Brechfa (Carmarthen)

☆ **Glasfryn Guest House and Restaurant**
SA32 7QY ☎ 01267 202306
www.glasfrynbrechfa.co.uk Map 146/526303
BB **B** ✕ £10-£15, 7-9pm D2 T1
Ⅴ Ⓑ Ⓓ 🍵🛁🛏 ★★★

Situated at the edge of the Brechfa Forest. Six miles from the A40. Ideal centre for walking, cycling and touring south, west and mid Wales. 15 minutes from National Botanic Gardens and Aberglesni Gardens (Garden Lost in Time). Licensed restaurant. Excellent home-cooked food. All rooms en-suite. Brochures available.

● Carmarthen
Trebersed Farm, St Peters, Travellers Rest, SA31 3RR ☎ 01267 238182
(Mrs Rosemary Jones) www.trebersed.co.uk Map 145,159/381200
BB **B** ✕ nearby D1 T1 F1 ♨(Carmarthen)
Ⓑ Ⓓ ⬤🍵🚗!🛁 ★★★

● Llandovery
Brecon Beacons
Cambrian Way

☆ **Llanerchindda Farm**
Cynghordy, SA20 0NB ☎ 01550 750274 (Nick & Irena Bointon)
www.cambrianway.com Map 160/808429
BB **B** ✕ £12, 7pm S3 D7 T6 F4 ♨(Cynghordy)
Ⅴ Ⓑ Ⓓ 🍵🛁🚗!🛁 Ⓜ ★★

Our Bed & Breakfast at a remote sheep farm 7 miles N.E. of Llandovery is a very popular base for walking clubs & groups.

With 42 beds in 20 mainly en-suite rooms, plus excellent facilities including drying room and map room with 20 well documented walks, we are understandably very popular.

Our special offer: Sun-Fri (5 nights) dinner & B&B – £ 166.50 (minimum 12), transport and packed lunches extra – single supplement in certain circumstances.

Email: nick@cambrianway.com.

☆ **Dan-y-Parc Farm Guest House**
Cynghordy, SA20 0LD ☎ 01550 720401 (Mrs Diane Brown)
www.danyparcholidays.co.uk Map 146,160/795378
BB **B** ✕ book first £15, 7pm S1 D1 T1 F1 ♨(Llandovery)
Ⅴ Ⓑ Ⓓ 🍵🛁🚗!🛁 ★★★

Beautifully situated 17th century farmhouse on the border of the Brecon Beacons National Park, and at the gateway of the Cambrian mountains.

Providing comfortable en-suite rooms with tea/coffee making facilities, hearty home cooked English or vegetarian breakfasts, home made evening meals. Also a woodland walk containing a waterfall and some of the oldest trees in Wales. In the vicinity, many waymarked routes. Pets are made very welcome.

● Llangadog

Brecon Beacons

▪🚍✕ Cynyll Farm, SA19 9BB ☎ 01550 777316 (Mrs Jackie Dare)
cynyllfarm@clara.co.uk   Map 146,160/718301
BB A ✕ book first £12-£13, approx 7pm   DI FI
Ⓥ Ⓑ Ⓓ ⊛ 🛏🛁☕🚗🅿 ★★★

▪🚍✕ Pen-y-Bont Guest House, SA19 9EN ☎ 01550 777126 (Maria Aldridge)
www.penybontguesthouse.co.uk   Map 146,160/719282
BB B ✕ book first £12, 7pm   D2 TI   Closed Nov-Feb   🚌(Llangadog)
Ⓥ Ⓑ Ⓓ ⊛ 🛏🛁☕🚗🅿 ★★★

● Pembrey (Burry Port)

▪🚍✕ The Old Vicarage, 125 Gwscwm Road, SA16 0AQ ☎ 01554 835389
(Ann Harrison) www.altouristguide.com/oldvicarage   Map 159/428012
BB B ✕ book first £8.50, 6:30pm   DI TI FI   🚌(Burry Port)
Ⓥ Ⓑ Ⓓ ⊛ 🛏🛁☕🚗🅿 ★★★

CEREDIGION

● Aberaeron

Ceredigion Coast Path

▪🚍✕ Llys Aeron Guest House, Lampeter Rd, SA46 0ED
☎ 01545 570276   www.llysaeron.co.uk   Map 146/459621
BB B ✕ nearby   SI DI TI   Ⓑ Ⓓ ⊛ 🛏🛁☕🚗🅿🛈📚 ★★★★

● Bow Street (Aberystwyth)

▪🚍✕ Garreg Lwyd, Penygarn, SY24 5BE
☎ 01970 828830 (Mrs A Edwards)   Map 135/625852
BB A/B ✕ nearby   SI DI TI FI   🚌(Aberystwyth) Ⓓ 🛏🛁☕📚 ★★

● Cellan (Lampeter)

▪🚍✕ Royal Oak, SA48 8JF ☎ 01570 493669 (Hazel Brookshaw)
www.stayatroyaloak.co.uk   Map 146/613494
BB B   TI FI   Ⓥ Ⓑ Ⓓ ⊛ 🛏☕🚗🛈📚 ★★★

● Lampeter

Black Lion Royal Hotel, High St, SA48 7BG
☎ 01570 422172 (Rob Jones)   Map 146/575481
BB C ✕ £10, 6-9pm   S8 D6 T2 F2   Ⓥ Ⓑ Ⓓ 🛏🛁☕ ★★★

● Llanon

Ceredigion Coast Path

▪🚍✕ Aromatherapy Reflexology Centre, The Barn House, Pennant Rd, SY23 5LZ
☎ 01974 202581 (Tony Rees)
www.aromatherapy-breaks-wales.co.uk   Map 135/513661
BB B ✕ nearby   S2 TI FI   Ⓑ Ⓓ ⊛ 🛏🛁☕🚗🛈📚 ★★

●Llechryd (Cardigan)

☆ **Glanhelyg**
SA43 2NJ ☎ 01239 682482 (Kath Sapey & Ann Williamson)
www.glanhelyg.co.uk   Map 145/211444
BB B ✕ £12.50, 7pm   S2 DI T2   Closed Dec-Jan
Ⓥ ⊛ 🛏📚

Victorian guest house set in 3 1/2 acres. Local footpaths. Close to Pembrokeshire Coast Path and Preselli Mountains. Full board available, including continental breakfast, packed lunch, gourmet vegetarian evening meal, use of lounge, kitchen and studio. Ideal for small groups.

● Pontrhydfendigaid (Ystrad Meurig)

Cambrian Way

☆ ▪🚍 **Black Lion Hotel**
Mill St, SY25 6BE ☎ 01974 831624 (Giles Polglase)
www.blacklionatbont.co.uk   Map 135,147/731666
BB B   ✕ £7:50, 6-9pm   D2 T2 FI
Ⓥ Ⓑ Ⓓ 🛏🛁☕🚗🛈🐕Ⓜ ★★★

The Black Lion Inn is set in a fold of the Cambrian Mountains, in an AONB close to Cors Caron Nature Reserve. Traditional welcome. Log fires and beamed ceiling. Fantastic walking on ancient paths. Guided/self guided walks arranged.

CONWY

● Betws-y-Coed

Snowdonia/Eryri

▪🚍✕ Glan Llugwy, LL24 0BN ☎ 01690 710592 (Graham & Jean Brayne)
jean@glanllugwy.fsnet.co.uk   Map 115/784565
BB B ✕ nearby   SI D2 TI FI   🚌(Betws-y-Coed)
Ⓓ ⊛ 🛏🛁☕🚗🅿 ★★

Bryn Bella Guest House, Lon Muriau, Llanrwst Rd, LL24 0HD
☎ 01690 710627 (Mark Edwards)   www.bryn-bella.co.uk   Map 116/800565
BB C ✕ nearby D5   🚌(Betws-y-Coed) Ⓑ Ⓓ ⊛ 🛏🛁☕🚗Ⓜ ★★★★

▪🚍✕ The Old Courthouse, Henllys, Old Church Rd, LL24 0AL
☎ 01690 710534 (Mark & Gillian Bidwell)
www.guesthouse-snowdonia.co.uk   Map 115/795568
BB B ✕ nearby   SI D6 T2 FI   🚌(Betws-y-Coed)
Ⓑ Ⓓ ⊛ 🛏🛁☕🅿Ⓜ ★★★

☆ **Fairy Glen Hotel**
Beaver Bridge, LL24 0SH ☎ 01690 710269 (Mr & Mrs B Youe)
www.fairyglenhotel.co.uk   Map 115/799547
BB B   ✕ book first £15, 7pm   SI D5 TI FI   Closed Nov-Feb
🚌(Betws-Y-Coed) Ⓥ Ⓑ Ⓓ 🛏🛁☕ ★★

Built in the 17th century., commended for its food and hospitality in the 21st century. The hotel where you can enjoy your walking, relaxation and food. Residents licensed bar. Private car park.fairyglen@youe.fsworld.co.uk

☆ ▪🚍✕ **Afon View 'Non Smokers' Guest House**
Holyhead Road, LL24 0AN ☎ 01690 710726 (Keith Roobottom)
www.afon-view.co.uk   Map 115/795562
BB B ✕ nearby   SI D2 T2 FI   🚌(Betws-y-Coed)
Ⓑ Ⓓ ⊛ 🛏🛁📚 ◆◆◆◆

A warm welcome awaits you from your hosts Keith & Teresa. Mountain bike hire is available nearby — secure overnight storage. You can choose from four-poster, twins, doubles and single rooms, all with en-suite shower. Guests who appreciate a relaxed, comfortable environment are well cared for here.

☆ The Ferns Non-Smokers Guest House

LL24 0AN ☎ 01690 710587 (Deborah & Ian Baxter)
www.ferns-guesthouse.co.uk   Map 115/795562
BB **B/C** ✕ nearby   D6 T1 F2   Closed Dec   ₩(Betws-y-Coed)
B D ⊗ ☜ ☕ ★★★

The Ferns Non-Smokers Guesthouse is conveniently situated in the village of Betwys. All rooms en-suite with TV, beverage trays, clocks & hairdryers. Ian and Deborah will make every effort to ensure that your stay is a comfortable one. Which?Recommended.

☆ Park Hill Hotel

Lanrwst Rd, LL24 0HD ☎ 01690 710540 (Jaap & Ghislaine Buis)
www.park-hill-hotel.co.uk   Map 116/801565
BB **B** ✕ book first £17, 7pm   D5 T4   ₩(Betws-y-Coed)
V B D ☜ ☕ 🚗 !   ★★★

"Our hotel is your castle". Family run hotel. Breathtaking views. Renowned for its informality, service and its teddybears. Indoor heated swimming pool with sauna, free and exclusively for guests, open 24h/day. Secluded carpark. Railway station and village 6 minutes walk.

● Conwy

Cambrian Way

☆ Glan Heulog Guest House

Llanrwst Road, LL32 8LT ☎ 01492 593845 (Stan & Vivien Watson-Jones)
www.walesbandb.co.uk   Map 115/779772
BB **B** ✕ nearby   D2 T2 F2   ₩(Conwy)
V B D ⊗ ☜ ☕ 🚗 ! ⚘   ★★★

Beautiful Victorian house coveniently situated in the World Heritage Town of Conwy. Non-Smoking en- suite rooms, centrally heated with TV, beverage trays, clock radio and hairdryers. Lounge and conservatory to relax in. Car parking.

● Llanfairfechan

Snowdonia/Eryri
Cambrian Way

🥾 Rhiwiau, Isaf, LL33 0EH ☎ 01248 681143 (Ruth Carrington)
www.rhiwiau.co.uk   Map 115/678732
BB **B** ✕ book first £8, 6:15pm   S3 D3 T4 F2   ₩(Llanfairfechan)
V B D ⊗ ☜ ☕ 🚗 !   ★★

🥾 Hafod Y Coed, Penmaen Park, LL33 0RN
☎ 01248 680404 (John & Helen Prichard)
www.hafodycoed.com   Map 115/687753
BB **B** ✕ nearby   D2 T1   ₩(Llanfairfechan)
B D ☜ ☕ 🚗 !   ★★★

● Trefriw

Snowdonia/Eryri

☆ 🥾 Crafnant Guest House

LL27 0JH ☎ 01492 640809 (Mike & Jan Bertenshaw)
www.trefriw.co.uk   Map 115/780631
BB **B** ✕ nearby   D3 T1 F1   Closed Dec-Jan   ₩(Llanrwst)
B D ⊗ ☜ ☕ 🚗 !   ★★★

Whether you've discovered the mountain lakes which nestle above our village, conquered Snowdon or just strolled in the stunning Conwy Valley then rest assured of the comfort and warm welcome of Crafnant House. All bedrooms have cast-iron beds with fresh white linen.

GWYNEDD

● Aberdovey

Snowdonia/Eryri

🥾 Awel Y Mor, 4 Bodfor Terrace, LL35 0EA
☎ 01654 767058 (Mrs Jennifer Johnson)
www.awelymor-aberdovey.co.uk   Map 135/612959
BB **B** ✕ nearby   S1 D1 T2 F3   ₩(Aberdovey)
B D ⊗ ☜ ☕ 🚗 ⚘   ★★★

● Bala

Snowdonia/Eryri

☆ 🥾 Abercelyn Country House

Llanycil, LL23 7YF ☎ 01678 521109 (Mrs Lindsay Hind)
www.abercelyn.co.uk   Map 125/914349
BB **B** ✕ book first £17.50, 7:30pm   D1 T1 F1
V B D ⊗ ☜ ☕ 🚗 ! Ⓜ   ★★★★   Guided walks.

Walker-friendly accommodation in a former Grade II listed rectory in own grounds. Home cooking using local produce. Visitors can be met by car. Drying room. Walking guides and maps. Guided walking. Self-catering available.

☆ Fronddew Country House

Stryd y Fron, LL23 7YD ☎ 01678 520301 (Paul Short)
www.fronderwhouse.co.uk   Map 125/915361
BB **B** ✕ £23.50   S1 D4 T1 F1   Closed Dec-Jan
V B D ⊗ ☜ ☕   ★★★★

Enjoying spectacular lake and mountain views, our early 17th century Dower house is an ideal base for touring and walking holidays. Fully refurbished. Off street parking. Imaginative cuisine and outstanding wine list. Close to many local walks and attractions.

Barmouth

Snowdonia/Eryri

Cambrian Way

The Gables, Mynach Rd, LL42 1RL
☎ 01341 280553 (Mrs D Lewis) Map 124/609166
BB **B** ✕ nearby S1 D2 F1 Closed Dec-Jan ⚡(Barmouth)
▣ ▣ ⊛ ⚑ ⚙ ⛊ ⚡ ! ⚐ ★★★

☆ Mynydd Ar Mor
Llanaber, LL42 1AJ ☎ 01341 281221 (June & Mike Goodwin)
enquiries@holidayinbarmouth.co.uk Map 124/602177
BB **B** ✕ book first £12, 6pm D4 T2 Closed Jan ⚡(Llanaber)
▣ ▣ ▣ ⊛ ⚑ ⚙ ⚡ ★★★

Mynydd Ar-Mor is a non-smoking guest house with 6 bedrooms, 3 en-suite, with stunning panoramic views across Cardigan Bay, mountain walks to the rear. Evening meals available. Low season £25-30 pppn.
enquiries@holidayinbarmouth.co.uk

Beddgelert (Caernarfon)

Snowdonia/Eryri

Cambrian Way

Plas Colwyn, LL55 4UY ☎ 01766 890458 (Lynda Osmond)
info@plascolwyn.co.uk Map 115/589482
BB **B** ✕ nearby S1 D2 T1 F2 ▣ ▣ ⊛ ⚑ ⚙ ⛊ ⚡ ! ⚐ ★★

Gwesty Plas Tan-Y-Graig, LL55 4LT ☎ 01766 890310 (John & Rae Duffield)
www.plastanygraig.co.uk Map 115/587483
BB **B** ✕ nearby D2 T2 F1 ▣ ▣ ⊛ ⚑ ⚙ ★★★

Blaenau Ffestiniog

Snowdonia/Eryri

Cambrian Way

☆ Cae Du
Manod, LL41 4BB ☎ 01766 830847 (Chris Carswell & Sue Ashe)
www.caedu.co.uk Map 124/709438
BB **B** ✕ book first £12 D2 T1 ⚡(Blaenau Ffestiniog)
▣ ▣ ▣ ⊛ ⚑ ⚙ ⚡ ! ★★★

Picturesque 16th century former farmhouse in magnificent mountain setting. Stunning panoramic views, comfortable en-suite rooms, log fires, 2 lounges, satellite TV, private parking. Beautiful mature gardens and ponds. Centrally located for exploring Snowdonia with varied walks direct from Cae-Du, guide if required. Great views, great walks, great home cooking, all make for ramblers to unwind with Chris and Sue. "It's our home – make it yours".

☆ Bryn Elltyd Guest House
Tanygrisiau, LL41 3TW ☎ 01766 831356 (Ann & Bob Cole)
www.accommodation-snowdonia.com Map 124/681448
BB **B** ✕ book first £10, 7.30pm S1 D1 T2 F1 ⚡(Blaenau Ffestiniog)
▣ ▣ ▣ ⊛ ⚑ ⚙ ⛊ ⚡ ! ⚐ Ⓜ ★★★ Guided walks.

Secluded mountain location in the centre of Snowdonia National Park, ideal for all outdoor activities. Sauna, drying room, evening meals and packed lunches. Discount for Ramblers and groups.

Conwy

Cambrian Way

☆ Sychnant Pass House
Sychnant Pass Rd, LL32 8BJ ☎ 01492 596868 (Bre Carrington-Sykes)
www.sychnant-pass-house.co.uk Map 115/754772
BB **C** ✕ £25, 7-8:30pm D2 T2 F6 ⚡(Conwy)
▣ ▣ ▣ ⚑ ⚙ ⛊ ⚡ ! ⚐ ◆◆◆◆◆

More than just an award winning Country House; it's a home that welcomes guests in a unique way. Lovely sittingrooms with comfortable sofas & beautiful pictures delight the eye; wonderful food served in the candlelit restaurant nourishes the body and a warm welcome embraces the spirit. Whether you stay in a suite or a standard room you will receive lots of little luxuries.
AA Best Guest Accommodation in Wales 2004.

Dolgellau

Snowdonia/Eryri

Tanyfron, Arran Road, LL40 2AA ☎ 01341 422638 (Elfed & Sue Rowlands)
www.tanyfron.co.uk Map 124/735176
BB **B** ✕ nearby D1 T1 F1 Closed Dec-Jan
▣ ▣ ⊛ ⚙ ★★★★

Y Goedlan, Brithdir, LL40 2RN
☎ 01341 423131 (Mrs G D Evans) Map 124/765184
BB **B** S1 D1 T1 Closed Dec-Jan
▣ ⊛ ⚙ ⚡ ★★★ Veggie breakfasts.

Clifton House Hotel, Smithfield Square, LL40 1ES
☎ 01341 422554 (Geoff & Teresa Challenor)
www.clifton-house-hotel.co.uk Map 124/728177
BB **B** ✕ £12, 6:30 onwards S1 D3 T3
▣ ▣ ▣ ⊛ ⚑ ⚙ ⚡ ! ◆◆◆◆

☆ Dwy Olwyn

Coed-y-Fronallt, LL40 2YG ☎ 01341 422822 (Mrs N Jones)
www.dwyolwyn.co.uk   Map 124/734183
BB A/B ✕ book first £11, 7pm   D1 T1 F2   Closed Jan
Ⓥ Ⓓ ⊛ 🐾♿ ⭐⭐⭐

"View of Cader Idris from Dwy Olwyn". A warm welcome awaits you in this comfortable guesthouse, set in an acre of landscaped gardens. Peaceful position only 10 mins walk into town. Ideal for touring Snowdonia NP, sandy beaches, gauge railways, RSPB sanctuary, picturesque walks including famous Precipice Walk above Mawddach estuary. Spacious bedrooms with colour TV, clock radio, hairdryer. Good home cooking. Lounge with selection of maps, guide books and leaflets. Cleanliness and personal attention assured.

☆ 🚶 Ivy House

Finsbury Square, LL40 1RF ☎ 01341 422535 (J S & M Bamford)
www.ukworld.net/ivyhouse   Map 124/727177
BB B ✕ book first £14.50, 6:30-7:30pm   D3 T2 F1
Ⓥ Ⓑ Ⓓ 🐾♿🚗⚡📷 ♦♦♦

At the centre of an idyllic walking area, a country town guesthouse, offering home made food: big breakfasts, evening meals and packed lunches. Fully centrally heated and licensed, all bedrooms have TV, hairdryers and tea/coffee making facilities, most en-suite. Email: marg.bamford@btconnect.com

● Llanberis (Caernarfon)
Snowdonia/Eryri

Mount Pleasant Hotel, High Street, LL55 4HA ☎ 01286 870395
www.waterton.org.uk/mph   Map 114,115/577602
BB B ✕ £12.50, 6-9pm   S2 D2 T1 F2   Ⓥ Ⓑ Ⓓ 🐾♿🚗⚡📷

Snowdon Cottage, 7 Pentre Castell, LL55 4UB
☎ 01286 872015 (Carol Anne Gerrard)   Map 115/585596
BB A ✕ nearby, 14pm   S1 D1 T1   Ⓥ Ⓓ ⊛ 🐾♿🚗⚡Ⓜ

● Llandanwg (Harlech)
Snowdonia/Eryri

Glanygors, LL46 2SD ☎ 01341 241410 (Gweneth Evans)   Map 124/570285
BB B ✕ nearby   D1 T1 F1   🚌(Llandanwg)
Ⓑ Ⓓ ⊛ 🐾♿⚡📷 ⭐⭐⭐

● Nantgwynant (Caernarfon)
Snowdonia/Eryri

Pen-y-Gwryd Hotel, Pen-y-Gwryd, LL55 4NT
☎ 01286 870211/870768   www.pyg.co.uk   Map 115/660558
BB B ✕ book first £20, 7:30pm
S1 D8 T6 F1   Closed Dec   Ⓥ Ⓑ Ⓓ 🐾♿ ⭐⭐

● Pant Glas (Garndolbenmaen)
Snowdonia/Eryri

☆ 🚶 Hen Ysgol (Old School)

Bwlch Derwin, LL51 9EQ ☎ 01286 660701 (Terry & Sue Gibbins)
www.oldschool-henyysgol.co.uk   Map 123,115/456474
BB B ✕ book first £12-£15, 7pm   D1 T1 F1
Ⓥ Ⓑ Ⓓ ⊛ 🐾♿🚗⚡📷 ⭐⭐⭐

A beautiful, historically 'Welsh Not' Country School provides a unique base for walking the re-opened network of paths linking Snowdonia with Lleyn Peninsular and Bardsey Island. Delicious home cooked evening meals and choice of breakfast menu. Call Terry or Sue for a brochure.

● Penrhyndeudraeth (Porthmadog)
Snowdonia/Eryri

☆ Talgarth

LL48 6DR ☎ 01766 770353 (Hilary & Paul Davies)
hilary@talgarthbb.freeserve.co.uk   Map 124/615398
BB B ✕ book first £10, 7pm   S2 D1   🚌(Penrhyndeudraeth)
Ⓥ Ⓓ ⊛ 🐾

Ideally situated in the walkers' paradise that is Snowdonia. Glorious views, friendly welcome. Warm & comfortable B&B with superb range of cooked food. Optional evening meal and packed lunches. Open all year round. Member of WTB Welcome Host scheme.

● Rhyd-Ddu (Beddgelert)
Snowdonia/Eryri & Cambrian Way

Ffridd Isaf, LL54 6TN ☎ 01766 890452 (Gina Kent)
www.snowdonia-b_and_b.co.uk   Map 115/576527
BB B ✕ book first £10, 7pm   D1 T1
Ⓥ Ⓓ ⊛ 🐾🚗   No single supplements.

● Trawsfynydd
Snowdonia/Eryri & Cambrian Way

🚶 Cae Gwyn Farm, LL41 4YE ☎ 01766 540245 (Yuki & Steve Barnett)
www.caegwynfarm.co.uk   Map 124/705306
BB B   S1 D1 T1   Ⓑ Ⓓ ⊛ 🐾♿🚗⚡

● Tywyn
Snowdonia/Eryri & Cambrian Way

Hendy Farm, LL36 9RU ☎ 01654 710457 (Anne Lloyd-Jones)
www.hendyfarmholidays.co.uk   Map 135/594013
BB B ✕ nearby   D2 T1   Closed Nov-Feb   🚌(Y)
Ⓑ Ⓓ ⊛ 🐾♿⚡📷 ⭐⭐⭐

🚶 Gwesty Minffordd Hotel, Talyllyn, LL36 9AJ
☎ 01654 761665   www.minffordd.com   Map 124/734115
BB C ✕ book first £22.95, 6-9pm   S1 D/S4 T/S2   Closed Jan
Ⓥ Ⓑ Ⓓ ⊛ 🐾♿🚗⚡📷 ⭐⭐⭐

MONMOUTHSHIRE

● Abergavenny

Brecon Beacons

Cambrian Way & Usk Valley Walk

🚂◀ The Guest House, 2 Oxford Street, NP7 5RP ☎ 01873 854823
(Jenny Taylor) theguesthouseabergavenny@hotmail.com Map 161/303147
BB **B** ✕ book first £ S1 D2 T2 F3 ⋙(Abergavenny)
Ⓥ Ⓓ ⊗ 🍵♨🚗❗🐾 ★

🚂◀ Park Guest House, 36 Hereford Road, NP7 5RA ☎ 01873 853715
(Neil & Julia Herring) www.abergavenny.net Map 161/303146
BB **B** ✕ nearby S1 D4 T1 F1 ⋙(Abergavenny)
Ⓑ Ⓓ 🍵♨ ★★

🚂◀ The Kings Head Hotel,Cross Str, NP7 5EU ☎ 01873 853575
www.kingshead.20fr.com Map 161/299141
BB **B** ✕ £6, 7-8:30pm S1 D1 T3 ⋙(Abergavenny)
Ⓥ Ⓓ 🍵♨ ★★

● Chepstow

Wye Valley Walk & Offa's Dyke

🚂◀ Upper Sedbury House, Sedbury Lane, Sedbury, NP16 7HN
☎ 01291 627173 (Christine Potts)
www.smoothound.co.uk/hotels/uppersed.html Map 172/547943
BB **B** ✕ nearby D3 T2 F1 ⋙(Chepstow)
Ⓑ Ⓓ ⊗ 🍵♨🐾 ★★

The First Hurdle, 9-10 Upper Church St., NP16 5EX
☎ 01291 622 189 (Jane Cooper)
www.thefirsthurdle.com Map 172,162/534939
BB **B** ✕ nearby S2 D5 T5 ⋙(Chepstow)
Ⓑ Ⓓ ⊗ 🍵♨

🚂◀ Lower Hardwick, Hardwick Hill, NP16 6PT
☎ 01291 620515 (Valerie Kells) Map 171/472984
BB **B** ✕ nearby F4 ⋙(Chepstow) Ⓑ Ⓓ ⊗ 🍵♨🚗❗Ⓜ ★★

● Llanellen (Abergavenny)

Usk Valley Walk & Cambrian Way

Yew Tree Farm B&B, NP7 9LB ☎ 01873 854307 (Liz Rose)
groseandcollanellen@ukonline.co.uk Map 161/286091
BB **B** ✕ book first £8 F1 Closed Nov-Mar
Ⓥ Ⓑ Ⓓ ⊗ 🍵♨🚗🐾 ★★

● Llanfihangel Crucorney (Abergavenny)

Brecon Beacons

Offa's Dyke

Penyclawdd Farm, NP7 7LB ☎ 01873 890591 (Ann Davies)
www.geocities.com/penyclawdd Map 161/312200
BB **B** ✕ nearby S/D/F1 D2 T2 F1 ⋙(Abergavenny)
Ⓑ Ⓓ 🍵♨🚗🐾 ★★★

● Llangattock-Lingoed (Abergavenny)

Brecon Beacons

Offa's Dyke

The Old Rectory, NP7 8RR ☎ 01873 821326 (Karen Ball)
www.rectoryonoffasdyke.co.uk Map 161/362201
BB **B** ✕ book first £11.50, 6:30-7pm S1 D2 T1
Ⓥ Ⓑ Ⓓ 🍵♨🚗❗ ★★★

● Llanthony (Abergavenny)

Brecon Beacons

Offa's Dyke & Cambrian Way

🚂◀ The Half Moon Hotel, NP7 7NN ☎ 01873 890611 (Christine Smith)
halfmoonllanthony@talk21.com Map 161/287276
BB **B** ✕ £5+, 7-8:30pm D4 T4 F1 Ⓥ Ⓑ Ⓓ 🍵♨❗🐾

● Monmouth

Offa's Dyke & Wye Valley Walk

🚂◀ The Riverside Hotel, Cinderhill Street, NP25 5EY
☎ 01600 715577 (Mr Gareth Collins)
www.riversidehotelmonmouth.co.uk Map 162/504123
BB **C** ✕ £6-£15, 7-9pm D6 T9
Ⓥ Ⓑ Ⓓ 🍵♨❗🐾 ★★★★

🚂◀ Penylan Farm, The Hendre, NP25 5NL ☎ 01600 716435
(Cathy & Dave Bowen) www.penylanfarm.co.uk Map 161/445162
BB **B** ✕ book first £12, 7:30pm D1 T1 F1
Ⓥ Ⓑ Ⓓ ⊗ 🍵♨🚗❗ ★★★

☆ 🚂◀ **Church Farm Guest House**
Mitchel Troy, NP25 4HZ ☎ 01600 712176 (Rosey & Derek Ringer)
www.churchfarmmitcheltroy.co.uk Map 162/492103
BB **B** ✕ book first £14, 7-7:30pm S2 D3 T2 F3
Ⓥ Ⓑ Ⓓ ⊗ 🍵♨🚗❗🐾Ⓜ ★★ See SC also.

Set in large garden with stream, a 16th century former farmhouse with oak beams and inglenook fireplaces. Excellent base for Wye Valley, Forest of Dean, Black Mountains. Central heating. Mainly en-suite bedrooms. Groups welcome (discounts available). Also Self-catering unit.

🚂◀ Whitecross House, Whitecross St, NP25 3BY
☎ 01600 716422 (Judith Perks)
judith@perks.dircon.co.uk Map 162/509129
BB **B** ✕ nearby S1 D1 T1 Ⓓ ⊗ 🍵♨🚗❗

🚂◀ Casita Alta, 15 Toynbee Close, Osbaston, NP25 3NU
☎ 01600 713023
http://bb.allcock.users.btopenworld.com Map 162/502143
BB **B** ✕ nearby S/D1 D/T1
Ⓥ Ⓑ Ⓓ 🍵♨🚗❗ ★★

● Pandy (Abergavenny)

Brecon Beacons

Offa's Dyke

Brynhonddu Country House B&B, Bwlch Trewyn Estate, NP7 7PD
☎ 01873 890535(Mrs Carol White)
www.brynhonddu.co.uk Map 161/326224
BB **B** ✕ nearby D1 T1 F1 Ⓑ Ⓓ 🍵♨🚗🐾 ★★

● Redbrook (Monmouth)

Offa's Dyke & Wye Valley Walk

Tresco, NP25 4LY ☎ 01600 712325 (Mrs M Evans)
Map 162/536101
BB **A** ✕ nearby S2 D1 T1 F1
Ⓥ Ⓓ ⊗ 🍵♨🐾Ⓜ

NORTH EAST WALES

● Afon-Wen (Mold)
Offa's Dyke & Clwydian Way
The Bungalow, CH7 5UB ☎ 01352 720338 (Mrs H Priestley)
hlpriestley@aol.com　Map 116/127716
BB **B**　✕ nearby　D1 T1　⬛ ☺ 🐾 🛁 🚗 ! 🛏

● Caerwys (Mold)
Offa's Dyke
Plas Penucha, CH7 5BH ☎ 01352 720210 (Mrs N Price)
www.geocities.com/plaspenucha　Map 116/108733
BB **B**　✕ book first £14.50, 7pm　S4 D2 T2
Ⓥ ⬛ Ⓓ ☺ 🐾🛁 🚗 ! 🛏 ★★★

● Corwen (Denbighshire)
Clwydian Way
Corwen Court Private Hotel, London Road, LL21 0DP ☎ 01490 412854
Map 125/080434　BB **A**　✕ book first £9, 7pm　S6 D4　Closed Dec-Feb
Ⓥ ⬛ Ⓓ 🐾 🛏

● Denbigh
Clwydian Way
Cayo Guest House, 74 Vale Street, LL16 3BW ☎ 01745 812686
stay@cayo.co.uk　Map 116/055663　BB **B**　✕ nearby　S1 D2 T3
⬛ ☺ 🐾 🛁 🚗 🛏　◆◆◆

● Llangollen
Clwydian Way & Offa's Dyke
Squirrels, Abbey Rd, LL20 8SP ☎ 01978 869041 (Mrs Lilian Speake)
www.squirrels-b-and-b.co.uk　Map 117/211423
BB **B**　✕ nearby　D3 T2　⬛ Ⓓ ☺ 🐾 🛁 🚗 🛏　★★★

> ☆ 🚶◀ **New Ross**
> Dinbren Rd, LL20 8TF ☎ 01978 861334 (Mr D Roberts)
> www.newrossllan.co.uk　Map 117/217418
> BB **B**　✕ nearby　D2 T1
> ⬛ Ⓓ ☺ 🐾 🛁 🚗 ! ★★★
>
>
>
> Set in a spectacular location by Offa's Dyke Path and overlooking Llangollen marina. The warm welcome and excellent breakfast inspired one visitor to comment "wonderful, friendly, relaxing B&B. Immaculate and with views to die for".

● Llangwm (Corwen)
Bryn Awel B&B, LL21 0RB ☎ 01490 420610 (Jenni Miller)
www.smoothhounds.co.uk/hotels/brynawel.html　Map 125/963439
BB **A**　✕ N　S1 D1 T1　Ⓓ ☺ 🐾 🛁 🚗 !

● Prestatyn
Offa's Dyke & Clwydian Way
Roughsedge Guest House, 26-28 Marine Rd, LL19 7HD ☎ 01745 887359
(Y Kubler)　roughsedge@ykubler.fsnet.co.uk　Map 116/066833
BB **B**　✕ nearby, 7pm　S2 D5 T2　〜〜(Prestatyn)
⬛ Ⓓ ☺ 🐾 🛁 🚗 !

PEMBROKESHIRE

● Amroth (Narberth)
Pembrokeshire Coast National Park
Pembrokeshire Coast Path
Ashdale Guest House, SA67 8NA
☎ 01834 813853 (Roy & Edith Williamson)　Map 158/160071
BB **B**　✕ book first £9.50, 6pm　S1 D4 T3 F0　Closed Dec-Feb
〜〜(Kilgetty)　Ⓥ　Ⓓ 🐾 🛁 🚗 !

● Bosherston (Pembroke)
Pembrokeshire Coast National Park
Pembrokeshire Coast Path
Trefalen Farm, SA71 5DR ☎ 01646 661643 (Marcia & Lawrence Giardelli)
trefalen@trefalen.force9.co.uk　Map 158/974939
BB **B**　✕ nearby　S3 D1 T2 F1　Ⓓ ☺ 🐾 🛁 🚗　★★Ⓦ

St Govan's Country Inn, SA71 5DN ☎ 01646 661643 (Warren Heaton)
trefalen@trefalen.force9.co.uk　Map 158/966947
BB **B**　✕ £8, 7-9pm　S1 D2 T2 F1　Ⓥ ⬛ Ⓓ 🐾 🛁　★★★

● Broad Haven (Haverfordwest)
Pembrokeshire Coast National Park
Pembrokeshire Coast Path

> ☆ 🚶◀ **Albany Guesthouse**
> 27 Millmoor Way, SA62 3JJ ☎ 01437 781051 (Mrs Morgan)
> www.albanyguesthouse.co.uk　Map 157/861138
> BB **B**　✕ nearby　S1 D1 T1　Closed Oct-Feb
> ⬛ Ⓓ 🐾 🛁 ! ★★★
>
>
>
> Albany is 2 min from beach and coastal path and 6 mins from cafes, pub, restaurant and shop. Ideal for walking, surfing, diving, birdwatching with local boat. Trips to bird sanctuary islands (puffins, razorbills and seals). TV and tea facilities in rooms. Parking.

● Croesgoch (St Davids)
Pembrokeshire Coast National Park
Pembrokeshire Coast Path
Torbant Farmhouse, SA62 5JN ☎ 01348 831276 (Mrs Barbara Charles)
www.torbantfarm.co.uk　Map 157/845307
BB **B**　✕ nearby　D2 T1　Closed Nov-Feb
⬛ Ⓓ ☺ 🐾 🛁 🚗 ! ★★★

● Dale (Haverfordwest)
Pembrokeshire Coast National Park
Pembrokeshire Coast Path
Allenbrook, SA62 3RN ☎ 01646 636254 (Elizabeth Webber)
www.ukworld.net/allenbrook　Map 157/811059
BB **B**　✕ nearby　S1 D1 T1 F1　Closed Dec
⬛ Ⓓ ☺ 🐾 🛁 🚗 ! ★★★★

Point Farm, SA62 3RD ☎ 01646 636541
www.pointfarm.info　Map 157/815053
BB **B**　✕ nearby　D2 F1　Closed Dec-Jan　Ⓓ ☺ 🐾 🛁 🚗 ! ★★★

● Dinas Cross (Newport)

Pembrokeshire Coast National Park

Dolwern, Feidr Fawr,, SA42 0UY ☎ 01348 811266 (Mrs Annette Keylock)
annette-keylock@lineone.net   Map 157,145/011390
BB **B**   ✗ nearby   SI D2 TI   B D 🍴☕🛏🚗! 🏠   ★★

● Dyffryn (Goodwick)

Pembrokeshire Coast National Park
Pembrokeshire Coast Path

Ivybridge, Drim Mill, SA64 0JT ☎ 01348 875366
www.ivybridge.cwc.net   Map 157/943371
BB **B**   ✗ book first £17.95, 6:30-7:30pm   SI D3 T3 F4   〰(Fishguard)
V B D 🍴☕🛏🚗!🏠   ★★★

● Fishguard

Pembrokeshire Coast National Park
Pembrokeshire Coast Path

🚶🛏◀ Cartref Hotel, 15-19 High Street, SA65 9AW ☎ 01348 872430
(Mrs Kristiina Bjorkqvist) www.cartrefhotel.co.uk   Map 157/956369
BB **C**   ✗ £14, 6:30-8:30pm   S4 D2 T2 F2   〰(Fishguard Harbour)
V B D 🍴☕🛏🚗!🏠   ★★

● Goodwick (Fishguard)

Pembrokeshire Coast National Park
Pembrokeshire Coast Path

🚶🛏◀ 6 New Hill Villas, SA64 0DS ☎ 01348 874076 (Anne Strawbridge)
garyann@glowinternet.net   Map 157/947385
BB **B**   ✗ nearby   DI FI   〰(Fishguard) B   D ⊗ 🍴☕🛏🚗! 🏠

☆ **Hope & Anchor Inn**

SA64 0BP ☎ 01348 872314 (Chris & Ulrika Burns)
hopeandanchor4@tiscali.co.uk   Map 157/945382
BB **B**   ✗ £8, 6-10pm   D2 TI FI   〰(Fishguard Harbour)
V B D 🍴☕🛏🏠   ◆◆

Small friendly inn on Coastal Path overlooking Fishguard harbour.
Hot and cold water in our bathrooms, shaver points, tea making facilities.
Restaurant for snacks or evening dinner.
Packed lunches. All rooms en-suite & TV's.
★★ WTB.
B&B £22.50 pp.

● Haverfordwest

☆ 🚶🛏◀ **Cuckoo Mill Farm**

Pelcomb Bridge, SA62 6EA ☎ 01437 762139 (Margaret Davies)
cmflimited@aol.com   Map 157,158/933172
BB **B**   ✗ £13-£15, 6-8:30pm   SI D2 TI FI   〰(Haverfordwest)
V B D ⊗ 🍴☕🛏🏠   ★★★

Mixed farm in central Pembrokeshire. Country walking. Six miles to coastal path. Meal times to suit guests. Excellent home cooking. Cosy farmhouse. Warm, well-appointed rooms. En-suite facilities. Gold Welcome Host.

College Guest House, 93 Hill St, St Thomas Green, SA61 1QL ☎ 01437 763710
(Colin Larby) www.collegeguesthouse.com   Map 157,158/951152
BB **B**   ✗ nearby   SI D2 T2 F3   〰(Haverfordwest)
B D 🍴☕🛏🚗! 🏠   ◆◆◆◆

● Manorbier (Tenby)

Pembrokeshire Coast National Park
Pembrokeshire Coast Path

Honeyhill, Warlows Meadow, SA70 7SX ☎ 01834 871906 (Susan Robinson)
honeyhillbandb@aol.com   Map 158/064983
BB **B**   ✗ nearby   SI D2 TI FI   〰(Manorbier)
B D ⊗ 🍴☕🛏!   ★★★

● Moylegrove (Cardigan)

Pembrokeshire Coast National Park
Pembrokeshire Coast Path

🚶🛏◀ Swn-y-Nant, SA43 3BW ☎ 01239 881244   ludbek@yahoo.com
Map 145/117446   BB **B**   ✗ book first £12   D2 TI   Closed Jan
V B D ⊗ 🍴☕🛏🚗!   ★★★

● Pembroke

Pembrokeshire Coast National Park
Pembrokeshire Coast Path

🚶🛏◀ High Noon Guest House, Lower Lamphey Road, SA71 4AB
☎ 01646 683736 (The Barnikel Family) www.highnoon.co.uk
Map 157,158/990011   BB **B**   ✗ nearby   S3 D3 TI F2   〰(Pembroke)
B D ⊗ 🍴☕🛏🚗! 🏠   ★★

● Roch (Dyfed)

Pembrokeshire Coast National Park
Pembrokeshire Coast Path

🚶🛏◀ Stackrock B&B, Church Rd, SA62 6BG ☎ 01437 710741
(Mike & Wendy Lort)   www.stackrock.com   Map 157/878218
BB **B**   ✗ nearby   DI TI   B D ⊗ 🍴☕🛏🚗!   ★★★★

● St Brides (Haverfordwest)

Pembrokeshire Coast National Park
Pembrokeshire Coast Path

Fopston Farm, SA62 3AW ☎ 01646 636271 (Mrs Bryn Price)
bryn.fopstonfarm@btopenworld.com   Map 157/798094
BB **B**   ✗ nearby   DI T2   Closed Oct-Mar   B D ⊗ 🍴☕🛏🚗!   ★★

● St Davids

Pembrokeshire Coast National Park
Pembrokeshire Coast Path

☆ **Ramsey House**

Lower Moor, SA62 6RP (Ceri & Elaine Morgan)
☎ 01437 720321   www.ramseyhouse.co.uk   Map 157/747250
BB **B**   ✗ book first £20, 7pm   D3 T3
V B D ⊗ 🍴☕🛏   ◆◆◆◆

Quality 4 star accommodation catering exclusively for adults. Quiet location situated just half mile from centre of St Davids, coastal path and cathedral. Ideal for walking, bird watching, watersports and beaches. Congenial relaxed hospitality and licensed bar complete your enjoyment.

Alandale Guest House, 43 Nun Street, SA62 6NU
☎ 01437 720404   (Rob & Gloria Pugh)
www.stdavids.co.uk/guesthouse/alandale.htm   Map 157/754256
BB **B**   ✕ nearby   SI D3 TI
Ⓑ Ⓓ ⊛ 🐾 ♿ 🚗 ! ◆◆◆◆

☆ Lochmeyler Farm Guest House
Llandeloy, Pen-y-Cwm, Solva, SA62 6LL ☎ 01348 837724 (Mrs M M Jones)
www.lochmeyler.co.uk   Map 157/855275
BB **B**   ✕ book first £15, 7pm   S2 D5 T4 F4
Ⓥ Ⓑ Ⓓ 🐾 ♿ 🏛 ★★★★★

15 en-suite non-smoking luxury bedrooms, TV & refreshment facilities. Centre St
David's peninsula. Ideal for exploring Pembrokeshire Coast Path & countryside.
B&B £25-35 pppn. Optional evening dinner £15 pp. Closed Christmas and New
Year. 10% discount on advance bookings for inclusive evening dinner, B&B for 7
nights or more. Email: stay@lochmeyler.co.uk

● **St Ishmael's (Haverfordwest)**
   Pembrokeshire Coast National Park
   Pembrokeshire Coast Path
Skerryback Farmhouse, Sandy Haven, SA62 3DN
☎ 01646 636598 (Mrs M Williams)
www.pfh.co.uk/skerryback   Map 157/852074
BB **B**   ✕ nearby   DI TI FI   Ⓑ Ⓓ ⊛ 🐾 ♿ 🚗 ! ★★★

● **Tenby**
   Pembrokeshire Coast National Park
   Pembrokeshire Coast Path
Sunny Bank, Harding Street, SA70 7LL ☎ 01834 844034 (Shirley Aston)
www.sunny-bank.co.uk   Map 158/131005
BB **B**   ✕ book first £16.50, 6-6:30pm   D3 TI FI   ⋙(Tenby)
Ⓥ Ⓑ ⊛ 🐾 ♿ ★★★★

● **Trefin (St Davids)**
   Pembrokeshire Coast National Park
   Pembrokeshire Coast Path
Bryngarw, Abercastle Rd, SA62 5AR
☎ 01348 831211 (Anthony & Judith Johnson)
www.bryngarwguesthouse.co.uk   Map 157/842325
BB **B**   ✕ book first £18, 7pm   D4 T2   Closed Nov-Dec
Ⓥ Ⓑ Ⓓ 🐾 ♿ ! 🏛 ★★★

🗪 Hampton House, 2 Ffordd-y-Felin, SA62 5AX
☎ 01348 837701 (Vivienne & Chris Prior)
viv.kay@virgin.net   Map 157/840324
BB **B**   ✕ nearby   SI DI TI
Ⓑ Ⓓ 🐾 ♿ 🚗 ! 🏛 ★★★   Veggie breakfasts.

POWYS

● **Boughrood (Brecon)**
   Wye Valley Walk
Balangia, Station Road, LD3 0YF ☎ 01874 754453 (M Brown)
carol@tamarisk20.fsnet.co.uk   Map 161/129387
BB **B**   ✕ nearby   SI DI TI   Closed Nov-Mar   Ⓓ 🐾 ♿ ! 🏛

● **Brecon**
   Brecon Beacons
   Usk Valley Walk
The Beacons, 16 Bridge Street, LD3 8AH
☎ 01874 623339 (Melanie & Stephen Dale)
www.s-h-systems.co.uk/hotels/beac.html   Map 160/042285
BB **B/C**   ✕ £7.95-£20, 6:30-9pm   D8 T2 F4
Ⓥ Ⓑ 🐾 ♿ 🚗 ! ★★★

☆ The Old Mill
Felinfach, LD3 0UB ☎ 01874 625385
Map 161/091332
BB **B**   ✕ nearby   DI T2   Closed Nov-Jan
Ⓑ Ⓓ 🐾 ♿ ★★★Ⓦ

A 16th century converted corn mill, peacefully
situated in its own grounds. Inglenook
fireplace, exposed beams, TV lounge, beverage
trays. Ideally situated for walks & touring the
Brecon Beacons NP & Black Mountains or just
relaxing. Local inn within walking distance. A
friendly welcome awaits you.

☆ 🗪 The Coach House
12-13 Orchard Street, LD3 8AN ☎ 07050 691216
www.coach-house-brecon.co.uk   Map 160/040284
BB **B**   ✕ £12, 6-8pm   S2 D4 T2 F2
Ⓥ Ⓑ Ⓓ ⊛ 🐾 ♿ 🚗 ! ◆◆◆◆

Superior, comfortable rooms with
en-suite facilities, television and
tea/coffee making facilities. A non-
smoking house with private parking.
"My tastes are simple. I am always
satisfied with the best"
– Oscar Wilde

☆ 🗪 Cantre Selyf
5 Lion St, LD3 7AU ☎ 01874 622904 (Helen Roberts)
www.cantreselyf.co.uk   Map 160/045285
BB **B**   ✕ nearby   D2 TI   Closed Dec-Jan
Ⓑ Ⓓ ⊛ 🐾 ♿ 🚗 ! ★★★★   Veggie breakfasts

17th century town house in central
quiet location. Elegant, comfortable
rooms all en-suite. Non-smoking,
own parking. Beautiful walled
garden. Close to restaurants and
pubs. A little bit of luxury after a
hard day's walking!

The Grange , The Watton, LD3 7ED
☎ 01874 624038 (Meryl, Ian & John)
www.thegrange-brecon.co.uk   Map 160/048283
BB **B**   ✕ nearby   D4 F4   Ⓑ Ⓓ ⊛ 🍴🛏📷   ★★★

Castle of Brecon Hotel, Castle Square, LD3 9DB ☎ 01874 624611
www.breconcastle.co.uk   Map 160/043288
BB **C**   ✕ book first £, 6-9pm   S1 D20 T/D16 F6
Ⓥ Ⓑ Ⓓ ⊛ 🍴🛏📷   ★★

The Borderers Guesthouse, 47 The Watton, LD3 7EG ☎ 01874 623559
www.borderers.com   Map 160/046283
BB **B**   ✕ nearby   D3 T3 F3   Ⓑ Ⓓ ⊛ 🍴🛏📷   ◆◆◆

🍴◀ Plas-y-Ffynnon, Battle, LD3 9RN ☎ 01874 611199 (Gill Badham)
gill@badhamg.freeserve.co.uk   Map 160/009310
BB **B**   ✕ book first £10   D3 T2
Ⓑ Ⓓ ⊛ 🍴🛏📷 ! Ⓜ

🍴◀ Wern Ddu Farm, Ffrwdgrech, LD3 8LF ☎ 01874 623009
www.wernddu.co.uk   Map 160/031265
BB **B**   D2 T1   Closed Nov-Dec   Ⓑ Ⓓ 🍴🛏📷

Canal Bank, "Ty Gardd", The Watton, LD3 7HG
☎ 01874 623464 (Peter & Barbara Jackson)
www.accommodation-breconbeacons.co.uk   Map 160/047281
BB **B**   ✕ nearby   D2 T1   Ⓑ Ⓓ ⊛ 🍴🛏📷 ! 🔔

☆ Lodge Farm
Talgarth, LD3 0DP ☎ 01874 711244 (Mrs M Meredith)
lodgefarm@bushinternet.com   Map 161/173344
BB **B**   ✕ book first £16, 7pm   D1 T1 F1
Ⓥ Ⓑ Ⓓ ⊛ 🛏📷   ★★★

Welcome to our 17th century farm house situated in the Brecon Beacons National Park, well placed for walking the Black Mountains and Brecon Beacons. En-suite bedrooms, tea-making facilities. Good, freshly prepared food including vegetarian. Non-smoking. FHB members.
Email: lodgefarm@bushinternet.com

● Builth Wells
Wye Valley Walk

☆ Dol-Llyn-Wydd Farmhouse
LD2 3RZ ☎ 01982 553660 (Biddy Williams)
Map 147/042488
BB **B**   ✕ book first £10, 7:30-8:30pm   S2 D1 T2   ⋙(Bluith Road)
Ⓥ Ⓑ Ⓓ ⊛ 🍴🛏📷 !   ★★

17th century farmhouse beneath the Eppynt Hills. Superb area for walking, touring, bird watching. Elan Valley, Black Mountains, Hay-on-Wye. 1 mile from Builth Wells, B4520 Upper Chapel, 1st left down lane – 200 yds, on left. Bike lockup garage. Wye Valley Walk.

🍴◀ Little Smithfield, Cwmbach, LD2 3RS   ☎ 01982 552973 (Mrs Philippa Wright)   andrew.wright91@virgin.net   Map 147/024548
BB **B**   ✕ book first £10, 7:30pm   S2 D2 F1
Ⓥ Ⓑ Ⓓ ⊛ 🍴🛏📷 ! 🔔   ★★★

● Buttington (Welshpool)
Glyndwr's Way & Offa's Dyke
1 Plas Cefn Holding, Heldre Lane, SY21 8SX ☎ 01938 570225 (M Broxton)
Map 126/266092   BB **A**   ✕ book first £6+, 6-7pm S1 D1 F1 ⋙(Welshpool)
Ⓥ Ⓓ ⊛ 🍴🛏 ! Ⓜ

● Capel-Y-Ffin (Abergavenny)
Brecon Beacons
Cambrian Way & Offa's Dyke
The Grange, NP7 7NP ☎ 01873 890215/157 (Griffiths Family)
www.grangeguesthouse.co.uk   Map 161/251315
BB **B**   ✕ book first £14, 7:45pm   S1 D1 T2 F2   Closed Dec-Feb
Ⓥ Ⓑ Ⓓ 🍴🛏📷 ! 🔔   ★

● Cemmaes (Machynlleth)
Glyndwr's Way & Cambrian Way
🍴◀ The Emporium, SY20 9PR ☎ 01650 511207 (Christine & Ian Yallop)
chrismy@btopenworld.com   Map 124,125/839061
BB **B**   ✕ nearby   S1 D2 T1   Ⓓ 🍴🛏📷 ! 🔔

● Crickhowell
Brecon Beacons
Cambrian Way
Dragon Hotel, High Street, NP8 1BE ☎ 01873 810362 (Andrew & Sian Powell)
www.dragonhotel.co.uk   Map 161/217183
BB **C**   ✕ £6-£15, 6:30-9:30pm   S3 D6 T6 F2   Ⓥ Ⓑ Ⓓ 🍴🛏 !   ★★

● Dinas Mawddwy (Machynlleth)
Snowdonia/Eryri
Cambrian Way

☆ Ty Derw
SY20 9LR ☎ 01650 531318 (Mair & Nick Godley)
www.tyderw.co.uk   Map 124,125/857136
BB **B**   ✕ £17.50, 7:30pm   D2 T1
Ⓥ Ⓑ Ⓓ ⊛ 🍴🛏📷 !   ★★★★★

A charming Victorian country house in the lovely Dyfi Valley just off the Cambrian Way.
Relax in our comfortable en-suite bedrooms and guests' sitting room, and enjoy good company and fine local produce at breakfast and, if you wish, dinner.

● Discoed (Presteigne)
Offa's Dyke

☆ 🍴◀ Gumma Farm
LD8 2NP ☎ 01547 560243 (Mrs Anne Owens)
www.ukworld.net/gummafarm   Map 137, 148/288651
BB **B**   ✕ book first £13.50, 6-8pm   S1 D1 T1   Closed Dec-Jan
Ⓥ Ⓑ Ⓓ 🍴🛏📷 ! 🔔   ★★★★

350 acre working farm accommodation at its best. 3 front rooms overlooking meadows and woodland. Peaceful. Guest lounge. Full breakfast. Antique furnishings. En-suite/private facilities. TV. Tea/coffee. All for £25. A perfect haven. Presteigne one mile. Brochures available.

● Dylife (Llanbrynmair)
Glyndwr's Way & Cambrian Way

☆ ☞◼ **Star Inn**
SY19 7BW ☎ 01650 521345
Map 135/863940
BB **B** ✕ £6.50, 7-9pm   SI D3 TI FI
Ⓥ Ⓑ Ⓓ 🐾🍴👜❗🛁   ◆◆◆

Set in breathtaking countryside. Superb food, real ales, residents' lounge, colour TV, showers/bath. Full central heating, excellent ambience, own tea & coffee making facilities, a warm & friendly welcome guaranteed.

● Glasbury (Hay-on-Wye)
Brecon Beacons & Wye Valley Walk

Aberllynfi B&B, HR3 5NT ☎ 01497 847107 (Catherine Sturgeon)
www.hay-on-wye.co.uk/aberllynfi Map 161/179390
BB **B** ✕ nearby   SI T2   Ⓓ ⊛ 🐾👜🚗 ❗

● Hay-on-Wye
Brecon Beacons & Offa's Dyke

Tinto House, Broad Street, HR3 5DB ☎ 01497 820590 (John Evans)
www.tintohouse.co.uk Map 161,148/228423
BB **B** ✕ nearby   D2 TI FI   Ⓑ Ⓓ ⊛ 👜❗🛁   ★★★

Fernleigh, Hardwick Road, Cusop, HR3 5QX ☎ 01497 820459
(Winnifred Hughes) Map 161,148/235422
BB **A** ✕ nearby   D2 TI   Closed Nov-Feb   Ⓥ Ⓑ Ⓓ ⊛ 🐾👜 Ⓜ

La Fosse Guest House, Oxford Road, HR3 5AJ ☎ 01497 820613
(Bob and Annabel Crook) www.hay-on-wye/lafosse.co.uk Map 161/232423
BB **B** ✕ nearby   D4 TI   Ⓑ Ⓓ ⊛ 🐾👜❗🛁   ★★

The Bear, Bear Street, HR3 5AN ☎ 01497 821302 (Jon Field)
www.thebear-hay-on-wye.co.uk Map 161,148/230424
BB **B** ✕ nearby   D2 TI   Ⓑ Ⓓ 🐾🍴👜 ❗

☞◼ Old Black Lion Inn, 26 Lion Street, HR3 5AD ☎ 01497 820841
www.oldblacklion.co.uk Map 161,148/231423
BB **C** ✕ £9+, 6:30-9:30pm   S2 D5 T2 FI   Ⓥ Ⓑ Ⓓ 🐾🍴👜❗★★★

Oxford Cottage, Oxford Road, HR3 5AJ ☎ 01497 820008 (Ed Moore)
www.oxfordcottage.co.uk Map 161,148/232423 BB **B**   D2 TI   Ⓓ ⊛ 🛁

☞◼ Baskerville Hall Hotel, Clyro Court, Clyro, HR3 5LE
☎ 01497 820033 www.baskervillehall.co.uk Map 161/208428
BB **C** ✕ £12, 7-9pm   S7 D10 TI2 F5
Ⓥ Ⓑ Ⓓ 🐾🍴🛁   See Groups also.

● Knighton
Glyndwr's Way & Offa's Dyke

The Fleece House, Market Street, LD7 1BB ☎ 01547 520168
(Mrs Dana Simmons) www.fleecehouse.co.uk Map 148,137/284723
BB **B/C** ✕ nearby   ⋙(Knighton) Ⓑ Ⓓ ⊛ 👜❗   ★★★
Advice, books & maps for local walks available

☞◼ The Plough, 40 Market Street, LD7 1EY ☎ 01547 528041
sarahscotford@aol.com Map 148,137/284723
BB **A** ✕ £3 (bar snacks), 7-9pm   S4 DI T3   ⋙(Knighton)
Ⓥ Ⓑ 🐾👜🚗❗🛁

Milebrook House Hotel, Milebrook, LD7 1LT ☎ 01547 528632
www.milebrookhouse.co.uk Map 148/315727
BB **C** ✕ £24.50, 7pm onwards   S2 D6 T4 FI   ⋙(Knighton)
Ⓥ Ⓑ Ⓓ 🐾👜🚗 ❗   ★★★★

George and Dragon Inn, 4 Broad Street, LD7 1BL
☎ 01547 528532   (Peter and Angela Vrettos)
www.thegeorgeknighton.freeserve.co.uk Map 148,137/286722
BB **B** ✕ £6-£12, 6-9pm   D2 T3   ⋙(Knighton) Ⓥ Ⓑ Ⓓ ⊛ 🐾👜❗

● Knucklas (Knighton)
Glyndwr's Way & Offa's Dyke

☆ ☞◼ **Belmont Cottage**
LD7 1PP ☎ 01547 529244 (Mrs Avril M Hoyle)
Map 148,137/251743
BB **B** ✕ book first £15, 7:30pm   SI DI T2   ⋙(Knucklas)
Ⓥ Ⓓ ⊛ 🐾👜❗🛁

A warm welcome awaits you in this 200 year old cottage. Cosy lounge for guests.

Near Offa's Dyke Pass and on Cycling Route 25.

● Llanbadarn Fynydd (Llandrindod Wells)
Glyndwr's Way

Hillside Lodge Guest House, LDI 6TU ☎ 01597 840364
(Mr W T & Mrs B Ainsworth) Map 136/085764
BB **B** ✕ nearby   TI F2   Ⓑ Ⓓ ⊛ 🐾👜🚗❗🛁   ★★★

● Llandrindod Wells

☞◼ Rhydithon, Dyffryn Road, LDI 6AN
☎ 01597 822624 (Mrs B J Jones) Map 147/058613
BB **B** ✕ book first £10, 6-8pm   SI TI FI   ⋙(Llandrindod Wells)
Ⓥ Ⓑ Ⓓ 🐾👜🚗❗🛁   ★★

☆ **Holly Farm**
Howey, LDI 5PP ☎ 01597 822402 (Mrs Ruth Jones)
www.ukworld.net/hollyfarm Map 147/049589
BB **B** ✕ book first £12, 7pm   D2 T2 FI   ⋙(Llandrindod Wells)
Ⓥ Ⓑ Ⓓ 🐾👜   ◆◆◆◆

Tastefully restored Tudor farmhouse on working farm in peaceful location. En-suite bedrooms with breathtaking views over fields and woods. CTV and beverage trays. Two lounges, log fires, delicious cuisine using farm produce. Excellent area for walking, birdwatching or relaxing. Near red kite feeding station. Weekly reductions. Packed lunches. Safe parking.
Call Mrs Ruth Jones for a brochure.

● Llangattock (Crickhowell)

Brecon Beacons

Cambrian Way & Usk Valley Walk

☆ ▪☞◀ **Usk View Cottage**
The Legar, NP8 1HL ☎ 01873 811480
Map 161/216179
BB **B** ✕ nearby S1 D1 T2 F1 Closed Dec
Ⓑ Ⓓ ⊛ 🐾 🛇 🚗 !

An attractive cottage in the Brecon Beacons. Ideal base for walking, cycling, paragliding, caving, etc. All rooms en-suite with tea/coffee making facilities and colour TV. Private car parking. Packed lunches on request. Mobile: 07745 569166

● Llangurig (Llanidloes)

Wye Valley Walk

▪☞◀ The Old Vicarage, SY18 6RN ☎ 01686 440280 (Margaret Hartey)
www.theoldvicaragellangurig.co.uk Map 147/912799
BB **B/C** ✕ book first £15, 7pm D3 T2 F1
Ⓥ Ⓑ Ⓓ 🐾 🛇 🎲 Ⓜ ◆◆◆◆

● Llanidloes

Glyndwr's Way

Lloyds Hotel & Restaurant, Cambrian Place, SY18 6BX ☎ 01686 412284
(Tom Lines & Roy Hayter) www.lloydshotel.co.uk Map 136/955844
BB **B** ✕ book first £26.50, 8pm S4 D3 T2 Closed Jan-Feb
Ⓥ Ⓑ Ⓓ ⊛ 🛇 ★★★

● Llanigon (Hay-on-Wye)

Brecon Beacons

Offa's Dyke & Wye Valley Walk

The Old Post Office, HR3 5QA ☎ 01497 820008 (Linda Webb)
www.oldpost-office.co.uk Map 161/213401
BB **B/C** D1 T1 F1   Ⓑ Ⓓ ⊛ 🛇 🎲 ★★★

● Llanrhaeadr-Ym-Mochnant (Oswestry)

☆ **Llys Morgan**
SY10 0JZ ☎ 01691 780345 (Mrs J Morgan)
e.b.morgan@dial.pipex.com Map 125/123261
BB **A** ✕ nearby D1 T1 F1
Ⓑ Ⓓ 🐾 🛇

An old vicarage where the bible was translated into Welsh by William Morgan in 1588. A charming, quiet and private historical house set in mature gardens. An ideal centre for outdoor pursuits, walking, fishing and sailing on Pistyll Rhaeadr, Lakes Vyrnwy and Bala.

Please mention **walk BRITAIN**
when booking your accommodation

● Llanwddyn (Oswestry)

Glyndwr's Way

☆ ▪☞◀ **The Oaks**
Lake Vyrnwy, SY10 0LZ ☎ 01691 870250 (Michael & Daphne Duggleby)
www.vyrnwyaccommodation.co.uk Map 125/017190
BB **B** ✕ nearby D1 T2
Ⓥ Ⓑ Ⓓ ⊛ 🐾 🛇 🚗 ! 🎲 ★★★

Located by Lake Vyrnwy on Glyndwr's Way. A warm and friendly welcome into a comfortable family home. Brilliant breakfasts. Excellent for walkers.
Email: mdugg99@aol.com

● Llanwrtyd Wells

▪☞◀ Neuadd Arms Hotel, The Square, LD5 4RB ☎ 01591 610236
(Lindsay Ketteringham) www.neuaddarmshotel.co.uk Map 147/879467
BB **B** ✕ £13.50, 6:30-8:30pm S7 D6 T8 F2 ▰▰(Llanwrtyd Wells)
Ⓥ Ⓑ Ⓓ 🐾 🛇 ! 🎲 Ⓜ ★

☆ ▪☞◀ **Belle Vue Hotel**
LD5 4RE ☎ 01591 610237 (Eileen & Bernie Dodd)
www.bellevuewales.co.uk Map 147/879467
BB **A/B** ✕ £4-£14, 6:30-9:30pm S4 D3 T8 F2 ▰▰(Llanwrtyd Wells)
Ⓥ Ⓑ Ⓓ 🐾 🛇 🚗 🎲 See Groups also.

Situated midway between Builth Wells and Llandovery on the A483 trunk road. Built in 1843 the Belle View Hotel is the oldest hotel in Llanwrtyd Wells. Combining village pub and local meeting place, which give this small, comfortable, family run hotel the charm and character of the friendly inhabitants of this town.

● Llanymynech

Offa's Dyke

Orchard Holidays, Unity House, Llandrinio, SY22 6SG ☎ 01691 831976
(Mrs Maxine Roberts) www.orchard-holidays.com Map 126/290160
BB **B** ✕ nearby S3 D2 T2 F1 Closed Nov-Feb
Ⓑ Ⓓ ⊛ 🐾 🛇 🚗 ! ★★

● Machynlleth

Glyndwr's Way

▪☞◀ Maenllwyd, Newtown Road, SY20 8EY ☎ 01654 702928 (Mrs M Vince)
www.cyber-space.co.uk/maenllwyd.htm Map 135/752008
BB **B** ✕ nearby D4 T3 F1 ▰▰(Machynlleth)
Ⓑ Ⓓ 🐾 🛇 🚗 ! 🎲 ◆◆◆◆

Dyfiguest, 20 Ffordd Mynydd, Griffiths, SY20 8DD ☎ 01654 702562
(Carol Handcock) www.dyfiguest.co.uk   Map 135/747012
BB **B**   ✕ book first £15, 7:30pm   DI   ∿(Machynlleth)
Ⓥ Ⓑ Ⓓ ⊛ 🐄 ♨ 🚗 ! 🛏   ★★★★

☆ ◄🍴 Talbontdrain Guest House
Uwchygarreg, SY20 8RR ☎ 01654 702192
www.talbontdrain.co.uk   Map 135/777959
BB **B**   ✕ book first £15, 7:30pm   S2 DI TI
Ⓥ Ⓑ Ⓓ ⊛ 🐄 🚗 ! 🛏

Remote and comfortable farm guesthouse.
Glyndwr's Way goes through our yard. Fantastic
food with second helpings. Really wonderful
walking country. Local walk maps and information.

Look at the website— you won't be able to resist coming!

● Montgomery
Offa's Dyke
◄🍴 Little Brompton Farm, SY15 6HY ☎ 01686 668371 (Gaynor Bright)
www.littlebromptonfarm.co.uk   Map 137/244941
BB **B**   ✕ book first £15, 6:30pm   SI DI TI FI
Ⓥ Ⓑ Ⓓ ⊛ 🐄 ♨ 🚗 ! 🛏   ★★★★

☆ ◄🍴 Hendomen Farmhouse
Hendomen, SY15 6HB ☎ 01686 668004 (Jo & Bruce Lawson)
www.offasdykepath.com   Map 137/218981
BB **B**   ✕ nearby   SI DI TI
Ⓑ Ⓓ ⊛ 🐄 ♨ 🚗 ! 🛏   ★★

Stay in Montgomery and walk the Dyke.
Transport of walkers between Knighton &
Llangollen & Glyndwrs Way.
Discounts for 3 nights. Owners are
walkers. Flexible breakfast times. 5 pubs
(1 with pool) nearby. Fabulous views.
Email: bruce.lawson@btinternet.com

◄🍴 Dragon Hotel, SY15 6PA ☎ 01686 668359 (Mark & Sue Michaels)
www.dragonhotel.com   Map 137/222964
BB **C** ✕ £7-£20, 7-9pm   S2 D9 T5 F4
Ⓥ Ⓑ Ⓓ 🐄 ♨ 🚗 ! 🛏   ★★★

● Presteigne
Offa's Dyke

☆ Carmel Court
King's Turning Road, LD8 2LD ☎ 01544 267986 (Marenee & Terry Monaghan)
monaghan@carmelcourt.freeserve.co.uk
Map 148,137/320639   BB **B**   ✕ nearby   SI D5 T3 F2
Ⓑ Ⓓ 🐄 ♨ ! 🛏   ★★

Former Carmelite
monastery, adjoining
original chapel. Shops,
hostelries, restaurants a
few minutes away —
Offa's Dyke and Mortimer
Trail just a little further!

● Rhayader
Wye Valley Walk

☆ The Horseshoe
Church Street, LD6 5AT ☎ 01597 810982 (Mrs P Bishop)
www.rhayader.co.uk/horseshoe   Map 147,136/969680
BB **B**   ✕ book first £12, 7pm   S2 D2 TI
Ⓥ Ⓑ Ⓓ ⊛ 🐄 ♨ 🚗 ! 🛏   ★★★

An 18th century Welsh stone house
in the heart of Red Kite country.
Four minutes walk from the
River Wye.
Excellent walking in the Eden Valley
and beyond.

Brynteg, East Street, LD6 5EA ☎ 01597 810052 (Mrs B Lawrence)
brynteg@hotmail.com   Map 147,136/972681
BB **A/B**   ✕ nearby   SI D2 TI
Ⓑ Ⓓ ⊛ 🐄 ♨ 🚗 ! Ⓜ   ★★★
Local footpath information.

● Talybont-on-Usk (Brecon)
Brecon Beacons
◄🍴 Gethinog, LD3 7YN ☎ 01874 676258 (Christina & Roy Gale)
www.gethinog.co.uk   Map 161/108233
BB **B**   ✕ book first £15, 7pm   DI TI
Ⓥ Ⓑ ⊛ 🐄 ♨ !

● Talyllyn (Brecon)
Brecon Beacons
Usk Valley Walk
◄🍴 Dolycoed, LD3 7SY ☎ 01874 658666 (Mrs Mary Cole)
Map 161/107271   BB **B**   SI DI TI   Closed Dec
Ⓑ Ⓓ ⊛ ♨ 🚗 🛏

● Welshpool
Glyndwr's Way & Offa's Dyke
Tynllwyn Farm, SY21 9BW
☎ 01938 553175 (Jane & Caroline Emberton)
www.tynllwynfarm.co.uk   Map 126/215086
BB **B**   ✕ book first £14, 6:30pm   DI T4   ∿(Welshpool)
Ⓑ Ⓓ 🐄 ♨ 🚗 ! 🛏   ★★★

Severn Farm, SY21 7BB ☎ 01938 555999 (T & J Jones)
www.severnfarm.co.uk   Map 126/231070
BB **B**   ✕ book first £9, 6:30pm   S2 DI TI F2   ∿(Welshpool)
Ⓥ Ⓑ Ⓓ ⊛ ♨ ! 🛏

◄🍴 Vine House, Oak Lane, Guilsfield, SY21 9NH
☎ 01938 554431 (Eve Pearce)
www.geocities.com/vinehouse2000   Map 126/217116
BB **B**   ✕ nearby DI TI   ∿(Welshpool)
Ⓑ Ⓓ ⊛ 🐄 ♨ 🚗 ! 🛏   ★★★

◄🍴 Ty-Isaf, Llanerfyl, SY21 0JB
☎ 01938 820143 (Sheenagh Carter)
sheen.carter@virgin.net   Map 125/024082
BB **B**   ✕ book first £10, 6:30-9pm   DI FI
Ⓥ Ⓑ Ⓓ ⊛ 🐄 ♨ 🚗 ! 🛏   ★★★

SOUTH WALES

● Cowbridge
Valeways Millennium Heritage Trail

☆ **Crossways Manor House**
CF71 7LJ ☎ 01446 773171 (Mandy Davies)
www.crosswayshouse.co.uk   Map 170/974741
BB **C**   ✗ nearby   D1 T1 F1
🅱 🅳 ⊛ 🐾 👶 🚗

A beautiful, historic country manor house in the heart of the Vale, country and coastal walks. 1 mile from the Roman market town of Cowbridge with its many small shops, tearooms, pubs and restaurants. A warm welcome and great breakfast. Self-catering also available.

● Llanmadoc (Gower)
⌕ Tallizmand, SA3 1HA ☎ 01792 386373
http://tallizmand.co.uk   Map 159/444933
BB **B**   ✗ book first £17, 6pm   S1 D1 T1
🆅 🅱 🅳 ⊛ 🐾 👶 🚗 🗟   ★★★Ⓦ

● Pontsticill (Merthyr Tydfil)
Brecon Beacons
Penrhadw Farm, CF48 2TU ☎ 01685 723481
www.penrhadwfarm.co.uk   Map 160/054109
BB **B**   ✗ nearby   S1 D2 T2 F4   〰(Pantyscallog)
🆅 🅱 🅳 🐾 👶 🚗 ! 🗟 Ⓜ   ★★★★★

● Port Eynon (Gower)

☆ ⌕ **Culver House Hotel**
SA3 1NN ☎ 01792 390755 (Mark & Susan Cottell)
www.culverhousehotel.co.uk   Map 159/468853
BB **B**   ✗ book first £16.50, 6.30-8pm   S3 D4 T3 F1   Closed Dec-Jan
🆅 🅱 🅳 🐾 👶 🗟   ★★

A family-run hotel with a warm friendly atmosphere, superb food and quality service. Most rooms have beautiful seaviews with en-suite facilities. Ideally situated for rambling the Gower peninsula. Groups welcome. Discounts available.

● St Brides Wentlooge (Newport)
Chapel Guest House, Church Road, NP10 8SN ☎ 01633 681018
chapelguesthouse@hotmail.com   Map 171/294822
BB **B**   ✗ nearby   S1 D1 T1 F1
🆅 🅱 🅳 ⊛ 🐾 👶 🗟   ★★★

● Welsh St Donats (Cowbridge)
Valeways Millennium Heritage Trail
Bryn-y-Ddafad, CF71 7ST ☎ 01446 774451 (Mrs June Jenkins)
www.bydd.co.uk   Map 170/024768
BB **B**   ✗ book first £12, 6-7:30pm   S1 D2 T1 F1
🆅 🅱 🅳 ⊛ 🐾 👶 🚗 !   ★★★★

● Ynysybwl
Brecon Beacons

☆ **Tyn-y-Wern**
CF37 3LY ☎ 01443 790551 (Mrs Hermione Bruton)
www.tyn-y-wern.co.uk   Map 170/065945
BB **B**   D2 T1
🅱 🅳 ⊛ 🐾 👶 🚗 ! 🗟   ★★★   See SC also

A Victorian mine manager's residence lovingly restored to its former glory. Offers a tranquil country retreat just 30 minutes from Cardiff. Spectacular walking. Phone for brochure.

SELF-CATERING

ANGLESEY

● Brynsiencyn

☆ **Cerrig Y Barcud Holidays**
☎ 01248 430056 (Julia Harfitt)
www.cerrigybarcud.co.uk
£150-£525   Sleeps 2-5. 4 cottages.
Tranquil location superb views.   ⊛   ★★★★★

Four high-standard, self-catering cottages, set in an Area of Outstanding Natural Beauty 300 metres from the Menai Straits. Superb panoramic views in all directions including Snowdonia. Quietly located yet convenient for all areas of Anglesey and North Wales. Email: Anglesey.selfcatering@virgin.net

---

● Llanerchymedd

☆ **Tyddyntruan Cottage**
☎ 01248 490078 (Jeni Farrell)
www.bryneglwyscottages.co.uk
£210-£588   Sleeps 6-10. 1 cottage, 1 farmhouse.
Beautiful houses, peaceful heart of Anglesey. 🗟   ★★★★

A warm welcome. Perfect location for exploring coastal and historic walks. Anglesey's Coast to Coast walk on the doorstep! Impressive stone farmhouse (sleeps 10) and pretty cottage (sleeps 6). Both offer a high standard of comfort and facilities.

CARMARTHENSHIRE

● Pendine
Sunnybank Cottage ☎ 01994 453431 (Sara Ellis)
£200-£480   Sleeps 4-5. 2 cottages.
Tranquil spot. Near coastal path. 🗟   ★★★ RA member.

CEREDIGION

● Aberporth

☎ 01239 810595 (Frances & Peter Miller) milldrove@aol.com
£180-£350   Sleeps 4. 2 cottages.
Rural setting. Walks & beach minutes away.   ⊗ ✍

☎ 01239 810387 (Jann Tucker) www.aberporth.com
£250-£950   Sleeps 4-8. 6 varying types.   Closed Dec
Close to Pembrokeshire Coast Path. ✍ ★★★★★

● Aberystwyth

☎ 01974 202877 (Mr & Mrs James) www.selfcatering-aberystwyth.co.uk
£175-£395   Sleeps 2-8 . 2 houses, 1 flat.
Open all year. Short breaks available. ₥(Aberystwyth) ✍ ★★★★

● Cardigan

☎ 01239 682931 (Sally Sparkes) glanafon.bach@virgin.net
£150-£320   Sleeps 2. 1 cottage.
Village location, linen, CH, log fire. ⊗ ★★★★

● Llwyndafydd

Tyhen Farm Cottages ☎ 01545 560346 (Roni Kelly)
www.tyhenswimminglessons.co.uk
£195-£655   Sleeps 2-6. 7 cottages.   Closed Nov-Jan
Private indoor heated pool & facilities. ⊗ ✍

● Machynlleth

☎ 01654 781335 (Magda Corser) www.kitevalleycottage.co.uk
£190-£415   Sleeps 2-5. 1 cottage, 1 flat.
Secluded hillfarm setting. Superb walkers base.
⊗ ₥(Dovey Junction) ✍ ★★★★

CONWY

● Llansannan
Snowdonia/Eryri

☎ 01745 870426 (Mr R Johnson) roger3103@yahoo.co.uk
£99-£329 Sleeps 2-6. 4 cottages.   Off beaten track. Idyllic. Beams, CH ✍

● Tal-y-Bont
Snowdonia/Eryri

The Lodge Hotel ☎ 01492 660534(Doug Barnett)
£308-£700   Sleeps 2-4. 4 cottages.
Large gardens and car park. ✍ ★★★

GWYNEDD

● Aberdaron

☆ **Wendy Hinchey**
☎ 01758 760664
wendyhinchey@aol.com
£300-£850   Sleeps 8 + cot. 1 cottage.
Glorious views from a luxury cottage. ⊗

Stunning sea and mountain views (Porth Neigwl) — National Trust land in AONB. Stone 300y/o luxury non-smoking cottage, large garden. Between Aberdaron and Abersoch, outstanding cliff/mountain walking. Recently refurbished to high standard.

● Abersoch

Crugeran ☎ 01758 730375 (Mrs Rhian Parry) www.crugeran.com
£150-£650   Sleeps 2-8. 4 cottages.
Four-poster beds, jacuzzi, baths. ⊗ ✍ ★★★★★

● Bala
Snowdonia/Eryri

☎ 01992 892331 (J H Gervis)
£200   Sleeps 2-8. 1 cottage. Isolated with mountain views, wood stove. ✍

Bala Holidays ☎ 01948 710777 (John & Ellen Dimelow)
www.balaholidays.co.uk   £150-£395 Sleeps 2-9. 2 apartments.
Three minutes from lakeside, drying cabinet. ✍ ★★★★

● Barmouth
Snowdonia/Eryri

☎ 01341 247033 (Val & Tom Bethell) bethellvt@btopenworld.com
£125-£225   Sleeps 2. 1 cottage. Closed Jan
Delightfully rural. Sea/mountain views. Peaceful ⊗ ₥(Dyffryn Ardudwy) ✍

● Beddgelert
Snowdonia/Eryri

☎ 01751 430624 (David Jackson) davjackson@supanet.com
£270-£395   Sleeps 4. 1 cottage.
Central heating, open fire, riverside location. ⊗ ✍

Glaslyn Leisure Ltd ☎ 01766 890880 (Mrs Joan Firth)
www.snowdonia-cottages.net   £275-£700 Sleeps 4-6. 5 cottages.
Excellent accommodation, village location. Families/groups. ⊗ ★★★★★

☎ 01675 430108 (Brigid Thomas) davidthomas279@hotmail.com
£150-£350   Sleeps 5-6. 1 cottage. Closed Aug
Village location. Modern kitchen. Two bathrooms. ✍ ★★★★

● Bethesda
Snowdonia/Eryri

Ogwen Valley Holidays ☎ 01248 600122 (Mrs Jill Jones)
www.ogwensnowdonia.co.uk   £160-£550 Sleeps 2-6. 1 flat, 1 cottage.
Situated in Ogwen Valley, beautiful mountain views. ✍ ★★★★

● Croesor
Snowdonia/Eryri

2 Tresaethon ☎ 01766 890354 (Anita Hartley) www.enjoysnowdonia.co.uk
£250-£400   Sleeps 4-5. 1 cottage.
Abundant walks, all levels from door. ⊗ ₥(Festiniog)

● Dolgellau
Snowdonia/Eryri

☆ **Brynygwin Isaf**
☎ 01341 423481 (Mr Gauntlett)
www.holidaysinwales.fsnet.co.uk
£132-£616   Sleeps 2-24. 2 cottages, 2 parts country house.
Walk guidesheets provided. Large bird-rich garden. ✍

Two self-contained sections of family country house built 1906 with large, comfortably furnished rooms, superb views, extensive garden and character cottages. 1 mile from Dolgellau. Over 30 walk guidesheets provided. Log fires. open all year. Children, pets welcome.
Email: holidays_wales@onetel.com

☎ 01341 430277 (Mrs O Williams)
£140-£170 Sleeps 6. 1 caravan. Closed Nov-Feb
Working farm. Estuary views, countryside walks. ⊗ 🏠

● **Llanberis**
   Snowdonia/Eryri

☆ **Wilson's Holidays**
☎ 01286 870261 (Lesley Wilson)
www.wilsons-holidays.co.uk
£395-£1,051 Sleeps 16. 1 cottage, 1 house.
Spacious, well equipped. Off road parking. 🏠 ★★★★

Halford Hill.
A seven bedroom detached house, in Llanberis, the village at the foot of
Snowdon. Three bathrooms (including a sauna room).

Large dining room, well equipped kitchen, log fire in lounge. Drying facilities.
Off road parking for five cars. Second house also available.

● **Llwyngwril**
   Snowdonia/Eryri
☎ 07746 399693 (Jonathan Highfield)
£200-£420 Sleeps 4. 1 cottage.
Sea and mountains within walking distance.
⊗ ᴡᴡ(Llwyngwril) 🏠 RA member

● **Porthmadog**
   Snowdonia/Eryri
Rhos Country Cottages ☎ 01758 720047 (Anwen Jones)
www.rhos-cottages.co.uk
£200-£1,000 Sleeps 2-8. 4 varying types.
Good walks from your door. 🏠 ★★★★★

MONMOUTHSHIRE

● **Monmouth**
Church Farm ☎ 01600 712176 (Rosey & Derek Ringer)
www.churchfarmmitcheltroy.co.uk
£150-£450 Sleeps 2-8. 1 barn conversion.
Wing of 16th century farmhouse. ⊗ 🏠 RA member. See B&B also.
Robin's Barn ☎ 01600 860058 (Jane McCord)
www.robinsbarn.co.uk
£200-£425 Sleeps 2-4. 1 barn conversion
Spectacular views over the Wye Valley. ⊗ 🏠 ★★★★

● **Tintern**
The Old Rectory ☎ 01291 689519 (Wendy Taylor)
www.tinternoldrectory.co.uk
£175-£400 Sleeps 2-5. 1 cottage, 1 apt.
Overlooking river Wye. Short breaks available.
⊗ 🏠 ★★★★-★★★★★

● **Trellech**
☎ 01600 860681 (Mrs S D M Poulter)
£150-£550 Sleeps 6. 1 cottage.
Characterful 17C stone property. Historic village.
🏠 ★★★★★

PEMBROKESHIRE

● **Broad Haven**
   Pembrokeshire Coast National Park

☆ **Timber Hill** (Leisure Ltd)
☎ 01437 781239 (John Bauer)
www.timberhill.co.uk
£280-£580 Sleeps 2-6. 12 lodges.
Quiet, beautiful valley. Adjacent coast path. ⊗ 🏠 ★★★★

David Bellamy Gold award (5 Year)
Quality self-catering canadian cedarwood
lodge in beautiful, peaceful valley.
A haven for birdlife, flowers and walks,
and set within 130 acres of the National
Park, with views of the famous Island of
Skomer and St Brides bay.

Excellent coarse fishing lake.
This is the perfect base from which to explore this lovely part of Pembrokeshire.
The coast path and beach are only a few minutes walk away.
Please send for brochure from resident proprietors,
John and Annette Bauer
08452 306090 Lo-call

Email: ra.@timberhill.co.uk

● **Haverfordwest**
   Pembrokeshire Coast National Park

☆ **Berry Hill Farm**
☎ 01437 776753 (Kevin Lindsell)
www.caravancampingsites.co.uk/prentals/lindsell.htm
£180-£360 Sleeps 6. 1 caravan.
Rural unique location. Panoramic Prescelli views. ⊗ 🏠

Farm sited luxury caravan on its own plot with
private car park. Equi-distant between
Haverfordwest and Broadhaven. Outstanding
panoramic views. Easy access to Pembrokeshire
Coastal Path. Ideal for those seeking privacy
and outdoor activities, including star-gazing,
but convenient access to town.

● **Porthgain**
   Pembrokeshire Coast National Park
Felindre Cottages ☎ 01348 831220 (Steve Craft) www.felindrecottages.co.uk
£170-£705 Sleeps 1-8. 3 cottages, 9 lodges.
Close to coast path and pub. 🏠 ★★★

● **St Davids**
   Pembrokeshire Coast National Park
Lower Moor Cottages ☎ 01437 720616 (Thelma M Hardman)
www.lowermoorcottages.co.uk £175-£995
Sleeps 2-10. 4 cottages. Beautiful location, near coast path.
⊗ ᴡᴡ(Haverfordwest) 🏠 ★★★★★ See Groups also.

● **St Dogmaels**
Trenewydd Farm Cottages ☎ 01239 612370 (Cheryl Hyde)
www.cottages-wales.com £190-£865 Sleeps 4-9. 5 cottages.
Coastal path, Preseli mountains, Bluestone country. 🐾 ★★★★★

● **Tenby**
Pembrokeshire Coast National Park
Cliff Cottage ☎ 01834 810002 (Neville Boughton-Thomas)
panoramicproperties@btinternet.com £200-£800 Sleeps 2-4. 3 flats.
All three properties have panoramic sea-views.
Ⓢ ᗰᗰ(Tenby) 🐾 ★★★★-★★★★★

POWYS

● **Brecon**
Brecon Beacons
Wern-Y-Marchog ☎ 01874 665329 (Ann Phillips) www.wernymarchog.co.uk
£100-£400 Sleeps 1-6. 1 bungalow, 1 apt.
Log fires. Short breaks. Doorstep walks. 🐾 ★★★★

● **Builth Wells**
The Old Court House ☎ 01591 610479 (Mrs Lewis)
£170 Sleeps 4-5. 1 cottage.
Traditional cottage overlooking village. Lovely views.
Ⓢ ᗰᗰ(Llangammarch Wells)

● **Erwood**
Brecon Beacons

☆ **High Valley View**
Mrs G Baynton ☎ 01452 313139
Sleeps 2-8   £300-£750
A large elevated stunning country home. 1 cottage
www.highvalleyview.co.uk Ⓢ 🐾

This large four bedroomed house is situated in an enviable location above the village of Erwood. The River Wye can be viewed from the house, which is exceptionally furnished within. Located near to Brecon, Hay-on-Wye and Builth Wells.

● **Lake Vyrnwy**
Snowdonia/Eryri

☆ **Eunant**
☎ 01691 870321 (Bronwen Davies)
eunant@terrafirmatravel.com
£226-£369 Sleeps 1-7. Gites.
Gorgeous lakeside scenery, edge of Snowdonia. 🐾

Lovely self-catering accommodation; large farmhouse, woodburning stove, spacious conservatory. Fabulous walking, cycling and fishing in this area of outstanding natural beauty, on the edge of the beautiful Berwyn hills, not far from Snowdonia. Castles, beaches and more...

● **Machynlleth**
Snowdonia/Eryri
☎ 01654 702952 (Lynn & John Williams)
www.lynn.john.williams.care4free.net
£170-£220 Sleeps 4-5. 1 cottage.
Local walks, wildlife, rivers, varied landscape.
Ⓢ ᗰᗰ(Machynlleth) 🐾 ★★★

● **Welshpool**

☆ **Orchard Holidays**
☎ 01691 831976 (Mrs Maxine Roberts)
www.orchard-holidays.com
£180-£285 Sleeps 2-16. 5 cottages & apts.   Closed Nov-Feb
Fishing , parking, fine views. Ⓢ ★★★

Birdsong is your alarm call. Choose to walk Offa's Dyke, Severn Way or Glyndwr's Way. Visit Powis Castle or relax in the tranquil gardens. Ideal touring base for Chester, mid-Wales coast, Snowdonia and Shropshire. B&B also available.
Email: info@orchard-holidays.com

SOUTH WALES

● **Pontypridd**
Brecon Beacons

☆ **Tyn-y-Wern Country House**
☎ 01443 790551 (Mrs Hermione Bruton) www.tyn-y-wern.co.uk
£195-£335 Sleeps 2-4. 2 lodges.
Beautiful location, Welsh valleys, spectacular walking.
Ⓢ 🐾 ★★★★ See B&B also.

Stylish conversion of old building offering modern facilities in tranquil country retreat just 30 minutes from Cardiff. Spectacular walking. Phone for further information. OS Map 170 - 065945
Email: tynywern2002@yahoo.co.uk

● **Port Eynon**
Bay View Farm ☎ 01792 390234 (Mrs Pat Jeffreys)
www.bayviewfarmgower.co.uk
£230-£600   Sleeps 4-6. 1 cottage, 1 wing of farmhouse.
Price includes c/h, sheets and duvets. Ⓢ ★★★★

● **Swansea**
Ivy Cottage ☎ 01792 371268 (Sian Owens) owenssian@hotmail.com
£200-£350 Sleeps 5. 1 cottage.
Situated on top of beach, Gower walks. Ⓢ 🐾 ★★

GROUPS

CARMARTHANSHIRE

Brecon Beacons
Cambrian Way

☆ Llanerchindda Farm (B&B/SC) Cynghordy, Llandovery SA20 0NB ☎01550 750274 • Map/Grid Ref: 160/808429 • www.cambrianway.com • 3 cottages • Min 12 max 42 • BB £28, SC £240 • ✕ 🐾 B D ⋙(Cynghordy) ⬥ 🚗 ★★★ Cambrian Way, Brecon Beacons • See B&B also.

Large farmhouse set high in the Cambrian mountain foothills with stunning views over the Brecon Beacons.
Popular with groups. Excellent facilities. Drying room, map room, licensed.
20 rooms (15 ensuite) sleeps up to 42. Famous home made food.
20 walks programmes including the Cambrian Way.
Email:nick@cambrianway.com

GWYNEDD

The Old School Lodge (SC) Deiniden, Caernarfon LL55 3HH
☎ 02186 879012 (The Booking Secretary)
www.oldschoollodge.org.uk   Map 115/584628
SC £1,480 Min 4, max 38 ✕ nearby B D ⊗

Please mention **walk BRITAIN**
when booking your accommodation

MONMOUTHSHIRE

Snowdonia/Eryri
Offa's Dyke

☆ **The Old Pandy Inn** (B&B)
Hereford Rd, Pandy, Abergavenny, NP7 8DR
☎01873 890208 (Alan Bridgewater)
www.theoldpandyinn.co.uk Map 161/335226
BB £14.50 Max 28 ✕ 🐾 B D ⊗ ! 🚗

Come walking in the Black Mountains and stay at the Old Pandy Inn.

Situated at the foot of the Black Mountains in Pandy, (OS 335226) Offa's Dyke path 400yds away. The market town of Abergavenny is nearby. The Black Mountain lodge is the ideal place to stay and recharge after a long day's walk.

We can accommodate large groups of up to 20 in three rooms and also have an en-suite room that sleeps 8 within the Inn. Our Inn offers cask ales and full range of day and evening meals. Mid week specials available.
Email: Pandyinn@beeb.net

Offa's Dyke

The Rickyard (SC) Wonaston, Monmouth ☎01600 740128
www.rickyardbunkhouse.co.uk Map 162/457124
Min 10, max 24 ✕ nearby 🐾
B D ⊗ ! 🚗 See Hostels also

Brecon Beacons

☆ **Ty'r Morwydd House** (B&B)
Pen-y-Pound, Abergavenny NP7 5UD
☎ 01873 855959 Map 161/298146
B&B £19 Min 12, max 75 ✗ 🐕
Ⓓ ⊗ 🚃(Abergavenny) ★★★

Come walking in the glorious Brecon Beacons and Black Mountains.

Stay in Abergavenny, an historic market town in the Welsh Marshes.

3 star hostel. 72 beds in twin and single rooms.
Full/half board accommodation. Bed & Breakfast. Packed lunches.
Good wholesome food. Self-catering barbecue. Self-catering available Christmas, new year and August.

Fax: 01873 855443
Email: enq@tyrmorwydd.co.uk

PEMBROKESHIRE

Pembrokeshire Coast National Park
Pembrokeshire Coast Path

Caerhafod (SC) Llanrhian, St Davids, Haverfordwest ☎ 01348 837859
(Siôn & Carolyn Rees) www.Caerhafod.co.uk Map 157/827317
SC £1,365-£1,610 5 ensuite units. Min 23, max 29.
✗nearby Ⓑ Ⓓ ⊗ ⚑ 🚗 ★★★ See Hostels also.

Pembrokeshire Coast National Park
Pembrokeshire Coast Path

High View (SC) St Davids ☎01437 720616 (Thelma Hardman)
www.lowermoorcottages.co.uk Map 175/740731
SC £395-£1,995 3 cottages. Min 2, max 16. ✗nearby
Ⓑ Ⓓ ⊗ ⚑ 🚗 See SC also

POWYS

Brecon Beacons

Baskerville Hall Hotel (B&B) Clyro, Hay-on-Wye ☎ 01497 820033
www.baskervillehall.co.uk Map 161/208428
BB £15 Min 4, max 100 ✗ 🐕 Ⓑ Ⓓ See B&B also.

Brecon Beacons

Capel-y-Ffin YHA (B&B/SC) Castle Farm, Capel-y-Ffin, Llanthay, NP7 7NP
☎ 01873 890650 www.yha.org.uk Map 161/250328
BB £23.50, SC £1,600-£2,600 Min 5, max 40
✗ 🐕 Ⓓ ⊗ ⚑ ★★ See Hostels also

☆ **Belle Vue Hotel** (B&B)
Llanwrtyd Wells ☎ 01591 610237 (Eileen & Bernie Dodd)
www.bellevuewales.co.uk Map 147/879467
BB £19.50 Min 10, max 24 🐕 🐕
Ⓑ Ⓓ 🚃(Llanwrtyd Wells) ⚑ 🚗 See B&B also

Situated midway between Builth Wells and Llandovery on the A483 trunk road. Built in 1843 the Belle Vue Hotel is the oldest hotel in Llanwrtyd Wells. Combining village pub and local meeting place and so giving this small, comfortable, family run Hotel the charm and character representative of the friendly inhabitants of this town.

HOSTELS, BUNKHOUSES & CAMPSITES

CARMARTHENSHIRE

Old Stable Bunkhouse (B) Rhiw-yr-Hwch, Llandovery
☎ 01550 720856 (Pauline Nut)
www.outdoorliteventures.co.uk Map 187/728357
Bednight £8 ✗ 🐕 Ⓓ ⊗ 🚃(Llandovery) ★★★

GWYNEDD

Snowdonia

Llwyn Celyn Bach (C) Llanberis ☎ 07769 420179 (Fiona Davies)
daviesllanberis@aol.com Grid Ref: SH573595
Camping £3 🐕nearby Ⓓ

MONMOUTHSHIRE

Offa's Dyke

The Rickyard (B) Wonaston, Monmouth ☎01600 740128
www.rickyardbunkhouse.co.uk Map 162/457124
Bednight £10 ✗nearby 🐕
Ⓑ Ⓓ ⊗ See Groups also

PEMBROKESHIRE

Pembrokeshire Coast National Park
Pembrokeshire Coast Path

☆ **Caerhafod** (IH)
Llanrhian, St Davids, Haverfordwest SA62 5BD
☎01348 837859 (Siôn & Carolyn Rees)
www.Caerhafod.co.uk   Map 157/827317
Bednight £12 ✗ nearby B D ⊗ ★★★ See Groups also

 Secluded superior 23 bed independent hostel facility overlooking the sea. Ensuite family rooms. Fully equipped kitchen-diner with patio. Near coastal path, cycle route & beaches.

Individuals, groups & families welcome. Welcome Host Gold Award. Linen provided. Laundry & drying facilities. Please phone for a brochure.

Pembrokeshire Coast National Park
Pembrokeshire Coast Path

Tycanol Farm (C/CB/B/IH/BB/OC) Newport ☎ 01239 820264
www.caravancampingsites.co.uk/pembrokeshire/tycanolfarm.htm
Map 157, 145/043396 Bednight £10 ✗ nearby B D

POWYS

Wye Valley Walk & Glyndwrs Way

The Bunk Barn (IH/BB) Beili Neuadd, Rhayader, LD6 5NS
☎ 01597 810211 www.midwalesfarmstay.co.uk Map 147/994698

Bednight £10 🐾 B D ⊗ ★★★
Wheelchair access

Brecon Beacons

Canal Barn Bunkhouse (B) Ty Camlas, Canal Bank, Brecon LD3 7HH
☎ 01874 625361 (Ralph Day)
www.canal-barn.co.uk Map 160/052280
Bednight £10-£50 ✗ nearby D ⊗ ★★★★

Brecon Beacons

Capel-y-Ffin (YHA) Castle Farm, Capel-y-Ffin, Llanthay, NP7 7NP
☎ 01873 890650
www.yha.org.uk Map 161, 250328
Bednight £10 Closed Dec-Jan
✗ 🐾 D ⊗ ★★ See Groups also

RANNOCH MOOR NEAR GLENCOE

SCOTLAND

Wild landscapes of mountain, loch and glen, majestic peaks, forests, wildlife and wide heather moorland. The highlands of Scotland offer some of the most remote landscapes in Europe. In some areas you can walk for days without meeting other hikers.

Southern Scotland is often overlooked, yet there are 2,800 miles of waymarked trails in Dumfries & Galloway and the Borders. The challenging Southern Upland Way stretches coast-to-coast through woodlands, rolling hills, historic towns and fishing-villages. St Cuthbert's Way traces the steps of the 7th century Saint's pilgrimage from Melrose to Holy Island (Lindisfarne). The Borders are scattered with castles, a testimony to past conflicts with its neighbours: Stirling Castle alone overlooks the site of seven battles.

A member says: "If you walk in Scotland on a brilliant sunny day, I would like to think there's nowhere comparable in the world. You're miles from anywhere, there's a great sense of freedom from being out on the hills, with views of sea, lochs and trees, there's a freshness about it, you feel entirely out in the wild though sometimes only 50 miles away from a populous place."

While the Central Belt is home to most of Scotland's five million population, there are still remote and rural areas that are easily accessible on a day trip from Edinburgh and Glasgow. The West Highland Way follows ancient drove roads from Glasgow through Loch Lomond & The Trossachs to Ben Nevis. You can extend the route from there along the Great Glen Way to Inverness or up to Cape Wrath. The new Cairngorms National Park is a great introduction to the Highlands and prized for its beauty and diverse wildlife.

There are also over 60 scheduled ferries to Scotland's islands, leading to walks in one of the sunniest places in Britain (Tiree) and one of the wettest (Skye).

New legislation in Scotland confirms that walkers have the right to roam almost everywhere as long as access is taken responsibly. There has never been a better time to visit Scotland.

PICTURES: WALKINGWILD.COM

Long Distance Paths

Cowal Way ....COW
Fife Coastal Path.........................FFC
Great Glen Way.......................GGN
Pennine Way ....PNN
Rob Roy Way ....RRY
Southern Upland Way ....SUP
Speyside Way..............................SPS
St Cuthbert's Way ....STC
West Highland Way ....WHL

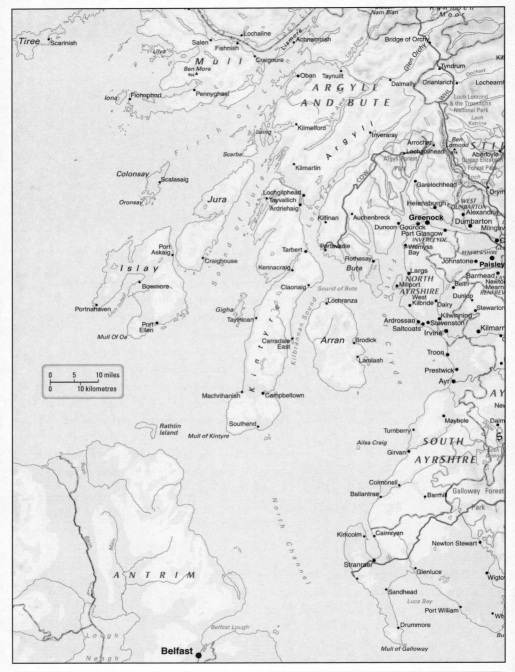

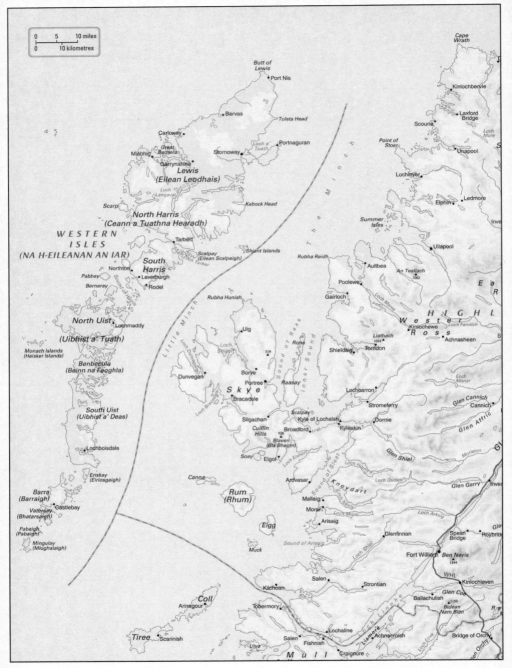

0   5   10 miles
0   10 kilometres

Cape Wrath

Butt of Lewis
Port Nis

Kinlochbervie

Barvas
Tolsta Head

Laxford Bridge

Carloway
Loch a' Tuath
Portnaguran
Scourie

Point of Stoer

Miábhig
Great Bernera
Garrynahine
Stornoway

Loch More

Lewis
(Eilean Leodhais)

Lochinver

Unapool

Elphin
Ledmore

Scarp

North Harris
(Ceann a Tuathna Hearadh)

Kebock Head

Summer Isles

Ullapool

WESTERN
ISLES
(NA H-EILEANAN AN IAR)

Tarbert

Rubha Reidh

Ea
R

Scalpay
(Eilean Scalpaigh)
Tarbert

Shiant Islands

South
Harris

Northton
Pabbay
Leverburgh
Berneray
Rodel

Aultbea

Poolewe

An Teallach
1063

HIGHL

Rubha Hunish

Gairloch

Wester
Ross

North Uist
Lochmaddy

Liathach
1054
Torridon
Achnasheen

Monach Islands
(Heiskor Islands)

Uig

Loch Snizort

Roba

719

Shieldaig

Benbecula
(Beinn na Faoghla)

Dunvegan

Borve
Portree

Raasay

Lochcarron

Loch Monar

South Uist
(Uibhist a' Deas)

Skye
Bracadale

Sligachan
Cuillin
Hills
Blaven
(Bla Bheinn)
Soay

Scalpay
Kyle of Lochalsh
Broadford
Kyleakin

Dornie

Stromeferry

Glen Cannich
Cannich

Lochboisdale

Elgol

Loch Eishort

Glen Affric

Eriskay
(Eiriosgaigh)

Ardvasar

Knoydart

Loch Quoich

Glen Shiel

Glen Garry

Barra
(Barraigh)

Canna

Rum
(Rhum)

Mallaig

Morar
Arisaig

Loch Arkaig

Spean
Bridge

Vatersay
(Bhatarsaigh)
Castlebay
Pabaigh
(Pabaigh)

Eigg

Glenfinnan

Mingulay
(Mìughalaigh)

Muck

Sound of Arisaig

Fort William
Ben Nevis
1344

WH

Kinlochleven

Coll

Arinagour

Kilchoan

Salen

Strontian

Glen Coe

Ballachulish

Bidean
Nam Bian

Bridge of Orchy

Tobermory

Tiree
Scarinish

Salen
Fishnish
Lochaline
Achnacroish

Ulva

Mull

Craignure

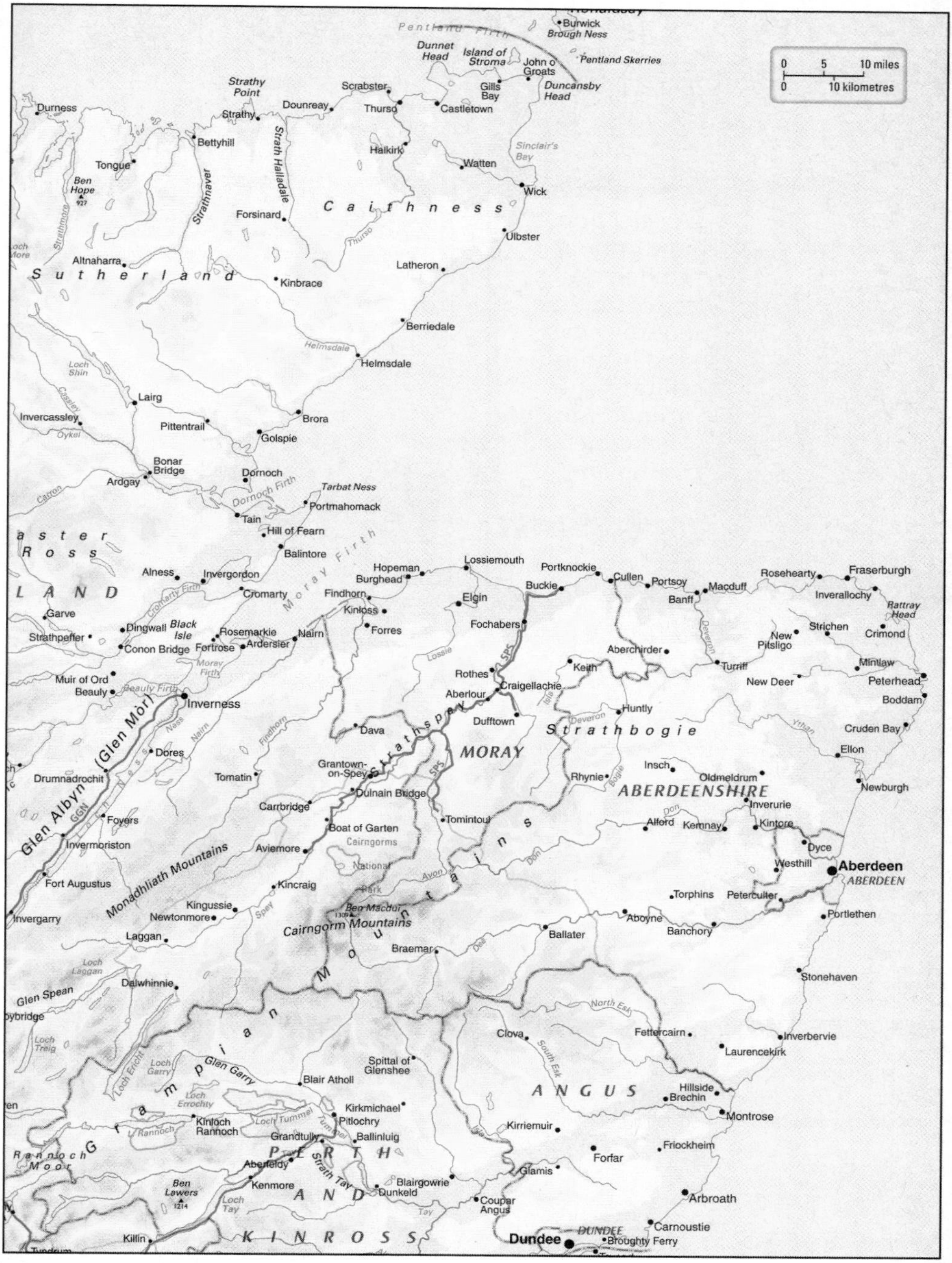
0 5 10 miles
0 10 kilometres
Pentland Firth
Burwick
Brough Ness
Dunnet Head
Island of Stroma
John o' Groats
Pentland Skerries
Duncansby Head
Strathy Point
Scrabster
Gills Bay
Durness
Dounreay
Thurso
Castletown
Strathy
Bettyhill
Strath Halladale
Sinclair's Bay
Halkirk
Tongue
Watten
Ben Hope 927
Strathnaver
Wick
Caithness
Forsinard
Strathmore
Thurso
Ulbster
Altnaharra
Latheron
Sutherland
Kinbrace
Berriedale
Helmsdale
Helmsdale
Loch Shin
Lairg
Cassley
Invercassley
Brora
Pittentrail
Oykel
Golspie
Bonar Bridge
Dornoch
Ardgay
Carron
Dornoch Firth
Tarbat Ness
Portmahomack
Tain
Hill of Fearn
Balintore
Moray Firth
Easter Ross
Alness
Invergordon
Hopeman
Burghead
Lossiemouth
Portknockie
Cullen
Portsoy
Rosehearty
Fraserburgh
Cromarty Firth
Cromarty
Findhorn
Buckie
Macduff
Banff
Inverallochy
Rattray Head
Garve
Kinloss
Elgin
Dingwall
Black Isle
Strichen
Strathpeffer
Rosemarkie
Nairn
Forres
Fochabers
New Pitsligo
Crimond
Conon Bridge
Fortrose
Ardersier
Aberchirder
Moray Firth
Lossie
Deveron
Muir of Ord
Rothes
Keith
Turriff
Mintlaw
Beauly
Beauly Firth
Craigellachie
New Deer
Peterhead
Aberlour
Inverness
Boddam
Glen Albyn (Glen Mòr)
Ness
Nairn
Findhorn
Dufftown
Huntly
Deveron
Dava
Strathspey
Strathbogie
Ythan
Cruden Bay
Dores
MORAY
Ellon
Grantown-on-Spey
Insch
Drumnadrochit
Tomatin
Rhynie
Oldmeldrum
Newburgh
Dulnain Bridge
ABERDEENSHIRE
Carrbridge
Inverurie
Foyers
Tomintoul
Alford
Kemnay
Kintore
Boat of Garten
Invermoriston
Aviemore
Cairngorms National Park
Dyce
Westhill
Aberdeen
ABERDEEN
Fort Augustus
Monadhliath Mountains
Kincraig
Avon
Don
Torphins
Peterculter
Kingussie
Ben Macdui 1309
Portlethen
Invergarry
Newtonmore
Spey
Cairngorm Mountains
Aboyne
Laggan
Ballater
Banchory
Braemar
Dee
Loch Laggan
Stonehaven
Dalwhinnie
Glen Spean
Grampian Mountains
North Esk
Loch Treig
Fettercairn
Clova
Inverbervie
Laurencekirk
Loch Ericht
Loch Garry
Glen Garry
Spittal of Glenshee
South Esk
Blair Atholl
ANGUS
Hillside
Brechin
Loch Errochty
Kirkmichael
Kinloch Rannoch
Loch Tummel
Pitlochry
Montrose
Rannoch
Tummel
Grandtully
Ballinluig
Kirriemuir
Rannoch Moor
PERTH AND KINROSS
Strath Tay
Isla
Forfar
Friockheim
Aberfeldy
Glamis
Kenmore
Blairgowrie
Ben Lawers 1214
Dunkeld
Loch Tay
Coupar Angus
Arbroath
Tay
Carnoustie
Killin
Dundee
DUNDEE
Broughty Ferry
SPS
GGN

SCOTLAND
LOCAL RAMBLERS CONTACTS

CENTRAL, FIFE & TAYSIDE
AREA SECRETARY
Mr David Galloway, 5 Doocot Road, St Andrews, Fife, Scotland, KY16 8QP
☎ 01334 475102
e-mail@davgal.fsnet.co.uk

GROUP SECRETARIES
Alyth & District Mrs N Bell, Lorne Villa, Kirkton Road, Rattray, Blairgowrie, PH10 7DZ
☎ 01250 874 301

Brechin Ms Ursula Shone, 4 Park Road, Brechin, Angus, DD9 7AF
☎ 01356 626087

Broughty Ferry Miss M Cameron, 19 Gillies Place, Broughty Ferry, Dundee, DD5 3LE ☎ 01382 776250

Dalgety Bay & District Marie Monaghan, 39 Steeple Crescent, Dalgety Bay, Dunfermline, Fife, KY11 9SY ☎ 01383 820632
www.dalgetybayramblers.org.uk

Dundee & District Mrs A C Cowie, 32 Ballindean Terrace, Dundee, Tayside, DD4 8PA ☎ 01382 507682

Forfar & District Mrs Judy Mcdade, 21 Duncan Avenue, Arbroath, DD11 2DA ☎ 01241 870695

Glenrothes Mr Doug Jolly, 16 Orchard Drive, Glenrothes, Fife, Scotland, KY7 5RG ☎ 01592 757039

Kirkcaldy Mr W H Gibson, Flat 5, 2 Darney Terrace, Kinghorn, Fife, KY3 9RF ☎ 01592 891 319

Perth & District Miss E J Bryce, 2 Hawarden Terrace, Jeanfield, Perth, PH1 1PA ☎ 01738 632645

St Andrews Ms P J Ritchie, 63 St Michaels Drive, Cupar, Fife, KY15 5BP
☎ 01334 653667

Stirling,Falkirk & District Ms J A Cameron, 17 Buchany, Doune, FK16 6HD ☎ 01786 841178

Tayside Trekkers Mrs M Nicol, 28 Provost Black Drive, Tayport, Fife, DD6 9HD ☎ 01382 550201
shelliwelly.aol.co.uk
www.taysidetrekkers.co.uk

West Fife Mrs M E Wrightson, 108 Coldingham Place, Garvock Hill, Dunfermline, Fife, KY12 7XS
☎ 01383 729 994

GRAMPIAN
AREA SECRETARY
Anne Macdonald, 64 Grant Road, Banchory, Aberdeenshire, AB31 5UU ☎ 01330 823 255
amacdonald@audit-scot.gov.uk

GROUP SECRETARIES
Aberdeen Miss A M Mitchell, 32 Gordon Road, Mannofield, Aberdeen, AB15 7RL
☎ 01224 322580
www.aberdeenramblers.org.uk

Inverurie Ms M T Corley, 60 Gray Street, Aberdeen, AB10 6JE ☎ 01224 318 672

Moray Mrs E M Robertson, Abbey Bank, Station Road, Urquhart, By Elgin, Moray, IV30 8LQ
☎ 01343 842489

Stonehaven Mrs Nan Byars, 15 Farburn Drive, Stonehaven, Kincardineshire, AB39 2BW
☎ 01569 764139

HIGHLAND & ISLANDS
AREA SECRETARY
Mr Brian Spence, 19 Redwood Avenue, Milton Of Leys, Inverness, IV2 6HA
☎ 01463 772602

GROUP SECRETARIES
Badenoch & Strathspey Libby Lamb, 19 Dalfaber Park, Aviemore, PH22 1QF
☎ 01479 810460
libby@raik.demon.co.uk

Inverness Ms J Mackenzie, 41 Ardholm Place, IV2 4QG
☎ 01463 230969

Lochaber & Lorn Mr K Van Rein, Glenduror House, Duror, Appin, PA38 4BS ☎ 01631 740395

LOTHIAN & BORDERS
AREA SECRETARY
Arthur Homan-Elsy, 55 Deanburn Road, Linlithgow, West Lothian, EH49 6EY ☎ 01506 842897
www.lothian-borders-ramblers.org.uk

GROUP SECRETARIES
Balerno Mr R J Bayley, 65 Silverknowles Drive, Edinburgh, EH4 5HX
www.lothian-borders-ramblers.org.uk/Balerno.htm

Coldstream Mrs M A Taylor, East Cottage, Lees Farm, Kelso Road, Coldstream, TD12 4LJ
☎ 01890 883137
www.lothian-borders-ramblers.org.uk/Coldstream.htm

East Berwickshire Mrs E Windram, 20 Hinkar Way, Eyemouth, Berwickshire, TD14 5EQ
☎ 018907 51048
www.lothian-borders-ramblers.org.uk/East_Berwickshire.htm

Edinburgh John Watt [acting], 17 Hillpark Avenue, Edinburgh, EH4 7AT ☎ 0131 539 3395
www.lothian-borders-ramblers.org.uk/Edinburgh.htm

Edinburgh Young Walkers Ms H K Brown, 20 Claremont Park, Edinburgh, EH6 7PJ
www.lothian-borders-ramblers.org.uk/Young_Walkers.htm

Linlithgow Mr J B & Mrs J G Davidson, 16 Friars Way, Linlithgow, EH49 6AX ☎ 01506 842504
www.lothian-borders-ramblers.org.uk/Linlithgow.htm

Livingston Mrs V Mcgowan, 4 Larbert Avenue, Deans, Livingston, EH54 8QJ ☎ 01506 438706
www.lothian-borders-ramblers.org.uk/Livingston.htm

Midlothian Walkers & Hillwalkers Miss L J Mckie, 48 The Square, Newtongrange, Dalkeith, Midlothian, EH22 4PX
www.lothian-borders-ramblers.org.uk/Midlothian.htm

Musselburgh Mr G C Edmond, 54 Northfield Gardens, Prestonpans, East Lothian, EH32 9LG
☎ 01875 810729
www.lothian-borders-ramblers.org.uk/Musselburgh.htm

North Berwick Mrs I R Mcadam, 23 Gilbert Avenue, North Berwick, East Lothian, EH39 4ED
☎ 01620 893657
www.lothian-borders-ramblers.org.uk/North_Berwick.htm

Tweeddale Mrs F Hunt, 8 Craigerne Drive, Peebles, EH45 9HN
☎ 07763 169896
www.lothian-borders-ramblers.org.uk/Tweeddale.htm

272

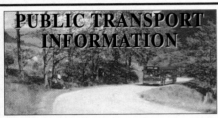

LOCAL RAMBLERS CONTACTS continued

STRATHCLYDE, DUMFRIES & GALLOWAY

AREA SECRETARY
Mrs E Lawie, Burnside Cottage,
64 Main Street, Glenboig,
Lanarkshire, ML5 2RD
☎ 01236 872959

GROUP SECRETARIES
Bearsden & Milngavie Mr N Weir,
24 Auldmurroch Drive, Milngavie,
Glasgow, G62 7SB
☎ 0141 956 1004
www.bearsden-and-milngavie-
ramblers.co.uk

Biggar Mrs I L Macdonald,
Tigh Na Cloich,
2 Glasgow Road, Lanark,
ML11 9UE ☎ 01555 661748

Clyde Valley Mr Harry Read,
6 Maybole Gardens, Hamilton,
Lanarkshire, ML3 9EU
☎ 01698 828207
www.cvramblers.supanet.com

Cumbernauld & Kilsyth
Mrs F Hardy-Smith, 78 Rannoch Drive,
Condorrat, Cumbernauld, G67 4EP
☎ 01236 782 117

Cunninghame Mrs M D Windsor,
1 Kildale Road, Kildale Court,
Lochwinnoch, PA12 4DF
☎ 01505 843626

Dumfries & Galloway Jean Snary,
7 Birchwood Place, Lockerbie Road,
Dumfries, DG1 3EB
☎ 01387 267450

Eastwood Mrs A P Fulton,
132 Greenwood Road, Clarkston,
Glasgow, G76 7LQ
www.eastwood-ramblers.org.uk

Glasgow Mr J Riddell,
61 Balcarres Avenue,
Glasgow, G12 0QE
☎ 0141 560 0722

Glasgow Region Under 40 First Footers (GRUFF)
Mr C M Duncan,
255 Eldon Street,
Greenock, PA16 7QA
☎ 01475 636515

Helensburgh & W Dunbartonshire
Una Campbell, 5 Dalmore House,
Dalmore Crescent
Helensburgh, G84 8GP
☎ 01436 673726
http://website.lineone.net/~g_flann

Inverclyde Mrs Hilary Graham,
Clune House, Clune Brae,
Clunebraehead,
Port Glasgow, PA14 5SW
☎ 01475 705569

Kilmarnock & Loudoun Ms M Bush,
14 Goatfoot Road, Galston,
Ayrshire, KA4 8BJ
☎ 01563 821331
margaret.bush@btinternet.com

Mid Argyll & Kintyre
Mrs Brenda Nicholson,
14 Wilson Road, Lochgilphead,
Argyll, PA31 8TR
☎ 01546 603026

Monklands Ms C Mcmahon,
4 Blackmoor Place,
New Stevenston,
Motherwell, ML1 4JX
☎ 01698 833983
www.monklandsramblers.org.uk

Paisley Ms M Docherty,
22 Douglas Road,
Renfrew, PA4 8BB
☎ 0141 561 4416

SLOW –
S Lanark Older Walkers
Ms M A Rankin,
18 Cherrytree Crescent, Larkhall,
Lanarkshire, ML9 2AP
☎ 01698 885995

South Ayrshire Mrs K Graham,
113 Logan Drive,
Troon, KA10 6QE
☎ 01292 311704

Strathkelvin Miss M Lang,
69 Redbrae Road,
Kirkintilloch,
Glasgow, G66 2DE
☎ 0141 776 4161

LOCAL RAMBLERS PUBLICATIONS

Easy Walks Around Milngavie
by Bearsden and Milngavie Ramblers and
East Dunbartonshire Council. Free leaflet
available from Milngavie Library,
☎ 0141 956 2776 (New this year)

Walk Strathkelvin
by John Logan (Strathkelvin Ramblers)
with introduction by Cameron McNeish,
historical essays by Don Martin and
nature notes by Ian McCallum,
ISBN 1 901184 44 7. Handsome
book of over 70 walks, mainly short
and easy walks taking half an hour to
two hours, plus longer walks in the
Campsies, canalside and disused
railway line trails, illustrated with
over 40 maps.
*£7.99 from Strathkelvin Ramblers, 25
Anne Crescent, Lenzie, Kirkintilloch G66
5HB (cheques to Strathkelvin Ramblers).*

---

millets® **stores in this region**

ABERDEEN	167/168 Union Street AB11 6BB	HAMILTON	17 Duke Street ML3 7DT
AYR	58 High Street KA7 1PA	INVERNESS	24 High Street IV1 1JQ
DUNDEE	23 Cowgate DD1 2MS	LOUTH	78 East Gate LN11 9PG
EDINBURGH	12 Frederick Street EH2 2HB	OBAN	71 George Street PA34 5NN
GLASGOW	71 Union Street G1 3TA	PERTH	182/186 High Street PH1 5PA
GLASGOW	Unit 2B Sauchiehall Street G2 2ER	STIRLING	20/22 Murray Place FK8 1DQ
GLENROTHES	56 Unicorn Way, Kingdom Centre KY7 5NU	BANGOR	261 High Street OX16 5DZ
GREENOCK	45 Hamilton Way PA15 1RQ	ELGIN	Unit 13 St Giles Centre IV30 1EA

BED & BREAKFAST

ARGYLL & BUTE

● **Arrochar**
Loch Lomond, the Trossachs & Cowal Way
Lochside Guest House, Main Street, G83 7AA
☎ 01301 702467 (Maria & Iain Gourlay)
www.stayatlochlomond.com/lochside   Map 56/299045
BB **B**   ✗ nearby   S1 D3 T1 F1   ⋘(Arrochar) Ⓑ   Ⓓ ♨   ★★★

● **Campbeltown**
⌲ White Hart Hotel, Main St, PA28 6AN
☎ 01586 522440 (Peter Stogdale)   www.whiteh.com   Map 68/718202
BB **C** ✗ £10, 5:30-9pm   S4 D6 T7 F3
Ⓥ Ⓑ Ⓓ 🐾♨🚗▪🍽🏕   ★★

● **Dalmally**
Loch Lomond & the Trossachs
Craig Villa Guest House, PA33 1AX   ☎ 01838 200255 (A W Cressey)
www.craigvilla.co.uk   Map 50/168273
BB **B**   ✗ nearby   D2 T2 F2   ⋘(Dalmally)
Ⓑ Ⓓ ⊗🐾♨▪   ★★★

Craigroyston, Monument Rd, PA33 1AA   ☎ 01838 200234
(Mrs Sandra Boardman)   www.craigroyston.com   Map 50/158271
BB **B**   ✗ book first £12, 7-8pm   S1 D1 T1   ⋘(Dalmally)
Ⓥ Ⓑ Ⓓ ⊗🐾♨🚗🏕   ★★★Ⓦ

● **Dunoon**
Bay House Hotel, West Bay Promenade , PA23 7HU   ☎ 01369 704832
(Rick & Linda Murry)   www.bayhousehotel.co.uk   Map 63/171763
BB **B**   ✗ £16, 6-7pm   S1 D1 T2 F2
Ⓥ Ⓑ Ⓓ 🐾♨🚗   ★★★

● **Helensburgh**
Loch Lomond & the Trossachs
Balmillig, 64B Colquhoun Street, G84 9JP   ☎ 01436 674922
(Anne & John Urquhart)   www.balmillig.co.uk   Map 56/297830
BB **B**   ✗ nearby   D1 T1 F1   ⋘(Helensburgh Central)
Ⓑ Ⓓ ⊗🐾♨▪   ★★★★

● **Kilchrenan (Taynuilt)**
⌲ Roineabhal, PA35 1HD   ☎ 01866 833207 (Maria Soep)
www.roineabhal.com   Map 50/033239
BB **C**   ✗ book first £30, 7pm   D2 T1   Closed Dec
Ⓥ Ⓑ Ⓓ 🐾♨▪🍽   ★★★★

● **Kilmichael Glassary (Lochgilphead)**
The Horseshoe Inn, PA31 8QA   ☎ 01546 606369
http://horseshoeinn.biz   Map 55/852930
BB **B**   ✗ £8, 6-9pm   D2 T2 F1   Ⓥ   Ⓑ🐾♨♨🏕   ★★

● **Oban**
Kathmore, Soroba Road, PA34 4JF   ☎ 01631 562104 (Mrs M Wardhaugh)
www.kathmore.co.uk   Map 49/860292
BB **B**   ✗ nearby   D4 T3 F2   ⋘(Oban) Ⓑ   Ⓓ ⊗🐾♨   ★★★

An Teallach, North Connel, PA37 1QX   ☎ 01631 710315 (Alan & Nan
Johnson)   anteallach@northconnel.freeserve.co.uk   Map 49/916348
BB **B**   ✗ nearby   D1 T1   Closed Nov-Mar   Ⓑ Ⓓ ⊗🐾♨

☆ **Lerags House**
Levags, PA34 4SE   ☎ 01631 563381 (Charlie & Bella Milley)
www.leragshouse.com   Map 49/842245
BB **C**   ✗ book first, 7:30-8:30pm   S1 D5 T1
Ⓥ   Ⓑ Ⓓ ⊗🐾♨🚗🏕   Price includes evening meals

Our intention for you while staying with us and experiencing our hospitality is to relax. The ambience throughout Lerags House is stylish, informal yet professional. But above all, you will feel at home. Exceptional flavours — excellent comfort — extraordinary beauty.

● **Tighnabruaich**
Cowal Way
The Royal at Tighnabruaich, PA21 2BE   ☎ 01700 811239
www.royalhotel.org.uk   Map 62/974721
BB **C**   ✗ £15, 6-9pm   D7 T3
Ⓥ   Ⓑ   Ⓓ🐾♨▪🍽   ★★★★

CENTRAL BELT

● **Aberdour (Fife)**
Fife Coastal Path
⌲ Aberdour Hotel, 38 High Street, KY3 0SW   ☎ 01383 860325
www.aberdourhotel.co.uk   Map 65,66/189852
BB **C**   ✗ £15, 6-9pm   D6 T6 F4   ⋘(Aberdour)
Ⓥ   Ⓑ   Ⓓ🐾♨▪   ★★★

● **Edinburgh**
Barrosa Guest House, 21 Pilrig Street, EH6 5AN   ☎ 0131 554 3700
(Miss Y Pretty)   Map 66/264753
BB **B/C**   ✗ nearby   D3 T3 F2   ⋘(Waverley) Ⓑ ♨🏕   ★★

Borodale, 7 Argyle Place, (off Melville Drive), EH9 1JU
☎ 0131 667 5578   (Mrs C A Darlington)
catherine@darlington496.freeserve.co.uk   Map 66/256724
BB **B**   ✗ nearby   S1 D1 T1 F1   ⋘(Edinburgh Waverley)
Ⓑ Ⓓ   ★★★

● **Glasgow**
⌲ Adelaide's, 209 Bath Street, G2 4HZ   ☎ 0141 248 4970
www.adelaides.co.uk   Map 64/584657
BB **C**   ✗ nearby   S2 D2 T2 F2   ⋘(Glasgow Central)
Ⓑ Ⓓ ⊗🐾♨▪   ★★

● **Haddington (East Lothian)**
⌲ Eaglescairnie Mains, Gifford , EH41 4HN
☎ 01620 810491 (Barbara Williams)
www.eaglescairnie.com   Map 66/516689
BB **B/C**   S2 D1 T1
Ⓑ Ⓓ 🐾♨🚗🏕   ★★★★

● **Longformacus**
Southern Upland Way
⌲ Whinmore, TD11 3NZ   ☎ 01361 890669 (June)
www.watch-fisheries.co.uk   Map 67,74/692573
BB **B**   ✗ book first £18, 7pm   S1 D1 T1   🐾♨🚗▪

● Rowardennan (Drymen)

Loch Lomond & the Trossachs
West Highland Way

Anchorage Cottage, G63 0AW ☎ 01360 870394
www.anchoragecottage.co.uk   Map 56/394947
BB **C**   D1 T2   Closed Oct-Mar   ⬚ Ⓓ ⊛ 🐾 ♨ 🚗

DUMFRIES & GALLOWAY

● Castle Douglas

Craigadam, DG7 3HU ☎ 01556 650233 (Celia Pickup) www.craigadam.com
Map 84/797728   BB **C**   ✗ book first £19, 6-8pm   D2 T4 F1
Ⓥ ⬚ Ⓓ ♨ 🚗 ! 🍴   ◆◆◆◆◆   See SC also.

🍴⊠ Buittle Bridge, East Logan, DG7 3AA ☎ 01556 660324
(Mrs Susan Matthews) Map 84/809640
BB **B**   ✗ £12, 7-8:30pm   D1 T1   Ⓥ   Ⓓ ⊛ 🐾 ♨ 🍴

The Kings Arms Hotel, Andrew Street, DG7 1EL
☎ 01556 502626 (Mr D Fulton) www.galloway-golf.co.uk   Map 84/763621
BB **C**   ✗ £10, 6-8:45pm   S2 D3 T4 F1   Ⓥ   Ⓓ 🐾 ♨ 🚗 ! 🍴   ★★

● Kirkcudbright

🍴⊠ Number 3 B&B, 3 High Street, DG6 4JZ ☎ 01557 330881
(Miriam Baker) www.number3-bandb.co.uk   Map 83,84/681509
BB **B**   ✗ nearby   D1 T2   ⬚ Ⓓ ⊛ 🐾 ♨ 🍴   ★★★★

● Lochmaben (Lockerbie)

Ardbeg Cottage, 19 Castle Street, DG11 1NY
☎ 01387 811855 (Bill Neilson) bill@neilson.net   Map 78/081826
BB **B**   ✗ book first £11, 6:30pm   D/T1 T1
Ⓥ ⬚ Ⓓ ⊛ 🐾 ♨   ★★★

● Moffat

Southern Upland Way

🍴⊠ Seamore House, Academy Road, DG10 9HW ☎ 01683 220404
(Heather & Allan Parkinson) www.seamorehouse.co.uk   Map 78/083055
BB **B**   ✗ nearby   D1 T3 F1   ⬚ Ⓓ 🐾 ♨ 🚗 ! 🍴   ★★★

🍴⊠ Morag, 19 Old Carlisle Road, DG10 9QJ ☎ 01683 220690
(Mrs L Taylor) morag_moffat44@btopenworld.com   Map 78/093046
BB **B**   ✗ book first £10, 5:30-7pm   S1 D2 T1
Ⓥ ⬚ Ⓓ ⊛ 🐾 ♨   ★★★

North Nethermiln, Old Carlisle Road, DG10 9QJ
☎ 01683 220325 (Heather Quigley) Map 78/093046
BB **A**   ✗ £8, 7-9pm   S/T1 D2 F1   Ⓥ   Ⓓ ⊛ 🐾 ♨ 🚗 !

● New Abbey

🍴⊠ Abbey Arms Hotel, 1 The Square, DG2 8BX ☎ 01387 850489
enquiries@Abbeyarms.netlineuk.net   Map 83/963662
BB **B**   ✗ £7.50, until 8pm   S1 D2 T5 F2
Ⓥ ⬚ Ⓓ 🐾 ♨ 🚗   ★★

● Newton Stewart

Kilwarlin, 4 Corvisel Road, DG8 6LN ☎ 01671 403047 (Mrs Hazel Dickson)
hazelkilwarlin@bushinternet.com   Map 83/409650
BB **B**   ✗ nearby   S1 D1 F1   Closed Nov-Feb   Ⓓ 🐾 ♨   ★★★Ⓦ

Benera, Corsbie Rd, DG8 6JD ☎ 01671 403443 (Mrs EM Prise)
ethel_prise@hotmail.com   Map 83/405655
BB **B**   ✗ nearby   D1 T1   Closed Nov-Mar
⬚ Ⓓ ⊛ 🐾 ♨ 🚗 !   ★★★

☆ 🍴⊠ **Sherwood**
4 Stronord, Palnure, DG8 7BD (Mrs G Pullen)
☎ 01671 401174   stronord@tiscali.co.uk   Map 83/450643
BB **A**   ✗ book first £6, 7pm   D1 T1
Ⓥ ⬚ Ⓓ ⊛ 🐾 ♨ 🚗 !

Galloway Forest trails direct from the door. Cairnsmore of Fleet opposite. Red squirrels are daily visitors along with numerous bird life. Come and enjoy Scotland's secret corner. Non-smoking, en-suite rooms.

● Wigtown (Newton Stewart)

☆ 🍴⊠ **Hillcrest House**
Madland Place, Station Rd, DG8 9EU   ☎ 01988 402018 (Deborah Firth)
www.hillcrest-wigtown.co.uk   Map 83/433550
BB **B**   ✗ book first £14, 7pm   D2 T2 F1
Ⓥ ⬚ ⊛ 🐾 ♨ 🚗 ! 🍴   ★★

Beautiful Victorian villa providing bright, spacious accommodation in Wigtown—Scotland's National Book Town. Perfect base for exploring the mountains, forests and coastline of this unspoilt and largely undiscovered part of SW Scotland.

HIGHLAND

● Altnaharra (Lairg)

☆ 🍴⊠ **Bed & Breakfast**
1 Macleod Crescent, IV27 4UG   ☎ 01549 411258 (Mrs M Smith)
www.altnaharra.net   Map 16/567352
BB **A**   ✗ £10, until 8pm   T2 F1
Ⓥ ⬚ Ⓓ 🐾 ♨ 🚗 ! 🍴   ★★★

Altnaharra is situated at the end of Loch Naver, with an overlook of Ben Klibreck, Ben Hope and Ben Loyal. With peace and tranquillity all around, it's ideal for walkers, climbers and cyclists. Email: info@altnaharra.net

● Aultbea (Achnasheen)

🍴⊠ Tranquillity, 21 Mellon Charles, IV22 2JN ☎ 01445 731241
(Mrs Pauline Bond) Map 19/849911
BB **B**   ✗ book first £15, 6.30pm   S1 D1 F1
Ⓥ ⬚ Ⓓ ⊛ 🐾 ♨ 🚗   ★★★

● Aviemore

Cairngorms
Speyside Way

🍴⊠ Ravenscraig Guest House, Grampian Road, PH22 1RP ☎ 01479 810278
(Jonathan Gatenby) www.aviemoreonline.com   Map 35,36/895131
BB **B**   ✗ nearby   S2 D3 T3 F4   〰(Aviemore)
⬚ Ⓓ 🐾 ♨ 🚗   ★★★

Ardlogie Guest House, Dalfaber Road, PH22 1PU ☎ 01479 810747
(Michael Willies)   www.ardlogie.co.uk   Map 35/897123
BB **B**   ✗ nearby   D4 F1   ⚡(Aviemore)
🔲 D ⊛ ⛊🐾🚲!🛏   ★★★   Guided walks.

Cairngorm Guest House, Grampian Road, PH22 1RP
☎ 01479 810630   (Gail and Peter Conn)
www.cairngormguesthouse.com   Map 35,36/895131
BB **B**   ✗ nearby   D5 T3 F2   ⚡(Aviemore)
🔲 D ⊛ ⛊🐾🛏   ★★★

● **Ballachulish (Argyll)**
Park View, 18 Park Road, PH49 4JS ☎ 01855 811560 (Mrs Diana Macaskill)
www.glencoe-parkview.co.uk   Map 41/080582
BB **B**   ✗ nearby   S1 D2 T1
D 🐾🚲🛏   ★★★Ⓦ   Veggie breakfasts

● **Dalwhinnie**
Cairngorms
The Inn at Loch Ericht, PH19 1AG ☎ 01528 522257
www.priory-hotel.com   Map 42/636842
BB **B**   ✗ £11.50, until 9:30pm   S2 D10 T13 F2   ⚡(Dalwhinnie)
Ⓥ 🔲 D 🐾⛊🚗!🛏   ★   Mountain bike hire available

● **Dornie (Kyle of Lochalsh)**
Highland Encounters, 5 Sallachy, IV40 8DZ (Monique & Skip)
☎ 01599 588228   www.highlandencounters.com   Map 25/911305
BB **C**   ✗ book first 7-9pm   D2 T2
Ⓥ D 🐾⛊🚗!   All meals included. Minimum 2 nights.

● **Drumnadruchit**
Great Glen Way

☆ Loch Ness Clansman Hotel
Loch Ness-side, IV3 8LA ☎ 01456 450326 (Mr Ian Miller)
www.lochnessview.com   Map 26/572349
BB **C**   ✗ £6-£12, 6:30-9pm   S2 D12 T6 F4
Ⓥ 🔲 D 🐾⛊🚗   ★★★

The only Loch Ness-side hotel.
Stunning views from the
observation lounge bar
and restaurant.
Free pick up for B&B from
Drumnadruchit (4 minutes) or
Abriachan/Lochlaite (5 minutes).

● **Durness (Lairg)**
Glengolly House, Durine, IV27 4PN ☎ 01971 511255 (Martin Mackay)
www.glengolly.com   Map 9/401678
BB **B**   ✗ nearby   D1 T1 F1
🔲 D ⊛ 🐾🚗   Veggie breakfasts.

For an explanation of the symbols
used in this guide see
Key to Abbreviations and Symbols on p 7

● **Forsinard (Sutherland)**
Station Cottage, KW13 6YT ☎ 01641 571262 (Susan Grimshaw)
www.scotland-index.co.uk   Map 10/891424
BB **B**   ✗ £10, 6:30-8:30pm   D1 T1   ⚡(Forsinard)
Ⓥ 🔲 D ⊛ 🐾⛊🚗!🛏

● **Fort William**
West Highland Way & Great Glen Way
Craig Nevis Guest House, Belford Road, PH33 6BU ☎ 01397 702023
www.craignevis.co.uk   Map 41/108741
BB **A/B**   ✗ nearby   S2 D3 T3 F2   ⚡(Fort William)
🔲 D ⊛ 🐾🛏

Glenlochy Guest House, Nevis Bridge, PH33 6LP
☎ 01397 702909 (Hugh MacPherson)
www.glenlochy.co.uk   Map 41/114742
BB **B**   ✗ nearby   S1 D7 T3 F2   ⚡(Fort William)
🔲 D ⊛ 🐾⛊🛏   ★★★

Alltonside Guest House, Achintore Road, PH33 6RW
☎ 01397 703542 (Elizabeth Ann Allton)
www.alltonside.co.uk   Map 41/085718
BB **B**   ✗ book first   D3 T2 F1   ⚡(Fort William)
Ⓥ 🔲 D ⊛ 🐾⛊🛏   ★★★

11 Castle Drive, Lochyside, PH33 7NR ☎ 01397 702659 (Mrs M Grant)
grantmoy@aol.com   Map 41/118758
BB **A**   ✗ book first £12   D1 T1   ⚡(Fort William)
Ⓥ 🔲 🐾⛊🚗!🛏   ★★★

☆ **Distillery House**
Nevis Bridge, PH33 6LR ☎ 01397 700103 (Stuart and Mandy McLean)
www.fort-william.net/distillery-house   Map 41/113744
BB **B**   ✗ nearby   S2 D3 T2 F1   ⚡(Fort William)
🔲 D ⊛ 🐾⛊🚗!🛏   ★★★★   See SC also.

Set in the grounds of the old Glenlochy
Distillery against the backdrop of Ben Nevis.
Lovely home cooked breakfast and well
equipped en-suite bedrooms. Recommended
in the Daily Mail article 'Great Glen Way'.
Enjoy a complimentary whiskey upon
arrival. Email: disthouse@aol.com

Ashburn House, Achintore Rd, PH33 6RQ
☎ 01397 706000 (Christine MacDonald)
www.highland5star.co.uk   Map 41/095732
BB **C**   ✗ nearby   S3 D3 F1   ⚡(Fort William)   🔲 D ⊛ 🐾⛊

● **Glenelg (Kyle)**
Marabhaig, 7 Coullindune, IV40 8JU
☎ 01599 522327 (Mrs Margaret Cameron)   Map 33/808189
BB **B**   ✗ book first £12, 6-8:30pm   D3 T1   Closed Jan
Ⓥ 🔲 D 🐾⛊!   ★★★

● **Kincraig (Kingussie)**
Cairngorms
Insh House, PH21 1NU ☎ 01540 651377 (Nick & Patsy Thompson)
www.kincraig.com/inshhouse   Map 35/836038
BB **B**   ✗ nearby   S2 D1 T1 F1   Closed Nov-Dec
🔲 D ⊛ 🐾⛊🚗!🛏   ★★★

● Kingussie
Cairngorms

☆ Ardselma
The Crescent, PH21 1JZ ☎ 07786 696384 (Valerie Johnston)
valeriedunmhor@aol.com   Map 35/757009
BB **B**   ✕ book first £12, 6-8pm   S1 D1 T3 F2   ᴁ(Kingussie)
Ⓑ Ⓓ 🐾🕯☕🚲🔔🧺

With views of the Cairngorms, Ardselma is quiet and peaceful, set in its private grounds of three acres with ample parking and safe bicycle storage. Large bedrooms, log fire sitting room, 5 min from train station and less from bus stop.

● Kinlochleven
West Highland Way

🖼◀ Hermon, 5 Rob Roy Rd, PH50 4RA ☎ 01855 831383 (Miss MacAngus)
h.macangus@tinyworld.co.uk   Map 41/189622
BB **B**   ✕ nearby   D1 T2   Closed Nov-Feb   Ⓑ Ⓓ 🐾🕯🚲🔔🧺

🖼◀ Edencoille Guest House, Garbhien Rd, PH50 4SE
☎ 01855 831358 (Elsie Robertson)   Map 41/181617
BB **B/C**   ✕ £15, 6:30-9pm   D2 T2 F2   Ⓥ Ⓑ Ⓓ 🐾🕯🚲🔔 ★★★

● Lochcarron (Strathcarron)
Aultsigh, Croft Road, IV54 8YA ☎ 01520 722558 (Ms M Innes)
moyra.innes@btinternet.com   Map 25/905400
BB **B**   ✕ nearby   D1 T1 F1   Ⓓ☕🐾🕯🚲🧺

● Lochinver (Sutherland)
🖼◀ Ardglas Guest House, IV27 4LJ ☎ 01571 844257
(Arthur & Meryl Quigley) www.ardglas.co.uk Map 15/093231
BB **B**   ✕ book first £9.50, 7pm   S1 D4 T1 F2
Ⓥ Ⓓ 🐾🕯🚲🚗 ★★★

Ardmore House, 80 Torbreck, IV27 4JB ☎ 01571 844310
(Mrs Sandra Macleod)   Map 15/069247
BB **B**   D1 T1   Closed Oct-Mar   Ⓓ☕🕯 ★★★★

● Melvaig (Gairloch)
Rua Reidh Lighthouse, IV21 2EA ☎ 01445 771263
www.scotland-info.co.uk/ruareidh.htm   Map 19/740919
BB **B**   ✕ book first £13, 7pm   D2 T2 F2   Closed Jan
Ⓥ Ⓑ Ⓓ☕🐾🕯🚲🧺Ⓜ ★★★★

● Nethy Bridge
Cairngorms
Speyside Way

🖼◀ Mondhuie, PH25 3DF ☎ 01479 821062 (David Mordaunt)
www.mondhuie.com   Map 36/991207
BB **A**   ✕ book first £10, 7:30pm   D1 T1   Closed Nov-Dec
Ⓥ Ⓓ☕🐾🕯🚲🔔🧺 See SC also.

● Newtonmore (Kingussie)
Cairngorms

🖼◀ The Pines, Station Rd, PH20 1AR ☎ 01540 673271 (Colin Walker)
http://ra.pinesnewtonmore.co.uk   Map 35/713986
BB **B**   ✕ book first £16.50, 7pm   S2 D2 T2   ᴁ(Newtonmore)
Ⓥ Ⓑ Ⓓ☕🐾🕯🔔🧺

☆ 🖼◀ Craigerne House Hotel
Golf Course Rd, PH20 1AT ☎ 01540 673281 (David & Jane Adamson)
www.craigernehotel.com   Map 35/716991
BB **B**   ✕ £20.50, 7-9pm   S1 D3 T6   ᴁ(Newtonmore)
Ⓥ Ⓑ Ⓓ🐾🕯🚗🧺

A detached Victorian villa with mature gardens commanding magnificent views of the Monadhliath and Cairngorm mountains and the Spey Valley. Only 100 yards from the centre of Newtonmore, "The Walking Centre of Scotland". Most rooms en-suite with tea/coffee making facilities.

● Spean Bridge
Great Glen Way

🖼◀ Mahaar, Corriechoille Road, PH34 4EP
☎ 01397 712365 (Isabel Muir)   www.mahaar.co.uk   Map 41,34/220816
BB **B**   ✕ book first £10, 6-8pm   S2 D1 T1 F1   ᴁ(Spean Bridge)
Ⓥ Ⓓ🐾🕯🚲🚗🧺 ★★★

🖼◀ Inverour Guest House, PH34 4EU ☎ 01397 712218 (Lesley Brown)
www.fort-william.net/inverour   Map 41,34/223816
BB **B**   ✕ book first £12.50, 7pm   S2 D3 T3 F1   ᴁ(Spean Bridge)
Ⓥ Ⓑ Ⓓ☕🐾🕯🚲🧺Ⓜ ★★★

☆ 🖼◀ Marlaw
3 Lodge Gardens, PH34 4EN ☎ 01397 712603 (Ros & Roy Griffiths)
www.marlawbandb.co.uk   Map 41,34/220816
BB **B**   ✕ nearby   D2 T1   ᴁ(Spean Bridge)
Ⓑ Ⓓ🐾🕯🚲🔔🧺

A modern centrally heated house with large gardens and well equipped rooms. Set in the grounds of Spean Lodge it is very close to all village amenities and ideally situated for the Great Glen Way and the Leanachan Forest trails.

● Torridon
Ben Bhraggie, Diabaig, IV22 2HE
☎ 01445 790268 (Mrs I Ross)   Map 24,19/802605
BB **A** ✕ book first £10, 7:30pm   S1 D1 T1   Closed Nov-Feb
Ⓥ Ⓑ☕🐾🕯🔔

Benview, Inveralligin, IV22 2HB ☎ 01445 791333 (Mrs Mary Mackay)
inveralligin@aol.com   Map 24/845577
BB **B**   D2 T1   Ⓓ☕ See SC also

● Ullapool
🖼◀ The Ceilidh Place Clubhouse, West Argyle Street, IV26 2TY
☎ 01854 612103   www.theceilidhplace.com   Map 19/126939
BB **B**   ✕ £20, 6:30-9pm   S4 T3 F4   Closed Nov-Mar
Ⓥ Ⓓ🐾🧺

● Urquhart (Moray)
Speyside Way

🖼◀ The Old Church of Urquhart, Parrandier, Meft Rd, IV30 8NH
☎ 01343 843063 (Andreas Peter) www.oldkirk.co.uk Map 28/284632
BB **B**   ✕ book first £11, 7pm   D1 T1 F1
Ⓥ Ⓑ Ⓓ🐾🕯🚲🔔🧺 ★★★★

ISLE OF ARRAN

● **Blackwaterfoot (Brodick)**
Lochside , KA27 8EY ☎ 01770 860276 (Marjorie Bannatyne)
george.bannatyne@virgin.net   Map 68,69/903268
BB **B**   ✕ book first £7, 6:30pm   S1 D2 T1 F1
Ⓥ Ⓑ Ⓓ 🛁 ♨ 🏇 ★★★   See SC also.

● **Brodick**

☆ **Rosaburn Lodge**
KA27 8DP ☎ 01770 302383
Map 69/009367
BB **B**   ✕ nearby   D3 T2
Ⓑ Ⓓ ⊛ 🛁 ♨ 🚗 !   ★★★

Beautifully located on the banks of river Rosa, nearest guest house to the Arran Hills. Comfortable bedrooms and bathrooms. Excellent breakfasts. Private parking.

ISLE OF BUTE

● **Port Bannatyne**
Russian Tavern at Port Royal Hotel, 37 Marine Rd, PA20 0LW
☎ 01700 505073 (Olga Crawford) www.russiantavern.co.uk
Map 63/071672   BB **B**   ✕ £18, 7-10pm   S1 D1 T2 F1   Closed Nov-Apr
Ⓥ Ⓑ Ⓓ ⊛ 🛁 ♨ 🏇

ISLE OF RAASAY

● **Skye & Lochalsh**

☆ 🛏◀ **Isle of Raasay Hotel**
IV40 8PB ☎ 01478 660222 (John & Rose Nicholson)
www.isleofraasayhotel.co.uk   Map 32,24/548365
BB **B**   ✕ £7.50, 6-8pm   S3 D4 T6 F3
Ⓥ Ⓑ Ⓓ 🏇 ♨ 🚗 ! 🏇   ★★★

Visit the undiscovered! Once you have seen the brochures you will be packing your bag. Call John or Rose. johnandrose@freeserve.co.uk

ISLE OF SKYE

● **Elgol**
Rose Croft, IV49 9BL ☎ 01471 866377 (Chris & Pauline Forrester)
www.rosecroftelgol.co.uk   Map 32/522142
BB **B**   ✕ nearby   D1 T1   Closed Nov-Apr
Ⓓ ⊛ 🏇 🚗 !

● **Portree**
Cuaig, 7 Kitson Crescent, IV51 9DP
☎ 01478 612273 (Catherine MacLeod)   Map 23/483483
BB **B**   S1 D1   Closed Nov-Apr   ⊛   ★★★

NORTH EAST SCOTLAND

● **Dufftown (Keith)**
Speyside Way
🛏◀ Errolbank, 134 Fife Street, AB55 4AQ
☎ 01340 820229 (Mrs J Smart)
jeandsmart@errolbank.freeserve.co.uk   Map 28/327397
BB **A**   ✕ nearby   S1 D1 F3   Ⓑ Ⓓ 🏇 ♨ 🚗 ! 🏇

● **Forfar**
🛏◀ Glencoul House, Justinhaugh, Murthill, DD8 3SF
☎ 01307 860 248 (Mrs Rosemary Kirby)
glencoul@waitrose.com   Map 54/464575
BB **B**   ✕ book first £10, 6-7:30pm   D1 T1
Ⓥ Ⓓ ⊛ 🏇 ♨ 🚗 ! 🏇 ★★★

● **Tomintoul (Ballindalloch)**
Cairngorms
Speyside Way
🛏◀ Morinsh, 26 Cults Drive, AB37 9HW
☎ 01807 580452 (Mrs Jean Birchall)
www.tomintoul-glenlivet.org.uk   Map 36/166189
BB **A**   ✕ nearby   S1 D1 T1   Ⓓ ⊛ 🏇 ♨ 🚗 ! 🏇
🛏◀ Argyle House, 7 Main Street, AB37 9EX
☎ 01807 580766 (Lin Forrester)
http://argyle.house.users.btopenworld.com   Map 36/170185
BB **A**   ✕ nearby   D2 T1 F2   Ⓑ Ⓓ ⊛ 🏇 ♨ 🏇 Ⓜ

PERTH & KINROSS

● **Balquhidder**
Loch Lomond & the Trossachs
Rob Roy Way
🛏◀ Kings House Hotel, FK19 8NY ☎ 01877 384646
www.kingshouse-scotland.co.uk   Map 51,57/543209
BB **B**   ✕ £13-£15, until 8:30pm   D5 T2   Ⓥ Ⓑ Ⓓ 🏇 ♨ !   ★★

● **Blair Atholl (Pitlochry)**
Dalgreine Guest House, Off St Andrew's Crescent, PH18 5SX
☎ 01796 481276   www.dalgreine-guest-house.co.uk   Map 43/878653
BB **B**   ✕ nearby   S1 D2 T2 F1   🚃(Blair Atholl)
Ⓑ Ⓓ ⊛ 🏇 ♨ 🚗   ★★★★

● **Blairgowrie**
🛏◀ Shocarjen House, Balmoral Rd , PH10 7AF ☎ 01250 870525
(Mrs Shonaidh Beattie) shonaidh.beattie@virgin.net   Map 53/180456
BB **B**   ✕ book first £8, 7pm   D1 T1
Ⓥ Ⓑ Ⓓ ⊛ 🏇 ♨ 🚗 ! 🏇   ★★★★

● **Crieff**
🛏◀ Galvelmore House, 5 Galvelmore St, PH7 4BY ☎ 01764 655721
(Katy Galbraith) www.galvelmore.co.uk   Map 52,58/862215
BB **B**   ✕ book first £15   D2 T1   Ⓥ Ⓑ Ⓓ 🏇 ♨ 🚗 !   ★★★

● Kirkmichael (Blairgowrie)

☆ ✉⊷◀ **Strathardle Inn**
PH10 7NS ☎ 01250 881224 (Jeff Ellis)
www.strathardleinn.co.uk   Map 52,53/082602
BB **B**   ✕ £6, 6:30-8:30pm   D3 T1 F1
Ⓥ Ⓑ Ⓓ 🐾🍵👜 ❗🚶

An enchanting, peaceful 18th century inn, set in the glorious Perthshire Highlands, offering comfortable en-suite accommodation, a cosy resident's lounge and a licensed bar and restaurant. There are over 80 Munros within easy reach and the Cataran Trail passes by the front door. Smoking is permitted in the bar only. The Inn is on the A924 between Pitlochry and Blairgowrie just outside the village of Kirkmichael.

● Perth

Beeches, 2 Comelybank, PH2 7HU ☎ 01738 624486 (Pat & Brian Smith)
www.beeches-guest-house.co.uk   Map 53, 58/124245
BB **B**   ✕ nearby   S2 D1 T1   🚌(Perth)
Ⓑ Ⓓ ⊛🐾👜 ★★★

● Pitlochry

✉⊷◀ The Atholl Centre, Atholl Rd, PH16 5BX ☎ 01796 473044
http://athollcentre.users.btopenworld.com   Map 52,53/941580
BB **B**   ✕ nearby   S1 D1 T4 F2   🚌(Pitlochry)
Ⓑ Ⓓ ⊛🐾   See Groups also. Guide dogs welcome.

● Stanley (Perth)

Glensanda House, Six Acres, Station Road, PH1 4NS ☎ 01738 827016
www.altouristguide.com/glensandahouse   Map 53/108334
BB **B**   ✕ nearby   S1 D1 T1   Ⓑ ⊛🐾👜 ★★★

SCOTTISH BORDERS

● Ancrum (Jedburgh)
St Cuthbert's Way

☆ **Cheviot View**
The Green, TD8 6XA ☎ 01835 830563 (Julie & Michael O'Sullivan)
www.cheviotview.co.uk   Map 74/626243
BB **B**   ✕ nearby   D1 T2
Ⓑ Ⓓ ⊛🐾👜🚗 ★★★

Enjoy friendly welcome and creature comforts of a traditional Scottish village. Super views and walks including St Cuthbert's Way. Good suppers nightly across the green. Stay two nights with car lifts for convenience. Tasty packed lunches and expert language tuition available.

☆ **Harden Vale**
Sunnyside, TD8 6UN ☎ 01835 830280 (Johan Hensens)
www.ancrumcraig.co.uk   Map 74/607245
BB **B**   ✕ nearby   T2 F1
Ⓑ Ⓓ 🐾👜 ★★Ⓦ

By the green in Ancrum village, five miles from A68, 1 mile from St Cuthbert's Way, and 100 yards from village pub serving real ales and excellent evening meals. Accredited Walkers and Cyclists Welcome Email: johan@ancrumcraig.co.uk

● Chesters (Hawick)

✉⊷◀ The Steadings, Roundabouts Farm, TD9 8TH
☎ 01450 860730   (Chris & Sandra Watts)
wattsca@madasafish.com   Map 80/623107
BB **B**   ✕ book first £10, 6-7pm   D2 T1
Ⓥ Ⓑ Ⓓ ⊛🐾👜🚗 ❗

● Galashiels (Selkirk)
Southern Upland Way

Ettrickvale, 33 Abbotsford Road, TD1 3HW ☎ 01896 755224 (Mrs S Field)
www.ettrickvale.co.uk   Map 73/499352
BB **B**   ✕ book first £7, 6-8pm   D1 T2
Ⓥ Ⓑ Ⓓ ⊛🐾👜 ★★★

✉⊷◀ Over Langshaw Farm, TD1 2PE
☎ 01896 860244 (Mrs Sheila Bergius)
www.organicholidays.com   Map 73/514390
BB **B**   ✕ book first £12, approx 7:30pm   D1 F1
Ⓥ Ⓑ Ⓓ ⊛🐾👜❗🐄 ◆◆◆

☆ **Ferniehirst Mill Lodge**
TD8 6PQ ☎ 01835 863279 (Alan & Christine Swanston)
http://ferniehirstmill.co.uk   Map 80/654171
BB **B**   ✕ book first £15, 7:30pm   S2 D2 T4
Ⓥ Ⓑ Ⓓ ⊛🐾👜🐄 ★

A chalet-style guesthouse set in its own grounds of 25 acres beside Jed Water. Large lounge. All rooms en-suite. Home cooking, including vegetarian. Dogs welcome. A country-lover's paradise. Email: ferniehirstmill@aol.com

● Jedburgh
St Cuthbert's Way

✉⊷◀ Riverview, Newmill Farm, TD8 6TH
☎ 01835 862145 (Elizabeth Kinghorn)
http://mysite.freeserve.com/riverviewbandb   Map 74/659227
BB **B**   D2 T1   Closed Nov-Mar   Ⓑ Ⓓ ⊛🐾👜🚗 ★★★

● Kelso

Border Hotel, Woodmarket, TD5 7AX
☎ 01573 224791 (E Galbraith)   BorderHotel@aol.com Map 74/728340
BB **B**   ✕ nearby   S3 D2 T1 F3   Ⓓ🐾🍵

☆ ▣◄ **Border Hotel**
The Green, TD5 8PQ ☎ 01573 420237
http://theborderhotel.com　Map 74/827282
BB **C**　✕ £7, 6-9pm　D2 T3 F1
Ⓥ Ⓑ Ⓓ 🐾🐾⛁🛏️

Attractive old coaching Inn. The Border Hotel is internationally known as the
end of the Pennine Way, and walkers can tactfully claim a free half pint on
completion with a copy of Wainwright's Guide. Also located on the popular
St Cuthbert's Way at the base of the Cheviots, we are a popular walkers hotel.
Chef proprietor uses local produce to create excellent meals.
Family run with local friendly staff.

● **Kirk Yetholm (Kelso)**
　Pennine Way & St Cuthbert's Way
▣◄ Blunty's Mill, TD5 8PG ☎ 01573 420288 (Gail Brooker)
Ggailrowan@aol.com　Map 74/825283
BB **B**　✕ nearby　T2　Ⓓ🐾🐾⛁🚗!🛏️Ⓜ　★★

● **Melrose**
　St Cuthbert's Way & Southern Upland Way
▣◄ Birch House, High Street, TD6 9PB ☎ 01896 822391 (Mrs Julie John)
birchhouse@melrose80.freeserve.co.uk　Map 73/547342
BB **B**　✕ nearby　S1 D1 T1　Ⓑ Ⓓ⊗🐾🐾⛁Ⓜ　★★★

▣◄ The George & Abbotsford Hotel, High St, TD6 9PD
☎ 01896 822308 (Philip & Janette Titley)
www.georgeandabbotsford.co.uk　Map 73/546340
BB **C**　✕ £7, 12-9pm　S6 D8 T15 F1　Ⓥ Ⓑ Ⓓ🐾🐾⛁!🛏️　★★

● **Morebattle (Kelso)**
　St Cuthbert's Way
▣◄ Linton Farm, TD5 8AE ☎ 01573 440362 (Mrs Mary Ralston)
ralston@ecosse.net　Map 74/773264
BB **A**　✕ book first £10　S1 D1 T1　Closed Nov-Feb
Ⓥ Ⓑ Ⓓ⊗🐾🐾⛁🚗!

● **Peebles**
Whitestone House, Innerleithen Road, EH45 8BD
☎ 01721 720337 (Mrs M Muir)
www.aboutscotland.com/peebles/whitestone.html　Map 73/251408
BB **B**　✕ nearby　S1 D1 T2 F1　Ⓓ⊗⛁Ⓜ　★★★

● **Selkirk**
▣◄ Ivy Bank, Hillside Terrace, TD7 4LT ☎ 01750 21270
(Mrs Janet MacKenzie) lannet@aol.com　Map 73/473286
BB **B**　✕ nearby　S1 D1 T1　Closed Jan
Ⓑ Ⓓ🐾🐾⛁🚗!🛏️　★★

● **Traquair (Innerleithen)**
　Southern Upland Way
The School House, EH44 6PL ☎ 01896 830425 (Mrs J A Caird)
www.old-schoolhouse.ndo.co.uk　Map 73/331344
BB **B** ✕ book first £12, 6:30pm　D1 T1 F1　Ⓥ Ⓓ🐾🐾⛁🚗!🛏️　★★

● **Walston (Carnwath)**
▣◄ Walston Mansion Farmhouse, ML11 8NF ☎ 01899 810334
(Margaret Kirby)　kirby-walstonmansion@talk21.com　Map 72/057454
BB **A**　✕ £9, 7pm　D1 T1 F2　Ⓥ Ⓑ Ⓓ🐾🐾⛁🛏️　★★★

STIRLING

● **Aberfoyle**
　Loch Lomond & the Trossachs
　Rob Roy Way
Corrie Glen B&B, Manse Rd, FK8 3XF ☎ 01877 382427
(Pauline & Steven Alexander)　www.corrieglen.com　Map 57/519003
BB **B**　D2 T1　Closed Dec-Feb　Ⓑ Ⓓ⊗🐾🐾⛁　★★★

☆ ▣◄ **Inchrie Castle**
The Trossachs, FK8 3XD ☎ 01877 382347
www.innscotland.com　Map 57/517007
BB **C**　✕ £15, 7-9pm　S6 D19 T17 F3
Ⓥ Ⓑ Ⓓ🐾🐾⛁🛏️　★★★

Surrounded by the stunning beauty
of The Trossachs, Inchrie Castle Inn
has a long and proud tradition of
all that is Scottish. A former keep,
it offers cosy lounges and a fine
restaurant serving only the best of
local produce.

● **Callander**
　Loch Lomond & the Trossachs
　Rob Roy Way
▣◄ Auchenlaich Farmhouse, Keltie Bridge, FK17 8LQ ☎ 01877 331683
(Rita Kyle)　www.incallander.co.uk/auchenlaich　Map 57/649070
BB **B**　✕ book first £10.50, 7-8:30pm　D2 T1 F2　Closed Jan
Ⓥ Ⓑ Ⓓ⊗🐾🐾⛁🚗!🛏️　Bicycle lock-up.

● **Crianlarich**
　Loch Lomond & the Trossachs
　West Highland Way

☆ ▣◄ **Suie Lodge Hotel**
Glen Dochart, FK20 8QT ☎ 01567 820417
www.suielodge.co.uk　Map 51/488278
BB **B**　✕ £6, until 8:30pm　S2 D3 T4 F1
Ⓥ Ⓑ Ⓓ🐾🐾⛁🛏️　★★

Delightful former shooting lodge in scenic
Glen Dochart surrounded by many Munros
and overlooking the river Dochart on the
A85. Comfortable accommodation, TVs,
clock radios in all rooms & CH. Relaxing bar
with open fire. Restaurant offering a wide
range of locally produced Scottish fare.

Drymen (Glasgow)
Loch Lomond & the Trossachs
West Highland Way & Rob Roy Way
Ceardach, Gartness Road, G63 0BH
☎ 01360 660596 (Mrs Betty Robb)   Map 57/477884
BB **B**   ✗ nearby   DI TI FI   Ⓓ ⊗ 🐾 🍴 ! 🛁   ★★

Hillview B&B, The Square, G63 0BL
☎ 01360 661000 (Mrs Irene Mullen)   Map 57/473885
BB **B**   ✗ nearby   SI DI TI FI
Ⓓ ⊗ 🐾 🛁 🍴 ! 🛁

Green Shadows, Buchanan Castle Estate, G63 0HX
☎ 01360 660289 (Gail Lisa Goodwin)
www.visitdrymen.co.uk   Map 57/460887
BB **B**   ✗ nearby   SI DI TI FI   Closed Dec-Jan
Ⓑ Ⓓ 🐾 🛁 🍴 !   ★★★

Falkirk
Ashbank Guest House, 105 Main St, Redding, FK2 9UQ
☎ 01324 716649 (Mrs Betty Ward)
www.bandbfalkirk.com   Map 65/922787
BB **B**   ✗ nearby   DI TI FI   🚌(Polmont)
Ⓑ Ⓓ ⊗ 🐾 🛁 🍴 !   ★★★

Inversnaid (Aberfoyle)
Loch Lomond & the Trossachs
West Highland Way
🚋🍴 Corriearklet B&B, FK8 3TU   ☎ 01877 386208 (Lorraine Martin)
www.corriearklet.scotbiz.net   Map 56/347094
BB **B**   ✗ £12.50, 6-8:30pm   DI TI FI
Ⓥ Ⓓ ⊗ 🐾 🛁 🍴 🛁   ★★

Lochearnhead
Loch Lomond & the Trossachs
Rob Roy Way

☆ **Lochearn House**
FK19 8NR ☎ 01567 830380 (Matthew & Dianne)
www.lochearnhouse.co.uk   Map 51/588239
BB **B**   ✗ book first £18, 6:30pm   D3
Ⓥ Ⓑ Ⓓ ⊗ 🐾 🛁   ★★★★

Set in the beautiful Scottish national park surrounded by lovely walks and on the national cycle route, Matthew and Dianne offer a warm and friendly welcome with excellent food and accommodation. 3 nights dinner and B&B special break from £99.00 pp.

Tyndrum
Loch Lomond & the Trossachs
West Highland Way
🚋🍴 Glengarry House, FK20 8RY ☎ 01838 400224 (Paul & Jen Lilly)
www.glengarryhouse.co.uk   Map 50/329302
BB **B**   ✗ nearby   DI TI FI   🚌(Tyndrum Upper)
Ⓑ Ⓓ ⊗ 🐾 🛁 🍴 !   ★★★   See SC also.

SELF-CATERING

ARGYLL & BUTE

● Dunoon
Loch Lomond & the Trossachs
Lyall Cliff ☎ 01369 702041 (Mr P Norris) www.lyallcliff.co.uk
£200-£550   Sleeps 4-8. 2 houses.
Beautifully situated spacious accommodation on promenade.
Closed Dec   ⊗

● Inveraray
The Anchorage ☎ 07751 105345 (Margaret Muir) www.scottishholidays.co.uk
£230-£350   Sleeps 6 +cot. 1 bungalow.
Loch-facing bungalow, cosy open fire.   ⊗ 🛁   ★★★

● Kilmelford
☎ 01866 844212 (Mrs G H Dalton) www.assc.co.uk/maolachy
£210-£320   Sleeps 1-2 +cot. 1 cottage.
Great walking amongst hills & forests.   Closed Nov-Feb   ★★★Ⓦ

● Oban

☆ **The Melfort Club**
☎ 01852 200257 (Carolyn Stoddart)
www.melfortvillage.co.uk
£325-£995   Sleeps 4-10. 32 cottages.
Local walks booklet available.   🛁   ★★★★

A small holiday village nestled in the hills and oak woods at the head of Loch Melfort, amidst some of the most beautiful scenery on the west coast of Scotland. A really relaxing holiday is guaranteed by the combination of beautifully furnished cottages, excellent leisure facilities and a friendly rural atmosphere.

CENTRAL BELT

● Biggar
Carmichael Cottages ☎ 01899 308336 (Richard Carmichael)
www.carmichael.co.uk/cottages
£180-£595   Sleeps 2-6 . 14 cottages & houses.
Great walking country. Lovely cosy cottages.   ⊗ 🛁★★-★★★★

Anglers Holiday Cottages ☎ 01899 308697 (John or Gwen)
www.anglersholidaycottages.co.uk
£225-£350   Sleeps 4. 1 cottage.
Location southern uplands. Fly-fishing, walks.   ★★★

● **Maybole**

☆ **Balbeg Holiday Lodges**
☎ 01655 770665 (Mrs L Sinclair)
www.balbeg.co.uk
£175-£1,400   Sleeps 4-16. 1 lodge, 2 cottages.
🈂 🐾 ★★★-★★★★

Quality self-catering accommodation in 300 acre country estate.
Excellent base for Galloway Hills (10 mins), within easy reach of Arran, Ben Lomond. Local walks from the front door.
The estate has two playparks, a nature pond, playing field and acres of woodland walks.
Email: info@balbeg.co.uk

DUMFRIES & GALLOWAY

● **Crocketford**
Craigadam ☎ 01556 650233 (Celia Pickup)
www.craigadam.com
£500-£550   Sleeps 6. 1 cottage.
Peacefully situated on organic sheep farm.
🈂 🐾 ★★★★ Access category 2. See B&B also.

● **Moffat**
☎ 0191 290 1461 (Mrs L Shilton) www.14ahighstreet.co.uk
£165-£300   Sleeps 2-5. 1 maisonette.
Excellent base for exploring southern Scotland.   Closed Dec-Jan 🈂

☆ **Holiday Elegance**
☎ 01784 740892 (Fran Considine) www.holidayelegance.co.uk
£240-£420   Sleeps 2-6. 1 apartment.
Luxury refurbished Victorian villa. Splendid views.
🈂 ★★★★

Spacious, elegant, two-bedroomed luxury apartment in prestigious former Victorian villa. Newly refurbished, furnished and equipped to a high standard. Splendid views. Wonderful walks. Overlooks Moffat town and the Moffat Hills. Private parking. Mobile tel: 07977 428223 Email: fran_considine@yahoo.com

---

● **Wigtown**

☆ **Duddingstone Lodge**
☎ 01671 830422 (Hazel Barnes)
www.duddingstonelodge.co.uk
£160-£210   Sleeps 3. 2 cottages.
Ideal for Galloway hills and coast.   🈂

Oak and Elm two cosy wee semi-detached cottages. Quiet location. Ideal base for Galloway Hills, spectacular coastline, numerous gardens and ancient sites. Wigtown, Scotland's National Book Town and Bladnoch Distillery (4 miles). Newton Stewart (10 miles). Torhouse Stones (1 mile).

HIGHLAND

● **Aviemore**
Cairngorms
English Charlie's ☎ 01479 810837 (Penny Weir) www.penspots.co.uk
£250-£350   Sleeps 6.1 flat.
Outstanding location for ramblers/pottery lovers.   🈂 🚶(Aviemore) 🐾

☆ **High Range Chalets**
☎ 01479 810363 (Mrs J Hyatt) www.highrange.co.uk
£210-£590   Sleeps 2-6. 8 chalets.
Peaceful complex with stunning mountain views.
🚶(Aviemore) 🐾 ★★★★

1-3 bedroom chalets sleeping 2-6, providing all that is necessary for your comfort. Situated in its own birch woodland park with magnificent views of the Spey valley and Cairngorm mountains. Five hundred yards from Aviemore centre. Ristorante, pizzeria and bar on site.

● **Boat of Garten**
Cairngorms
Aldon Lodge ☎ 01479 831462 (Mairi Gordon) http://aldonlodge.co.uk
£195-£310   Sleeps 5. 1 house.
Scenic location on Speyside Way. 🚶(Boat of Garten)

● **Fort Augustus**
☎ 01809 501287 (Miss J Ellice) www.ipw.com/aberchalder
£200-£1,400   Sleeps 2-12. 3 varying types.
Deer stalking and fishing.   🈂 🐾

● **Fort William**
Distillery Cottages ☎ 01397 700103 (S Mclean) www.distillerycottages.co.uk
£240-£490   Sleeps 2-4. 3 apartments.
West Highland Way and Ben Nevis.   🈂 🚶(Fort William) 🐾   ★★★
See B&B also.

● **Inveralligin**
Benview ☎ 01445 791333 (Mrs Mary Mackay) inveralligin@aol.com
£200-£330   Sleeps 2-6. 1 cottage.
Ideally situated for climbing and walking.   See B&B also.

● **Invergarry**

☆ **Ardochy House Cottages**
☎ 01809 511292 (Mr C Sangster)
www.ardochy.ukgateway.net
£190-£440   Sleeps 4-6. 3 cottages.
Variety of walks and Munros nearby.   🈂 🐾

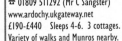

3 traditional cottages grouped around a cobbled courtyard and facing south over Loch Garry and the mountains beyond. Most bedrooms en-suite. C/H in season. Open fire or stove. Drying facilities. Forest and mountain walks and many Munros nearby. Short breaks available.

● Kingussie
Cairngorms

☆ **Landseer House**
☎ 01926 640560 (Mary E Wheildon)
www.carrickhousekingussie.co.uk
£195-£600   Sleeps 5-6 + cot. 2 houses.
For Scotlands mountain peaks & rushing rivers. 〰(Kingussie) ★★★

 Landseer House & Carrick House, 2 comfortable 3-bedroom traditional granite houses at the foothills of both the Cairngorm and Monadhliath mountains offer a splendid base from which to explore the many outdoor activities, spot the wildlife and encompass the district's peace and tranquility. Email: m_e_wheildon@hotmail.com

---

● Lochaline
Rahoy Estate ☎ 01967 421287 (Paul Smith) www.rahoy-estate.com
£185-£330   Sleeps 4. 4 cottages.
Peace and tranquillity close to nature.

● Nethy Bridge
Cairngorms
Speyside Way
Mondhuie ☎ 01479 821062 (David Mordaunt) www.mondhuie.com
£95-£275   Sleeps 3-6. 2 chalets. Owner is a mountaineer.   Closed Nov
〰(Nethy Bridge)   See B&B also.

☆ **John Fleming**
☎ 01479 821643
www.holiday-cairngorm.co.uk
£140-£550   Sleeps 2-7. 4 cottages, 2 bungalows.
Traditional stone-built cottages in large garden. ★★★

 Warm comfortable highland cottages in secluded garden of lawns and mature woodlands, by the Abernethy Reserve one mile from Nethy Bridge in sight of the Cairngorms. Footpaths and bicycle tracks lead directly into the forest and on to the mountains.

● Newtonmore
Cairngorms

☆ **Inveralder Holiday Homes**
☎ 01540 673575 (Alex Gillies)
£175-£395   Sleeps 4-6. 5 cottages.
Cottages are "home from home".
〰(Newtonmore)

 Our quality holiday cottages offer the perfect blend of comfort and value for money, each well equipped and can sleep either four or six. Many of our guests return year after year. You are advised to book early to avoid disappointment.

Crubenbeg Holiday Cottages ☎ 01540 673566 (Jennifer Graham)
www.crubenbeg.com   £240-£450   Sleeps 2-5. 8 cottages.
The walking centre of Scotland. Closed Nov-Jan   ★★★★

● Ullapool
Corran Self-catering ☎ 01854 612501 www.corranullapool.co.uk
£350-£550   Sleeps 6. 1 house.
Traditional village house, hills, sea views

☆ **Mrs P Campbell**
☎ 01854 612107
www.ullapool.co.uk/customhouse
£180-£300   Sleeps 2-4. 1 cottage.
Quiet conservation area, near shops/harbour. Closed Nov-March

 One self-catering cottage sleeping 2-4 people. This cottage is part of a modernised listed sandstone property in a quiet conservation village close to shops, restaurants, the harbour, sea and hills.

ISLE OF ARRAN

● Blackwaterfoot
Lochside ☎ 01770 860276 (Mrs M Bannatyne)
george.bannatyne@virgin.net
£220-£380   Sleeps 2-6. 2 cottages.
Centrally heated, near beach/village. Aga.   See B&B also.

ISLE OF MULL

● Salen
Kilmore House ☎ 01631 770369 (Sarah Scott) www.glenaros.co.uk
£180-£450   Sleeps 4-7. 5 cottages. ★★

ISLE OF SKYE

● Carbost
Forester's House ☎ 01478 640320 (R Van Der Vliet)
bluelobster_grula@yahoo.com   £500-£600 Sleeps 6. 1 cottage.
Walks start from doorstep. Private location.

● Edinbane
☎ 01470 582285 (Mrs Barbara Herbert) www.islandview-skye.co.uk
£165-£275   Sleeps 4. 1 apartment.
Superb sunsets, loch & mountain views. Closed Nov-Mar

NORTH EAST SCOTLAND

● Aboyne
Cairngorms
Glendarven House, Dr Moira Milne ☎ 01339 881601
www.glendavanhouse.com
£800-£1250   Sleeps 10. 1 lodge.
Victorian shooting lodge in nature reserve   ★★★★ RA member

● Kintore

Kingsfield House ☎ 01467 632366 (Mrs J Lumsden)
www.holidayhomesaberdeen.com
£275-£475   Sleeps 4 + cot. 1 cottage.
Tranquil position overlooking fields.   Closed Dec-Feb ★★★★

● Strathdon
Cairngorms

☎ 01956 51371 (M Debremaeker)
£300-£350   Sleeps 4. 1 property.
Scandinavian house in idyllic secluded situation. Closed Nov-Feb

● Tomintoul
Cairngorms

☆ R M Clifford
☎ 01425 277644
robert.clifford@talk21.com
£400-£800   Sleeps 10. 1 house.
★★★★ RA Member

Well appointed modernised former
hunting lodge, large garden, stunning
views, fantastic walks, close to Speyside
Way. Four double rooms each with
en-suite plus two single rooms.
All linen and towels included.

PERTH & KINROSS

● Aberfeldy

Garth House ☎ 01887 830515 (Lady Eveline Bright)
www.garthhouse.co.uk
£215-£650   Sleeps 5-10. 2 apartments.   Well situated for hill walking.

☆ Gamekeepers Cottages & Norwegian Lodges
☎ 01764 652586 (Stephen Brown)
www.monzievaird.com
£335-£880   Sleeps 2-8. 23 lodges, 1 cottage.
★★★★Ⓦ

Gamekeeper's Cottage and Norwegian Lodges in a designated designed landscape.
Beautiful, mature and extensive grounds.
Private and well spread out.
Elevated positions with magnificent views.
Large local path network on our doorstep.
Fishing, horse riding and many other local activities.

● Glenshee
Cairngorms

☆ Finegand Cottages
☎ 01250 885234 (Mrs Shona Haddon) www.finegandestate.com
£153-£388   Sleeps 2-7. 4 cottages.
Individually sited, well equipped, magnificent views.
★★

4 individual traditional highland cottages
in this beautiful glen with its winding
river. South edge of Cairgorm National
Park: 17 Munros nearby; historic walks
such as the Cateran Trail and Lairig Guru.
Small trout loch and wonderful bird life.
Email: finegand@tesco.net

● Pitcairngreen

☆ The Bield
☎ 01738 583606 (Shonagh Mahon)
Mahon4theBield@aol.com
£280-£400   Sleeps 2-4. Converted coach house.
Outstanding quality, renovated within. Mezzanine gallery.

Quality renovated coach house on village
green — when linked with ensuite rooms in
Georgian main house provides group
accommodation for 8-10. Self-catering or
Bed & Breakfast. Gateway to the highlands
and easy access to all the beauty
of Perthshire.

SCOTTISH BORDERS

● Jedburgh

☆ Tweed Cottage
☎ 0191 272 0013 (Helen Grayshan)
tweedcottage@hotmail.com
£180-£540   Sleeps 4 + cot. 1 cottage.
Modern style, fully equipped, facilities nearby.   ★★★★

Cottage with lovely views, peaceful setting, five minutes
walk from town in the heart of the borders.
High standard of comfort.
Facilities include TV, video, CD, dishwasher, private
parking, open plan lounge, veranda for outdoor dining,
linen, towels and electricity all included.

STIRLING

● **Killin**
Loch Lomond & the Trossachs

☆ **Wester Lix Cottages**
☎ 01567 820990 (Mrs Gill Hunt)
www.westerlix.co.uk
£350-£995 Sleeps 4-8. 5 cottages.
Decking, sauna. Loch view. Central location. 🏠 ★★★

5 cottages in a peaceful retreat located in a remote and secluded forest clearing, but at the same time within easy reach of nearby villages and local amenities. Features of the location include our own private loch fed from the burn that runs through the site.

● **Tyndrum**
Loch Lomond & the Trossachs
Glengarry House ☎ 01838 400224 (Paul & Jen Lilly)
www.glengarryhouse.co.uk
£200-£300 Sleeps 4-6. I chalet. West Highland Way, plenty of Munros.
ᴡ(Tyndrum Upper) ⊛ 🏠 ★★ See B&B also.

GROUPS

ISLE OF EIGG

☆ **Glebe Barn Field Centre & Independent Hostel** (B&B/SC)
PH42 4RL ☎ 01687 482417
www.glebebarn.co.uk Map/Grid Ref: 39/483853
B&B £19 Bednight £9 Min 14, max 24
✕ (groups only) 🐾 D ⊛ ! 🚗 See Hostels also

The Glebe Barn Hostel & Outdoor Centre is a conversion of a 19th century barn with magnificent views across the mainland. We provide comfortable self-catering accommodation for large groups, families and individual backpackers.

PERTH & KINROSS

The Atholl Centre (B&B/SC) Atholl Rd, Pitlochry PH16 5BX
☎ 01796 473044 (Jean Marzetti) http://athollcentre.users.btopenworld.com
BB £20, SC £1,540 Min 2, max 34 ✕ 🐾 ᴡ(Pitlochry)
B D ⊛ See B&B also

HOSTELS, BUNKHOUSES & CAMPSITES

HIGHLAND

Bunroy Park Camping Site (C) Roy Bridge, Inverness-shire
☎ 01397 712332 www.bunroycamping.co.uk Map 41/274806
Camping £4.50pn Closed Nov-Feb
🏕nearby ᴡ(Roy Bridge) ★★★★

Sail Mhor Croft Hostel (IH) Dundonnell, Ross-shire IV23 2QT
☎ 01854 633224 www.sailmhor.co.uk Map 19/064983
Bednight £9.50 D ⊛

Shemas Backpackers Lodge (IH) Mallaig, Inverness-shire ☎ 01687 462764
Bednight £13 ✕nearby ᴡ(Mallaig) D ⊛

Sleeperzzz.com (IH) Rogart Station, Sutherland ☎ 01408 641343
(Kate Roach) www.sleeperzzz.com Map 16/725019
Bednight £10 ✕ nearby ᴡ(Rogart) Railway carriages! D ⊛

ISLE OF EIGG

Glebe Barn Field Centre & Independent Hostel (IH/OC) PH42 4RL
☎ 01687 482417 www.glebebarn.co.uk Map 39/483853
Bednight £10-£12 Closed for individual bookings Oct-Apr
D ⊛ See Groups also

PUBS & TEAROOMS

PERTH & KINROSS

● **Birnam (By Dunkeld)**
☕ Katie's Tearoom, Perth Rd, PH8 0AA
☎ 01350 727223 (Katie Dalgliesh)
www.birnamautopoint.co.uk Map 52,53/030419
✕ ᴡ(Dunkeld) V ♨ ⊛ ⑧(☺) Internet access.

STIRLING

● **Balmaha**
Loch Lomond & the Trossachs
West Highland Way
🍷 Oak Tree Inn, Balmaha, G63 0JQ
☎ 01360 870357 (Linda Gow)
www.oak-tree-inn.co.uk Map 56/421907 ✕
V ♨ ♪ (Recorded) L G ⊛ ⑧(D) ↵

WALKING HOLIDAYS
BRITAIN

Byways Breaks, 25 Mayville Road, Liverpool L18 OHG Tel 0151 722 8050 Web www.byways-breaks.co.uk Self-led walking & cycling holidays. Flexible routes, comfortable accommodation, luggage transported. Covers: Shropshire, Welsh borders, Offa's Dyke, Cheshire

Bob Close Coach Assisted Walking Holidays, 40 Spring Hill, Kingswood, Bristol, BS15 1XT. Tel 01179 672459 Fax 01179 671986 Web www.bobswalkingholidays.co.uk Coach assisted walking holidays. Long distance walks 7-8 days. No leader. Choose your distance. Youth Hostel accommodation. Small friendly groups. Coach carries your luggage. Covers: UK

Tread Suffolk, French's Farm, Debach, Woodbridge, IP13 6BZ Tel 01473 277126 Fax 01473 737756 Email maggie@treadsuffolk.co.uk Web www.treadsuffolk.co.uk Guided walking breaks. Farmhouse based, transport to walks, friendly atmosphere. Covers: East Suffolk, Coastals, Rivers, Market towns

Instep Linear Walking Holidays, 35 Cokeham Road, Lancing, West Sussex, BN15 0AE Tel 01903 766475 Fax 01903 766475 Email walking@instephols.co.uk Web www.instephols.co.uk Coast to Coast Merchandise, Tee & Sweatshirts, Badges, Videos, Maps, Guide Books. Covers: Cumbria, The Dales, North Yorkshire

Wycheway Country Walks, 39 Sandpiper Crescent, Malvern, Worcestershire WR14 1UY Tel 01886 833828 Email enquiries@wychewaycountrywalks.co.uk Web www.wychewaycountrywalks.co.uk Guided & self-guided walking holidays, Monarch's Way, Cotswold Way, Teme Valley. Covers: England and Wales, focus on Herefordshire & Worcestershire

Walking Support- Booking and Guiding Service, 2 Wembley Terrace, Melrose, Roxburghshire TD6 9QR Tel 01896 822079 Web www.walkingsupport.co.uk Booking & guiding service for walkers, supported with comprehensive route websites. Covers: Scotland and North England

celtic trails – a different walking experience

"A wonderful getaway experience in every aspect. Spectacular walking and scenery, excellent accommodation; first-class organisation and service " **Experience the difference**

The best Independent Walking holidays in England, Scotland and Wales - and some in Europe too! **Please visit us at www.bestbritishwalks.com** For help and information please contact us at tel .**01600 860846;** fax. **01600 860843;** e-mail. **info@bestbritishwalks.com**

Celtic Trails

ENGLAND

Archaeology Holidays – Lindum Heritage, 7 Ridgeway, Nettleham, Lincolnshire, LN2 2TL Tel 01522 851388 Email info@lindumheritage.co.uk Web **www.lindumheritage.co.uk** Archaeology and history short breaks, historic setting. Excavation. Free brochure. Covers: Archeology, history, UK holidays, short breaks

Bath & West Country Walks, Osmington, Brewery Lane, Holcombe, Bath BA3 5EG Tel 01761 233807 Email info@bathwestwalks.com Web **www.bathwestwalks.com** Guided and self-guided walking holidays. Enquire about Rambler's group rates. Covers: Cotswolds, Exmoor, Mendip Hills, Somerset, Wiltshire

Footprints of Sussex, Pear Tree Cottage, Jarvis Lane, Steyning, West Sussex BN44 3GL Tel 01903 813381 Fax 01903 816533 Web www.footprintsofsussex.co.uk 7/9 night holidays on the South Downs Way, including baggage transfers Covers: South Downs

Overdale, 29 Howard Ave., West Wittering, Chichester PO20 8EX Tel 01243 670233 Email alan.bloss@btinternet.com Web **www.walkoverdale.co.uk** Itineraries designed to your own specification in regions of your own choice. Route planning, accommodation, luggage transfer, supporting information. Covers: N and S Downs, Wye Valley, Pembs. Coast or your own choice

Curlew Guided Walking, 26 De Vitre Cottages, Ashton Road, Lancaster LA1 5AN Tel 01524 35601 Email curlewgw@globalnet.co.uk Web **www.users.globalnet.co.uk/~curlewgw** Walking holidays and short breaks, comfortable accommodation and transport included. Covers: Lake District, Yorkshire Dales, Hadrian's Wall and other areas of Northern England

Orchard Trails, 5 Orchard Way, Horsmonden, Tonbridge, Kent TN12 8JX Tel 01892 722680 Fax 01892 722680 Email Grabham@btinternet.com Web **www.kent-esites.co.uk/orchardtrails** Unescorted walking/cycling holidays. Kent and East Sussex. Luggage transported. Covers: Kent, East Sussex

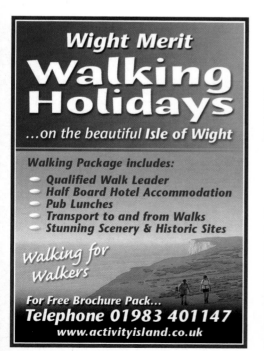

ENGLAND continued

Celtic Trails, PO Box 11, Chepstow, Monmouthshire, NP16 6ZD. Tel 01600 860846 Fax 01600 860843 Email info@bestbritishwalks.com Quality walking holidays, luggage transfer, short breaks. High standard service and organisation. Covers: Cotswold Way, Hadrians Wall Path, Dales Way, Norfolk Coast Path, South West Coast Path, Exmoor and Dartmoor, Offa's Dyke Path, Wye Valley Walk

Pace the Peaks, Cumbria House, 1 Derwentwater Place, Keswick, Cumbria, CA12 4DR Tel 017687 73171 Email cathy@pacethepeaks.co.uk Web www.pacethepeaks.co.uk Explore the Lakeland Fells with Cathy. Guided Walking and Navigation for individuals and groups. Accommodation at Cumbria House, Keswick. Covers: Lake District, Cumbria

Brigantes Walking Holidays, Rookery Cottage, Kirkby Malham, Skipton, N.Yorks BD23 4BX Tel 01729 830463 Fax 01729 830463 Self-guided walking holidays and baggage couriers throughout Northern England. Covers: Northern England

WALES

Dragon Trails, Myrtle Cottage, Welsh Newton Common, Monmouth, Wales NP25 5RT Email **richard@dragontrails.com** Tel 01989 770606 Guided walking on West Wales coast, full board in beautiful country house. Pembrokeshire Coast, Preseli Hills, Teifi Valley

Hillscape Walking Holidays, Blaen-y-ddôl, Pontrhydygroes, SY25 6DS Tel 01974 282640 Web **www.wales-walking.co.uk** Self-guided walking specialists. 40 various routes. Exceptional 3-star hospitality/ accommodation. Covers: Cambrian Mountains, Cambrian Way, Ceredigion Coast

Edge of Wales Walk, 1 Dolfor, Aberdaron, Gwynydd, LL53 8BP Tel 01758 760652, Fax 01758 760582 Email enquiries@edgeofwales.co.uk Web **www.edgeofwales.co.uk**. Walking holidays on the Llŷn Peninsula – Accommodation, transport, luggage transfer. Covers: The Llŷn Peninsula in North Wales

Celtic Trails, PO Box 11, Chepstow, Monmouthshire, NP16 6ZD. Email **info@bestbritishwalks.com** Tel 01600 860846 Fax 01600 860843 Quality walking holidays, luggage transfer, short breaks. High standard service and organisation. Pembrokeshire Coastpath, Offa's Dyke, Wye Valley Walk, 3 Castles Walk, Glyndwrs Way, Snowdonia Trail & Northern Cambrian Way

SCOTLAND

Celtic Trails, PO Box 11, Chepstow, Monmouthshire, NP16 6ZD. Email **info@bestbritishwalks.com**. Tel 01600 860846 Fax 01600 860843 Quality walking holidays, luggage transfer, short breaks. High standard service and organisation. Covers: West Highland Way, Great Glen Way. Rob Roy Trail, Cataran Trail, St Cuthberts Way, Southern Upland Way.

SCOTLAND continued

Lomond Walking Holidays

(est.1996) Guided, fully supported, all inclusive walking holidays in Scotland and Northern England from £299

West Highland Way fully inc 7 days £399 • Great Glen, Speyside, St Cuthbert's, • Rob Roy and Hadrian's Wall trails • Cape Wrath Trail & Scottish 2 week coast to coast Guides, luggage transfers, mini-bus backup, quality accom. Also mountain walking • April-October 2005 Brochure • 5 Burnside, Kippen FK8 3EF • 01786 870456 www.walkingholidaysuk.com • Paul@milligan.force9.co.uk

GLEN AFFRIC WALKING FESTIVAL 3-5 JUNE 2005

12 low level and 6 hill walks (including several Munros) in the National Nature Reserve Wildlife, bird watching, conservation, heritage, evening entertainment

Contact: GLEN AFFRIC WALKING FESTIVAL, c/o P. Lebrun 1 Shenval, Glenurquhart, IV63 6TW Tel/fax: 01456 476 363 Email: lebrunshenval@hotmail.com www.glenaffric.info

About Argyll Walking Holidays, Letters Lodge South, Strathlachlan, Argyll PA27 8BZ Tel 01369 860272 Fax 01369 860272 Email info@aboutargyll.co.uk Web www.aboutargyll.co.uk Guided walking holidays designed for people who like to explore the beautiful countryside and discover the secrets of its history and wildlife. Covers: South-West Highlands & Islands of Scotland.

North-West Frontiers, Tigh na Creig, Garve Road, Ullapool, IV26 2SX Tel 01854 612 628 Fax 01854 612 628 Email info@nwfrontiers.com Web www.nwfrontiers.com Guided small group walking & special interest holidays in NW Scotland since 1986. Covers: Scottish Highlands & Islands, Orkney, Shetland, Faroes

IRELAND

USEFUL CONTACTS
NATIONAL GOVERNMENTS

CABE
(Commission for Architecture and the Built Environment)
☎ 020 7960 2400
www.cabe.org.uk

CABE Space
(Parks and public open spaces)
www.cabespace.org.uk
Non-departmental public body championing the creation of great buildings and public spaces.

CADW – Welsh Historic Monuments
☎ 029 2050 0200
www.cadw.wales.gov.uk
Guardian of the built heritage in Wales.

Countryside Agency
☎ 01242 521381
www.countryside.gov.uk

Countryside access helpline:
☎ 0845 100 3298
www.countrysideaccess.gov.uk

Walking the way to Health Initiative:
☎ 01242 533258
www.whi.org.uk

Countryside Council for Wales – Cyngor Cefn Gwylad Cymru
☎ 0845 130 6229
www.ccw.gov.uk

Countryside code website:
www.codcefngwlad.org.uk
Wildlife conservation authority and advisor on sustaining natural beauty, wildlife and the opportunity for outdoor enjoyment in Wales and its inshore waters, including overseeing National Trails.

Directgov
www.direct.gov.uk
Principal internet portal for government departments and services.

UK Resilience
(emergency information):
www.ukresilience.info

DCMS (Department for Culture, Media and Sport)
☎ 020 7211 6200
www.culture.gov.uk

Defence Estates
(manages MoD lands)
☎ 0121 311 2140
www.defence-estates.mod.uk
Information on access to MoD lands and contact telephone numbers for details of firing times.

Defra
(Department for Environment, Food & Rural Affairs)
☎ 0845 933 5577
www.defra.gov.uk

Conservation Walks register:
countrywalks.defra.gov.uk
Lists walks in England on countryside managed under environmental schemes providing public access.

Department for Transport (DfT)
☎ 020 7944 8300
www.dft.gov.uk

Highway Code online (rules and advice for all road users):
www.highwaycode.gov.uk

In Town Without My Car (Car-free day):
www.itwmc.gov.uk

English Heritage
☎ 0870 333 1181
www.english-heritage.org.uk

Hadrian's Wall Unit:
☎ 01434 605088
Responsible for protecting many of England's historic buildings, landscapes and archaeological sites, including many properties open to the public.

English Nature
☎ 01733 455000
www.english-nature.org.uk
Champions the conservation of wildlife and natural features.

Environment Agency
Head Office:
☎ 0870 850 6506
Midlands Region (for Severn Way information): ☎ 0870 850 6506
www.environment-agency.gov.uk
Responsible for protecting and enhancing the environment, including maintaining flood defences and rivers.

Forestry Commission
☎ 0845 367 3787
www.forestry.gov.uk
Protects and expands Britain's forests and woodlands and increases their value to society and the environment, both by managing its own woodlands and making grants to other landowners. Work in England, Scotland and Wales is now devolved.

Highway Authorities: see Local Authorities (p 304)

Historic Scotland
☎ 0131 668 8600
www.historic-scotland.gov.uk
Agency of the Scottish Executive that safeguards Scotland's built heritage.

MAGIC
(Multi-Agency Geographic Information for the Countryside)
www.magic.gov.uk
Project to create a single website for rural and countryside information about England on the web, including mapping boundaries of protected areas. Partnership of the Countryside Agency, DEFRA, English Heritage, English Nature, the Environment Agency, Forestry Commission, ODPM.

Met Office
☎ 0870 900 0100
www.metoffice.com
Official weather service with very informative website.

Ministry of Defence: see Defence Estates

NATIONAL GOVERNMENTS continued

**National Assembly for Wales –
Cynulliad Cenedlaethol Cymru**
☎ 029 2082 5111
www.wales.gov.uk

NHS (National Health Service)
☎ 020 7210 4850
www.nhs.uk

NHS Direct (medical advice and
information): ☎ 0845 4647

**Office of the Deputy Prime
Minister**
☎ 020 7944 4400
Deals with planning, regional and local
government.
www.odpm.gov.uk

Ordnance Survey
☎ 0845 605 0505
www.ordnancesurvey.co.uk
*Buy a map on www.ramblers.org.uk and the
Ramblers' Association earns a commission to
help fund its work for walkers at no extra*

*cost to you. Government mapping agency,
with products including large scale maps
for walkers. Promotes navigation courses
in association with Expedition Company.*

**Scottish Avalanche Information
Service**
www.sais.gov.uk
Forecasts for five key climbing areas in
Scotland during the winter season.

**Scottish Environmental
Protection Agency**
(SEPA)
☎ 01786 457700
www.sepa.org.uk
Aims to provide an efficient and
integrated environmental protection
system that will both improve the
environment and contribute to
sustainable development.

Scottish Executive
☎ 0131 556 8400
www.scotland.gov.uk

Scottish Natural Heritage
☎ 0131 447 4784
www.snh.org.uk
Responsible for the care, improvement
and responsible enjoyment of Scotland's
natural heritage.

**Sports Council for Wales –
Cyngor Chwaraeon Cymru** and
Welsh Institute for Sport
☎ 029 2030 0500
www.sports-council-wales.co.uk

Sport England
(English Sports Council)
☎ 0845 850 8508
www.sportengland.org

SportScotland
(Scottish Sports Council)
☎ 0131 317 7200
www.sportscotland.org.uk

Outdoor Training Centre:
☎ 01479 861256
www.glenmorelodge.org.uk

AREAS OF OUTSTANDING NATURAL BEAUTY AND FOREST PARKS

Arnside/Silverdale AONB
Management Service
☎ 01524 761034
www.arnsidesilverdaleaonb.org.uk

**Association for AONBs –
Cymdeithas dros AoHNE**
☎ 01451 862007
www.aonb.org.uk

Blackdown Hills Project
☎ 01823 680681
www.blackdown-hills.net

Cannock Chase AONB
☎ 01889 882613
Museum of Cannock Chase:
☎ 01543 877666
Visitor centre:
☎ 01543 876741
Forest centre (Forestry Commission):
☎ 01889 586593
www.cannockchasedc.gov.uk/
cannockchase/countryside.htm

Chichester Harbour Conservancy
☎ 01243 512301
www.conservancy.co.uk

Cornwall AONB Partnership
☎ 01872 322350
www.cornwall-aonb.gov.uk

Chilterns Conservation Board
☎ 01844 271300
www.chilternsaonb.org
Chiltern Society:
☎ 01494 771250
www.chilternsociety.org.uk

**Clwydian Range –
Bryniau Clwyd**
☎ 01352 810614
www.denbighshire.gov.uk
(under Countryside Services)

Cotswolds AONB Partnership
☎ 01451 862000
www.cotswoldsaonb.com

**Cranborne Chase &
West Wiltshire Downs** AONB
☎ 01725 516925
www.dorsetcc.gov.uk/cranborne
chase

Dedham Vale & Stour Valley
Countryside Project
☎ 01473 583176
www.dedhamvalestourvalley.org

Dorset AONB Partnership
☎ 01305 224279
www.dorsetaonb.org.uk

East Devon
AONB Partnership
☎ 01395 517557
www.eastdevonaonb.org.uk

East Hampshire: see South Downs
under National Parks

Forest of Bowland AONB
☎ 01772 534140
www.forestofbowland.com

Gower AONB
☎ 01792 635741
www.goweraonb.org

High Weald AONB
☎ 01580 879500
www.highweald.org

Howardian Hills AONB
☎ 01653 627164
www.howardianhills.org.uk

Isle of Anglesey – Ynys Môn
AONB – AHNE
☎ 01248 752429
www.anglesey.gov.uk

Isle of Wight AONB
☎ 01983 823855
www.wightaonb.org.uk

Isles of Scilly AONB
☎ 01720 423486
www.ios-aonb.info

Kent Downs AONB
☎ 01622 221522
www.kentdowns.org.uk

Kielder Partnership
☎ 01434 220643 www.kielder.org

Lincolnshire Wolds
Countryside Service
☎ 01507 609740
www.lincswolds.org.uk

Llyn Planning and Economic
Development Department
☎ 01758 704083
www.gwynedd.gov.uk

Malvern Hills AONB
☎ 01684 560616
www.malvernhillsaonb.org.uk

Mendip Hills
Charterhouse Centre
☎ 01761 462338
www.mendiphillsaonb.org.uk

Nidderdale AONB Project
☎ 01423 712950
www.nidderdaleaonb.org.uk

Norfolk Coast Partnership
☎ 01328 850530
www.norfolkcoastaonb.org.uk

North Devon Coast and
Countryside Service
☎ 01237 423655
(Includes Braunton Burrows Biosphere
Reserve)
www.northdevon-aonb.org.uk

North Pennines AONB Partnership
☎ 01388 528801
www.northpennines.org.uk

North Wessex Downs AONB
☎ 01488 685440
www.northwessexdowns.org.uk

Northumberland Coast AONB
Countryside Services
☎ 01670 534088
www.northumberland.gov.uk

Quantock Hills AONB
☎ 01278 732845
www.quantockhills.com

Shropshire Hills AONB
☎ 01588 674080
www.shropshirehillsaonb.co.uk

Solway Coast Discovery Centre
☎ 016973 33055
www.solwaycoastaonb.org.uk

South Devon AONB
☎ 01803 861384
www.southdevonaonb.org.uk

South Hampshire Coast AONB
☎ 023 8028 5356
www.hants.gov.uk/coast

Suffolk Coast and Heaths
Project
☎ 01394 384948
www.suffolkcoastandheaths.org

Surrey Hills AONB Partnership
☎ 01372 220653
www.surreyhills.org

Sussex Downs: see South Downs
under National Parks

Tamar Valley Service
☎ 01579 351681
www.tamarvalley.org.uk

Wye Valley AONB
☎ 01600 713977
www.wyevalleyaonb.co.uk

COMMUNITY FORESTS

Forest of Avon
Ashton Court Visitor Centre
☎ 0117 953 2141
www.forestofavon.org.uk

Central Scotland Forest
☎ 01501 822015
www.csct.co.uk

Forest of Marston Vale
The Forest Centre ☎ 01234 767037
www.marstonvale.org

Forest of Mercia Chasewater
Country Park ☎ 01543 370737
www.forestofmercia.co.uk

**Great Western Community
Forest** ☎ 01793 466324
www.forestweb.org.uk

**The Greenwood Community
Forest** Partnership Team Office
☎ 01623 758231
www.greenwoodforest.org.uk

Mersey Forest
☎ 01925 816217
www.merseyforest.org.uk

National Forest
☎ 01283 551211
www.nationalforest.org

Red Rose Forest Dock Office
☎ 0161 872 1660
www.redroseforest.co.uk

South Yorkshire Forest
☎ 0114 257 1199
www.syforest.co.uk

Greensites website:
www.greensites.co.uk
South Yorkshire interactive environmental
website with walking information.

Tees Forest
☎ 01642 300716
www.teesforest.org.uk

Thames Chase Forest Centre
☎ 01708 641880
www.thameschase.org.uk

**Watling Chase Community
Forest**
Countryside Management Service
☎ 01992 555256
http://enquire.hertscc.gov.uk/
cms/wccf/default.htm

ENVIRONMENT & COUNTRYSIDE

BEN
(Black Environment Network)
☎ 01286 870715
www.ben-network.org.uk
Promotes equality of opportunity with
respect to ethnic communities in the
preservation, protection and development
of the environment.

BTCV
(British Trust for Conservation
Volunteers)
☎ 01302 572244
www.btcv.org
The UK's largest practical conservation
charity helping volunteers take hands-on
action to improve the rural and urban
environment including improving access to
the outdoors. Also runs Natural Breaks
conservation holidays.

**Campaign to Protect Rural
England** (CPRE)
☎ 020 7981 2800
www.cpre.org.uk
Promotes the beauty, tranquillity and
diversity of rural England by encouraging
the sustainable use of land and other
natural resources in town and country.
See also Campaign for the Protection of
Rural Wales, ruralScotland.

CPRW/YDCW (Campaign for the
Protection of Rural Wales – Ymgyrch
Diogelu Cymru Wledig)
☎ 01938 552525
www.cprw.org.uk
Aims to help the conservation and
enhancement of the landscape,
environment and amenities of the
countryside, towns and villages of rural

Wales. See also Campaign to Protect Rural
England, ruralScotland.

ENCAMS
(Environmental Campaigns)
☎ 01942 612639
www.encams.org.uk
Environmental charity aiming to achieve
litter free and sustainable environments by
working with community groups, local
authorities, businesses and other partners.
Formerly Keep Britain Tidy campaign; also
runs Keep Wales Tidy and Keep Scotland
Beautiful.

**Environmental Transport
Association** (ETA)
☎ 0800 212810
www.eta.co.uk
Campaigns for a sound and sustainable
transport system and provides an

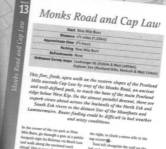

environmental alternative to the other motoring organisations.

Everyone campaign: See Scottish Environment LINK

Friends of the Earth England, Wales and Northern Ireland
☎ 020 7490 1555
www.foe.co.uk
Scotland: ☎ 0131 554 9977
www.foe-scotland.org.uk
The world's largest federation of environmental campaigning groups.

Greenpeace UK
☎ 020 7865 8100
www.greenpeace.org.uk
Researches and campaigns on the environment using non-violent direct action.

Groundwork UK
☎ 0121 236 8565
www.groundwork.org.uk
Federation of trusts working in poor areas to help build sustainable communities through joint environmental action.

IWA
(Inland Waterways Association)
☎ 01923 711114
www.waterways.org.uk
Campaigns for the conservation, use, maintenance, restoration and development of inland waterways in England and Wales. See also Scottish Inland Waterways Association.

John Muir Trust
☎ 0131 554 0114
www.jmt.org
Conserves and protects wild places by acquisition; currently owns seven areas in the Scottish Highlands and Islands totalling 20,000ha/50,000 acres.

Keep Britain Tidy: See ENCAMS

National Trust
☎ 0870 609 5380
Wales: ☎ 01492 860123
www.nationaltrust.org.uk
Protects, through ownership, countryside, coastline and historic buildings in England, Wales and Northern Ireland.

National Trust for Scotland
☎ 0131 243 9300
www.nts.org.uk
Protects, through ownership, countryside, coastline and historic buildings.

Open Spaces Society
☎ 01491 573535
www.oss.org.uk
Works to protect common land and footpaths in England and Wales.

***rural*Scotland**
(Association for the Protection of Rural Scotland)
☎ 0131 225 7012
www.aprs.org.uk

ELECTRONIC MAPS

Anquet Maps
☎ 0845 270 9020 www.anquet.co.uk

Hillwalker (ISYS)
☎ 0845 943 1533 www.hillwalker.org.uk

memory-map
☎ 0870 740 9040
www.memory-map.co.uk

TrackLogs
☎ 01298 872537 www.tracklogs.co.uk

For Ordnance Survey maps: see National Governments

Scotland's rural champion. See also Campaign for the Protection of Rural Wales, Campaign for the Protection of Rural England.

RSPB (Royal Society for the Protection of Birds)
☎ 01767 680551
Scotland: ☎ 0131 311 6500
Wales: ☎ 029 2035 3000
www.rspb.org.uk
Works for a healthy environment rich in birds and wildlife, including managing over 150 nature reserves.

Scottish Environment LINK
☎ 01738 630804
www.scotlink.org
Everyone campaign
www.everyonecan.org
Voluntary organisations working together to care for and improve Scotland's heritage for people and nature. Also manages the LEARN project. See also Wildlife and Countryside Link.

Scottish Inland Waterways Association
www.siwa.org.uk
Coordinates the conservation and use of the waterway network. See also IWA.

Scottish Wildlife Trust
☎ 0131 312 7765
www.swt.org.uk
Protects all forms of wildlife and the environment, with over 120 reserves. Part of The Wildlife Trusts network.

Transport 2000
☎ 020 7613 0743
www.transport2000.org.uk
National campaign for environmental and sustainable transport.

Way to go campaign:
www.way-to-go.org.uk
Joint campaign to pressure the

government to put more emphasis on walking, cycling and public transport in its next transport plan, supported by various organisations including the Ramblers' Association.

Wildlife and Countryside Link
☎ 020 7820 8600
www.wcl.org.uk
Liaison service for all the major non-governmental organisations in the UK concerned with the protection of wildlife and the countryside. See also Scottish Environment LINK.

Wildlife Helpline National Service
☎ 01522 544245
www.wildlifehelpline.org.uk
Information on the identification of British wildlife and wild flowers and contacts for wildlife organisations.

Wildlife Trusts
☎ 0870 036 7711
www.wildlifetrusts.org
Partnership of 46 local groups throughout Britain and junior group Wildlife Watch protecting wildlife in town and countryside, and maintaining 2,400 nature reserves.

Woodland Trust
☎ 01476 581111
Scotland: ☎ 01764 662554
Wales: ☎ 01686 412508
www.woodland-trust.org.uk
Protects Britain's native woodland heritage by conserving and managing over 1,000 sites, all with public access, and creating new woodlands. Also conservation holidays.

WWF-UK
☎ 01483 426444
www.wwf.org.uk
Aims to conserve and protect endangered species and address global threats to nature.

NATIONAL PARKS

Association of National Park Authorities
☎ 029 2049 9966
www.anpa.gov.uk

Brecon Beacons – Bannau Brycheiniog Visitor centre (Mountain centre)
☎ 01874 623366
www.breconbeacons.org

Brecon Beacons Park Society – Cymdeithas Parc Bannau Brycheiniog
☎ 01639 730179
www.breconbeaconspark society.org

The Broads Broads Authority
☎ 01603 610734
www.broads-authority.gov.uk

Cairngorms National Park Authority
☎ 01479 873535
www.cairngorms.co.uk

Council for National Parks
☎ 020 7924 4077
Wales office:
☎ 029 2045 0433
www.cnp.org.uk
Works to protect and enhance the National Parks of England and Wales, and areas that merit National Park status and promote understanding and quiet enjoyment of them for the benefit of all.

Cymdeithas Eryri – Snowdonia Society
☎ 01690 720287
www.snowdonia-society.org.uk
Works to protect Snowdonia National Park. See also Snowdonia – Eryri

Dartmoor
☎ 01822 890414
www.dartmoor-npa.gov.uk

Dartmoor Preservation Association (DPA)
☎ 01822 890646
www.dartmoorpreservation.com
Aims to protect, preserve and enhance the natural beauty, cultural heritage and scientific interest of Dartmoor, and to preserve public access and commoners' rights.

Exmoor Dulverton Visitor Centre
☎ 01398 323841
www.exmoor-nationalpark.gov.uk

Friends of the Lake District
☎ 01539 720788
www.fld.org.uk
Cares for the countryside and wildlife of the Lake District.

Lake District Brockhole Visitor Centre ☎ 015394 46601

Loch Lomond & The Trossachs National Park ☎ 0845 345 4978
www.lochlomond-trossachs.org

New Forest Lymington Visitor Information Centre
☎ 01590 689000
www.thenewforest.co.uk
The New Forest was designated as a national park in June 2004, and it is expected to open in 2006.

North York Moors
Moors Information Centre:
☎ 01439 772737
Park Information Centre:
☎ 01845 597426
www.moors.uk.net

Northumberland National Park Authority
Once Brewed Visitor Centre
☎ 01434 344396
www.northumberland-national-park.org.uk

Peak District National Park Authority
☎ 01629 816200
www.peakdistrict.org
Visitor information:
www.visitpeakdistrict.com

Pembrokeshire Coast – Arfordir Penfro Visitor Centre ☎ 01437 720392
stdavids.pembrokeshirecoast.org.uk

Scottish Council for National Parks ☎ 01505 682447
www.scnp.org.uk
Works to protect and enhance National Parks in Scotland and to promote the case for new national parks.

Snowdonia – Eryri Information Centre ☎ 01690 710426.
See also Cymdeithas Eryri – Snowdonia Society.

Society of Sussex Downsmen
☎ 01273 771906
www.sussexdownsmen.org.uk
Aims to preserve and protect the South Downs.

South Downs
Sussex Downs Conservation Board:
☎ 01243 558700

East Hampshire: ☎ 023 9259 1362
www.vic.org.uk
These two adjoining AONBs work to protect, conserve and enhance the natural beauty of the South Downs. A public consultation is currently being carried out on government proposals to designate this area as a national park, with a decision expected in 2005.

South Downs Campaign
☎ 01273 563358
www.southdownscampaign.org.uk
Grouping of organisations including the Ramblers campaigning for the adoption of the South Downs as a National Park.

Yorkshire Dales
☎ 01969 650456 or ☎ 01756 752748
Visitor centre, Hawes
☎ 01969 667450
www.destinationdales.org

MISCELLANEOUS

BBC
(British Broadcasting Corporation)
☎ 0870 010 0222
www.bbc.co.uk
Excellent online news service at
www.bbc.co.uk/news

British Red Cross
☎ 020 7235 5454
www.redcross.org.uk
Cares for people in crisis by supporting the statutory rescue, health and welfare services, and providing first aid training.

GSM Association
☎ +353 (0)1 269 5922
Mobile phone providers' trade association for Britain and Ireland.
www.gsmworld.com

RADAR (Royal Association for Disability and Rehabilitation)
☎ 020 7250 3222
Minicom 020 7250 4119
www.radar.org.uk
Run by and for disabled people to campaign and advise on disability issues

St Andrew's Ambulance Association
☎ 0141 332 4031
www.firstaid.org.uk
Scotland's premier provider of first aid training and services.

St John Ambulance
☎ 0870 010 4950
www.sja.org.uk
St John Supplies (trading arm):
☎ 020 7278 7888
www.stjohnsupplies.co.uk
Leading first aid, transport and care charity in England, Northern Ireland, Channel Islands and Isle of Man.

St John Ambulance Wales
☎ 029 2062 9308
www.stjohnwales.co.uk
Teaches first aid and life-saving skills in Wales.

TRANSPORT AGENCIES AND OPERATORS

British Waterways
☎ 01923 226422
www.britishwaterways.co.uk
Leisure information on waterways
including walking:
www.waterscape.com
Responsible for the maintenance and
safety of most of Britain's canal network:
over 3,200km of waterways, including
towpaths.

National Rail Enquiries
☎ 0845 748 4950, textphone 0845 605 0600
www.nationalrail.co.uk
Rail tickets: **www.thetrainline.com**

Taxi information for all stations in
mainland Britain **www.traintaxi.co.uk**
Taxi phone numbers including
by SMS and WAP
www.cabnumbers.com

Public transport websites gateway
www.pti.org.uk

National Express
(England, Wales, international)
☎ 0870 580 8080, textphone 0121 455 0086
www.nationalexpress.com
Citylink (Scotland): ☎ 0870 550 5050
www.citylink.co.uk

Network Rail
☎ 0845 711 4141
www.networkrail.com
National Rail Enquiries
☎ 0845 748 4950
www.nationalrail.co.uk
Not-for-profit company managing the
day-to-day running of the infrastructure of
Britain's national rail network.

Transport for London
☎ 020 7222 1234
www.tfl.gov.uk/walking
Walking leaflet orders: select Leaflets and
Information on walking website or
☎ 0870 240 6094
Public transport enquiries: use journey
planner at **www.tfl.gov.uk**

Traveline
☎ 0870 608 2608
Textphone 0870 241 2216
www.traveline.org.uk
Bus, metro/underground, tram/light rail
and ferry information. Website links to all
available journey planners.

Tripscope
Helpline ☎/minicom 0845 758 5641
www.tripscope.org.uk
Provides travel advice and transport
information for people with disabilities.

TOURISM

Tourist Information
For your local tourist or visitor
information centre, see your phonebook.
The local centre can give you numbers of
centres in other areas, or you can find a
full list at **www.visitbritain.com**

VisitBritain
☎ 020 8846 9000 (not an information line: for
tourist information please visit the VisitBritain
website and look up your nearest centre)
www.visitbritain.com
Aims to build the value of inbound
tourism throughout Britain and to grow
the domestic market for the benefit of
England. Website has visitor information
including a database of Visitor Information
Centres.

VisitScotland
(Scottish Tourist Board)
Visitor information and accommodation:
☎ 0845 225 5121 or 01506 832121
www.visitscotland.com
Walking Wild
Walking in Scotland website:
www.walkingwild.com

**Wales Tourist Board – Bwrdd
Croeso Cymru**
Information and booking line: 0870 121 1251,
minicom 0870 121 1255
www.visitwales.com

The Power of **Lightweight**

trekking & outdoor footwear

Promenade Gtx
This lightweight, Italian made ladies' boot
offers the ideal level of support for low level
trekking, approach routes and day hiking.
The full Goretex liner ensures it is fully
waterproof. Also available in sage/grey.

WALKING AND OUTDOOR ACTIVITIES

Backpackers Club
www.backpackersclub.co.uk
Promotes and encourages backpacking for the benefit of its members.

BMC (British Mountaineering Council)
☎ 0870 010 4878
www.thebmc.co.uk
Protects the freedoms and promotes the interests of climbers, hillwalkers and mountaineers.

British Horse Society
☎ 0870 120 2244
www.bhs.org.uk
Works to improve the welfare of horses through education, training and promoting the interests of horse riders and owners, including defending bridleways.

British Orienteering Federation (BOF) ☎ 01629 734042
www.britishorienteering.org.uk

British Upland Footpath Trust (BUFT) ☎ 0870 010 4878
Aims to improve the quality and standard of footpath works and deal with erosion problems on upland paths.

British Walking Federation (BWF)
www.bwf-ivv.org.uk
British affiliate of the International Volkssport Federation, organising non-competitive walking events.

British Waterways: see Transport

Byways and Bridleways Trust
www.bbtrust.org.uk Aims to protect Britain's ancient minor highways, publishes *Byway and Bridleway* magazine.

Camping and Caravanning Club
☎ 024 7669 4995
www.campingandcaravanningclub.co.uk
Runs 90 members' sites throughout the UK, offers technical advice and membership benefits.

Confraternity of St James
☎ 020 7928 9988
www.csj.org.uk
Promotes modern use of the old European pilgrimage routes of Saint James/Santiago de Compostela.

CTC (Cyclists' Touring Club)
☎ 0870 873 0060
www.ctc.org.uk
Campaigning for cyclists' rights, lobbying government and other agencies to promote, invest in and facilitate cycling, also organises club activities.

Defence Estates for walks on MOD lands: see National Government

Disabled Ramblers
☎ 01628 621414 (Dr M Bruton)

website.lineone.net/~disabledramblers
Aims to improve countryside access for disabled people and organises regular rambles and visits. See also Scottish Disabled Ramblers.

Duke of Edinburgh's Award
☎ 01753 727400 Publications: ☎ 0131 553 5280
www.theaward.org
Operates a challenging and rewarding personal development programme for people aged 14-25.

Fieldfare Trust
☎ 0114 270 1668
www.fieldfare.org.uk
Works with people with disabilities and countryside managers to improve access to the countryside for everyone.

Gay Outdoor Club (GOC)
☎ 01522 804596
http://goc.net
Organises walking and other outdoor activities for lesbian, gay, bisexual and transgender people across the UK.

Go Outdoors (Outdoor Industries Association) ☎ 020 8842 1111
www.go-outdoors.org.uk
Trade body for manufacturers and retailers of outdoor clothing and equipment in Britain and Ireland.

Green Space (Urban Parks Forum)
☎ 0118 946 9060
www.green-space.org.uk
Helps those committed to the planning, design, management and use of public parks and open spaces.

Hillphones   www.hillphones.info
Recorded information on deer stalking between August and October in selected areas to assist those planning walks and climbs. Provided in conjunction with the Mountaineering Council of Scotland.

Institute of Public Rights of Way Officers (IPROW)
☎ 0700 078 2318   www.iprow.co.uk
Professional body for local authority rights of way officers in England and Wales; also run a variety of training courses.

Living Streets (Pedestrians' Association) ☎ 020 7820 1010
www.livingstreets.org.uk
Defends the rights of pedestrians and campaigns for living streets.

See also Walk to School, Walking Bus

London Walking Forum: see Transport for London

Long Distance Walkers Association
www.ldwa.org.uk

Works to further the interests of those who enjoy long distance walking, including documenting the long distance path network in its *Handbook* and *Strider* magazine.

Mountain Bothies Association (MBA)
www.mountainbothies.org.uk
Maintains around 100 simple, unlocked shelters in remote country.

Mountain Rescue Committee of Scotland ☎ 01360 770431
www.mrc-scotland.org.uk
Representative and coordinating body for mountain rescue in Scotland.

Mountain Rescue Council
www.mountain.rescue.org.uk
Secretary: ☎ 01457 869506
Handbook: eveburton@chinley35.fsnet.co.uk
Official coordinating body for mountain rescue in England and Wales.

Mountaineering Council of Scotland (MCS)
☎ 01738 638227
www.mountaineering-scotland.org.uk
Representative body for climbers, walkers and others who enjoy the Scottish mountains.

Paths for All Partnership
☎ 01259 218888
www.pathsforall.org.uk

Paths to Health:
www.pathstohealth.org.uk

Partnership of 17 Scottish organisations working to create path networks for walkers of all abilities to walk, cycle and ride for recreation, health and sustainable transport. Also coordinates local Paths to Health walking for health schemes in Scotland.

Railway Ramblers
www.railwayramblers.org.uk
Discovers and explores old railway lines and promotes their use as footpaths and cycleways.

Red Rope
☎ 01274 493995 (Titch Kavanagh)
www.redrope.org.uk
The socialist walking and climbing club.

Scottish Avalanche Information Service: See SportScotland

Scottish Disabled Ramblers
☎ 01337 858699
www.scottishdisabledramblers.org.uk
Fostering health by outdoor interests and appreciation of the countryside. See also Disabled Ramblers

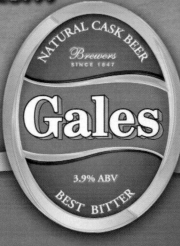

ScotWays (Scottish Rights of Way and Access Society) ☎ 0131 558 1222
www.scotways.com
Works for the preservation, defence, restoration and acquisition of public rights of over land in Scotland, including public rights of way.

Sensory Trust ☎ 01726 222900
www.sensorytrust.org.uk
Works to make green space accessible to as many people as possible.

Sustrans (Sustainable Transport)
☎ 0845 113 0065
www.sustrans.org.uk
Works on practical projects to encourage people to walk and cycle more; champions the National Cycle Network, some of which includes off-road mixed use routes also suitable for walkers (more information on the website).

SYHA (Scottish Youth Hostels Association) ☎ 0870 155 3255
www.syha.org.uk

Hostel holidays and courses:
www.hostelholidays.com
Providers of budget accommodation and countryside activities. See also YHA

Wainwright Society
www.wainwright.org.uk
Set up in commemoration of renowned hillwalker and author A Wainwright.

Walk to School (National Walking to School Initiative)
www.walktoschool.org.uk
International Walk to School Day:
www.iwalktoschool.org
Encourages walking to school and promotes National Walk to School Week. Partnership of TravelWise, Living Streets and Dorset County Council.

Walking Bus
☎ 0870 420 3236
www.walkingbus.org
Information about walking buses (schemes in which groups of children walk to school according to a set route and timetable).

Walking-Routes
www.walking-routes.co.uk
Extensive links to sites with online route descriptions.

Walking the way to Health Initiative – Cerdded Llwybr Iechyd
England: contact the WHI team at the

Countryside Agency: ☎ 01242 533258
www.whi.org.uk

Wales: contact the WW2H/CLLI team at the Countryside Council for Wales:
☎ 0845 130 6229
www.ww2h.org.uk or
www.clli.org.uk

Scotland: see Paths for All Partnership (Paths to Health)

Joint initiative of the Countryside Agency, CCW and British Heart Foundation using walking to improve the health of people in England who currently get little exercise

Walking Wild: see VisitScotland under Tourism

Way to Go: see Transport 2000

YHA England & Wales (Youth Hostels Association)
☎ 0870 870 8808
Walking holidays and accommodation booking: ☎ 0870 241 2314
Edale Activity Centre:
☎ 01433 670302
www.yha.org.uk
Providers of budget accommodation and countryside activities. See also SYHA.

OUTSIDE GREAT BRITAIN

EUROPE
European Ramblers Association
(ERA) c/o Klub Ceskych Turistu, Archeologická 2256, CZ-155 00 Praha 5 - Luziny
☎ +420 2 5162 7356
www.era-ewv-ferp.org
Federation of 26 national organisations including the Ramblers' Association working for walking and climbing, protecting the countryside and creating international long distance paths (E-Paths). The website is a good source of information on walking in Europe and member organisations' contact details.

Hostelling International
(International Youth Hostels Federation) 2nd Floor Gate House, Fretherne Road, Welwyn Garden City, AL8 6RD, UK
☎ +44 (0)1707 324170 www.iyhf.org
(has links to national sites)

CHANNEL ISLANDS
Alderney Tourist Information
☎ 01481 822333
www.visitalderney.com

Guernsey Tourist
☎ 01481 723552
www.visitguernsey.com

Herm Tourist Information
☎ 01481 722377
www.herm-island.com

Jersey Tourist Information
☎ 01534 500700
www.jersey.com

Sark Tourist Information
☎ 01481 832345 www.sark.info

NORTHERN IRELAND
Countryside Access and Activities Network for Northern Ireland
☎ 028 9030 3930
www.countrysiderecreation.com
Responsibilities include the province's network of 14 Waymarked Ways.

Northern Ireland Tourist Board
Ireland Welcome Centre (information)
☎ 029 9024 6609
www.discovernorthernireland.com

London: information available from Fáilte Ireland (see Republic of Ireland)

Ordnance Survey of Northern Ireland ☎ 028 9025 5755
www.osni.gov.uk

Translink
☎ 028 9089 9400
Enquiry line ☎ 028 9066 6630
www.translink.co.uk
Operates integrated public transport services including Northern Ireland Railways, Citybus and Ulsterbus

Ulster Federation of Rambling Clubs ☎ 028 9066 6358

REPUBLIC OF IRELAND
Fáilte Ireland (Tourism Ireland)
☎ +353 (0)1 602 4000
www.ireland.ie

Walking website:
www.walking.travel.ie

CIE (Córas Iompair Éireann)
☎ +353 (0)1 703 2358
Rail enquiries ☎ +353 (0)1 836 6222
Bus enquiries +353 (0)1 836 6111
www.cie.ie
Operates integrated public transport services including Iarnród Éireann (Irish Rail), Bus Éireann and Dublin Bus

Mountaineering Council of Ireland
☎ +353 (0)1 625 1115
www.mountaineering.ie

National Waymarked Ways Advisory Committee
Irish Sports Council:
☎ +353 (0)1 860 8800
www.walkireland.ie

Ordnance Survey Ireland – Suirbhéireacht Ordanáis Éireann
☎ +353 (0)1 802 5300
www.osi.ie

ISLE OF MAN
Manx Footpaths Conservation Group
manxfootpaths.iomonline.co.im

VisitIsleofMan – Cur jee shilley er Ellan Vannin
☎ 01624 686801
www.visitisleofman.com

LOCAL AUTHORITIES

In this section we list councils in Britain with primary responsibility for footpaths, to whom footpath or access problems should be reported. Many of them also promote walking locally and can provide information about walking routes, parks and countryside areas.

Reporting path and access problems helps us keep the network open and free from obstruction. You can send your report either to the local Ramblers' Association Area, so the local footpath officer can take the matter up with the council. Or you can report the problem directly to the local authority, but please send a copy to the local Ramblers contact too.

If you wish, use the Path Problem Report Form on p 23. You can request further forms from Ramblers' Association offices and you can also report problems on the footpath campaign pages on our website. Otherwise, don't forget to report what the problem is, where it is and when you noticed it.

ALPHABETICAL ORDER

Councils covering only a part of an historic county are listed under the council area's name, not the county's name: for example, West Dunbartonshire is listed under 'W'.

ENGLAND

In most of England the council with responsibility for footpaths – the 'highway authority' – can either be a county council, unitary authority or metropolitan borough council. These councils are also 'surveying authorities', with responsibility for maintaining the official 'definitive' map of public rights of way. In national parks, the national park authority often takes over responsibility for footpaths: look under National Parks in Useful Contacts. Highway authorities and national park authorities are also responsible for setting up local access forums under the Countryside and Rights of Way Act 2000 (see p 13). Path problem reports should be addressed to the Public Rights of Way Officer.

Barking and Dagenham
(Outer London Borough)
Civic Centre, Dagenham RM10 7BN
☎ 020 8592 4500
www.barking-dagenham.gov.uk

Barnet (Outer London Borough)
Hendon Town Hall, The Burroughs, London
NW4 4BG ☎ 020 8359 2000
www.barnet.gov.uk

Barnsley (Metropolitan Borough)
Town Hall, Barnsley S70 2TA ☎ 01226 770770
www.barnsley.gov.uk

Bath & North East Somerset
(Unitary Authority)
Trimbridge House, Trim Street, Bath BA1 2DP
☎ 01225 477500
www.bathnes.gov.uk

Bedfordshire (County Council)
County Hall, Cauldwell Street, Bedford
MK42 9A, ☎ 01234 363222
www.bedfordshire.gov.uk

Bexley (Outer London Borough)
Civic Offices, Broadway, Bexleyheath DA6 7LB
☎ 020 8303 7777
www.bexley.gov.uk

Birmingham (Metropolitan Borough)
The Council House, Victoria Square, Birmingham
B1 1BB ☎ 0121 303 9944
www.birmingham.gov.uk

Blackburn with Darwen
(Unitary Authority)
Town Hall, Blackburn BB1 2LX ☎ 01254 585585
www.blackburn.gov.uk

Blackpool (Unitary Authority)
Municipal Buildings, PO Box 77, Town Hall
Blackpool FY1 1AD ☎ 01253 477477
www.blackpool.gov.uk

Bolton (Metropolitan Borough)
The Wellsprings, Bolton BL1 1US
☎ 01204 333333
www.bolton.gov.uk

Bournemouth (Unitary Authority)
Town Hall, Bourne Avenue, Bournemouth
BH2 6DY ☎ 01202 451451
www.bournemouth.gov.uk

Bracknell Forest (Unitary Authority)
Market Street, Bracknell RG12 1LR
☎ 01344 424642
www.bracknell-forest.gov.uk

Bradford City
(Metropolitan Borough)
City Hall, Channing Way, Bradford BD1 1HY
☎ 01274 435681
www.bradford.gov.uk

Brent(Outer London Borough)
Town Hall, Forty Lane, Wembley HA9 9EZ
☎ 020 8937 1234
www.brent.gov.uk

Brighton & Hove (Unitary Authority)
Town Hall, Bartholomew Sq, Brighton BN1 1J
☎ 01273 290000
www.brighton-hove.gov.uk

Bristol City (Unitary Authority)
The Council House, College Green, Bristol
BS1 5TR ☎ 0117 922 2000
www.bristol-city.gov.uk

Bromley (Outer London Borough)
Civic Centre, Stockwell Close, Bromley
BR1 3UH ☎ 020 8464 3333
www.bromley.gov.uk

Buckinghamshire (County Council)
County Hall, Aylesbury HP20 1UA
☎ 01296 395000
www.buckscc.gov.uk

Bury (Metropolitan Borough)
21 Broad Street, Bury BL9 0AW
☎ 0161 253 5000
www.bury.gov.uk

Calderdale (Metropolitan Borough)
Northgate House, Halifax HX1 1UN
☎ 01422 357257
www.calderdale.gov.uk

Cambridgeshire (County Council)
Shire Hall, Cambridge CB3 0AP ☎ 01223 717111
www.cambridgeshire.gov.uk

Camden (Inner London Borough)
Camden Town Hall, Judd Street, London
WC1H 9JE ☎ 020 7278 4444
www.camden.gov.uk

Cheshire (County Council)
Goldsmith House, Hamilton Place, Chester
CH1 1SE ☎ 01244 602424
www.cheshire.gov.uk

City of London: see Corporation of
London; see also London

Cornwall (County Council)
County Hall, Truro TR1 3AY
☎ 01872 322000
www.cornwall.gov.uk

Corporation of London
Guildhall, London EC2P 2EJ ☎ 020 7606 3030
www.cityoflondon.gov.uk

Coventry (Metropolitan Borough)
Council House, Earl Street, Coventry CV1 5RR
☎ 024 7683 3333
www.coventry.gov.uk

Croydon (Outer London Borough)
Taberner House, Park Lane, Croydon CR9 3JS
☎ 020 8686 4433
www.croydon.gov.uk

Cumbria (County Council)
The Courts, Carlisle CA3 8NA ☎ 01228 606060
www.cumbria.gov.uk

Darlington (Unitary Authority)
Town Hall, Darlington DL1 5QT ☎ 01325 380651
www.darlington.gov.uk

Derby (Unitary Authority)
The Council House, Corporation Street, Derby
DE1 2FS ☎ 01332 293111
www.derby.gov.uk

Derbyshire (County Council)
County Offices, Matlock DE4 3AG
☎ 01629 580000
www.derbyshire.gov.uk

Devon (County Council)
Lucombe House, Topsham Road, Exeter EX2 4QW
☎ 01392 382000
www.devon.gov.uk

Doncaster (Metropolitan Borough)
2 Priory Place, Doncaster DN1 1BN
☎ 01302 734444
www.doncaster.gov.uk

Dorset (County Council)
County Hall, Dorchester DT1 1XJ
☎ 01305 251000
www.dorset-cc.gov.uk
See also Bournemouth, Poole

Dudley (Metropolitan Borough)
Council House, Priory Road, Dudley DY1 1HF
☎ 01384 818181
www.dudley.gov.uk

Durham (County Council)
County Hall, Durham DH1 5UB ☎ 0191 383 3000
www.durham.gov.uk

Ealing (Outer London Borough)
14-16 Uxbridge Road, London W5 2HL
☎ 020 8825 5000
www.ealing.gov.uk

East Riding of Yorkshire
(Unitary Authority)
County Hall, Beverley HU17 9BA
☎ 01482 393939
www.eastriding.gov.uk

East Sussex (County Council)
County Hall, St Anne's Crescent, Lewes BN7 1UE
☎ 01273 481000
www.eastsussexcc.gov.uk

Enfield (Outer London Borough)
Civic Centre, Silver Street, Enfield EN1 3XA
☎ 020 8379 1000
www.enfield.gov.uk

Essex (County Council)
County Hall, Chelmsford CM1 1LX
☎ 01245 492211
www.essexcc.gov.uk

Gateshead (Metropolitan Borough)
Civic Centre, Regent St, Gateshead, NE8 1HH
☎ 0191 433 3000
www.gateshead.gov.uk

Gloucestershire (County Council)
Shire Hall, Gloucester GL1 2TH ☎ 01452 425000
www.gloucestershire.gov.uk

Greater London: see London

Greater Manchester: see
Manchester

Greenwich (Inner London Borough)
Woolwich Town Hall, Wellington Street, London
SE18 6PW ☎ 020 8854 8888
www.greenwich.gov.uk

Hackney (Inner London Borough)
Town Hall, Mare Street, London E8 1EA
☎ 020 8356 3000
Parks office: Greenway Close, London N4 2EY
☎ 020 7923 3644
www.hackney.gov.uk

Halton (Unitary Authority)
Municipal Building, Kingsway, Widnes WA8 7QF
☎ 0151 424 2061
www.halton.gov.uk

Hammersmith and Fulham
(Inner London Borough)
Town Hall, King Street, London W6 9JU
☎ 020 8748 3020
www.lbhf.gov.uk

Hampshire (County Council)
Mottisfont Court, High Street, Winchester
SO23 8ZF ☎ 0800 028 0888
www.hants.gov.uk

Haringey (Outer London Borough)
Civic Centre, High Road, London N22 4LE
☎ 020 8489 0000
www.haringey.gov.uk

Harrow (Outer London Borough)
Civic Centre, Station Road, Harrow HA1 2XF
☎ 020 8863 5611
www.harrow.gov.uk

Hartlepool (Unitary Authority)
Civic Centre, Hartlepool TS24 8AY
☎ 01429 266522
www.hartlepool.gov.uk

Havering (Outer London Borough)
Town Hall, Main Road, Romford RM1 3BB
☎ 01708 434343
www.havering.gov.uk

Herefordshire
(Unitary Authority)
35 Hafod Road, Hereford HR1 1SH
☎ 01432 260000
www.herefordshire.gov.uk

Hertfordshire (County Council)
County Hall, Hertford SG13 8DQ
☎ 01438 737555
www.hertscc.gov.uk

Hillingdon (Outer London Borough)
Civic Centre, Uxbridge UB8 1UW ☎ 01895 250111
www.hillingdon.gov.uk

Hounslow (Outer London Borough)
Civic Centre, Lampton Road, Hounslow TW3 4DN
☎ 020 8583 2000
www.hounslow.gov.uk

Hull: see Kingston upon Hull

Isle of Wight (Unitary Authority)
County Hall, Newport PO30 1UD ☎ 01983 821000
www.iow.gov.uk

Isles of Scilly
Town Hall, St Mary's TR21 0LW ☎ 01720 422537
www.scilly.gov.uk

Islington (Inner London Borough)
222 Upper Street, London N1 1XR
☎ 020 7527 2000
www.islington.gov.uk

Kensington and Chelsea
(Inner London Borough)
Town Hall, Hornton Street, London W8 7NX
☎ 020 7937 5464
www.rbkc.gov.uk

Kent (County Council)
County Hall, Maidstone ME14 1XQ
☎ 0845 824 7247
www.kent.gov.uk/countrysideaccess

Kingston upon Hull (Unitary Authority)
Guildhall, Hull HU1 2AA ☎ 01482 300300
www.hullcc.gov.uk

Kingston upon Thames
(Outer London Borough)
Guildhall, Kingston upon Thames KT1 1EU
☎ 020 8547 5757
www.kingston.gov.uk

Kirklees (Metropolitan Borough)
Market Street, Huddersfield HD1 1WG
☎ 01484 221000
www.kirkleesmc.gov.uk

Knowsley (Metropolitan Borough)
Muncipal Buildings, Archway Road, Huyton
L36 9UX ☎ 0151 489 6000
www.knowsley.gov.uk

Lambeth (Inner London Borough)
Town Hall, Brixton Hill, London SW2 1RW
☎ 020 7926 1000
www.lambeth.gov.uk

Lancashire (County Council)
County Hall, Fishergate, Preston PR1 8XJ
☎ 0845 053 0000
www.lancashire.gov.uk

Leeds (Metropolitan Borough)
Civic Hall, Calverley Street, Leeds LS1 1UR
☎ 0113 234 8080
www.leeds.gov.uk

Leicester (Unitary Authority)
New Walk Centre, Welford Place, Leicester LE1 6ZG,
☎ 0116 254 9922
www.leicester.gov.uk

Leicestershire (County Council)
County Hall, Glenfield, Leicester LE3 8RJ
☎ 0116 232 3232
www.leics.gov.uk

CONFORM ABLE
by SIDAS

STEP-IN+
TREK

Go further.

Thermo Adaptation Possible

HEAT

Foot•Body Support

Antivibration

Transflux Construction

Improved shock absorption:
The heel bone is the softest bone in the body and strikes the ground 4,000 times each day. Conform'able Step-in+ foot beds are designed to cradle the heel bone thanks to the deep heel cup and improve shock absorption using double EVA foam.

Better support and fit:
The unique Conform'able 3D shape supports all 3 arches in each foot preventing tiredness and collapsing. The support can be adjusted to suit your feet!

More stability:
The 26 bones in the foot are controlled by muscles. We know fatigue will set in with exercise, so give your feet some help with a proper base of support and fit a Step-in+ footbed.

Your feet and body will feel better!

steve.couper@sidas.co.uk
tel: 07909 966 076
fax: 01539 725 817
www.sidas.com

Lewisham (Inner London Borough)
Town Hall, London SE6 4RU ☎ 020 8314 6000
www.lewisham.gov.uk

Lincolnshire (County Council)
County Offices, Newland, Lincoln LN1 1YL
☎ 01522 552222
www.lincolnshire.gov.uk
See also North Lincolnshire, North East
Lincolnshire

Liverpool (Metropolitan Borough)
Municipal Buildings, Dale Street, Liverpool
L69 2DH ☎ 0151 233 3000
www.liverpool.gov.uk

London Greater London Authority and
Mayor of London (strategic only):
City Hall, The Queen's Walk, London SE1 2AA
☎ 020 7983 4000
www.london.gov.uk

Luton (Unitary Authority)
Town Hall, Luton LU1 2BQ ☎ 01582 546000
www.luton.gov.uk

Manchester (Metropolitan Borough)
Town Hall, Albert Sq, Manchester M60 2LA
☎ 0161 234 5000
www.manchester.gov.uk

Medway (Unitary Authority)
Civic Centre, Strood, Rochester ME2 4AU
☎ 01634 306000
www.medway.gov.uk

Merton (Outer London Borough)
Civic Centre, London Road, Morden SM4 5DX
☎ 020 8274 4901
www.merton.gov.uk

Middlesbrough (Unitary Authority)
Municipal Buildings, Middlesbrough TS1 2QQ
☎ 01642 245432
www.middlesbrough.gov.uk

Milton Keynes (Unitary Authority)
Civic Offices, 1 Saxon Gate, Milton Keynes
MK9 3HG ☎ 01908 252406
www.mkweb.co.uk/countryside

Newcastle (Metropolitan Borough)
Civic Centre, Barras Bridge, Newcastle upon Tyne
NE99 1RD ☎ 0191 232 8520
www.newcastle.gov.uk

Newham (Outer London Borough)
Town Hall, London E6 2RP ☎ 020 8430 2000
www.newham.gov.uk

Norfolk (County Council)
County Hall, Martineau Lane, Norwich NR1 2DH
☎ 0844 800 8020
www.norfolk.gov.uk

North East Lincolnshire
(Unitary Authority)
Municipal Offices, Town Hall Square, Grimsby
DN31 1HU ☎ 01472 313131
www.nelincs.gov.uk

North Lincolnshire (Unitary Authority)
Pittwood House, Ashby Road, Scunthorpe DN16
1AB, ☎ 01724 296296
www.northlincs.gov.uk

North Somerset (Unitary Authority)
Town Hall, Weston-super-Mare BS23 1UJ
☎ 01934 888888
www.n-somerset.gov.uk

North Tyneside (Metropolitan Borough)
Forum House, Segedunum Way, Wallsend
NE28 8LX ☎ 0191 200 5000
www.northtyneside.gov.uk

North Yorkshire (County Council)
County Hall, Northallerton DL7 8AH
☎ 01609 780780
www.northyorks.gov.uk

Northamptonshire (County Council)
County Hall, Northampton NN1 1DN
☎ 01604 236236
www.northamptonshire.gov.uk

Northumberland (County Council)
County Hall, Morpeth NE61 2EF ☎ 01670 533000
www.northumberland.gov.uk

Nottingham (Unitary Authority)
The Guildhall, South Sherwood Street, Nottingham
NG1 4BT ☎ 0115 915 5555
www.nottinghamcity.gov.uk

Nottinghamshire (County Council)
Trent Bridge House, West Bridgford, Nottingham
NG2 6BJ ☎ 0115 982 3823
www.nottinghamshire.gov.uk

Oldham (Metropolitan Borough)
Civic Centre, West Street, Oldham OL1 1UG
☎ 0161 911 3000
www.oldham.gov.uk

Oxfordshire (County Council)
County Hall, New Road, Oxford OX1 1ND
☎ 01865 792422

Peterborough (Unitary Authority)
Town Hall, Peterborough PE1 1PJ ☎ 01733 747474
www.peterborough.gov.uk

Plymouth (Unitary Authority)
Civic Centre, Plymouth PL1 2EW ☎ 01752 668000
www.plymouth.gov.uk

Poole (Unitary Authority)
Civic Centre, Poole BH15 2RU ☎ 01202 633633
www.poole.gov.uk

Portsmouth (Unitary Authority)
Civic Offices, Guildhall Square, Portsmouth
PO1 2BG ☎ 023 9283 4092
www.portsmouth.gov.uk

Reading (Unitary Authority)
Civic Centre, Reading RG1 7TD, ☎ 0118 939 0900
www.reading.gov.uk

Redbridge (Outer London Borough)
Town Hall, High Road, Ilford IG1 1DD
☎ 020 8854 5000
www.redbridge.gov.uk

Redcar and Cleveland
(Unitary Authority)
Langbaurgh Town Hall, Fabian Road, South Bank,
Middlesborough TS6 9AR ☎ 01642 444000
www.redcar-cleveland.gov.uk

Richmond upon Thames
(Outer London Borough)
Civic Centre, 44 York Street, Twickenham TW1 3BZ,
☎ 020 8891 1411
www.richmond.gov.uk

Rochdale (Metropolitan Borough)
Electric House, Smith Street, Rochdale OL16 1YP
☎ 01706 647474
www.rochdale.gov.uk

Rotherham (Metropolitan Borough)
Civic Building, Walker Place, Rotherham S65 1UF
☎ 01709 382121
www.rotherham.gov.uk

Rutland (Unitary Authority)
Catmose, Oakham LE15 6HP ☎ 01572 722577
www.rutnet.co.uk/rcc

Salford (Metropolitan Borough)
Civic Centre, Chorley Road, Swinton, Salford
M27 5DA ☎ 0161 794 4711
www.salford.gov.uk

Sandwell
(Metropolitan Borough)
PO Box 2374, Oldbury B69 3DE ☎ 0121 569 2200
www.sandwell.gov.uk

Sefton (Metropolitan Borough)
Balliol House, Balliol Road, Bootle L20 3AH
☎ 0151 934 4040
www.sefton.gov.uk

Sheffield (Metropolitan Borough)
Town Hall, Sheffield S1 2HH ☎ 0114 272 6444
www.sheffield.gov.uk

Shropshire (County Council)
Shire Hall, Abbey Foregate, Shrewsbury SY2 6ND
☎ 0845 678 9000
www.shropshire-cc.gov.uk

Slough (Unitary Authority)
Town Hall, Bath Road, Slough SL1 3UQ
☎ 01753 552288
www.slough.gov.uk

Solihull (Metropolitan Borough)
Council House, Solihull B91 3QT ☎ 0121 704 6000
www.solihull.gov.uk

Somerset (County Council)
County Hall, Taunton TA1 4DY ☎ 01823 355455
www.somerset.gov.uk

South Gloucestershire
(Unitary Authority)
The Council Offices, Castle Street, Thornbury
BS35 1HF ☎ 01454 868686
www.southglos.gov.uk

South Tyneside
(Metropolitan Borough),
Town Hall & Civic Offices, Westoe Road, South
Shields NE33 2RL ☎ 0191 427 1717
www.southtyneside.info

Southampton (Unitary Authority)
Civic Centre, Southampton SO14 7LY
☎ 023 8022 3855
www.southampton.gov.uk

Southend on Sea (Unitary Authority)
Civic Centre, Southend-on-Sea SS2 6ER
☎ 01702 215000
www.southend.gov.uk

Southwark (Inner London Borough)
Town Hall, Peckham Road, London SE5 8UB
☎ 020 7525 5000
www.southwark.gov.uk

St Helens (Metropolitan Borough)
Town Hall, Victory Square, St Helens WA10 1HP
☎ 01744 456000
www.sthelens.gov.uk

Staffordshire (County Council)
Martin Street, Stafford ST16 2LH ☎ 01785 223121
www.staffordshire.gov.uk

Stockport (Metropolitan Borough)
Town Hall, Edward Street, Stockport SK1 3XE
☎ 0161 480 4949
www.stockport.gov.uk

Stockton-on-Tees (Unitary Authority)
Municipal Buildings, Church Road
Stockton-on-Tees TS18 1LD ☎ 01642 393939
www.stockton.gov.uk

Stoke-on-Trent (Unitary Authority)
Civic Centre, Glebe Street, Stoke-on-Trent
ST4 1RN ☎ 01782 234567
www.stoke.gov.uk

Suffolk (County Council)
8 Russell Road, Ipswich IP1 2BX ☎ 01473 583000
www.suffolkcc.gov.uk

Sunderland (Metropolitan Borough)
Civic Centre, Sunderland SR2 7DN
☎ 0191 553 1000
www.sunderland.gov.uk

Surrey (County Council)
County Hall, Kingston upon Thames KT1 2DN
☎ 0845 600 9009
www.surreycc.gov.uk

Sutton (Outer London Borough)
Civic Offices, St Nicholas Way, Sutton SM1 1EA
☎ 020 8770 5000
www.sutton.gov.uk

Swindon (Unitary Authority)
Civic Offices, Euclid Street, Swindon SN1 2JH
☎ 01793 463725
www.swindon.gov.uk

Tameside (Metropolitan Borough)
Council Offices, Wellington Road, Ashton-under-
Lyne, Tameside OL6 6DL ☎ 0161 342 8355
www.tameside.gov.uk

Telford & Wrekin (Unitary Authority)
Civic Offices, Telford TF3 4LD ☎ 01952 202100
www.telford.gov.uk

Thurrock (Unitary Authority)
Civic Offices, New Road, Grays RN17 6SL
☎ 01375 652652
www.thurrock.gov.uk

Torbay (Unitary Authority)
Civic Offices, Torquay TQ1 3DR ☎ 01803 201201
www.torbay.gov.uk

Tower Hamlets
(Inner London Borough) Town Hall, 5 Clove
Crescent, London E14 2BG ☎ 020 7364 5000
www.towerhamlets.gov.uk

Trafford (Metropolitan Borough)
Town Hall, Talbot, Stretford M32 0YX
☎ 0161 912 2000
www.trafford.gov.uk

Wakefield (Metropolitan Borough)
County Hall, Bond Street, Wakefield WF1 2QL
☎ 01924 306090
www.wakefield.gov.uk

Walsall (Metropolitan Borough)
Civic Centre, Walsall WS1 1T, ☎ 01922 650000
www.walsall.gov.uk

Waltham Forest
(Outer London Borough)
Town Hall, Forest Road, London E17 4JF
☎ 020 8496 3000
www.lbwf.gov.uk

Wandsworth (Inner London Borough)
Town Hall, Wandsworth High Street, London
SW18 2PU ☎ 020 8871 6000
www.wandsworth.gov.uk

Warrington (Unitary Authority)
Town Hall, Warrington WA1 1UH
☎ 01925 444400
www.warrington.gov.uk

Warwickshire (County Council)
Shire Hall, Warwick CV34 4RA ☎ 0845 090 7000
www.warwickshire.gov.uk

West Berkshire (Unitary Authority)
Council Offices, Faraday Road, Newbury RG14 2AF
☎ 01635 42400
www.westberks.gov.uk

West Sussex (County Council)
County Hall, Chichester PO19 1RH
☎ 01243 777100
www.westsussex.gov.uk

Westminster (Inner London Borough)
City Hall, Victoria Street, London SW1E 6QP
☎ 020 7641 6000
www.westminster.gov.uk

Wigan (Metropolitan Borough)
Town Hall, Library Street, Wigan WN1 1YN
☎ 01942 244991
www.wiganmbc.gov.uk

Wiltshire (County Council)
County Hall, Bythesea Road, Trowbridge BA14 8JN
☎ 01225 713000
www.wiltshire.gov.uk

Wirral (Metropolitan Borough)
Town Hall, Brighton Street,
Wallasey CH44 8ED
☎ 0151 606 2000 www.wirral.gov.uk

**Windsor and Maidenhead Royal
Borough** (Unitary Authority)
Town Hall, St Ives Road, Maidenhead SL6 1RF
☎ 01628 798888
www.rbwm.gov.uk

Wokingham (Unitary Authority)
Shute End Offices, Wokingham RG40 1GY
☎ 01189 778731
www.wokingham.gov.uk

Wolverhampton
(Metropolitan Borough)
St Peters Square, Wolverhampton
WV1 1SH ☎ 01902 556556
www.wolverhampton.gov.uk

Worcestershire (County Council)
County Hall, Spetchley Road, Worcester WR5 2NP
☎ 01905 763763
www.worcestershire.gov.uk

York City (Unitary Authority)
Guildhall, 9 St Leonard's Place, York YO1 1QN
☎ 01904 613161
www.york.gov.uk

Yorkshire, South: see Barnsley,
Doncaster, Sheffield
Yorkshire, West: see Bradford,
Calderdale, Kirklees, Leeds, Wakefield

WALES

The council with responsibility for footpaths, or 'highway authority', is always the unitary authority. These councils are also 'surveying authorities', with responsibility for maintaining the official 'definitive' map of public rights of way. Path problem reports should be addressed to the Public Rights of Way Officer unless another department is shown.

Blaenau Gwent
Municipal Offices, Civic Centre, Ebbw Vale
NP23 6XB ☎ 01495 350555
www.blaenau-gwent.gov.uk

Bridgend
Civic Offices, Angel Street, Bridgend
CF31 1LX ☎ 01656 643643
www.bridgend.gov.uk

Caerphilly
Council Offices, Nelson Road, Tredomen,
Ystrad Mynach CF82 7WF ☎ 01443 815588
www.caerphilly.gov.uk

Cardiff
County Hall, Atlantic Wharf, Cardiff
CF10 4UW ☎ 029 2087 2000
www.cardiff.gov.uk

Carmarthenshire
County Hall, Carmarthen SA21 1JP
☎ 01267 234567
www.carmarthenshire.gov.uk

Ceredigion
Penmorfa, Aberaeron SA46 0PA
☎ 01545 570881
www.ceredigion.gov.uk

Conwy
Bodlondeb, Conwy LL32 8DU
☎ 01492 574000
www.conwy.gov.uk

Denbighshire
Council Office, Wynnstay Road, Ruthin
LL15 1YN ☎ 01824 706000
www.denbighshire.gov.uk

Flintshire
County Hall, Mold CH7 6NB
☎ 01352 752121
www.flintshire.gov.uk

Gwynedd
Swyddfa'r Cyngor, Caernarfon LL55 1SH
☎ 01286 672255
www.gwynedd.gov.uk

Isle of Anglesey
Swyddfa'r Sir, Llangefni LL77 7TW
☎ 01248 750057
www.anglesey.gov.uk

Merthyr Tydfil
Civic Centre, Castle Street, Merthyr Tydfil
CF47 8AN ☎ 01685 725000
www.merthyr.gov.uk

Monmouthshire
County Hall, Cwmbran NP44 2XH
☎ 01633 644644
www.monmouthshire.gov.uk

Neath Port Talbot
Civic Centre, Neath SA13 1PJ
☎ 01639 763333
www.neath-porttalbot.gov.uk

Newport
Civic Centre, Newport NP20 4UR
☎ 01633 656656
www.newport.gov.uk

Pembrokeshire
County Hall, Haverfordwest SA61 1TP
☎ 01437 764551
www.pembrokeshire.gov.uk

Powys
County Hall, Llandrindod Wells LD1 5LG
☎ 01597 826000
www.powys.gov.uk

Rhondda Cynon Taff
The Pavillions, Cambrian Park,
Clydach Vale CF40 2XX
☎ 01443 484400
www.rhondda-cynon-taff.gov.uk

Swansea
County Hall, Oystermouth Road, Swansea
SA1 3SN ☎ 01792 636000
www.swansea.gov.uk

Torfaen
Civic Centre, Pontypool NP4 6YB
☎ 01495 762200
www.torfaen.gov.uk

Vale of Glamorgan
Dock Offices, Barry Docks, Barry CF63 4RT
☎ 01446 700111
www.valeofglamorgan.gov.uk

Wrexham
Wrexham LL11 1WF
☎ 01978 292000
www.wrexham.gov.uk

SCOTLAND

The council with responsibility for footpaths is known as the 'planning authority', and is always the unitary authority. There is no requirement for councils to keep official maps of paths. Path problem reports should be addressed to the Director of Planning.

Aberdeen
Town House, Broad Street, Aberdeen AB9 1AQ
☎ 01224 522000
www.aberdeencity.gov.uk

Aberdeenshire
Woodhill House, Westburn Road, Aberdeen
AB16 5GB ☎ 0845 606 7000
www.aberdeenshire.gov.uk

Angus
The Cross, Forfar DD8 1BX
☎ 0845 277 7778
www.angus.gov.uk

Argyll and Bute
Kilmory Castle, Lochgilphead, Argyll PA31 8RT
☎ 01546 602127
www.argyll-bute.gov.uk

Clackmannanshire
Council Offices, Greenfield, Alloa FK10 2AD
☎ 01259 452000
www.clacks.gov.uk

Dumfries & Galloway
Council Offices, English Street, Dumfries
DG1 2DD ☎ 01387 260000
www.dumgal.gov.uk

Dundee
Council Offices, 21 City Square, Dundee DD1 3BY
☎ 01382 434000
www.dundeecity.gov.uk

East Ayrshire
Council Offices, London Road Centre, London
Road, Kilmarnock KA3 7DG ☎ 0845 724 0000
www.east-ayrshire.gov.uk

East Dunbartonshire
Council Offices, Tom Johnston House, Civic Way,
Kirkintilloch G66 4TJ ☎ 0141 578 8000
www.eastdunbarton.gov.uk

East Lothian
Council Buildings, Haddington EH41 3HA
☎ 01620 827827
www.eastlothian.gov.uk

East Renfrewshire
Council Offices, Eastwood Park, Rouken Glen
Road, Giffnock G46 6UG ☎ 0141 577 3001
www.eastrenfrewshire.gov.uk

Edinburgh
City Chambers, High Street Edinburgh EH1 1YJ
☎ 0131 200 2000
www.edinburgh.gov.uk

Falkirk
Municipal Buildings, Falkirk FK1 5RS
☎ 01324 506070 www.falkirk.gov.uk

Fife
Fife House, North Street Glenrothes KY7 5LT
☎ 01592 414141
www.fife.gov.uk

Glasgow
City Chambers, George Square, Glasgow G2 1DU
☎ 0141 287 2000
www.glasgow.gov.uk

Highland
Glenurquhart Road, Inverness IV3 5NX
☎ 01463 702000
www.highland.gov.uk

Inverclyde
Municipal Buildings, Clyde Square, Greenock
PA15 1LX ☎ 01475 717171
www.inverclyde.gov.uk

Midlothian
Midlothian House, 40 Buccleuch Street
Dalkeith EH22 1DJ ☎ 0131 270 7500
www.midlothian.gov.uk

Moray
Council Offices, High Street, Elgin IV30 1BX
☎ 01343 543451
www.moray.gov.uk

North Ayrshire
Cunninghame House, Friar's Croft,
Irvine KA12 8EE ☎ 01294 324100
www.north-ayrshire.gov.uk

North Lanarkshire
Civic Centre, Motherwell ML1 1TW
☎ 01698 403200
www.northlan.gov.uk

Orkney Islands
Council Offices, School Place, Kirkwall
Orkney KW15 1NY
☎ 01856 873535
www.orkney.gov.uk

Perth & Kinross
Council Offices, 2 High Street, Perth
PH1 5PH ☎ 01738 475000
www.pkc.gov.uk

Renfrewshire
Municipal Buildings, Cotton Street
Paisley PA1 1BU
☎ 0141 842 5000
www.renfrewshire.gov.uk
See also East Renfrewshire

Scottish Borders
Council Headquarters, Newtown St Boswells,
Melrose TD6 0SA
☎ 01835 824000
www.scotborders.gov.uk

Shetland Islands
Town Hall, Lerwick ZE1 0HB ☎ 01595 693535
www.shetland.gov.uk

South Ayrshire
Council Offices, Wellington Square, Ayr KA7 1DR
☎ 00845 601 2020
www.south-ayrshire.gov.uk

South Lanarkshire
Council Offices, Almada Street, Hamilton
ML3 0AA ☎ 01698 454444
www.southlanarkshire.gov.uk

Stirling
Council Offices, Viewforth, Stirling FK8 2ET
☎ 0845 277 7000
www.stirling.gov.uk

West Dunbartonshire
Council Offices, Garshake Road, Dunbarton
G82 3PU ☎ 01389 737000
www.west-dunbarton.gov.uk

West Lothian
West Lothian House, Almondvale North,
Livingstone EH54 6QG ☎ 01506 777000
www.westlothian.gov.uk

Western Isles – Eilean Sir
Council Offices, Sandwick Road, Stornoway
HS1 2BW ☎ 01851 703773
www.w-isles.gov.uk

I found a breathtaking reason not to take the shortcut

Every step you take on your walking holiday in Ireland will bring you further into the rich, picturesque landscape. Savour nature's beauty whether it be alone or as part of a group. On your way you'll find good accommodation whatever your budget, where you can rest your weary legs and sample some of the local culinary specialities.

For your free walking information pack call 0845 7700 350 or visit www.walking.ireland.ie
www.discovernorthernireland.com
www.tourismireland.com

The island of memories **Ireland**

The companies listed here have chosen to advertise with us and their inclusion should not imply any recommendation by the Ramblers' Association

SouthWestWalks Ireland, , 6 Church Street, Tralee, Co.Kerry, Ireland Tel 066 7128733 Fax 066 7128762 Email swwi@iol.ie Web **www.southwestwalksireland.com** Ireland's premiere Walking Holiday operator, offering comprehensive programmes, Guided & Self-Guided. Covers: Ireland-North, South, East & West

Carmels, Glendalough, Annamoe, G.Wicklow, Ireland Tel 0404 45292 Fax 0404 45297 Email **Carmelsbandb@eircom.net** Well established home set in the heart of the Wicklow Mountains. Covers: Glendalough, Wicklow

Cliffords B&B, Main St. Waterville Co Kerry Tel 066 9474283 Fax 066 9474283 Email **cliffordbandb@eircom.net** Overlooking the sea, packed lunch, luggage transfer available, drying facilities

Creveen Cottage, Healy Pass Road, Lauragh, Co.Kerry Tel 00 353 64 83131 Email info@creveenlodge.com Web **www.creveenlodge.com** Idyllic location. Breathtaking views. Mountains. Spectacular walks. Covers: Near Beara Way

Tír Na Hilán Cottages, Teernahillane, Castletownbere, Co. Cork, Ireland Tel 00 353 27 70108 Email info@tirnahilan.com Web **www.tirnahilan.com** ITB approved SC Cottages, pony riding, 2.5miles ex CTBere town. Covers: Beara Way Walking Trail

Crockuna Cottage, Largynaseeragh, Glencolumbkille, Co. Donegal, Republic of Ireland Tel 00353 69 85255 Fax 00353 69 85285 Email hughstancliffe@eircom.net Web **www.crockunacottage.com** Comfortable bungalow near Ardara. Sleeps 4. Magnificant walking. Available all year.

Four Winds, Annascaul, Co.Kerry, Ireland Fax 066 91 57174 Bed - breakfast also self catering cottage. Covers: Dingle Peninsula

The island of memories **Ireland**

INDEX